IP AND OTHER THINGS

The Rt Hon Professor Sir Robin Jacob has been variously a leading member of the Intellectual Property Bar, a High Court judge and, as Lord Justice Jacob, a judge in the Court of Appeal of England and Wales. His primary area of expertise is intellectual property (IP) rights. He chose to leave the Court of Appeal in March 2011 to take up his current position as the Sir Hugh Laddie Chair in intellectual property at University College London. Besides teaching and writing he still sits occasionally in the Court of Appeal, sits as an arbitrator, provides expert evidence, chairs the Advisory Committee on the Appointment and Training of the Judges of the Unified Patent Court and often advises the UK Government and EU Commission on IP matters. These essays and speeches, selected from his published and unpublished writings and lectures, illustrate the breadth of his learning in IP and other matters. They are written in typically straightforward and entertaining style and, in the case of the older essays, include a commentary of what has happened since they were first published. They will be of interest to any lawyer, law student or scholar interested in the development of IP law in the past quarter century or so.

IP and Other Things

A Collection of Essays and Speeches

Robin Jacob

•HART•
PUBLISHING
OXFORD AND PORTLAND, OREGON
2017

Hart Publishing
An imprint of Bloomsbury Publishing Plc

Hart Publishing Ltd
Kemp House
Chawley Park
Cumnor Hill
Oxford OX2 9PH
UK

Bloomsbury Publishing Plc
50 Bedford Square
London
WC1B 3DP
UK

www.hartpub.co.uk
www.bloomsbury.com

Published in North America (US and Canada) by
Hart Publishing
c/o International Specialized Book Services
920 NE 58th Avenue, Suite 300
Portland, OR 97213-3786
USA

www.isbs.com

First published in hardback, 2015
Paperback edition, 2017

British Library Cataloguing-in-Publication Data
A catalogue record for this book is available from the British Library.

ISBN: PB: 978-1-50991-838-6
HB: 978-1-84946-595-3

Typeset by Compuscript Ltd, Shannon
Printed and bound in Great Britain by
Lightning Source UK Ltd

Preface

Richard Arnold said: 'Why don't you put some of your pieces into a book'? That gave me the confidence to think it might be worthwhile. Since I had written a few bits outside the world of IP of which I was (perhaps conceitedly) proud, I went for an eclectic mix. Also I had some stories to tell, so there is also a bit of autobiography here. Hence the title. Rather than just print the pieces as they were I thought it might be more interesting in some cases to add some footnotes in italics and a postscript. The idea was to give my 'then and now view' or put in 'what has happened since.' This involved more than I thought it would. I hope readers will be able to distinguish new from old easily—the key is that stuff in italics (save for case names) is new.

When I was at the Bar I did not do much lecturing or writing, save for textbook work. All I can recall of substance is a talk in 1980 at the Max Planck Institute (no one remembers much of what I talked about but everyone remembers that I brought my notes out of a plastic bag printed with a large Union Jack!) and the Herschel Smith lecture in 1992. I can't remember any others before I became a judge in 1993. In the early years thereafter I found myself doing a few. The first big one was at the biennual European Patent Judges' Symposium of the EPO. The UK was host and did it at the Patent Office in Newport. We all stayed in a terrible hotel called the Angel next to old Cardiff Arms Park. Wendy and I arrived the day the conference started but poor Judge Ford had come the day before. A false alarm got all the guests into the streets of Cardiff at 4 am—we learned that Judge Ford was to be seen in rather 1950s pyjamas. Willie Aldous, the senior patent judge, had told me it was the duty of the junior judge to write a paper—so I did. It was about the fiction that adding 'for' some new purpose you could confer novelty on an old product. I was against it then but time has shown that it sort of works even though it is intellectually dishonest! A little later, in 1996, Hugh Hansen made contact and asked me to come to New York for his Fordham IP conference in 1997. I have included the paper here. By then I was on the conference circuit and have never really been able to get off. I have made friends all over the world through it. If only it paid too!

Quite a lot of the pieces were published and I have tried to say where and when. I decided years ago that I would never assign my copyright or grant an exclusive licence—all I would grant was the right of first publication. I am glad I did that. I wrote to all the publishers of pieces here out of courtesy. Most replied to wish me well but one or two did not. Suppose I had had to ask for permission? Not unlike an orphan work problem—but with my own work! I thank all those publishers who did reply for their courtesy and will not name the inefficient non-repliers.

Why the cover picture? I first thought of IP related pictures—trade marks the subject of big cases, a picture of the hepatitis C virus (*Chiron*, my last case at the Bar), a line of music from a copyright case and so on. A bit hackneyed. Then I thought: why not use one of Wendy's pictures? There is no point in having a wife who is a Vice-President of the Royal Water Colour Society and going elsewhere. She has done some lovely Venice pictures and Venice is the spiritual home of patents. It had, in 1474, the first ever patent *law* (as opposed to individual monopoly grants by kings or princes)—all the basic elements are there, novelty/obviousness and enablement, as well as recitals explaining the justification for the system, which is as true now as it was then. And, through the annual meetings on the spartan Isola di Servolo in the middle of the Lagoon, much of the best work for creating the new Unitary Patent Court was done. It was done by judges and practitioners. Would that the politicians had been confined there (Lennie Hoffmann called it Alcatraz) until they came up with a better system than the one they threw together in great ignorance.

Thanks. My first are above all to Wendy who has put up with me all these years. None of this would have been possible without her. Other are to Kashif Syed who undertook a first sort of what might be publishable and what not, and then most especially to my research assistant Bhaavin Wallia. Not only did he find stuff I needed almost in an instant but he drove me to get on with it—sometimes I felt I was working for him. From further back in time I want to record my gratitude to the great teachers I had, and most especially Bill Cornish at the LSE, Anthony Walton (my pupil master) and Thomas Blanco White, my head of chambers.

Bentham House,
University College London
January 2015

Contents

Part I

Introduction

1

*Addresses of Welcome for Mr Justice Jacob**

In the High Court of Justice—Chancery Division

Before: Mr JUSTICE JACOB

1 OCTOBER 1993

ANTHONY *WALTON*, QC: If your Lordship pleases. A speech of welcome to a new judge would normally be very brief. As one Lord Chief Justice said to somebody in my position: 'Do hurry up. Our smiles of welcome are beginning to run out of sincerity.' But on this occasion I can inform my Lord, with my hand on my heart, that everything we say is going to be absolutely sincere, because the Bar in general and the Patent Bar in particular is always keen to welcome a good judge.

A vacancy having occurred, it is a very natural thing to appoint a patent man, in accordance with the well-known patent maxim 'Obvious to try', which has sometimes the unfortunate and sinister echo 'With what expectation of success?'

Here I think we have to be extremely careful and divide a judge's functions into what he does and how he does it. As to what he does,

* *These are reported at [1993] FSR 764 and were transcribed by Marten Walsh Cherer. Quite stupidly the Internet version of the FSR omits speeches of welcome or valediction to judges yet they are often huge fun—Westlaw are a grey lot.*

now we all know what a good judge is. When you come into court, the good judge smiles and says: 'Well, Mr Walton, I have read all the papers in the case and subject, of course, to anything your opponent may say, I think you have made out your case for the relief'.

When your opponent speaks, he looks terribly bored or, preferably, he goes to sleep, waking up at intervals to ask your opponent questions which cannot readily be answered and, when it is your turn, he says: 'I need not trouble you, Mr Walton. Take your relief'.

That is the good judge but, unfortunately, your Lordship has been sitting as Tribunal in various capacities in other jurisdictions and ugly rumours have been reaching us that you not only listen to what they say on the other side but you actually make notes of what they are saying.

Jacob J: Don't worry, Mr Walton. I cannot read them.

Anthony Walton, QC: As one disgruntled practitioner complained to me after appearing before your Lordship: 'The trouble with young Jacob is he is too damned judicial'. However, my Lord, take courage. You and I can think down the years of the steady stream of ornaments to the Bench, who very successfully managed to overcome this handicap, and there can be no doubt that the mantle[1] of one or other of them will fall upon the shoulders of my Lord.

The second thing is the way a judge actually does it. Now it has been said many times, and it will he said many times in the future, we do not have an inquisitorial system; we have a gladiatorial system, an adversarial system in which the judge is a referee, sending people off and deciding whether a goal has been scored. He has a laid-back, non-interventionist attitude. Here my Lord's track record is quite impeccable and right at the outset we can give him a starred first. Alike as my pupil, then as my junior and finally in collaboration in writing various books of one sort or another, your Lordship invariably took a laid-back and relaxed position.

You never wanted to spoil any of my fun by looking up the cases or drafting any of the documents. You let me have all the fun. You always took a great interest in the cases we were in together. When

[1] *This was a hidden reference to the fact that my red robes (complete with dinner stains from the Lord Mayor's banquet), which were given to me by Frank Brady, Aldous J's clerk, belonged originally to Lloyd-Jacob J, a judge who was not greatly respected by the Bar. When I went to the Court of Appeal I sold the robes and sent Frank the money, £1000.*

you and I were briefed in the case, never one day went by but at some stage or other you would put your head round the door asking how I was getting on, usually shaking your head very sadly and moving rapidly on.[2]

So the prognosis for my Lord being a good judge is obviously very great; but from a good judge the Bar is entitled to expect certain things and we do hope that you will hear our petition, our prayer, our entreaty. Steadily down the years you and I have encountered a whole series of beautiful points on which the grasp of intellectual property law manifested by other judges has not been very great. There are questions like 'What is a trade mark actually for?'[3] 'What is the difference between "adapted to distinguish" and "capable of distinguishing"?' 'What, if anything, is the meaning of section 4 of the 1938 Act?' 'How far can you take *Bismag v. Amblins*?'[4] 'Is the *Electrolux* decision logical?'[5] 'What constitutes use in public?' 'How does one interpret the Protocol on interpretation?' and many, many other points, which my Lord will realise have been undecided down the ages.

There will be a magnificent opportunity for my Lord to decide these points once and for all and our humble petition is this: 'For God's sake, don't do it!' Think of all us poor working boys at the Bar with our livings to earn. I know what my Lord will say: 'There are plenty of Euro-points, good juicy incomprehensible points'. Yes, it is very true, but they of have a habit getting decided—wrongly of course, but they do have a habit of getting decided.

The points I have mentioned and many others my Lord can think of are the good solid dependable points, the Gödel Undecidable points,

2 *I fear this is all true!*

3 *Does anyone actually know? In my foreword to Jeremy Phillips' 2003* Trade Mark Law: A Practical Anatomy, *I said 'some basic questions of trade mark law remain uncertain and probably always will be. [Jeremy] makes you understand that trade mark law has a lot in common with quantum mechanics. Each has at their heart an uncertainty principle'. And that was before the ECJ started inventing imprecise and elusive functions of trade marks.*

4 *The case that decided comparative advertising using a Part A registered trade mark was not allowed. As Walton prophesied, the extent to which it is allowed was bound to be controversial, the subject of uncertain law and the source of good fees for lawyers,* cf Case C-487/07 *L'Oréal v Bellure* [2009] ECR I-5185, Case C-533/06 *O2 v Hutchison 3G* [2008] ECR I-4241, Case C-236/08 *Google France v Louis Vuitton* [2010] ECR I-2417 and Case C-323/09 *Interflora v Marks and Spencer* [2011] ECR I-8625.

5 *Electrolux Ltd v Electrix Ltd* (No 2) [1954] 71 RPC 23. *Electrolux was about what constituted bona fide use of a trade mark to save a mark from a non-use attack. Again the law under the Directive has been uncertain—see Case C-40/01 Ansul BV v Ajax* [2003] ECR I-2439 *and Case C-259/02 La Mer Technology v Laboratoires Goemar* [2004] ECR I-1159.

the points which, like 'Schweppervescence',[6] have lasted the whole of our careers through. They have bought our first second-hand car; they have sent our children to school; but properly managed they will set up the usual endowment fund for our grandchildren. It would be most unkind if my Lord was to take these points away from us.

That only leaves, with great respect, a word of advice. During the course of our cases, you and I together, we have met many judges who were less than satisfactory; judges who favoured a particular type of litigant; judges who disfavoured a particular cause of action; judges who believed six impossible witnesses before breakfast; judges who—well, what is the good of beating about the bush—found against us. Their venial decisions are set out in the Law Reports and there will come a time (there is bound to come a time) when these Law Reports are presented to my Lord as precedents and your Lordship will be tempted, your Lordship will be sorely tempted, not merely to distinguish them but to say outright that they were wrongly decided in the light of all common sense and higher authority.

My respectful word of advice is this. My Lord, do not misunderstand me: I am not suggesting that my Lord should resist the temptation. None of the other judges do, so why should your Lordship? No, no, no; my simple advice is this. For the honour of the Patent Bar do try and keep the grin off your face.

My Lord, welcome home!
[*Cries of 'Wonderful!' and 'Well done!'*]
Jacob J: Thank you, Mr Walton.

Michael Silverleaf Esq: May it please you, my Lord. With your Lordship's permission, I would like to add a few words of welcome on behalf of the members of the junior Bar. It is traditional on these occasions to indulge in a little reminiscence, so I hope you will forgive me for recalling the occasion on which we met. I was a new and freshly scrubbed pupil and your Lordship was instructed as junior to Mr Gratwick on an important and difficult matter of breach of confidence. Your Lordship was then responsible for my first gainful employment at the Bar by paying me to devil the extensive legal research required. Your Lordship was a successful junior and, of course, far too busy to undertake it. This was my first contact with

[6] *A reference to a successful and attractive advertising campaign in the 1950s and '60s for Schweppes soft fizzy drinks: 'Schweppervescence lasts the whole drink through'.*

your great generosity in promoting new members of the Bar and getting their practices off the ground.

Shortly after this you took Silk and you have since then, to my knowledge, always been ready with a recommendation of a new barrister and generous with praise of the work done as a result. I and many other of today's juniors owe you a considerable debt for putting them forward and giving them such a helping hand. This is an important and valuable virtue, not often found in those who have already achieved success.

It is a curiosity of the English legal system that the most able and successful advocates are elevated to the Bench. It is they who are, by definition, least likely to adapt easily from the hurly-burly of preparing and putting forward a case to listening patiently and carefully to arguments which are often erroneous or inapplicable to the facts of the instant case.

Jacob J: What were you saying, Mr Silverleaf?

Michael Silverleaf Esq: My Lord, the temptation to interfere must be curbed.

The greater curiosity is that the transition is nearly always made with complete success and, as a result, the quality of the English judiciary is recognised worldwide.

Your Lordship fits the mould perfectly and we welcome the opportunity to watch you undergo the classic transition of poacher into gamekeeper, although in your Lordship's case it is more a question of Robin Hood being transformed into the Sheriff of Nottingham. My Lord, I am sure it is a transition which your Lordship will make without any effort.

Personally, I am very much looking forward to appearing before your Lordship. In saying that I know I speak for us all. We welcome you wholeheartedly to your new role and wish you a long and successful career.

Simon Cooke Esq: My Lord, may I on behalf of my side of the profession and, in particular, on behalf of the Patent Solicitors Association, welcome you to the Bench.

In the early days you personally caused me a great deal of trouble. For instance, in *Olin v Biorex*, you had a hand in the beautification of a certain Dr Simpkins, later you helped to woo the ego of Lord Diplock in the battle of the *GE* Trade Mark; and, much more recently, you winkled an amazing judgment out of the Court of Appeal in *Genetech*.

However, having had you on my side in recent actions, I have learned, maybe rather late in the day, to value your counsel and friendship. Sadly, we lose your great ability as an advocate but, happily, we look forward to accurate and speedy resolution of disputes by you in the future.

It is indeed a blessing to have two specialist judges again, because we can now tell clients that delays are less likely and that the United Kingdom is and will continue to be *the* forum for the settling of IP disputes.

We wish you a long and happy tenure of office.

Jacob J: Thank you, Mr Cooke.

John Brown Esq: My Lord, I am honoured to address you in your court when we are not on appeal from the Patent Office. On behalf of the President and the Council of the Chartered Institute, we congratulate you on your appointment.

We normally feel at the Chartered Institute a great loss when somebody resigns from the Institute. However, when somebody resigns for the reasons that your Lordship resigns, we feel very happy.

My Lord, we wish you a very long and successful career on the Bench. We trust that your judgments are not too critically reviewed and viewed by your previous compatriots.

Jacob J: Thank you, Mr Brown.

Mr Walton, it is 26 years almost to the day that I became your pupil. You bear a very heavy responsibility. But for you I would not be here and I would like those to know that if I ever should fall into error it is not my fault but yours. Don't blame me; blame Walton!

You will also know that my appointment is as a general Chancery judge. Some of you may just wonder whether I have had any appropriate training, experience or testing for the job, so I thought I might as well tell you. Let us be frank, for these are the days when everything should be in the open.

Testing: I was given a medical. They tested my hearing but not my listening; my eyesight but not my insight; my blood pressure but not in the presence of an aggravating counsel; my heartbeat but not my heart; my blood but not my bloodiness. They did not test my patience, understanding, temper, memory, clarity of thought or expression. My attention span was of no interest to them at all, and there was no investigation of my judgment.

As to experience, Mr Walton, you will be glad to know l have got some. I have done a whole week Deputy Judging. I am afraid I never sat in the Patents County Court, but there you are.

As to training in these other matters, I have had none really. I was wondering whether the Lord Chancellor's Department were looking at my schooling and university, looking for precedents in other judges who had been to the same school and college, and so on, and there is one who went to the same school, the same college and university. Maybe that is why they picked me. The other judge was Judge Jeffreys. Mr Walton, there you have it. You have got me with all that training.

I think there may be another reason why the Chancery Division is going to have me thrust upon it. They want a fresh approach—somebody who does not know anything about it at all.

The Chancery Bar must be quaking with uncertainty, and that is fair enough because I am quaking with uncertainty as well. As to the Patent Bar, of course they know me better and I hope they are quaking with certainty.

What will I make of this job? I do not know. My current ambition is simply to take it on a case-by-case basis and try and get each one done right and quickly and fairly. If I can, what I want to achieve is at least that some losing parties behave like one I acted for in front of Graham J. When we had lost, I said to him 'Well, we could appeal that; it might work'. He said: 'No, I'll take the opinion of that bloke'. If I can do that, then I think I am doing reasonably well.

Mr Walton, this is a very happy occasion for me. Very remarkably, there are present in court all those, except l think, Mr Blanco White, whom I joined in Chambers in 1967; all the barristers, my clerk Sidney Leigh, yourself, Kynric Lewis and Julian Jeffs, and I have to thank them, through you, again for all their help. Most of my pupils are here, many of my grandpupils and some of my great-grandpupils; and we all are well.

On a personal note, my wife and my sons are here and my father, my mother and my brothers, and even my cousin from San Francisco.

There are many others here from the Bar, solicitors and patent agents. I rather think I worked with each and every one of them and probably against each of them. I want to thank, through you, all of them for coming today. I want to thank them for all the fun we had over the years. I hope it will be as much fun up here—but I have a sneaking suspicion it will not be quite as good: but now is the time to put a bit back.

Mr Walton, I propose to try and do my best. Thank you very much.

Part II

General Non-IP

2

Pieces for My Almae Matres

Trinity College and LSE

I WENT TO three schools: a 'free thinking' school in Hampstead (King Alfred), a Comprehensive School (Mount Grace in Potters Bar) and finally St Paul's School. I only left Mount Grace because I wanted to go to Cambridge to read science; in 1953 you had to have Latin to go to Cambridge—whatever subject you were going to read. The science master (a lovely Indian chap) sadly told me I had to go to somewhere that did Latin. I scraped into St Paul's, doing the Scholarship exam. Although I didn't get one (not surprising since the exam included Latin, which I had only tried to learn for a month), I did do well in maths—so well taught at Mount Grace. St Paul's was organised in much the same way as Mount Grace, namely on a football league system (three up and three down) with setting for languages and maths. Mount Grace was probably the better of the two at the time. And it had girls!

I quite luckily got into Trinity College Cambridge from St Paul's.[1] *I read Natural Sciences Parts I and II. After that I went to the London School of Economics (LSE) and Grays Inn at the same time. I have written pieces for both Universities (and am proud to be an Honorary Fellow and Governor of the LSE). Here they are:*

[1] *I failed to get into UCL (University College London) where I hold my present Chair!*

AFTER DINNER SPEECH TO THE TRINITY COLLEGE CAMBRIDGE LAWYERS ASSOCIATION[2]

My Lords Ladies and Gentlemen,

Whenever there is a gathering of Trinity men and women there is apt to be a certain aura of how shall I say—smugness. We all just know we went to the finest College not just in Cambridge, or England but the world. How often does that comforting thought—'Trinity has more Nobel prize-winners than France—or Oxford for that matter'—come to mind?

Yet to some like me it is a bit of a delusion—basking in reflected glory only. I read natural sciences and got a double third—rather far from those Trinity Nobel prizewinning scientists.

I switched to law after leaving Trinity mainly because of Trinity's lawyers, both dons and undergraduates—they all were having such fun. I always admired the lawyer undergraduates—they did no work for most of the year and effortlessly collected firsts and 2.1s. We scientists had nine o'clock lectures six days a week. The lawyers could not even miss nine o'clock lectures for there were none to miss. The earliest lecture a lawyer could miss was at 10, and not even then every day of the week and never on a Saturday. The lawyer undergraduates debated topics such as *The Wagon Mound* and *Re Polemis*—which seemed so much easier than physics. And they spoke with such affection for their dons, Tony Jolowicz, Eli Lauterpacht and Tony Weir prominent amongst them. They made law infectious and I am grateful to them for catching the infection.

My friends even lured me sometimes to work in that little law library in Bishops Hostel. There, as a physics avoidance exercise, or as a work substitute, I read the odd case recommended by my lawyer friends. I still remember two of them.

One, I recall, was about whether someone could be an accomplice to a crime if the principal, by reason of duress, had committed no crime. The case involved a man, a woman and an Alsatian dog. It was called *Rex v Bourne*. My Girton girlfriend asked whether Rex was the name of the dog.

[2] *9 March 2009.*

Another case was called *Smith v Hughes*. It was about whether there had been an offence of soliciting in the street. Let me read a bit to you from [1960] 1 WLR 830:

> [T]he magistrate found, inter alia, that on January 9, 1960, between 12.40 a.m. and 1.0 a.m. the defendant solicited men passing in the street for the purposes of prostitution from a closed ground-floor window of No. 39 Curzon Street (the window being some 3 feet from some 4 feet high railings which bounded the pavement on the side of the premises). The defendant's method of soliciting the men was (i) to attract their attention to her by tapping on the window pane with some metal object as they passed in the street in front of her and (ii) having so attracted their attention, to invite them in for a price which she indicated by extending three fingers of her hand and indicating the correct door of the premises. On one occasion the price so indicated by the defendant was agreed and the man entered the premises, leaving some 15 minutes later. On another occasion, the price so indicated by the defendant was not agreed by the man concerned who, in his turn, made a counter-proposal as to price by extending two fingers of his hand. That counter-proposal was not accepted by the defendant and that man walked away.

She was acquitted on the grounds that being behind a window is not being in or on the street.

But back to Trinity and greatness. I looked up to our great lawyers. There are no Nobel prizes for law. And anyway Nobel prizes only started in 1901. So there are no Trinity lawyer Nobel prize-winners.

But there were some who would have got the prize if it had been awardable.

I mention, first, Francis Bacon. He was not only Lord Chancellor, but Treasurer of this Inn [The dinner was in Gray's] three times. His statue stands outside our Hall. He went up to Trinity in 1573 at the age of 12 and joined this Inn when he was 15. His philosophy was advanced for its age—a typical Trinity man—and one that espoused what we now call the scientific method. Two other things: when he was impeached for taking money from two litigants, his defence was that he decided the case on the merits and anyway found against them; and he died in pursuance of science, catching a fever after getting too cold trying to stuff chickens with ice to see if they could be preserved—a kind of early Dr Birdseye.

Next Bacon's contemporary, Sir Edward Coke. He went up to Trinity in 1567 leaving in 1570 without a degree. The DNB [*Dictionary of National Biography*] does not say why. His *Commentaries* and reports made a secure foundation for the future of the common law, both here and, later, in the US. His fierce defence of the independence of the judiciary was and remains vital—even now our politicians often do not understand it, as for example when the Home Secretary wanted to meet the Law Lords.[3] It is worth reminding ourselves of Coke's words in refusing to allow the King to take part in a case:

> God had endowed His Majesty with excellent science, and great endowments of nature; but his Majesty was not learned in the laws of his realm of England ... which law is an act which requires long study and experience, before that a man can attain to the cognizance of it.

Even at 76 he played a great part in the Petition of Right. His contribution to democracy and rule of law was Nobel-prize worthy.

So also was the contribution of Thomas Erskine. For it was he who laid down another foundation stone of liberty: the independence of the Bar and the right of an accused to be represented. He matriculated in 1776 when he was 36 having had a career both in the Navy and Army. The point was that those who had a degree could be called more quickly. Moreover as the son of a nobleman he was entitled to a degree without examination, so he did not have to be in residence. His career at the Bar was meteoric. Famously he defended Tom Paine on a charge of libel (criminal libel it must have been) for publishing *The Rights of Man*. And in the course of that he famously said:

> From the moment that any advocate can be permitted to say, that he *will* or will *not* stand between the Crown and the subject arraigned in the court where he daily sits to practise, from that moment the liberties of England are at an end.

So we can justly claim that Trinity lawyers played a major part in establishing freedom under the law.

Another Trinity lawyer did not come into the same class: Judge Jeffries of the bloody assizes. He went to Trinity in 1662 (interestingly from my personal point of view, also my school, St Paul's) and became Lord Chief Justice in his 30s. Following the Monmouth rebellion he was in charge of the West Country assizes at which the alleged rebels were charged. Starting in Winchester on 26th August 1685 and ending in Wells on 23rd September more than 1,400 prisoners were tried. Ultimately 300 were executed, 800–850 were transported and others died in prison of goal fever. The King made Jeffries Lord Chancellor for his efforts, but after the Glorious

[3] *See footnote 6 to Chapter 6 'Be Ye Ever So High'.*

Revolution he was caught trying to escape the country and ended his days in the Tower.

Other famous Trinity lawyers of history include Chief Justice Tindall, James Scarlett, later Lord Abinger, Lord Cottenham and Lord Lyndhurst. Moreover we have had great academics: a top two of the nineteenth century, Pollock and Maitland, were Trinity.

In the twentieth century we have Lord Slynn, the first English judge in the ECJ [European Court of Justice] and Lord Justice Scrutton. He read Moral Sciences, whatever that may mean. He was described as 'lanky and uncouth, and was thought to be the only Englishman who had never shaved in his life'. It is said that when he was appointed to the High Court bench the Master of Trinity, JJ Thompson said 'I remember Scrutton. No imagination'. That may have been true, but he knew a lot about charterparties.

Overall we can say this: that without the Trinity lawyers of the past the world would be a poorer place.

What then of now—well the general pattern has been stable for some time. Three or four Trinity judges in the CA [Court of Appeal] one or two in the Lords, a fair scattering at first instance and mass of talented Trinity lawyers out there in the professions. TCC law is as good now as it ever was. No change there then: *Semper Eadem*.[4]

I give you the toast. TCC.

Comment

Actually I was not all that happy at Trinity. College was fun but the work was too hard for me. I tried but found the science difficult. In retrospect I don't think we were taught at all well—we were not one of those years whose intake which, for reasons no one can control or predict, take off. By the middle of my second year I decided I had to quit science. I had little imagination. The University had no useful advice, though they did hand me a boring pamphlet from the Chartered Institute of Patent Agents. It portrayed the career of a patent agent as one of excruciating dullness. So I turned to what many friends had in mind and what my Dad had done—become a barrister. I remember phoning home from a telephone box on the edge of Parker's Piece. Dad was delighted—he had never tried to steer me and here I was choosing to go that way.

[4] *The College motto—'Always the same'.*

I joined Grays Inn in the summer of 1962 and started the necessary dining (you had to get in three years' worth before you could be called to the Bar). I joined some of the parties from Cambridge who went down to London to dine (three dinners for one legal term) in one of the Inns. I felt at home even before I started learning any law. Yet rather than change to law for my third year, I elected to do Natural Sciences Part II (mainly physics). I am afraid I ended up with a double third—one of my enduring sorrows. But I am far from sorry that I tried.

When I came down I went to a crammer to do the Bar Part I exams (they correspond roughly to what is now called the 'conversion course'). You mug up a great deal of law and splurge it out on exam day—not so different from what barristers actually do: mug a case up and splurge it out before the judge. Grays Inn had a 'student advisor', a nice old gent from King's College called Jimmy Wellwood. Dad said I should go and see him. 'What for?' I asked. 'I don't know,' said Dad, 'but there can't be any harm.' So I went.[5] Jimmy said, 'You should do a law degree—there is an evening LLB course at the LSE.' I went home thinking this was ridiculous. When I told Dad he said, 'Yes, I'll pay.' I said, 'But I'm already doing Bar Part I.' Dad said I could at least try to do both, and I agreed.

It was the best thing that ever happened to me work-wise. Within a day or two (I started late in the term) I found myself in a contract class of eight graduates given by an assistant lecturer called William Cornish. He taught me for three of the four years of the evening degree. I have never recovered, I am glad to say. The LSE was transformative. It had brilliant teachers, including some young barristers such as Lord-Chancellor-to-be Derry Irvine. And I found myself in a quite the opposite sort of year from my Cambridge year—almost everyone in the year was infected with the joy of learning the law. The final year,'66–'67 was particularly hard for I did a pupillage, my finals for the degree[6] and got married. The earlier, intervening year '65–'66, I spent doing my LSE Part I exams, a Grays Inn Scholarship exam (I got one but I missed the top one by missing a point in the viva) and teaching law part-time at Kingston College of Technology—to business students. Joe Harper who gave me the job says there was a complaint about one of my contract lectures.

[5] *It is a good rule to try things out even if you see no point before you do.*

[6] *I had done my Bar exams in 1965 and was called to the Bar in June that year. Crikey! It will be 50 years next year.*

Apparently (I have no memory of it) I taught the facts of Carlill v Carbolic Smoke Ball Company *by saying 'Mrs Carlill, the plaintiff, wrote a letter to the directors of the company. It said:*

> *Dear Sirs,*
> *Your advertisement promised £100 to anyone who caught flu when using your product. Well I have been smelling your balls for three months and have caught the flu. Please may I have my £100?'*

The complaint about me was rejected. I hope it would be now, but one can't be sure.

FOR *OBITER*[7]

From my room at the top of the West Building of the Royal Courts of Justice I can see bits of the LSE. So I haven't come very far since I graduated in 1967. The fact that *Obiter* has been revived is welcome news—and of course I agreed to write for it when your editor asked. I owe a lot to LSE—and to the students' Law Society, which I chaired in 1966. The editor suggested I should write about 'the role and obligations of a judge'. But that sounds a bit heavy; if you want to know about that, read Lord Bingham's 'The Business of Judging' and, if not, read it anyway.

What I thought I would try and do is to contrast what I do now, what I did at the Bar and what I did as a law student. Curiously I have concluded that what I do now is closer to being a law student than being a barrister.

I begin with a story—a true story told me by Judge Gerald Butler (also of LSE). When he was at the Bar he went into Sweet & Maxwell's bookshop (then at the bottom of Chancery Lane—it is now, as one would expect, a restaurant). He met Geoffrey Lane, then a Lord Justice of Appeal (and future Lord Chief). Lane was looking at the Nutshell on Landlord and Tenant. When asked why he said, 'I'm sitting with two Chancery chaps tomorrow on a landlord and tenant case and don't know anything about it. I'm trying to mug up so I don't look too stupid. But don't tell Bessie!' [This last was an RAF expression from the war—meaning keep quiet—Lane was a bomber pilot].

[7] *When I was at the LSE we had a student law magazine called* Obiter. *Apparently it fell by the wayside for a bit but some students in the late '90s revived it and asked me (then a Chancery judge) to write a piece for it.*

That encapsulates a lot of judging. Both sides know a lot more about the case than you do. Your first job is to try to understand what the problem you are supposed to solve is. And often you start with very little background knowledge. Then you are in just the same position as the law student. She starts with no knowledge of a particular subject, tort say. She has to learn the basic rules (as to foreseeability, remoteness and so on). Being at the LSE she will be taught to question those rules (Why are they what they are? Should they be what they are? Do they need modifying?) and she has to apply them to problems. True they are problems set by lecturers and professors rather than real life—but that is a trivial difference—especially since most problems set in university are variants of real life cases. She has to predict what the judge will do. And the judge has to decide using the established rules to fashion answers for new situations.

Being a fighting lawyer involves some of those skills—but it involves more. You have to think of arguments—and in our system particularly—about evidence. The great Southern General, Jackson, who won so many battles, when asked the secret of his success said: 'I get there the fastest with the mostest.' So with law cases—our system requires the parties to bring their evidence to court—the court does not go out and get it. So you have to think about witnesses and documents a lot. You are essentially creative. The same goes for the applicable law. I used to tell my pupils that law books (especially reports) should be seen not as repositories of learning and scholarship—they contain the swords (and shields) you are going to use in battle. Some lawyers take all this too far—they see things so aggressively that they are unable to put themselves in the position of the judge. Rambo lawyers are one of the menaces out there—in other systems as well as ours. So they never know when to quit—in poker terms betting on their clients' cases (and with their clients' money!) when they have only got a pair. Good lawyers know when to quit as well as when to fight.

Now the sort of thing I have just described is hardly possible to teach outside practice. Whereas what a judge does—at least once the facts are decided—is possible for law students to follow. We are doing nearly the same job—only the judge has been doing it a lot longer than the student.

Both of us need to understand *and question* the existing rules. Keep doing that and LSE law graduates will remain some of the best in the land. And I hope the judges can keep up.

3

*Knowledge of the World and the Act of Judging**

LORD CHIEF JUSTICE Hewart once famously said 'Justice must not only be done but must manifestly and undoubtedly be seen to be done'.[1] Did he require more than was necessary? Is it enough if justice is seen to be done: never mind if it is actually done? A purist might say not. But hear me out. In ancient China it is said there was a mythical one-horned beast called the *xiezhi*—the beast of justice. You put the plaintiff and defendant on either side of it. The one it touched with its horn lost. Not only was this much quicker and cheaper than all our current procedures, but it satisfied the population. Justice was seen to be done. From the point of view of society all was well. The same went for trial by ordeal, whether of fire, water, knives or some other horror—a process carried out not only in mediaeval Europe but in many other countries and cultures.

Behind these methods of trial was the notion of a God directing justice. Judges derived their authority from God and did not need to explain themselves very much. Incidentally we still have vestiges of that—most particularly in the taking of the oath. Swearing to tell the truth by Almighty God is the default method for a witness—and it can still actually work. I once had a young Muslim man, made to lie by his overbearing and dishonest father, choke as tried to take the oath on the Qur'an.

* *A paper given to the Congrés de La Magistrature (about 500 Canadian judges) (Québec City, November 2008).*

[1] *R v Sussex Justices, Ex parte McCarthy* [1924] 1 KB 256, [1923] All ER 233.

Thing have moved on. Society now expects the act of judging to be carried out by a rational process of assessment and weighing of evidence: not only in relation to fact finding, but also in relation to the interpretation of the rules of law itself. For justice to be seen to be done, the modern judge must give reasons—to explain to a critical public why he or she decides a case. And most particularly, for justice to be seen to be done, the judge must explain why the losing party lost—which involves stating and answering that party's main points.

What can best place a judge to carry out this task? I start by saying what will not do—pomposity. A judge is a person of power and authority. There is a real danger it can go to his or her head. Common lawyers even have a word for this—'judgitis'. I do not know whether other legal systems have a similar special word: whether they do or not I am sure they know the phenomenon.

In the early years of the Industrial Revolution and well into the twentieth century, in my country and I suspect most other common law countries, society placed the judge on a particularly high pedestal. Society itself encouraged judgitis. They even wanted it so that it could be ridiculed, as they still do. Here is a story from the Edwardian era about a particularly pompous, self-important man called Mr Justice Darling. A celebrity of the time was a music hall artist called George Robey—a household name. There came a case where FE Smith—later Lord Chancellor—was before Mr Justice Darling. He mentioned George Robey in the course of his address. 'Who is George Robey?' asked Mr Justice Darling. FE Smith smiled: 'Oh my Lord, he is the darling of the music halls.'

Judgitis continued. In 1936, Chief Justice Hewart, in his speech to the Lord Mayor's Banquet, said: 'Her majesty's judges are satisfied with the almost universal admiration in which they are held.' And the press said nothing.

These days I believe that judgitis is a disease somewhat under control—though no one should ever think it can be eliminated and the fight against it must go on. It is I think a personal fight for each judge.

The next thing to be avoided—an aspect of judgitis—is to appear unworldly. As if the things that are part of the life of the ordinary citizen are below his or her exalted status. Legend has it that a judge in the 1960s once asked 'Who or what are the Beatles?' It was a legend—the story is attached to no particular judge, but it was credible. The press have told the story often since and will continue to do so.

So judgitis and remoteness are undesirable attributes. What about those which are desirable? Following the theme of 'appearance' with which I started, a modern judge must at least appear to have knowledge of the world—I suppose we all ask teenage children or grandchildren about the names of popstars and celebs so as to at least appear 'with it'. In a music case involving Bruce Springsteen, when his counsel got up, I said, 'Now I am supposed to ask, who is Bruce Springsteen,' in a what, with hindsight, seems a rather pathetic attempt to show I was at one with the common man.

But appearing to be at one with the common man—to be 'with it'—is not enough either. The judge must be more than superficially worldly—he (by which I include she) should in fact be so. Sometimes judicial reasoning explicitly appeals to knowledge of the world. Long ago, in 1877, Lord Justice James asked this question in a passing off case: 'Now, what could have been the only motive which can be suggested to a man of the world by a man of the world of the Defendants in doing that'?[2] And in considering whether a magistrate was right to hold that what was really a permanent garage was not a 'structure' because it was made of canvas on a fixed frame, Lord Goddard said:

> I think, therefore, that we must hold that the magistrate did not direct himself properly in this matter. Had he asked himself, as a man of the world, as an ordinary citizen—the man on the Stoke Newington bus—whether it was a structure, I think that he must have come to the conclusion that this was a structure.[3]

And of course the favourite child of the common law, the reasonable man—the man on the Clapham omnibus[4]—*le bon père de famille* as you say in Quebec—is a man of the world.

So, from the point of view of public acceptance of what we do, we must seem to be in touch—to have knowledge of the world. How is that to be achieved? The only really effective way to seem to be something is to be it. In reality it is not enough to seem to be in touch. You can't get away with pretending all the time. So a judge actually does require knowledge of the world.

This truth has important implications in at least two ways: how judges are to be chosen, and whether and if so how they are to be trained.

I start with judge appointment. The biggest difference across the world is between systems which have career judges and those which

2 *Orr-Ewing v Johnson* (1877) 13 Ch D 434, 451.
3 *LCC v Tan* [1954] 1 WLR 371.
4 Attributed to Lord Bowen.

have judges appointed from practising lawyers. I once discussed this with a distinguished German lawyer who was about 50 years old at the time. I said: 'Would you like to be a judge?' After a long pause he said: 'You know, I have never thought about it—because it is not possible in Germany.' Then, after another pause, he added: 'But, yes.' I thought what a pity. The German judicial system was the loser. I have had similar discussions with French lawyers—with much the same response. The divide broadly follows the divide between common law and civil law countries. A few countries, eg Holland, have a mixture between career-only and bar-appointed judges. Some throw in appointment of academics.

As regards knowledge of the world, I suspect few would challenge the proposition that a bar-appointed judge is likely to be better placed than a career judge. A judge whose only worldly experience is school, law at university, judge school, judicial continuing education and actual judging is not given much of a chance to learn the ways of the world. That is not to say that there are not many fine civil law judges for there are. But it is surely easier to judge if one has experience of actual clients and of actual case preparation. The best gamekeepers were once poachers; as the saying goes 'set a thief to catch a thief'. There is confirmation from the opposite perspective: a good friend of mine, Jan Brinkhof, was the widely respected President of the Court of Appeal in the Hague. In his early 50s he changed course, becoming a practising lawyer for the first time. He says he was surprised to learn what real clients (and opponents) were like, that he wished he had had such experience when he was a judge. Another judge I know, Judge Lv Guo Quang, Vice President of the Shanghai No 2 Intermediate People's Court, spent three years during the Cultural Revolution out in the country planting vegetables and studying the Little Red Book. He did not like it much, but the knowledge of the world he gained has surely helped him as man and as judge.

I turn to the process of judicial appointment. I can only really talk about what we do in England and Wales (remember Scotland is different). Other countries will have different systems but I suspect all of them have moved or will have moved along similar lines. In England it was once simple and cheap—but far from 'transparent'. A man from the Lord Chancellor's Office went round the judiciary and a few select others (eg the Chairman of the Bar) and took what were called 'soundings'. The Lord Chancellor then made an appointment. Formally it was by the Queen—in the case of Court of Appeal and

House of Lords judges on the recommendation of the Prime Minister. That is how it was done when I was appointed 15 years ago. Moreover there was no requirement of any prior training or judicial experience by way of sitting as a deputy judge. Other countries worried about this sort of thing earlier. Here is a story from the USA: Chief Justice Burger held a conference about judicial appointments where the need for prior assessment and training was discussed. A man from the Lord Chancellor's department was there as an observer. He was heard to murmur: 'I don't see the problem. All we do is take a barrister and turn him round.'

Now things are different. There is political if not public pressure for greater openness and for diversity. A Judicial Appointments Commission was established in April 2006. It has a lay Chairman and 14 Commissioners, five judicial, five professional and four lay. The presence of the lay members shows something significant about a public perception that judges should have knowledge not merely of law but of the world. You would not sensibly put lay people on a panel choosing a brain surgeon or a professor of physics—though I dare say sometimes it is done. The Commission has explicit goals of equal opportunities and diversity of race and sex, though at the same time the ultimate criterion is merit. It goes about its work in an elaborate and necessarily bureaucratic way. People have to apply to be judges—even write an essay about why they think they would be good at it. Consultation forms are sent here there and everywhere—followed by elaborate short-listing and interviews. It costs nearly £9m a year to run—and that does not include any of the time put in by consultees.

Are English judges any more aware of the world, more diverse, as a result of all this? Not so far. It is early years but the number of women or black or Muslim appointees remains low. It will change in the future—simply because more able lawyers of these groups are coming through to appointable age. For myself I doubt whether the expensive change from secret soundings has produced any better, or indeed, different results. What has changed is perception—the appointees are seen to be chosen more fairly and to be more 'of the world' than in times past.

Before finishing with judicial appointment I end with a question to which I do not know the answer. I have noticed that the proportion of women judges in Canada seems to be much higher than that in England or indeed anywhere else in the common world I have been. I do not know why and would like to. I would add that there is a very high proportion of women judges in France. One judge told me why. She said, 'We are paid very badly—like nurses—so we 'ave 'usbands who earn the money.'

Next, and briefly, judicial training. Some countries have long had a substantial continuing programme of judicial training. Germany, which spends more on its judiciary per head of population, has two permanent judicial training facilities for its judges. In England we once had none. Now we have a Judicial Studies Board with an annual budget of about £8m—which of course does not include the cost of training provided by judges. This body clearly helps a lot with judicial awareness—and provides an important means of keeping judges in touch. Other countries are increasing judicial training—both of a formal kind and the informal kind provided by things such as this conference.

Of course none of this can really make us men or women with great knowledge of the world. It can help somewhat, but really it all depends on the individual. We can but do our best to remain aware, to listen, to read. And the wider our experience the more we can develop what I think is a key attribute—the ability to put yourself in the place of the other man or woman, whether they be litigant or witness or anyone else. This attribute—empathy—is precious; beyond just the courts it is one of the greatest protections against cruelty and one of the greatest forces for peace. The truth is that knowledge of the world, that is to say of others, is, or ought to be, an aspiration for everyone, whether they are judges or not.

POSTSCRIPTS

1. *Another Judgitis story. In the mid-eighties I was in Chambers at lunchtime when some solicitors rang up in a bit of a panic. They acted for Penguin Books who were about to publish a biography of the new football 'superstar' Paul Gascoigne—known as 'Gazza'. The book was not 'authorised' and was simply called 'Gazza'. The solicitors had just been told that Mr Gascoigne was going to apply for an* ex parte *injunction at 2 pm. Would I go over and help prevent its grant? Off I went. We found ourselves before the Honourable Mr Justice Harman, a very good judge but one who did suffer both from judgitis and a love of headline*

grabbing. Michael Silverleaf, my opponent, opened. It went something like this:

Silverleaf: *My Lord I appear for Mr Paul Gascoigne, perhaps the most famous person in the country today.*

Harman J: *Really? He can't be as famous as the Duke of Wellington was in his time.*

Silverleaf: *He probably is more so, as the evidence will show. He is known as 'Gazza', a unique name.*

Harman J: *No it isn't. There is an opera of that name, the 'Gazza Ladra'. I think it means 'silken ladder'.*

Jacob: *No, my Lord, it means 'Thieving Magpie', by Rossini.*

The farce continued a little while longer before Harman J, rightly, threw the application out. I am quite sure Harman J worked his jokes up before he came into court. The case is a good example of the overreaching ambitions of the world of celebrity. It is preposterous to suggest that the law (whether passing off or registered trade marks or anything else) can prevent the publication of a biography of a person by simply using their name. So in a sense Harman J was right to portray the whole thing as ridiculous. The press reported it by suggesting that Harman J said he hadn't heard of Gazza, but they made that bit up—it made a better story.

2. *Women as judges. I have a few comments on this subject. I begin by saying where I am coming from. My mother was a feminist and my father took no fewer than six women pupils before his appointment as a Master in 1956. The story of the first of these is worth reading. In those days there were no such things as 'pupillage committees'. You just applied to individual barristers to be their pupil (and were supposed to pay 100 guineas). There was undoubtedly prejudice, though far from total. The story is told in my Dad's own words in Chapter 5 ('My Dad and Gray's Inn').*

   The story of the first woman at the Patent Bar is worth telling too. Mary Vitoria had a PhD in chemistry but had decided to study law and had taken a law degree. She had got a job as a lecturer at Queen Mary College (as it was then called) down the Mile End Road (as the Law Department was then situated). In about 1977 she applied to me for a pupillage but with no intention of actually going to the Bar. I took her on and quickly found she was both brilliant and very fast. Towards the end of her year she asked whether she could join chambers. I told the others, there was no real problem (though one member of chambers raised the lavatory objection!). So Blanco White, head of chambers) told the clerks:

Blanco White: *Sydney, we are thinking of taking on Miss Vitoria.*
Sydney: *No sir.*
Blanco White: *Why not?*
Sydney: *She wouldn't get any work.*
Blanco White: *Well ... never mind.*

To be fair to Sydney he belonged to a different era, having first come into the Temple as a very junior clerk in 1925. And once Mary was taken on, Sydney treated her just as he treated all other young juniors, with respect, care and encouragement. Two years after she was taken on the then junior clerk John Call (still in chambers now, having taken over from Sydney as Senior Clerk in about 1976), said to me: 'I don't know what we'd do without Mary!' She was the first woman silk at the Patent Bar. When Mary was taken on she was the sole woman in a set of about eight. Now there are 30 of whom seven are women—more to the junior end of chambers though one has taken silk. They are inundated with work.

There might have been an earlier woman at the Patent Bar. For Margaret Thatcher, like Mary, had a PhD in chemistry and after call to the Bar (unlike Mary she did not get a first in the Bar Final) applied for pupillage in patent chambers. She certainly applied to what we in our chambers called 'the politician's chambers' (both Sir Lionel Heald QC, a Conservative Attorney-General, and Sir Stafford Cripps KC, a Labour Chancellor of the Exchequer, were there). Whether she applied to my chambers is not clear. Sydney said she did but was not convincing about it. Blanco White and Walton said she did not. Almost certainly she was refused at the Patent Bar because of her sex. In the end she got a pupillage in tax chambers with John Brightman and later, when Prime Minister, appointed him to the Court of Appeal and then the House of Lords.

There is much debate these days about whether there should be some sort of positive discrimination. As I pointed out in my Quebec lecture, we have a much lower proportion of women judges than they do in Canada. I asked why? Rosalie Abella's witty answer ('we do it on merit') I do not think is the real reason. That reason lies partly in the structure of the English and Welsh profession—in particular the divided profession which they hardly have in Canada. For, however much a set of chambers may support women members (eg as we do with rent and expenses 'holidays' for women with babies), the reality is that barristers are sole practitioners. They develop and maintain their individual reputations with solicitors by being there and doing their jobs well. If you are not there (the reason does not matter—a baby, a sabbatical, illness or anything else), your name with your key customers is bound to fade—out of sight out of mind as the saying goes. Vigorous positive action by way of promotion when you return can help but you are very apt to have fallen behind those who did not have time off. Lord Sumption was against positive discrimination in his Bar Council Law Reform Lecture, saying that we should just let things develop.[5] *Lady Hale was for what she called 'affirmative action' but against positive discrimination in her Kuttan Menon Memorial Lecture 'Equality in the Judiciary'.*[6] *But what is the difference? Lord Neuberger said we should do more, but it is not clear what, in his Rainbow Lecture 2014 on diversity.*[7] *As for myself, I think we should just let things develop. Even since Lady Hale's lecture only two years ago, the number of women judges in the Court of Appeal has gone up by four (from four to eight out of 38; percentages—especially to decimal points—are not a good way to present these sort of figures). And notice that most of the eight are in the lower age bracket so the proportion will continue to grow.*

Nor do I espouse the suggestion of a career judiciary. That in my opinion is the sure way to devalue our judiciary. None of my continental friends in the judiciary think it a good idea, as I recounted in my Quebec lecture. Napoleon gave it to them (or largely did so). It is not the pragmatic English way.

Finally I would add this: of much more concern than proportions of women in the judiciary is the problem of making it possible for the impoverished young to become lawyers. That really matters for it is no good having a 'diverse' bench consisting of close to equal numbers of men and women if they all come from the same class of society. The reality is that it is much harder now for those from low-income families to become lawyers than it was in the 1960s and 1970s. That is where the focus should be.

[5] 15 November 2012.

[6] 21 February 2013.

[7] Lord Neuberger suggested that there might be some bias in chambers against women for the pragmatic reason that the mentality of most chambers is very much skewed in favour of barristers who are available for solicitors all the time. I think the problem is not so much attitudes in chambers but the 'out of sight out of mind' problem.

4

My Dad and Gray's Inn[*]

THE EDITOR ASKED me to do an obituary of my father, Honorary Master Sir Jack IH Jacob QC. But many obituaries appeared in the press and specialist legal periodicals. To write yet another could add little about his formal achievements—besides, writing an obituary for his father is not really a son's job. *Graya* deserves something different. About five years ago, when his last and paralysing illness was well upon him, the family asked him to dictate memories. I thought that it might be better for his own words to appear in *Graya*—I am sure that is what he would have wanted.

They need a brief introduction. My father was one of 10 children (nine boys) born into an extraordinarily narrow community, the Sephardic, Jewish, British, people of the International Settlement of Shanghai. His parents had come, via India, from Baghdad. It was an arranged marriage, recorded in the British Consulate, which was an imposing building by the park which famously had the notice 'no dogs or Chinese'. My grandfather was 35, my grandmother 15. Dad was the third son, born when she was 18.

He was brought up as a religious Jew. But the most formative influence on him was the Shanghai Public School for Boys. It was built at the turn of the century and manned by Oxbridge teachers it looks rather like UCS [University College School] in Hampstead. It was really an old-style grammar school, not as 'classy' as the Cathedral school. Schooling was based on the Empire—and it was at school

[*] *Graya* (2002)

that the idea of becoming a lawyer in England came to him. This is what he said:

> Of course I couldn't stay and have lunch at school as it wasn't kosher, in fact the very opposite. There was a very obnoxious smell of roast pig. [Later my father enjoyed ham and bacon.] After the morning session at school, I used to rush home for lunch. It would be all ready for us and would consist of a substantial meal. In particular, on Mondays we had a milk lunch, on Thursdays a Chinese lunch. As soon as we got home, we ate it and then rushed back to school. We used to travel by train. We would stand on the platform where the driver was and talk to him as he was controlling the tramcar. When it reached the end, we ran off the tram and into school. I remember on one occasion when one of the other boys was standing by the tram driver. We were discussing what we were going to do after school. I told them I wanted to become a lawyer. Most of them could not believe that. Most of them wanted to become engineers. I said that if that was what they wanted to do then that was very good as well. It was when I was talking to the boys on the train that I first thought of the idea of becoming a lawyer or a student in London.

As the boys grew up a possibility for one of them to go to London emerged. The eldest, Isaiah, was expected to remain. The next, Joseph (who Dad said was the cleverest, spoke eight languages and was once described to me in Hong Kong by an old schoolmate 'as the best Bridge player in the world') was not trusted to be a good Jewish boy. So, my Dad got the chance. Here is how he told it.

> My school reports were not all that brilliant, in fact I was more in the middle of the school class than otherwise. There were of course, exceptions to this, the most important of which were the views of Mr Bennett who was then my form master. In December 1924, he added the following to the report: 'would do well at an English university'. This message came whilst my mother and father were sitting on the floor mourning the death of my father's mother. My mother read it and was most struck by it. She kept on referring to it and took into account the fact that by this time she knew that I wanted to go to university.

My father brought that school report to England. I still have it. He arrived here in 1926. He could not afford Oxbridge. Initially he went to the LSE on the grounds that it was the only London college to accept fees in instalments. He changed to UCL (University College London) upon getting a scholarship there. He joined Gray's:

> So far as the Bar was concerned, it was necessary to become a student of one of the four Inns of Court and be admitted by one of them. On the basis of the papers that I read about all this, it was less expensive for me

> from the money point of view to join Gray's Inn rather than the other Inns of Court. This was because Gray's Inn permitted a student to become a member of the Inn by letting two householders warrant your good behaviour as a student, whereas in the other Inns you were required to deposit £100 as a guarantee for good behaviour. I was able to get two householders to stand in as guarantors of my good behaviour. They were rabbis at the two synagogues that I knew about, Lauderdale Road synagogue and the old synagogue in the City of London. Both came up to the Inn separately and signed up guaranteeing good behaviour and agreeing to pay a penalty of £100 for misbehaviour.

The first person my father saw in the Inn was a junior clerk—Mr Davies. When I first went to the Inn, in 1963, he was the first person I saw too. Dad was interviewed:

> My application to join Gray's Inn faced a real set back when the Under Treasurer required me to attend before him. When I attended upon the Under Treasurer of Gray's Inn, he greeted me very nicely and asked me a number of questions about myself and my family. Then, out of the blue, he asked me to spell the word 'certificate'. When I had spelt it he burst out laughing and he said to me that I had got it wrong in my application. What I had written was 'certericate'. It would have been a great pity to be refused entry to Gray's Inn or suffer delayed entry simply because of the misspelling of one very common word. Anyway, I was admitted to the Inn in September 1927.

The last time he lunched in the Inn was in the autumn of 1997. We sat on High Table. He realised it was about 60 years since he had first come into Hall. Actually, of course, the Hall he first entered was the original Elizabethan one. But to him it was the same room: he pointed out where he had first seen a young student standing in the doorway to the right at the back of Hall—the young Patrick Devlin who had a presence even then.

My father loved Hall. He told me how, in the War, he came the morning after the firebombs fell, to see the smouldering ruin—and cried. He had his 90th birthday party in Hall. And we held the Gathering to celebrate his life there—as he would have wanted. It was a non-religious celebration, for my father had ceased to believe shortly after he arrived in England:

> I immediately started to eat my dinners although at that time I was refraining from eating meat. Dinners consisted mainly of curry dishes. I then started not to worry about what I was eating. At one stage during the eating of dinners at Gray's Inn I had their meat dishes as well.

Dad got a first at London University and a 2.1 in the Bar exams. He won some important scholarships:

> I must have been able to pick up the law quickly because as it happened I won the Arden scholarship and also the Cecil Peace prize. The amount of money was quite considerable for that period. The Peace prize was £100 and the Arden scholarship £160 per year for three years. There was a stipulation for the Arden that the prize money should be used in England. This was an argument that I used when I had to explain to my parents and family why it was that I stayed in England.

I once saw a letter from Glanville Williams who was runner up for the Peace Prize. It asked Dad whether he would send him a copy of the winning essay, offered to return it (no photocopies then!) and pay the postage. There was a return letter too: containing a detailed critique! Sadly, the letters, and the ever-so-badly-typed essay, have gone missing.

Dad remembered his Call night:

> I was called to the Bar on 28th November 1931. It was a great occasion for me. I had to hire an evening dress. I remember that I enjoyed my food and drink immensely. I think it was on that occasion that I became drunk for the first time. I stood on the table and addressed the gathering after the Masters had left the dining room in Hall and at some stage, when I was a bit beyond it, I got very drunk and they put me under the tap for a while. When I awoke the next morning I had a pretty sore head to look after.

He got a pupillage with a man called Richard Levy. It is a reflection of the times that Levy advised my father to change his name so as not to sound Jewish:

> He said to me, 'Jacob you are just about to enter that great profession and there are good chances for doing well but I want to suggest to you that you change your name from Jacob to some other, non Jewish, name'. He said to look at himself. He would have done much better if he had changed his name when he came to the Bar. He would have taken Silk much earlier. I would be able to get a larger and better practice if I changed my name from Jacob. I was very taken aback by this suggestion and said I just could not understand it. He then said that I should consider it and come back to him. I did this. The more I thought about it, the more absurd and silly became the suggestion, and I decided to take no step at all to change my name, even my middle name is 'Hai' (Hebrew for 'life'). I went and told him so and he accepted what I said. I told my family about this and both my father and mother were very thrilled and happy that I should have resisted the temptation of considering such an absurd suggestion.

Stories about the law and people in it enable one to reach back, as it were, into time. This, for example:

> I had a most singular distinction during my pupillage of addressing the Court of Appeal consisting of Lord Justice Scrutton, Lord Justice Greer and I forget who the third Judge was. Richard Levy had to leave the brief and apologised for leaving the court and putting me in as a substitute. I addressed the court as best I could and when it was all over I asked Serjeant Sullivan, who was there, what he thought about my performance. He said it was very good but somewhat 'circumlocutionary'. I remember that word now. I will never forget it.

Dad went into practice but almost as he did the dark shadow began to grow in Germany. He was well aware what was happening. I skip to 1939:

> I was one of those who thought the War was necessary. After a few days, indeed on Thursday 7th September 1939 I went to volunteer to join the army at South Kensington. At that time, Rose was staying with me and we both thought it would be a just war, and although it meant me being separated if I was taken into the army, Rose was enthusiastic about me joining. On my interview on that occasion, I was interviewed and asked the date and place of my birth. When I replied that l was born in Shanghai they wanted to know where my parents were born. I told them Baghdad, which was, of course, in Iraq. The answer to me was 'I'm Very sorry, I can't do anything for you, you will have to go to the Iraqi embassy and get their permission to enrol.' This let me off joining at that time. I was very glad to be able to walk out of the interview more or less a free man. It is quite an experience to look back on it and to think that I could have been enrolled with a view to becoming an officer. I would have lost the opportunity of marrying Rose and bringing up a family. It was a great escape but not one that I had wanted or contrived. I well remember walking up past Hyde Park Gardens and taking a bus, sitting on the top deck feeling free and indeed thinking that perhaps that idea had not been well founded. At that time there were many people around me taking steps to get out of the war.

Dad told me that at the time of that interview he also had a medical and was graded C3 for bad eyesight and flat feet. In late 1940 he got his call-up papers, was graded A1 and was drafted into the Army:

> It was a very cold winter in 1940–1 and we did a lot of exercises in order to keep warm. After 4 to 6 weeks of initial training we were sent to Tidworth on Salisbury Plain. There were a lot of new barracks and on the second day of arriving we had to report to the CO who was an Irishman from the Enniskillen Regiment. We were stood outside his door and kept waiting for

> about two hours in that awful cold. He came out and made us open ranks so he could pass through. He asked each man what he did in civilian life. I remember watching that and decided to make the most of my own reply. When he asked me I shouted at him 'barrister at law sir'. He walked away about 2 or 3 paces and then came back and asked 'Which Inn?' as though to catch me out. I replied 'Gray's Inn sir'. He told the sergeant to take my name and number. A few days later I was sent for. He said, 'Jacob, are you really a barrister?' When I said yes, he said that was what he wanted to do in life but his family wanted him to be a soldier. He thought that he might have been a very good barrister. Then he said he had a lot of very important courts martial work to do and asked if I would help him. Of course I said yes. He pulled up a chair next to his and told me to sit on it.
>
> I then started to work with him and was able to see the working of the Unit from the inside. The sergeant major would come in in the mornings to report how many people were on charges and what the charges were about. After 2 or 3 weeks the CO said to me that discipline was difficult and asked if I minded sitting in the room next door. This went on until my time at Tidworth ran out. I asked for leave and was given a pass for 3 or 4 days. I went to London and did some work in the courts. I, rather stupidly, appeared in the uniform of a private. I was also rather stupid in wanting to do that work because I would be paid a fee and pay tax on it. I should have said that I was retired from the Bar and then the fees that I got would be tax free.

Dad was commissioned in the Royal Army Ordnance Corps. He was based in the War Office. He took part in the planning of D-Day:

> The main job was to organise the 21st Army Group for the invasion. This involved using a completely new organisation. Here's what we had to do: prepare proposals for the number and types of Units; compose the First Army Group and liaise with Lord Montgomery. The proposals we made would be circulated to the members of the committee which was responsible for the effectiveness of the 21st Army Group. We had to work out the number and types of Units and make proposals for the organisation or reorganisation of Units. This had to go before a committee to approve or amend as necessary. Sometimes this consisted of five members and sometimes of three, depending on the importance of Units being examined. My job was to present and persuade the committee to accept the proposals. What you would find was that the proposals were always subjected to a certain amount of criticism which you had to meet and overcome; it was much like going before the Judge or Master in Chambers. If the proposal was for the Unit to be under the command of a major, the argument would be that a captain would do, or if the proposal was for a sergeant major, a sergeant would do. This applied equally to the ordnance requirements

> of the Units under discussion. We found that it was always the Treasury representative who would argue for the lower grade.
>
> People working on the formation of the 21st Army Group knew, of course, the dates of the intended in invasion. It had to be ready by that day and the date of invasion was fixed for 5th June 1944 which was, by coincidence, the date of my birthday. As it happened the invasion took place on 6th June 1944. It was a little ironical that on that day I had a meeting with representatives from different parts of the War Office. The main topic was to fix the salary of a staff captain and staff officers at the War Office.

After the War, Dad came back into practice. Things were hard—I remember him marking Bar correspondence courses. But things got better. There is one last story of his which I know he would particularly have wanted telling:

> By about 1948 my work increased sufficiently to warrant the clerk agreeing for me to take pupils. I then took pupils until I was appointed Master. I had in all just over 20 pupils of whom six were women. I had an interesting experience when I was first asked to take a woman pupil. She was the wife of one of the solicitors who came to me. She had been to Cambridge. Her name was Estelle Stanley. When she applied to me I immediately told her that I would do it. Then I was faced with the blank objection of the head of chambers who was then also the Chairman of the Bar Council. When I told him that I wanted to have a woman pupil he said 'I don't think you can really'. I asked 'why not?' He replied 'where would she go' I countered, 'where we go'. He told me that other members of chambers would not agree. I said that I would ask each of them individually. He said 'don't do that, it will be all right with them but what about the clerk? He won't like it'. I said that I would talk to him. He said 'don't do that, I'm sure he wouldn't like it'. In the end I said I would have to tell everybody, particularly this girl, that the Chairman of the Bar Council does not wish to have a woman pupil in his chambers. 'Oh,' he said, giving up the ghost, 'we will arrange for her to come'. In due course I had a further five women pupils, one of whom was Estelle's sister Poppy (now Poppy Jolowicz, wife of Master Jolowicz).

One of Dad's pupils (and then fellow member of Chambers) was Louis Blom-Cooper. It was Louis who saw the job of Master of the Supreme Court advertised, not in a newspaper but on a notice board in Middle Temple. Lord Goddard LCJ appointed Dad. In those days the appointment lay with the Chief Justice and Master of the Rolls in turns. Goddard asked Dad how old he was. Dad said 49. The Chief said, 'You've got a long run.' How right he was.

Before long Dad, very much taking his initial guidance and inspiration from another QB Master, Master Diamond (father of Master of the Bench Tony Diamond), launched the career for which most remember him. His name was on the back of the White Book for 31 years. He invented the study of Civil Procedure and became a Professor at his old college, UCL. But all these are things which appeared in the public obituaries. I have one last story about Dad and the Inn—it is not greatly to its credit. You may wonder why my father was an Honorary Master of the Bench. The answer is that in those days there was a rigid policy of not making a Master of the Supreme Court a Bencher. So Dad, notwithstanding his achievements and international fame, was excluded. Rumour has it there was a tremendous row, with one eminent Bencher threatening to resign if nothing was done. Shortly before that time someone had the idea of creating a new class of Bencher, Honorary Bencher. This was, as now, really for distinguished foreign lawyers or politicians. They settled on that for Dad, though I have to say he would have liked to be a 'proper' Bencher. I am glad to say that such a daft policy was abrogated some time ago—indeed the current Senior Master was embenched by the Inn just a few years ago. Dad was glad to learn of that.

5

*'Be Ye Ever so High, the Law is above You': What that means in Practice**

THE STRIKING SENTENCE in my title was written in the seventeenth century. It was a time when the Kings of England thought that they had a God-given right to rule. And that the laws of England were for their subjects, not for them. We had a revolution, a short republic and then a return of Kings. But when they returned it was on terms: that the laws were made by Parliament not the King alone, and that the laws were administered by independent judges.

The key parts of that model: that laws are made by a parliament and administered by independent judges is the model of the Western world. It has proved itself, both by creating free societies and by creating the framework in which commerce and commercial transactions can prosper. It has created the framework for innovation and for consumer protection.

This model means that no one can do what they like. Even the most powerful government, Prime Minister, President, Emperor or corporation must stay within the law. If he she or it fails to do so then injured citizens or companies can take them to court for an order to redress the wrong.

And that redress is administered by independent judges. Critical here is a fearless non-corrupt judiciary. I am proud to say that not only has no one ever tried to bribe or influence me, but that I have never heard of such a case in my country. It was not always so. Only

* *A paper for the St Petersburg Forum, May 2011.*

when two things were firmly established did we get to that state. First is that a judge cannot be dismissed save for good cause. And second, that the judges are properly paid.

Corruption was driven out in that way. Low-paid judges mean two things: the danger of temptation is high. And just as important, society does not hold judges in high esteem—an important part of the rule of law.

Now the rule of law can mean that sometimes governments do not like what judges do. We in our country have found politicians—even Ministers—complaining about our decisions. But it does not matter. We do what we do, administer the law.

I want to conclude with a passage from a famous judgment. In the War, when you and we together faced a total evil, our government was, naturally, suspicious of recent immigrants from continental Europe. Many were refugees, but, the suspicion was, some might be spies. There was a power to lock people up if they were potential spies. It said the Minister could do so if he had 'reasonable cause' to do so. But who was judge of reasonable cause? The Minister himself. If so his power was quite unrestrained. Could the Minister lock anyone up without charge and for an indefinite time by saying 'I have reasonable cause, but I am not telling anyone what it is?' The case came before our courts and I am afraid to say that they said 'yes'.[1] But in our highest court there was a dissenting judgment from a judge called Lord Atkin. This is what he said:

> In England, amidst the clash of arms, the laws are not silent. They may be changed, but they speak the same language in war as in peace. It has always been one of the pillars of freedom, one of the principles of liberty for which on recent authority we are now fighting, that the judges are no respecters of persons and stand between the subject and any attempted encroachments on his liberty by the executive, alert to see that any coercive action is justified in law.

Lord Atkin's view was that the phrase 'reasonable cause' in the statute at hand indicated that the actions of the Secretary were meant to be evaluated by an objective standard. As a result, it would be within the court's purview to determine the reasonableness of the Secretary's actions.

It is now settled law that Lord Atkin was right. Not even in time of war can the government lock people up without giving a reason. That

[1] [1942] AC 206.

has carried down to the present day—where there are similar fears about potential terrorists. Can they be locked up without knowing why and with no prospect of challenge? In the early 2000s the UK government passed a law saying foreign (but not British) suspects could be locked up for a long period without the government having to say why. Our Supreme Court (then called the House of Lords) said that would not do—effectively following Lord Atkin. One of the judges (Lord Hoffmann) said this:

> I said that the power of detention is at present confined to foreigners and I would not like to give the impression that all that was necessary was to extend the power to United Kingdom citizens as well. In my opinion, such a power in any form is not compatible with our constitution. The real threat to the life of the nation, in the sense of a people living in accordance with its traditional laws and political values, comes not from terrorism but from laws such as these. That is the true measure of what terrorism may achieve. It is for Parliament to decide whether to give the terrorists such a victory.[2]

The government did not like it, but it had to accept what the judges decided.

Finally a word about what the rule of law means to citizens as between themselves. They can go about their daily business knowing what the rules are and that they will be enforced fairly. Thus for instance, contracts can be made and acted upon because the judges are there.

POSTSCRIPT

1. *I delivered this in St Petersburg in May 2011. Immediately after me, an American, Mary Patrice Brown, Vice Deputy of the US Attorney General, made the same point about even the highest being below the law in a particularly effective and personal way. One day in May 1974, she came back from High School, turned on the television and saw the impeachment proceedings of the President of the United States, Richard Nixon. She was very moved, realising with visceral force, the fact that all were below the law, that it was the law which protected people from arbitrary government. That decided her to be a lawyer.*

[2] *A(FC) v Secretary of State for the Home Office* [2004] UKHL 56 at [97].

2. *I am not sure how much good these talks did. If you have grown up in a system without the rule of law you cannot and do not necessarily and naturally feel that is how it should be: the rule of law is not self-evident to all. Judge Learned Hand put it this way when he famously said: 'Liberty lies in the hearts of men and women; when it dies there, no constitution, no law, no court can save it'.*[3] *There has been many a Constitution of a dictator which proclaims liberty, justice, equality and such high objects. And yet I do not quite go along with Hand. For I believe there is something about being a judge which at least inclines the person concerned to independence—merely to do a political master's bidding (or what you think would be his bidding) is contrary to intellectual honesty, and that goes against the grain for most people.*
3. *I have seen a good sign of this in China. In 2012 I was asked to join a delegation of European Commission officials who had arranged to meet members of the IP Chamber of the Supreme Court of China. The Commission had a concern that the Supreme Court was not properly (in its view) enforcing trade mark law in that it was (in its guidance notes for lower courts)*[4] *suggesting that there might be co-existence of trade marks. This suggestion was supposed by the Commission to be that the Court, in deciding a case, should take into account the co-existence of the plaintiff's and defendant's marks in the period from issue of proceedings to trial. The Commission had asked for the meeting.*[5] *I think the Court should have refused, and I hope there will never be another like it. The Commission brought senior people*

[3] *'The Spirit of Liberty' delivered to a vast crowd in Central Park NYC on 'I am American Day,' 21May 1944.*

[4] *The Chinese Court issues these independent of actual judgments. This makes sense in a country so vast, even though there is a bit of blurring of the legislative with the judicial functions. And particularly so given that China is building an IP system almost from scratch, starting only in 1994.*

[5] *In itself a failure by civil servants to understand the nature of the rule of law—in the UK, for example, the judges would never meet the government to discuss the principles by which they decide cases. The UK Home Secretary, Charles Clarke, tried a similar thing in 2005 when he wanted to influence the Law Lords' decisions in asylum cases. Lord Bingham rebuffed him summarily, Bingham lecture to Grays Inn 10 November 2005. I later found myself on a panel with Charles Clarke. He had left office but remained unrepentant—he just could not see that the rule of law could not allow the judges to meet a Minister one week to discuss policy and have to consider that policy in a case the next. It is quite alarming when our politicians do not feel the rule of law.*

from two companies (Lacoste and Hugo Boss, in the latter case the CEO) in effect to lobby for big brands. There was even a scarcely veiled threat to take China to the World Trade Organization as being in breach of TRIPS (Agreement on Trade-Related Aspects of Intellectual Property Rights). A German judge (Judge Lieber from Munich) came too. Both he and I became increasingly embarrassed. I said there were cases in English law allowing for co-existence.[6] *The Chinese judges repeatedly said they were not applying a co-existence doctrine as suggested by the Commission, that the relevant date for deciding liability was when the proceedings commenced. It was quite clear that they were acting independently of any central or party control. At lunch the Chinese judges (Chief Judge Kong Xiangjun and Judge Wang Yanfang) were sitting by themselves. I went over, we chatted for a bit, then the Chief Judge invited me to dine with them in the Supreme Court and asked me to invite Judge Lieber too. We made friends over that dinner, which began by Judge Lieber making a very formal apology for the conduct of the officials. I am glad to say that both judges are now members of the Advisory Board of UCL's IBIL (Institute of Brand and Innovation Law). So the meeting was not a total failure. I believe the Chinese judiciary will increasingly be independent as time goes on.*

[6] GE Trade Mark *[1973] RPC 297. The ECJ has confirmed that there can be such cases.* Budejovicky Budvar v Anhauser-Busch *Case C-482/09 [2011] ECR I-1000.*

6

*Court-Appointed Experts v Party Experts: Which is Better?**

THE EDITOR HAS asked me to comment on the Davies J v Heerey J debate.[1] Before I do so I begin with some of my favourite quotes about expert evidence.

James Fitzjames Stephen in 1859:[2]

> [Would it be] desirable to withdraw from the jury the consideration of scientific evidence, and to constitute some other tribunal, whose decisions upon scientific points should be binding on them?

Sir George Jessel:[3]

> Now, in the present instance, I have the evidence of experts on the one side, and on the other, and, as usual, the experts do not agree in their opinion. There is no reason why they should. As I have often explained, since I have had the honour of a seat on this bench, the opinion of an expert may be honestly obtained, and it may be quite different from the opinion of another expert, also honestly obtained. But the mode in which evidence

* *This was first published in (2004) 23* Civil Justice Quarterly, *400–07.*

[1] *The debate—well worth reading—is also in vol 23 of the* CJQ, *at 396 (Heerey) and 386 (Davies). It was about some proposed rules for expert evidence in the Queensland Supreme Court. As recounted in the debate it seems that Queensland was proposing to enact a rule whereby a single court-appointed expert would be the norm, party-experts being only allowable by the court for cause. The Queensland rules as actually enacted did not go that far. Party-experts are allowed as of right provided there is a report in time and so on. The rules do encourage single court-appointed experts by way of cost sanctions and other devices. Whether in the event they made much difference to Queensland litigation I do not know. I doubt it.*

[2] 'On Trial by Jury and the Evidence of Experts', *Proceedings of the Juridical Society* (1858–1863) vol II p 236. Stephen answered his question 'no'—saying that provided special juries and proper defence funds were made available 'Our system of trial by jury would be the most perfect that could be—as it is now the best that has been—devised for the trial of the most delicate and complicated cases which could be made the subject of criminal proceedings'. I am grateful to Sir Louis Blom-Cooper QC who unearthed this remarkable article.

[3] *Thorne v Worthing Skating Rink* [1877] 6 Ch. Div. 415 (a patent case).

is obtained is such as not to give the fair result of scientific opinion to the court. A man may go, and does, sometimes to half a dozen experts. He takes their honest opinion: he finds three in his favour and three against him; he says to the three in his favour: 'Will you be kind enough to give evidence?' He pays the ones against him their fees and leaves them alone; the other side does the same. It may not be three out of six; it may be three out of fifty … I am sorry to say the result is that the court does not get the assistance from the experts which, if they were unbiased and fairly chosen, it would have a right to expect. Then it is said sometimes, why does not the Court appoint an expert of its own?—a course which is sometimes taken by the Court. It is very difficult to do so in cases of this kind. First of all the Court has to find out an unbiased expert. That is very difficult. The Court does not know how many of these experts have been consulted by the parties, either in the case of this particular patent or of a similar patent. It may turn out that a particular expert has been largely employed by the particular solicitor on the one side or the other in the case, and it is so extremely difficult to find out a really unbiased expert and a man who has no preconceived opinion or prejudice, that I have, hitherto abstained from exercising the power which, no doubt, the Court has of selecting an expert to give evidence before the Court. That being so, it throws the Court on its own limited resources, and they are always limited with respect to subject-matter of the patent, a matter which depends on a very great variety of circumstances; and although the Court does derive, no doubt, a great deal of knowledge from the evidence of experts, yet of course, as we all know, in a subject-matter with which a person is not familiar from long training serious mistakes may be made which will not be made.

Mr Learned Hand:[4]

> The trouble with all this [ie party experts subject to cross-examination] is that it is setting the jury to decide where doctors disagree.

Judge Learned Hand:

> The system which submits such questions to the decision of laymen upon the evidence of partisan experts apparently satisfies the profession.[5]

[4] 'Historical and Practical Considerations Regarding Expert Testimony' [1901] *Harvard Law Review* 40, originally published in the obscure *Albany Medical Annals*. This astonishing essay was written when Hand was only 28. He traces the way the procedure of the common law evolved from earliest times—ending up with what he regarded as the absurd practice of calling hired experts before a lay jury on complex scientific questions. He never changed his mind.

[5] *Elyria Iron & Steel v Mohegan Tube* 7 F 2d 827 (2nd Cir 1925). It still satisfies a lot (perhaps most) of American trial lawyers—even in patent actions of the utmost complexity. The lesson here is surely that a longstanding legal culture and tradition can lead lawyers to favour a legal procedure, which the rest of the world thinks is irrational.

Mark Twain:[6]

> An expert is some guy from out of town.

So, disquiet about the way we go about things is very old. Davies J has some heavy hitters on his side in criticising the conventional approach. The problems with the pure adversarial system can be listed:

(1) party selection of experts means all counter- or neutral opinions are suppressed (Jessel objection 1);
(2) party experts are apt to be biased;[7]
(3) rival expert views are apt to polarise the position of the parties thus rendering compromise more unlikely;
(4) costs are substantial—each side needs to hire at least one professional and each side needs to instruct technically lay lawyers to cross-examine the opposite expert;
(5) there can be substantial repetition of background material thereby increasing costs;
(6) the tribunal (whether judge or jury)[8] is a technically lay body trying to decide between detailed matters of expertise (the Hand objection);
(7) extremely complicated cases may be beyond the powers of a lay tribunal to resolve fairly.[9]

It is an extraordinary fact that no one bothered much about these difficulties for many, many years. So far as England and Wales is concerned even the element of surprise was retained in the civil courts until the early 1980s when, for the first time, expert evidence was deployed in a written report in advance of trial. When I started at the Patent Bar the first time (apart from making shrewd guesses)

[6] This is widely attributed to him, but I cannot find the source. In looking, I found this (in a piece about learning to ride a 50in wheel penny farthing bicycle): 'in a few more days [after leaving hospital] I was quite sound. I attribute this to my prudence in always dismounting on something soft. Some recommend a feather bed, but I think an Expert is better'.

[7] For extreme cases see *Cala Homes (South) Ltd v Alfred McAlpine Homes East Ltd (No 1)* [1995] FSR 818, 841–44; *Pearce v Ove Arup* [2001] EWHC 455 (Ch). The problem can be exacerbated by 'coaching' (what the Americans call 'woodshedding') by lawyers. Good experts resist this.

[8] Although this is the *Civil Justice Quarterly* it should be remembered that the problem of expert evidence is even more acute in criminal trials where there is much more element of surprise and a lay jury.

[9] A jury does not have to give reasons but a judge in deciding to choose between two opinions really has to get immersed in the technology—as Heerey J notes, in one patent case the Court was supposed to understand post-doctoral technology.

the defendant heard the patentee's technical case was when it was outlined in counsel's opening speech followed by the patentee's expert giving his evidence by way of question and answer in evidence in chief. The defendant's counsel had to cross-examine at once. No one now would call that rational or fair yet it was done for centuries.[10]

In comparatively recent years the courts themselves began to try and ameliorate the problem. But it was not until *Whitehouse v Jordan*[11] that the courts in this country started spelling out even the need for the expert's evidence to be, and to be seen to be, the independent product of the expert, uninfluenced as to form or content by the exigencies of the litigation.[12] It took another 10 years for the matter to be dealt with in more detail in *Ikerian Reefer*.[13] Similar concern in the US led to the Supreme Court Decision in *Daubert v Merrell Dow*,[14] which made inadmissible 'expert' evidence unless it was 'supported by appropriate validation on good grounds "based on what is known"'. Only in the new Civil Procedure Rules was the duty of the expert to the court finally set out.

What then of the alternative—the court-appointed expert? Well again there are a host of objections:

(1) How does the court find the 'right' person?
(2) How does that person receive the 'right' instructions, both factually and as to what question or questions he/she should be answering?[15]
(3) What if a party considers that the court expert has got it wrong—either factually or as a matter of professional opinion? Can he cross-examine, or call contrary expert evidence?
(4) Is not the court expert really made the judge—moreover a judge who does not hear (or have to hear) rival contentions?

[10] In the criminal courts things are at still a more primitive stage—though recent miscarriage of justice cases (eg Sally Clarke, but there are plenty of others) may compel the Criminal Procedure Rules Committee to come up with something much more along the lines of current civil procedure (exchange of expert reports, meetings of experts) and so on.

[11] *Whitehouse v Jordan* [1981] 1 WLR 246.

[12] *per* Lord Wilberforce at 256.

[13] *National Justice Compania Naviera SA v Prudential Assurance Co Ltd (The Ikarian Reefer) (No 1)* [1993] 2 Lloyds Rep 68.

[14] *Daubert v Merrell Dow* (1993) 109 US 579.

[15] Only a small amount of practice shows that experts, party or court, are very apt to answer questions of their own choosing rather than the issue in the case, eg in a professional negligence case they will set out what they would have done, rather than answering the well-known *Bolam* test approved in *Whitehouse v Jordan* [1981] 1 WLR 236.

If one looks at the Davies/Heerey debate—essentially about court or party experts—one can see how well each identifies the problems of the other side. The knight's squire in *The Seventh Seal* comes to mind: 'Every way you turn, your backside is still behind you'. Just so with the court expert or party expert debate: all the virtues of one system lead to defects addressed by the other.

MERELY A PIOUS HOPE?

Is the expert's duty to the court merely a pious hope, as Davies J contends? It is true that it is a duty with no real legal sanction. You cannot (save perhaps in a wholly unlikely case—perhaps a forged set of experimental results) prosecute an expert for perjury.[16] Nor can you sue him for false evidence.[17] Indeed since in most cases the key part of an expert's evidence is of opinion[18] it would be close to impossible to prove that he did not actually hold that opinion.[19] It may be that some professional bodies will take disciplinary action against an expert who was found to have been too partisan by a court. But professional bodies are not really equipped for this—do they retry the case if the expert defends himself by saying he was right?[20]

So Davies J is right up to a point—the point being that there are no legal sanctions against an out-of-order expert witness. But I think he is too dismissive of the duty. Other mechanisms do in practice help enforce the duty:

(a) First it is not the case that most experts are partisan, saying whatever they like to support their side's case. On the contrary most experts (particularly those who give evidence regularly)

[16] Nor are proceedings for contempt realistic, notwithstanding the fact that CPR r 32.24 envisages possible action by the Attorney General if a witness statement is made without an honest belief in its truth.

[17] *Paimano v Raiss* [2001] Lloyd's Rep PN 341, [2001] PNLR 21 (absolute privilege in respect of expert's evidence). There may be limits here—if a party relies on an expert's advice to bring or continue with litigation, that advice may not be evidence at all—and so negligent or reckless advice at that stage may be actionable. *Since that was written, Jones v Kaney [2011] EKSC 13 has changed things—there is no absolute privilege protecting an expert from negligent expert evidence.*

[18] Though of course he may incidentally give evidence of fact: for instance experiments conducted for the litigation (or even not) or evidence of a medical examination.

[19] It is easy enough to say that the state of a man's mind is as much a fact as the state of his digestion—but proving it when it is an opinion is another matter.

[20] I cannot see how they can avoid this: but a retrial is nonsense—not least because the parties are not there. Moreover the expert may well want to rely on privileged matter on which he based his opinion.

genuinely do try to help the court. For an expert to be reminded of his duty to be independent (and to swear that he has been and that he genuinely holds the opinions expressed) is not just a ritual of no meaning. In the great majority of cases this has a real effect. Anecdotally most practising lawyers and judges in England and Wales would say that the quality of expert evidence has improved since the introduction of the express duty by the Woolf rules.

(b) Secondly, there is the real sanction of a serious slagging off by the judge if the expert is found to have breached his duty. True it is that legally this may go no further.[21] But the practical effect may be serious: the expert if he gives evidence regularly is unlikely to get much more work of that sort.[22]

(c) Thirdly, he will probably find it difficult to hold his head up amongst his professional colleagues—in real life to lose the respect of one's peers is perhaps the greatest sanction of all.

In this regard it is worth discussing the recent development in the UK of quasi-professional associations of those who give expert evidence on a regular basis. The Expert Witness Institute[23] has about a 1, 000 active expert witness members[24] and is growing. The function of such bodies goes well beyond acting as a trade union providing a source of names of suitable experts for lawyers. By courses, lectures, seminars and newsletters, experts are trained in the court process, how to write reports, and how to comply with the duty. They have disciplinary procedures of their own.

It is also worth mentioning another recent development in the UK—the notion of accreditation. This has been driven mainly by a series of miscarriages of justice in criminal law. The Council for the Registration of Forensic Practitioners has been set up. This is not the place for a detailed discussion of accreditation.[25] I confine myself to saying that I think it has formidable difficulties: a professional body

[21] Though there is the possibility of disciplinary action by a professional body, as I have said.

[22] Even if he fails to tell future instructing lawyers he is likely to get found out—a prudent lawyer will search the name of his expert (and that of the other side) through one of the case-law databases.

[23] Of which I have been a Governor since its foundation. Its website is www.ewi.org.uk. There is also the essential private Academy of Experts. It is not possible to know the size of its active membership, though it is clearly substantial.

[24] From many different fields: doctors, accountants, surveyors are typical, but more esoteric fields (eg floor laying) are represented too.

[25] *It still isn't—but it is worth noting that the accreditation idea has advanced somewhat over the 10 years since this paper—but is far from fully formed or in operation.*

can provide supervision of an expert's expertise. But what mechanism or body can be devised for dealing with an expert's expertise as a witness? The notion, which some have, that courts should not allow non-accredited experts to give evidence, is entirely impractical. There are kinds of case where real experts only give evidence as experts once or rarely in their life (the typical patent action). To ask an FRS (Fellow of the Royal Society) to become 'accredited' so he can give evidence would put him off altogether. And there are many other sorts of expert who would never get involved in any accreditation process—unless it were essentially so crude as to be near valueless.[26] So I think the notion of accreditation alone is unlikely really to raise standards. The truth is that it is criminal procedure, and particularly as to how expert evidence is adduced and decided, which needs a total revision—mere accreditation will not solve the problem.

EXPERTS' MEETINGS AND JOINT REPORTS

These, along with written expert reports, have become routine in civil litigation. There can be few judges or practitioners who do not think this has improved the quality of justice. They often save time—and I think serve to produce a fairer result. Like Heerey J, when I was at first instance, I found experts' meetings particularly useful in the case of accountants.[27] Davies J does not dispute any of this: his objection is that by the time they start happening—well after the proceedings have commenced—positions have polarised, and costs have been run up and so become part of the dispute. Both judges are right—whether the Queensland proposal will help remains to be seen.

THE HOT TUB

This uniquely Australian idea has not yet travelled, so far as I know.[28] I can see no formal reason why it should not happen in England

[26] EWI has a crude accreditation process for admission to membership—no one would pretend that it is or could operate as a high-level process whereby the wheat is really sorted from the chaff.

[27] Perhaps because their reports often condescend to unnecessary detail. Meetings certainly get rid of quibbles—and are apt to achieve some resolution of bigger points.

[28] *It has travelled a bit now and has been used mainly experimentally in England and Wales by some specialist circuit judges. I have had experience of it in two arbitrations. In both cases it was very successful. I think we should use it much more.*

and Wales. Obviously the lawyers would hate it—what, leave cross-examination of the enemy's expert to your own expert? There may be other objections too—good and fair experts are not necessarily also good debaters. Nonetheless I should like to see it tried here. I doubt it will ever save much costs—after all it happens at trial, which is too late from that point of view.

ASSESSORS WITH JUDGE

Heerey J suggests they have a real part to play in the case of highly complex technical cases, and I rather agree—indeed I think the Patents Court (or Court of Appeal) might well appoint scientific advisors more frequently.[29] At least a perceived danger is that the assessor will become the real judge—the very thing that happens with single-experts. Plainly the assessor system would be unnecessary if there were a single expert, whether appointed before or after proceedings start—for there would be no technical dispute before the court.

THE NEW QUEENSLAND RULES

The idea here—and it is I think original—is to get a single expert in *before* the proceedings are started. The thinking is that at that point costs have not been run up and positions have not polarised. In practice the procedure already exists in this country informally: anecdote says that solicitors on both sides in smallish claims often agree an expert to produce a report before proceedings start. Will the Queensland rule work? Well in a sense it is bound to if the court simply says that no other expert evidence may be called. The same is true if there is a single joint expert appointed after proceedings have started.

Whether this is really 'fair' is more doubtful. I think it is undeniable that the 'justice' will be rougher for each individual case. That may not matter—the trade-off is speed and much reduced cost. Overall the benefit could well be worth it in smaller disputes. Certainly (as in the case of all experts) it will be vital that the expert knows exactly what it is he or she is supposed to be doing.

[29] He or she does not have to be a Nobel prize winner—what is wanted is someone to help the court understand the technology.

MY OPINION

Where do I stand? Well I think it worth examining my own experience before answering. Much of my life at the Bar was concerned with high-technology patent cases. To conduct these one had to be trained in the technology by an expert. There would be many conferences where the basic background material had to be taught before one could even begin to grapple with the disputed technology. In 1969 Graham J endorsed the production of a 'primer' setting out the basic undisputed technical background of the dispute.[30] When the matter comes before the judge in a patent action (scientifically numerate but not an expert in the particular technology) each side is well prepared. Experts on both sides attend throughout trial. And the experts are really that—top people in their field.[31] All this is about as good as the adversarial system can get. But at what cost? In big-money cases this Rolls Royce procedure may be the best that can be devised.[32]

I also had one other really valuable experience—of appearing as Counsel to a tribunal[33] concerned with two technical matters.[34] The Committee was presided over by Sir John Badenoch,[35] an eminent doctor. I well remember his nervousness before the inquiry started—there were going to be lots of lawyers representing all sorts of different people, patients, engineers, architects, doctors, and so on. Was he going to be able to control it? His reaction later was deeply instructive: 'there is no substitute for the time-honoured method of question and answer'. But again there was a lot at stake. And it worth noting that though the Committee's job was inquisitorial, that made little difference to the expense or the way expert evidence was handled. The Committee's report contains a deeply instructive explanation of how it went about its task.[36]

[30] *Olin Mathieson Chemical Corp v Biorex Laboratories Ltd* [1970] RPC 157—the primer is set out as an appendix. This was an early version of that part of a joint expert report setting out matters not in dispute.

[31] In my last case as counsel, *Chiron v Murex*, no fewer than three Nobel prize winners were engaged as experts—two were actually called.

[32] It is certainly better than the US system of putting all this before a jury.

[33] The Committee of Inquiry into the Outbreak of Legionnaire's Disease in Stafford in April 1985.

[34] What flaw or flaws in its construction or maintenance caused Stafford General Hospital to emit the bacterium and was there a proper medical response to the outbreak?

[35] Whose son, James Badenoch QC, is Chairman of the Institute of Expert Witnesses.

[36] Cmnd.9772.

I do not think one can escape from the fact that testing evidence—expert or fact—by cross-examination is the best way humans have devised for trying to get at the truth. When conducted on a fully funded basis by skilled properly instructed cross-examiners you will get as close as can be done. But the cost (both in time, of individuals and in getting to a hearing, and in money) is immense. So I think it impractical and unconstructive to insist on this procedure for all cases—compromises have to be made.

Thus, when a lot is at stake, I side with Heerey J. The single expert, whether appointed before or after proceedings have started, is likely to produce a less unreliable result. Moreover he is less likely to be perceived as 'fair'. On the other hand, Davies J has a point too: the new Queensland rules may prove to provide overall[37] a fairer and cheaper system for lower-cost cases. I look forward to seeing how it works in practice.[38] Of one thing I am sure. There is no 'perfect' way of going about expert evidence.

[37] I emphasise that I am speaking statistically here—the justice is likely to be rougher this way.

[38] *Remarkably neither I nor my research assistant, Bhaavin Wallia, have been able to find out how the Queensland Rules have worked in practice.*

Part III

General IP

7

*Intellectual Property in the House of Lords**

FINAL APPEAL, BY Louis Blom-Cooper and Gavin Drewry, was published in early 1972. I had a small hand in it: the Acknowledgements include the statement 'Mr Robin Jacob initiated us into the mysteries of patent, trade mark and copyright law'. *Final Appeal* did not use the term 'intellectual property'. It was hardly ever used then, and insofar as it was, it meant only copyright and like rights (matters of the 'intellect' rather than vulgar trade). The term 'industrial property' was used for patents and industrial designs. IP, nationally and internationally, was something of a commercial and legal backwater. We did not know then that it was about to grow into the giant it has now become—occupying a key position worldwide. Decisions of important national courts in the field of IP are now studied all over the world the moment they appear. A House of Lords decision (or even the fact that leave to appeal has been given) will be the subject of almost immediate comment and discussion across the Internet well before anything appears in any legal journal concerned with IP (there are many of these now, virtually none then). So it is that the international importance of the judicial House of Lords in IP has grown since *Final Appeal*. Most importantly of all this has been in the field of patents, as I shall discuss more fully later.

My main task for *Final Appeal* was to produce a potted summary[1] of each of the IP cases for Part B entitled 'The House of Lords in

* *Chapter 39 in* The Judicial House of Lords 1876–2009, *edited by Louis Blom-Cooper, Brice Dickson and Gavin Drewry, pp 711–28. This is a very special book, organised by Sir Louis Blom-Cooper. Anyone who loves the common law should get it. Almost every chapter is a gem. I confess I am rather proud of this one.*

[1] This was an invaluable exercise for a young barrister, providing a sure foundation for practice. For the present task I have been similarly (but more ably) assisted by James Whyte, a barrister of 8 New Square, Lincoln's Inn. I am very grateful.

Action 1952–68'. The summaries were used by whoever wrote the actual text. Perhaps it was Louis, but he feigns not to remember. This time I got to write the text.

What I intend to do is review what I see as the key features and cases following those considered in *Final Appeal*—those from 1969 to 2007. But I must start by going back in time to consider the place of the House of Lords in IP up until the pre-*Final Appeal* period, until 1952. By and large it performed a valuable and cohesive function. Thus patent law was developed for the capitalist economy during the nineteenth century into a workable body of rules even before the partial codification in 1932[2] of the grounds of invalidity and its complete codification in 1949.[3] Prior to then the substantive governing law was essentially still the Statute of Monopolies 1624. And the rules for determining the scope of a patent or what amounted to infringement remained uncodified until the new European system took over in 1977.[4] So it fell to the judges—ultimately the House of Lords—to work out the rules. Key figures in this process were the two IP giants of the early twentieth century, Lords Parker and Fletcher Moulton. They each had a special interest in IP.[5] (It seems to be a feature of the House of Lords that from time to time a member of the Court takes a shine to the subject, particularly patents.)[6] Lord Parker created the modern law of passing off in *Spalding v Gamage*.[7] He, along with Fletcher Moulton LJ in the Court of Appeal, also created the cautious British approach to the registrability of trade marks.[8] The '20s to '50s were fairly quiescent for IP. The '30s saw some hostility, particularly to patents.[9] The '40s and '50s, particularly under

[2] By the Patents Amendment Act 1932.

[3] By the Patents Act 1949.

[4] The year of implementation of the European Patent Convention.

[5] Fletcher Moulton piloted the Trade Marks Act 1905 through the House of Commons and is said to have drafted much of it himself. Parker chaired a wartime committee to look into the alleged deficiencies in UK patent law. There was a perception that pre-War Germany had used the patent system so as to advantage its (particularly chemical) industry as against British industry by suppressing UK manufacture. I am not convinced of that, but it was wartime.

[6] Lord Reid, Lord Diplock and Lord Hoffmann are more recent examples of this.

[7] *Spalding v Gamage* (1915) 32 RPC 273, building on 19th-century HL cases, *Reddaway v Banham* [1896] AC 199, *Powell v Birmingham Vinegar* [1897] AC 710 and *Montgomery v Thompson* [1891] AC 217. Lord Parker's key contribution was to identify that the action protected not property in a name or trade mark but the goodwill attached to a name or trade mark.

[8] *W&G du Cros Appn* [1913] AC 83 and *per* Fletcher Moulton LJ in *Crosfield's Appn* (1909) 26 RPC 837.

[9] For instance the patent for the pentode valve was struck down as being too wide, *Mullard v Philco* (1936) 53 RPC 323, a decision which is generally regarded as wrong or, at best, unsatisfactory.

Lord Russell and Simmonds, continued a restrictive approach to the scope of patents—one which we now regard as unsatisfactory: in particular the approach consisting of regarding the claims as so distinct from the context of the specification and the drawings that the latter should only be considered as an aid to construction where there is ambiguity of claim[10] has long gone. Much the same has, of course, applied generally to questions of construction of all sorts of documents—'strict' has given way to 'purposive'.

I turn to the period under review. First, some statistics. In the 16 years reviewed in Final Appeal there were 24 IP cases in the House of Lords; in the subsequent 38½ years (1969–mid 2008) 55 if one counts a few cases which might be called borderline IP.[11] Of these 26 were on patents, 12 on copyright, nine on registered trade marks, two on passing off, two on registered designs and four on breach of confidence. Numbers have not been significantly on the increase, notwithstanding the increased importance of the subject. But the actual numbers do not tell the full story, particularly for patents. The cases heard have, in the main, had more legal significance than many of the cases in the earlier period.[12] Then it was not difficult to get leave to appeal, often from the Court of Appeal. Being under the naïve impression that only questions of important legal principle came before the House, when, as a pupil in 1967, I asked my master, Anthony Walton what principle was involved in *Ransburg v Aerostyle*[13] where the CA had given leave, his answer summed up the ease with which leave could then be obtained: '£100,000 worth of principle'. By contrast, in the period under review I cannot think of a single case where the mere amount of money involved has been enough to get leave. Big money cases did not get leave unless there was an element of public interest, for instance an important question of law. So although the rate of cases has been fairly constant, their importance has been more significant.

A change during the review period has been the length of hearings. At the beginning of the review period, IP appeals, and particularly patent appeals, were apt to take a long time. Hearings were often five days or more. In 1963 Lord Reid had protested about the length

[10] An approach endorsed by the House of Lords in *EMI v Lisson* [1939] AC 83.

[11] In particular 4 cases concerned with breach of confidence.

[12] Many of the cases—particularly patent cases—though reported, were seldom, if ever, cited, even in cases under the old law, deciding, as they did, no important question of law.

[13] *Ransburg v Aerostyle* [1968] RPC 217.

(19 days) of *van der Lely v Bamfords*[14] but nothing really changed for a long time. Even in 1980, *Catnic v Hill & Smith*,[15] concerning a simple mechanical invention, took 10 days. By the '90s and '00s hearing times were somewhat down even though the technical subject matter was much more complex. Most notably, the key case of *Kirin-Amgen v Transkaryotic Therapies (No 2)*[16] had only nine hearing days. The subject matter, recombinant technology, was vastly more complicated than that in *van der Lely* (a hay rake) and the law was also much more complex (European and American authorities were considered in detail).

Another feature of IP cases in the review period has been the low level of dissenting opinions, particularly in relation to cases involving substantive IP law.[17] There have been no dissents in such cases since 1974.

The figures include three appeals from Scotland.[18] There is no leave requirement for these. It is doubtful whether two of the cases would have got leave if they had been English or Northern Irish. The third, *Johnstone*, raised an important point of trade mark law[19] (though in a criminal context, the point is of wider significance) but these days, with the last word on trade marks now lying with the ECJ, the decision cannot be ultimately determinative.

Next a bit about the leading personalities. The review period commenced with what can fairly be called Lord Reid's court. He presided in nearly all IP cases until his retirement in December 1975. You cannot get a better picture of Lord Reid in action than to read the vivid report of argument in *GE TM*.[20] I well remember his way of asking a seemingly innocuous question to which counsel gave the self-evident answer. That would be followed by similar question with the same

14 *van der Lely v Bamfords* [1963] RPC 61.

15 *Catnic v Hill & Smith* [1982] RPC 183.

16 *Kirin-Amgen v Transkaryotic Therapies (No 2)* [2005] RPC 9.

17 Lord Diplock dissented in *American Cyanamid v Upjohn* [1971] RPC 425 and Lords Reid and Morris in *Bristol Myers (Johnson's) Appn* [1974] AC 646.

18 *Buchanan v Alba Diagnostics* [2004] RPC 34; *Redrow Homes v Bett Bros* [1999] AC 197 and *R v Johnstone* [2003] FSR 42.

19 Does the defendant's use have to indicate trade origin to infringe? The ECJ is still working its way on this topic, see eg, Case C-206/01 *Arsenal TM* [2002] ECR I-10273, Case C-2/00 *Hölterhoff v Freisleben* [2002] ECR I-4187 and most recently Case C-533/06 *O2 v Hutchison Case C-533/06, (2008)*—see also [20] of the AG's opinion to the effect that the case law on this topic is all at sea.

20 *GE TM* [1973] RPC 297. The argument was reported by Peter Prescott who, working from the transcript, captured all the key interchanges, generally with the exact words. It reads like a play.

result. Then the old man, looking surprisingly small for a man of his height, would lean forward with his hands clasped together just below his chin, his eyes bright behind those round spectacles: 'Very well then, so does it follow that ...?' A pit opened up.

Lord Diplock was the next dominant Law Lord in IP. He gave the leading (often the only) speech time and time again. His interest in IP probably stemmed not only from the fact that he had a degree in chemistry, but also from the fact that his father had been a patent agent. He even, whilst a Law Lord, sat as a judge of first instance in a patent trial.[21] Even his last 'speech' was in a patent case, being delivered posthumously by Lord Fraser in *Allen & Hanbury v Generics*.[22] After Diplock it fell to Lord Oliver, with less evident enthusiasm for the subject, and Lord Templeman, with enthusiasm to cut back IP rights,[23] to take the lead roles. When Lord Hoffmann arrived in the House of Lords in 1995 he immediately took over and has given the leading speech in nearly every IP case since.[24] We may expect Lord Walker and Lord Neuberger each to take a similar interest in IP and take over as the leading IP judges of the new Supreme Court when Lord Hoffmann retires, as he must in May 2009.[25]

I turn now to consideration of the cases. They are of two sorts, those about the core rules of IP law and those which, although having an IP right in the background, were really about some more general question.

THE GENERAL CASES

Norwich Pharmacal

I begin with perhaps the most important case of all, *Norwich Pharmacal v Customs & Excise*.[26] I will tell the whole story: it is one

[21] *Standard Fabrics v Reeves* [1972] RPC 47.

[22] *Allen & Hanbury v Generics* [1986] RPC 203.

[23] He realised, that, particularly in the field of 'soft IP' (a patent lawyer's term for rights in non-technical subject-matter such as copyright and trade marks) the new enthusiasm for IP was getting out of hand with a resulting risk of overprotection and the stultification of proper competition.

[24] They include all 9 patent cases and the only copyright case of importance, *Designers Guild v Russell Williams* [2001] FSR 11.

[25] Both sat on a number of IP cases, including patent cases, both at first instance and in the Court of Appeal.

[26] *Norwich Pharmacal v Customs & Excise* [1974] AC 133.

worth telling and if I not do it here it may never be told. It is difficult, if not impossible, to remember or even picture procedural law before the era of the *Norwich*, *Anton Piller* and *Mareva* orders. They all emerged in the early '70s. The seminal case was *Norwich*, changing as it did the whole ethos of what remedies a court could grant.

It started in 1967 when I was Anthony Walton's pupil. The drug company *Smith Kline & French* had an exclusive licence under *Norwich Pharmacal*'s patent for a chicken food additive called furazolidone. SK&F noticed that statistics of imported products published in the 'special chemical register' by Customs included furazolidone. Clearly it infringed the patent.[27] The amounts and dates of import but not the names of the importers were published. SK&F asked Customs for the names. Customs said it could not and would not supply them. It could not because the names were confidential to the supplier of the information and moreover by implication statute[28] precluded disclosure. It would not because if it did supply the names that would imperil the integrity of the special chemical register in that dishonest people would lie about what they were importing. SK&F went to Anthony Walton. He suggested the thing to do was to sue Customs claiming it was infringing because the infringing product passed through its control. This was seen as a long shot but the idea was to bring some pressure on Customs, possibly to get the names on discovery of documents and somehow make use of them, or even to lose but make some political capital out of that with a view to getting legislation to deal with this manifest injustice. The idea of an action for discovery as such was so alien that it never crossed the mind of anyone.

An action for infringement was started in 1969. It was not pursued with great enthusiasm given its prospects. But one day, looking through 4 Chancery Division reports for something wholly unconnected with this case, Walton's eye accidentally, and serendipitously, fell upon page 97, the 1876 case of *Orr v Diaper.* There it was, or seemed to be, an order for discovery of the name of a trade mark infringer. The order was against a shipper of goods bearing a spurious trade mark to find out who the exporter was. The Norwich writ was amended to include a claim for discovery. Customs listed documents which would disclose the names, but claimed Crown privilege.[29]

[27] Save on the improbable hypothesis that it was SK&F product bought in the UK, exported and re-imported.

[28] In the shape of s 3 of the Finance Act 1967.

[29] As public interest immunity was called in those days.

So a summons for inspection was issued. It came before Graham J. He, the practical business-minded judge that he was, held that discovery should be given, against the arguments of Mr Templeman QC and Mr Jean-Pierre Warner for the Crown. The Court of Appeal reversed Graham J with a resounding thump—there was no such thing as an action for discovery against anyone who was not himself a wrongdoer and in any event the information both could not as a matter of law and should not on the grounds of Crown privilege be disclosed. Lord Denning MR's judgment was particularly conservative—even accepting the argument that the Crown should protect wrongdoers in the interests of keeping the statistics accurate.[30] Leave to appeal was refused.

So it was on an application for leave that the case first reached the House of Lords. As I recall it the oral argument lasted for most of the day. It was in the Moses room rather than one of the two usual Committee rooms. Oddly, what interested the three law Lords[31] who heard it most was the point about whether statute precluded disclosure. Leave was given.

Thus the stage was set for a right royal battle. By then Mr Templeman had gone to the bench and Mr Warner to be the UK's first Advocate-General in the ECJ. The new Crown team were Peter Oliver QC leading, as first junior, Mr Peter Gibson. By then the amount of legal research which had been done was truly massive. We had trawled the English Reports, early American and Commonwealth authorities and the leading textbooks of the nineteenth century. All the authorities had been photocopied and put in five large, bound, volumes.[32]

Walton decided to start with the statutory prohibition/Crown privilege points—these were seen as the soft target because the idea of the Crown protecting wrongdoers was obviously unattractive. The plan failed at the first moment. Before he had got further than 'May it please your Lordships I appear with ...' Lord Reid interrupted: 'Mr Walton, there are two points in this case. Their Lordships would like you to start with the question of whether there is an action for discovery'. Clearly there was some scepticism about this. Walton

[30] The dishonest infringing importers might lie if they knew their identify might be exposed.

[31] Lord Cross was one, I cannot remember the other two.

[32] Not just ringbinders. Photocopying a few, unreported, cases had been done once or twice before but this was an exercise on a different scale. It was, I believe, the first time reported authorities had ever been photocopied. Before that the House and counsel all worked with actual volumes of reports.

embarked on the exercise taking them through the detailed stuff we had found. There was much intervention. Some progress seemed to be made but not, it seemed, enough when Peter Oliver got up on, I think, the third day. At some point thereafter, either the Thursday or the following Monday, Lord Kilbrandon did not appear—he was sick. Lord Reid said the court would press on with four. So Peter Oliver finished his response on the discovery appeal and Walton had about a day and a bit to reply. By now they were really interested. At about midday on the Wednesday of the second week the argument on this point was complete. We were turned out of Committee room Number 1 while the four debated what do. Lunch came and went. We all walked up and down that corridor, seemingly for ever. At about quarter to four the door was flung open and the usher called 'Counsel'. In we went. Lord Reid said: 'Mr Walton and Mr Oliver. Their Lordships are evenly divided. Lord Kilbrandon will be better by Monday. We would like you to re-argue the question. The rest of us will endeavour not to interrupt'.

After that it was all downhill. After the action for discovery the other point was easy. In the result it was a 5:0 decision.

I, and all others in the case, long wondered which two changed their minds. None of us ever found out. A possible mind-changer was Lord Cross. A few days after the argument was over counsel got a letter from him.[33] He had discovered a case of 1887 in the Supreme Judicial Court of Massachusetts, *Post v Toledo*,[34] which he thought supported the existence of the action. If I were asked to speculate now as to the other mind-changer I would say Lord Morris. He had played a lesser part in the debate, and I think, by nature, was rather more conservative than the others.

Norwich set in train a whole series of cases about the limits of the rule itself (journalists' sources, malicious informers and so on); it changed the very notion of using litigation to obtain information.[35]

[33] I do not know many times such a post-hearing letter had happened before.

[34] *Post v Toledo* (1887) North Eastern Reporter 540. The judgment was by Associate Justice Holmes, the future Justice Holmes of the US Supreme Court. Actually Peter Prescott's (he was second junior) researches had already found this case but we did not cite it because we thought it distinguishable on the grounds that the defendant was in effect a wrongdoer. We were not so purist as to say that it did not help after Lord Cross had found it and though it was in our favour!

[35] A quick early example was *D v NSPCC* [1978] AC 171, where a mother, wrongly accused of child abuse, sought an order that the identity of the informer be disclosed by the NSPCC. The HL refused the order on the ground of public interest—the doctors, teachers, relatives and neighbours who are the regular informants to the NSPCC of cases of suspected child abuse

It changed lawyers' attitudes to creative procedural litigation. If this unthinkable thing could be done, why not others? So came *Anton Piller*,[36] *Mareva*,[37] orders against third-party banks for production of documents,[38] passport seizure orders where an alleged debtor was likely to abscond[39] and others. I do not think any of these things would have happened as quickly or even at all but for the sea-change brought about by *Norwich*.

American Cyanamid v Ethicon[40]

This was Lord Diplock at his most prescriptive, indeed virtually legislative. Until the 1960s interlocutory injunctions in patent cases were seldom granted. The general practice was, unless the patent was old and well established, to refuse an injunction where counsel asserted that validity was to be challenged. That changed essentially when the business-minded Graham J went on the bench. The rule became, broadly, that if the plaintiff could establish a 'strong prima facie case'—ie show that he was likely to win—he would get an injunction.

Now that was all very well for simple patent cases. The court could realistically form such a view.[41] But when you tried to work out who

would all dry up if their names could come out. Curiously a recent author, Ruth Costigan, has asserted that 'there is no appellate authority on whether a public interest defence can defeat a *Norwich Pharmacal* claim', 'Protecting Journalists' Sources' *Public Law*, autumn 2007, 464 at 475. She cites a Court of Appeal case where the point was assumed, *Mersey NHS Trust v Ackroyd* [2003] EMLR 36. Is *D* so old that everyone has forgotten it? And is *Norwich* itself no longer read? for in *Norwich* the question of public interest was a live defence, only failing on the merits?

[36] *Anton Piller KG v Manufacturing Processes Ltd & Ors* [1976] Ch 55. I am quite sure this would never have happened but for *Norwich*. Following *Norwich*, record companies who were facing the new phenomenon of piracy quickly sought disclosure orders against retailers as to their sources. It usually turned out that by the time action against these was taken they said they had nothing left and had only sold a few. The need to 'get in there' provoked legal research by Hugh Laddie in the 19th-century cases for a justification for such an order. About 8 were granted in favour of record companies until the Chancery judges decided that the order needed the sanction of the Court of Appeal. The 9th case, where it was refused, *Anton Piller* happened not to be a record piracy case. It was one of breach of confidence. When taken to appeal, Lord Denning MR was much in favour of the order (the contrast with his attitude to *Norwich* is marked). And so it was that the name of this obscure German company entered the language of the law.

[37] *Mareva v International Bulkcarriers* [1975] Lloyds Rep 509.

[38] *Bankers Trust v Shapira* [1980] 1 WLR 1274.

[39] *Bayer v Winter (No 1)* [1986] FSR 323, CA.

[40] *American Cyanamid v Ethicon* [1975] AC 396.

[41] See eg *Carroll v Tomado* [1971] RPC 401, about a simple and short patent for a domestic plastic-coated wire frame 'airer/drier'.

was really likely to win in a high-tech case of some complexity with conflicting expert evidence on affidavit, the job of assessing who was likely to win became impossible. *American Cyanamid* was such a case. The parties put piles of affidavits before the court and, over many days, argued about whether or not there was a 'strong prima facie' case. Graham J held there was. The Court of Appeal held there was not, following an eight-day hearing. The case came before the House (the House having given leave) with an estimate of 12 hearing days. It took three. The House, through Lord Diplock, took both sides by surprise by refusing to go much into the question of how strong the plaintiff's case was. Instead he decided to lay down completely general rules about the grant of interlocutory injunctions. He set aside the 'strong prima facie case' rule and set out the well-known formula, which I summarise here:

(1) Has the plaintiff 'any real prospect of success'?[42] If no, no injunction; if yes:
(2) Would damages be an adequate remedy and could the defendant pay? If both yes, no injunction; if either no, injunction
(3) Would the defendant, if ultimately successful, be adequately compensated under the plaintiff's undertaking as to damages and could the plaintiff pay? If yes to both, injunction; if either no.
(4) How tips the 'balance of convenience? Injunction or not depends on how the balance tips, a multifactorial assessment.
(5) If the factors are 'evenly balanced' preserve the status quo by granting an injunction.

There are two other important points. First Lord Diplock went out of his way to say that, if damages were an adequate remedy and the defendant could pay, there should be no injunction 'however strong the plaintiff's claim appeared to be'. Secondly he allowed that the court could consider who would be the likely winner only as an item in step 4 (balance of convenience) where 'it is apparent upon the facts as disclosed by evidence as to which there is no credible dispute that the strength of one party's case is disproportionate to that of the other party'.

Following *Cyanamid* (another IP word to have entered the language of the law) there have been I do not know how many decisions trying to work out the implications. Often you see courts struggling

[42] Which means 'Is there a serious question to be tried?'

to get out of the *Cyanamid* straightjacket, trying to grant or withhold an injunction depending on the merits of the case. I have long thought that this decision was wrong and harmful. The apparent logic is itself deeply flawed. Here are some of my objections:

(1) It makes no sense to withhold an injunction 'however strong the plaintiff's claim appears to be'.
(2) The whole exercise gives neither side much of a basis to settle the case since the court is going out of its way not to give a clue as to who it thinks has the better case.
(3) The questions of whether damages would be an adequate remedy or whether the undertaking as to damages would be adequate are themselves difficult to assess. The court is led into considering a whole lot of 'what if' scenarios.
(4) Likewise investigations about whether a party has enough money to pay involves speculation both as to how much would be involved and as to the financial standing of the party concerned. There can be and often is a mini-trial about this.
(5) The test is apt to tilt things in favour of plaintiffs—to get past the first hurdle is relatively easy and then you are mainly into questions of money rather than legal merits.
(6) You can tilt things back in favour of defendants by taking a wide view of what is meant by damages being an 'adequate remedy'. Some judges have taken that to mean 'capable of assessment' in the sense that the court could come up with a figure. But in reality assessment of damages is apt to be a complicated and to some extent broad-brush exercise.[43] Trying to put someone back in the financial position they would have been but for an infringement, or but for the fact they were 'wrongly' injuncted, is a task to be avoided if one can.

So far as I know, no other jurisdiction in the world considers the prospects of ultimate success at trial as such a minor factor at the interlocutory stage. *Cyanamid* has not taken root in any common law country. And I am not surprised. I think it a pity that the Civil Procedure Rules did not do away with *Cyanamid*.[44] And it would be a good thing if the House of Lords in its dying days or the new

[43] See, eg, the assessment of damages for patent infringement in *Gerber v Lectra* [1995] RPC 383, [1997] RPC 443 (CA).

[44] But then the CPR in the main just restate the old rules in language which is more prolix although supposed to be more 'user friendly'.

Supreme Court in its early days reconsidered it. Of course there will be cases where one cannot realistically express a view on the merits, cases where there is an acute conflict of evidence or cases where the whole thing is too complicated,[45] but it makes no sense in other cases to demote the ultimate merits. You are more likely to get an unjust result if you do.

LB Plastics v Swish[46] and *British Leyland v Armstrong*[47]

The House does not come well out of this pair of cases. Following the Design Copyright Act 1968, a general realisation grew that copyright law could be used to prevent the copying of most industrial artefacts. The basic reasoning was simple:[48] most things are first designed by drawings. Copyright will subsist in these, in those days for 50 years from the year of death of the author for things with no eye appeal and 15 years from first marketing of articles which had eye appeal. It is an infringement of the copyright in a drawing to copy it. That includes copying it indirectly and in three-dimensions by copying the designer's article, itself made from the drawing.

Such had been the position established by the cases in the lower courts when *LB Plastics* reached the House. It was about a 'knock-down drawer system'. The defendants had based their rival system on that of the plaintiffs. Their drawers would fit those of the plaintiffs. They had denied copying. If one looks at the actual pictures of the two sides' articles set out in Reports of Patent Cases one can see why—the individual parts are very different in appearance. The main point argued was that the only feature actually copied was an unusual feature called 'a reverse countersink'. The House treated the case as mainly being about burden of proof—once you have proof of some copying and some visual identity, the burden of proof shifts to the defendant to prove that he did not copy. The trial judge held the defendants were liars and the House had little sympathy for them.

This 'main' argument meant that the most important point did not get the attention it deserved and should have had. Was this bizarre

[45] Patent cases can often be of this sort—*Cyanamid* was.
[46] *LB Plastics v Swish* [1979] RPC 551.
[47] *British Leyland v Armstrong* [1986] AC 577.
[48] This is not the place to go into the detailed provisions or the cases.

rule of copyright, creating effectively perpetual protection against copying of most mechanical items, right? It was argued that if and to the extent the defendants had copied, all they had taken was the 'idea'. The argument was brushed aside. It was advanced briefly by junior counsel for the respondents. It was not considered significant enough even to be summarised in the report of argument.

It seems fairly clear that the House[49] did not appreciate what was really at stake: should copyright confer the extraordinary degree of protection which the lower courts had established in the '70s? It treated the case as mainly one about fact and onus of proof. To be fair, that may well be because of the way it was argued.

When the rule started to become established, manufacturers realised they could use it to maintain monopolies in spare parts.[50] So they did, either reserving the market in spares to themselves or licensing others to make spares on payment of substantial royalties. In the motor car business one of those manufacturers[51] was British Leyland. Armstrong, who made spare exhaust systems for BL cars, refused to take a licence saying they did not need to do so for a variety of reasons. Those reasons included technical arguments under copyright law, an alleged implied licence to repair, custom and usage under the law merchant, and that enforcement of the copyright would be contrary to the competition rules of the EEC.

All these reasons had failed up to the Court of Appeal decision. Most were re-run before the House. In addition it was invited to reverse *Swish* using the 1966 Practice Direction even though it had been decided only a few years before. By a majority of four to one it refused to do so. Lord Griffiths alone was prepared to hold that *Swish* had missed the point:

> I am equally satisfied that it was not the intention of Parliament to bestow upon a manufacturer through the draughtsman in his drawing office protection for a purely functional object that could not be obtained through either patent or design copyright legislation.

What the majority did (Lords Templeman and Bridge, Lords Scarman and Edmund-Davies effectively concurring) was truly remarkable. All the appellants' arguments were rejected, but the House found

[49] Which consisted of Lords Wilberforce, Hailsham, Salmon, Fraser and Keith. None of these had much experience of IP.

[50] *British Northrop v Texteam Blackburn* [1974] RPC 57.

[51] Ford and Volvo were others and had their own litigation against spare part makers.

a new one of its own.[52] And it did so without hearing argument on the point or giving the respondents an opportunity of commenting on the argument or the authorities used to justify it. If a lower court had done that it would have been rightly castigated. I doubt that the present House of Lords would do anything similar—Article 6 is now in everyone's minds. The contrast with Lord Cross's letter in the *Norwich* case stands out.

The explanation for this extraordinary case undoubtedly lies in the Lords' hostility, particularly that of Lord Templeman and Lord Bridge, to over-powerful monopoly rights. Actually the pricing and availability (short and long term) of spares is a very complicated economic matter,[53] much more suitable for investigation and control by industry self-regulation[54] or competition authorities[55] than the blunt instrument of an IP court concerned, as it must be, with black or white rules of law. Most would say now that the House should have left the problem to the legislature, as indeed it was invited but refused to do.

Polaroid (Land's) Patent[56]

I put this in mainly for fun, but also to ask rhetorically, why is this not done more often, not only by the House of Lords but by other appellate tribunals? Leave had been given by the Court of Appeal. These are the speeches in full:

> Lord Diplock: My Lords, the reasons given by Buckley, LJ, for the Court of Appeal, from which this appeal to your Lordships' House is brought,

[52] The point was based on a supposed inherent 'right to repair' coupled with a borrowing from land law rules and cases under which a grantor of a right may not derogate from his grant. It has not received much acceptance since. Parliament changed the law of copyright in 1988 so as to remove the most over-protective aspects of copyright law. The Privy Council in *Canon v Green Cartridge* [1997] AC 728 (via Lord Hoffmann, who else?) cut the doctrine back and made it fairly clear that it thought *Leyland* an aberration: 'it is of course a strong thing (not to say constitutionally questionable) for a judicially-declared head of public policy to be treated as overriding or qualifying an express statutory right'.

[53] For instance the supplier of spare parts will only be interested in those which are profitable, but an original equipment manufacturer as a practical matter will probably have to maintain supplies of all parts, most of which would be unprofitable in a stand-alone market.

[54] eg a code under which spares for a particular model will be made available for a fixed period after the model becomes obsolete.

[55] And was a live subject at the time with a Competition Act investigation into Ford's pricing and spare parts policies.

[56] *Polaroid (Land's) Patent* [1981] FSR 578.

are, in my opinion, obviously right and expressed in terms so clear and convincing that I do not think I can improve upon them. I would dismiss this appeal.
Lord Russell of Killowen: I concur.
Lord Lowry: I also concur.
Lord Emslie: I too concur for the same reasons.
Lord Bridge of Harwich: My Lords, I concur.

I love the little elaborations in the concurring speeches too.

PATENT LAW

The House of Lords has served patent law well over the review period. I start with what is generally the most important question in a patent case, the scope of the monopoly covered by the patent. The 1960s, which ended the period covered by Final Appeal, left some unfinished business about this. There had been two 3:2 decisions, *Van der Lely*[57] and *Rodi*.[58] The majority view in each case was that the monopoly was confined to that which was covered by the claims properly construed. Moreover claim construction required a strict approach. The minority view was that patent law should prevent what Lord Reid called 'sharp practice',[59] namely taking the idea of the claim without falling within its strict meaning as a matter of language.[60] In the jargon of the time this was called the 'doctrine of pith and marrow'. The majority view did not formally say that the doctrine was dead, but it was, given the strict constructionalist approach, as a practical matter impossible to imagine a case where it would apply.

Lord Diplock, in *Catnic v Hill & Smith*[61] resolved this old problem, created a more liberal approach to claim construction but went on to create a new puzzle which came to be known as the 'Catnic questions'. He resolved the old problem by declaring, with a Stalinesque rewriting of legal history, that there never had been a doctrine of pith and marrow, that the differing opinions given in the two great cases of the '60s were simply about construction of the patent claims. They

[57] *Van der Lely v Bamfords* [1963] RPC 61.
[58] *Rodi & Weinenberger v Henry Showell* [1969] RPC 367.
[59] *Van der Lely* (n 57) at 77.
[60] In the case in point, the claim was directed at a hay rake device constructed so that you could take the 'hindmost' wheels off the frame and attach them to the front. The alleged infringement worked in exactly the same way save that you took the foremost wheels off and attached them to the rear.
[61] *Catnic v Hill & Smith* [1982] RPC 183.

obviously were not. No one could or had ever read them that way,[62] including the lower courts in *Catnic* itself. That resolved the matter for the time being—all was just a question of claim construction.

The advance Lord Diplock made in claim construction was to require a much more intelligent approach. The emphasis was to be on how 'those likely to have a practical interest in the subject matter of [the] invention' would read the claim in context. 'A patent specification should be given a purposive construction rather than a purely literal one derived from applying to it the kind of meticulous verbal analysis in which lawyers by their training are too often tempted to indulge'. Lord Diplock went on to elaborate this with a series of questions about what was to be done if there was 'a variant' from a particular descriptive word used in a claim. This was the least successful part of his speech. The questions were not easy as they stood. Hoffmann J tried to restate them in *Improver v Remington*.[63] The order was bit more logical, but nonetheless the approach was too complicated—it involved considering first the acontextual meaning of the word.

When he reached the House of Lords, Lord Hoffmann took the opportunity of not so much rejecting the *Catnic* questions as elegantly making them irrelevant. This was in *Kirin-Amgen*. Catnic had been the last case concerned with scope of patent monopoly under the common law. In 1978 the European Patent Convention ('EPC') came into effect, implanted in UK law by the Patents Act 1977. This was a messy attempt to reconcile the perceived English and German approaches to the problem. The perceived English approach was strict constructionism of the kind which had been the approach in the '30s until, at the latest, the early '70s—read the claim as a freestanding piece of language, resorting to context (specification and drawings) only in the case of ambiguity. The perceived, indeed actual, German approach was to use the claims only as a guideline. The compromise was provided by Article 69 of the EPC and a Protocol upon it. Article 69 says:

> The extent of the protection conferred by a European patent ... shall be determined by the terms of the claims. Nonetheless, the description and drawings shall be used to interpret the claims.

[62] How could you with passages such as 'I am not suggesting that the doctrine of pith and marrow is dead' (per Lord Morris in *Rodi* (n 58) at 384).
[63] *Improver v Remington* [1990] FSR 181.

The Protocol, in summary, rejects both approaches to construction. The approach of Article 69 is to be one which 'combines a fair protection for a patentee with a degree of certainty for third parties'.

Lord Hoffmann provided a masterful analysis of the whole subject of determination of scope of patent. He covered not only the European rules but contrasted (and criticised) the US rules, which clearly include a 'doctrine of equivalents'.[64] His intended audience was not just the UK. He was seeking to persuade other European judges to eschew woolly rules—a doctrine of equivalents which meant that some things just outside the claim were also within the monopoly. He was warning of the consequences of such an approach. One can confidently expect *Amgen* to form part of the future debate about scope of patents for many years to come. The battle is not yet over. Many Continental judges think there is a 'doctrine of equivalents' though there is nowhere near a consensus as to what it is. For the present, the UK rule is:

> The determination of the extent of protection conferred by a European patent is an examination in which there is only one compulsory question, namely that set by Art. 69 and its Protocol: what would a person skilled in the art have understood the language of the claim to mean?

Lord Hoffmann has also now tackled all the other major areas of patent law, namely the most important questions concerning validity. The requirements of novelty[65] and sufficiency[66] have been clarified. His last contribution to patent law was his consideration of obviousness in *Conor v Angiotech*.[67] Two experienced patent judges (Nicholas Pumfrey at first instance) and a Court of Appeal including me were reversed, Lord Hoffmann preferring the opinion of the Dutch court, which had held the patent valid. It is perhaps too early to say how important this decision is: on one view he has endorsed the patentability of what in essence is a research programme to find out if the idea works.[68]

[64] Under this there can be infringement by something which is *outside* the language of the claim properly construed. Some equivalents will do, but others not: which? The problem is what are the limits of the doctrine? It is still not settled in the US and may never be. Lord Hoffmann thought probably not: 'once the doctrine is allowed to go beyond the claims, a life of its own is exactly what it is bound to have'. And 'American litigants pay dearly for results which are no more just or predicable than could be achieved by simply reading the claims'.

[65] *Merrell Dow v Norton* [1996] RPC 76; *Synthon v SmithKline No* 2 [2006] RPC 10.

[66] *Biogen v Medeva* [1997] RPC 1.

[67] *Conor v Angiotech* [2008] UKHL 49.

[68] *The Supreme Clourt has carried this further in Human Genome Sciences v Eli Lilly [2011] UKSC 51. Maybe there is a good policy justification for this (who would otherwise do the research?) but it is difficult to reconcile with the idea that a patent should teach something practical.*

Finally on the subject of validity Lord Oliver's contribution in *Asahi*[69] is worthy of mention. For the House clearly and finally decided that under the EPC, the old common law muddled thinking about prior disclosure or commercialisation (the problem was which really mattered?)[70] had been superseded by a new rule: only a prior disclosure (whether by use or in a document) which *enabled* a skilled person to perform an invention counted as novelty destroying.

One other contribution of Lord Hoffmann needs mentioning—the judicial teach-in. In *Kirin-Amgen* he arranged for the panel, in advance of the hearing, to have technical seminars about recombinant technology from Professor Yudkin of Oxford University. The parties consented to this so there could be no objection. But the technique is clearly of general application to high-technology cases and may come into more general use even if they object.[71] Some purists might question the court being taught in private in this sort of way, but I think that is unrealistic—provided any genuine point of difficulty pointed out by the 'teacher' is raised with the parties, that should satisfy any fair-minded observer as to the openness and fairness of the trial.[72]

The result of all this vigorous activity in relation to core patent law is twofold: first the House of Lords in its last years has established clear, practical and sensible rules which are likely to serve UK law for some years ahead. Secondly, in the event that a truly European (either EU or freestanding) patent court is established, these decisions will form valuable contributions to what will be a new, European, jurisprudence in patent law. If such a court comes,[73] then, as has already happened with trade marks and will happen with registered designs, the position of 'top' court for IP will be passed on. The recent decisions and a few more would be the last of a UK-only final court of appeal.

[69] *Asahi Kasei Kogyo's Appn* [1991] RPC 485.

[70] The split decision and varied reasoning in *Bristol Myers (Johnson's Appn)* [1974] RPC 646 shows the problem of trying to reconcile distinct grounds of attack, prior disclosure and prior secret commercialisation.

[71] The Court of Appeal recently sat with a scientific advisor who provided similar pre-hearing instruction in a case concerning computer modelling of rock drill bits, *Halliburton v Smith* [2006] EWCA Civ 1715.

[72] If a court cannot use a live teacher, is it precluded from reading books or searching the Internet? All these things must surely be open to a court, provided that any point emerging is put to the parties.

[73] It is possible in the next 10 years or so, but given that the project is already 50 or so years in the making, one should not hold one's breath.

As regards non-core patent subjects, the House has also been active in the review period. The ragbag of subjects covered, important though they are, do not warrant detailed coverage here, particularly since in most cases they are about now-repealed or obsolete provisions of the Act.

REGISTERED TRADE MARKS

In the review period the House considered nine trade mark cases. Seven of these were concerned with the provisions of the 1938 Act, repealed in 1994 and replaced by new, EU-based legislation. In the early part of the period Lord Diplock took a commanding position. His speech in *GE TM*[74] is a genuine masterpiece, outlining the early nineteenth-century law of trade marks in the common law and at equity. It is about the need for accommodation of marks independently developed in small markets but which come into conflict later. Much of what he says is of value for today in the wider context of the European Union where conflicting trade marks can and do emerge perfectly lawfully in different Member States. His speech is still considered by European trade mark jurists today.

Also of interest is Lord Diplock's speech in *SK&F's TM*.[75] An application to register as trade marks the appearance of a number of pharmaceutical capsules succeeded. The appearance was fancy, the system of colouring being to have one end of a particular colour, the other transparent through which you could see small spheres, some white, some coloured (like hundreds and thousands). Again his speech is a masterpiece. Clearly the panel that, 10 years later, vehemently rejected the registration of the shape of a Coca-Cola bottle,[76] thought *SK&F* wrongly decided. But by then, as has already been observed, an anti-monopoly mood had set in. Actually the requirements of industry do extend, in appropriate cases, to registration of shapes and containers. The European Trade Marks Directive explicitly allows this.[77] The consequence, thus far, of allowing registration of shapes as famous as that of the Coca-Cola bottle, has not been the

[74] *GE TM* (n 20).
[75] *SK&F's TM* [1976] RPC 511.
[76] *Coca-Cola's TM Appn* [1986] RPC 472.
[77] EC 89/104 but only where the 'sign' is distinctive, see Arts 2, 3.1(b).

disaster for proper competition which Lord Templeman thought it would be.

Conservatism was also displayed in *York Trailer Holdings Appn*.[78] Most people who have driven behind large lorries will have seen the trade mark York. Yet registration of the mark was refused. Lord Wilberforce gave the leading speech. It followed the official line that registration might be a restriction upon competition—a trailer maker or trader in York might be put in difficulty. Personally I thought this a bit of nonsense, though I had advanced the official line. Again the new European law has swept this on one side.

PASSING OFF

The review period contains just two passing off cases. The first, *Erven Warninck v Townend*,[79] decided that where a number of traders use a common term for their product (in the case concerned, 'advocaat', in the case approved, 'champagne') they can each sue a third party who deceptively uses the name for the non-genuine thing (egg-flip or 'Spanish champagne'). Lord Diplock laid down a five-fold test which, in retrospect, was not particularly successful. So the later decision, *Reckitt & Colman v Borden*,[80] went back to the 'classical trinity', reputation, misrepresentation and damage. The only remarkable thing about the case was that the plaintiffs had been able to prove all three in relation to a lemon-shaped container of lemon juice.[81]

COPYRIGHT

The review period covers 11 cases involving copyright. The first[82] was something of a disaster jurisprudentially. The issue was whether the prototype for a mass-produced sofa was a 'work of artistic

[78] *York Trailer Holdings Appn* [1984] RPC 231.
[79] *Erven Warninck v Townend* [1979] AC 731.
[80] *Reckitt & Colman v Borden* [1990] RPC 341.
[81] I also got some personal satisfaction persuading my other former pupil master, Lord Bridge. He did not like it—'If I could find a way of avoiding this result, I would'. And 'with undisguised reluctance I agree with my noble and learned friends that this appeal should be dismissed'.
[82] *Hensher v Restawile* [1976] AC 64.

craftsmanship.' All five members of the court agreed it was not. But their reasons were, to put it bluntly, all over the shop. No one, here or abroad,[83] has been able to reconcile the speeches. The most interesting is that of Lord Simon of Glaisdale who traced the phrase back to the arts and crafts movement of the late nineteenth century.

CBS v Amstrad[84] was about the provision of means (double-headed tape recorders) for copying. Could phonographic copyright owners sue the sellers of such machines because it was near certain that the machines would be used to copy recordings still in copyright? Not surprisingly the answer was no, but the problem has not gone and will not go away. Increasingly those who provide the means for copyright infringement, particularly on the Internet, are likely to be made or held liable, either by courts determining existing law or by legislation. If the only way to stop piracy is to shoot the messenger, the messenger is likely to be shot.

The only other copyright case I wish to mention is *Designers Guild v Russell Williams*.[85] It was about a fabric design. The trial judge, disbelieving the defendants' claim of independent derivation, held that they had infringed. The Court of Appeal reversed on the grounds that none of the detail had been taken. The House, led by Lord Hoffmann, restored the trial judge's decision. It laid down that this sort of decision is not to be interfered with unless the judge was plainly wrong. Some members of the Patent Bar, including one who is now a senior judge, are still surprised by the result. Some indeed say that, like *LB Plastics*,[86] the case is really authority for the proposition that liars lose.

DESIGNS

Early in the review period the House decided *Amp v Utilux*.[87] Purely functional articles (connecting parts to go inside a washing machine), having no 'eye appeal' could not be registered as designs.

[83] Particularly Australia where the same phrase appears in their Copyright Act.
[84] *CBS v Amstrad* [1988] AC 1013.
[85] *Designers Guild v Russell Williams* [2001] FSR 11.
[86] *LB* Plastics (n 46).
[87] *Amp v Utilux* [1972] RPC 103.

The reasoning is elegant, particularly that of Lord Reid, but the result was wholly unintended. For if an article could not be registered as a design, ordinary copyright protection would run for the life of the author plus 50 years. This is what upset the House so much in *Leyland*. Whether, if the House had realised the consequence, it would have so held, remains a matter of conjecture.

CONCLUSION

The House has generally served IP well, and has particularly served patents very well. IP law is a lot better off for the second tier of appeal.

8

Intellectual Property and Competition Law: Can Economists Help?[*]

TO WRITE FOR Joachim's Festschrift is indeed an honour. But what subject should I choose? Well he has guided and tended Germany's law of trade marks and competition law for many years with great success—keeping both in balance. What do these subjects have in common? When you think about it the answer is obvious—behind each of them is largely economic policy. So I thought I would write about the intersection between intellectual property law and competition law and whether economics (or rather economists) have anything useful to say about either of these subjects.

I will come to the relationship between IP law and competition law later. But before I do so it is important to get a historical perspective. For well before there was anything which could remotely be called a distinct competition law, some of its underlying philosophy began to shape what came to be called (but only in the last 30 years) intellectual property law.

I take some examples from patent law, copyright law and trade mark law. They are all English—mainly because I do not know much about other laws. The English attitude has always rather favoured a strongly competitive market—as made sense for a trading nation. In this connection it must be remembered that English history, although including two revolutions (the second being essentially peaceful), has

* *This was first published as a chapter in W Büscher, W Erdmann, M Haedicke, H Köhler and M Loschelder (eds),* Festschrift für Joachim Bornkamm zum 65. Geburtstag *(CH Beck, 2014).*

been more evolutionary than most if not all continental European countries. There was never a huge structural change such as those brought about by the French Revolution or the various upheavals across Europe in the nineteenth century. Nor has there been a substantial process of federalisation with the emergence of a modern state in the comparatively recent past (eg Germany, Italy). Such processes inevitably involve a new look and reformulation of laws covering a range of subjects which need to be federal. IP law and unfair competition, and competition law are just the sorts of law which require reformulation if you are going to create a federal state from constituent parts each with its own laws on the subject.

I start with patent law. In the time of Queen Elizabeth I[1] of England and Wales[2] the country began its transformation from a state on the edge of continental Europe (whose main powers were France, Spain and the Netherlands) into a major trading and naval power with interests in colonisation around the world. The beginnings of what was to become the British Empire really go back to this time. The Crown (the name by which the government was and is often known) needed money—not least, for instance, in relation to a war in Ireland. Taxes had displaced the feudal system of rendering services to a lord who in turn had to render services upwards and so on ultimately to the Sovereign. But taxes did not produce enough. Also by then people were making substantial money by trade, by buying and selling. It was natural for the Crown to devise other ways of raising money. Raising this from rich traders became attractive. One of these ways was via patents—legal monopolies—sold by the Crown. Such monopolies in a time of increasing trade were obviously valuable: traders would buy them to keep out the competition. By then the grip of the older scheme of control over various trade by associations of traders—mediaeval guilds or what we would perhaps now call cartels, was weakening. The Crown considered itself free to sell monopolies in any sort of trade, new or old. Whilst she was alive, no one dared challenge Elizabeth's power to do this. She sold monopolies of all sorts. But the rising mercantile classes began to resent these legal interferences in their freedom to trade. So in the year of her death, there was a legal challenge to the Crown's right to

[1] 1533–1604, ruler for 45 years.
[2] But not Scotland which was then a separate state.

sell monopolies. The matter came to a head in the Case of Monopolies, *Darcy v Allen*,[3] decided shortly after she died.

This is the case that everyone remembers. The patent monopoly under challenge in the common law court of King's Bench was for 'the whole traffic in playing cards'—an old trade. It had been the subject of monopoly for some time (with re-issued patents) and Darcy got it re-issued to him 'in consideration of his long and acceptable services to the Crown'. The Court held the patent invalid. The various reports of the case are neither complete nor consistent with one another. But none of that matters. The folk memory of the case is the common law suspicion, even hostility, towards monopolies over trade. The saying 'all monopolies are odious' come from that case.[4] It has oft been repeated. For instance the Constitution of the State of Maryland of 1776 says that 'all monopolies are odious, contrary to the spirit of a free government and the principles of commerce, and ought not to be suffered'.[5] And Justice Millar in the US Supreme Court in 1884 said 'I hold it to be an incontrovertible proposition of both English and American public law, that all mere monopolies are odious, and against common right'.[6]

The common law position was affirmed by the Statute of Monopolies 1623. It did so in gloriously sweeping language:

> All Monopolies, and all Commissions, Grants, Licences, Charters and Letters Patents heretofore made or granted, or hereafter to be made or granted, to any Person or Persons, Bodies Politick or Corporate whatsoever, of or for the sole Buying, Selling, Making, Working or Using of any Thing within this Realm, or the Dominion of Wales ... or of any other Monopolies, or of Power, Liberty or Faculty, to dispense with any others, or to give Licence or Toleration to do, use or exercise any Thing against the Tenor or Purport of any Law or Statute ... and all Proclamations, Inhibitions, Restraints, Warrants of Assistants, and all other Matters and Things whatsoever, any way tending to the Instituting, Erecting, Strengthening, Furthering or Countenancing of the same or any of them ... are altogether contrary to the Laws of this Realm, and so are and shall be utterly void and of none Effect, and in no wise to be put in Use or Execution.

[3] *Darcy v Allen* (1601) 11 Co Rep 84. A very full discussion of the case is by Matthew Fisher of UCL, 'The Case that Launched a Thousand Writs, Or All that is Dross? Reconceiving Darcy v Allen: The Case of Monopolies' [2010] *Intellectual Property Quarterly*, 1.

[4] Coke's report, (1602) 11 Co Rep 84b, at 88b.

[5] Maryland Declaration of Rights, Art 41. Still in force!

[6] *Butchers' Union Slaughter-House & Live-stock Landing Co v. Crescent City Live-stock Landing & Slaughter-House Co* (1884) 111 US 746

Section 6 provided the exception allowing patents for inventions. It said that section 1:

> [S]hall not extend to any letters patents (b) and grants of privilege for the term of fourteen years or under, hereafter to be made, of the sole working or making of any manner of new manufactures within this realm (c) to the true and first inventor (d) and inventors of such manufactures, which others at the time of making such letters patents and grants shall not use (e), so as also they be not contrary to the law nor mischievous to the state by raising prices of commodities at home, or hurt of trade, or generally inconvenient (f): the same fourteen years to be accounted from the date of the first letters patents or grant of such privilege hereafter to be made, but that the same shall be of such force as they should be if this act had never been made, and of none other

As early as then there was provision about what was to become a key aspect of explicit competition law when it first began to emerge at the end of the nineteenth century:[7] the 'raising of prices at home or hurt of trade'. The inherent conflict between patent monopoly—one of the key purposes of which is to enable the owner to make a larger profit than he could without the monopoly, to charge higher prices—and the notion of free competition keeping prices down, is exposed but not resolved in the very statute itself. We have not come much nearer to resolving the conflict down to this day!

I turn to trade marks and unfair competition. Because of the common law's bias in favour of free competition, it never saw (and still does not)[8] the need for any general law of unfair competition. Indeed it was surprisingly late[9] that the law even developed a civil remedy for a competitor against a trader who used dishonest false or misleading badges.[10] The law only really came to create a right of action for this sort of conduct in the nineteenth century. But the courts were

[7] Firstly in the USA with the Sherman Antitrust Act 1890.

[8] See *L'Oréal v Bellure* [2007] EWCA Civ 968, [135] *et seq*. Of course big brand owners always want such laws—and then label almost any form of competition that even refers to their brand as 'unfair'. Their constant well-organised and powerful pressure with little by way of organised resistance (as also in the case of copyright) means that IP rights are apt to be extended from time to time. Policymakers giving way to lobbying is part of the nature of the IP system. As the saying goes 'constant dripping wears away a stone'.

[9] After all counterfeiting and false trade marking are universal and go back at least to the time of the ancient Greeks in the West and the early Chinese Empire in the East. As long as trade or manufacture exists there will be cheats.

[10] The common law built upon the tort of deceit concluding by 1915 that the action to protect property in goodwill, see *Spalding v Gamage* (1915) 32 RPC 273 Equity (the law separately administered by the Court of Chancery until 1875), created a property in a trade mark which had been put into use—see for its history *General Electric's TM* [1973] RPC 297.

not willing to extend to rights to some sort of generalised unfair competition. For instance the courts recognised as long ago as 1930 that honest comparative was lawful, both at common law and in respect of the statutory right conferred by a registered trade mark.[11]

Next copyright. As is well known the first statute protecting copyright anywhere in the world was the so-called Statute of Anne of 1709. Prior to that there was some sort of protection via royal grants and the once powerful but increasingly weakened Stationers Company. This was essentially a cartel of booksellers—what we now call publishers. It was they who claimed and lobbied for protection most, as is still the case now.[12] And it was the publishers who tried to get the common law to recognise a perpetual copyright even when statutory copyright expired. The case was *Donaldson v Beckett*[13] (1774). Given the common law's bias against monopoly it is not surprising that the claim was rejected. Lord Camden, for instance, was graphic in his condemnation: '[the] perpetuity now contended for is as odious and as selfish as any other, it deserves as much reprobation, and will become as intolerable. Knowledge and science are not things to be bound in such cobweb chains'.

Part of the reasoning, still relevant today, was that it was not for the common law to add to the copyright of limited term provided by statute. The common law would today take the same view, for instance in relation to designs: there is a design registration system. If a man fails to register his design in time, then the law, with its bias in favour of free competition, will not step in to help him when he did not help himself. The contrast with German unfair competition is stark. A recent instance demonstrates this well. The design of the actual iPad was not registered (amazingly enough). Apple had a registered design of what might have been an early prototype but it

[11] *Irving's Yeast Vite v Horsenail* (1934) RPC 110. The big brand owners successfully lobbied Parliament about this—with the result that the Trade Marks Act 1938 made it unlawful to use a trade mark (technically only so-called Part A marks, but most were) in comparative advertising, *Bismag v Amblins (1940) 57 RPC 209*.That continued to be the law until the Trade Marks Act 1994 implemented the Trade Marks Directive. Even as a young common lawyer I just could not see that this restraint of competition made sense. Yes the competitor was 'riding on the coattails' but he was honest and the consumer was given a fair choice. The protection of the investment into creating goodwill had to give way to the competition.

[12] Not many authors pressed for the absurd extension of copyright term from 50 to 70 years from year of death of the author. Some of their heirs did—naturally wanting an extension of their free lunches.

[13] *Donaldson v Beckett* (1774) 2 Brown's Parl Cases 129, 1 Eng Rep 837; 4 Burr 2408, 98 Eng Rep 257.

was quite different from the iPad.[14] The Oberlandsgericht Düsseldorf held it was not infringed by certain Samsung tablets but nonetheless granted protection under unfair competition law.[15]

I come at last to the relationship between IP rights and competition law. It has not been and never will be a happy one. Their basic philosophies are in conflict. On the one hand IP in all its forms is based on an exclusive right—the right to stop others doing something. On the other hand competition law favours competition in all its forms. It views monopolies with distaste at best. IP lawyers call IP rights 'protection'; competition lawyers call them 'monopolies'. I think this conflict is unfortunate, with a bit of fault on either side of the line, but, I have to say, more on the part of competition lawyers. Too often they overlook the fact that IP law itself has a built-in accommodation in respect of competition. Thus the very reason that you cannot patent that which is old or obvious in view of what is old is so that patent law does not interfere with competition in any existing artefact or process. It does interfere with what, but for invention, would not exist to be traded or used at all. The danger, exemplified by the Commission's pointless and damaging pharma sector inquiry of a few years ago,[16] is forgetting that we are looking at the unpredictable and hugely dynamic business of innovation. Classical competition law is ill-equipped to do this. It is constructed around cartels and abuse of de facto monopoly power. So when it comes to monopolies actually recognised by the law it struggles.[17]

So also, I am afraid, for many economists, many of whom have large input into the application of competition law and increasingly into IP policy. A recent extreme example comes from the USA. Here is what two economists recently said: 'The best solution is to abolish patents entirely through strong constitutional measures and find other legislative instruments, less open to lobbying and rent-seeking, to foster innovation whenever there is clear evidence that laissez-faire under-supplies it'.[18] They are not the first to say this sort of

[14] See the corresponding English Court of Appeal decision, which contains illustrations of all the designs involved, [2012] EWCA Civ 1339.

[15] OLG Düsseldorf, Urteil vom 31 Jan. 2012, Az I 20 U 126/11 and I 20 U 157/11.

[16] I criticised it heavily when it presented its preliminary conclusions on 18 November 2008, ec.europa.eu/competition/sectors/pharmaceuticals/inquiry/jacob.pdf. The inquiry cost the industry a huge amount—estimates are of the order of €400,000 and nothing or virtually nothing came out it.

[17] See for example my 2008 Burrell Lecture [2008] *CIPA Journal* 144.

[18] M Boldrin and D Levine, *The Case against Patents*, September 2012, http://research.stlouisfed.org/wp/2012/2012-035.pdf.

thing. Indeed patent abolitionists have come and gone over the years ever since the Industrial Revolution got going.[19] And they actually had their way in late-nineteenth-century Holland where the system was abolished for about thirty years.[20] Similarly the Swiss patent system was deliberately very weak so as to keep it essentially patent free.[21] Today Philips in Holland and Swiss pharma companies are all patent giants. The economists never ask why—they miss the big picture. I have often wondered why. The only reason I can offer is that they want to measure things which are inherently unmeasurable. They are either too complex or there is no reliable thing to measure[22] at all, or both. I believe the time has come for economists themselves to make a real study of the limits of economics in the field of intellectual property. I am not saying that their work has no value, but I do think it should be confined to that which really works. Otherwise there is a real danger that policy will be made on the basis of work which has an inadequate basis in commercial reality. Following Boldrin and Levine, for instance, would almost surely lead us into a dark age where investment in innovation died or at least became moribund.[23]

It follows from this that we cannot rely on economists to provide much help with the difficult interface between IP law and competition law. We will have to carry on with what we have done in the past, using the common sense and experience of wise men such as Joachim Bornkamm. That's going to be a better way than relying on uncertain formulae based on simplified assumptions and uncertain data.

[19] The story is well told by Mark Janis, 'Patent Abolitionism' (2002) 17 *Berkeley Technology Law Journal* 899.

[20] A Mr Philips was able to make light bulbs free from the Edison patents.

[21] Hence the setting up of chemical companies in Basel next to the German border. German law at the time did not protect substances in themselves—only processes and did not protect products made abroad by the patented process.

[22] Economists use 'proxies', things they can measure which they take to correspond to things they can't. But I have never seen a convincing one yet! For instance, some are using number of citations in patent searches as a way of estimating so-called 'patent thickets'. This entirely overlooks really important things like width of claim, whether the claims cover anything anyone actually wants to do and whether the patent is valid. It is a counting exercise which gives virtually no insight into reality and certainly less than any competent patent lawyer or attorney could give.

[23] Abolitionists say that people will still have bright ideas. And so they may, but there is a lot more to bringing a bright idea to market than just having the idea. Generally it requires developmental research and risk.

POSTSCRIPT

I stand by this. The more I look at competition law, the more I think it is unable to cope with IP rights, especially patents. Inventive industries are in competition not merely in their current goods, but even more so in invention itself. Unlike people who have de facto monopolies in what might be called staple commercial products (potatoes or cement, for example), innovative companies cannot rely on their current monopolies to stay in business. They live by a different rule: innovate or die. And they can only innovate if they charge enough to sustain current research and development.

9

*Woolly Lines in Intellectual Property Law**

IT IS A pleasure and a privilege to write for Josef Straus's *Festschrift*. He has for many years (is he really 70?) been a force for a rational and clear approach to IP law (both substantive and procedural) and particularly patent law. I hope he approves of what I say.

It goes without saying that we are all in favour of 'legal certainty', just as we are all in favour of motherhood and apple pie. People even speak of a 'principle of legal certainty'. But how certain can laws be? And how far have legislators (and judges) in fact sought to give us clear rules which can be readily and predictably applied? It is this subject, in the context of IPRs (intellectual property rights) which I have chosen to discuss.

I begin with why. First it is important to note that IPRs are in their nature intangible. They are exclusive rights—rights to stop other people doing things.[1] To be more precise, they are rights to go to court for an order that the defendant should not do acts protected by the right and for a financial remedy for any past such acts. If he fails to stop, then he will be liable to various sorts of enforcement. Ultimately in some countries that might mean sending him to prison.[2]

* *First published in* Patents and Technological Progress in a Globalized World: Liber Amicorum Joseph Straus *(Springer, 2009).*

[1] One of my favourite quotes from an old barrister is: 'we are the grit in the wheels of industry'.

[2] Some countries have a system of fines, sometimes payable to the right owner. In others there is fine payable to the state. In my country we use the grandiose name 'contempt of court' for breach of a court order. In practice the remedy may run from merely paying the costs of contempt of court proceedings to imprisonment for up to 2 years, depending on the flagrancy of the breach and whether or not the defendant has a track record of breach—'form' as the criminal lawyers would call it.

So IPRs, unlike rights over physical things, can only be enforced by going to court. That means, in any case of uncertainty, at the very least the taking of legal advice by both sides. And of course a lot more if people decide to fight.

The next thing to observe is that the kind of activities which can be protected by IPRs range hugely—from things which may be trivial (for instance, in my country, copyright in a mundane letter) to things of enormous commercial (and even human) significance (for instance a major pharmaceutical drug). Although some legal cultures attach more significance than others to notions of creativity and IP rights as an expression of personality, fundamentally IPRs are important for their *economic* effects in a competitive economy. Rights in inventions, designs and artistic works are the mainsprings of different sorts of creativity. Rights in trade marks are vital for competition to work effectively—both to enable consumers to exercise choice properly and to suppress dishonest trading.

So it is pretty important that IPRs should be clearly defined. People—mainly business people—need to know what they can, and cannot do. IPRs normally have a core—an umbra—where it is easy to say what is protected: exact copies of a copyright work, or counterfeit trade marks, or an article unarguably covered by the language of a patent claim are examples of this. On the other hand there are things clearly outside an IPR—a quite different trade mark, a quite different painting, or a quite different article from that covered by the patent claim. The trouble comes with things in between: those outside the umbra but arguably within the penumbra of the right. It is that penumbra which causes all the difficulty. I call this a 'woolly line'. 'Fuzzy line' or 'a grey area' conveys the same notion. The opposite is what has come to be called a 'brightline'.

The wider its woolly edges, the more an important IPR is likely to be litigated. This is for the simple reason that there is room for divergent opinions as to the 'right' answer. And because what the right protects is commercially valuable, competitors will want to come close if they can. Now I do not subscribe to the view that it is pointless for SMEs[3] to go to the expense and trouble of patenting because they can never afford the litigation which may be required to enforce the patent. This is because in my entire experience at Bar and Bench I have never come across a case where a large company has

[3] Small and medium-sized enterprises.

deliberately flouted a patent or any other IPR which is clearly valid and infringed.[4] I am not so naïve as to suppose this is because there is a deep well of morality in large companies. It is simply that they cannot afford the risk.

But when it comes to woolly lines things are different. Then the deep pocket (and available management and other resources) of the large company will favour it against the SME. In practice a large company will more readily risk moving into a woolly line of an SME's IPR than the other way round. The large company can afford the litigation costs, management time and risk of losing so much more readily.

The result is this: woolly lines in IPR are unfair; they favour large enterprises against smaller ones. Some may say so what, or does it really matter? Well I think it does. The economic reasons are simply stated. Competition (including competition in innovation) is a mainspring of the economy. Few innovations, even in trade marks, are complete departures from that which went before. Most innovation is incremental only. For competition to flourish competitive enterprises have a reasonable need to come somewhat close to what is on the market already. If you have to stay well away from all the woolly lines of IPRs of all those already on the market, particularly those of the big companies, you will find it difficult to compete or even do anything. And, most seriously, you are likely to find your ability to innovate hampered. So woolly-lined IPRs can be a threat to competitive innovation and particularly innovation by SMEs.

A good historical example of the suppression of innovation by a woolly IPR line is the use by the powerful Birmingham businessman Matthew Boulton of the James Watt patent in the early days of steam. The first steam engines (Newcomen) very wastefully condensed the steam (at close to atmospheric pressure) inside the cylinder by injecting cold water. Watt's idea was to condense the steam in a separate condenser—this avoided heating and cooling the main cylinder and piston. Trevithick of Cornwall saw that if you used high pressure ('strong steam') you could simply do away with condensing the steam at all. But until expiry of the Watt patent (it had been extended through clever manoeuvring) Boulton's lawyers asserted that this different idea was covered by the Watt patent. The woolly line of Watt's patent makes this arguable.[5] Boulton demanded, and

[4] And plenty of cases where they have refrained.

[5] There were no patent claims in those days. The whole point of claims is to have certainty as to the scope of the monopoly.

through the threat of legal action got, payments on the basis of the saving of coal compared with Newcomen engines.[6] And he claimed the patent covered 'strong steam' devices. There is no doubt that this held up the development of steam really until final expiry of the Watt patent. Only with strong steam could engines become efficient enough and small enough to be mobile.

Important postscript: I am now quite satisfied that this paragraph was completely wrong—I had picked it up from some anti-patent writings by Boldrin and Levine. Boulton never asserted or tried to assert the patent against 'strong steam'. There was never even cause to do so. The real reason for the delay in its introduction (and the doing away with Watt's idea of a separate condenser) was purely technological: you had to be able to contain the steam at high pressure which meant having the ability to do so with sufficient confidence that it was safe. I am grateful to two articles[7] which, instead of working by prejudice and assumption, went back to the original sources and utterly demolished the idea of the 'hold-up' of the advent of strong steam because of patents. There is a moral here—check your sources—particularly if it is economists with a personal theory to support! See also Chapter 23 on 'Patent Thickets'.

The moral objection to woolly lines is also powerful. Laws (in the widest sense including, therefore, the litigation system which enforces them) ought not to favour the strong against the weak, the rich against the poor.

For all these reasons I am, in principle, against woolly lines and in favour of brightlines for IPRs. Legislators and judges (for judges do make law, albeit as Justice Holmes famously said, 'incrementally') should strive to avoid the former and achieve the latter. I am not saying woolly lines are wholly unavoidable—in the nature of things some important lines are inherently so. But one should lean against them wherever possible.

I am going to examine some individual woolly lines laid down by both legislators and judges, but before I do so, I make this general observation. There are several sorts of woolly line. Firstly there can be imprecision as to what the law (the legal rule) actually is.

[6] This particularly mattered for the mines of Cornwall. Cornwall has no coal and so the cost of transport from Wales made it very expensive.

[7] *G Selgin and J Turner, 'Strong Steam, Weak Patents, or, the Myth of Watt's Innovation-Blocking Monopoly, Exploded' (2011) 54(4)* Journal of Law and Economics; *G Selgin and J Turner, 'Watt Again? Boldrin and Levine Continue to Exaggerate the Adverse Effect of Patents on the Progress of Steam Power' (2009) 5(3)* Review of Law and Economics.

Normally that sort of imprecision can be sorted out by a judicial decision of a senior court. But secondly, although a legal rule may be tolerably clear in itself, the rule itself may impose a woolly line. This latter sort of case is sometimes inevitable. By way of example consider trade mark law. No one doubts that it should make a defendant's use for his own goods of a trade mark which is confusingly similar to a registered mark an infringement. You cannot allow a competitor of Kodak to use Kodok. So you can lay down a legal rule to the effect that confusingly similar marks must not be used for the goods of the registration. But that rule involves a question of fact—you have to decide when one mark is so close to the other as to be likely to cause confusion. In borderline cases the unpredictability lies in the facts, not the legal rule. But there are other legal rules which are *unnecessarily* woolly. It is these I believe should be avoided—by legislators and courts alike.

What follows is an examination of some of the lines in IPRs and discussion of their wooliness or non-wooliness.

WOOLLY LINES IN PATENT LAW

First consider the major rules about validity. To be valid a patent must be novel, non-obvious, and enabling (sufficient). It must also not be for unpatentable subject matter.[8] How woolly are these rules?

The first of them, novelty, is a fairly precise requirement. The patent must not cover that which is old in the sense that the invention was previously made available to the public. The English case of *General Tire v Firestone*[9] contains the best formulation I know in a case of alleged novelty destruction by a prior publication (by far the most common type of case):

> If the prior inventor's publication contains a clear description of, or clear instructions to do or make, something that would have infringed the patentee's claim if carried out after the grant of the patentee's patent, the patentee's claim will have been shown to lack the necessary novelty,

[8] ie be 'capable of industrial application' and not be excluded by any specific rule of law, such as that laid down by Art 52 European Patent Convention (EPC).

[9] *General Tire v Firestone* [1972] RPC 457, 485. See also *Synthon v SKB* [2006] RPC 323, [2005] UKHL 59 where Lord Hoffmann summarised the law of novelty thus: 'anticipation requires prior disclosure of subject-matter which, when performed, must necessarily infringe the patented invention'.

> that is to say, it will have been anticipated … if carrying out the directions contained in the prior inventor's publication will inevitably result in something being made or done which, if the patentee's patent were valid, would constitute an infringement of the patentee's claim, this circumstance demonstrates that the patentee's claim has in fact been anticipated.
>
> If, on the other hand, the prior publication contains a direction which is capable of being carried out in a manner which would infringe the patentee's claim, but would be at least as likely to be carried out in a way which would not do so, the patentee's claim will not have been anticipated, although it may fail on the ground of obviousness. To anticipate the patentee's claim the prior publication must contain clear and unmistakeable directions to what the patentee claims to have invented [citations]. A signpost, however clear, upon the road to the patentee's invention will not suffice. The prior inventor must be clearly shown to have planted his flag at the precise destination before the patentee.

Perhaps some room for wooliness still exists however. Consider this example. Suppose a piece of prior art has two components nailed together and the patent claim says they should be 'fixed together'. No one would doubt that the claim lacks novelty. But suppose the patent claim says the components should be screwed or riveted together. What then? It depends on how you believe the piece of prior art should be read. Some may say that although it only mentions fixing by nails, it clearly teaches by implication fixing by any suitable means. Others would say nails means nails only, and that fixing by any other means, although ever so obvious, is not as such disclosed.[10] Fortunately this possible difference seldom matters,[11] and I know of no case where anything turned on it. So by and large the novelty rule is non-woolly, both as a rule of law and in its application.

Obviousness is another matter—it is an inherently woolly test. Let me explain why. It is clearly the case that you need an inventive step for a good patent. All patent laws provide for this in one way or another—even the 1474 Statute of Venice said the idea had to be

[10] Judge Rogge argued for a wider view in his lecture to the 8th Symposium of European Patent Judges, 1996, 'The Concept of Novelty with Particular Regard to Conflicting Patent Applications', 28 IIC 6/1997 at p794. His example was a prior art description of a soup recipe which did not mention the addition of salt. Would a later patent claim for the same recipe but with the addition of salt be anticipated? Judge Rogge thought yes, but I am not so sure. Obvious, certainly, but why not new?

[11] In particular, normally objection of obviousness will also be available. However it can matter in the case of co-pending applications.

'ingenious'. Our present system translates the requirement into one of non-obviousness.[12] But how do you judge this? The line is inherently rather woolly. Lord Hoffmann in *Biogen v Medeva*[13] rightly said that the application of the test for obviousness is 'simply one of degree'.[14] The standard is simply not otherwise. From time to time courts and patent offices try to find or create a brightline rule for obviousness. Such attempts, to my mind, are doomed to failure. Thus, questions such as 'obvious to try with a realistic (or good) expectation of success' or the more elaborate 'Cripps question'[15] or the 'problem/solution approach' of the European Patent Office (EPO) or a 'teaching, suggestion or motivation' test[16] are all very well when applied to some sorts of case, but they just do not fit for all kinds of case.[17] This is hardly surprising—the statutory test is simply this: 'was the invention obvious?' All sorts of factors must be assessed before coming to the overall *value judgement* conclusion about this. I think there is a real danger in trying to create a brightline.[18] If you approach the question purely intellectually and try to use some other test as a result, you will overlook the economic balance which the patent system requires—protection for inventions but none for the obvious. For myself, I think the late TA Blanco White QC put his finger on what really matters. Has the inventor made 'a useful addition to the stock of human knowledge?'[19]

Obviousness, then, is inherently somewhat woolly. It just can't be helped. To some extent the same goes for insufficiency. Again it goes

[12] I tend to think that the older, German concept of 'inventive height' was a better conceptual approach, but it is too late now to make this explicit. It is probably implicit all the same: is this an idea clever enough to warrant a patent is something most judges will have in mind.

[13] *Biogen v Medeva* [1997] RPC 1.

[14] Hence his laying down the rule that an assessment by a first-instance judge should not readily be disturbed. 'Where the application of a legal standard such as negligence or obviousness involves no question of principle but is simply a matter of degree, an appellate court should be very cautious in differing from the judge's evaluation'.

[15] 'Was it for all practical purposes obvious to any skilled chemist in the state of chemical knowledge existing at the date of the patent ... that he could manufacture valuable therapeutic agents by making the higher alkyl resorcinols?' The question was coined by Sir Stafford Cripps in *Sharpe & Dohme v Boots* (1928) 45 RPC 153, 173. There is a world of difference between 'could' and 'should' and much inwardness in the word 'valuable'. See the discussion of this question by Graham J in *Olin Mathieson v Biorex* [1970] RPC 157, 188.

[16] Rejected by the US Supreme Court in *KSR v Teleflex*, 30 April 2007.

[17] For instance the problem/solution approach requires a problem. But not all inventions are solutions to problems. Only if you artificially create a problem for the purposes of applying the approach can it begin to work. But that depends on how you state the problem.

[18] The Australian High Court, for instance, in *Hässle v Alphapharm* (2002) 312 CLR 411 followed a 'directly led to' test which gives so little room for obviousness as to make almost anything not actually old, patentable.

[19] TA Blanco White, *Patents for Inventions*, 4th edition (Stevens, 1974) §4–211.

without saying that a patent must teach the skilled man how to perform the invention. But how much teaching he needs involves an identification of the skills of the 'person skilled in the art' and is to some extent a question of degree.

What then of the test for infringement—the test by which you decide the scope of the patent? Here it is clear that judges in different countries disagree about what is to be done. There is general agreement that you first decide on the meaning (in the English lawyer's word, 'construe') of the claim. There is now, in Europe at least, though I think it is more general, agreement that you do not read the words in isolation—you read them in the context of the specification and drawings.[20] When you see a word or phrase in a claim, you consider what it is *for.* But, as is well-known, some say that you go further—that there is a 'doctrine of equivalents'. It is founded, perhaps, on the notion that somehow taking the inventor's idea or part of it ought to be caught even if the defendant is just outside the claim. There is no space to go far into this. What I think one can fairly say is that those who think there is or should be such a rule are far from agreed as to what it is or should be. So, in virtually all legal systems of which I am aware which claim to have such a doctrine, it is impossible to find out exactly what the rule is. As Lord Hoffmann said in *Kirin-Amgen v Transkaryotic Therapies*,[21] 'once the monopoly had been allowed to escape from the terms of the claims, it is not easy to know where its limits should be drawn'.

In short, a doctrine of equivalents is a judge-made fuzzy line. I think it is a mistake for that reason alone[22]—a mistake which we do not need and which does not advance the proper function of the patent system. Both patentees and the public should work on the firm principle that the patent claim is there to define the monopoly. It is not to teach the invention. It is to be read with the eyes of a skilled man who knows that the patentee is intending to set out his monopoly in this place. A doctrine of equivalents is an unnecessary woolly line. And because it will always involve extra argument and extra evidence, it is a line which increases the cost of litigation which in turn will favour the big against the little.

[20] Art 69 EPC says you must.

[21] *Kirin-Amgen v Transkaryotic Therapies* [2004] UKHL 46, [2005] 1 All ER 667, [2005] RPC 9.

[22] There is another: it may impede innovation.

I pass to one other woolly line in patent law—that about what sort of thing cannot be patented. Possibly deliberately there is no definition of 'invention' in the European Patent Convention (EPC). But there are exclusions. An examination of the *travaux préparatoires* shows a complete absence of any clear thinking about these. It was going to be left to the Judges (including the EPO in this context) to decide what the limits were. Have they done a good job? It is not for me, a judge, to opine definitively. The EPO thinks it is doing a good job.[23] I have doubts—not only as to whether the EPO is getting it right, but as to whether anyone is. I think the line is fuzzy: what is 'technical' (a test often asked) is an easy question to ask but not to answer. Nor is there any clear policy thinking by the judges who have to draw the lines. Or much in the way of evidence to assist them in their policy decisions. Are patents for business methods or computer programs a good way of encouraging progress or do they stand in the way of it? I do not actually know and I do not think anyone else does either. All too often you hear the assertions of those who do not doubt—believers that patents for such things are, or are not, good. So there it is—a woolly line drawn by the law itself and then its interpreters.

So, so far as patents are concerned, there are some inevitable woolly lines and a few unnecessary ones. Overall I would say it is not that bad.

WOOLLY LINES IN TRADE MARK LAW

Things are very different in trade marks. The subject is littered with woolly lines, many of which are made by the legislature and its interpretation by the ECJ. As I have said, the question of whether one mark is confusingly similar to another is inherent in the subject and cannot be avoided. But those responsible for the legislation actually made things much harder. The result has been that since 1994 (is it only 14 years since it all started?) there have been so many references from national courts plus the many appeals to the ECJ. Over the previous century and a bit,[24] in the UK the House of Lords took

[23] The then President of the EPO, M Pompidou, declined the suggestion I made judicially in *Aerotel* [2006] EWCA Civ 1371, [2007] RPC 7 that the Enlarged Board of Appeal should be consulted. So we press on with the uncertainty.

[24] The first UK registration Act was 1875.

only a few trade mark cases—perhaps 25 or 30. And when a point was decided it was decided. By contrast I suppose we are already near to 100 references from national courts quite apart from the mass of appeals from OHIM (Office for Harmonization in the Internal Market) Boards of Appeal. And far from the rules becoming clearer, the opposite seems to be happening. Even as I write I am preparing for a hearing about repackaging and parallel imports Despite two references to the ECJ, the parties are in dispute as to the effect of the answers—each says they mean that they have won!

I have a little, but not much, sympathy with all this. For trade mark law has aspects which remind you of quantum physics and particularly Heisenberg's principle of uncertainty: the more you clarify one aspect the woollier become others. Truly I think with confidence that no one will ever come up with a clear vision of what a trade mark is or is for. Of course we can all agree about the core concept—an identifier of trade origin. But the edges will remain forever woolly.

Having said that, however, there are a serious number of unnecessary woolly lines created by the legislation. When it was drafted Member States each had about 100 years' or more experience of their individual trade mark laws. The major problems thrown up by experience were known. Yet the legislation addresses none of them. It ought to have done. Not even the basic question of whether or not the defendant must be using the mark as a trade mark for his goods was addressed.[25] Similarly the vexed question of use in comparative advertising was left alone. It really should not have been left to European industry to pay for the ECJ to try and sort out that sort of question.

Sometimes it is said that it cannot be helped—that the legislation is a compromise. But I do not think that is a proper explanation of the failure to address these basic points. For in most cases there is no evidence of any competing positions taken by different Member States. There simply was no compromise—just a failure to think and draft properly.

Let me take just a couple of other examples from the legislation. One of the types of infringement provided for is similar mark/similar goods.[26] But what on earth is one to do about 'similar goods'? It is an

[25] Only now is the Court feeling its way to an answer—see Case C-48/05 *Adam Opel*, Case C-2/00 *Hölterhoff v Freiesleben* [2002] ECR I-4187, [2002] FSR 52. What these cases show is that the crude assumption of the Directive, that 'same mark, same goods' must be confusing and so must automatically be an infringement will not work for some situations. The Court has begun to write down the assumption.

[26] Directive 89/104, Art 5(1)(b).

inherently woolly concept. What was the point of having it? Why not limit a trade mark owner's rights to the goods or services for which he is registered?

And the Court has not helped. In *Canon*[27] it seemed to hold that the more famous a mark the wider is the scope of 'similar goods',[28] thus making a woolly line even woollier and one which expands or contracts depending on the fame of the mark at any one time.

Another example of wooliness inbuilt into the legislation is its use of the test of 'without due cause takes unfair advantage of ... the trade mark' as part of the extended form of protection conferred by Art 5(2) of the Directive. This is posed for the case where a mark has a reputation and the defendant uses it (or a similar mark) for dissimilar goods or services.[29] I focus on the word 'unfair'. It is reasonably easy to decide whether the defendant's mark takes advantage of that of the trade mark owner. But when does the advantage become 'unfair'. Is honest comparative advertising 'unfair'. Some say it is—even saying truthfully 'Robin's film is half the price of Kodak and just the same' takes advantage of fame of Kodak. Kodak might say it also is unfair because it relies upon the tremendous reputation it has built up over the years—a 'free riding'. It was not allowed under prior UK law.[30] It is almost certainly allowed now, following the Comparative Advertising Directive.[31] But a test as imprecise as 'unfair' is dangerous—particularly across Europe where different judicial cultures as to freedom to compete abound. What is 'unfair' to one man is just fair competition to another. The Court of Justice will have to try to sort out what is meant by unfair and will have to grapple with the problem in the pending references from my Court in *O2 v Hutchison*[32] and *L'Oréal v Bellure*.[33] I do not envy them the job for, try as they might, I think the test will remain forever woolly.[34]

[27] Case C-39-97 *Canon*,[1998] ECR I-5507.

[28] That is how most English lawyers read it. I have been told that in OHIM they do not so read it—I do not blame them for ignoring it. What the Court said is impractical for a working office—which needs to develop and have an objective standard reached by collection of decisions on where the line is to be drawn—to de-woolly the line as far as possible.

[29] The Court has decided the test also applies for similar goods, plugging a blunder in the legislation, see Case C-292/00 *Davidoff v Gofkid* [2003] ECR I-389.

[30] Section 4(1)(b) of the Trade Marks Act 1938, *Bismag v Amblins* (1940) 57 RPC 209.

[31] Reg 97/55 amending 84/850.

[32] *O2 v Hutchison* [2006] EWCA Civ 1656, [2007] RPC 407.

[33] *L'Oréal v Bellure* [2007] EWCA Civ 968, [2008] ETMR 1.

[34] *This all proved too true. The comparative advertising was permitted in* O2 *(C-533/06) but not in* L'Oréal *(C-487/07). And then the ECJ had to back-peddle in* Google *(C-236/08) and* Marks & Spencer *(C-323/09).*

UNFAIR COMPETITION LAWS GENERALLY

That brings me to consider the more general subject of laws directed at unfair competition generally. We can all agree that a trader who deceives the public ought to be stopped. That is clearly 'unfair'. But to what extent should the law go further? I am no great expert, but it is generally known that many countries have some sort of law aimed at 'unfair' competition and that some of the laws, as applied, do go further than merely stopping deceptive or misleading activities. I freely confess that I do not know why. We have specific laws aimed at creating monopolies or quasi-monopolies as exceptions on the grounds of public interest to the general rule that competition should be free. The exceptions each have a rationale, encouragement of innovation and investment (patents), protection of creativity (copyright and designs) and so on. Why add anything to these? If you do, you are almost certain to add a woolly-lined rule. And you are leaving it to judges who are not necessarily the best persons to make policy.

Judicially I put it this way in *L'Oréal*:

> [161] So, I think the tort of passing off cannot and should not be extended into some general law of unfair competition. True it is that trading conditions have changed somewhat over time—but I cannot identify any particular change which makes a general tort of unfair competition desirable, still less necessary. If the courts (or indeed Parliament) were to create such a tort it would be of wholly uncertain scope—one would truly have let the genie out of the bottle. Accordingly I would dismiss the 'unfair competition' appeal.

I would add that I find it most interesting that Germany rewrote its unfair competition law in 2004. As I understand it, it was with the very purpose of reigning in and tightening up the woolly and over-broad lines of the previous law. Sensible indeed in my view.

Before passing from this topic I wish to add one other thing—the danger of the use of the word 'misappropriation'. The concept is inherently woolly. This is what I said about it in *L'Oreal*:

> [160] Some commentators, generally those who support some wider tort, use the word 'misappropriation' of goodwill to designate it, see e.g. Hazel Carty, *The Common Law and the Quest for the IP Effect*, [2007] IPQ 237. I am not sure where I first saw the word used in this context, though I believe it to have come from the USA. I wish to state that I think it very unhelpful. We are all against misappropriation, just as we are all in favour of mother and apple pie. To use the word in the context of a debate about

the limits of the tort of passing off and its interface with legitimate trade is at best muddling and at worst tendentious.

Extra-judicially I adhere to that view.

WOOLLY LINES IN COPYRIGHT LAW

The most famous of these is the idea/expression dichotomy. No amount of legislation can make this precise. Judge Learned Hand said of it:[35] 'Nobody has ever been able to fix that boundary and nobody ever can'. All that can say is that the court is left with a sort of value judgement—if too much detail is taken then there will be infringement, if hardly any, then just the legitimate taking of an idea.

Another area of copyright law where there may be difficulty due to wooliness relates to 'originality'. There are actually two sorts of possible wooliness. First there is the law: what is meant by 'original?' Will 'sweat of the brow' alone do, as the English did, thus giving copyright to things like telephone books, TV programme listings and football fixture lists? If not, what more is needed? Is the court to decide what art is? The second woolly line is factual—just how close can a copyist go? One test for this, sometimes applied by a court when it is feeling moralistic, is 'anything worth copying is worth protecting'.[36]

Another famous woolly line is the 'fair use' exception to copyright infringement. If you set that as the standard for escaping infringement you will, as the US cases show, never come to an end of it. Almost certainly for that reason the English copyright legislator has always tried to tie down fair use to something more specific. So there is a long list of specific exceptions. Which is the better approach? The danger of a general 'fair use' is its wooliness, the danger of specific exceptions is that a deserving new kind of activity (home transfer of format, tape to DVD or loading from your own CD to iPod) will have no exception unless and until it freshly legislated.

[35] *Nichols v Universal Pictures* (1930) 45 F(2d) 119.

[36] *University of London Press v University Tutorial Press* [1916] Ch 601 about copyright in examination papers. The expression is sometimes used to justify the subsistence of copyright and sometimes to justify a finding of infringement. Either way it proves too much.

WOOLLY LINES IN DESIGN LAW

Design laws differ markedly from country to country and even within a country. In my lifetime the UK has had a whole host of them. This tells you something: that the legislator has no clear view as to what should, and should not, be protected. Wooliness is an inevitable result. For the sake of convenience and intelligibility across Europe I propose to consider just the new European registered design legislation, Reg 6/2002.

This legislation is strewn with woolly lines. There is first the 'individual character' test. Recital 4 puts it this way:

> [W]hether the overall impression produced on an informed user viewing the design clearly differs from that produced on him by the existing design corpus, taking into consideration the nature of the product to which the design is applied or in which it is incorporated, and in particular the industrial sector to which it belongs and the degree of freedom of the designer in developing the design.

That raises a host of imprecise concepts: 'existing design corpus', 'informed user', 'industrial sector to which it belongs'. I recently struggled with some of this in *Proctor & Gamble v Reckitt.*[37]

Could the legislature have done better? I rather think so but in the end it may not matter. For in my experience in the end in design cases the court tends to go by gut reaction rather than the precise legal language of the law. Maybe one should not say that, but then, why not?

CONCLUSION

This short overview of some IPR woolly lines is intended to do a number of things. Most importantly it is to alert legislators to concentrate hard on avoiding them for all the reasons I identify at the outset. Secondly, and almost equally importantly it is to urge judges to do the same thing in their decisions. Thirdly, it is to invite academics and other thinkers to identify IPR woolly lines, especially unnecessary ones to guide future reform. Fourthly, it is to suggest that readers themselves think about other woolly lines, whether they are inevitable or whether they could be brighter and if so how.

[37] *Proctor & Gamble v Reckitt* [2007] EWCA Civ 936.

10

*IP Law: Keep Calm and Carry On?**

MR BENTHAM. THIS is *your* annual lecture. This University claims you as its intellectual father—a UCL website says 'spiritual father', but I am sure you would not think the word 'spiritual' to be appropriate for the Godless Institution of Gower Street. Actually your only connection to UCL was slight. You were 80 when it opened its doors in 1828. But you did put up £100[1] as shareholder. Nonetheless we think of you as hovering around and variously approving and disapproving of what we do. And we like to think that you agree you got good value for your £100 even if it was not in cash. What happened to the shares I wonder?

Mr Bentham,[2] although this is primarily your lecture, I hope you do not mind this audience eavesdropping—especially because your Association forms part of it. I want to tell you in a short space of time where the subject now called Intellectual Property has got to since your days, and particularly how people are trying to shape it now. I will aim a few criticisms of some things on my way.

Mr Bentham, you will not mind my being a bit critical—after all you were not slow in coming forward yourself. A man who can criticise the notion of inalienable and fixed natural rights by saying 'natural rights is simple nonsense: natural and imprescriptible rights,

* *First published in (2013) 66(1)* Current Legal Problems *379–99, based on the 2013 Bentham Association Presidential Address and my inaugural lecture as the Sir Hugh Laddie Professor in Intellectual Property Law.*

[1] About £7000 in today's money on an RPI basis.

[2] All quotations from Jeremy Bentham and the detail in the footnotes about them were kindly provided by Michael Quinn, a senior Research Associate of the UCL Laws Bentham Project.

rhetorical nonsense, nonsense upon stilts'—as you did[3]—can hardly mind another chap having a bit of a go, even if nowhere near as brilliantly as you.

So, Mr Bentham, here goes.

The term Intellectual Property did not exist in your time. And it has only come to be a general umbrella name for the laws about copyright, patents, trade marks, designs and trade secrets in the last 30 years or so.[4] An innocent might think there is no harm in having a general name for all these laws. I doubt whether you would have made the same mistake. It depends on how much one overestimates the capacity for people—especially journalists, politicians and civil servants—to think and reason rationally. For by giving these rather disparate subjects a single name people tend to think they are the same or same sort of thing, that the reasons for them are the same and that the same rules should and even do govern them all.[5] Journalists typically talk about 'copyrighting a trademark', 'patenting a name', 'registering a copyright', and so on.[6] Politicians likewise muddle the rights up. For instance, successive Prime Ministers Brown and Cameron each commissioned a review of the whole of intellectual property. Brown commissioned Gowers,[7] Cameron, Hargreaves.[8] Quite why journalists were chosen for this task is a mystery. Both were given only about 18 months. Not surprisingly both paid little attention to patents, designs, or trade marks for these would have been beyond their comprehension in the space of time allowed. They concentrated on copyright.

[3] J Bentham, 'Nonsense upon Stilts, or Pandora's box opened, or The French Declaration of Rights prefixed to the Constitution of 1791 laid open and exposed—with a comparative sketch of what has been done on the same subject in the Constitution of 1795, and a sample of Citizen Sieyès' in P Schofield, C Pease-Watkin and C Blamires (eds), J Bentham, *Rights, Representation, and Reform: Nonsense upon Stilts and Other Writings on the French Revolution* (OUP, 2002) 317–401, 330 [written 1795].

[4] J Hughes, 'A Short History of Intellectual Property in Relation to Copyright' (2012) 33 *Cardozo Law Review* 1293.

[5] There is another danger too, stemming from the use of the word 'property'. The key indication of 'property' is the right of the owner to keep others off. All very well and good for ownership of land, but the subjects of IP are much more nuanced than that, involving a balance between the owner and the public, a balance largely (but not exclusively) dictated by economic considerations. The danger is too much 'property thinking': M Lemley, 'Property, Intellectual Property, and Free Riding' (2004–05) 83 *Texas Law Review* 1031.

[6] Of course they did it before, but it seems to have got worse after the umbrella name came in.

[7] *Gowers Review of Intellectual Property* (HMSO 2006) www.hm-treasury.gov.uk/d/pbr06_gowers_report_755.pdf.

[8] *Digital Opportunity: A Review of Intellectual Property and Growth—An Independent Report by Professor Ian Hargreaves* (2011) www.ipo.gov.uk/ipreview-finalreport.pdf.

Actually, Mr Bentham, as you would have seen from the outset, the subjects need clear thinking, not muddle. Giving them a common name has hindered rational thought.[9]

Mr Bentham, one might perhaps be led to believe that something like rational thought is being put into policymaking these days. For policymakers are apt to say that their thinking should be 'evidence based'. It is a new, fashionable phrase. Professor Hargreaves' very first recommendation said:

> Government should ensure that development of the IP System is driven as far as possible by objective evidence. Policy should balance measurable economic objectives against social goals and potential benefits for rights holders against impacts on consumers and other interests. These concerns will be of particular importance in assessing future claims to extend rights or in determining desirable limits to rights.[10]

All very laudable, but what does it mean? What is a 'measurable economic objective'? How do you measure—indeed can you measure—such things as the benefits provided by trade mark rights, patents, copyrights, or design rights? What is 'objective evidence'? There is an implicit assumption that if you can't measure something, it doesn't exist or is not important.

I take just one example: parody and copyright. Our law has no exception to copyright infringement allowing for parody. One might have thought that a self-evident defect—a harmful interference with liberty of expression. Pursuant to recommendations from Gowers, and again from Hargreaves, the UK Intellectual Property Office consulted. Did it consult about liberty and freedom of expression? No—because you can't measure these. Instead it asked daft questions such as 'What is the value of the market for parody works in the UK and globally?' Believe me, Mr Bentham, they really did ask that.[11] And even got a tiny answer from a small study of parodies of pop songs on YouTube.[12] It showed just what one would expect—that parody has had no detectable effect on sales of the original.

[9] WR Cornish, *Intellectual Property: Omnipresent, Distracting, Irrelevant?* (OUP, 2004) 2–5 (arguing that while 'IP' may now be a 'convenient genus, ... its various species remain distinct').

[10] *Hargreaves Report* (n 8) 8.

[11] UK Intellectual Property Office, *Consultation on Proposals to Change the UK's Copyright System* (2011) 87, Q 79; www.ipo.gov.uk/consult-2011.copyright.pdf. Almost unbelievably the UK IPO had only just consulted on the parody exception: *Taking Forward the Gowers Review of Intellectual Property: Proposed Changes to Copyright Exceptions* (2008) 31–32; www.ipo.gov.uk/consult-copyrightexceptions.pdf. Why two consultations remains a mystery.

[12] K Erickson, M Kretschmer, D Mendis, 'Copyright and the Economic Effects of Parody: An Empirical Study of Music Videos on the YouTube Platform and an Assessment of the

Mr Bentham, the government accepted Hargreaves' recommendation that policy should be evidence based. But it has since gone on to do just the opposite. Without any 'objective evidence' and contrary to the recommendation of the earlier Gowers report, which was supported by Hargreaves, the government voted for the EU legislation,[13] which increased the term of protection for sound recordings from 50 years to 70 years from publication. Is there really a class of pensioner rock performer who will be on the poverty line without this extension? Or will performers perform more or better by knowing that the term of protection is 70 rather than 50 years? Commissioner Barnier of the European Commission asserted such nonsense,[14] though it flies in the face of common sense. That says that only a few recordings more than 50 years old still matter and that the makers of those that do are very rich already.[15]

Further, without any evidence of any sort, objective or otherwise, the government is currently pushing through legislation[16] which will extend the term of protection for artistic works which have industrial application from 25 years from first sale to 70 years from the year of death of the author—averaging something like a century of protection. For instance, Lucienne Day fabric designs and George Nelson clocks and, maybe, classic designs of chairs—Mies van de Rohe, Charles Eames, and so on[17]—will remain the exclusive right of successors

Regulatory Options', Project Report (IPO, 2013); www.ipo.gov.uk/ipresearch-parody-report3-150313.pdf.

[13] Directive 2011/77/EU of the European Parliament and of the Council of 27 September 2011 amending Directive 2006/116/EC on the term of protection of copyright and certain related rights.

[14] 'Today's decision to increase the term of protection for musicians' copyright from 50 to 70 years will make a real difference for performers. With increasing life expectancy, the previous 50-year protection term was clearly insufficient. Despite the fact that their music and songs are still popular, today many performers are left without income when they are older. The increase to a 70-year term means performers can still receive remuneration when their music is played once they have retired': statement by Commissioner Michel Barnier, 12 September 2011; www.ec.europa.eu/commission_2010-2014/barnier/headlines/news/2011/09/20110912_en.htm.

[15] The economic evidence suggests the same, just as one would expect: Centre for Intellectual Property and Information Law, University of Cambridge, *Review of the Economic Evidence Relating to an Extension of the Term of Copyright in Sound Recordings* (2012); www.cipil.law.cam.ac.uk/policy_documents/gowers_cipilreport.pdf.

[16] Now enacted by the Enterprise and Regulatory Reform Act 2013, s 74. This repeals the Copyright Designs and Patents Act 1988, s 52. Put crudely, s 52, subject to exceptions (eg works of sculpture), limited the term of protection for industrially applied artistic works to 25 years from first marketing.

[17] It depends on whether they are 'works of artistic craftsmanship'. The test for a 'work of artistic craftsmanship' is murky at best: *George Hensher Ltd v Restawile Upholstery (Lancs) Ltd* [1976] AC 64. And besides, the UK might have to adopt a wider test, if (which seems wrong in law) the EU Directive requires this. I am grateful to Professor Lionel Bently of Cambridge University for providing me with his insight into this subject.

in title to the long-dead designers. Why, a citizen might ask, should these undeserving successors get this monopoly? All the more so because protection will be wide: infringement of copyright extends to a reproduction of a substantial part. This means protection for not merely more or less exact copies but also to virtually any variant based on the original. I do not think the government even appreciates that copyright gives wider protection than the law of registered designs. Opposition from all the professors of copyright law in this country,[18] opposition from established British manufacturers of old design classics, opposition from many in the field of design itself, has been set at naught by the government. Instead it has listened to the lobbyists. Perhaps also it is acting out of a craven fear, never articulated or reasoned in the open, that it could be sued under the *Francovich*[19] principle by the undeserving if it does not give them what they want. The professors say that view of the law is wrong and have yet to see any reasoned opinion saying otherwise. This sort of thing is too important to be based on unpublished legal opinions from unknown civil servants. Much more important is the impediment to young modern designers which will be caused if they cannot safely design things which are inspired by the designs of yesteryear. IP policy should be looking to encourage creativity now over rewarding that of the long past. And surely it matters that companies in this country who are currently making here perfectly lawful copies of these old designs will have to shut down or move out of Europe altogether.

Another example. There are calls from a small minority of noisy lobbyists to make patent and design infringement a crime. Both the European Commission[20] and the UK Intellectual Property Office consulted[21] as though they thought this idea might be in the slightest degree sensible. Neither organisation looked at the experience of history, or the practicalities, or the common sense of the idea.

Patents and crime. The last criminal prosecutions for infringement of a patent for an invention in this country were in the time of James I. They were mainly, you may not be surprised to hear, in Star Chamber.

[18] See their letter to *The Times*, 31 July 2012.

[19] Case C-6/90 *Francovich v Italian Republic* [1991] ECR I-5357.

[20] COM(2005) 276/1, Proposal for a European Parliament and Council Directive on criminal measures aimed at ensuring the enforcement of intellectual property rights. This would have applied to both patents and designs. It was eventually dropped: Withdrawal of Obsolete Commission Proposals, OJ C252/7, 18 September 2010.

[21] The UK consultation was confined to designs: UK Intellectual Property Office, *Consultation on the Reform of the UK Designs Legal Framework* (2012) 21–23; www.ipo.gov.uk/consult-2012-designs.pdf. The consultation consisted of a series of extremely leading questions.

The last prosecution in a common law court was in 1617. It was of Sir Hugh Myddleton, the genius behind the New River Project. He was a Goldsmith—and indeed became Royal Jeweller to James I. He and others were charged with infringing a patent for some way of making gold thread. The case got mired in complexity. Myddleton alleged the patent was invalid. The prosecution went to sleep.[22] From then on no prosecution for infringement of an invention patent was ever brought. The driving force for innovation provided by patents throughout the Industrial Revolution and right through until now evidently did not need the criminal law. So why would criminalising patent infringement help now?

And how, you ask, Mr Bentham, would it work? After all, questions of the scope of patents and of their validity are complicated and often involve much science and technology. And remember that many patents are invalid or unduly wide—for no patent office can act as better than a rather coarse filter. Is a jury to decide on patent infringement and validity? I know they do that in civil suits in the USA.[23] It is an object lesson in what not to do—evidence-based policy would do well to study it. It is a major cause of the expense of litigation in the USA. The US courts have had to devise complicated procedures such as so-called Markman[24] hearings and elaborate summary judgment procedures to get round or minimise the problems caused by jury

[22] Technically infringement of a patent was contempt of a royal command: *Halsbury's Laws of England*, 3rd edn, vol 10, para 1053; I Hawk PC c 6; 2 BL CLE 141; *Dudley's Patent* (1622) 1 Webst PC 15; *Goldsmid v Great Eastern Railway Co* (1883) 25 Ch D 511 (infringement of a patent for a market right in Spital Square). The *Myddleton* case was a prosecution by way of criminal information by Yelverton A-G in the Court of Exchequer: SR Gardiner, 'On Four Letters from Lord Bacon to Christian IV King of Denmark, together with Observations on the part taken by him in the grant of monopolies made by James I' (1867) 41 *Archaelogia* 219, 242. As far as I know the most recent discussion of the common law crime of infringement is to be found in a very odd and obscure place, namely Schedule II to the Appellants' printed case to the House of Lords in *Norwich Pharmacal Co v Commissioners of Customs & Excise* [1974] AC 133 (available in Lincoln's Inn Library). I was junior in the case. The point never came into play in the oral argument or in the judgments. It arose in the following way. The Customs were arguing that discovery of the name of a wrongdoer was contrary to law and anyway involved what is now called public interest immunity and was then called Crown privilege. The patentees said 'but suppose the Mona Lisa had been stolen and Customs found it on a search. Surely it could tell the police and the Louvre and identify the culprit?' Customs responded by saying that perhaps there was an exception for crime. And the Appellants said: 'But patent infringement *is* a crime'.

[23] Borrowing from English procedure in your time, Mr Bentham. It is frozen in time by the Seventh Amendment to the US Constitution: 'In suits at Common Law, where the value in controversy shall exceed twenty dollars, the right of trial by jury shall be preserved, and no fact tried by a jury, shall be otherwise reexamined in any court of the United States, than according to the rules of the common law'.

[24] *Markman v Westview Instruments Inc* 517 US 370 (1996). The Supreme Court held that interpretation of patent claims was a matter of law and so not a matter for the jury.

trial. Do we really think that innovation will be promoted by criminalising patent infringement?

Now, the notion of making patent infringement an offence will probably get nowhere for the present. But one can be far from confident that will be so in the case of infringement of design, registered or not. For the clamour of the minority for this is much noisier than for patents. The government is consulting[25] in terms which suggest that it thinks this is a good idea[26]—an 'evidence base' being something, it seems, that you measure by noise not content. Well, you, Mr Bentham, of course appreciate that for any criminal law to work, a major requirement is that it should be simple and straightforward—something that Old Bailey juries, magistrates, and dare I say it, average Crown Court judges, can grasp readily. The offences must be, in the words of Lord Nichols, 'simple for local weights and measures authorities to enforce and for magistrates and jurors to understand'.[27]

Is there any real evidence that this could be done well for design infringement? Are the rather sophisticated tests for infringement and validity suitable for a jury? It can make no sense for Apple and Samsung[28] or Proctor & Gamble and Reckitt[29] to fight it out via a prosecution in Snaresbrook Crown Court by a weights and measures inspector. 'Ah,' say the proponents of criminality, 'but what about the little man whose design is ripped off? He can't afford to go to the civil courts. So let's make it criminal and the State will look after him.'[30] The same logic would apply to breach of contract or any other civil wrong. Mr Bentham, why can't they see the absurdity of all this? What is the point of even consulting when the answer is plain?[31]

[25] See n 21. Subsequent to the delivery of this lecture, the government has indeed given way to the lobbyists. It proposes to make deliberate design infringement a crime: see *The Consultation on the Reform of the UK Designs Legal Framework Government Response* (2013); www.ipo.gov.uk/response-2012-designs.pdf; and the Intellectual Property Bill tabled on 10 May 2013. The government has counted submissions ('the majority'), listening to clamour and not reason. The proposal is something of a legal shambles since only deliberate copying will come within the provision, yet copying is not an ingredient of design infringement at all. The IP professors, the IP Bar Association and the IP Federation (representing many major companies) are all opposed.

[26] One is reminded of Ambrose Bierce's definition of 'consult' in the *Devil's Dictionary*: 'to seek another's approval of a course already decided on'.

[27] *R v Johnstone* [2003] UKHL 28, [2003] 1 WLR 1736 [25].

[28] *Samsung Electronics (UK) Ltd v Apple Inc* [2012] EWCA Civ 1339, [2013] FSR 9.

[29] *Procter & Gamble Co v Reckitt Benckiser (UK) Ltd* [2007] EWCA Civ 936, [2008] Bus LR 801.

[30] The government has ignored the seismic change in the Patents County Court under Judge Birss as he then was.

[31] It is really worrying that far from being plain to the government it has accepted the clamour of what is obviously in reality a minority view.

I would add that even the evidence base for the proposal, that little men's designs are being ripped off on a vast scale, is itself almost non-existent. The government commissioned an investigation—but that did not even really try to find out whether there is really a mass of clear cases of infringement of registered or indeed unregistered design rights which go unchallenged in the civil courts for lack of funds.[32] You can't and mustn't just count people who claim to be victims of this sort of copying—you need to know whether there really was an infringement. There is no substitute for examining the detail. Anyone with experience in IP will tell you that unsophisticated victims of competition are often apt to say their rights have been infringed when they have no rights or there is obviously no infringement. If you were to look for the detail you would have to look for cases of pure design infringement—design infringement alone. For if there is also trade mark infringement or copyright infringement or both (as with most counterfeits) then there are already on the statute book straightforward criminal offences to use against fraudsters.[33] There would be no point in adding design infringement to such cases.

Mr Bentham, I am far from saying that there is no place for criminal law in IP infringement. But it should be confined to simple cases and those where there is a clear public interest in criminality being punished—generally the sort of thing that involves deception of the public—in short, fraud. That is where it is now. It should stay that way. It works reasonably well, and only goes wrong when prosecuting authorities try their hand at more complex IP infringements as they do from time to time.[34]

That leads me to trade marks. You, Mr Bentham, were rightly concerned with the deception of the public which could come about by false marking of products. You wrote that you favoured a 'Faculty of obtaining protection for the reputation of superior workmanship by a man's registering his name and marks as put upon his goods; counterfeiting the same to be thereupon punishable as forgery'.[35] (Incidentally, as far as I know, that was the first proposal

[32] See UK Intellectual Property Office, *Consultation on the Reform of the UK Designs Legal Framework: Summary of Responses—December 2012* (2012) 12–14; www.ipo.gov.uk/response-2012-designs-summary.pdf.

[33] Trade Marks Act 1994, s 92.

[34] eg *R v Higgs* [2008] EWCA Crim 1324, [2009] 1 WLR 73, and *R v Gilham* [2009] EWCA Crim 2293, [2010] Crim LR 407.

[35] J Bentham, 'Proposals Relative to Divers Modes of Supply', Bibliothèque de Genève Ms Dumont 72, unnumbered folio, copied from a missing Bentham manuscript written in 1794.

for a general register of trade marks.) And as far as crime is concerned, dealing with some sorts of trade mark infringement in that way makes sense—dishonest people to be dealt with by the criminal courts. But any type of IP infringement not involving dishonesty should be treated like other infringements of private rights—as a matter for the civil courts. And all the more so now that Judge Birss, helped by sensible rule changes derogating from the mistaken Woolf idea that all courts should have the same rules, has made the Patents County Court fit for purpose.

Mr Bentham, you were in favour of a proprietary right in a trade mark. But you must be astonished at where this simple idea has got to now. You can no longer honestly sell a lawful copy of something by using its trade mark to tell the consumer that your product is what it is—a copy.[36] You can't import into the EU genuine goods bearing the mark of a trade mark owner unless he says you can.[37] You wouldn't believe it, Mr Bentham, but whether or not a man could put on a toy model of a motor car the trade mark which appeared on the real thing was the subject of a serious case.[38] In the end it was held that you can—the worrying thing is not the result but that any different result could seriously have been contemplated.

The Court of Justice of the EU (CJEU) has, as far as trade marks are concerned, been quite unable to produce simple and clear interpretations of trade mark law. Instead we have a vast number of cases, many inconsistent with others. The number of references about trade marks to the CJEU since the system started less than 20 years ago is nearing 150. To these must be added a greater number of appeals from the Court of First Instance or General Court. By way of contrast, the House of Lords heard just 17 trade mark cases in the period 1900 to 1994 and the law was largely settled. The fact is that trade mark law has become unpredictable.

The Minister who introduced the Bill for the new trade mark law to Parliament in 1992 asserted that it would save British industry £30 million a year.[39] He said he got this figure from industry, but detail was never given. It has certainly not proved true. I suspect the trade

[36] Case C-487/07 *L'Oréal SA v Bellure NV* [2009] ECR I-5185.

[37] Case C-355/96 *Silhouette International Schmeid GmbH & Co KG v Harlauer Handelsgesellschaft mbH* [1998] ECR-I-4799.

[38] Case C-48/05 *Adam Opel AG v Autec AG* [2007] ECR I-1017.

[39] HC Debs, 18 April 1994, vol 241, cols 658–88.

mark departments of most companies are at least 50 per cent larger now than they were before the new system.[40] All this could have been predicted—modesty aside, I did just that.[41] You did not need economists to work this out—all you needed was a bit of thinking about what was being introduced. For instance, it was and is very obvious that a system where use or intention to use a trade mark counts for little is bound to end up with bureaucratic conflicts between mark owners and a clogged register—as has happened.[42]

Mr Bentham, a cynic might conclude that the trade mark system was devised to give life to a perverted view of your great utilitarian principle. Not 'the greatest good for the greatest number', but 'the greatest good for the greatest number of trade mark lawyers'.

Mr Bentham, copyright. In your day, this was a pretty limited right compared with what we have now. The Statute of Anne in 1709/10 had created the world's first form of statutory copyright. It was originally only for 'books and other writings', but by your time had been extended to engravings (thanks to Hogarth), prints, lithographs, and works of sculpture.[43] The copyright had essentially a term of 14 years from publication, with a second term of 14 years if the author had survived the first. The battles to extend the statutory term were yet to come—as they did in the next century.[44]

Let me remind you of some of what you wrote about copyright. Firstly, in relation to a case called Millar v Taylor,[45] in 1769. It was about whether a common law right of property in the nature of copyright could exist, given that Parliament had created a statutory copyright. The court said 'yes'. Evidently you did not think much of this, for this is how you referred to the case:

> The case of literary property so thoroughly agitated not many years ago in Westminster Hall presented a curious spectacle: Advocates in multitudes

[40] That is anecdotal—I routinely ask those in large trade mark departments of industry.

[41] In the Preface to D Kitchen and J Mellor (eds), *The Trade Marks Act 1994: Text and Commentary* (Sweet & Maxwell, 1995).

[42] Ask any practising trade mark attorney—whose views from the coal face are worth a lot more than anything else, such as the Max Planck Institute for Intellectual Property and Competition Law, *Study on the Overall Functioning of the European Trade Mark System* (2011); http://ec.europa.eu/internal_market/indprop/docs/tm/20110308_allensbach-study_en.pdf.

[43] See *Primary Sources on Copyright (1450–1900)*, commentaries by Professor Ronan Deazley; www.copyrighthistory.org.

[44] L Bently, '*R. v The Author*: From Death Penalty to Community Service' (2008) 32 *Columbia Journal of Law and the Arts* 1. For the battles that led to the 1842 extension to 42 years or life plus 7, see C Seville, *Literary Copyright Reform in Early Victorian England: The Framing of the 1842 Copyright Act* (CUP, 1999).

[45] Court of Justice (1769) 4 Burr 2303, 98 ER 201.

> and all the Judges in and out of office talking about property in general, not one of them knowing what it was nor how it was created: it was an assembly of blind men disputing about colours.[46]

Of course, only a few years later, in *Donaldson v Beckett*,[47] the House of Lords reversed *Millar*—a decision of which I suspect you approved. Judges creating rights on the hoof was not your sort thing.

You had a much more limited notion of the scope of protection for copyright than we do now. You thought that copyright protected only the written form of words as they would be said aloud:

> The party favoured in the Law of Copy-right is the party who has first made a set of visible marks that are the signs of the audible signs in question; I mean either that party himself, or such other person as, by an act of conveyance, he has put into his place.
>
> The object not to be published in this case is not the ideas but the sounds—the spoken language; primary signs of those ideas. Translation into another language may by possibility be so made, at least if the discourse translated be a very short one, as to suggest precisely the same ideas as the original. Yet to publish the translation I suppose *would* not, certainly *need* not be consider'd as an invasion of the Copy-right to the work. Why? Because here the primary audible signs suggested by the secondary visible signs in question are different.
>
> Yet to publish a Copy of the same work in short hand I suppose would: especially were the use of short hand to become general. Why? Because here the primary audible signs suggested by the secondary visible signs in question are the same.[48]

Mr Bentham, dare I suggest that with hindsight you might accept you got this wrong? If one is going to protect an author's work, does it matter how it sounds?

No matter, I shall not embarrass you more. What I really want to draw to your attention is how far-reaching copyright has become. Hugh Laddie, the great man after whom my Professorial Chair is named, drew attention in his 2007 inaugural lecture to the irrational

[46] J Bentham, 'Manual of Political Economy', UCL collection of Bentham manuscripts (henceforth 'UC') xvii 49, reproduced in W Stark (ed), *Jeremy Bentham's Economic Writings* (George Allen & Unwin, 1952–54) vol 1, 265n. The dating of manuscripts written for 'Manual of Political Economy' is problematic, but their composition can certainly be limited to the period 1790–95. The text suggests that Bentham was in court and heard the argument.

[47] *Donaldson v Beckett* (1774) 2 Bro PC 129, 1 ER 837.

[48] J Bentham, 'Preparatory Principles Inserenda', UC lxix 180, written in or about 1776.

term extension from 50 to 70 years from the year of death of the author for ordinary copyright in things like literary, musical, dramatic and artistic works.[49] That happened in the 1990s.[50] I have already mentioned the 70-years-from-publication term now given to copyright in sound recordings.[51] The types of work protected have expanded greatly too. Performing rights in copyright works now exist (you noted they did not in your time). There are rights in photographs, films, sound recordings, performances, computer programs, and so on. Common sense says the period for these is too great, perhaps for some kinds of work more than others—computer programs are a clear example. But common sense and copyright have long been strangers one to another.

Critics of the corresponding US law also extending copyright term from 50 to 70 years from the death of the author called it the Mickey Mouse Act—for Mickey Mouse was about to go out of copyright without term extension.[52] I suspect we will hear soon about moves to extend the term of copyright even further—for otherwise Mickey will enter the public domain.

Mr Bentham, one can expect lobbyists to prevail over sense again unless something happens. The forces for term extension have proved victorious nearly every time—ever since the great 1830s debates featuring Lord Macaulay and Serjeant Talfourd. In copyright there is

[49] Sir Hugh Laddie, 'The Insatiable Appetite for Intellectual Property Rights' (2008) 61 *Common Legal Problems* 401.

[50] Implementing Council Directive 93/98/EEC of 29 October 1993 harmonizing the term of protection of copyright and certain related rights, replaced by Directive 2006/116/EC of the European Parliament and of the Council of 12 December 2006 on the term of protection of copyright and certain related rights.

[51] Implementing Directive 2011/77/EU of the European Parliament and of the Council of 27 September 2011 amending Directive 2006/116/EC on the term of protection of copyright and certain related rights. This change will come into effect in November 2013; see the UK IPO website for details: www.ipo.gov.uk/c-policy-copyterm.htm.

[52] Created as 'Steamboat Willie' in 1928, the cartoon would initially have benefited under the US Copyright Act 1909 from two 28-year terms (taking it to 1984). During the second term, the US Copyright Act 1976 was passed, the effect being to extend the term for works-for-hire to 75 years, thus until 2003. The 1998 Copyright Term Extension Act added another 20 years (to 95 years), taking this to 2023. Disney died in 1966, and so under EU law protection would last until 2036 (though the principle of comparison of terms should mean it is not protected for longer in Europe than it is in its country of origin). For general discussion of the status of Mickey Mouse, see D Hedenkamp, 'Free Mickey Mouse: Copyright Notice, Derivative Works and the Copyright Act of 1909' (2003) 2 *Virginia Sports and Entertainment Law Journal* 254 (discussing whether Mickey Mouse is actually in the public domain). Of course, trade mark protection means that certain uses of Mickey Mouse might be preventable long after copyright lapses.

something of a law of nature—lobbying prevails over sense. Lord Macaulay called copyright a 'tax on knowledge' and reasoned thus:

> It is good that authors should be remunerated, and the least exceptionable way of remunerating them is by a monopoly. Yet monopoly is an evil. For the sake of the good we must submit to the evil: but the evil ought not to last a day longer than is necessary for the purpose of securing the good.[53]

Macaulay by and large lost.[54] Unless Joe Public stands up and says 'enough is enough', it will happen again.

It would matter much less if the extended term provided only very narrow protection—to the very thing the subject of protection. For then embellishment, variation, homage, building on, or transformation would all be lawful—but there is no sign of that. As I have pointed out, copyright extends to copying of a substantial part.[55] So the reality is that copyright will increasingly be a dead hand on creativity rather than a force encouraging it.

Before I part from copyright, you will be interested to know of one of the justifications used by those who favour extensive and long copyright rights. Borrowing from some of the thinking about natural rights of your time, civil law lawyers see copyright as an extension of the personality of the author, not merely as an economic right.[56] This gives rise to the notion of inalienable so-called 'moral rights'. You would call this an example of 'nonsense on stilts'. You are right—and especially about inalienability, which is not called for by the Berne Convention.[57]

Mr Bentham, I turn to patents for inventions. Here the forces of irrationality are driving the other way: there is currently a significant anti-patent brigade.[58] You knew quite a lot about patents. You would of course have been well aware of the doings of Mr Boulton and Mr Watt.[59] You would have known not only of Watt's big invention

[53] Speech delivered to the House of Commons on 5 February 1841.

[54] Though the initial extension was much watered down, and Macaulay himself favoured extension, proposing 42 years or life: Hansard, HC Debs, 3rd series, vol 61, 1393 (1842).

[55] Or 'any original part' if the Directive 2000/31/EC of the European Parliament and of the Council of 8 June 2000 on certain legal aspects of information society services, Article 2, applies generally to copyright. See Case C-5/08 *Infopaq International A/S v Danske Dagblades Forening* [2009] ECR I-6569.

[56] See E Adeney, *The Moral Rights of Authors and Performers: An International and Comparative Analysis* (OUP, 2006).

[57] Berne Convention for the Protection of Literary and Artistic Works, Article 6 *bis*.

[58] eg NS Kinsella, 'Against Intellectual Property' (2001) 15 *Journal of Libertarian Studies* 1. Stephan Kinsella is Director of the Center for the Study of Innovative Freedom, information relating to which is online at www.c4sif.org/about/.

[59] See eg E Robinson, 'James Watt and the Law of Patents' (1972) 13 *Technology and Culture* 115.

of the separate condenser, but also of his many other inventions, such as the fly-ball governor and the sun and planet gear. You would have known how Boulton and Watt made it possible to provide power far away from coalfields—most importantly to the Cornish tin mines. And you would have known how Boulton used the patent system to protect the results of his investment in Watt's research. Moreover, your own brother Sam was an inventor and engineer and must have talked with you about patents.[60] He later became an important figure in creating the Portsmouth Block Factory for making pulley blocks for the Navy by machinery rather than by hand.[61] A key inventor of these was Marc Brunel, Sam's business partner and the father of Isambard Kingdom.

Here are two passages of what you wrote about patents:

> An invention will not be brought to light and practiced except in as far finds a person willing as well as able to bring it to maturity and to practice it.
>
> A man will not be at the trouble and expense of bringing to maturity [an] invention unless he has the prospect of an adequate satisfaction, at least of such a satisfaction as to his eyes appears an adequate one, for his trouble and expense.[62]

You went on to reason that fame and glory might be enough for a few inventors but even such an inventor would need a sufficient fortune to 'enable him to bestow on the object in question the measure of labour and expense ... which appears likely to be requisite to the accomplishment of the object'.[63]

You concluded in the early 1790s:

> So long as men are governed by unexamined prejudices and led away by sounds, it is natural for them to regard Patents as unfavourable to the encrease of wealth. So soon as they obtain clear ideas to annex to these sounds, it is impossible for them to do otherwise than recognize them to be favourable to that encrease: and that in so essential a degree, that the security given to property can not be said to be compleat without it.[64]

[60] On 30 March 1794, Bentham complained to a correspondent that in making preparations for the building of the panopticon pentitentiary: '*Patent* has been added to *Patent* (an object of itself of between 600 and 700 pound:)': AT Milne (ed), *The Correspondence of Jeremy Bentham Volume 5: January 1794 to December 1797* (Athlone Press, 1981) 24.

[61] A ship of the line needed 1,500 plus copious spares. Sam's blocks would have played an important, but silent, part in the battle of Trafalgar.

[62] J Bentham, 'Manual of Political Economy', UC xvii 46 (reprinted in *Jeremy Bentham's Economic Writings* (n 46) vol 1, 261–62).

[63] J Bentham, 'Manual of Political Economy', UC xvii 46–47 (reprinted in *Jeremy Bentham's Economic Writings* (n 46) vol 1, 262).

[64] J Bentham, 'Manual of Political Economy', UC xvii 48 (reprinted in *Jeremy Bentham's Economic Writings* (n 46) vol 1, 265).

Mr Bentham, nothing that has happened since suggests you were in any way wrong. Patents for inventions and the knowledge they can be obtained and relied upon to protect the investment and research that went into making and developing them have been really important drivers from the beginning of the industrial revolution to now.[65]

Mr Bentham, I do not claim that there can be no innovation without a patent system. That would be to overstate things. Again an example: some of the listeners (not you for obvious reasons) may have taken their car to the continent by ferry. If so, very likely it was on a fast-moving catamaran. What not many know is that most of these high-speed catamaran ferries around the world were made in Hobart, Tasmania. They are of the order of 100m in length and capable of carrying 400 cars and 100 people. They are the brainchild of a genius called Robert Clifford,[66] who developed them starting in the early 1990s. Yet all his innovations have been unprotected by patents. He says, 'well, if they copy what I did 5 years ago it doesn't matter.' But he didn't need patents for other reasons. Firstly, his fabrication techniques with the very light but difficult material aluminium are an art which cannot readily be copied. Secondly, it is not that easy to copy a very expensive thing like a catamaran. You can hardly just go out and buy one to take apart. Thirdly, there are limits to what you can learn from an examination—you can see how a thing is shaped in a particular way, but not why. However, even in the case of Robert Clifford I suspect a few patents (for instance on the device which reduces roll) might have made him even stronger.

Take industries which have received much media prominence: the pharma industry and the mobile phone industry. They are both highly patent based and they are both highly innovative. They would not, as many of them do, spend 20 per cent of their income[67]—income, mark you, not profit—on R&D without the security of property

[65] There have always been sceptics: eg HI Dutton, *The Patent System and Inventive Activity during the Industrial Revolution, 1750–1852* (Manchester University Press, 1984); C Macleod, *Inventing the Industrial Revolution. The English Patent System, 1660–1800* (CUP, 1988). But, Mr Bentham, once you have worked with industry and seen the living patent system, as I have been fortunate to do, there really can be no doubt that it drives innovation.

[66] See A Mant, *The Bastard's a Genius* (Allen and Unwin, 2010).

[67] For pharma, see the largely hostile European Commission, *Pharmaceutical Sector Inquiry Final Report* (2009) 30, which gives a figure of 17%; http://ec.europa.eu/competition/sectors/pharmaceuticals/inquiry/staff_working_paper_part1.pdf. My own experience is higher. This comes from figures provided in evidence, first in Patents Act 1949, s 41 compulsory licence-cases and later in licence of right cases following the Patents Act 1997, which provided for extension of patent term from 16 to 20 years with the last four years being licence of right. For mobile phones, the figures come from my informal inquiries from large companies.

provided by a patent. Ask them. Or imagine you are a small inventor who wants to raise some money to develop an invention and bring it to market. You want to borrow some money or sell shares in your company. Will anyone put up the money if your idea, if it proves successful, can be copied at low cost?

Mr Bentham, the reasoning is simple, and rather short. I do not see how it can be refuted. Nor did you. Yet there are people out there who want to abolish patents altogether, or at least curtail them—especially important patents. They are, in your words, 'governed by unexamined prejudices'. Here, for instance, are two prominent American economists writing in September last year:

> The best solution is to abolish patents entirely through strong constitutional measures and find other legislative instruments, less open to lobbying and rent-seeking, to foster innovation whenever there is clear evidence that laissez-faire under-supplies it.[68]

In a 2008 book[69] they argued that (1) patents neither increase invention, nor adequately reward inventors; and (2) patents simply create a market in patents and in associated legal services. They assert that most research in economics indicates that patents do not work. Mr Bentham, research which produces a manifestly absurd conclusion must be flawed. An engineer or scientist is taught not only how to do calculations but to check the end result to see if it makes sense. It seems otherwise with some economists. I suggest there is a very real need for serious work to be done on the limits of what economics can tell us in the field of IP. At least one, George Priest, says that economic analysis of IP lacks an empirical basis, is 'founded on little more than assumptions', and consequently 'has taught us almost nothing'.[70] Much of the working of IP law may be beyond

Published figures include Qualcomm Inc, *Annual Report for 2012* 36: 20% of turnover; www.files.shareholder.com/downloads/QCOM/2502788657x0x523322/6EBEB924-8E0D-4829-B233-2ED3D7FD3625/2011_Annual_Report_on_Form_10-K.pdf. More generally, the 20 companies with the highest spend on R&D, including their expenditure as a percentage of turnover, were identified in a 2012 study by Booz & Co, *The Global Innovation 1000: Making Ideas Work* (2012); www.booz.com/media/file/BoozCo_The-2012-Global-Innovation-1000-Study.pdf. The figures for percentage of turnover on R&D spend are somewhat, but not by much, below 20%.

[68] M Boldrin and DK Levine, 'The Case against Patents' Federal Reserve Bank of St Louis Working Paper 2012—035A September 2012; www.research.stlouisfed.org/wp/2012/2012-035.pdf.

[69] M Boldrin and DK Levine, *Against Intellectual Monopoly* (CUP, 2008).

[70] Professor of Law and Economics at Yale University. See G Priest, 'What Economists Can Tell Lawyers About Intellectual Property' (1986) 8 *Research in Law and Economics* 19: 'in the current state of knowledge, economists know almost nothing about the effect on social welfare of the patent system or of other systems of intellectual property'.

the analytical tools of economists: if that is so, then they are no better placed to give policy advice than a rational thinker such as you, Mr Bentham.

Some economists, for example, worry about the current mobile phone patent wars (as they call it). They talk about patents causing 'hold up'. But can they not see that which is evident to everyone else—that innovation in the mobile phone industry is proceeding at a simply astonishing pace, that this innovation has to be paid for, and that those who are paying for it expect to get their investment back through sales of improved products and licence fees from others? Can they not see that the fierce competition in the industry is in new and improved products? The extraordinarily fast shifts in market leadership are innovation driven, all that IP being generated to get a return.[71]

The misplaced worry about the so-called wars is also based on massively incomplete evidence—it can only be based upon the public litigation because only that is visible. What the worrying economists cannot see and have no knowledge of are the much larger class of cases where patent licences are negotiated and work quietly for the benefit of the parties and the consuming public. Nor do they understand that litigation itself is, as my father once put it, adapting the words of von Clausewitz—'the continuation of negotiation by other means'.[72]

Moreover, the abolitionists offer no serious alternative: government awards to inventors have never worked, from the time John Harrison was nearly cheated out of his award for the chronometer,[73] through the Soviet system of awards for inventors, down to now.

There is nothing new about patent abolitionists. Evidently they existed in your day, Mr Bentham, for you would not otherwise have spoken of men governed by unexamined prejudices. In the nineteenth century there was a considerable anti-patent movement.[74] Part was inspired by the terrible procedures for getting a patent, involving as

[71] Some doubt that patents are important here: eg J Bessen and MJ Meurer, *Patent Failure: How Judges, Bureaucrats and Lawyers Put Innovation at Risk* (Princeton University Press, 2008). And it is true that many patents turn out to be invalid. But you only have to ask anyone in the industry (and I frequently do) how important the patents are and how important the patent incentive, and you get the same answer—they really, really matter. Only an economist would say the entire industry is suffering from a delusion. Actually, the insiders say, everyone knows which patents really matter.

[72] Dad used that in discussion with me—whether he wrote it anywhere I do not know.

[73] JR Siegel, 'Law and Longitude' (2009) 84 *Tulane Law Review* 1. The story is well told in D Sobel, *Longitude* (Penguin, 1996).

[74] See eg F Machlup and E Penrose, 'The Patent Controversy in the Nineteenth Century' (1950) *Journal of Economic History* 1; M Coulter, *Property in Ideas: The Patent Question in Mid-Victorian Britain* (Thomas Jefferson University Press, 1991).

they did the payment of a host of fees to various leech-like officials with obscure titles. Dickens' narrator in *A Tale of a Poor Man's Patent*, written in 1850, concludes 'that the whole gang of Hanapers and Chaff-Waxes [people who took fees] must be done away with and that England has been chaffed and waxed sufficient'.

A writer under the pseudonym Vindicator had attacked the procedure with considerable force[75]—and there were reforms starting in 1835 with more important changes in 1852 and culminating in the Patents Act 1883.

But there was more to abolitionism than just the problems of bad procedure. In other European countries there were abolitionist movements. Indeed the Dutch abolished patents from 1869 to 1912, and the Swiss had no effective patent law until 1888. The consequences are not uninteresting. Holland had not taken a major part in the Industrial Revolution and the patent-free period enabled it to catch up. The most notable example was that of Mr Philips who made light bulbs free of the Edison and Swan patents. Now Philips are one of the most patent protected innovators in Europe. Hoffmann-La Roche (1896), Sandoz (1886), Geigy (earlier in dyestuffs), and CIBA (1884) all started up in Basel next to the German border, so that they could make and sell into Germany, whose patent system did not then provide adequate protection in respect of imported products made abroad by a patented process.[76]

Mr Bentham, note that the abolitionists of the nineteenth century were economists associated with free trade. *The Economist* magazine, founded in 1843, advocated abolition of the Corn Laws and patents for inventions. It is no coincidence that today's abolitionists are economists too. Patents don't fit their world view. And because competition law is largely driven by economists, competition authorities show signs of becoming anti-patent too. Examples are the recent absurd but vastly expensive[77] pharma industry sector inquiry of the

[75] MJ Janis, 'Patent Abolitionism' (2002) 17 *Berkeley Technology Law Journal* 899. This article contains much of value and much of what I cite in the following footnotes comes from it.

[76] E Schiff, *Industrialization without National Patents: The Netherlands, 1869–1912; Switzerland, 1850–1907* (Princeton University Press, 1971); DS Ritter, 'Switzerland's Patent Law History' (2004) 14 *Fordham Intellectual Property, Media and Entertainment Law Journal* 463.

[77] Some lawyers from big pharma have told me they reckon it cost the industry £250 million. The Commission has never said how many people it put onto the inquiry, but it cannot have been fewer than 30 and may well have been 50 or more. The whole story, starting with dawn raids as if the respondents were all crooks, followed by incessant written questions often asking things that had already been answered, ought to be investigated and told. I think that dawn raids without any judicial warrant are not a proper way of proceeding.

European Commission,[78] and its even more recent interest in, and threat of such an inquiry into, the mobile phone industry.[79] They should leave well alone.

Not all of today's abolitionists are as total as Boldrin and Levine. They are apt to say they are in favour of patents, but then suggest there are problems and chip away at various aspects of patent protection. For instance there has been much recent talk about 'patent thickets' and that something (it is not clear what) should be done about them.[80]

Here is the sort of emotive description used:

> [A] dense web of overlapping intellectual property rights that a company must hack its way through in order to actually commercialize new technology.[81]

[78] *Pharmaceutical Sector Inquiry Final Report* (n 67). Essentially the Commission found nothing—though it remains suspicious of settlement agreements between big pharma and generics and 'monitors' all such settlements. The Commission (like many competition lawyers) cannot get its head round the fact that in the real commercial world patents are not simply good or bad. That can only be determined by litigation to the death—and settlements are intended to avoid just that. If the patent were litigated and turned out to be good, the patentee would be worse off than his settlement agreement. But if it were invalid, the patentee would be better off. The settlements (even reverse payment settlements) represent a middle ground. I think there is a lot to be said for making anyone who wants to say the settlement is anti-competitive prove not only that the patent is invalid, but also that it was obviously invalid to both sides—for then the settlement would be sham.

[79] Those in the industry have told me that this was mentioned by a Commission official at a conference in early 2012. However, the prospect of such an inquiry has receded for two reasons. First is that the Commission has taken action against Samsung and Motorola asserting that the mere claim for an injunction in legal proceedings for infringement of a standards-essential patent amounts to an abuse of monopoly (Samsung on 31 January 2012, Motorola on 6 May 2013). Second is that the German courts have now raised essentially the same questions by a reference to the CJEU: Case C-170/13 *Huawei Technologies*. What the court will make of it is anyone's guess.

[80] eg B Hall, C Helmers, G von Graevinits and C Rosazza-Bondibene *A Study of Patent Thickets: Final Report Prepared for the UK Intellectual Property Office* (2012); www.elsa.berkeley.edu/~bhhall/papers/HHvGR_Patent_Thickets_FIN_29Oct12.pdf. Their conclusion is that 'Econometric analysis of the probability of entry into patenting by technology area shows that the density of a patent thicket is associated with reduced entry into patenting in the technology area in the data set used for this study'. Well, wouldn't you expect a lot of patents in fast-moving technology? And if you are an outsider wanting to start for the first time in that area, shouldn't you have to pay to use other people's inventions made at their risk and cost? Or you could try inventing around—one of the points of the patent system. The European Patent Office's Economic and Scientific Advisory Board also published a study on thickets in March 2013: *Report of Workshop on Patent Thickets* (2013); http://documents.epo.org/projects/babylon/eponot.nsf/0/B58781F239B083CEC1257B190038E433/$FILE/workshop_patent_thickets_en.pdf. Its conclusion (at 5) is that they are not a problem per se. Insofar as they are a problem, that problem can be solved or alleviated by '(1) improvements in the granting process; (2) improvements in dispute resolution; (3) improvements in standards related IP management; (4) improvements in transparency; and (5) market-based incentives'.

[81] C Shapiro, 'Navigating the Patent Thicket: Cross Licenses, Patent Pools, and Standard-Setting' in AB Jaffe et al (eds), *Innovation Policy and the Economy* (MIT Press, 2001).

> [A]n overlapping set of patent rights which require innovators to reach licensing deals for multiple patents from multiple sources.[82]

Hargreaves even went so far as to assert (without proof) that patent thickets 'obstruct entry to some markets and so impede innovation'.[83]

Well there is nothing new here. A nineteenth-century abolitionist, Macfie, complained in 1865:

> In the manufacture with which I am connected—the sugar trade—there are somewhere like 300 or 400 patents. Now, how are we to know all these 400 patents. How are we to manage continually, in the natural process of making improvements in manufacture, to know which of these patents we are conflicting with? So far as I know, we are not violating any patent; but really, if we are to be exceedingly earnest in the question, probably we would require to have a highly paid clerk in London continually analysing the various patents; and in every year, by the multiplication of patents, this difficulty is becoming more formidable.[84]

What these economists who worry about thickets forget is that good patents are meant to be a barrier to entry. They forget, too, that the phenomenon of thickets is as old as the hills; and the reality—that so-called thickets appear in fast-moving innovative industries just as truffle flies appear over truffles. They even forget that merely counting patents, or counting in a more sophisticated way as the recent study commissioned by the UK Intellectual Property Office did,[85] will not tell you much about what important monopolies outsiders seeking entry might face. Some patents have wide important claims, others only narrow ones. Economists never get as far as claims or validity—another example of working on the principle that if you can't measure something then it isn't important.

Now I am not saying that the patent system does not have problems—it does, but they are none of the problems identified by economists. The problems are much more practical—cost, expense and procedure. It is these we should focus on. We are not doing very well here—the proposed new unitary patent and court promise disaster in my opinion—but this is a subject for another day.

[82] *Hargreaves Report* (n 8) 18.

[83] *Hargreaves Report* (n 8) 5.

[84] G Macfie, 'Is the Granting of Patents for Inventions Conducive to the Interests of Trade?' [1865] *Transactions of the National Association for the Promotion of Social Science* 661, 666, quoted in Janis (n 75) 936.

[85] *A Study of Patent Thickets,* Final report prepared for the UK Intellectual Property Office, Bronwyn Hall, Christian Helmers, Georg von Graevenitz, Chiara Rosazza-Bondibene, 9 October 2012.

Mr Bentham, 'Keep Calm and Carry On' was a phrase used on a poster designed by the Ministry of Information just before the Second World War. It was in fact never publicly used, but the discovery of a small stash of posters in 2000 was publicised on the TV programme *The Antiques Roadshow*, and this sparked interest. The phrase has become iconic and has been widely parodied. Someone has successfully persuaded the European trade mark office[86] to register it as a trade mark—an example of the sort of absurdity highlighted by Sir Hugh Laddie in his inaugural lecture. I suppose there is also a now a respectable argument that the five-word phrase is a copyright work, short though it is. After all, our Court of Appeal (not including anyone here) held that an 11-word newspaper headline could be a copyright work, depending on how creative it was.[87]

I pass these matters by to concentrate on the message. Should we keep calm about IP and carry on, or should we worry? I think the answer is a bit of both. We should keep calm about mistaken alarmists such as the abolitionists and over-zealous competition lawyers, but we should be vigilant about curbing the excessive growth of copyright and design law. As for trade mark law, we can only despair.

Mr Bentham, thank you for listening.

POSTSCRIPT

1. *The shrillest voice sort of won in relation to criminalisation of design infringement, though in the end it was reduced to deliberate infringement and confined to registered designs only. It should not do much harm (or any good).*
2. *Other topics of this general lecture are considered more fully in other chapters (Chapter 19—'Grasshoppers' (regarding pay for delay), Chapter 23—'Patent Thickets' and Chapter 8—'Can Economists help?').*

[86] EU009455619. There are various UK registrations too, all by the Keep Calm and Carry On Beverage Co Ltd.

[87] *Newspaper Licensing Agency Ltd v Meltwater Holding BV* [2011] EWCA Civ 890, [2012] Bus LR 53. The case went on appeal (sub nom *Public Relations Consultants Association Ltd v Newspaper Licensing Agency Ltd*), but not on this point, and the Supreme Court referred questions to the CJEU: [2013] UKSC 13.

11

*Is Intellectual Property the Grit in the Wheels of Industry?**

I begin with three stories from the past and a speech in a House of Lords debate in 1841.

Filippo Brunelleschi was the first person in Europe to be granted a patent for an invention. He was the genius who designed and constructed the great dome of Santa Maria del Fiore, Florence cathedral. The city fathers gave out the architectural work by a series of competitive tenders. When he tendered, Brunelleschi was fearful that others would steal his ideas and get the work. So he generally tendered without saying how the job was going to be done. For instance, he was frightened about disclosing how he was going to raise the many tons of stone needed to create the great dome. It nearly cost him the work. By and large he was lucky in that, although he never explained how he was going to do a thing, he got the job anyway. But late in the project he was so concerned about piracy that he procured from the city fathers a patent, granted in 1421. He wanted 650 tons of a pure white marble called Bianchi Marmi for the eight great ribs of the cupola. It was to come from a quarry at Carrera, some 65 miles away. The cheapest way to bring the marble was via the Arno, if it could be done. But the 50 miles from Pisa to Florence was most troublesome—the Arno was tideless, prone to silting and also to flooding. Brunelleschi devised some sort of barge to solve the problem. He was given a three-year patent—a term which was extended at least once because the invention had not been put into use. Brunelleschi's patent does not disclose the details of his design, but informed guesses have been made. It was probably some sort of vast amphibious raft provided with giant wooden wheels to deal

* *The Gray's Inn Reading, Gresham College (25 June 2002).*

with shallows. We know the Florentines called it *Il Badalone*—'the Monster'. Eventually *Il Badalone* was constructed and loaded with 100 tons of Bianchi Marmi. It set off from Pisa. It sank or became stranded less than halfway to Florence. The marble was lost. Brunelleschi's attempts to salvage it failed. I expect it is still there.

Thus the modern intellectual property system began with a flop. It has certainly moved on since then. The first British patent was more of a success. It was granted to a Dutchman, John of Uthnam, in 1449. He had special techniques for making stained glass windows. He was given a monopoly plus also certain tax advantages in return for which he had to make the stained glass windows of Eton College and a now defunct Cambridge college. Notably, he also had to train apprentices in the new techniques. Here is what his patent said:

> [A]nd because the said art has never been used in England and John intends to instruct divers lieges of the king in many other arts never used in the realm beside the said art of making glass, the king retains him therefore for life at his wages and fees and grants that no liege of the king learned in such arts shall use them for a term of twenty years against the will and assent of John, under a penalty of £200, whereof two parts shall be rendered to the king and one part to John, any liege who cannot levy that sum to suffer imprisonment without delivery save by the king's special command.

I do not think history records what John's invention was. Certainly his patent did not say. I say 'invention' because, until 1977, British law treated the person who first brought an idea from abroad here as much an inventor as if he had devised it himself.

My third story is later in time—well after the early Renaissance and at the beginning of the Industrial Revolution. It is of the Boulton and Watt patent for a steam engine.

I have cut this out. I had been beguiled by the theory that the Watt patent had held up innovation. That was a serious blunder—see Chapter 23 on 'Patent Thickets'. I deeply regret spreading this mythical nonsense further.

My piece of Parliamentary debate relates to the fierce arguments in the 1840s about the length of term of copyright. By 1840 the term was 28 years from publication or until the year of death of the author, whichever was the longer. It was thought too short. A Bill was introduced into the Commons by Serjeant Talfourd to make the term 60 years from the death of the author. Lord Macauley opposed this vehemently in the Lords. Here is some of what he said:

> It is good that authors should be remunerated, and the least exceptionable way of remunerating them is by a monopoly. Yet monopoly is an evil. For

> the sake of the good we must submit to the evil: but the evil ought not to last a day longer than is necessary for the purpose of securing the good.

He went on to point out that the balance between the evil of monopoly and the good of authors' remuneration shifted in favour of the evil of the longer the term:

> A monopoly of 60 years produces twice as much evil as a monopoly of 30 years and thrice as much evil as a monopoly of 20 years. But it is by no means the fact that a posthumous monopoly of 60 years gives to the author thrice as much pleasure and thrice as strong a motive as a posthumous monopoly of 20 years.

He went to give an example. The quote is a little long, but delicious:

> Dr Johnson died 56 years ago. If the law were what my honourable and learned friend wishes to make it, somebody would now have the monopoly of Dr Johnson's works. Who that somebody would be, it is impossible to say: but we may venture to guess. I guess, then, that it would have been some bookseller, who was the assignee of another bookseller, who was the grandson of a third bookseller, who had bought the copyright from Black Frank, the Doctor's servant and residuary legatee in 1785 or 1786. Now, would the knowledge that this copyright would exist in 1841 have been a source of gratification to Johnson? Would it have stimulated his exertions? Would it have once drawn him out of his bed before noon? Would it have cheered him in a fit of spleen? Would it have induced him to give us one more allegory, one more life of a poet, one more imitation of Juvenal? I firmly believe not.

What can we learn from these bits of history in a modern context? Well, actually rather a lot. I start with John's patent. A major purpose of the grant of John's patent was in part the same as the purpose of a patent today, namely that disclosure of an invention should be given in return for a time-limited monopoly. John was to disclose to apprentices—the modern way is to disclose in the patent itself. By and large the system works well. Disclosure of inventions still lies at the heart of the system but a little less so than it was. Under our old law, the rule was that if you commercialised an invention, even by a single sale, prior to seeking a patent, the patent was no good—it was not novel. You could not even secretly work the invention without making any subsequent patent invalid. The common law encouraged, as far is it could, early disclosure in the trade-off between incentive to invent and monopoly. Now the rule is different. Only a disclosure which enables a skilled man to work the invention invalidates. A product can be in all the shops, but unless you can work out how it is made, there can be a subsequent patent. The balance shifted towards monopoly—as it has in almost every aspect of intellectual property over the last 30 years, both in terms of legislation and judicial decisions, particularly, so far as the latter are concerned, in the USA.

Disclosure now leads to a new problem—information overload. By 2001 the European Patent Office had grown from nothing in 1977 to a staff of over 5,000 and an annual income of about nearly €1 billion. In 2001 it received 110,000 patent applications. Now we all know that there are many ideas which seem bright at the time but subsequently turn out to be useless or worse. That is very true of patents and patent applications. Applications are examined for novelty and inventive step. Some fail at that stage. Others are granted but, for one reason or another, the idea is not considered worthwhile protecting. The number of patents which are renewed by the payment of fees to the end of their maximum life, 20 years, is but a small proportion of those filed. So there are many, many patent specifications out there but no one to tell you which ones are commercially important, or even which ones actually work as promised. Many patents are for ideas no better or more practical than was Brunelleschi's for *Il Badalone*.

It remains the case, however, that industry must read all patent applications relevant to its activities. It must do so to see whether anything it does or is proposing to do infringes or will do so. In that regard alone, I was told that BP estimated over half the resources of its patent department were devoted to that task. The applications must also be read to learn of new ideas—the system there serving its intended purpose—the same purpose expressed in John of Uthnam's patent.

In passing it may be worth noting a second-order effect, not intended in the time of Brunelleschi or John of Uthnam. Important commercial monopolies create an incentive to design around them. This incentive is additional to the incentive provided by the prospect of a patent monopoly. Glaxo's Zantac (ranitidine) was at one point the top selling pharmaceutical in the world. It was the result of an inventive design around SmithKline's cimetedine patent. The incentive to design around was one of the spurs of the men of Cornwall faced with Boulton and Watt—*again wrong!*.

On any basis, therefore, the patent system has a substantial 'transaction cost'—a happy phrase of economists. All patent offices, patent agents and patent lawyers are part of that transaction cost.

Indeed you are hearing from a transaction cost at this very minute. So great has been the growth of intellectual property law in the last 40 years that I dare take a guess. It is that more than half of all intellectual property lawyers of the world who have ever lived are still living and probably still in active practice.

I wish to say some more about transaction costs. Intellectual property rights, unlike say rights in land, are apt to be fuzzy at the edges. For instance whether an invention is obvious, whether a word or phrase in a patent claim has a wide or narrow meaning, whether one trademark is confusingly similar to another, whether a substantial part of a copyright work has been taken, are all matters on which reasonable minds can differ. In the competitive world served by intellectual property rights, attention is particularly focussed on these fuzzy edges. If you want to make something competitive with a patented product it is upon those fuzzy edges that you focus. And uncertain laws again increase transaction costs. They also increase the power of the skilful right holders—just as the uncertainty of Boulton and Watt's rights did so many years ago.

How I milked this wrong example!

It is for that reason that I think judges should, so far as they can, strive to keep the edges of IP rights sharp. That has not always been done. I give a recent example—one where the ECJ differed from me. Under European trade mark legislation you infringe a registered trade mark if you use it or a confusingly similar mark for the goods for which it is registered. But you also infringe if you use it, or a confusingly similar mark, for 'similar goods'. So, if Kodak is registered for film, the registration protects the mark used for similar goods, probably, for instance, video tape but not, say, for socks. Now what I held was that the concept of 'similar goods' was independent of the nature or fame of the mark. The ECJ, on a reference from Germany, differed. It held that the more famous a mark the wider the ambit of 'similar goods' for which there was protection. This is to make a fuzzy rule fuzzier. The result has been, as any trade mark practitioner will tell you, increased uncertainty and therefore cost.

I turn to another area where width of IP rights has become a topic of major debate. Many are saying that the patent system here is a substantial hindrance to progress—more than a bit of grit in the wheels—something like a large lump of concrete. I refer to the so-called patenting of genes.

It has become possible to identify stretches of DNA which code for particular proteins. DNA has a double helix structure. Along each strand of the helix are points of attachment to one of four different chemical groups, A, T, G or C. As you go along the strand you can have any one of the four groups at each position. So you can have a code—for instance AGTCC ... It is now known how that code works—when the gene is switched on, as they say, it tells various chemicals in the cell to make a particular protein. So, by identifying the code you can identify the protein. And (ignoring complications) you can work backwards from the protein to the code.

The use of these techniques has enabled scientists to put copies of particular genes into bacteria (and indeed animals) so that they produce a particular protein. For instance the protein erythroproietin (epo) is made this way. Epo is an immensely valuable drug for the treatment of anaemia—it is also misused by racing cyclists, weight lifters and other athletes. What happened was this. Natural epo is present in minute traces in human urine. Vast quantities of urine were used by a man, appropriately named Dr Goldwasser, to isolate a small amount of epo. Analysis of this made it possible to work out what a bit of the genetic code—the gene—for making it was. That in turn enabled scientists to find the rest of the gene, isolate it, and put it into bacteria. The bacteria are then allowed to breed, making epo, much as yeast makes alcohol.

The resulting patent has been the subject of much litigation. It is currently being studied by our Court of Appeal—precisely on the question of its appropriate breadth. Our House of Lords had to conside related question concerning the breadth of the Patent for the Hepatitis B vaccine—and held it too wide.

The problem with these gene patents is indeed their width. For once you have isolated a gene you set about patenting it, not in the body (which is old) but when isolated or contained in some new carrier or cell. The width of such a patent is potentially enormous—it will almost certainly cover the product of any further research based on the gene.

It has also become possible to identify particular genes which are associated with particular diseases. The precise mechanism by which the gene either causes the disease (for instance Huntington's disease) or causes a predisposition to a particular disease (for instance breast cancer) remains unknown. But you can at least produce testing kits for the disposition and even, perhaps, for the disease. Just as in the time of Boulton and Watt the problem is width of monopoly and perceived width of monopoly. I take a prominent example. A company called Myriad connected with the University of Utah has two patents on two genes known to be associated with breast cancer. The genes are called BRCA1 and 2. It is using the patents to insist upon control over the testing of patients for the gene. It is even, as I understand it, saying only it can carry out the tests. Moreover many scientists fear that the patents impede research into breast cancer. They may be legally wrong about that (in Europe, at least, there is a reasonable research exemption to infringement) but it is the perception that matters. Boulton and Watt's grim-faced process servers from Birmingham have their modern-day equivalents, sharp-suited patent lawyers from New York or London, or open-necked ones from California. They act on a global basis.

I don't think I was entirely wrong about the Myriad patents. They caused huge concern, a concern which led to the US Supreme Court decision in relation to these patents that isolated gene claims were mere discoveries and unpatentable but that claims for the corresponding cDNA were. The decision was illogical: an isolated gene was new and could not be made before the invention. It is more than a 'discovery' for it is a working molecule—a thing.

An associated problem with gene patents is the absence of any ability to 'design around'. I observed earlier that a clear second-order effect of patents is as a spur to find something different. But gene patents are not like that. Your genes are the only genes in town. This again makes one wonder whether the patent system is too powerful in this area of human endeavour.

I turn to other IP rights more generally. Before the 1960s there were just three forms of these, patent for inventions, registered design right and registered trade marks—with the latter went passing off rights or like rights in other countries going by the name of 'unfair competition'. Each country had its own system. Now things are very different. As part of the drafting process for the Civil Procedure Rules, which are to have a Part 63 'Intellectual Property', it became necessary to list out the various types of right to which the rules might apply. Here it is:

> Patents (whether granted by the EPO in Munich or the British Patent Office), copyright, design right (whether under our own 1988 Act or the Community Regulation), registered designs (whether granted under the British System or the forthcoming European system), registered trade marks (whether granted by the UK Registry or the Office for Harmonization of the Internal Market in Alicante), rights in performances, rights in semiconductor topographies, plant variety rights, moral rights, database rights, rights to prevent unauthorised decrypting, and passing off.

There are other candidates too—cases about the taking of technical trade secrets and possibly Competition Act cases. This is an awful lot to try to know about if you are a lawyer. It is industry which has to pay for that knowledge.

Industry also has to pay for lawyers to know about much more than their own country's laws and procedure. This is because trade is so globalised. This has had its effect on IP law—it too is being globalised. That is particularly apparent within the European Union. We now have European Union Trade Marks, we are about to have European Union Registered and unregistered Design Rights. There is an incomplete European Patent system. Under this, laws have been harmonised, there is a central granting authority but the result of a grant is a bunch of parallel national patents which can only be litigated in national courts. The EU is pressing to create a unitary EU patent to be enforced by a new, EU court. It would be the first truly federal court of Europe. Industry, by and large, supports this—provided there is a judicial system which can be relied upon.

On a world scale there have been massive developments too. Most prominent so far is the Agreement on Trade-Related Aspects of Intellectual Property Rights of 1994 [TRIPS]. This forms part of the WTO Agreements. For practical purposes if a nation wishes to trade it has to conform to these agreements and to TRIPS. For the first time ever there are international rules requiring member states to have basic IP laws. For instance, by incorporation of the Berne Convention, TRIPS requires members to have copyright laws protecting 'literary and artistic works' for a minimum of 50 years from the end of the author's death. Such works are defined very widely by Berne, but TRIPS goes on expressly to include computer programs too. Some might say it thus ensures the domination throughout the world of the big software companies for the foreseeable future.

I have not time to say all that I would wish about TRIPS. I will just say this. To require nations such as Bangladesh, upon pain of trade sanctions, to have substantial intellectual property laws and a system of enforcement of such laws is to ask for the impossible. Although TRIPS provided some leeway for compliance, that leeway is nowhere near enough. It is hardly surprising that it causes much resentment. Mark Twain's Connecticut Yankee at the Court of King Arthur said that 'A country without a patent office and good patent laws was just a crab that couldn't travel any way but sideways or backwards'. That is not true for third world countries. They may be crab-like but it is not the absence of a patent office which is the cause. And even the

Connecticut Yankee had in mind a system of laws which encouraged local exploitation of inventions.

This brings me to the other feature of TRIPS worth mentioning: its major departure from the driving force of John of Uthnam's patent. His patent was created so as to encourage exploitation within the realm. TRIPS and the modern worldwide patent system do not do that. They provides the monopoly but not the local industry to go with it. So it does not create an incentive to invest in third world countries. Again that is resented and again that is hardly surprising. There are perhaps limited exceptions in the case of medicines. And there can simply be such powerful political forces that patent laws are swept aside—as happened in the case of the anti-AIDS drug patents in South Africa.

One of the features of all these developments has been what one might call the 'ratcheting up' of rights. Let me give the paradigm example. For reasons which are not clear, the Austrians and Germans, but no one else in Europe or elsewhere, had settled on a term of copyright which was 70 years from the year of death of the author. The rest of the world had, for most of the last century, had a life-plus-50-year period. I have never found the justification for that period, still less the German one. The latter is supposed to have something to do with giving a reward not just to the author, but to his children and grandchildren on the grounds that his children somehow lost out due to the Great War. Whatever the reason, the disparity in term was seen as distorting the common market, as it did. The solution was to ratchet up all copyrights to life plus 70 years. It was done with hardly any debate at the time. No doubt so far as our government was concerned it was worthwhile—British copyrights, what with British pop music and the predominance of English as an author's language, are worth proportionately more than continental copyrights. No one cared about Joe Public.

No one has justified, or could, justify this on the grounds of encouragement of authors. It is a pity that Lord Macauley was not around to oppose any of this. Actually, so far as I can see, no one was—not even that the extension was retrospective with only a limited exception for those who had started exploiting a work whilst it was out of copyright. Thus this year we have had the James Joyce copyrights held to be partly in force—the Joyce estate is concerned to preserve the purity of his work. One day people will be able to do with it as they want.

The US has followed this ratcheting up by the EU. It too extended copyright term to 70 years. Promotion of this was largely by the vested interests of Hollywood and the record industry—the inheritors of the mantles of Lord Macauley's booksellers. Even now the Supreme Court is considering whether the extension, either prospective or retrospective, squares with the Constitution.[1]

Here are another pair of cases where there is pressure to ratchet rights upwards. First from the US. The US courts have increasingly been prepared to hold that particular types of subject matter are patentable—'anything under the sun made by man' is the test. So, in the US, both computer programs and business methods are patentable if they are new and non-obvious. You can have a new and improved insurance policy or even, so far as I can see, method of stacking oranges on a barrow.[2]

So far as computer programs are concerned, no one asks whether they need the patent system for their encouragement. They already have copyright. No one could say that the rate of technical improvement in that area has been slow—do we really need patents too? As for business methods, competition lies at the heart of all business. Businesses supply products or services, they do not supply themselves. It is very difficult to see the economic justification for business method patents. There is pressure from the US for the EU to have both sorts of patent—to ratchet up.[3]

There is ratcheting-up pressure the other way too. The EU has created a curious sort of right called a database right. Actually there are two sorts of rights in databases—a copyright and a freestanding right. The former is directed at copying from a compilation of information. The latter is directed at extraction of information from a database. The theory is easy: it costs a lot to put a database together. So copying or its use should be protected. There are substantial problems to be resolved as to the limits of these rights. But it is clear that there are few defences inside those limits—nothing like a fair use doctrine exists. The Europeans are pressing the Americans to ratchet up their law to have database rights. The Americans are resisting. They have judicially recently abandoned copyright in mere sweat and

[1] *It held 7-2 that the 1998 Sonny Bono Copyright Term Extension Act was not unconstitutional,* Eldred v Ashcroft *537 US 186 (2003).*

[2] *The US Supreme Court has now cut down this expansionist view. See* Association for Molecular Pathology v Myriad Genetics *569 US __133 S Ct 2107 (2013) and* Alice Corp v CLS Bank International *134 S Ct 2347 __(2014).*

[3] *Following* Alice *(2013), it looks like the US has backed off business method patents—a good thing too.*

toil works such as telephone directories. Many in the US are alarmed at the notion of these database rights, which, if taken to their logical conclusion, certainly reach into many activities which people take for granted. The problem is exacerbated by the fact that in reality database rights are perpetual—for they undergo constant revision thereby creating fresh rights. Again no one has asked Macauley's basic question. Is the cost of the monopoly worth it?[4]

I could go on, taking you through other rights which have been created, reinforced or extended. Why, for instance, was the term of a UK-registered design extended in 1988 from 15 to 25 years? But I believe I have said enough to paint a picture of increasing and more complex IP rights on a global scale. We have moved a long way from Brunelleschi's first patent. But I rather think we have not thought many of these rights through. We have been taken with the word 'protection', which sounds good, and forgotten its obverse, 'monopoly', which sounds bad. We have in place such a complicated and expensive set of laws for intellectual property that one can see there is much grit. It is time to try to find out how much of that grit is worth it. And I suggest it is certainly time to stop putting more grit into the machine, at least until we can know more about what we have done so far.

[4] *The European Database right turned out to be largely a damp squib as the Commission's own report concluded:* DG Internal Market and Services Working Paper, 'First evaluation of Directive 96/9/EC on the legal protection of databases *(Brussels, 12 December 2005).*

12

Towards a European Civil Procedural Code[*]

'NO MAN BUT a blockhead ever wrote, except for money.' So said Dr Johnson. What would he have called a man who lectured, except for money—a 'double blockhead' perhaps? For such a man then to choose an impossible subject renders him some kind of triple-blockhead. You see before you such a man.

The title of this lecture is 'Towards a European Civil Procedural Code'. There has been a blunder—there should have been a question mark, or even, perhaps, an exclamation mark, or, more probably, both. How come I should choose such an impossible subject?

The explanation lies in a combination of several factors: my legal background, recent developments in Europe concerning enforcement of intellectual property rights, and my father's influence. First it is necessary to understand my background. Many of you will know that for most of my legal time I have been involved in the law of intellectual property—patents for inventions, trade marks, copyright for things artistic and industrial designs. All these have certain characteristics in common. They are completely incorporeal. They are essentially legal rights to stop others doing something—indeed a wise old member of chambers used to say 'we are the grit in the wheels of industry'. To work they depend upon effective legal action. To be even more precise they depend upon a legal structure which can and does provide effective legal action.

[*] *I gave this speech at the Upjohn Lecture in 1998, first published in* The Law Teacher, *vol 32, pp 136. I have had the honour of being the Honorary President of the Association of Law Teachers for about 20 years. My father was the second Hon President and he too gave the Upjohn lecture.*

Let me go into more detail, taking patents as the paradigm example. A patent is a legal monopoly. The claims of the patent are a description in words which defines that monopoly. The monopoly must not cover anything which is old or obvious in view of what is old. If it does, then the patent is bad—invalid as the lawyers slightly more pompously call it. Plainly there are genuine borderline cases where there can be argument over the scope of meaning of the claim or whether the claim is bad because it covers that which is old or obvious. Such cases, if they matter commercially, come to court and are the bread and butter—some would say Château d'Yquem and pâté de fois gras—of patent lawyers. But the vast majority of cases are such that there is little room for serious debate—the patent is fairly clearly good (or bad) and the claim fairly clearly covers (or does not cover) what the patentee's competitor does. Such clear cases should not have to come anywhere near a court system. There is seldom any point in the patentee suing on a rotten case if the system delivers him a swift uppercut when he tries.

So, it is certain that industry needs a patent enforcement system which is predictable, quick and reliable. Without this, patents turn into instruments of oppression, producing not only injustice in individual cases, but overall a great hindrance to innovation and investment. Within the UK we have gone some way towards this desideratum. Patent actions take only about a third of the trial time they took in the 1970s—and come to trial about twice as fast. You can now get an average case on within a year without straining the system—and often urgent cases can be decided more quickly, sometimes within six months, or even less. These changes were brought about by changes in procedure—and in particular by the court taking, and being willing to take, a more active role in the management of cases. I confess that I, and my brother patent judges, actively enjoy this role.

Thus far I have not mentioned one further characteristic of intellectual property laws—and it is this characteristic which brings me nearer to my subject. Intellectual property laws are, or at least hitherto have been, territorial. You get a patent or a copyright or a trade mark for a particular country. Historically each country (or at least each industrial country) had its own patent office, its own patent laws, and its own legal system for the enforcement of its patents. You could not and cannot get a world patent. All you can do is get a US patent, a British patent, a German patent, a French patent and so on. So if there was an alleged infringement going on in a number of countries, you had to (and, by and large, still have to) go to the legal system of each country to enforce that country's patent. The result was and is expense for industry. Moreover you could (and can) get a patchwork of results, a win here, a loss there and so on. This is not as bad as it might seem at first sight. Most parallel patents are not litigated in all possible countries. But no one can say there is not a problem. The important message is that intellectual property rights are not like many other matters with an international element. You cannot, for instance, litigate the same contract dispute in a whole variety of parallel actions in different countries, though of course you can have a dispute about where a contract dispute should be litigated.

Now there has been a lot of progress towards harmonisation of substantive patent laws. The cost of obtaining patents in different countries, with each national office doing its own examination and with variants of national substantive law and even different periods for the life of a patent, in the 1960s and 1970s, led many European countries (and not just the then members of the Common Market) to a new European Patent Convention—the EPC. This did two major things. It required members of the convention to have common substantive rules as to patentability. And it set up the European Patent Office in Munich. No attempt was made to abolish national patent offices, but, from when the Convention came into force (June 1977) the laws of each member state as to patentability were to be the same. And formally they are. The way the EPO works is that if you apply there you get, if the application succeeds, a bundle of patents for all the countries you designate. In law they are treated just the same as if they had been granted by the patent office of each designated country. They are national patents, though they have sister patents, in exactly the same terms, governed as to their validity by national laws which are all supposed to be in exactly the same terms.

Also in the 1970s, there was another convention. This was for Common Market members only—the Community Patent Convention. This also sought to do two things: to harmonise laws as to infringement and, much more ambitiously, to set up a unitary patent for the Common Market. Harmonising the substantive infringement laws turned out to be no problem. Most if not all European Union countries have brought their laws into alignment with the Convention and hence with each other. But the other half of the Community Patent Convention, the creation of a unitary patent for the Common Market, proved too difficult. And an attempt to revive the idea in the late 1980s failed. It failed because industry—the would-be customers—found it too expensive on translation requirements and, note this, because it said it did not trust the judicial arrangements. These were, crudely, the use of a national court, with a Community hat on, and a common court of appeal. Industry feared inexperienced courts with power to revoke a patent Community wide. Note how the proposal contained nothing about a common code of procedure—each court was going to use its own national procedures and the court of appeal would, unless it allowed everyone to start again with fresh evidence and arguments, have to work on the material gathered by the court below, whatever that might have been.

The result of all this is that we now have in Europe harmonised substantive laws on patentability and infringement. And throughout Europe we have patents whose terms are identical but which are legally distinct. How were they to be litigated? From the inception of this position in 1978 until the early '90s, the received view and the accepted practice was that there could be parallel actions, on infringement and validity, running in different European countries. That is how it worked. A patentee could sue on his European Patent (UK) in the English courts for infringements going on in England, in France on his European Patent (France) for French infringements, on his European Patent (Germany) in Germany for German infringements and so on. Each country applied its own national procedures. Under this system you can, and do, get different results in different countries. And you have no common ultimate judicial authority. Even so the differences are not always significant: for instance as between here and Germany it is no longer easy to say which country would go which way in marginal cases. No one should think that the position is wholly chaotic, but, in what was increasingly really becoming a common market, it was (and is) a serious matter if a patent action succeeds in one country but fails in another. The market thus fragmented is bad for industry. In some cases, if an important part of the market is cordoned off by a patent injunction on a particular product, the company concerned may decide it is not worth selling in Europe at all. I shall call the procedural set up of each country doing its own thing the Classical Model.

Things did not stay with the Classical Model, however, though it still generally prevails. Two developments ran in parallel. First the Dutch courts, initially in trade marks and then in relation to other intellectual property rights, decided, in the late 1980s they had power to enforce foreign intellectual property rights. This initially caused enormous alarm. Here, was a court prepared to grant Europe-wide, indeed worldwide, injunctions provided an allegedly infringing article was sold in Holland. The seller, and then his supplier were joined in the proceedings. For example, the court asserted a power to order a factory, say in Scunthorpe, to stop making a product in infringement of a UK patent, just because the product was, inter alia, exported to Holland I propose to call a scheme whereunder courts simply assert the right to enforce foreign intellectual property rights the Unrestrained Dutch Model. If completely uncontrolled the dangers are obvious: worldwide scrambles for injunctions, anti-suit injunctions and so on. Could the US courts, for instance, keep out if the courts of major European countries started injuncting US companies from conducting activities not only in Europe but also in the US itself? Recognising the problems, the Dutch courts themselves pulled back, not only in restraining their activity to Europe alone, but also to plain cases and, in the latest development, in effect to cases where the main defendant is Dutch. A major factor in their thinking has been the Brussels Convention of 1968.

This Convention was simply ignored by intellectual property lawyers for many years. But in the 1990s it has become the source of the second development: an attempt to use its rules to decide where intellectual property disputes should be decided on a pan-European basis. Now I said that the intellectual property lawyers had ignored it for years. This was mainly through sheer ignorance—it never darkened my door when I was in practice. But there was more than that: the Convention was and is extremely unsatisfactory as an instrument for dealing with intellectual property rights. Let me explain why. It is essentially an allocation instrument. What it seeks to do is to set up a scheme of rules for where a particular dispute is to be litigated. It in no way seeks to harmonise the rules of litigation within a country. The general idea is simple enough. Article 2 provides the basic rule—the defendant is to be sued in his home country. But there are exceptions. In particular the defendant can be sued in the country where the damage occurs. And once you have got one defendant properly sued you can join other related defendants into those proceedings. Thus you got the absurdity of a case such as *Pearce v Ove Arup*.[1] The plaintiff was an architect. He said a firm of Dutch architects had infringed his plans in designing Rotterdam town hall. He wanted

[1] *Pearce v Ove Arup* [2001] EWHC Ch 455.

to sue them. The natural forum by any standards was Holland: the town hall was there, the alleged acts of copying were there and the primary infringer, the Dutch architects, were there. Yet the plaintiff contrived to sue in England. He did so by the expedient of joining in the consulting engineers. They of course had to make their own copies of the architect's drawings to add structural detail. And so technically they would infringe if the architects had infringed. They did their work in England. So, under Art 2 of Brussels, they could be sued here. Then it was easy to join the architects and Rotterdam town Council. Why did he want to do this? Because he could get legal aid here. And he would also get the benefit of the unjust legal aid rule that successful defendants do not get their costs from the plaintiff or the legal aid fund.

So Brussels may be turned on its head for intellectual property cases: all the plaintiff had to do was to find *a* defendant in the forum of his choice, sue him and then join in all the others. In particular all he had to do was to find a seller of the goods concerned, sue him as an infringer and then he could join in the real defendant. The Brussels Convention, designed to prevent forum shopping, was and is being used for just that. Counter-tactics were devised—in particular the idea of the potential defendant suing in the forum of his choice for a declaration of non-infringement came into play. The games of tactics and counter-tactics involve use of the Convention's rules to allocate cases to particular countries. Because the Convention can be used by a plaintiff in the way I have described, its essential purpose is being diverted. The reason is not hard to see. The Convention presupposes a single dispute, a breach of contract or a tort, and sets out to allocate one country's courts for resolution of that dispute. It is not really framed for disputes which involve parallel wrongs in different countries, of which intellectual property disputes and libel are examples. I shall call a system of European intellectual property litigation based on the current Brussels convention the Brussels/Dutch Model.

Now I must mention a further complication. Under Art 16(4) of Brussels, questions of the validity of a registered intellectual property right—a patent, a registered trade mark or the like, are given to the court of the country concerned on an exclusive basis. And of course if a right is invalid, it does not exist and cannot be enforced. Does that mean that if a defendant says the right is invalid, the whole case must be heard where validity is challenged? That would be a return to the Classical Model. Mr Justice Laddie and the Court of Appeal in

Fort Dodge say yes. The Dutch courts think no. And the European Court of Justice will have to decide in a year or so. It must choose between the Classical Model and the Dutch/Brussels model.

It is self-evident that neither of these solutions, and still less the Unrestrained Dutch Model, are any good for a market which is increasingly really becoming a common market—a market in which national boundaries simply do not matter to traders. Next year that market will largely be covered by a common currency, which will make the current position even more ridiculous. If the Dutch/Brussels Model prevails, forum shopping will become the vogue. Indeed it already has as Dutch Rambo lawyers (the phrase of a prominent Dutch patent agent) toured the world advertising Holland as the place to get pan-European injunctions. If the Classical Model prevails we face a fragmentation of the market. A point of crisis has, I believe, been reached. Innovative European industry does not have to hand a rational litigation system. Not surprisingly it is complaining. It is complaining about the cost and the uncertainty. It wants a single system for litigating patents in Europe. And that system must be reasonably cheap and speedy and it must be predictable.

Now the European Commission is currently proposing a partial solution—the creation of a European Union Patent. As I have said before similar proposals did not work before because of translation costs and the problem of 'judicial arrangements'—the phrase it uses for a system of litigation. Increasingly European industry is also complaining of the costs of translations and it may be that some pragmatic solution will be reached. It is not easy for one whose native tongue is English to comment. I merely observe that some industries in some European countries are suggesting a move to a single language. Perhaps surprisingly Swiss and some parts of French industry are supporters of this: they say they have to do business in the rest of the world and for that purpose they have to translate to English anyway.

Let me turn back to that phrase of the Commission 'judicial arrangements'. It is an anodyne expression—and it is too glib. It suggests that forming a suitable judicial system is just a question of arranging things. I say it is not. It is a formidable task. All the evidence shows that this is so. I will give a series of examples.

I have mentioned the first already—the failure of the 1975 Community Patent Convention and the failure of the revamped version of that in 1989. The second example is contained within the files of the Commission itself. Over 10 years ago my father had, lying on his desk, a letter from Sir Leon Britton.[2] It spoke of a Commission project to produce a code of civil procedure. A little work was done but not much. I gather that from time to time someone at the Commission brings out the papers, dusts them down, looks at them and then puts them away—too difficult. My third example is the working of the European Patent Office itself. There is a so-called 'opposition' procedure whereunder, within nine months of the grant of a patent, people can apply for its revocation. The framers of the Convention envisaged a relatively informal and speedy system. But the result has proved to be most unhappy. Here is not the place to dwell on the problems. It suffices to say that even appeals are taking over two-and-a-half years to come to a hearing and that it will not be long before a patent (the term of which is 20 years) will still be under opposition when it expires. Any new system must avoid the problems encountered by the EPO. My fourth example, still in the field of intellectual property, is trade marks. Although there is now a European Trade Mark Office and the laws of national marks have been brought into line pursuant to a Directive, most practitioners have serious misgivings about the arrangements for litigation. More generally much of European commercial law is being harmonised and in due course the pressure to create a European legal dispute resolution system will increase.

Why is the task of making suitable 'judicial arrangements' so hard? The question is, I think, very important. We need to know the answers because I think, if there is going to be a solution which is accepted by European industry it must be one that takes into account deep current differences between nations. And the answer or answers are very revealing. I think the first and principal answer is this: that the real difference between the legal systems of different countries lies not in their substantive law but in their procedural law, including in that their system of judges. Most of were told when we were young that the big difference between the common law and that of the civil law systems lay in the fact that the common law was based on judge-made law contained in precedent laid down through the ages whereas civil law systems were derived from a code, for instance the Napoleonic Code. I think that, although true in principle, was highly misleading. And to the extent it was true at all, it has increasingly become less

[2] *Then a European Commissioner.*

so. In my practice as a barrister and in increasing contacts with continental lawyers, I have learned that they too essentially have a case-law-based system, whatever the theory. If the German higher courts interpret the law in a particular way, lower courts follow. If you think about it this must be so—particularly given the general nature of the codes we are talking about. If the courts kept coming to different conclusions when applying such a code you would get chaos—which is something all judges strive to avoid. A typical example, with which we are more familiar because European Union law is part of our law, which shows what actually happens with a generalised code is to be found in the case of the European Court of Justice. It in practice provides a judge-made law, just in the same way as the common law. People speak of this case or that just as they do of English cases. They even use their names or shortened forms of them,. Every student of European law knows about *Cassis de Dijon* for instance, just as every student of our tort law knows about *Donoghue v Stevenson*. True it is that precedents are not strictly binding and that final courts are not bound by their own previous decisions, but these are differences which count for little in the everyday application of the law.

Turning back to patent law, you can see how true what I say is. We now have harmonised patent law and patents expressed in exactly the same terms. So the differences between different countries are purely judicial and procedural. Yet the differences between different countries are still profound. We use our common law method, with its emphasis on discovery, oral evidence and argument. The parties produce their experts and the judges are experienced patent lawyers, with either a formal background in science or years of experience of patent law with the concomitant picking up of technical expertise. It is expensive, which may not matter in very big cases but certainly does in smaller ones. And, though I have not time to go into this, the same is largely true of trade marks. Each other country has its own system. Let no one assume that civil law countries all have similar legal procedures. They do not. For instance in Germany, for historical reasons, the question of validity is treated as a matter for a federal court whilst infringement is treated as a civil wrong—a matter for the state courts. Germany has thus developed a specialised Federal Patent Court staffed by experts who mainly come from the Patent Office and are accompanied by a lawyer judge. Their infringement courts (by custom, mainly the courts of just three of the *Länder*, ie states) are staffed by lawyers. Holland has a specialised patent court, but the judges rotate in and out of it. Of course they use a different procedure yet again. France has its own way based essentially on its normal civil procedures, with only limited specialisation at the Court of Appeal level. Italy has regional courts and so on. Each country has its own way of dealing with patents, that way coming under the general system of that country's court and procedural system with more or less modification. Likewise judges vary from those very experienced in patent matters (England and Wales, but not Scotland or Ireland), Germany, Sweden, Holland are examples) to those who seldom, if ever, see patents at all.

So the first reason is the deep differences in national legal procedures. Although the Common Market is now about 40 years old, and we have been in it for 25 years, national legal procedures have remained virtually untouched by it, so resistant are they to change.

The second reason is, I believe, that the importance of legal procedures and the judicial system is consistently and seriously underestimated by everyone, but particularly by politicians, civil servants and business. They have all consistently taken the view that harmonising substantive law is the important thing—the procedures by which that harmonised law is actually to work have seemed the lesser problem. Lawyers and law schools are at fault too. Notwithstanding the work of my father in his time, civil procedure remains very much an orphan subject for academics. Comparative civil procedure is hardly a subject at all. Yet its study, in a practical and non-academic way, is vital if the current muddle-headed assumption that procedure is really not a problem is to be displaced. I think there is a deep need for lawyers with considerable practical experience to become involved in this. The problem with purely academic study is that it is really difficult to understand how a system works simply by reading or indeed studying in great detail the rules. Unless you have played some chess or Monopoly, a study of the rules alone would give you no real idea of the game.

The third reason is that, until recently at least, judges themselves have remained supremely ignorant of what brother national judges have been doing in their own countries. Indeed that remains the general position. In patents there has been a change: pursuant to what in future may be seen as an inspired seminal development, the European Patent Office instituted a biennualmeeting of European patent judges. We have been exposed to each other's ideas. We have begun to learn what we each do and how we do it. We have, above all, learned respect for each other and some of us have become good friends. It remains the case that we still have much to learn from each other. We try to do that via informal meetings of some of us between the bennial meetings. Many of us believe that the judges themselves must take an active part in forging a uniform code for the litigation of European patents.

Now I have mentioned earlier the Brussels Convention with its system of dispute forum allocation. And I have briefly described how it is not working, and cannot really ever work for parallel rights in different countries. Allocation is not the way of the future—one day it may be seen for what it is at best—an interim measure. Things are not stable as they are. Something of a crisis is upon us. The imperative of the Common Market of the European Union dictates that in the end we shall have common courts for that common market. History will force the countries of Europe to start forging a European system of litigation. And for a beginning it is intellectual property—with patents at the fore—where the need is greatest. The time has come to create a court system with a full procedural code for the litigation of patents in Europe. This is of course much less ambitious than the Commission's original plan for a general code of European Civil procedure. But you have to start somewhere and the place to start is where the need is greatest. I believe that to be in the field of patent litigation. That need has got to overcome the deeply ingrained historical differences of procedure across Europe. If you like there are two forces at work: the deep needs of European industry to have a rational dispute resolution system forcing the pace one way, and the inertia of history, language and above-all legal culture resisting that force. Resources, more than are being devoted at the moment, should be allocated to serious work on the project. It is no good just saying 'we need adequate judicial arrangements' and hoping it will all turn out in the wash.

Let me assume for a moment that what I say is accepted. What should happen next? Obviously there would have to be proper legal basis for setting up a European patents court. Existing treaty arrangements would, it seems, require that it be part of the Court of First Instance of the European Court. I wonder whether this is a good idea. That court may not have the necessary machinery for dealing with the sometimes complex technical questions which can arise. I think we have to look to a new Treaty—perhaps the next updating of the Rome Treaty. For make no mistake, to try to fudge this project will mean it will not work. It is clear that unless it is attractive to users, they will simply shop elsewhere. And on any view the existing scheme of national patents (including patents granted by the European patent office) will have to continue.

So assume there is no legal restraint on what is set up—a treaty setting out to create a court system which really works. There is much to be thought about. I believe the judges will have to be scientifically competent. For a busy patent court to have judges who have no technical background, either by formal degree or by years of experience, would be to hamper it at the outset. In practice I see no alternative to the use, to a large extent, of patent-experienced national judges, initially at least on a part-time basis. One of the possible problems with the use of the Court of First Instance is that it may not be possible under existing treaties to borrow judges in this way. In practice I think it would also be a good thing if the court could 'go on circuit'. It would not seem too remote—just as the judges of assize went out across our country so I think the possibility of a European patent 'assize' should be considered. It may also be that electronic techniques would allow the court in many cases to convene electronically.

There is the major question of how the court is to get its information. Is it to be from experts called by the parties or from its own expert or from some sort of hybrid system? You find here exact echoes of the current debate over the function of experts in the post-Woolf era of our own system of litigation. For myself I think there is a lot to be said for the hybrid idea and for flexibility. Expert 'opinion' baldly stated is seldom useful—for instance if an expert said the patent claim was obvious and no more, one would have no way of testing that opinion. So whether the expert is called by the parties or the court there must be some way of testing the opinion. But I cannot see that our present English way of testing the opinion by extensive cross-examination could survive unmodified into a European system. I am not sure it will survive here either, for that matter. At least in some cases the Court can and must take steps to control it—otherwise cases can take a disproportionate amount of time. It is in practice perhaps the single most time-costly matter in a patent action. And I am by no means sure that we get significantly different results from those of other countries, though we of course sometimes differ. The fact is that obviousness, for example, is a matter over which opinions can and do differ.

Or take the question of discovery. I think the power of the court to order discovery is important. But it is not so critical that it should be ordered on a routine basis for all aspects of any case. It is particularly important when a defined and clear issue of fact is involved and there is a conflict of evidence over it. Beyond that, however, it often proves to be a waste of time—and indeed may serve to distract attention from what really matters.

What about witnesses? Should it be the court or the parties who call them? Should the prime questioner be the court or the parties? Again I am not sure that our technique of evidence in chief and cross-examination is the only way. An amalgam of the two techniques might well work well. It all depends on what the point is. If you are testing the veracity of a man alleged to be a liar, then our technique of cross-examination by a well-prepared hostile lawyer may well be better than questions by the court. But far from all cases involve that sort of point.

How much should the proceedings be oral and how much written? Even in our own system the principle of orality is being limited. Evidence in chief has become written and courts are increasingly moving to limit the time spent on all aspects of trial (or appeals for that matter). Interestingly I think the result has been to improve the quality of justice. People with limited time must concentrate on the bits of the case which matter most. Any European court would have to have serious control over the time spent on oral proceedings—otherwise it could be buried under its caseload.

Then there are other questions: what about legal costs? Who can appear? Note that the battles between the Bar and solicitors have their equivalents in other countries—indeed in some places they seem more intense, for instance the rivalry between German patent agents and German lawyers.

There are also more complex questions involving interface with national law. This court would not have any machinery of its own for enforcement—there would be no tipstaff to enforce orders and indeed it may well be questioned whether our concept of contempt of court (which has no parallel on the Continent) should apply. So how are its orders to be enforced? By national procedures simply being added on? Or should there be some uniform sanction which national courts are asked to enforce? And what about other remedies such as damages or an account of profits? Will it be for the court to evolve European rules as to how these are assessed?

The time has come for serious debate on such matters. I think, like it or not, we are at the beginnings of a code for European civil procedure. And I think it will be intellectual property which, perforce, will lead the way. Serious consideration should be given to setting up an international conference which has the objective of creating a new legal system and code of procedure. And preparations for such a conference should start soon. I only hope that we can create something which truly represents the best sort of amalgam of the varying civil procedures around Europe. Europeans deserve no less.

POSTSCRIPT

It has all taken longer than I thought and than it should have done. Neither has it been done as well as it could have been. But for the first time a European procedural code is coming into existence for a European federal court—the Unified Patent Court (UPC). And for the first time there will be a uniform procedural code for this court—see Chapter 25: 'The Perfect Patent Court'. This piece is interesting for its date—just before things began to happen. Quite a lot of what I said there has come to pass.

13

*International Intellectual Property Litigation in the Next Millennium**

LAST YEAR MY friend Judge Randall Rader chose the topic 'The Coming Decades of World Intellectual Property Law'—a big subject. I was also asked to choose a big picture topic. Randy will obviously have covered all that can said about substantive world IP law. So I have been left with what I would have chosen anyway: what is so often seen as the Cinderella of the law—courts and legal procedure.

Many of you are students. It is the way of most law teaching to concentrate on the basic rules of law. Procedure is seen as mere machinery. In fact, as you get into practice, you will discover that procedure dominates all. Substantive law is the skeleton, procedure is the flesh, blood and nervous system of the law—that which gives it life. This great practical truth is almost universally ignored by civil servants and legislators—often leaving judges and litigants with what we in England call a shambles. My theme is that we have managed to achieve a shambles in international IP litigation, that very probably things are going to get worse before, well into the next millennium, things get better.

Let us first take stock of where we are. In the last century each country began to develop its own IP laws. You in the US put the right to a patent and a copyright into your Constitution, copyright laws began to develop (though in the US you remained essentially international pirates as Dickens and others complained bitterly)[1].

* *This was first published in (2000) 32(3)* Case Western Reserve Journal of International Law *507–16 and based on the Deioma Lecture (October 1999).*

[1] 'But he is in the trade of importing works from the United States of America. Anyone in the trade must be taken to know that works of American origin are piratical' *per* Sir George Jessel MR in *Cooper v Whittingham* (1880) 15 ChD 501.

Each nation-state went its own way. At the end of the century the great international treaties of Paris and Berne came into being. These did not seek to bring laws into line, they set forth the principles of equality of treatment (so that in each nation-state foreigners got the same rights as citizens) and the principles of recognition of dates of filing.[2] From then on, for most of the century things proceeded on a nation-state basis—if you wanted to complain about an IP violation in a particular country you went to the courts of that country and nowhere else. In theory this was untidy and could lead to multiple litigation, but in practice it really was not that bad. People seldom litigated in more than two or three countries. And—after all—who better to judge whether the patent governed by the law of a particular state was infringed than the courts of that state? And if a court was to say that a violation was to stop, could it really be right that a court from some other country should say stop? In concrete terms would it be politically acceptable, for instance, for a court in Düsseldorf or Tokyo to order a factory in Cleveland or Detroit to close because of a violation of a US patent? So, with very limited exceptions, all the courts of the world regarded it as none of their business to deal with violations of foreign IP rights.

Things began to change, almost imperceptibly at first, some time after the creation of the Common Market in 1953 with just six countries. The first real change began when the European Court of Justice began to create the concept of European exhaustion of IP rights, starting with *Deutche-Grammophon v Metro*[3] and culminating in *Merck v Stephar*.[4] It was becoming apparent that IP laws, as purely local rights, were becoming inappropriate for single markets which crossed national borders. But even by 1980 the perceived view and actual practice remained that national IP rights had to be litigated in the nation concerned. No one who practised in IP had noticed the

[2] You in the US persisted (as you do today) with the individualistic first-to-invent rule which is perceived by the naïve as helping small inventors but which in practice costs many Americans proper protection outside the US because, relying on the rule, they prior publish themselves thus making their own publication prior art in the rest of the world (first-to-file) countries. *It was another 12 years before the AIA, subject to an unclear grace period, got rid of this rule. There is now some pressure on Europe to have a grace period—but before that could even be considered seriously you would have to know what it was—6 months, a year, what about prior use as opposed to mere publication and so on? If there is to be one it would only make sense if it were internationally agreed so that inventors everywhere knew where they stood and knew that it worked universally. As things are, only a fool or an ignoramus would rely on the US or (different) Japanese grace period instead of working on first to file.*

[3] *Deutche-Grammophon v Metro* [1971] ECR 731.

[4] *Merck v Stephar* [1981] ECR 2063.

European Convention on Jurisdiction and Enforcement of Judgments in Civil and Commercial Matters of 1968—the Brussels Convention. This Convention (to which the UK acceded in 1982 and which other non-EU countries have also joined via the Lugano Convention) is basically about where you litigate a single dispute, typically a contract or tort claim. For instance, there was a case where someone in Germany allowed a poisonous discharge to get into the Rhine causing damage in Holland. Could the plaintiff sue in Holland?[5] The draftsmen of the Convention knew virtually nothing about IP—and did not bother to ask industry.

At the time of the Brussels 1968 Convention, European IP laws were not at all harmonised—the position was still that each country had its own patent offices and own laws and own courts. In the 1970s, under pressure from industry, the European Patent Convention came into being. This set up the European Patent Office, granting a bundle of patents in identical terms for all the countries designated by the patentee. At the same time the parties to the Convention were required to bring their substantive patent laws into line with the Convention. It was now beginning to be rather silly to have exactly parallel patents, subject to exactly parallel laws, litigated in different courts. An attempt was made in 1975 to provide for a litigation system for the Community (the Community Patent Convention). But for two main reasons (translation costs and judicial arrangements) it was not acceptable to the users—nor was a later 1989 revision any more acceptable.

It was the Dutch IP lawyers who actually decided to read the Brussels Convention. Its provisions opened up the possibility of trying to litigate parallel rights in just one court. But, as I shall show, it does not work at all well. I turn to the Convention.[6]

The basic rule is that a defendant is to be sued in his home country—his country of domicile (Art 2). There are exceptions, however. Under Art 5(3), in the case of tort, delict and quasi-delict, a defendant can be sued in the courts of the country where the harmful event occurred. And, most significantly, if there are number of defendants, they can all be sued in the country of domicile of any one of them (Art 6).

It is these basic provisions which enable the right holder to turn the Convention on its head. The reason is that anyone who sells or deals

[5] See Case 21/176 *Reinwater (Bier v Mines de Potasse d'Alsace)* [1976] ECR 819.

[6] *This has been replaced by a Regulation, the latest version of which is 1215/2012. The numbering has changed (why do they do that?).*

in goods covered by the right is in law an infringer. This is true for the whole range of IP rights, not only patents. So you can, in general, find a seller and hence an infringer in any country of the common market. And once you have got a seller in the country where you want to sue, you can not only sue him, but also join in his supplier and ultimately the manufacturer who is generally the real defendant. Under the philosophy of the Brussels Convention he would normally expect to be sued at home. But he finds himself playing away instead. One reason for this is that the Convention has set its face against any doctrine of *forum conveniens*—there is no room for jurisdiction being conferred on the country which has the most connection with the alleged infringement.

Of course defendants do not like this. So they have been taking evasive steps by way of seeking declarations of non-infringement and bringing revocation proceedings in the country of their choice. Instead of waiting to be sued, they start the litigation. And of course generally speaking a potential defendant can always do this: he knows what he is proposing to do before the plaintiff can ever start proceedings against him. Once he has started these proceedings in the country of his choice he invokes Art 21 of the Convention, which says that where there is a *lis pendens* in the courts of one country, the courts of all other countries must stay the action.

There is another kind of evasive action too—in the market place. We have seen it happen in Holland where, at least in the early days of the pan-European injunction, some companies simply took special care to ensure that they did not start any new activities in Holland. That was the advice that the Chief Patent Agent of Akzo gave to his company—advice which at the time was startling.

A particular form of exploitation of the *lis pendens* rule has been described as the 'Italian or Belgian torpedo'. The idea is to get the case well away from any country which might grant a pan-European injunction and to bog it down. If you sue for a declaration for non-infringement in a court which is very slow you may well achieve this. A recent example of the firing of a Belgian torpedo by a potential defendant is *Sepracor v Hoechst Marion Roussel*.[7] My brother judge, Mr Justice Hugh Laddie, acidly observed of the current position that 'a less sensible system could not have been dreamt up by Kafka'.[8]

[7] *Sepracor v Hoechst Marion Roussel* [1999] FSR 746.
[8] ibid, para 14.

What has also been put into practice is early attacks on the validity of the patent. Before saying more about such tactics it is necessary to go back to the Brussels Convention. This has not thought out IP rights well. Some are registered and some are not—patents on the one hand and copyright on the other are examples. In some cases the rights are closely allied, for instance registered trade marks and unfair competition rules. Under the Convention, in the only place where IP rights are considered, questions of validity of registered rights are the subject of the exclusive jurisdiction of the country concerned (Art 16(4)).

What then of a patent action in which validity is contested? Does Art 16(4) mean that it can only be fought in the country of the patent? Under Art 19 a court shall of its own motion declare that it has no jurisdiction over a matter in which the courts of another state have exclusive jurisdiction. Invalidity of a patent is often a major defence to a claim. In many cases it is really the only defence. The English courts have said that where validity is contested then, by a combination of Arts 16 and 19, the English court has exclusive jurisdiction—the *Coin Controls* case.[9] The Dutch courts thus far have said that is wrong: the court forms a view as to whether or not the challenge to validity is likely to succeed.

The European Court of Justice will have to decide. But no solution is satisfactory. On the one hand the purely national position means, in principle, multiple litigation on exactly parallel rights and laws. Yet the Dutch solution, coupled with Italian torpedoes and national applications for revocation, is inherently unstable—and gives the whip hand to those who are best advised. If the position is truly that the courts of any country can order that factories in other countries close down many would say that there is a breach of comity. And as a practical matter you are finding more and more unseemly scrambles between parties for getting the litigation in the forum of their choice.

A good example of the latter occurred in England. A man sued three defendants, namely a firm of Dutch architects, their client the town Council of Rotterdam and the consulting engineers who happened to be British. The claim was that the architects had infringed the plaintiff's copyright in architectural plans when designing the new town hall of Rotterdam. So, apart from the fact that the consulting

[9] *Coin Controls v Suzo* [1997] FSR 660; principle affirmed by CA in *Fort Dodge v Akzo Nobel* [1998] FSR 222.

engineers were domiciled in the UK, the whole case was based on what happened in Holland. Why did the plaintiff sue in England? The answer is twofold—first he wanted to play 'at home' and, more significantly, he could get legal aid if he did so. I think this case (*Pearce v Ove Arup*[10]) is a vivid example of what is not right under the Convention.[11]

There are other problems with litigating in one country about infringement of a foreign IP right. For instance, what is the position about damages? Does the court award these on the basis of its own principles or the principles of each of the countries the subject of the litigation. Is it necessary that there is a home patent or other IP right at all? What about the principles of provisional relief, provided for by Art 24? For example, in England comparatively short periods of delay will result in denial of an interlocutory injunction. Holland is more relaxed. Can it really be right that a party in England can be made the subject of a Dutch temporary restraining order (or the alternative a *kort gedding*) when he could not be subject to such an order in his home country?

You may well think from what I have told you that we have made rather a mess of things in Europe. Now why am I telling you in the US all this? The answer is not merely that as IP lawyers you have to know what is going on in other industrial countries and regions. There is more. Quite unbelievably, there is currently an international negotiation going on intended to lead to a treaty which will impose a similar shambles on the world, including the US. Let me tell you about it. The proposed convention is called the Hague Convention. Its latest proposals for IP are modelled on Brussels. You have before you the June 1999 draft. There is to be a meeting this month for the negotiators to give its final approval, following which there is intended to be a diplomatic conference. It has been under discussion for some time.

[10] *Pearce v Ove Arup* [1999] FSR 491.

[11] *I also disagree with the decision of the UK Supreme Court in* Lucasfilm v Ainsworth *[2012] 1 AC 208. The Court held that a UK citizen could be sued in the UK for an alleged infringement of US copyright for simply selling Star Wars helmets from this country to customers in America. He was doing nothing wrong by UK law—just going to the post office to post the goods to the US. How the Supreme Court could assert, as Lord Collins did that 'There are no issues of policy which militate against the enforcement of copyright' I do not know. Here was an Englishman going about his business lawfully in England and accepting orders from the US. Was he really supposed to check on the laws of every country that wanted to buy his products? Did it not matter that this was long-arm US jurisdiction or that the US courts would not enforce UK copyright if the position were the other way round?*

Under Art 3 the basic rule is similar to that of Art 2 of Brussels—except wider, giving the plaintiff a range of choices based on the idea of suing the defendant 'at home'. Article 9 widens the choice considerably—to any place where there is a 'branch, agency or any other establishment of the defendant'. That may include, I suppose, subsidiary companies. Article 10 approximates to of Art 5 of Brussels. Article 10(3), however, may (see the draft) limit the power to seek worldwide relief save where the *plaintiff* has its habitual residence or seat in that state. This seems to allow the plaintiff to get worldwide jurisdiction in the courts of its seat, provided it can get jurisdiction over the defendant—a job that may not be too difficult in many situations. Otherwise the rule does help, effectively preventing claims for worldwide relief in cases where the basis for jurisdiction is the place of the damage.

Article 13 provides for exclusive jurisdiction. Registered IP rights are dealt with in Art 16(4)—copied from Brussels. The same problem as exists under Brussels is in the draft—what if the defendant counterclaims for invalidity? Can the infringement action still go in a country other than the country of the registered right? Unlike Brussels, however, there is no unifying court for this proposed treaty—so courts in different countries can come to different results with no one to say one is right and one is wrong. Article 23 contains the *lis pendens* rule—which corresponds to Art 21 of Brussels and gives rise, within Europe, to the Italian torpedo. If we enact this treaty as it stands the search will be on by potential defendants for the slowest jurisdiction in the world in which the potential plaintiff can be sued.

The proposed Hague Treaty may not quite go so far as to include a provision corresponding to Art 6 of Brussels—the article which, until recently, the Dutch courts thought enabled them to get pan-European jurisdiction if an infringing product was on the market in Holland: at present the question of multiplicity of defendants remains to be considered. The game in Holland, as I have told you, was to sue the seller, and then use Art 6 to join in the manufacturer. The Dutch Court of Appeal has recently qualified this on the 'spider in the web' theory—you can only sue for pan-European relief if the infringement was organised from Holland. No one knows whether that rule will withstand further appeal or will be approved by the European Court of Justice.[12] What they will put into Hague concerning multiple

[12] *It did not survive. See* Roche v Primus, GAT v LUK *in the ECJ, Cases C-529/03 and C-4/403 July 2006.*

defendants could be important if it ultimately applies to all or some IP rights.

I hope you will agree with me that the proposed Hague agreement is extremely badly thought out so far as IP laws are concerned. Why is this? Well, I am reminded of WC Fields, who borrowed from the German of Bismarck: 'If you approve of sausages and laws you should never see them being made'. So far as I can see there has been no debate about, and no consultation concerning, the Hague proposals. There is no discussion in the IP journals. The whole thing has been thought up by academics and civil servants. I hope the users will wake up and be heard soon. I expect they will want Hague to leave enforcement of their registered IP rights at least (patents designs and trade marks) alone, for instance by adding to Art 13 infringement as being a matter for exclusive jurisdiction.[13]

Attempts to give jurisdiction to the courts of any particular country for worldwide infringements of related but not identical IP rights will not work. The Hague or Brussels solutions produce more problems than they solve—problems of scrambles for jurisdiction, Italian torpedoes, and, above all, general uncertainty.

What, then, do I see as an answer in the next millennium? I will begin within Europe. Here we have harmonised IP laws a lot (particularly patents and trade marks) and will harmonise more. Thus they are truly parallel rights. And we have the embryonic beginnings of a federal state—for example European law is superior to national law in any area where they conflict. Moreover we have two European courts, the European Court of Justice (for the European Union) and the European Court of Human Rights. On top of that we have the concept, increasingly becoming a reality, of a common market. A common market requires common IP laws (which, as I say, are increasingly becoming so) and the logic of the whole thing is slowly and inexorably a common court. There is discussion of the problem of 'judicial arrangements' (as the Commission calls the problem) now. It is unfocused and incomplete—the current suggestion is along the lines of trial at national court level and appeal to a common court. That will not work—the users have said so unanimously. They will not apply for Community Patents if that is the judicial system. For trade marks they are willing to put up with the idea—but then they will also keep their trade marks registered in national offices

[13] *In the end the ill-thought-out Hague proposal died. But some of its thinking continued, as in* Lucasfilm, *see n 11.*

until they see how things go. For patents they ask questions of this sort: how can you have an appeal court working on a trial record of a French, Greek or Swedish trial system? Some countries do not even have a proper record and allow all sorts of new material on appeal—a different concept from a common law appeal. Even in the US, I have heard it said that the Federal Court of Appeal finds things unsatisfactory because of regional differences. And yet the Federal courts are supposed to operate using a common set of procedural rules—the Federal Rules of Procedure. How much bigger this problem would be in Europe. Potential users ask about the expertise of the court or how it is to deal with expert evidence. They want nothing of the delays inherent in many national systems. You can go on and on as to why you cannot use national courts for European patents.

I think the only real way forward will be the creation of a true European Court of First Instance and Appeal. It will come to pass in patents, I believe fairly soon in the next millennium—despite all the problems of language and cost. European patent judges meet regularly, we have the manpower and the experience. It is the way forward. Once it works for patents (perhaps by 2020),[14] other rights may be treated the same way.

What about the world position? I do not see Hague providing any useful answer by way of a single litigation forum. It would do much better to keep IP (or at least major IP such as patents and trade marks) out of its system and leave the nation-state litigation systems in place. I think that is what will happen even if governments sign up to a Brussels-type variant—the users will complain so much that the agreement will not come into force. The way forward for the world will be twofold. First, some major companies who cannot wait for governments will form quasi-arbitration agreements—by this I mean they will agree amongst themselves that if there is a patent dispute they will not litigate in multiple countries but will either go to a true arbitration, or will use the courts of some country they respect and abide by the result for the world. I hear tell that some companies have agreed to such a system already—promoted by Proctor & Gamble.[15]

As time goes on, however, it may be that, if the European solution works out as I suggest it may, the world will realise that at least for IP the days of the nation-state are over and truly international courts

[14] *I wasn't far off—my best guess now is 2017.*

[15] *This initiative did not really take off.*

will be created. This is not without growing precedent—the tribunals of the WTO and the increasing number of war crimes tribunals are but a part of globalisation from which IP will not be able to stand apart.

Well, you asked for a big picture. If I am right, you who are students are all going to need passports and doubtless many of you will succeed and at the same time enjoy yourselves. When, towards the end of your careers, you look back, I hope you will do as David Deioma has done. He came to visit me in London this summer. I asked him why he had founded this series of lectures. He said he wanted to put back something for all the pleasure and interest IP had given him. Remember that when you have seen IP into the next millennium.

14

The Convergence of European Intellectual Property Law?[*]

INTELLECTUAL PROPERTY HAS long been a major concern and potential obstacle for the commercial integration of the EU. This piece seeks to consider how far we have come on the road to a uniform approach to IP law across the EU. I propose to examine it at two levels, first on the EU-wide level as created by the European Union[1] and then at the level of national courts. I am going to suggest that in recent years most (not all) national courts have been doing a better job at convergence than those concerned with the formal higher level of convergence, namely the European Commission in drafting EU IP laws and the Court of Justice of the European Union[2] in interpreting them.

THE EU LEVEL

It is worth recalling some of the history. Before what is now called the European Union began, each European state had its own IP laws, patent and trade mark offices and courts. To be a practitioner you did not have to know much about what went on elsewhere. Businesses which depended on IP had to have separate advisors in each country. Fragmentation of Europe ruled, as it had done for hundreds of years.

[*] *For the Festschrift of the President of the Austrian Supreme Court, Imgard Griss (Jan Sramek Verlag, 2011).*

[1] I shall call it the EU even though in earlier times the less ambitious phrases 'European Communities' and 'European Economic Communities' were used.

[2] As we must, post Lisbon, learn to call the European Court of Justice—there's law reform for you.

By the time Irmgard Griss became a judge, in 1979, things had begun to change. The EU had expanded from its original six Member States to nine in 1973 and to twelve in 1975. The European Court of Justice had begun to try to deal with some of the problems of IP law as it affected the common market. Initially it rather made a mess of things. *Sirena*[3] was its first significant IP case in 1969. The muddled reasoning[4] in that case has never been applied again and is long forgotten. In the 1970s the Court was hostile to IP and trade marks in particular:[5] trademarks are 'distinguishable ... from other forms of industrial and commercial property, inasmuch as the interests protected by the latter are usually more important, and merit a higher degree of protection, than the interests protected by an ordinary trade-mark'. IP rights were seen as divisive of the Common Market and, as such, needed to be curtailed if they interfered with the single market. Abandoning *Sirena* reasoning, the Court realised that by using the intellectually dishonest but effective fiction of a distinction between an IP right and its exercise, a rule in favour of free movement of goods, based on first marketing in the common market, could be devised.[6] It was necessary for the Court also to say (which was obviously also not really true) that an IP right was a measure 'equivalent to a quantitative restriction on imports'.[7] The point of the rule was to prevent IP rights, only national in extent, from dividing the common market. It meant overruling IP rights.

In its pursuit of a Common Market the 1970s Court went too far. Thus in *HAG I* it simply overruled a trade mark right because it had once had a common origin,[8] a decision which it later, when it

[3] Case 40/70 *Sirena v Eda* [1971] ECR 69, [1971] CMLR 260.

[4] Based on a fictitious notion of a market-dividing contract when all there was was an assignment made years before the common market ever existed.

[5] *Sirena* (n 3) para 7. Can this really be the same institution as that which has gone so protectionist as to object to honest comparative advertisements, *L'Oréal?*

[6] It first appeared in a competition case, *Consten and Grundig v Commission* [1966] ECR 429, 345. It was applied to stop IP rights interfering with free movement of goods marketed by the right holder in *Deutsche Grammophon v Metro* [1971] ECR 487 (copyright), *Centrafarm v Winthrop* [1974] ECR 1183 (trade marks) and *Centrafarm v Sterling Drug* [1974] ECR 1147 (patents).

[7] The key was the use of Art 30 of the Rome Treaty (now Art 34 of the Consolidated Treaty on the functioning of the EU). It provides: 'Quantitative restrictions on imports and all measures having equivalent effect shall, without prejudice to the following provisions, be prohibited between Member States'. Noone would ordinarily call an IP right a 'measure'. It is a private right—moreover one which is not in any way 'quantitative'. . See the scathing attack on the notion by that great Anglo-German jurist Dr FA Mann, *Industrial Property and the EEC Treaty* (1975) 24 *ICLQ* 31.

[8] Case 192/73 *Van Zuylen Frères v HAG AG ('HAG I')* [1974] ECR 731, [1974] 2 CMLR 127.

was becoming more pro-IP, overruled.[9] And in *Merck v Stephar*[10] it held that a patent right was exhausted within the EEC by the patentee marketing his product in a country where he had no patent—no right to exhaust. That was manifestly unfair because, open to generic competition in the place where he sold his goods (unpatented there), the patentee could not get any reward for his invention. Later, as a judge,[11] I tried to get the Court to change its mind, but it held it was too late.[12]

Turning back to earlier times, Austria joined the EEC in the 1975 enlargement. Irmgard—is one surprised?—of course already had the foresight to realise that, in the wider Europe to be, she had to be more than just an Austrian lawyer. One of the best ways to do that was to learn about another and different legal system. So when Austria joined, she was in Harvard learning to understand the common law—and a rather different method of learning to think about legal problems. Her wider perspective thus gained has stood her, and Austria, well.

In those early days the EU did not seek to legislate in the field of substantive IP law at all. The European Patent Convention of 1973, setting up not only the European Patent Office but also the substantive rules of patentability was, and remains, a non-EU international treaty. The Commission tried to create common rules for infringement and an EU patent court via the 1975 Community Patent Convention. It failed, hardly surprisingly since there was virtually no consultation with users. A revised attempt in 1989 failed for the same reasons. The 1975 Convention did contain some substantive rules about infringement (the definitions of infringement, contributory infringement, and the exceptions to infringement). Many EU countries adopted these as part of their new patent laws, but there was no obligation to do so and the rules were not laws of the EU.

Thus copyright, trade marks and designs laws in the 1970s continued to be purely national in nature. Inherently they potentially divided the common market. So it is not surprising that in the 1980s the Commission and Council began to set about creating EU-wide

[9] Case C-9/93 *HAG II* [1994] I ECR 2789, one of the very few instances where the Court has openly admitted it got it wrong last time—a much clearer thing to do than what it normally does, namely just to pretend earlier, inconsistent, decisions never happened.

[10] Case 187/80 *Merck v Stephar* [1981] ECR 2063

[11] I was counsel for the UK in *Merck v Stephar.*

[12] Joined Cases C-267/95 and C-268/95 *Merck v Primecrown* [1996] I-062285. It was a close-run thing, for A-G Fenelly advised that *Merck* should indeed be overruled.

rules as to IP laws. The 1970s had seen failure with patents so maybe trade marks would be easier. They were thought to be and harmonisation happened, with the Directive of 1989[13] followed by the Regulation.[14] These two harmonised substantive trade mark law and created an EU-wide trade mark right. I am afraid I do not regard the legislation as successful. It failed to deal with basic and obvious questions of trade mark law—must there be use as a trade mark to infringe?, what about comparative advertising?, how easy should it be to obtain registration of common surnames or well-known places?, what amounts to non-use (particularly is use in a small corner of the EU enough to keep a mark for the whole of it alive) and so on. The list is endless. Nor do I think the ECJ has coped well with it. The result has been harmonisation of a sort - harmonised uncertainty! Not even procedurally was the system thought out rationally. No one would rationally have three levels of appeal for a trade mark opposition, yet that is exactly what was provided for by way of appeals from OHIM.

Here is what I wrote about the position in 2005:[15]

> The Directive of 1989 and its subsequent implementation changed all that. Trade mark law has become much more complicated, and, I am afraid to say, much more uncertain. Although it has never been possible to say *exactly* what a trade mark is or what it is for, it was possible to approximate towards it. Einstein once said that physics consisted of a series of approximations towards the truth. The same was somewhat true of the legal meaning of trade mark which developed under the old law—it became more precise without every actually achieving precision. Now we have moved back a lot ...
>
> As I observed in an earlier Preface, the Directive seems to have been written on the basis that there were no lessons to be learned from history. All the experience of trade mark problems learned in the member states over the previous 100 years or so was ignored. So the Court of Justice had to start from scratch—using a document which did not itself provide clear answers to any of the well-known problems (e.g., fundamentally, must a defendant be using the mark complained of as a trade mark, what is meant by 'distinctive', what amounts to use and so on). The mass of cases in the last 11 years (by way of reference and appeal from OHIM) proves

13 89/104/EEC.

14 Regulation 40/94.

15 Preface to *Kerly's Law of Trade Marks and Trade Names*, 14th edn (Sweet & Maxwell, 2005).

> the uncertainty of the Directive itself. But it also shows the Court itself has no clear views of trade mark law—look for instance at the *Chiemsee, Baby Dry, Doublemint and Sat.2* series of cases ...
>
> Unfortunately, despite all the cases the clear impression one has is that things are less certain now than before. All too often the rulings of the ECJ in this area of law (I find the contrast, with e.g. VAT where the rulings are pretty clear, remarkable) are not sufficiently precise for the needs of industry. A trade mark is a guarantee of origin? Yes but infringed if it is used on imports unless there is express permission; yes, but infringed if a notice of intention to parallel import from within the EU is not given in time? And how can a mere colour ever really alone guarantee origin? What is the point of protecting a part of an advertising slogan? And is that really a guarantee of origin?
>
> I do not know the reasons for the less-than-perfect guidance coming from the ECJ. Part of it is undoubtedly the fact that the Judges are not trade mark specialists and trade mark law is unexpectedly full of pitfalls, inherent ambiguities and complex concepts. Part of it may be that it is very difficult without experience to take a holistic approach (for instance what counts as use for infringement should be the same as that which counts as use for the purpose of validity).

Since I wrote that, things have remained uncertain. The tsunami of references and appeals to the Court continues.[16] And the Court has become, in my view, over-protective of trade marks—much more protective than the courts of the USA, or the common law courts around the world.[17] I said so in my judgment in *L'Oréal v Bellure*.[18] Why should a man not honestly say his perfume smells like a famous brand if it does? Most commentators I have seen and spoken to agree.[19] We have not seen the last of this.

[16] Running at about 10–15 a year in trade marks. The UK Intellectual Property Office maintains a really useful list of pending IP references to the Court. Got to www.ipo.gov.uk and search for 'Policy' under which there is a link to these lists. *And it continues still!.*

[17] India, Australia, Canada, Singapore (now a hub of IP for Asia) and so on. I am not familiar enough with the attitude of the courts of China, Japan or South America to know what their approach to honest comparative advertising is.

[18] *L'Oréal v Bellure* [2010] EWCA Civ 535.

[19] Including a number of continental, especially German, lawyers. An example the other way, of a supporter of the ECJ decision, is Gert Würtenberger whose opinion in (2010) 5(10) *Journal of Intellectual Property Law and Practice* complains that my criticism overlooks the interests of the trade mark owner. What interest, I ask, given that neither the owner's sales nor his image is affected? Mr Würtenberger identifies none other than that the newcomer gets an advantage from the expensive fame of the brand. Why is that an interest which should be protected as such in a competitive market? The brand owner may not like being copied, but IP law is not there to protect against copying as such.

The story in other IP subjects is similar: poorly drafted legislation followed by uncertainty and problems with uncertain ECJ rulings. Take just two more examples: supplementary protection certificates (SPCs) and designs. The Court is currently under a small deluge of references about SPCs,[20] the legislation for which shows small sign that those who drafted it had a firm grasp of either patent law[21] or pharmaceutical regulatory law and practice. As for designs, I had cause to examine the legislative history of the Designs Directive[22] and Regulation.[23] I found myself writing this:[24]

> [43] Since in relation to all three points I shall be referring to the *travaux* it is convenient at this point to relate the general history leading up to the Regulation. I am afraid that I am repeatedly reminded of what Bismarck said: 'To retain respect for sausages and laws, one must not watch them in the making'.

I know that all this sounds like a complaint. That is because it is. I think the time has come to recognise that IP law requires careful draftsmanship and courts which specialise in it. This means that the Commission cannot carry on preparing draft legislation 'in house' after a consultation on principles and then get it through the Council and Parliament. Widespread consultation is needed—not only on the principles, but also on the details of any draft legislation. To its credit the Commission has been doing just that[25] in relation to the proposed European Patent Court (and possible EU) patent.[26] Get together a team of experts (judges, academics and practitioners) and you will address the practical and substantive problems in time to deal with and reduce subsequent uncertainty. Carry on as we have been doing

[20] Three in 2010 alone. They raise fundamental questions about the working of this enormously important area of law, questions which were obviously foreseeable and which should have been addressed in the legislation.

[21] Did they know, for instance, that a patent for substance A is infringed if substance A is mixed with substance B? Had they appreciated that Swiss-form claims—and now claims for 'A for the treatment of disease X' are novel? *The SPC reference deluge continues and the Court decisions become less and less intelligible. What, for instance, is a national court (or patent office) to make of the latest test emerging from the CJEU, namely whether the claims relate 'implicitly but necessarily and specifically to the active ingredient in question', Case C-493/12* Eli Lilly v HGS [2013] EUECJ. *This is close to gibberish. Patent claims are there to define a monopoly. A product is either within the claim or not. Claims do not 'relate' to products. That is not their purpose or function.*

[22] 98/71/EC.

[23] Reg 6/2002.

[24] *Green Lane Products v PMS International* [2008] EWCA Civ 358.

[25] With a draft Statute and draft Rules of Court.

[26] I am not convinced we need this yet. Get a court going for a number of countries first and worry about the theoretically tidy but largely practically unimportant EU patent later.

and the uncertainty will continue. The price of uncertainty is a lack of competitiveness—people who do not know what they can or cannot do generally play safe—most especially if they are SMEs.

THE NATIONAL COURT LEVEL

I turn to what the national courts have been doing. They have no mandate to harmonise, yet they have become, to some extent, not only a force for harmonisation but a force for convergence—for certainty. This has come about, I believe, because the IP judges of Member States have come to know and respect one another.[27] The harmonisation is most explicit between the courts of Germany, Holland, and England and Wales.[28] My former court put it this way when we decided to follow German case law about secondary infringement of patent:[29]

> [79] Advocates should recognise that where a point of patent law of general importance, such as the construction of a provision which by Treaty (either the EPC or the Community Patent Convention) is to be implemented by states parties to those conventions, has been decided by a court, particularly a higher court, of another member state, the decision matters here. For, despite the fact that there is no common ultimate patent court for Europe, it is of obvious importance to all the countries of the European Patent Union or the parties to the Community Patent Convention ('the CPC'), that as far as possible the same legal rules apply across all the countries where the provisions of the Conventions have been implemented. An important decision in one member state may well be of strong persuasive value in all the others, particularly where the judgment contains clear reasoning on the point.
>
> [80] Broadly we think the principle in our courts—and indeed that in the courts of other member states—should be to try to follow the reasoning of an important decision in another country. Only if the court of one state is convinced that the reasoning of a court in another member state

[27] Through the important biennual European Patent Judges' Symposium sponsored by the EPO since 1982, the biennual European Trade Mark and Designs Symposium sponsored by the OHIM, the annual Venice Symposium sponsored by the EPO and the European Patent Lawyers Association (EPLAW) and many other international events to which various European patent and trade mark judges go. Notably there is not the same amount of contact in the field of copyright and related rights.

[28] It includes others too, of course. For instance I followed the well-articulated reasoning of the Austrian Court in *Proctor & Gamble v Reckitt Benckiser* [2007] EWCA Civ 936 at para 61.

[29] *Grimme v Scott* [2010] EWCA Civ 110.

> is erroneous should it depart from a point that has been authoritatively decided there. Increasingly that has become the practice in a number of countries, particularly in the important patent countries of France, Germany, Holland and England and Wales. Nowadays we refer to each other's decisions with a frequency which would have been hardly imaginable even twenty years ago. And we do try to be consistent where possible.
>
> [81] The Judges of the patent courts of the various countries of Europe have thereby been able to create some degree of uniformity even though the European Commission and the politicians continue to struggle on the long, long road which one day will give Europe a common patent court.

I wish that judges of other EU countries would, or could[30] join in more. Europe needs reliable and predictable IP laws. In the end that can only be achieved, even if the legislation is good,[31] by judges working with respect for each other.

Of course even if judges do work together, there will be a long way to go. In particular the Anglo-Saxon common law approach to IP laws is driven by essentially economic criteria only. The general thought is 'monopolies are prima facie bad. An IP right is an exception and therefore requires not only justification but to be kept strictly within that justification'. In many continental countries the approach to IP laws has a much higher 'moral' element, for instance deprecating copying as such or regarding something like copyright as imbued with the author's personality. Ideas such as *droit de suite* and *droit morale*[32] come from that tradition. These differences in legal culture will, at best, take a long, long time to fade—for IP law to converge and to reach a rational, predictable steady state.

Such a state is what both judges and legislators should be aiming for. As things are, we under the Chinese curse: we live in interesting times.

[30] There is a particular problem with France, whose judiciary do not readily refer to case law at all. This is part tradition and part, as I understand it, because it is seen as a constitutional matter: thinking derived from the time of the Revolution, that there is not, or ought not to be, case law.

[31] As, for instance, the substantive law provisions of the European Patent Convention largely are.

[32] These rights, however theoretically good, do not produce much income for artists—particularly the poor ones they are supposed to benefit. Artists who have become rich and famous benefit, but laws which are expensive to run and really benefit only the rich are, I suggest, not helpful.

15

Community Intellectual Property Law in English Courts[*]

IT IS NOT given to all to enjoy writing an essay. But when Francis Jacobs and Mads Andenas ask, you do not have much choice. So here goes. In part this is an essay of personal reminiscence and in part a commentary on some bits of the law. It is a bit of a ramble. I hope it is not too idiosyncratic.

THE BEGINNING

Intellectual property law has burgeoned since the early 1970s. Before then it was an unfashionable and rather dull area of law, typically involving half-hearted disputes in the patent office. The High Court was fairly moribund as far as IP was concerned.[1] But, just as we joined the Common Market (or just before) the sleeping giant awoke. People found they were able to turn to the law to prevent a variety of competition. Thus copyright entered the field of industrial design, copyright was used for the first time effectively to prevent copying of dresses and so on. IP lawyers began to devise new procedural remedies, first the *Norwich* order and, a few years later, the *Anton Piller*.

Thus IP law and Community law were ready to meet when we joined the Common Market on 1 January 1973. And it was IP cases which featured most prominently in the UK courts so far as

[*] *First published in Mads Andenas and Francis Jacobs (eds),* European Community Law in the English Courts *(Clarendon Press, 1998) chapter 15, pp 209–22.*

[1] In 1963 Lloyd-Jacob J spoke of the 'somewhat exiguous list of the assigned judge', *Terrapin v Builders' Supply* [1963] RPC 301, 307. Only a handful of copyright cases were reported in the decade 1960 to 1970. And one only has to look at the thickening of volumes of the Reports of Patent Cases in 1972 to give an approximate date to the IP explosion.

Community law was concerned. I think the first time the Rome Treaty was referred to in any English Court was an IP case, *Lerose v Hawick*.[2] It is now long forgotten and of no importance save that it was the first. The case was heard on 29 November 1972, a month before the UK joined. The plaintiff sought an interlocutory injunction to restrain copying of a fabric design. The defendant argued that an injunction would have the same effect as an agreement not to use that design and that such an agreement would fall foul of Art 85. So there would be a defence after 1 January. At the time I knew nothing about the Common Market. There was a very new junior in chambers who claimed he did and so, for the first time in my career I was given a junior. His name was HIL Laddie. He was going to argue this point and was all full of enthusiasm and authorities. But Whitford J did not call upon us. He did not think an injunction was the same as an agreement and that was that.

INFRINGERS' DEFENCES

Lerose v Hawick was a foretaste of what was to come. Defendants in IP cases began habitually to rely on the Treaty. Almost invariably such reliance was ultimately unsuccessful. I think it remains the case that even today, save in relation to goods put in free circulation in the Common Market by the IP right holder, no defence of Community Law has ever succeeded in the English courts. I do not find this particularly surprising since in most cases if there is no defence to an infringement claim apart from the Treaty, it is not self-evident that the Treaty should somehow come to the rescue.

I will trace this 'infringer's defence' through some of the cases. I think it was next tried (November 1974) in a passing off case, *Löwenbraü München v Grunhalle Lager International*.[3] This was in the early days of 'foreign' beers. The plaintiffs, a large German brewery, were the only people to use the word 'Löwenbraü' in the UK, though it was in fairly common use by others in Germany. Here, I suspect, only a few of those who knew the mark knew also that it meant Lion Brew, but no matter. The defendants wanted to use 'Grunhalle Löwenbraü'. There was evidence that the name would deceive here, albeit not in Germany where there were a number of

[2] *Lerose v Hawick* [1974] RPC 42.
[3] *Löwenbraü München v Grunhalle Lager International* [1974] RPC 492.

Löwenbraü beers, differentiated by additional names. The defendants were enjoined on an interlocutory basis. Graham J was able to distil from the existing community authority a doctrine of exhaustion but not a proposition that if the plaintiff cannot object in law to an act done in one part of the Community he cannot object anywhere. The only surprising thing about the case is that anyone ever thought the contrary might be arguable. Graham J also refused a reference under Art 177. I think this was the first time anyone in the English courts had sought a reference,[4] again IP law leading the way.

EMI v *CBS*

At any rate Graham J certainly was not afraid to make a reference. He did so shortly thereafter (March 1975) in *EMI v CBS*.[5] This was the second reference from the UK. Again a plain infringer tried to resort to the Treaty as an excuse. EMI held the registered trade mark Columbia in all nine of the then members of the Common Market. But, as a result of history, CBS held the mark in the USA and some other countries. EMI sued in the UK, Denmark and Germany to prevent US Columbia records from being imported or sold. Shortly before then the Court of Justice had given its (as we now know) erroneous decision in *HAG I*[6] to the effect that where a mark had become divided within the EEC, then, even if there was no connection between the respective owners, neither could enforce its mark against the other.[7] CBS argued that this 'common origin' doctrine applied even where the mark had been divided between the EEC and some third country. A few years earlier the Court had indicated a less-than-friendly attitude towards trade marks in *Sirena*.[8] CBS clearly hoped

4 See *Van Duyn* v *Home Office* [1974] 1 WLR 1107, 1116: 'There appears to have been so far only one case in this country in which the court has been asked to make a reference, namely that of *Löwenbraü*' *per* Pennycuick J.

5 *EMI v CBS* [1976] RPC 1.

6 *Van Zuylen v Hag*, Case 192/73 [1974] ECR 127.

7 Even at the time I wondered who had really won the case. True it was that the Belgian plaintiffs could not enforce their mark against German HAG in Belgium or Luxembourg. But they got the right to enter Germany under the mark, until, of course *HAG II*.

8 *Sirena Srl v Eda Srl and others* [1971] ECR 69, 82, para 7: 'The exercise of a trade-mark right is particularly apt to lead to a partitioning of markets, and thus to impair the free movement of goods between States which is essential to the Common Market. Moreover, a trade mark right is distinguishable in this context from other rights of industrial and commercial property, inasmuch as the interests protected by the latter are usually more important, and merit a higher degree of protection, than the interests protected by an ordinary trade mark'.

that the Court would have the same attitude towards the EMI rights. But it did not, holding that CBS should obliterate Columbia.[9]

I was the junior for *EMI* before Graham J. I was led by one TH Bingham QC. He suggested that another junior from his chambers be added to the team because that junior knew rather a lot about EEC law. I supported the idea with vigour because this was all a new world. Thus in the ECJ you will see that one Francis Jacobs was the first junior. I think this was his first active involvement in a trade mark case. The fundamental lack of logic of the common origin rule which we were up against in *EMI* clearly rankled with him: it was Advocate General Jacobs who wrote the opinion in *HAG II*,[10] which led to the reversal of *HAG I*. That opinion is, in my view, essential reading for anyone concerned with trade marks. And it is a delight. I hope that if and when the ECJ comes to consider the 'extended' view of trade mark rights espoused by some (but not all)[11] in the Netherlands,[12] it will receive the same level of assistance. It would be a shame if the Court moves from the 'less worthy of protection' view of the 1970s to an 'over-worthy of protection' view.

There are a couple of other reminiscences of the *EMI* case. The day before the hearing Tom Bingham wanted to go to the court room just to get the feel of where he would be the next day. It was nice to know he felt nervous. We got into the chamber and he stood at counsel's rostrum, just getting the feel. One of our party pointed out that the seats (upholstered and clad in white leather—or perhaps, more likely, imitation leather) for the parties and spectators were provided with ash trays. Tom said: 'Well if you take a job lot of aeroplane seats, you must take them as they come'. At the actual hearing there were counsel for the parties from both Denmark and Germany (whose courts had followed Graham J and made references in parallel cases). The Danes, fearing that interpreters would not render Danish into the other languages well, asked the leave of the Court to address it in English.[13] Our side's Danish counsel's speech consisted of taking

[9] *EMI v CBS* [1976] ECR 811.

[10] Case C-10/89 *CNL-SUCAl v Hag GF* [1990] 1 ECR 3711.

[11] As I know from discussion with some Dutch judges.

[12] See *Wagamama v City Centre Restaurants* [1995] FSR 713; Kamperman Sanders, 'The Wagamama Decision: Back to the Dark Ages of Trade Mark Law' [1996] *European Intellectual Property Review* 3; P Prescott, 'Think before you Waga Finger' [1996] *European Intellectual Property Review* 315; and Kamperman Sanders, 'The Return to Wagamama' [1996] *European Intellectual Property Review* 521.

[13] *The current President of the CJEU will not allow advocates to address the Court in other than their own language (or, perhaps, French). Just stupid and anti-European—we need a common language.*

an LP in its sleeve, approaching the judges closely and showing how small obliterations of the mark Columbia could be done. It worked—the decision was that CBS should obliterate. In retrospect, what was remarkable about the case was the real fear that the Court had such a down on trade marks that it would let the American Columbia in without any reciprocity from the US.

CRITERIA FOR A REFERENCE: *BULMER v BOLLINGER*

I return to IP law in the English Courts. It was in another IP case, *Bulmer v Bollinger*,[14] that the Court of Appeal first considered the criteria for making a reference to the Court of Justice under Art 177. The English makers of 'champagne cider' and 'champagne perry' sued the French champagne houses for a declaration that these names were lawful. The champagne houses counterclaimed for passing off. The action was proceeding when the UK joined the EEC. The champagne makers sought to add a claim to the effect that the use of 'champagne', except for the real thing, was contrary to EEC law. They also sought a reference. It was refused by Whitford J and by the Court of Appeal. Lord Denning MR gave guidelines which concentrated on the word 'necessary': 'The point must be such that whichever way it is decided it is conclusive'. There was also great emphasis on deciding the facts first. Since then, it has generally been recognised that these guidelines were somewhat restrictive, but I think it fair to say that at least until recently our courts have been more reluctant than some continental courts to make a reference, perhaps because of this decision. It was in this case that Lord Denning spoke of the Treaty in graphic terms: 'When we come to matters with a European element, the Treaty is like an incoming tide. It flows into the estuaries and up the rivers. It cannot be held back'. And:

> In future, in transactions which cross the frontiers, we must no longer speak or think of English law as something on its own. We must speak and think of community law, of community rights and obligations and we must give effect to them. This means a great effort for the lawyers. We have to learn a new system. The Treaty, with the regulations and directives, covers many volumes. The case law is contained in hundreds of reported cases both in the European Court of Justice and in the national

[14] *Bulmer v Bollinger* [1974] Ch 401.

> courts of the nine. Many must be studied before the right result can be reached. We must get down to it.
>
> In the task of interpreting the Treaty, the English judges are no longer the final authority. They no longer carry the law in their breasts. They are no longer in a position to give rulings which are of binding force. The supreme tribunal for interpreting the Treaty is the European Court of Justice, at Luxembourg.

One sometimes wonders why it has taken some politicians so long to realise the truth of what Lord Denning said.

Diverting a little, it is worthwhile recording the ultimate fate of the champagne producers' plea. It failed.[15] And in due course the champagne growers got the regulations changed in their favour.

THE TIN CAN LITIGATION

Another 'first' for IP law is that it was in an IP case when the Court of Appeal considered the Treaty for the first time. The case was *Appln des Gaz v Falks Veritas*.[16] It was another infringer's defence case. Lord Denning began his judgment thus: 'This is the first case in which in this court we have had to consider the Treaty of Rome. It comes about because of a tin can'. In the early 1970s the power of copyright in industrial drawings was becoming widely appreciated. The plaintiffs were seeking to enforce the copyright in their drawing of the Camping Gaz tin to prevent the defendants making copies of their cans. The defendants sought to amend an existing defence which put copyright in issue and alleged estoppel by alleging breach of the Treaty. Both Arts 85 and 86 were relied upon. The judgment of Lord Denning contains a number of passages which, in retrospect at least, were too wide, eg:

> In the ordinary way, the national courts of various member states can protect and enforce patents, trade marks, copyright and trade names by their own laws with their own remedies as they always have done ... But the national courts should not enforce such rights in any case where such enforcement would impede the free movement of goods within the community between one member state and another.

15 *Bulmer v Bollinger* [1978] RPC 79, 110.
16 *Appln des Gaz v Falks Veritas* [1974] Ch 381.

Amendment was allowed, even though the Court recognised that there would be a large burden of discovery. This broad-brush approach was, of course, an enormous invitation to infringers. Just pleading a breach of Arts 85 and 86 became a vogue. The difficulties of pleading were significant and they themselves became the subject of contests. The first of these was in the same case. The defendants had asserted a dominant position and its abuse in only general terms. Whitford J held the plea as it stood to be speculative and ordered proper particulars, *Appn des Gaz v Falks Veritas*.[17]

And the tin can managed to bother the Court of Appeal thrice more before it faded from view. First the plaintiffs, Gaz, seem to have been so concerned by the Euro-defences that they dropped their claim for an injunction and damages for infringements after UK entry into the EEC—and indeed for a slightly earlier period being that between the issue of the Writ (in mid-1972) and entry. They just claimed damages for past infringements.[18] On that basis they successfully sought to evade the need to give discovery concerning their alleged dominant position and breaches of Art 85. There was a bizarre argument in the Court of Appeal to the effect that somehow the Treaty was retrospective, but it did not wash. The decision of the Court of Appeal[19] is of no interest. What is of interest is the constitution of the Court, namely Viscount Dilhorne, and Lords Edmund-Davies and Scarman. I have never heard of an all-Law Lord Court of Appeal before or since. Maybe Lord Woolf should try borrowing some Law Lords now to help with the current backlog in the Court of Appeal.

Gaz, having got the Euro-law out of their own claim, found the defendants wriggling by other means to get it back in. The defendants sued Gaz for breaches of Arts 85 and 86. Their first attempt was held wholly embarrassing,[20] a decision upheld by the Court of Appeal. They returned to the fray with a new writ, joining in not only Gaz, but Gaz's UK distributors, for whom I appeared. The pleading was complicated, prolix and muddled, with important allegations called 'particulars' buried away. Whitford J struck it out. However

[17] *Appn des Gaz v Falks Veritas* [1975] FSR 363.

[18] This may still have been a hefty claim, going back for some six years before the Writ and including the then permissible but outrageous claim for damages for conversion. If ever the claim had come to trial there would have been a beautiful point about whether the gas inside the cylinder, perforce of the shape of the cylinder, was an infringing copy.

[19] [1978] 1 CMLR 383.

[20] ibid 30.

the defendants found a friendly Court of Appeal who allowed them to re-plead,[21] much to my annoyance—after all we had got the Court to hold that the existing pleading was no good. As I recall it, even though they finally got a pleading allowed to go ahead, they ended up paying for the entire costs of the exercise. My submission to the Court on costs was 'if you get the Court of Appeal to draft your pleadings, you ought to pay'. The Court particularly went out of its way to say that it did not necessarily agree with Lord Denning in the first tin can case when he said:

> Arts. 85 and 86 are part of our law. They create new torts or wrongs. Their names are 'undue restriction of competition within the Common Market'; and 'abuse of dominant position within the common market.' Any infringement of those articles can be dealt with by our English courts. It is for our courts to find the facts, apply the law, and use the remedies which we have available.

Again one sees the general view of the 1970s, that Euro-points should all be treated with care, avoiding deciding anything if at all possible.

THE COURTS SMELL A RAT: '*NEXUS*' ARRIVES

I think the tin can litigation died thereafter, on what basis I do not know. It was left to other defendants in other cases to try to plead Euro-defences. The courts started to be suspicious. In *British Leyland v TI Silencers*[22] Walton J said of a pleading which in effect asserted no more than that an injunction would interfere with inter-State trade:

> These are really some of the most audacious allegations that I have ever seen, because what they amount to is a positive pleading that if the plaintiffs obtain the relief sought in the action, the defendants will be debarred from continuing to do a whole series of wrongful acts which they should never have been doing anyhow. Whatever else it is, the Treaty of Rome is not intended to be a pirate's charter.

And, in *ICI v Berk*[23] the plaintiffs were suing in passing off. Their claim was that the exact imitation of their pills—pink pills—amounted to a misrepresentation. The alleged abuse was the charging of unfair

[21] ibid 87.
[22] *British Leyland v TI Silencers* [1979] FSR 591, 598.
[23] *ICI v Berk* [1981] 2 CMLR 91, [1981] FSR 1.

prices, which was said to affect trade between Member States. Sir Robert Megarry V-C struck the defence out. He said: 'The English courts must be ready to scrutinise a Euro-defence with care, notwithstanding any apparent complexity, and should not adopt the attitude, whether overt or covert, that because it is a Euro-defence it must at least be arguable'. And:

> I do not think it could be said that a person in breach of some statutory or other prohibition thereupon becomes an outlaw, unable to enforce any of his rights against anyone. If the plaintiffs are imposing unfair selling prices … I cannot see this breach of Art. 86 means that the defendants are thereby set free from any liability to the plaintiffs if they, the defendants, commit the tort of passing off (or indeed, any other tort) against them … Further, if the defendants are right, the ability of the plaintiffs to sue them for passing off will exist and be destroyed in accordance with the prices which for the time being the plaintiffs are charging, coming and going as the plaintiffs charge a fair price or charge a price that is unfairly high or unfairly low, with all the problems that would arise from prices which are in a twilight zone of merely possible or arguable unfairness.

He particularly identified what he called (and has come to be generally called) the *nexus* point. He said that there was no nexus between the alleged overcharging (the alleged abuse) and the alleged passing off.

He further doubted whether there was an effect upon trade between Member States and the alleged overcharging but did not base his decision on that ground. Jumping ahead, that is indeed a formidable ground on its own in an alleged overcharging case. It was the ground of strike-out in *Chiron v Murex (No 2)*.[24] The plaintiffs had a patent on hepatitis C testing kits. The defendants alleged abuse of Art 86 by overcharging and refusal to license. It was not possible to point to a link between the allegedly high prices and an effect on inter-State trade, so the pleading failed. Other pleadings have suffered a similar fate on *nexus*.[25]

ARTICLE 177: AGAINST WHAT COURT IS THERE 'NO JUDICIAL REMEDY?'

Incidentally, it was the *Chiron* case which highlighted a procedural problem about references under Art 177. What happens when the

[24] *Chiron v Murex (No 2)* [1994] 1 CMLR 410, CA.
[25] eg *Duracell v Ever Ready* [1989] RPC 731.

Court of Appeal finally deals with a Euro-point and refuses leave to appeal? Since the House of Lords may yet give leave to appeal one cannot say the decision of the Court of Appeal is that of the court of final resort (ie in the language of Art 177, the 'court or tribunal of a member State against whose decisions there is no judicial remedy under national law'). The defendants in *Chiron* sought a reference from the Court of Appeal but were refused. They went to the House of Lords for leave to appeal, which was itself refused. They did not at that point ask for a reference. Instead they went back to the Court of Appeal and asked for a reference there. It was refused on the grounds that they were asking the wrong court, the Court of Appeal itself being *functus officio*. It may seem a pity that a procedural blunder defeated the application for a reference, but I do not think so.[26] I think the 'overcharging' defence ought to be no sort of defence at all. It is essentially hypocritical: what the defendant wants to do is charge just under the allegedly over-high price. He has no real interest in lower prices.

WHAT IS AN UNFAIR PRICE FOR PATENTED GOODS?

Conceptually I think there are real problems with any allegation of 'overcharging' for patented goods. The whole point of a patent monopoly is to enable the patentee to charge more. Even in a context where overcharging is a statutory ground for a licence ('where a demand for the product in the UK is not being met on reasonable terms'[27]) it is extremely difficult to say a price is 'too much'. In *Research Corpn's Patent*[28] the patented drug cost eight times as much as an unpatented drug which was therapeutically equivalent. But the unpatented drug had terrible side-effects, which meant that the patient had to be an in-patient, whereas this was not so when the patented drug was used. In truth using the patented drug was cheaper. Hoffmann J refused to find overcharging. In *Chiron*, as I recall it, the use of the test cost about £2 per blood donation whereas other, unpatented tests for other diseases were about 50p. But the saving in increased medical costs alone from people who did not get hepatitis C as a result of the use of the test was some five

[26] I try to disregard the fact that I was, for some time, including the initial successful strike-out in the CA, counsel for *Chiron*.

[27] Patents Act 1977, s 48(3)(b)(i).

[28] *Research Corpn's Patent* [1990] RPC 663.

times the cost of testing the blood supply for hepatitis C. It is too often easy, after the event, to say, as did the burghers of Hamlyn Town, 'A thousand guilders! Why, take fifty'. It is not uninteresting to note that so far as I know there has been no case decided anywhere (including direct complaints or action by the Commission) holding simply that a patentee has been overcharging and is thereby in breach of Art 86.[29] There may, of course, be cases of overcharging (Art 86 specifically contemplates 'imposing unfair ... prices') but, absent some very extraordinary case, a claim of 'overcharging' should be regarded with very considerable suspicion.

THE CURRENT STATUS OF 'BREACH OF ART 85 OR 86 DEFENCES'

Finally, I believe that there is a lot to be said for Staughton LJ's approach in *Chiron No 2*:[30]

> For my part, I consider that the time has come when these questions should be resolved, as they must be sooner or later. The nettle should be grasped now. Otherwise this and other cases concerned with intellectual property will be encumbered at trial with a great deal of evidence about market, dominant position and abuse which may be wholly unnecessary.
>
> In the ordinary way, I consider that the remedy for abuses such as are alleged in this case is not to refuse relief to the holder of the patent against the infringer. That could be altogether lacking in proportionality ... There are other remedies available.

However the majority of the Court in *Chiron No 2* did not support this, leaving it uncertain as to whether the ultimate legal position is as summarised by Hoffmann J in *Pitney-Bowes v Francotype-Postalia*:[31]

> It is sufficient that the existence of the intellectual property right creates or buttresses the dominant position which the plaintiff is abusing. The remedy contemplated by the court is that the plaintiff may have to be deprived of the means of maintaining his dominant position.

It is certainly time that the courts decided the point: they may be guided by US experience where anti-trust defences, once all the rage,

[29] In one of the few cases to go to trial on this point, *Hoover v Hulme* [1982] FSR 565, Whitford J had no difficulty in rejecting the defence of overcharging, even though the plaintiffs' prices were higher than those of the defendants by quite a bit. The plaintiffs lost for other reasons, as I remember to my discomfort.

[30] *Chiron No 2* [1994] FSR 187.

[31] *Pitney-Bowes v Francotype-Postalia* [1991] FSR 72.

have largely faded away. Further I have heard little of such defences even being raised, still less having any success, in other countries of the EC. This too is an important consideration. It is, of course, more attractive for a defendant to plead abuse here than on the Continent: it costs him little and he can put the plaintiff to enormous discovery.

BEYOND THE 'SUBJECT-MATTER?'

I turn to another kind of Euro-defence. This is really an assault on the kind or width of an IP right itself. The argument goes something like this: an IP right is a measure 'having equivalent effect' under Art 30. So unless Art 36 provides an exception, an IP right may not be used to affect inter-State trade. Article 36 provides for the 'protection of industrial and commercial property'. It is for Community law to decide the proper limits of this. It does so by the concept of the 'specific subject' of a right. If a national IP law purports to go beyond this, then to that extent it is not within Art 36 and the free circulation permitted by Art 30 prevails. For many years such arguments were tried. The leading English case rejected it at Court of Appeal level, *British Leyland v Armstrong*,[32] Oliver LJ saying:

> What the defendants have to say in this case is either that English copyright is not 'industrial or commercial property', or that the right which the statute confers upon the owner of artistic copyright to prevent copying by or from three-dimensional reproduction is not within the 'specific object' of the property rights. The former proposition is hopeless, having regard to the GEMA case[33] and, as regards the latter, the only argument which can be adduced to support is that the copyright owner does not have that protection in other countries of the Community.
>
> That appears to me to be a hopeless proposition, because the object of the property right can, as I see it, be judged only by the domestic law which creates it.

And Fox LJ said:[34]

> It seems to me that, in the absence of any specific assumption or provision in the Treaty of Rome (and there is none) one can only ascertain the rights which constitute the specific subject-matter of copyright by looking at the national law.

[32] *British Leyland v Armstrong* [1984] FSR 81, 616.
[33] Joined Cases 55 and 57/80 *Musik-Vertrieb Membran v GEMA* [1981] 1 ECR 147.
[34] *British Leyland v Armstrong*, 633.

A reference was refused and the point never got off the ground in the House of Lords because the House divined a defence under English law of a positive right to mend.[35] However, I have always wondered whether the Court of Appeal was right.[36] I said so in *Kerly*,[37] where I particularly wondered whether the rule that the holder of a Part A mark could prevent honest comparative advertising would stand up in the ECJ. It seems to me that the ECJ must have the ultimate say in whether or not a right (or a particular aspect of a right) can properly be regarded as within Art 36. Thus in *BAT v Commission ('Toltecs')*[38] it was held that the taking of infringement proceedings under a dormant registered mark (permitted by national law[39]) was a misuse of rights. I am far from saying that the ECJ has a swingeing power to cut back national IP rights. It plainly has not, and has refused to do so in a number of cases.[40] Only the *Magill* case[41] stands out as one where a national IP right was held as going too far.

PENNEYS

Next I go back to a little more reminiscence. What follows is not a pretty story. The youngest son of Garfield Weston (the chairman of the giant ABF food and other business group) set up a clothing store business in Ireland (where he lived with his Irish wife). He called it

[35] [1986] AC 577.

[36] And Whitford J went even further in *Parker Knoll v Knoll Overseas* [1985] FSR 349, 366. He held that even if Community law in effect modified what amounted to an infringement, that would be no defence to a defendant in a motion for contempt for breach of an injunction restraining infringement. The proper remedy would be to seek modification of the injunction. That can hardly be right, although the sensible course might well be to apply for modification before embarking on what would be a breach by the rules of national law.

[37] *Kerly's Law of Trade Marks and Trade Names,* 12th edn (Sweet & Maxwell, 1986) 221.

[38] Case 35/83 *BAT v Commission ('Toltecs')* [1985] ECR 363.

[39] And so 'commercial or industrial property' by national law.

[40] eg '*Quattro*', Case 317/91 *Deutsche Renault v Audi* (question of confusion a matter for national law provided there is no arbitrary discrimination). Personally I rather wish something could be done about what seems the over-protective view of the German courts in respect of trade marks. Surely it is taking a dim view of the intelligence of the average German to hold that *Terrapin* is confusingly similar to *Terranova* (permitted by the ECJ, [1976] ECR 1039), or that *Racoon* and *Dragon* are deceptively similar, even if one assumes that Germans do not speak English [1996] GRUR 414? Other cases showing the reluctance of the court to interfere with a national right are Case 35/87 *Thetford v Fiamma* [1988] ECR 3585, [1990] Ch 339 (UK rule, that older-than-50-year patents do not novelty-destroy a patent, permissible even though other Member States do not have such a rule) and Case 238/87 *Volvo v Veng* [1988] ECR 6211. In the latter case (where I appeared for the defendants, though I was unable to get to the hearing), I thought there was a real chance that the ECJ might say 'hold on—50 years plus life of author for spare parts based on a copyright with no inherent artistic merit') but it did not.

[41] Case T-69/89 *Radio Teleis Eireann* [1991] II ECR 485.

Penneys, I think innocently. The company prospered and was on its way to becoming the Marks & Spencer of Ireland. Penneys branched out to England and Scotland. The giant US store group JC Penney got to hear of the Irish Penneys. It had no shops in Europe but did have some slight use of its name on imported goods. It felt obliged to protect its name. It was almost certainly too late to sue in Ireland but it sued in England[42] and Scotland. I was the junior in the English case. JC also sued in Hong Kong (successfully claiming that a reputation amongst suppliers was enough for a passing-off action)[43] and commenced various rectification proceedings against an assortment of ABF registered marks in an assortment of countries. In addition JC applied for a number of ABF marks in countries where ABF did not have registrations and these were opposed. Much money was spent on litigation, which ultimately covered 14 countries. There was a Scottish trial which lasted six weeks. Before judgment was given there the parties entered a settlement agreement. It was a simple deal: the Irish Penneys were to give up all use of the word on goods and all use of the word outside Ireland. They could carry on with the shop name in Ireland. And some money passed. Irish Penneys agreed never to attack JC's European trade mark registrations and, for ever outside Ireland, not to use the word as a trade mark or for shops. There were some worries at the time that this agreement might fall within Art 85(1) so the agreement was made conditional upon approval by the Commission. JC's US lawyers (who had a Brussels Office) said they knew what they were doing and arranged a meeting. We all polled up in the Commission building in Brussels (the one they had to pull down). We met the relevant official—I will not name him but he has long been a prominent member of DG4. He said there was a problem—the Commission will not give an exemption or negative clearance for agreements conditional upon approval by the Commission.[44] He added that otherwise he could not see a problem. We all went out to discuss the position. The discussion was over a Brussels lunch and involved myself and my solicitor, ABF's company secretary, JC's in-house European lawyer and a lawyer from the Brussels firm representing them. By now we were good friends with JC and it was a good lunch. The JC in-house lawyer for Europe, having

[42] The interlocutory proceedings are reported at [1976] FSR 367, CA.

[43] [1979] FSR 26.

[44] I have never seen any justification for this. I can understand the Commission not dealing with a purely academic agreement, but one that takes effect if approved is more than this. Parties ought to be able to avoid any risk of a violation of Art 85(1) if they so wish.

heard the assurance to the effect that there was no problem other than the fact that it was conditional said he would agree to make the agreement unconditional and ABF did likewise. We took the agreement back to the Commission in the afternoon and went home, thinking the job was done.

Nothing was heard for a couple of months and then a letter came raising objections to the agreement. Both we and JC were shocked. The objection was that it was anti-competitive because our side were agreeing for ever not to use Penneys outside Ireland. That this agreement was the result of a serious settlement of litigation counted for nothing. Nor did commercial reality impinge: if we were giving up Penneys then obviously we would be using a new name and mark and once that was in use, we would have no conceivable commercial interest in going back or attacking the JC registrations. We all went back to Brussels, JC including in their team Oliver Axter, a sixth-generation patent lawyer from Düsseldorf with whom it was a pleasure to work. We went to see the official concerned, I and Oliver representing the two parties, once enemies but now friends and facing a common enemy. The official refused to budge. It did not bother him that the agreement had been made unconditional on the basis of his promise that he foresaw no problem. We were given an appointment with another official. The alternative was for the parties to take the Commission to the ECJ—something the lawyers could not face taking to their management who thought this mad litigation had been settled. So we took up the further appointment and hammered out a modification to the agreement in an all-day meeting with the Commission. It was JC which had to 'give way', losing ABF's agreement not to use the mark for ever. I had the idea of a five-year keep-out period, basing this on the period of five years' non-use as a ground for removal of a registered mark which was the prevalent period in Member States, based on the Paris Convention.[45] The Commission bought this and gave a negative clearance.[46]

I think the costs of this perfectly pragmatic settlement were wholly disproportionate. It reflected no credit on the Commission at all. I heard that the JC man in Europe lost his job as a result of relying on the Commission's assurance. If true, that was terribly unfair. It may well be that there ought to be an Ombudsman to deal with maladministration within the Commission. There is an interesting

[45] Art 5C(1).
[46] [1978] FSR 385.

postscript: the new name used by the Irish Penneys was (and is) Primark. It has been successful and the view within the company later was that the new name helped contribute to the success by quite a way. For myself I learned not to put my faith in Princes and to realise that the Commission had a lot to learn by way of fairness and by way of appreciating the true commercial significance of things like no-challenge clauses. I also learned that one had to be very careful in settling a case. I am glad to hear that in general the view is that things are rather better now—certainly the rigid view of no-challenge clauses has gone. One other postscript is that JC, having got the rival Penneys out of the way, never did open up stores in the UK (nor, I believe, other European countries). And, of course, Irish Penneys[47] never did attack any of the Penney registrations.

FREE MOVEMENT

The last subject I wish to touch upon is free movement. By and large it was not the English courts which were involved in the cases leading up to the rule in *Merck v Stephar*:[48]

> The proprietor of an industrial or commercial property right protected by the law of a Member State cannot rely on that law to prevent the importation of a product which has lawfully been marketed in another State by the proprietor or with his consent.

As it happens I was counsel in *Merck*.[49] I thought (and still think) there was an injustice. The patentee had no Italian patent and sold there in competition with others, naturally at a reduced price compared with the price in countries where he had a patent. His goods, bought in Italy, were taken to Holland (where he had a patent) and sold there. The court, abandoning any fair notion of exhaustion of rights,[50] permitted this. I have always thought this was an unnecessary development of EC law. The rule went no further in the 1980s—for instance, on an English court reference it was held that it did not apply to goods sold under a compulsory licence.[51] As a judge,

[47] *Still a large chain in Ireland—I wonder whether they ever think of changing the name to Primark!.*

[48] *Merck v Stephar* [1981] ECR 2063.

[49] For the UK government, intervening.

[50] There was no Italian right to be exhausted.

[51] Case 19/84 *Pharmon v Hoechst* [1985] ECR 2281.

I asked the Court to reconsider *Merck* in *Merck v Primecrown*.[52] The Advocate-General recommended its reversal, but I was not altogether surprised to find that the Court thought it too late to do so.[53] I doubt whether, if the point had been new, the court would have so held. It has developed a less hostile and more rational attitude to IP laws in the 1980s.[54]

By way of conclusion it is apparent that IP Euro-law in the English courts has been an active and fertile field. I believe we have contributed well to the general development of Community law. I hope we can continue to do so in the future.

POSTSCRIPT

1. *Although Euro-defences to IP claims are out of fashion it remains the case that it still has not been decided that they do not work. The most recent case in which the defence was considered was* Intel v Via *[2002] EWCA Civ 1905 where a Court of Appeal, reversing an excellent decision of Lawrence Collins J, again held that such a defence was arguable. I dislike that sort of decision: courts are paid to decide things, especially points of law, not to decide merely that a point of law is arguable.*
2. *There is another story related to the* EMI *case. On the evening before the hearing we were in the bar of the Holiday Inn. Tom told us he had just had judgment from the Court of Appeal in a case called* D v National Society for the Prevention of Cruelty to Children, *D being a mother of a small child. Someone (let us call him or her X) had told the NSPCC that she was abusing the child and the inspector had come in (the law allowed) but allegedly in an offensive and frightening manner. The allegation was completely untrue. She sued, claiming the NSPCC had been negligent and that she had suffered nervous shock. What she really wanted, however, was to know who X was, someone*

[52] *Merck v Primecrown* [1995] FSR 909.

[53] Cases C-267-8/95, 5 December 1996.

[54] *cf* the attitude in *Ideal Standard, IHT International Heiztechnik v Ideal-Standard* [1995] FSR 59, which surely would have gone the other way in the 1960s, 1970s and early 1980s, quite apart from the 'common origin' doctrine. I confess I was surprised by the result in any event. An assignment of a trade mark for only some of the countries of the EC is bound to be market divisive and I would not have seen a lot of harm in saying it did not really work.

she knew, a vindictive neighbour or relative? That she sought as part of discovery—and also as the name of a wrongdoer under the recently established Norwich Pharmacal *principle. The application had first come before my father, the Senior Master. He granted the order (later he said he was wrong but Lord Diplock, who had presided in the House of Lords when the case got there, told him: 'You were right at your level'). The High Court judge overruled Dad and the Court of Appeal had restored his order. Tom was really upset in that bar. He could see as clear as daylight that if informers could be named, then they would not inform and the NSPCC's extensive child protection activities would virtually come to an end. This really mattered. I remembered some stuff from our* Norwich Pharmacal *researches (see Chapter 7) and said I was pretty sure that there was something in the nature of a discretion to refuse disclosure in the public interest. I told Tom that. About a month later he rang and asked me whether I would be his junior in the House of Lords—the greatest compliment of my legal life. I of course said yes (though neither of us would take a fee). There was quite a lot of research to be done. It all paid off—the NSPCC won hands down in the Lords,* D v NSPCC.[55] *One other thing: whilst the case was on its way to the House of Lords my brother published an article strongly criticising the Court of Appeal decision. It was cited by Lord Edmund-Davies. So in a way it was Jacob Brothers 2: Jacob Dad 1. Our Mum said we were ganging up on him.*

[55] D v NSPCC *[1978] AC 171.*

16

The Relationship Between European and National Courts in Intellectual Property Law[*]

OF RELATIONSHIPS BETWEEN COURTS BELOW AND APPEAL COURTS IN GENERAL

AN OLD, WISE American trial judge had inscribed on his desk, 'Remember, the most important guy in court is the guy who's going to lose'. A court of appeal judge could, and should, add 'And the most important guy outside court is the judge we are going to reverse'. The thought behind these stories contains two important truths: that civility between courts and being seen to be fair really matters. The losing litigant will be much more likely to feel he has had justice if the judge articulates his key arguments before explaining why they are wrong. And the reversed judge will respect a court of appeal which explains his error rather than simply ignores what he said altogether or still worse is unnecessarily rude.

Here are some stories illustrating these points from my own experience. First, the losing litigant. In 1972 I appeared for a one-man company which had a patent on an airer/drier.[1] One infringer appeared and lost before Graham J.[2] Then another with something more arguably outside the claim. We sued but lost on that one, Graham J explaining why although the case was finely balanced, he thought the better view was in favour of the defendant. I said to the client: 'This is a runner in the Court of Appeal but with no guarantee of success'.

[*] *First published in Justine Pila and Ansgar Ohly (eds),* The Europeanisation of Intellectual Property Law: Towards a Legal Methodology, *chapter 10 (Oxford University Press, 2013).*

[1] A frame for hanging washing to dry. It could either stand upright or hook onto a bath.

[2] *Carroll v Tomado* [1971] RPC 401.

He said: 'No, I'll take the opinion of that bloke'. A judge can hardly have a finer tribute.[3]

The second is more personal, being about how a judge reacts when a higher court disagrees. More specifically it is about how I have felt when my judgments have been disagreed with by a higher court. Although I speak of my own reactions, I know that other judges treated similarly feel the same. I have two examples. My first comes from the judgment of the ECJ in *L'Oréal v Bellure*.[4] The issue was straightforward enough: is it a trade mark infringement for the alleged infringer to say truthfully that his goods are the same or close to the same as those sold under a well-known, much more expensive brand? For instance the defendants were saying truly that '*Stitch* No. 7 smells like *Trésor* [the well-known brand]'. I, in writing the lead judgment in the Court of Appeal,[5] referring the questions to the ECJ, took considerable care to set out why the case was being referred and how important the question was.[6] It is important to accept and appreciate that in all these cases the merchant who uses such a list does so to promote his product So there is a kind of 'free riding'. Although that expression has crept into European Trade Mark law (see also *Mango v Diknak* [2005] ETMR 5 at [19]) it is, to me at least, subtly and dangerously emotive: it carries the unwritten message that it ought to be stopped. That is far from being necessarily so. The needs of proper competition and lawful free trade will involve an element at least of 'free riding'. The problem for trade mark law is where to draw the line between permissible and impermissible 'free riding'. Using the epithet does not solve the problem.[7]

The ECJ ruled just under two years later. It is hardly a secret that I did not and do not agree with the ruling, see my judgment after the referral.[8] Now is not the place to go into the details. What matters for present purposes is the ECJ's complete failure to consider or deal with the important questions of principle which I had gone out of my way to identify for it. What is legitimate competition and what not (and if not why not) required much more analysis, as I was trying to say. The judgment is as if these passages had never been written—and for all anyone knows they had indeed never even been read by the

3 After all judging is perhaps the only trade where 51% customer satisfaction is scoring high.
4 Case C-487/07 *L'Oréal v Bellure*, 18 June 2009.
5 [2007] EWCA Civ 968, [2008] RPC 196.
6 Paras [26–28].
7 Para 27.
8 [2010] EWCA Civ 535.

Court. Its judgment just amounted to a crude condemnation—almost tirade—of 'riding on the coattails'. Such a form of judgment—ignoring entirely the court below—does not engender respect, yet respect is vital for the proper functioning of any court system.

The criticism is not solely aimed at the ECJ for the same sort of thing can and does happen domestically. For example the Supreme Court decision in *Lucasfilm v Ainsworth*[9] reversing a unanimous decision of the Court of Appeal of which I was a member. We had decided that an owner of a foreign copyright could not sue a defendant in this country for infringing that foreign copyright. We were reversed. So any British exporter is liable to be sued here for infringing a copyright by the law of the country to which it exports. Taking an order over the Internet, going to the local post office and posting the goods is enough if the foreign law of copyright law says that is an infringement. It makes no difference where the property passes or that all the exporter did was perfectly lawful by the law of this country. I thought we gave powerful reasons as to why this should not be permitted. But the decision reversing us ignored them. Bizarrely it even said there were no policy reasons for withholding jurisdiction. Tell that to any British exporter!

What is important to appreciate is not that a judge does not like being reversed, for few do.[10] It is when he or she is reversed without his or her judgment being considered fairly. I did not mind, for instance, when the House of Lords reversed our decision in *Yeda v Rhone-Poulenc*.[11] Once one saw the point (which was not argued before us)[12] the answer is plain. My reaction was 'dammit, I should have seen that'. And I would not have minded much if in *Lucasfilm* we had been reversed on the work of sculpture point—there were good arguments either way and they were fully considered. The problem lies with those cases where the higher court leaves the judge(s) below with the reaction was 'Did they even read what I wrote?'[13]

[9] Decision in *Lucasfilm v Ainsworth* [2012] 1 AC 208.

[10] There are cases where he or she feels they have to follow a precedent even though it leads to what he or she thinks is an unjust result. Then, if the higher court reverses the precedent or finds a way round it, the judge is actually quite happy.

[11] *Yeda v Rhone-Poulenc* [2008] RPC 1, [2007] UKHL 43 overruling the basis of our decision in *Markem v Zipher* [2005] RPC 31, [2005] EWCA Civ 267 (though the case would have gone the same way under the principles applied by the HL in *Yeda).*

[12] Either in *Yeda* or *Markem.* That is not an excuse. I still feel rather stupid for not seeing it myself.

[13] I fear there may be some first instance judges whose reaction to being reversed by a Court of Appeal decision to which I was party may be the same! Sometimes one is too pressed to be courteous.

OF RELATIONSHIPS BETWEEN THE NATIONAL COURTS OF DIFFERENT EUROPEAN COUNTRIES

Here I begin, oddly enough, with the relationships between the courts of the three UK jurisdictions, England and Wales, Scotland and Northern Ireland. They are, perhaps surprisingly to an outsider, rather meagre. I used to say that the only time one met a Scottish judge was at an international conference. That was and is still basically true. Most Scottish judges have never met more than a few English judges and I suspect quite a few have never met any. And vice versa. There are no regular meetings of the judges from the three jurisdictions. Sometimes there is a social or semi-social event.[14] But nothing by way of serious meetings. Work-wise we only know each other[15] through judgments when they are cited to us.[16]

I think that is a pity—for experience has shown that getting to know the judges of other jurisdictions has done more for harmonising law than I could have imagined before I had taken part in it. Regular symposia between the common law (I would include Irish) judges would bring huge benefits.

I have talked about the experience of meeting judges from other jurisdictions. The principal vehicle so far as I am concerned has been the biennual European Patent Judges' Symposium. These were started by the European Patent Office in 1984. They move between different members of the European Patent Union.[17] By 1994 I was a judge and went to my first Judges' Symposium. It was the UK's turn and it chose the Patent Office in Newport as the venue with the judges staying in Cardiff. For the first time I met other European judges.[18] Previous English patent judges had gone to the earlier Symposia but with the exception of William Aldous they had done little to forge links with

[14] Basically only one: the Lord Chancellor's Breakfast in Westminster Hall following the Service for the Opening of the Legal Year in the Abbey. A few Scottish and Northern Irish judges are invited. This year Mr Justice Langstaff had the great idea of inviting the Celtic judges and English and Irish judges to a dinner on the night before the opening.

[15] I had one personal exception: I, along with Brian Gill, now the Lord President, were co-Deputy-Chairmen of the Copyright Tribunal when it started in 1989. We have kept in contact ever since.

[16] And that is not very often in my experience.

[17] One of the questions we all ask as a Symposium comes towards its end is 'where next time?'. I have been to Newport Wales, Stockholm, Madrid, Thessaloniki, Lisbon and Bordeaux. This year it is in Dublin and I missed Copenhagen and Luxembourg.

[18] Interestingly on that occasion three Chinese judges came; few, if any, realised how quickly China would come to embrace IP. It was unimaginable that the Chinese Patent Office would become one of the great Offices by the mid-2000s. It has a way to go of course, but is well on the path.

other European judges. For me it was an eye-widening experience. When you get to know people and discuss things with them, your respect for them grows. We found that we got on, despite language difficulties. For instance, I remember Judge Gisbert Steinacker of the Oberlandsgericht, Düsseldorf, saying in 1998 (Madrid Symposium): 'Once when someone told me there was an English decision on the point, I said "thank you" and put it down. Now I read it'. And Judge Steinacker came from an older background and had but limited English. Change was happening amongst Europe's patent judges. They were beginning not only to know each other, but as a result to respect each other and to look at each other's judgments.

My own speech at that 1998 Symposium was mainly about the creation of a European patent court but it contained a section on how European patent judges should treat each others' judgments. *See Chapter 34, Paper for the Ninth (Madrid) Symposium of the European Patent Judges 1998.*

Quite a lot of that has come to pass. I think some continental judgments have become more explicit—at least I find the translations so.[19] I can say, however, that at least some English judgments are written with an eye on foreign readers. Length is a problem we should keep an eye on.[20]

Dissemination of judgments has of course become common, though not in the end so much by way of paper reports as via the Internet. For instance, the EPO keeps a database of national judgments, the IPKat blog tells everyone of any important IP judgment almost at once, and there are more formal, powerful, databases such as DARTS and Kluers.

Consultation amongst judges has become quite common. Mainly between the Dutch, English and German judges but also with some French judges. I do not wish to be misunderstood here. We do not ask each other what to do. It is not a case of secret consultation with someone who is not part of the court. We do ask what the solution would be in that judge's country and whether there is any case law. There is no more, indeed rather less, consultation than takes place between English judges who discuss a case informally. It is the arguments before the court which in the end count. However, the case

[19] Though I still have trouble with the terse style and conclusionary form of some French judgments, particularly of the Cour de Cassation. Judgments in German cases which the court knows will be important have become much more intelligible—though there is a non-English opinion that they should become even more English in style—see paper by Dieter Stauder given to the Utrecht Patent Law conference, 11 January 2011.

[20] *I fear things are getting worse.*

law of other countries can be of assistance and a general discussion around a legal problem is helpful.

The importance of decisions of the courts of other members of the EPC has itself been judicially recognised. Perhaps the most explicit recognition came in *Grimme v Scott* where, in the course of our joint judgment, Etherton LJ and I said:

> [79] Advocates should recognise that where a point of patent law of general importance, such as the construction of a provision which by Treaty (either the EPC or the Community Patent Convention) is to be implemented by states parties to those conventions, has been decided by a court, particularly a higher court, of another member state, the decision matters here. For, despite the fact that there is no common ultimate patent court for Europe, it is of obvious importance to all the countries of the European Patent Union or the parties to the Community Patent Convention ('the CPC'), that as far as possible the same legal rules apply across all the countries where the provisions of the Conventions have been implemented. An important decision in one member state may well be of strong persuasive value in all the others, particularly where the judgment contains clear reasoning on the point.
>
> [80] Broadly we think the principle in our courts—and indeed that in the courts of other member states—should be to try to follow the reasoning of an important decision in another country. Only if the court of one state is convinced that the reasoning of a court in another member state is erroneous should it depart from a point that has been authoritatively decided there. Increasingly that has become the practice in a number of countries, particularly in the important patent countries of France, Germany, Holland and England and Wales. Nowadays we refer to each other's decisions with a frequency which would have been hardly imaginable even twenty years ago. And we do try to be consistent where possible.
>
> [81] The Judges of the patent courts of the various countries of Europe have thereby been able to create some degree of uniformity even though the European Commission and the politicians continue to struggle on the long, long road which one day will give Europe a common patent court.[21]

The point made in [80] was in fact a point I made orally at the 1978 Madrid Symposium. I remember it well for it provoked rather a storm. A lot of judges said they agreed. Then the French judges said they could not refer to judgments of other courts—that indeed they could not even refer to other French judgments. I thought they

[21] *Grimme v Scott* [2010] EWCA Civ 1110. *Readers will note the parallel to what I had said at the 1998 Madrid Symposium—see Chapter 34.*

said it was contrary to French law, but I am not sure for I have since seen a few French judgments which do refer to other judgments. The general notion is this: the law, *la loi*, is the written law made by the legislature. It is not for judges to take over and interpret that—otherwise you are getting a law made by judges. The idea seems to have come from the Revolution (so much in France still does). The thought was something like this:[22] that if judges paid attention to (or still worse followed) decisions of other judges they were not properly applying the law as laid down by the people's representatives. Under the *Ancien Régime* things had been different. The judges were seen as lackeys of the King and their use of previous decisions to justify their decisions was to be eschewed.[23]

I have to say I think that has been a pity. French judges have not played as much a part in the increasing cohesion of European patent judges as they might have done. There are signs of change for the future—some discussion now takes place[24] and that can only be good.

OF RELATIONSHIPS BETWEEN THE EUROPEAN PATENT OFFICE AND NATIONAL COURTS

Procedural Law

Those who created the European system were not experienced in litigation—and, sadly, left Europe with a significantly imperfect system. The EPO's internal system of opposition has major failings. The first instance (opposition division—OD) is not regarded as a true judicial panel—and whilst it contains the examiner who granted the patent probably cannot be. The system of appeal is largely treated as a fresh first instance—with liberal admission of new evidence and fresh arguments. The practice of deciding only one point at a time leads to 'ping pong': if the Board of Appeal decides the OD was wrong to revoke a patent on one point (not uncommonly on an 'added matter', an objection the OD routinely considers first), the case gets sent back

[22] I am no scholar and this may be all wrong, but it sounds right and there has to be a reason why only in France is the idea that a judge should pay attention to earlier decisions of other judges frowned upon.

[23] How perfectly Enlightenment—and how unrealistic!

[24] Not so long ago I was asked by one French judge how a particular problem would be solved under English law. I know she asked the same question of patent judges in other countries too.

for the next point to be considered. If the Board on appeal from that considered the OD got that wrong, there is yet a further remission.

There are other failings too. It costs comparatively little to oppose—low fees and no award of costs against you if you lose. So you only have your own attorney costs. There is no sanction in costs or otherwise for multiple citation of prior art—it is cheaper to cite art than to read it carefully, decide which are your best few points and run just those. So cases are full of points, good bad and indifferent. Further you have to oppose within nine months of grant. That leads to two things. First is that the Office does absolutely nothing with a case until the nine months is over. So even if you oppose on day one, you cannot speed things up.[25] Moreover, none of the rules provide for times to be truncated—only lengthened, which happens with regularity because no one has appreciated that whilst it is always easier in the short term to put things off the long-term effect is to slow the system down.

It is true that the Boards of Appeal are willing to try to speed things up and that they are willing to work with national courts to achieve this.[26] But that does not speed up the whole opposition process or avoid things like 'ping pong'. So the upshot is that the EPO opposition system is ponderously slow. That has a knock-on effect on litigation in national systems where validity is in issue and one side or the other wants the case on early even though there is an ongoing opposition in the EPO. The Germans are apt to stay things.[27] We do the opposite—broadly only staying where a result in the EPO is within sight.[28] Other countries vary in their practices.

The problem of the two systems of national courts and the EPO running side by side leads to another complication. If the national

[25] By contrast a UK revocation action could well be nearing trial if it was started on the day of grant—in exceptional cases it might even be over.

[26] See eg *Eli Lilly v Human Genome Sciences* [2009] EWCA Civ 168 where the English Court of Appeal asked the Boards of Appeal to speed things up. The Board was willing but one party refused and sat on its right to file at the last minute—the result was a lost date for the hearing of the English appeal. The last-minute date could not be brought forward under the EPC Rules. No rational litigation system would be so hidebound that times cannot be truncated.

[27] That itself may encourage oppositions: you oppose to stay the German litigation.

[28] The detailed factors to be taken into account were identified in *Glaxo Group v Genentech* [2008] EWCA Civ 23, [2008] FSR 18. A recent case where a stay was granted was *Danisco v Novozymes* [2011] EWHC (Pat), [2012] FSR 21. The EPO opposition was relatively close to determination.

court goes first it must decide the case on the claims as they stand (or as proposed to be amended if the national court can allow patents to be amended).[29] If it decides the patent is valid and infringed what is the position if the patent is either wholly revoked or amended so that what was alleged to infringe does not on the claims as amended in the EPO? Again things vary across Europe. The English position is clear, subject to any change which may be made by the Supreme Court.[30] It is that once there is a final binding decision[31] to the effect that a patent is valid, has been infringed and that the patentee is entitled to compensation, the parties are bound by that decision. It is *res judicata*. It makes no difference if the patent is subsequently revoked. The cause of action for patent infringement has been substituted by the judgment, *Unilin v Berry*.[32] It makes no difference that the amount of compensation has not yet been determined.[33] In other countries the *res judicata* rule only applies once the amount has been determined and actually paid.[34]

Substantive Law

As regards substantive law the relationship between national courts and the case law of the Board of Appeal of the EPO is rather more satisfactory. In the absence of a full European patent court, the Boards of Appeal are the closest thing to it. Because consistency is so important, the higher UK courts have for at least 20 years made it plain that the principles laid down in the decisions of the Boards

[29] Some, like the UK, allow this. Others do not.

[30] The point is pending before the Supreme Court now in *Virgin Atlantic v Contour*—the Court of Appeal judgment is [2009] FSR 15, [2009] EWCA Civ 1513. *The Supreme Court reversed the Court of Appeal, overruled an earlier Court of Appeal decision which had never been questioned in a hundred years and to my mind seriously disturbed the certainty which early final judgment gives,* Virgin Atlantic v Zodia *[2013] UKSC 46.*

[31] ie one in which there is no longer any possibility of appeal.

[32] *Unilin v Berry* [2007] FSR 25.

[33] As is customary the general practice in the UK, as in most other European countries (contrast the US) is to decide liability (validity and infringement) first, only going on in a follow-up proceeding to work out quantum if that proves necessary. In practice in most countries the parties settle after the first stage.

[34] eg Holland, s 75(6) of the Patent Code, and Germany. In a landmark decision of the Cour de Cassation it was decided that a party who had paid damages for patent infringement could not claim restitution if the patent was subsequently revoked in other proceedings, *Reginald Wehrkamp-Richter v Louis Paul Guita*, 17 February 2012.

of Appeal should be followed in the UK courts. I put it this way in *Actavis v Merck*:[35]

> [46] Our courts would normally follow such settled jurisprudence. That would be in accordance with what Lord Hoffmann said in *Merrell Dow Pharmaceuticals v Norton* [1996] RPC 76 at 82:
>
> > ... the United Kingdom Courts ... must have regard to the decisions of the European Patent Office ('EPO') on the construction of the EPC. These decisions are not strictly binding upon courts in the United Kingdom but they are of great persuasive authority; first, because they are decisions of expert courts (the Boards of Appeal and Enlarged Board of Appeal of the EPO) involved daily in the administration of the EPC and secondly, because it would be highly undesirable for the provisions of the EPC to be construed differently in the EPO from the way they are interpreted in the national courts of a Contracting State.
>
> [47] Nicholls LJ (as he then was) said the same thing perhaps with even greater force in *Gale's Application* [1991] RPC 305 at 322:
>
> > *[Quotation omitted]*
>
> [48] Mr Prescott put the point so colourfully in his skeleton argument that it is worth repeating:
>
> > Now, you cannot have 34 [the current number of EPC members] ships steering in the same convoy unless there is something like a commodore. That is why Mustill LJ in *Genentech Inc's Patent* [1989] RPC 147, 266 referred to the Board of Appeal of the European Patent Office as 'the central decision making body of the European patent system' [which] must be hearkened to with particular attention'.
>
> [48] In saying our courts would and should normally follow the settled jurisprudence of the EPO it should be understood, of course, that they are not bound do so. In the unlikely event that we are convinced that the commodore is steering the convoy towards the rocks we can steer our ship away. Technically we are not in the same position as we are in the case of decisions of the European Court of Justice (see further below). And of course if there is no clear message from the commodore or he gives mixed messages we must decide our own course anyway.

The courts of other countries of the European Patent Union also follow EPO jurisprudence.[36] Its 'White Book' (*Case Law of the Boards of Appeal of the European Patent Office*, currently in its

[35] *Actavis v Merck* [2008] EWCA Civ 444.
[36] See, eg, *Walzenformgebungsmaschine*, GRUR Int. 2010, 761.

sixth, 2010 edition) is a must-have for any European patent judge or patent practitioner.

The use of case law is not entirely one way—national courts looking to the Boards. Sometimes the Boards of Appeal refer to and rely on decisions of national courts. But that is very rare—most experienced national patent judges think it is too rare. For experienced patent judges (particularly in non-bifurcated systems) are somewhat closer to the commercial reality of a case than the Boards. They, in the nature of things, inhabit a somewhat isolated world. In particular how a patent might be enforced is always a live question for a national judge, and that can influence how you think about validity for things like 'use' claims.

There is one other thing to say about the relationships between national courts and the Boards. As I have said, those who created the system had little idea of litigation. Nor did they really understand case law. They put in place the strange system of Enlarged Boards of Appeal[37] rather than a proper final appeal court which could control its docket. A matter can be referred to the Enlarged Board 'in order to ensure uniform application of the law, or if a point arises.[38] But the reference can only be made by a Board of Appeal or the President—and the latter only on a point of law 'where two Boards of Appeal have given different opinions on that question'. A restrictive view about the power to refer is taken by the Enlarged Board so references by the President are particularly limited, the Enlarged Board in *G0003/08* drawing a purposeless distinction between 'legal development' and 'conflicting decisions'.

For present purposes, however, all that can be noted is that the Enlarged Board can, and generally does, include one national judge.[39] Although the term of appointment is three years, in practice it will be seldom that a national judge even sits on more than one case. The EPO practice is simply to work its way through a rather long list of national judges who have been appointed. The 'national judge' provision in practice had little effect, and none of an institutional kind.

Finally I should mention the Court of Appeal's attempt to invent something like a reference system. In *Aerotel and Macrossan*[40] we

[37] References can only be made to it by the President of the EPO.

[38] Art 112(1) EPC. Art 112a provides for the possibility of something like a real appeal in cases of serious procedural violation (they are set out in the Article). Before the amendment in 2000 not even these could be challenged.

[39] EPC Art 11(5).

[40] *Aerotel and Macrossan* [2006] EWCA Civ 1371.

proposed some questions for the President to ask about the patentability of computer programs. We said:

> [75] It is formally no business of ours to define questions to be asked of an Enlarged Board of Appeal. What we say now is only put forward in case the President of the EPO finds it helpful. If he thinks it pointless or arrogant of us to go this far, he is of course entirely free to ignore all we say. Nonetheless in the hope that there is a spirit of co-operation between national courts and the EPO we ventured to ask the parties what questions might be posed by the President of an Enlarged Board pursuant to Art.112. As we have said the British Comptroller of Patents has encouraged us in this course.

What actually happened after was that I immediately sent a copy of the judgment given on 27 October 2006 to the then President of the EPO, Alain Pompidou. He replied on 23 November 2006:

> Thank you very much for bringing this judgment to my attention. The EPO not only closely monitors developments in the case law of its own boards of appeal but is also very interested in developments in the case law of national courts.
>
> The matter of referring questions relating to excluded subject-matter to the Enlarged Board of Appeal of course has been and will be discussed internally, and I am sure that your judgment will form a valuable contribution to the discussion.

But he made no reference to the Board. The next President, Alison Brimelow did so on 22 October 2008. I was disappointed at the outset. The questions referred were not the pragmatic ones we and the Comptroller had devised in *Aerotel.* They were the extraordinarily convoluted ones in *G0003/38*. Moreover the basis for the referral, conflicting Board decisions, was not very well explained—I thought we had done that in the Appendix to *Aerotel.*

In the end, therefore, the exercise came to nothing. I doubt any national court will try again. Which is a pity.

OF RELATIONSHIPS BETWEEN NATIONAL COURTS AND THE COURT OF JUSTICE OF THE EUROPEAN COMMUNITIES

This is a big subject. I do not propose to discuss the procedure whereby a national court can make a reference for a preliminary ruling to the

CJEU[41] save to draw attention to the fact that the CJEU itself provides guidance on the procedure both as to the steps taken and how courts should make references. This is in the form of an *Information Note*.[42] What I will discuss are two things: when a court should make a reference, and how the CJEU deals with them. Both topics are dealt with in other, better-researched and more comprehensive works.[43] My discussion will be rather eclectic.

First, then, when should a court make a reference? One would think that is simple: a reference is needed when the law is unclear and clarity is needed to decide the case. That is what Art 234 of the Lisbon Treaty[44] says:

> The Court of Justice of the European Union shall have jurisdiction to give preliminary rulings concerning:
>
> (a) the interpretation of the Treaties;
> (b) the validity and interpretation of acts of the institutions, bodies, offices or agencies of the Union.
>
> Where such a question is raised before any court or tribunal of a Member State, that court or tribunal may, if it considers that a decision on the question is necessary to enable it to give judgment, request the Court to give a ruling thereon.

The trouble is that these days there is so much EU law—and so much of it ill-drafted—that it is seldom one can say a point is clear. Points which one judge may think are clear others do not. A good recent example is *Neurim v the Comptroller-General of Patents*.[45] Arnold J had upheld the Patent Office's refusal to grant a Supplementary Protection Certificate. He thought the point *acte clair*. We in the Court of Appeal thought his logic was near faultless but that the result was so absurd that there had to be something wrong. We devised something. The CJEU agreed and came up with a sensible answer, albeit somewhat ignoring things it had said in some earlier cases.

So if every referable case was referred the result would be even greater overload of the CJEU than there is now. That was a concern

[41] It is provided for in CPR Part 68.

[42] 2005/C 133/01—printed in the White Book along with the CPR and its Practice Direction.

[43] eg A Arnull, *The European Union and its Court of Justice* (Oxford University Press, 2006).

[44] Art 267 in the consolidated version.

[45] *Neurim v the Comptroller-General of Patents* [2011] EWCA Civ 228, [2011] RPC 19 (CA); Case C-130/11 19 July 2012, CJEU.

in the 1970s[46] and remains one now. Moreover, there would be delay in any event—and sometimes (perhaps quite often) it is better to give the parties a result with a hope and expectation of ending the litigation than trying to get perfection (or rather a decision of the ultimate court, which may be far from perfection).[47]

Thus there is a problem. It has a variant too. Should a first instance judge refer or should he or she leave that to the Court of Appeal? Again this is not easy. On the one hand, if the first instance judge refers time will or may be saved; on the other, if the Court of Appeal refers the case is likely to have been refined so that the reference is more precise.[48]

I think it impossible to formulate clear rules about when to refer and when not. I do not think I am alone. Judge Joachim Bornkamm of the Bundesgerichtsthof has said his court could refer almost all cases that come to it (he is President of the division that deals with trade marks and competition law). It is all a judgment call—a multi-factorial decision.

My other topic. How the questions should be framed and how the CJEU deals with them? In this country rather a lot of effort goes into formulating these. Sometime too much effort and argument between the parties can lead to questions which are too long, too many and too complex. I believe in keeping things simple and I think that involves the court itself doing a bit of preliminary work by making a first draft in the judgment deciding to refer.[49] I did that, for instance, in *Budejovicky Budvar v Anheuser-Busch*[50] for it was obvious that these warring parties could never produce an agreed set of questions.

I turn finally to how the Court answers the questions. It is not very satisfactory. It seldom actually answers the questions sent.[51] Indeed, I cannot recall an occasion when it did. Too often we get the formula 'By its first question (or 'by its first and third questions') the referring court is essentially asking …' and a different question is posed and then answered. It does not always matter—the question

[46] See *Bulmer v Bollinger* [1974] RPC 401, 422 *per* Lord Denning MR.

[47] 'Right because it is final, not final because it is right' as the old saying goes.

[48] Not always. I always regret not referring *Philips v Remington*. I gave a full judgment dealing with all the points in issue [1998] RPC 283. It went to the Court of Appeal, [1999] RPC 809, which referred questions. I think they were not that well framed and certainly added nothing. The ECJ took nearly four years to come up with an answer. Not satisfactory.

[49] Though of course any party suggesting or asking for a reference ought itself at the outset to produce a first draft. Too often they don't.

[50] *Budejovicky Budvar v Anheuser-Busch* [2009] EWCA 1022.

[51] So all or a lot of the trouble that goes into formulating them with precision is wasted.

actually asked is covered. But it can matter, with the result that there is real dispute on the return of the case to the national court about what the oracle really meant. With respect I think the CJEU should give the national courts a little more credit: the questions posed will normally have been carefully crafted for the case concerned. After all the CJEU's primary task is to answer the questions sent it.

Another concern, particularly strong in intellectual property[52] is that the answer is not enough to solve the case. I said this in *L'Oréal*:

> [2] Not for the first time in intellectual property cases (e.g. *British Horseracing Board v William Hill* [2005] EWCA (Civ) 863, [2005] RPC 883, *Arsenal v Reed* [2003] RPC 696, [2003] EWCA Civ 696 and *Boehringer Ingelheim v Swingward* [2004] EWCA Civ 129, [2004] ETMR 90) the Court's judgment has left enough room for the parties to disagree about what it means. It is such a disagreement which comes before us now.

It was intended as a minor rebuke—almost a request, for answers clear enough to prevent this sort of subsequent fight. I do not know whether it has worked. I leave that to the reader to try to find out.

[52] The Court has no member experienced in this field of law—and is rather weak on commercial law generally.

17

Article for The House*

THE COALITION'S PROGRESS on intellectual property ('IP', ie patents, trade marks, copyright and designs, and related subjects)—and what more could be done to improve policy in this area—all in 500 words!

I remind readers that some big parts of IP are largely out of the government's hands. Patent law is governed by the European Patent Convention (a non-EU Treaty) and trade mark and design law by EU law (as befits a common market) and some aspects of copyright law are also laid down at EU level. But there are some matters left to domestic law and other matters are at an EU level under discussion now.

Early on the government asked Professor Hargreaves to review IP. He reported in May 2011. His first recommendation was that:

> Government should ensure that development of the IP System is driven as far as possible by objective evidence. Policy should balance measurable economic objectives against social goals and potential benefits for rights holders against impacts on consumers and other interests. These concerns will be of particular importance in assessing future claims to extend rights or in determining desirable limits to rights.

The government said it accepted Hargreaves—and in part, it has, for instance in relation to assisting the creation of a 'digital copyright exchange'. Similarly, largely sensible consultations have been going on about minor amendments to copyright law.

But in three important respects the government reneged on its acceptance of its commitment to 'objective evidence'. It gave in to lobbying from those who scream loudest.

* *This is a magazine for the House of Commons managed by cross-party MPs and senior Parliamentarians. This piece appeared in November 2013.*

Example 1: The 25-year period of protection from first marketing given to industrial designs by copyright law ought to be enough. After all patents for inventions only get 20 years from filing (not marketing). And registered designs get 25 years. But lobbyists for 'classic' (ie 'old' designs, such as Lucienne Day fabric designs and maybe classic furniture eg Charles Eames) persuaded the government to extend the term to 70 years from the year of death of the author. No regard was paid to the effect on the freedom of young designers who need to draw inspiration from the past. And no regard was paid to those British companies who honestly made reproductions of these old classics. Some are closing down or moving out of Europe. Industry, the IP profession and academics all opposed this.

Example 2: Criminalising infringement of registered design. Opposed by all the professions (Bar, solicitors and patent attorneys), most of industry (eg the IP Federation) and supported only by a shrill lobby group called ACID. There is no evidence that it will do any good but a lot that it will do harm. The government is pushing this through now. MPs would do well to read the evidence about this and reject it.[1]

Example 3: Term extension of copyright in sound recordings from 50 to 70 years. All government advice (eg Hargreaves and the earlier Gowers report) was against this. Yet the government supported it in Brussels. If copyright lasts too long it becomes a dead hand on creativity and an unjust reward for the descendants of the creators. The government should have said so.

Moral: If you say you will act by objective evidence, you should stand by your word.

[1] *They didn't but it was watered down so as to require intent, rather a nonsense given that intention is irrelevant to infringement of registered design.*

18

*Industrial Property—Industry's Enemy?**

THIS IS THE second Stephen Stewart memorial lecture. I am honoured to be asked to give it. I wish he was here to discuss with us the problems upon which I touch this evening. He would have had a lot to say.

When I was asked for a title I gave my answer instantly over the telephone. The sponsors, Butterworths, in due course e-mailed back. Did I mean 'industrial property' or had the word 'intellectual' got garbled over the telephone? I e-mailed back the word 'industrial'. I will tell you why at the outset.

The general area of law now called 'intellectual property' is in the main a law conferring private rights on one party to prevent competition from others. It is fundamentally about industry—an economic law—a law that controls or forms the base for industrial activities. To call it 'intellectual' is misleading; it takes one's eye off the ball. 'Intellectual' confers a respectability on a monopoly which may well not be deserved. A squirrel is a rat with good PR. 'Intellectual Property' is perhaps a phrase coined by the same PR agent for monopolies? One senior member of chambers used to say when I was starting out: 'We are the grit in wheels of industry'. That was perhaps too cynical a view, but it is right to say that so-called IP is the law of private monopolies affecting industry in its widest sense. It should be viewed in that light.

Last year Sir Hugh Laddie's lecture was confined to copyright. He called it 'Copyright—Over Strength Over Regulated and Over Rated'. The title was meant to contain a question mark but it was clear from his lecture that he regarded copyright as having gone too

* *First published in (1997) 1* Intellectual Property Quarterly *3–15 and based on the Stephen Stewart Memorial Lecture on 7 November 1996.*

far. He pointed to its entry into the control of industrial design, to the vast period of copyright protection of 50 years from the death of the author being increased to the even vaster period of 70 years from death, to the extraordinary remedies of additional damages, to the danger then threatened of the government regarding the very laws of the land as being property to be charged for, and to the low level of originality required by our law. Fortunately the government has now retreated somewhat and as a result it is to be hoped that modern methods of containing and displaying statutes—CD ROMs, and on-line services—will not be imperilled by threats of government applications for injunctions. But that is a matter of concession only. Even so it remains the case that transcripts of reserved Court of Appeal judgments bear the doubtful, but menacing, claim 'Crown Copyright' on their title page.

Sir Hugh indicated his own considerable unease at the present scope of copyright. The question I put before you today is whether that unease should apply to other areas of IP, and if so what should be done? Are IP laws, originally intended to strengthen creativity, innovation, investment and enterprise, getting out of hand? I not only share Sir Hugh's unease about copyright—I think there is justification for unease over the whole range of the subject. I indicated my unease in my Foreword to this Institute's Newsletter in January this year. I said: 'However justified the cry "what we need is protection" may be for an anti-AIDS campaign, it is not self-evident for a process of the creation of new or escalated kinds of monopoly'. Sir Hugh and I are not alone. The next Newsletter of this Institute found Lord Hoffmann also raising questions about where IP is and is going.

What I propose to do this evening is to examine some current topics in the field of industrial property, generally focusing on particular examples. There will be a constant theme—IP rights need properly researched legal and economic information before they are imposed. I also propose to mention one or two hobby horses of my own.

I begin with where Sir Hugh left off. He ended his lecture by giving the Fosbery flop as an example of a case where not all copying is bad and that sometimes copying and developing is good. He thought that was self-evident. But inside a year two young and bright American lawyers, Scott Kieff[1] and Rob Kunstadt had suggested,[2] in an article

1 *Scott is now a judge of the International Trade Commission.*

2 The *International Law Journal*, 20 May 1996. At the time of writing they were Associates with a well-known UK firm of intellectual property lawyers and are now Law Clerks to that

entitled 'It's Your Turn, but My Move', that novel athletes' moves (leading for instance to being able to pitch a baseball 10 per cent faster) are patentable. They argue that there is no difference in principle between this and any other innovation—particularly, in the case of sports innovations in equipment. They also suggest that copyright may have a part to play in sports—regarding movements as something like choreographed movements of dance. Looking at some Olympic so-called sports one can see their point. Similarly, even if it seems difficult to imagine a new way of heading a soccer ball, it is not difficult to imagine a new way of celebrating a goal. Indeed sometimes it seems that that is the primary occupation of some players. Kieff and Kunstadt finally suggest that there might be some trade mark or like protection available to novel athletic moves. The important point to note about their article is that it is not absurd—legally speaking. This sort of 'protection' is coming within the range of the guns of IP. And I suggest that it is doing so because people have stopped asking what IP is for and whether it is doing any good.

Another example from the field of patents. As many of you will know the Federal Court of Appeal in the USA has held in *re Alappat*[3] that computer programs as such are, essentially, patentable. And there is complaint from the USA that the EPC forbids the patenting of programs as such. This is despite the protection given by copyright and the fudges which allow hardware when programmed to be patentable in some circumstances. Now what is instructive if one reads the Federal Court judgments—both the majority and the powerful dissent of Chief Judge Archer, is the lack of any measurements to support or refuse protection. One finds economic assertions made but not justified. Likewise when the British Patent Office held a Symposium in 1994 on legal protection for software-related innovation, whilst there was a majority in favour of patents for computer programs, the *reasons* for the majority view remain essentially assertion of benefit rather than proof. Some may intuitively feel that the computer program industry has in no way needed a patent incentive to encourage innovation. It has and continues to blossom at an astonishing rate. And the problem of properly defining claims and searching prior art might (as Archer CJ suggests) prove to be a mighty hindrance to the

great judge and jurist Judge Giles Rich of the Federal Court of Appeal for the 10th Circuit. I am grateful to the authors for sending me a copy of their article and I hope they will forgive my using it as an example of IP law going too far.

[3] *re Alappat* 33 F 3d 1526 (1994).

industry. Likewise the combination of protection with the adoption of standards (eg the increasing dominance of Windows) may suggest that the anti-monopolists—the anti-trust brigade—should step in. The truth seems to be that no one actually knows. What is certain is that the protagonists of 'protection' have a loud voice. But then they would, wouldn't they—for they are principally the lawyers of the big battalions.[4]

My next example in the field of patents is one which I mentioned some time ago in my Herschel Smith lecture. This is the problem of 'undue' width. As you will know the 1949 Act and its predecessors (ultimately the common law) explicitly contained the notion that you cannot patent more than you have invented. In the language of the 1949 Act a claim had to be 'fairly based' on the matter disclosed in the specification. Under Art 84 of the EPC a claim has to be 'supported by' such matter, but—and this is surprising to many—once a patent has been granted there is no objection to validity as such upon this ground. One has an intuitive feeling that something ought to be done about it. And now something has. It has taken 20 years for the ingenuity of the EPO and, last week, our House of Lords, to get round the problem by a hardly self-evident stretching of the Convention. The arguments are roundabout and over-elaborate ways of dealing with the perceived problem of undue width. Both the EPO and the courts (look, for instance, at what can only be described as soul-searching by the Court of Appeal in *Genentech*) are worried by over-large claims. They have been, until last week, finding ways of cutting them back based on an intuition of an economic harm caused by over-large claims. Last week that which was intuitive and unexpressed was, for the first time, made explicit. Lord Hoffmann in *Biogen* expressly looked at an economic analysis of over-large claims in holding that the Patents Act permits claims to be struck down on this ground.[5] The analysis was American. I am not aware of any European analysis of the problem, which I think is considerably under-researched. Further, I believe that so far as our IP jurisprudence is concerned, this is the first time a court has looked at

[4] *It is only recently that the Americans have woken up to problems with software patents—especially for business methods involving the use of programs. The Supreme Court has cut them back in* Alice Corporation Pty Ltd v CLS Bank International, et al *134 S Ct 2347). I remain doubtful that they have served the purpose of furthering innovation.*

[5] *This ground came to be known as 'Biogen insufficiency'. It is not entirely clear that it still exists in the same way because Biogen turned on the form of the claim, see* Generics v Lundbeck *[2009] UKHL 12 upholding a Court of Appeal which included Lord Hoffmann and me, [2008] EWCA Civ 311.*

an economic analysis in deciding what the law should be. I very much doubt that one study is enough. Is undue width really a problem, and if so in respect of what sorts of claim? Surely it is not beyond the wit of modern research techniques to find out. Or must judges (and Patent Offices) go on working largely by intuition? The investigation should be how actual supposedly over-large claims actually affect industry's behaviour. There will be an economic angle to this too—do the owners of over-large claims make too much money from them?

My next patent example relates to the much discussed 'use' or 'for' claims. The Enlarged Board of Appeal of the European Patent Office, in *MOBIL/Friction reducing additive*[6] approved a claim in the form 'Use of compound X as a friction reducing additive in a lubricant'. This was so even though it was known to add X to a lubricant for the purpose of rust inhibition. No one knew that X also reduced friction until the patentees found that out. It is not my intention to go into the merits of this decision now. Why should I when the House of Lords skirted the point in *Merrell Dow*? My point in referring to the case tonight is to look at the real justification for the decision. This was an inarticulate major premise in the decision itself. It was made articulate by one member of the Board later. Mr Paterson, in a lecture to the 1994 European Patent Judges' Symposium, said:[7] 'Use claims provide protection for research into the further properties of known products, especially chemical and pharmaceutical products'. Now what I want to know is whether what is implied by that assertion is true. The editors of the European Patent Office Reports said when they reported the case: 'Claims of this type, now that they have been formally sanctioned by the Enlarged Board of Appeal, may be expected to proliferate'. Well have they?[8] Is it really the case that research on 'inherent' results of old processes is impeded by lack of prospects of a patent? Has the decision in *MOBIL* made the slightest difference to the direction of research? The decision is now six years old and one ought to be able to find out. In the words of *Private Eye*, I think we should be told. Similar questions arise in relation to the effect of the second medical use type of claim. This has been established much longer. So firm results should be discoverable.[9]

[6] *MOBIL/Friction reducing additive* [1990] OJ EPO 93, (1991) 22 IIC 85, [1990] EPOR 73.

[7] (1996) 27 *International Review of Intellectual Property and Competition Law* 179, 181.

[8] Only cases where a simple process claim is not available would count. Just tacking on a use claim when you have a valid process claim would not be relevant evidence of anything other than sensible precautions by patent agents.

[9] *By and large the decisions seem to have worked even though there are illogicalities.*

At this point I propose to take a diversion from my main theme tonight to put forward a proposal. The need for it is exemplified by *MOBIL*. It is self-evident that there are intellectual and practical difficulties with *MOBIL*-type claims from the infringement point of view. Mr Paterson suggests that infringement would involve what he calls 'an element of subjectivity'—but that is not readily to be found in the provisions of the Community Patent Convention (CPC), from which most, but not all, national laws of infringement are derived. It is easy enough for the EPO to side-step the difficulties. It is not an infringement court. And the Enlarged Appeal Board is not staffed by judges. One of the things I would like to see is a change in the composition of the Board. I think its legal members should be national judges with patent experience. The Board sits on comparatively few cases a year and so the judges could go 'on circuit' for the short periods necessary. They would have the expertise and experience to consider how claims would be treated in national courts. The decisions of a Board so composed would be likely to command respect throughout Europe and to have a significant effect on the harmonisation of the European patent system. As Mr Paterson observed in his discussion of *MOBIL*:[10]

> Since the legal framework within which the EPO works is not exactly equivalent to the framework within which each national court works, the achievement of a harmonised European patent system in the absence of a truly integrated system cannot be easy.

I believe my proposal, if implemented, would result in a significant degree of harmonisation of the patent system. Judges who work together are much more likely to think together or at least along closely similar lines. So not only would the opinions of the Enlarged Board have an enhanced status, but in other areas of law, both substantive and procedural, an increased mutual understanding and a common approach would be likely to emerge. I think from my own experience that the meetings of European patent judges, which been organised by the EPO have shown the way. I am glad to say that I think I have benefited very much from such meetings. I know Sir Hugh agrees and I hope and believe our European colleagues from other countries feel the same way.

My last patent example relates to employee inventions. Sections 39–42 of the Patents Act 1977 provide for employee inventions in

[10] *Mobil* (n 6) 190.

various ways. In particular there is provision for what is called 'compensation' for an employee who has made an invention which is of outstanding benefit to his employer. If the invention was patented then the employee is to get a 'fair share' of the benefit. The thinking behind the provisions was in part that employees would have a greater incentive to invent and in part some sort of general equitable fairness. There are similar provisions in Germany. I have a number of questions. Does the UK system work? How many employees are getting compensation? How much is being paid? I suspect the answers are 'few' and 'little'. Certainly there are few reported cases on the provisions and I can hardly believe that this is because most of the claims are resolved without any formal dispute. Assuming the provisions have failed, does this matter? Is the incentive theory valid? Is more paid in Germany, as I believe it is? What is the effect in research departments in Germany, and particularly are there fights to be named as inventor? What about US and Japanese company employee inventors? Is the whole theory of the thing a mistake? It is only hard research, not speculation, which can begin to answer these questions. Yet they are important. If a system of extra reward for successful inventions was a real and effective spur to employee inventors then surely, if our existing provisions do not work, they should be made to. And if such a system is not effective or is not shown to be so, then let us get rid of it as having been no more than an emotive but ultimately pointless scheme.[11]

I wish next to consider proposals for *droit de suite* and second-tier protection.

The part dealing with droit de suite *is omitted. Its substance and a later commentary are in Chapter 40 'The Globalisation of Copyright'.*

So I think the Commission and Council should have courage. First they should establish on the basis of facts a real need for harmonisation. If such a need really exists, then harmonisation down is the right way unless it can be shown that there is a real economic need for this right. The presumption should be *against* imposing or extending monopolies or like rights. Only harmonise up if a serious economic case for it is proved. Some might say that a good example of this was the introduction of Supplementary Protection Certificates (SPCs) increasing the term of protection for inventions such as pharmaceuticals which, for regulatory reasons, could not be marketed for

[11] *We still do not know whether this is really a good idea!*

most of the term of the normal patent life. SPCs encouraged investment in underdeveloped inventions and one can intuitively feel that they are probably justified on that ground.

Let me consider harmonisation further. Assume a policy of complete harmonisation for IP laws throughout the Union. Each country at present has its own laws. A thorough policy of harmonisation carried only upwardly would require all countries to have a monopoly or like law if any one of them did. Thus our design law, both registered and unregistered, has no exact counterpart in other countries. Must our law be imposed on them to achieve harmonisation? And other countries have their laws of unfair competition of varying strength. Must the strongest of these be imposed on the whole Union? In some countries the legal procedural system makes it easier to obtain interlocutory injunctions than in others. Should we all grant such injunctions because one country does? And even that might not be enough. Why should parties be allowed to patent in only some countries of the Union? Surely if they patent in one, for the sake of harmonisation they ought to be compelled to patent in all—even if they can't afford it.

I return to *droit de suite. Omitted here—see Chapter 40.*

The conclusion is simple: the case for *droit de suite* is not made out. There has been nowhere near enough research or economic analysis. There ought to have been. One should not go about making Community-wide monopoly or like rights without proper in-depth economic and quantitative studies. The Commission should go back to the drawing board. It should be looking at abolishing *droit de suite*—at harmonising down or simply leaving things as they are. It is a nice emotional idea, but in practice it may be worse than useless.

I turn to another proposal which I think suffers from exactly the same defects of inadequate research. This time that research is not merely inadequate in economic terms, but also in legal terms. I refer to the proposal for 'second-tier protection' or 'utility models' or 'petty patents'. I prefer the last of these terms—the word 'patent' conveys more properly what is being discussed—a monopoly right of some sort.

The general thought behind the idea is something like this: some ideas or mechanical designs are not inventive enough to be patentable. And anyway the costs and time of getting a patent are both substantial. So the patent system is not available for these 'petty' inventions. The problem is particularly significant for small and medium-sized enterprises (SMEs): all too often they find their ideas copied and as a result they cannot find the capital necessary for investment. So what is needed is some lesser right than a full patent, a right which costs less, for instance because there is no examination.

It seems to follow from the above as night follows day that there should be a cheap system of petty patents. Indeed one can hardly imagine how so many countries have got on without such a system. Yet I have to say that it is my belief that the imposition of a petty patent system would cost us Europeans dearly. I say that from my many years' experience in practice and my more limited experience on the Bench. I am well aware that many lawyers may say otherwise. I suggest, however, that lawyers can only contribute to part of the debate—and probably the lesser side of it. When I set out the reasoning for the system, almost every statement leading to the conclusion was an economic, not legal, assertion of fact.

First, consider the position of SMEs. Why should they be the winners if petty patents become possible Europe-wide? Big industry will take these out more readily than small industry—especially if they are cheap. A competent corporate patent department will not only apply for patents to cover the company's products—it will surround the patents with an outer defence wall of petty patents. A small man wishing to innovate will be able to get his petty patent cheaply—but will not know, unless it is searched, whether it is any good. And if he wants to market his new product he is likely to have to search not only for patents, but for petty patents too. And if the latter are unexamined, then he will have to take advice as to their scope and validity. The advice will include the cost of searching. And who will get the best advice—the big company or the little company? You will notice that I have here specifically included the costs of lawyers and patent agents in the costs of the system. They are all, of course, loveable and especially deserving people. But in economic terms they are a compliance cost of the IP system. Industry has to pay for them. So far as I can see compliance costs have not been taken into account at all.

Next consider the position of the courts. The suggested petty patent is to be invalid if it is very obvious. But a patent is invalid if it is obvious and in practice a patent has to be pretty obvious before it is revoked these days. Under the old German national patent system a patent had to have sufficient 'inventive height'—which may have involved more than mere obviousness. Anecdotally they had a higher standard than we did in the UK: in other words obviousness was easier to establish in Germany than here, both in the respective Patent Offices and the courts. That may have been enough to leave some room for a petty patent in Germany. But anecdotally at least, the EPO has not required the same inventive height as was formerly the case in Germany. And I for my part cannot see any room for clear water between current standards of obviousness for patents and some lesser standard for a petty patent.

In reality a petty patent will be just an unexamined patent, but with a lesser term, a less well-defined scope and of very uncertain validity. It is likely to be a millstone round the necks of European industry, especially small and medium-sized industry.

What then does one say about the fact that a number of EU countries have a petty patent system? Well, I do not think we have anywhere near enough information about how they work in practice. It is no good just looking at the substantive law. That is the easy thing to do—you look at the formal provisions of the law. Apart from commissioning a report from an economic research institute in Germany, that is all that the Commission have done. What one wants to know is how the various systems actually affect research, innovation and investment. How they actually affect big companies and little companies. Before one embarks on an EU-wide imposition of second-tier protection these questions must be answered and answered satisfactorily and not by assertion. If one does not do that one is embarking again on a harmonisation-up exercise without any or any sufficient justification.

This is no trivial matter. If this system is imposed on Europe and it turns out to be mistaken, it will be very, very difficult to go back. Petty patents, once granted, will not be removable. It really is worth organising a detailed study of what is best to do. The existing studies suffer from a number of defects. I will return to this point shortly.

In this country we have no experience of a petty patent system as such. But we did have something slightly comparable and indeed have it still. Mechanical inventions are often embodied in copyright drawings and, such was the overarching nature of copyright protection during the 1970s and early 1980s, that in practice copyright in industrial designs operated as a partial petty patent system preventing close copying of industrial artefacts. Again I have a question. What good or harm did the system do? Surely we can have more concrete answers than 'it prevented unfair copying'. Did the system encourage innovation or investment? Or did it unduly cushion companies into lazy reliance on the protection given so that their need to beat others in the market by novel design was reduced? Are there no ways of finding out by research?

Incidentally the repeal of the existing system and its replacement with a weaker and shorter system of protection is one of the few examples of a reduction in IP rights in recent times. I commend it as showing that harmonisation up is not the only way. You can reduce IP rights.

I said I would return to the existing studies. The Commission based its work on a study done in Germany by the well-respected IfoInstitute. That study, the Commission's green paper, has been examined here for this Institute[12] by Dr Margaret Llewellyn. I have to say that Dr Llewellyn's excellent work really shows beyond doubt that the case for imposition of a second-tier system of some kind is far from made out. In part this is because the Commission has taken the Ifo results further than they will legitimately go and in part because the original study is, I am afraid, rather too limited. If a system of such potential for impeding European industry is to be imposed, I believe that a much fuller and deeper study is called for. That such a study would be expensive is as nothing compared with the cost if the system is mistakenly imposed.

There is another reason for waiting. As you will know there are advanced proposals for a European Union registered design system. I do not have the time to go into this. In principle again it seems a good idea. What worries me is that it is to be added to other systems of 'protection'. It will undoubtedly cover some of the ground of a second-tier system, however theoretical the different sorts of right are supposed to be. And in our country it will add to unregistered design right. In others it might be added to unfair competition or like rights. Let us see how this goes before rushing into second tier too.[13]

Next I turn to trade marks. The Trade Marks Directive and the corresponding national legislation (ours is the 1994 Act) have sought to harmonise in part European trade mark law. But at the same time there are many who seem to think that it has also taken trade mark law well beyond anything conventionally recognised as such. Let me give you two examples.

First 'Association'. Can there be infringement if a defendant's trade mark merely brings to mind the plaintiff's, even though no one thinks the defendant's goods or services have any trade connection with the

[12] *ie the Institute of Intellectual Property—now wound up because the things it did (seminars and research) have been taken over by the universities.*

[13] *In the end, the proposal for petty patents died. But it shows signs of coming to life again and I fear the fight to stop it will have to happen all over again.*

plaintiff? Those who have read *Wagamama*[14] and the articles and counter-articles in the *European Intellectual Property Review* by Mr Peter Prescott QC and Dr Kamperman Sanders will be familiar with the problem and will, I hope, forgive me for briefly summarising it. It arose in *Wagamama* in the following way. Wagamama is a well-known Japanese noodle bar. The defendants intended to open an Indian restaurant called 'Rajamama'. The plaintiffs proved that a significant number of people would think that Rajamama was not only an Indian version of Wagamama but also that it formed part of the same enterprise. So there was passing off. Laddie J also held that there was trade mark infringement because Wagamama was a registered mark. He could have stopped there. But, given that the subject matter of the dispute was restaurants, he made a meal of things. He went on to consider what the position would be if people thought no more than that Rajamama was a sort of Indian Wagamama but did not think it was commercially connected with it. He said there would be no infringement in those circumstances. He held that the phrase in the Trade Marks Directive 'a likelihood of confusion on the part of the public which includes the likelihood of association between the sign and the trade mark' meant only that a kind of association which led to confusion was an infringement.

Emotive language characterised the subsequent debate. Dr Kamperman Sanders started it by calling his first article[15] 'Back to the Dark Ages'. He asserted that a trade mark is more than a trade mark. He asserted a 'Modern understanding that the trade mark itself embodies value as a conveyor of goodwill and quality, publicity or life-style'. He coupled this with an assertion that any association with the plaintiff's mark ought therefore to be stopped as endangering this value. I believe that real trade marks are a good deal more robust than that. There was some 'association', for some, with Mr Stringfellow's nightclub when McCains called their chips 'stringfellows' but there was no damage of any kind. Kit Kat and KiteKat have lived side by side for years. The tons of annual Kit Kat sales say that no one worries about the association with cat food. Mr Peter Prescott QC hit back at Dr Kamperman Sanders with an equally emotively entitled article 'Think before you Waga Finger'.[16] And Dr Kamperman

[14] *Wagamama Ltd v City Centre Restaurants plc* [1995] FSR 713.

[15] A Kamperman Sanders, 'Back to the Dark Ages of Trade Mark Law' (1996) 1 *European Intellectual Property Review* 3.

[16] P Prescott, 'Think Before You Waga Finger' (1996) 1 *European Intellectual Property Review* 317.

Sanders replied with a more moderately entitled article 'The Return to Wagamama',[17] which was in its content fairly heated.

It is not necessary to go into the details further today. What I wish to say is you can approach this question practically or in an abstract manner. My contribution to the debate is to ask, what can be proved as a practical matter for both sides? In particular I suggest that the extended view of trade mark protection favoured by some theorists requires justification as a practical matter. The extension of monopoly rights by assertion of damage without proof will not do. Purely theoretical or abstract arguments have no place in forming the rules of IP.

Can research help here? Is there anything which can be measured or shown justifying the extended view? If not, then it should not prevail. Once could investigate, for instance, what trade marks in the 'Dark Ages' were damaged by the kind of association favoured by the wide school of thought. If none, or only a few, can be found, that would militate against the extended view of 'association'. After all the traditional view of what trade marks do has, I believe, served industry well for a long time. Going further may well represent an unwarranted interference with the rights of others, another burden on industry. That burden relates not only to what cannot be done, but to the enormous costs of finding suitable marks. Compliance costs are an important matter all too often overlooked in considering what the law should be. What is the compliance cost of the extended view?

Trade mark law has changed out of all recognition since this was written nearly 20 years ago. It has become both much more protective and much more obscure. I do not think there is any credible evidence that this has done any good for trade, as opposed to trade mark lawyers.

My next example relates to 'distinctiveness'. It is clear that under the new law containers may be registered as trade marks. This was barred under our old law of registered trade marks, but the law of passing off could clearly protect a distinctive container, as the Jif lemon case revealed. So far I have no problem. My problem starts when one sees what the UK Registry appears to be doing and what I fear the European Trade Mark Registry may do. People are coming along with funny-shaped bottles. They say: that's an unusual shape, a distinctive shape. So put my new bottle on the register. This,

[17] A Kamperman Sanders, 'The Return to Wagamama' (1996) 1 *European Intellectual Property Review* 521.

if followed through, will turn the trade marks registries into designs registries—nay better than designs registries for the monopoly given is permanent. I believe (and this is a mere non-judicial opinion without argument) that mere unusualness in a container shape does not make it *a priori* capable of distinguishing for trade mark purposes. Distinctive does not mean unusual, it means doing the job of being a trade mark. Whether or not a funny shape does that job can only be established by use and recognition as a trade mark. But suppose I am wrong. Does it matter if funny-shaped bottles can be registered on the nod for permanent monopolies? I think we need research here too.[18]

I have covered a lot—probably too much—ground tonight. But I want to conclude by considering where this seemingly unstoppable drive for more monopoly has come from and how I see things developing.

So far as the drive is concerned I have to say that I think that too much of it has come from lawyers. Professor Goodhart summed it up in the title of his Chorley lecture this year: 'Economics and the Law: Too Much One Way Traffic'. Why has the traffic been one way in the case of IP rights? These rights are complex not only in law, but even more so in their practical operation. They are not readily understood even by businessmen, still less the general public. Businessmen have a terrible tendency to let policy be decided by lawyers. The attitude is: we have got an IP department: why keep a dog and bark yourself? The answer is that it is generally a mistake to let your dog run your affairs.

Also I think there is a psychological trick at work here: it is somehow much more interesting to think about how you are going to stop others than to think about others stopping you. It is more fun to be a plaintiff than a defendant. And use of words like 'protection' rather than monopoly encourages such thinking.

Further there is the fact that lawyers' studies of the problems can be over-academic. Often they are studied because they are intellectually interesting rather than because they are important. Thus, the differences, if any, between the German and British approach to patent infringement remain the subject of almost perpetual debate. Yet this can only be of significance in marginal cases. It is a minor problem compared with a new second-tier system or what the rules for a European Design System should be. And I have to say that

[18] *See Chapter 38.*

I think even economists and other observers often look at problems or do studies at too general a level to be helpful in deciding what IP laws should actually be. You can try to consider what IP rights are worth in a general sort of way. But detailed research aimed at specific topics—eg the significance of use claims—is rare indeed.

As to the future, I think things are looking up. Economists are looking more carefully at legal rules and lawyers are looking beyond the law. It is my hope that we will see very rapid progress in this area and that future legislation and, perhaps, judicial decisions will be founded upon a more solid basis than has been the case in recent years. If that can be achieved IP will be the friend of industry, not its enemy.

POSTSCRIPT

I am now sure that I was wrong in thinking that economists could help, see Chapter 8. Things did not look up.

Part IV

Patents

19

Competition Authorities Support Grasshoppers: Competition Law as a Threat to Innovation[*]

AESOP TOLD THE fable of the ant and the grasshopper. In the summer the ant works, gathering and storing food against the coming winter. The grasshopper laughs and sings, living only for the day. Those who innovate are the ants: using part of the income of today to build for the future. The grasshoppers are those who look only for profits for today and do not contribute to the future. In my opinion competition authorities are favouring grasshoppers, positively helping them sing in the summer (ie gather in profits now) and saying 'do not worry, sing away. When winter comes we will make the ants feed you'. The danger to innovation is all too obvious for those who can see: it pays to be a grasshopper rather than an ant—better to be a copyist than an innovator.

I shall demonstrate this by reference to the competition authorities' conduct in relation to two industries heavily dependent on innovation: pharma and telecoms. Let us recall some basics.

BASICS: IP LAW ITSELF HAS INBUILT REGARD TO THE NEED FOR COMPETITION

IP rights are exceptions to the general Western model of free competition, are justified by the advantages they provide to society outweighing the advantages provided by uncontrolled free competition. Some types of IP are completely uncontroversial. Thus no one contests that

[*] *This was first published in (2013) 9(2)* Competition Policy International.

the law should prevent one trader from falsely representing his goods or services to be that of another. He may compete with another, but not by lying to the public. Where trade mark law goes further—for instance by preventing a man from honestly comparing his goods or services with another—controversy begins. But the debate takes place within the context of the nature of the IP right itself—competition is taken into account in the legal assessment of the extent of the right. Competition law just does not come into it.

As regards patent law its very basic rules are built round the idea of free competition. You cannot patent that which is old or obvious. Why not? Because otherwise you would interfere with free competition. Nor can you patent more than you have invented. Why not? Because you would monopolise that which should be free for others to explore. A patent term is limited by the rather crude 20-year (actually 21-year if you use the priority system well) term. Why is it term-limited? Because a longer monopoly would interfere with free competition.

Thus patent law rights and concepts are riddled with non-interference with competition. What you can patent is the practical application of new and ingenious ideas. You get a monopoly but it is a monopoly in something which would not have existed (or existed as soon) but for your inventive contribution. The law interferes not with ordinary competition but with competition in something which would not have existed but for the inventor.

The availability of a future monopoly is a major driver for innovation. It is no good bemoaning this reality. It is no good advocating abolition and replacement of the patent system with some alternative such as state-sponsored research rewards. It has been tried (for instance in the Soviet Union) and has not worked. There is of course much government- or charity-supported research, particularly in the field of medicines. But the reality is that the patent system remains the bedrock of future research both for new medicines and new medical devices. Indeed it is unfortunate that patent law does not go further in some cases—particularly in not really providing adequate protection for future uses of known medicines. Abolitionist or dilutionist economists have been around a long time—since the mid-nineteenth century at least. All the current talk of thickets, 'hold-up' and the like has happened before—and fortunately largely been seen off. True it had its successes—eg patents were abolished from 1869 to 1912 in Holland.

THE APPROACH OF COMPETITION AUTHORITIES

Given that patent law is so aware of competition, why is it that competition authorities wish so much to restrict patent rights further? Or, what amounts to the same thing, the enforcement or attempted enforcement of patents? I think there are several, interrelated, reasons.

First is that they are largely staffed by somewhat theoretical economists. They have not only a very imperfect understanding of how the patent system actually works, but also similar lack of understanding of how business—particularly innovative business—works and is financed. Patent monopolies do not fit their models of competition. These models look to the present, not the future. Of course current patent monopolies interfere with current competition. They make current prices higher than they would be in a state of perfect competition—some economists' ideal market. That some patents cover important products which do not have any or any significant alternative makes them worse in their eyes because such patents can and sometimes do command markets in an 'inelastic good'—something for which there is no substitute.

This view easily gains ill-informed populist support. Politicians always jump on a bandwagon when they see one. Who is not in favour of lower prices? Anyone who stands in the way of these—such as a patentee—is a bad guy. But deep down what the competition authorities are doing is pushing for instant gratification in the shape of lower prices[1] to consumers now at the expense of the benefits of delayed gratification in the shape of innovation for the future. I shall demonstrate this by reference to two of the most important subject-matters of patent protection: pharma and telecoms. In both of these industries the competition authorities have weighed in heavily in favour of the copyists and against the inventors. In so doing they are in conflict with other agencies who support innovation (see for instance the recent highly pro-IP report from the OHIM)[2] and more seriously in conflict with innovating companies. They play the part of the Mayor of Hamlyn town.

[*Quote from Browning's poem omitted. See it in Chapter 20 'Pharma-sector Inquiry'*, p 233.]

[1] Or what they believe will be lower prices.

[2] 'Intellectual Property Rights Intensive Industries Contribution to Economic Performance and Employment in the EU'.

THE PHARMA-SECTOR INQUIRY

This went in two stages—first a preliminary report in 2008 and then a final report in 2009. What led to the inquiry in the first place I do not know. But the manner in which it was conducted was a disgraceful use of the Commission's powers. For it began with simultaneous dawn raids on major pharma companies throughout Europe. To my mind dawn raids without a judicially issued search warrant and without any justifiable suspicion that evidence would be destroyed are strongly reminiscent of a lawless regime. A Commission official at a conference I was at recently described dawn raids as 'normal'! That itself is shocking to anyone who cares about civil liberties.

The preliminary report was appalling. It revealed a vast ignorance on the Commission's part as to how the patent system actually works. In introducing it, the then Commissioner, Neelie Kroes, said on 28 November 2008:

> Several of the most damaging practices which delayed or blocked market entry of competitors include:
>
> 1. *Patent clustering*, where a company forms a dense network of patents around a medicine. The worst example we found of this method was 1300 separate patent filings, across the EU, for a single medicine.
> 2. A *large number of litigation cases* over patents, which originator companies invoked against generic companies. On average, these cases took three years to resolve, and originator companies lost a clear majority of cases.
> 3. *Patent settlements* which constrain market entry of generic companies, and sometimes involve direct payments from originator companies to generic companies. In total, these payments amounted to more than € 200 million
> 4. *Interventions before regulatory bodies*, which have to approve generic products and decide on their pricing and reimbursement status. These interventions slow down the approval process by 4 months on average.
>
> Where successful, these practices result in significant additional costs for public health budgets—and ultimately consumers—and reduce incentives to innovate.

That was entirely nonsense. I go through the four points.

Of course there is patent clustering—there always has been. Some now speak of 'thickets' and postulate that there are: 'a dense web of overlapping intellectual property rights that a company must hack its way through in order to actually commercialize new technology'[3] or 'an overlapping set of patent rights which require innovators to reach licensing deals for multiple patents from multiple sources'.[4] This is said to lead to 'hold-up'—economists are fond of emotive tags. But there is no evidence of any such thing. Just look at fast innovative industries and ask, if things are moving so fast, 'where is this is "hold-up"?' In the real world clusters of patents are and always have been a sign of a technology in a state of high inventiveness—not hold-up. Edison surrounded himself with a thousand patents, the sewing machine wars of the 1850s and '60s were replete with patents[5] and even Boulton, the business genius who, with Watt, was a key figure of the Industrial Revolution, used the patent system with clusters.

Kroes' second point 'a large number of litigation cases' was simply wrong: most pharma patents, like most patents in general, are not litigated. But that some are is hardly surprising. There is a lot of money involved. Generic companies naturally challenge big pharma patents if there is a realistic possibility of winning. Equally naturally big pharma sues on its patents if there is a realistic possibility that they may be held valid. This sort of patent fight is and always has been a normal part of the pharma industry.

Her third point, patent settlements restraining generic entry, is uncommercial and unrealistic. The sort of thing the Commission is worried about is a deal between a patentee and a generic company by which they settle a dispute about the validity of a patent by agreeing a date, somewhere between the date of the agreement and the date of expiry, upon which the generic may enter the market. Economists have another emotive tag: 'pay for delay'. The theory is that it is anti-competitive because the generic agrees not to enter the market earlier than the agreed date. But the theory ignores reality. And for three distinct reasons.

First, put aside the rare case where the patent is surely invalid and the patentee knows that. The normal case is where there is real uncertainty about validity. Neither side knows who would win the

[3] C Shapiro, 'Navigating the Patent Thicket: Cross Licenses, Patent Pools, and Standard-Setting' in AB Jaffe et al (eds), *Innovation Policy and the Economy* (MIT Press, 2001).

[4] *Hargreaves Report*, 'Digitial Opporrtunity: A Review of Intellectual Property and Growth', May 2011, para 2.11 p 18.

[5] See A Mossoff, The Rise and Fall of the First American Patent Thicket: The Sewing Machine War of the 1850s' (2009) 53 *Arizona Law Review* 165.

prospective legal battle, which, if it takes place, will be expensive and time consuming. If the patent is valid then the agreement, far from being anti-competitive is pro-competitive—it allows entry earlier than expiry. If the patent is invalid then agreement delays entry—by that generic company alone. But at the time of the agreement no one knows whether it is or is not valid. That could only be determined by the end of final appeals in the very battle the agreement is designed to avoid. At the very least the Commission, if it wants to prove that such an agreement is in fact anti-competitive, must itself prove the patent invalid.

The second reason is the real danger of deterring bona fide settlements. If these agreements are treated ipso facto as anti-competitive there is only one alternative: litigation to the death. The Commission has never really been able to cope with the commercial settlement of IP disputes where one party agrees not to do something.[6] It is time the Commission understood that settlement of IP disputes often involves one party agreeing not to do something. If that settlement is genuine and not bogus the Commission should keep out. If the Commission wants to prove that the agreement is bogus, a sham to cover what is in reality a market-sharing agreement, then the onus must lie on it to prove it.

The third reason why this sort of agreement is not anti-competitive is that it in no way affects the right of any other generic to challenge the patent and to try to enter the market meanwhile. An agreement with just one generic cannot seriously affect the potential market in the drug concerned at all. You simply can't 'pay for delay' by a deal with one company if anyone else who wants to sell the generic medicine is free to challenge the patent and try to enter the market meanwhile (subject to an interim injunction[7]). The position in Europe is not the same as in the US where a first generic may in some cases get a limited period of exclusivity (see below).

The Commissioner's fourth reason, interventions in the courts with decisions of regulatory bodies, is equally fallacious. The report itself concedes that about a third of these interventions are justified. Moreover, the rule of law requires that the legality of actions of administrative authorities must be open to challenge. Just because pharma

[6] In the 1970s I was involved in a Commission attack on a bona fide settlement of a trade mark dispute where the defendant agreed not only to change its name, but not to use the plaintiff's name, p 175–8.

[7] Which can only be obtained on the terms that the patentee must compensate the defendant if in the end the patent is found invalid.

companies try to do this sometimes unsuccessfully is hardly a reason for saying they are doing anything wrong. The Directorate-General for Competition (DG Comp) is saying that the very act of going to court is wrong—a point to which I return.

In the end the Sector Inquiry fizzled out but not before a very large amount of public and pharma company money was wasted. The Commission has, to its undemocratic shame, never said how much it cost the public purse. It is difficult to imagine that it involved fewer than 30 expensive officials for a year. A better estimate might be 50. As for the industry costs, even after the initial raids, each company was swamped with ill-thought-out questions on a weekly or more frequent basis. It must have cost the industry as a whole of the order of half a million euros. A scandal that has not had the publicity it deserved.

All that is left is 'monitoring' of pharma settlements—this is largely to save face. For hardly any have been challenged—save for the ongoing investigation of the *Servier* case where there may be a case to answer because it seems possible that it knew full well that the patent it sought to enforce was invalid. The law may have something to say about that, but it is not clear that it is competition law: how can there be an abuse of monopoly when the complaint is that there was no monopoly only a purported one?

The final report was accompanied by a statement from Commissioner Neelie Kroes. She said: 'There is something rotten in the state [of the pharmaceutical industry] ... Makers of original medicines are actively trying to delay the entry of generic medicines on to their markets' (18th July 2009). Others may think there is something ill—a wrong mindset—within the Competition Directorate revealed by this. It was a wholly unjustified slur on the whole innovative pharma industry: an industry which acted in a perfectly rational and legally justified way; an industry which spends (with great risk) 17 per cent of its *income from prescription medicines*[8] on trying to find new or better medicines for humanity.

Notice also that nowhere in its inquiry did the Commission look to see what profits were being made by the grasshoppers—the generic companies whose very business depends on the inventive work of the ants.

I have just one thing to add by way of postscript in relation to this sorry story. As I have said the Commission clearly knew almost

[8] *The figure will be higher for patented prescription medicnes.*

nothing about how the patent system worked. This is hardly surprising—it has no staff of its own experienced in this. True it is that it sought some assistance from the EPO who sent a very able patent examiner to assist. But patent examiners are not the people to ask about the commercial working of the system after patents are granted. Their experience is about examining for validity, not the commercial exploitation or enforcement of patents. Once a patent is granted it goes out into the wide world and leaves the Office which gave birth to it in ignorance of its life as an adult.

THE FTC AND PHARMA

The competition authorities in the US, particularly the Federal Trade Commission, have been somewhat less aggressive to innovative pharma in the US—there has been nothing like the full-blooded assault on a whole industry by DG Comp. But the same tendencies are there as is demonstrated by *FTC v Actavis*[9]—about 'pay for delay'.

Before I discuss the US further it is vital to notice a huge difference between generic entry in the US and in Europe. In the US the first generic is given a special position by the Hatch-Waxman Act. It is not only allowed to enter the market with regulatory authority without having to undergo a duplicative application process (Europe is in broadly the same position), but in addition it gets a 180-day monopoly as the first generic allowed on the market. Europe has no equivalent of the latter: any generic with regulatory approval can come on the market once the patent is out of the way by expiry or earlier revocation. A 'pay-for-delay' agreement in the US can even set the date of permitted entry as the date of expiry of the patent and yet make commercial sense because the generic may still get a six-month, very worthwhile monopoly. In Europe that simply could not happen. The first generic gets no *legal* advantage from being first.

There is another significant difference between Europe and the US. In Europe there is no 'standing' requirement for a party who wishes to ask a court to revoke a patent. Anyone can challenge at any time. Any generic feeling itself impaired by a patent can attack it well ahead of its intended marketing. It is for that reason that the UK has a 'clear the way' rule about interim injunctions. A pharma patent holder will normally get such an injunction against a generic company about to

[9] *FTC v Actavis* 570 US ___ (2013).

come onto the market but which failed to attack the patent earlier.[10] In the US there is a 'standing' requirement before a party can seek a declaration of invalidity:[11] a generic company cannot, well before it intends to market, ask a court to clear the way.

I turn to *Actavis*. Solvay (the patentee) had made a reverse payment to Actavis in return for Actavis agreeing not to enter the market for a set term and settling the ongoing patent litigation the key issue of which was the counterclaim for invalidity. The Federal Trade Commission (FTC) said this was a violation of antitrust laws. It took a brutal, simplistic per-se anti-patentee stance:

> A payment from one business to another in exchange for the recipient's agreement not to compete is a paradigmatic antitrust trust violation. The question presented here is whether such a payment should be treated as lawful when it is encompassed within the settlement of a patent infringement suit. The answer to that question is no.

Throughout the argument there was simply no discussion of the effect sought by the FTC—less income for pharma companies with the inevitable depressing effect on research funding.

The Court came up with an unsatisfactory result: in effect 'that it all depends'. It rejected the FTC black and white position that all pay-for-delay settlements are inherently bad and rejected the alternative view that provided the settlement was of a bona fide dispute, antitrust law had no place. It chose a middle ground, that each case should be judged by a 'rule of reason'. But no one knows what that means with the result that the case (and others) is ongoing with much uncertainty. There is much to be said for the dissenting opinion of Roberts CJ to which two other members of the court assented.

For present purposes there are two things to note: first is that the FTC intervention has made it much more difficult to settle bona fide patent litigation between big pharma and generics. And secondly it was essentially anti-patent: the sooner patent protection falls away the better, was the driver behind the FTC's approach. The result is less protection for the innovator companies: they are likely to have less income to fund their future research. It would have been much better for our future medicines if the FTC had left well alone. I hope the

[10] *Novartis v Hospira UK* [2013] EWCA Civ 583.

[11] The US does not actually have a formal revocation proceeding. 'Standing' requires that the patentee has in some way indicated that it will try to enforce the patent. Merely owning it is not enough. Makes no sense to me: a patent is a running public claim to a monopoly, the public should be able to attack it at any time.

same sort of thing does not spread to Europe (where, as I explained above) things are different.

PATENTS AND TELECOMS: STANDARD ESSENTIAL PATENTS (SEPs)

I turn to the other area where the regulatory authorities' interventions are mistaken and dangerous for innovation. It concerns so-called 'standard essential patents' (SEPs). Many industries find it necessary to develop technical 'standards' so that the products of one company can work with those of others. Standards are very old—standards for things like telephones go back to the nineteenth century and for gramophone records not much later. Today we have many more standards—for broadcasting, blue-ray, CDs, DVDs and so on. Most prominent are the standards for mobile phones. Over the years inventors have allowed their inventions to be used for standards without any problem. The general nature of the system is that all parties allow use of their patented inventions, either via licensing or a patent pool.

In particular for mobile telephony the standards are set by an industry-wide organisation called the European Telecommunications Standards Institute (ETSI). It is ETSI which sets the standards for 3G, 4G and the future 5G, 6G … It works this way. ETSI members get together to settle on the standard. It is a hugely complicated process requiring many thousands of engineers' hours. The aim is to make the standard work as well is possible—the better it does the more the market will want the parties' products.

DG Comp suspects that manufacturers vie to get their particular patented solution made part of the standard with a view to a large income stream later. It did a study which showed that there was a spike in patent applications shortly before a meeting to set standards—and drew the inference from that. Again this shows a lack of understanding of the patent system—you have to apply for a patent before you disclose your invention (as you will at ETSI) or your patent will lack novelty. It makes entire sense to apply for your patent just before you disclose because then you can put the most information about your invention into your patent—also important for validity (insufficient disclosure being a ground of invalidity). I do not believe there is any evidence to support the Commission's hypothesis—the competition is between qualities of solutions to get the best standard—the best standard is the motivation.

ETSI members must make a FRAND (Fair Reasonable and Non-Discriminatory) commitment to ETSI—to offer licences under their patents for use with the standard on FRAND terms. Other standard bodies sometimes use the acronym RAND. The commitments are not the same for all standards.[12]

No one checks whether declared patents really are essential—or even reads the patents or patent applications. You could even declare a patent on a rubber boot as essential and it would be recorded as such. Broadly over-declaration is a good thing—much better to err on the side of that than on the side of under-declaration with the result that an undeclared patent might cover the standard.

The wording of the commitment to ETSI is that the patentee will give: 'an irrevocable undertaking in writing that it is prepared to grant irrevocable licences on fair, reasonable and non-discriminatory terms and conditions under such IPR to at least the following extent'(then follow manufacture and use details). Note particularly that it is the patentee who says he is willing to grant a licence on FRAND terms. It follows as night follows day that if he makes an offer which is FRAND compliant he has complied with his commitment. The licensee has but to accept the offer and the grant is made. The position of the would-be licensee—whether or not he is a 'willing licensee' in some sort of loose sense or is prepared to enter into negotiations—is quite irrelevant.

So what happens if an SEP patentee sues someone on his patent? The Commission takes the view that the *very act of asking for an injunction in his claim* is an abuse of monopoly—for which the patentee can be fined and enjoined. Here is the press release in *Motorola v Apple*:[13]

> The European Commission has informed Motorola Mobility of its preliminary view that the company's seeking and enforcing of an injunction against Apple in Germany on the basis of its mobile phone standard-essential patents ('SEPs') amounts to an abuse of a dominant position prohibited by EU antitrust rules. While recourse to injunctions is a possible

[12] And it may not be a mere difference in wording: there may be a real difference between a commitment actually to grant a licence on RAND or FRAND terms, and a commitment to offer a licence on such terms. The difference is that a commitment to grant leaves it open as to who is to determine the terms. The commitment to offer FRAND leaves it to the *patentee* to determine the terms of his offer—anything within the range of FRAND will comply with his commitment.

[13] 6 May 2013.

> remedy for patent infringements, such conduct may be abusive where SEPs are concerned and the potential licensee is willing to enter into a licence on Fair, Reasonable and Non-Discriminatory (so-called 'FRAND') terms. In such a situation, the Commission considers at this stage that dominant SEP holders should not have recourse to injunctions, which generally involve a prohibition to sell the product infringing the patent, in order to distort licensing negotiations and impose unjustified licensing terms on patent licensees. Such misuse of SEPs could ultimately harm consumers.

One can hardly believe how wrong this is:

1. It is saying that merely going to court to ask for an order is an abuse of monopoly. That breaches two important principles:
   (a) First at a very high level it breaches the right of a party's access to the courts contained in Art 6 of the European Convention on Human Rights (ECHR) and well recognised in cases such as *Golder v UK*. The Commission is in effect standing with a shotgun at the courthouse door and saying 'if you go in there and dare even ask for an injunction we will shoot you'. Contrast that with the European Court of Human Rights in *Golder*:

   > The principle whereby a civil claim must be capable of being submitted to a judge ranks as one of the universally 'recognised' fundamental principles of law; the same is true of the principle of international law which forbids the denial of justice. Article 6(1) must be read in the light of these principles. Were Article 6(1) to be understood as concerning exclusively the conduct of an action which had already been initiated before a court, a Contracting State could, without acting in breach of that text, do away with its courts, or take away their jurisdiction to determine certain classes of civil actions and entrust it to organs dependent on the Government. Such assumptions, indissociable from a danger of arbitrary power, would have serious consequences which are repugnant to the aforementioned principles and which the Court cannot overlook.

   (b) Secondly, still at a high level, it breaches the principle of sincere co-operation in Art 4(3) of the bedrock Treaty on European Union. This provides:

   > 3. Pursuant to the principle of sincere cooperation, the Union and the Member States shall, in full mutual respect, assist each other in carrying out tasks which flow from the Treaties.

The Commission is in substance saying 'we do not trust the Member States' courts—they might grant an injunction which we think would be an abuse of monopoly. We, an administrative agency know better'. So much for 'mutual respect'.

2. It is on the facts perfectly ridiculous—to suppose you can bully Apple or the Chinese companies ZTE or Huawei[14] by a mere application to court shows a profound ignorance of how real big businesses or indeed courts work. If these companies have a defence of abuse of monopoly they will surely deploy it with maximum force before the national courts. None of these companies needs the Commission to defend them.
3. It is virtually a per se rule—for although there is some concession in the case of a defendant who might be impecunious, it is difficult to see how that could work in practice. Suppose the patentee considered the defendant impecunious but the Commission thought otherwise? The fact that the Commission is taking the part of such big companies itself demonstrates the essentially per se nature of its position.
4. It overlooks the fact that before the court decides whether or not to grant an injunction it will not only hear the parties but could hear the Commission too. For the Commission has a right to intervene.[15] Surely the Commission should take the least intrusive course of intervening rather than threatening fines?
5. It ignores the fact that litigation is a way of bringing things to a head. The pressure of a date in court is not a pressure to do a non-FRAND deal but a pressure to do a deal. All defendants string things out if they can. Litigation is a continuation of negotiation by other means.
6. The Commission's focus on a 'willing licensee' is entirely misplaced. Defendants will always say they are willing to negotiate—that really means stringing things out for as long as possible and paying as little as possible in the end. That is not a criticism—it is a sensible commercial tactic if you can get away with it. There may of course be negotiations, but the only thing which matters legally is whether the patentee has made a FRAND offer.

[14] These are all latecomers to mobile telephony and have no or hardly any SEPs themselves. Moreover it seems they are not contributing to 4G, 5G and so on: all published figures show they have very few SEPs between them.

[15] Art 335 of the Treaty on the Functioning of the European Union.

The focus should be on that, not what the defendant says is FRAND or whether he says he is willing to negotiate. The whole concept of a 'willing licensee' is amorphous and impossible to pin down.

7. It asks the question of 'abuse' at the wrong time—before the court is asked to make its decision. It treats an application for an injunction as if it were an injunction. When the court comes to make its decision it will have evidence from both sides and can decide what to do.[16]
8. It ignores the fact that if the patentee has made no offer *when the court makes its decision* the court will surely refuse an injunction because the patentee has committed to make a FRAND offer—a commitment which the industry accepts is binding on all never mind any legal theory which might suggest otherwise.
9. It assumes that a declared SEP is in itself market dominant. But a declared SEP may not be essential at all—many are not. And even those essential once may cease to be so because ways round have been devised.
10. If the patentee has made an offer, it can be examined to see whether it is FRAND or not. That can be determined by the court if necessary but there may be better ways such as arbitration by an expert panel. Meanwhile the court may make an interim order requiring the defendant to pay a minimum to the patentee, and the disputed difference into escrow. A solution I favour.
11. It ignores the reality that if the patentee is deprived of any right to an injunction or possibility of one, defendants will simply fight infringement and validity patent by patent. If they lose, why then all they have to pay is damages to be assessed on FRAND terms—this is 'reverse hold-up'. The Commission's actions support just that. How much have Apple, Huawai and ZTE paid anyone for use of the standards on which they have been able to build their businesses?
12. It ignores the reality that this industry is one of the most competitive in the world—which company will be leader in even three years' time? The competition is in products and innovation. Where is there a competition law problem?
13. Is any of this in the consumer's interest? If the non-innovators have to pay only little and late (which is the effect of the

[16] There is no suggestion of ex parte injunctions in this field.

Commission's position) does anyone think it will be passed on to the public? No, it will mean that the profits of these companies will be greater at the expense of the ant innovators who made the grasshoppers' business possible.

I suspect the Commission knows it is on shaky ground. For it is pursuing an insidious course of negotiating with patentees to get them to agree to limit their rights to go to court. It recently[17] issued a press notice:

> The Commission has concerns that Samsung's seeking of injunctions against Apple in the European Economic Area (EEA) on the basis of its mobile SEPs may have amounted to an abuse of a dominant position prohibited by EU antitrust rules (see IP/12/1448). To remedy these concerns, Samsung has offered to abstain from seeking injunctions for mobile SEPs for a period of five years against any company that agrees to a particular licensing framework. Interested parties can now submit their comments within one month. If the Commission concludes, in light of the comments received, that the commitments address the competition concerns, it may decide to make them legally binding on Samsung.
>
> Seeking injunctions before courts is generally a legitimate remedy for patent holders in case of patent infringements. However, access to patents which are standard-essential is a precondition for any company to sell interoperable products in the market.
>
> The Commission considers that the seeking of an injunction based on SEPs may constitute an abuse of a dominant position if a SEP holder has given a commitment to license its SEPs on Fair Reasonable And Non-Discriminatory (FRAND) terms and where the company against which an injunction is sought is willing to enter into a licence agreement on FRAND terms.
>
> The Commission is concerned that the seeking of injunctions in such circumstances could allow Samsung to impose royalty rates or other licensing terms, such as broad cross-licenses, which a licensee would not agree to, absent the threat of having its products excluded from the market. This may unduly distort licensing negotiations and cause harm to consumers by increasing prices, reducing product choice and stifling differentiating innovation in the markets for smartphones and tablets.

This is trying to create precedent by a creeping process. Undertakings of this sort imply that they are necessary to avoid a breach of competition law. They are well attacked by Professor Marsden in

[17] 17 October 2013.

a recent article—'Soft Law. The Emperor's Clothes Laid Bare: Commitments Creating the Appearance of Law while Denying Access to Law'.[18]

The Commission is aiming to extract the undertaking by the threat of fines. Companies are really frightened of the Commission:[19] it behoves it to use its powers with care. It does not have to threaten fines. It could simply have said to Samsung and Motorola, 'Let us go to court and test the legality of your actions. We will levy fines only if we win and you carry on regardless.'

But I think there comes a time to stand up—not to pay Danegeld. Companies should say to the Commission, 'See you in court. You can't use your powers to deny access to the courts. You can't allege abuse of monopoly, hold-up and the like based on a theory which is unsubstantiated on real facts but is obviously wrong given the rate of innovation in this sector. You should not be protecting those who contributed virtually nothing from the inventions which make up the standards. Leave it all to the Courts; they can enforce the FRAND obligations.'

One other matter: the Commission's current stance may have an unintended consequence—that it becomes a FRAND-determining tribunal. On 21 November 2013 it was announced that Sierra Wireless had complained to the Commission that Nokia would not grant it a FRAND licence. What if Nokia's response is that it had made an offer which was FRAND compliant? The Commission would be forced to decide one way or the other. Surely the Commission is not the right tribunal for determining whether an offer is or is not FRAND? Yet it could find itself in a mire of complaints and counter-complaints.

All of the above applies in the US, mutatis mutandis. The FTC and Justice Department successfully persuaded President Obama to veto the import ban on certain Apple products which the International Trade Commission (ITC), following a reasoned decision of its administrative court, held infringed a valid patent of Samsung. The theory was that the patent was subject to a FRAND declaration. The ITC court had not accepted the FRAND defence. To an outsider it looks awfully like a government overruling a court decision—something rather incompatible with the rule of law.

[18] *CPT Antitrust Chronicle*, October 2013 (1).

[19] Not surprisingly. I heard that one pharma company which wanted to resist the dawn raid of the pharma inquiry by challenging it in court, was threatened with a fine if it chose to do that.

I end with this. The competition authorities' anti-patentee actions penalise those who made the inventions in the past. In the language of economists the costs of making and developing those inventions (and all the abortive research and development) are 'sunk' costs—money already spent. If you say those sunk costs produce results of little value today, you degrade the incentive to sink costs today—to do research for the inventions of tomorrow. In the case of patents for standards, you are threatening not only invention, but the very process of standardisation. If the pharma companies have less income we will have fewer new medicines in the future; if those who create the inventions for new and faster standards see the prospect of proper reward degraded then the rate of progress to 5G, 6G ... will diminish. Such is the public demand for more and faster capacity the result could well be that existing standards will not cope—the result would be that either our phone connection will clog up or the price of connection will have to go up to reduce demand.

The competition authorities should cease harassing inventive industries and let the patent system do the job it was designed to do. Leave the ants alone.

POSTSCRIPT

1. *I am sorry that my hope (not I am afraid my expectation) was confounded. The European Competition Authority took up the cudgels in a big way, fining Lundbeck and some generic companies for their pay-for-delay settlement of litigation in June 2013. Commissioner Almunia, predictably claiming to be the champion of cheap medicines, said: 'Agreements of this type directly harm patients and national health systems, which are already under tight budgetary constraints. The Commission will not tolerate such anticompetitive practices'. How was he to know whether the patent was valid or not? If it was valid, then patients and national health systems benefitted from the deal. Things would be different if the patent was clearly invalid and the parties knew that.*
2. *The fine was huge—€93.8 million for Lundbeck alone. Much better spent on pharma research than on the Commission. Also I wonder whether a body which fines and gets to keep the fine can possibly be fair or seem to be fair.*

3. *I have thought a bit more about enforcement of SEPs. As I see it there is simply no need for competition authorities to get involved. The next chapter (a paper that I circulated at the 'Patents in Telecoms' Symposium, which I organised with George Washington University in November 2014) explains why.*
4. *We may shortly know what the CJEU thinks about SEP enforcement. The omens are not good for the A-G's November 2014 opinion in* Huawei v ZTE *(Case C-170/13) does not mention it explicitly. All is not lost—for the A-G does say that taking legal action on an SEP is not itself an abuse of a dominant position—which is not consistent with the Commission's black and white, doctrinaire view that going to court to ask for an injunction on an SEP was ipso facto an abuse unless the defendant was dilatory.*

20

Patents and Pharmaceuticals— A Paper given on 29 November 2008 at the Presentation of the Directorate-General of Competition's Preliminary Report of the Pharma-sector Inquiry

I BEGIN BY qualifying myself to speak. From the late '60s a significant part of my work has involved the pharmaceutical industry: first when I was a barrister and from 1993 as a judge. I have been in, and presided over, many battles about pharmaceutical patents. Those battles have not only been about validity and infringement but about other, economic matters too. Thus until 1977 the UK law[1] allowed anyone to apply for a compulsory licence under a patent for a medicine. And until then a patentee who had not got adequate remuneration from his patent before the normal date of expiry (16 years from application) could apply to the court for an extension of term—a much more sophisticated equivalent of a supplementary protection certificate. It was more sophisticated because it involved a deep inquiry into how much money the patentee had made in its capacity as a patentee. And after 1977, when the term of patent went up to 20 years, pre-1977 patents got four more years but subject to a licence of right. Both sorts of licence involved deep inquiries into costs and profits in order to set the royalty rate.

[1] s 41 of the Patents Act 1949.

Over the years I have seen bad behaviour by both big pharma companies and generic companies. I am neither pro nor against either of them. I am a judge. My job is to decide who is right in fact and law.

I begin with two quotations. The first is from *The Pied Piper of Hamelin*:

> 'If I can rid your town of rats
> Will you give me a thousand guilders?'
> 'One? fifty thousand!'—was the exclamation
> Of the astonished Mayor and Corporation.

Later, when the rats had all been drowned, the Mayor said:

> So, friend, we're not the folks to shrink
> From the duty of giving you something to drink,
> And a matter of money to put in your poke;
> But as for the guilders, what we spoke
> Of them, as you very well know, was in joke.
> Beside, our losses have made us thrifty.
> A thousand guilders! Come, take fifty!

So it is with pharmaceuticals. Before the invention of a new drug we would willingly pay for it. After the risk and investment have produced a new medicine there is a great temptation to say the price is too high.

My second quotation is from a 1947 small booklet[2] by TA Blanco White:[3]

> There is ... a way in which a monopoly in an important invention may be kept alive after the patent has come to an end, and that is by patenting large numbers of minor improvements to the original invention ... Provided the patented improvements represent genuine development over the period during which the original patent is in force, and provided they are patented with determination and persistence, by the time the original patent expires a would-be imitator should be faced with this situation: that the article described in the original specification is too inferior to contemporary designs to be commercially saleable, while he cannot imitate the newer models without risking an action for infringement of so many of the improvement patents, that he would almost certainly lose in respect of some patent or other. Even if he were to win the action on enough of the patents to let him go on manufacturing without any fundamental change in his design, the cost of fighting and losing the action as a whole would still take much of the profit out of his venture. For this reason the

[2] TA Blanco White, *Patents and Registered Designs* (Stevens, 1947).

[3] Later QC, one of the most influential writers and thinkers about IP law in the post-War era.

> existence of a mass of improvement patents is often a sufficient deterrent to would-be imitators. The original manufacturer's position need not deteriorate with further lapse of time: he should always be some years ahead in design so far as patentable improvements are concerned, while the loner he keeps the field to himself the greater the advantage he has in manufacturing experience. His monopoly will last until some competitor comes along with the skill needed to 'design round' the more dangerous patents and the courage to fight a patent action if necessary; how long this will be will depend as usual on the importance of the market covered by the monopoly, as well as on the rate at which he continues to devise new patentable improvements. In the past, such monopolies have sometimes lasted a long time.

This passage demonstrates that there is nothing new about what the Commission calls 'patent clusters'. Nor that they are confined to pharma patents. On the contrary, any experienced patent lawyer will tell you that clusters of improvement patents are a feature of nearly all industries. It is a bit worrying that the Commission seems to think that it has discovered something new and special to the pharma industry.

I now proceed to some sure foundations, essential for understanding this industry. The following matters are really beyond any reasonable argument:

1. Most pharmaceuticals cost very little to make. All you need per dose is a very small amount (typically, say, 10 mg) of a chemical itself fairly easy to make. A kilogram of active material will be enough for 100,000 doses. Putting it in picturesque terms: drugs cost tuppence a bucket and a bucket is enough for a nation.
2. So the selling price of a patented medicine is way, way above its manufacturing cost. Unlike, for instance, an engineering product, a patented medicine cannot be and simply is not priced on the basis of cost of manufacture plus a mark up.
3. Patented medicines are priced taking into account the current cost of research and development. To that are added overheads, marketing costs, the small amount of manufacturing costs and a profit. On a more sophisticated analysis one adds in the cost of capital employed The key thing for the purposes of the present debate is this: the income produced by the sales of today's patented medicines pays for the ongoing R&D, which may lead to new and better medicines.

   The Commission in some places talks about 'recouping' investment. That can be misunderstood. No one can or could run a research-based pharmaceutical company on the basis of trying to work out how much it cost to invent and develop a drug and get a return on that. The pharma industry is the same as most of us: current income must pay for current research and all the other things a company does (promotion, cost of capital employed, cost of overheads, dividends, etc etc).

The most important figure in the Preliminary Report is that current R&D costs are 17 per cent of *turnover*. That is much higher than most if not all other industries. I am sorry that the interim report somewhat belittles the figure by adding that only 1.5 per cent is 'basic research'. I am not sure I know what is meant here, but it does not matter. It is no good finding a potential suitable molecule. Unless you spend the money and time to find out if it really works and is safe, it is no use. Assuming the figure is indeed 1.5 per cent, it would come to nothing without the remaining 15.5 per cent.

4. It is the patent system that has made the advances in medicines possible. Although economists sometimes debate whether the patent system is useful generally, no one has ever seriously challenged its place for medicines. And that is because it is so obvious that without a reliable patent monopoly there is simply no incentive to invest. The entire period of the command economy of the Soviet Union did not produce, so far as I know, any major pharmaceutical product. And in the West, even in those rare cases of an important invention being made at a university (eg the cephalosporin antibiotics) or by a small inventor or company (eg the anti-epilepsy drug sodium valproate), it has been the pharmaceutical industry which has undertaken the risk of the considerable costs of development.
5. Promotional expenditure is indeed higher than R&D at 23 per cent of turnover.[4] There is perhaps an innuendo that it is too high—and for the whole industry. Such an inference should be rejected. Firstly such promotion should not be thought of as analogous to promotion to the public, of a cosmetic, for instance ('Because you're worth it'). Promotion aimed at consumers is typically

[4] *Of course 'promotion' of medicines is largely really education of doctors. That is not to say that there are not egregious examples (paid-for conferences in luxury resorts) but to a large extent the pharma industry has cut back on this sort of thing. And the figure of 23% for new medicines is put in perspective when one realises that the figure is much higher for less worthy things such as cosmetics and perfumes—see Chapter 36 'Trade Marks: Reality or Illusion'.*

a greater proportion of turnover. But more significantly we are here concerned with promotion to the medical profession. It is essential that the benefits and side-effects are well communicated. Experience over the years shows that this is not easy. The profession is conservative and it takes a lot to persuade a doctor to prescribe a new medicine. Of course there have been glaring examples of over-elaborate promotion. For instance I can remember an article in the early 1970s, by Bernard Levin in *The Times*, attacking the promotion of a new drug called 'Nobrium'. But merely stating the average figure is miles from suggesting any breach of competition law rules. It is not for the Commission to tell drug companies how to promote their products, any more than it is for the Commission to tell companies in other sectors how to do so.

6. Moreover, the nature of the investment is risky. Most research leads nowhere. The few winners must pay for all the losers. And in recent years the number of really important drugs coming forward seems to be diminishing. It is in the nature of investors—human that they are—that the higher the risk the more reward is needed to persuade them to put their money up.
7. The time of true monopoly is likely to be very limited. Although the term of all patents is the same—20 years from application—in reality a new drug is unlikely to get more than 10 or 11 years even with the supplementary protection system. Personally I do not think that is enough time to encourage the risk and expense involved in seeking further medicines, but that is beside the point. The short period may help explain some of the conduct by way of 'evergreening' the subject of the Commission's inquiry, but it is more likely that it would happen whatever the period of full protection.
8. Generally speaking, in Europe, drug prices are the subject of high-level negotiation between powerful players. In my country and Spain, for example, it is essentially a matter between the companies and the government. Governments have traditionally shied away from attacking patents or getting involved in disputes about validity of bad pharma patents. I do not know why; they are, after all, the customers.
9. The generic companies have no or very limited research costs. Nor do they undertake anything like the risk involved in original research. Nor do they promote their product, save to the limited extent of trying to persuade doctors to promote generically—something which is much more powerfully pressed by governments.

10. That is not to say that generic companies do not perform a useful function. On the contrary once a patent has expired these companies will enter the market and cause prices to fall. The more companies enter the market the faster the prices fall. And when a product comes off patent it is right that prices should fall.
11. Generic companies are not actually in favour of low prices. Just as in the case of the big research-based companies, they are in business for a profit. The lower the prices the less the profit. It is human nature for a generic company to want to be close to a high price. That is why, for instance, we often receive evidence from generic companies about how important it is that they should be first in the market. This can happen, for instance, where a generic company believes for one reason or another that it is ahead of all the others. If it can be first it can and very likely will set its initial price at something like 10 per cent below the patentee's. That will very likely take a substantial portion of the market and with a very large profit margin.

    Generic companies have traditionally, and not surprisingly, waved the flag of 'lower prices'—the position has been so throughout my entire career. They never talk about the profits they themselves make. The Commission has not inquired into how many multi-millionaires have made their money by selling 'me-too' pharmaceuticals with no corresponding research benefit.
12. There can be little doubt that a number of drug companies have sought to protect their market monopolies beyond the life of their basic patent by spurious or near spurious patents—a process generally called evergreening. And there is no doubt that, as the Canadian Supreme Court recently observed,[5] 'Evergreening is a legitimate concern'.
13. Legal questions in the pharma industry are nearly always about the validity of patents rather than their scope. This is because there is seldom a real argument about the extent of protection. The claims are clear—normally to a class of chemical compounds or often to a particular compound. This has important consequences as regards the question of how these questions are to be resolved.

[5] *Apotex v Sanofi*, 6 November 2008, *per* Rothstein J at [96].

14. Finally the whole subject of patents and medicines and medical treatments is fraught with emotion and, dare I say it, irrational prejudices. Some say: 'How can big pharma charge the ill for medicines that are so cheap to produce? Down with these greedy companies.' We even have in the European Patent Convention a specific exclusion from patentability of methods of medical treatment, which has led to a lot of convoluted quasi-nonsensical reasoning by way of trying to get round the rule as far as possible. Personally I think the rule should go. If you want better methods of medical treatment, the patent system is the way to encourage it.

I turn to some of the subjects raised by the inquiry:

1. 'Raising the bar'. The idea here is that Patent Offices should do better—that they should get closer to the ideal of granting all good patents and refusing all bad ones. How that is to be achieved given the ever-rising flood of applications and the ever-increasing importance of Chinese prior art, I have no real idea. Pharmaceutical patents are only a minor proportion of the total numbers of applications. Patent Offices have limited resources: they have no mandate and should have no mandate to examine pharma patents by different standards from those for other subject matters.

   Here I should point out that the phenomenon of patents for trivial or non-inventions is by no means confined to those for pharmaceuticals. Far from it. Anyone with experience of other fields, for instance telecom- or computer-related inventions, would be familiar with abundant examples. No doubt if there were more co-operation between Patent Offices around the world on things like searches, some savings and perhaps improvements could be made. But I think it is unrealistic to suppose that we can go back to the pre-EPC days when passing the German or Dutch Offices (and their examination procedures were very slow) was a kind of hallmark of a good patent.

   Moreover I am wholly unconvinced that even giving more time for an examiner to consider an application would make much a difference in the pharma field. Let me explain why by reference to a recent case in our courts. Simplifying a little, a pharma company had a patent taken out in 1980 over a basic valuable new compound. It got the product onto the market very quickly—in 1987. In 2000 it took out a new patent covering what it said was a new crystalline form said to be particularly useful for formulation. You could not tell from reading the old patent anything about the crystalline form. So you could not tell that the later patent was in fact for the old product. It is not surprising the patent was granted. The Office had no choice. In England the patent was knocked out by the High Court in fairly short order and my court, the Court of appeal, upheld the result soon after.

This is important. Fiddling with the law will not make any difference to the reality: it is for this reason that one cannot ever expect the grant of a patent by a Patent Office to be also a certificate of validity. It never has been and never will be. In truth a Patent Office is a kind of coarse filter—rejecting clearly bad cases but having to allow those which may be good.

One should not feel too depressed by this major truth—particularly in the pharma industry where the legal costs of both innovating companies and generic companies are only a minor proportion of what is at stake.

2. I wish to emphasise that the phenomenon of evergreening is not confined to the pharma field. Nor is it new. Far from it. Every patentee of a major invention is likely to come up with improvements and alleged improvements to his invention. By the time his main patent has expired there will be a thicket of patents intended to extend his monopoly. Some will be good, others bad. It is in the nature of the patent system itself that this should happen and it has always happened. There is nothing new about evergreening, only the name and the implication which flows from the word, that there is something sinister going on and that it has only recently been discovered. My quotation from Blanco White shows this.

   I would add that the particular figure of 'up to 1,300' patents for a cluster needs more detail. I do not believe it to be typical. In any event one needs to divide the figure by 27 (for the membership of the EU). But whether the patents are good or bad is not mentioned. For all we know they are for perfectly good inventions, perhaps only incremental. It has never been the law that patents are refused for incremental non-obvious improvements. Nor should it be.

3. I have mentioned that some have proposed changes to patent law. Let me examine those proposals in more detail:
   (a) It is suggested there should be an obligation upon the patentee to disclose all information known to it material to patentability.

This has never been the law. Moreover it is impossible to see how it can work satisfactorily or at a reasonable cost. Must there be disclosure of all the patentee's documents and legal advice? Is there to be cross-examination of the patent agent? What is the cost of the proposal?—every case could involve complicated questions of what the patentee knew, when it knew and what it should have known. They have some of that in the US—something which contributes to the extreme cost of litigation there. Nor is the proposal necessary—if there is material which is a clear knock-out it will normally emerge in the course of a proper and ordinary search. So far as pharma is concerned I know of no case where material prior art was hard to find.

(b) It is suggested that better third-party participation should be available at the pre-grant stage. Already third parties can submit prior art to the Office at that stage—and make observations. But, unless you beef up the whole process—in effect introduce pre-grant opposition—it just will be of little use. And a long time ago the founders of the EPC rejected—rightly in my view—pre-grant opposition. We had it in my country and the grant of patent rights would be held up for years.

Moreover the proposal is unlikely to be used by generic companies. Currently they do not or seldom oppose a patent at a time where there is no product on the market protected by it, The reason is simple. You have to oppose (ie apply for revocation) within one year of grant. Grant, even if delayed, is likely to be within at the worst about eight years from application. At that stage the basic product will probably not be on the market. And if it is—because the patent is a late evergreener—the generic companies (and governments) have another remedy—attack it in the courts. Of course if the evergreening patent is applied for when a financially attractive product is on the market, generic companies may oppose. If they do they have a fair point that the period of opposition is likely to be long.

(c) It is suggested current opposition proceedings should be faster. With that I wholeheartedly agree. I have said so for years. But the problem is quite general, and far from being confined to pharmaceuticals. I would favour an in-depth study of the practice and procedures of the EPO—along with education of the profession as to how such speeding up could be achieved.

(d) There is complaint that courts are willing to grant interim injunctions. So they are: I have little sympathy with the complaint for two reasons. First, generic companies can attack validity earlier than they do—'clear the way' as I put it in one of my judgments. There can be no interim injunction if they take that elementary course. Second, I have long wondered why perhaps the most affected party—the paying ultimate customer, normally a government—does not intervene when the injunction is sought: to say it wants to be compensated if it turns out that the patent is no good and there never should have been an injunction.

5. There is a suggestion that pharma companies have used litigation against regulatory authorities in order to hold up authorisation. Again this is nothing new. Similar actions were taken in the 1970s.[6] Sometimes the companies are right even if they are, more often than not, wrong. To say they should not go to court on a weak case would be a serious threat to access to justice.
6. Generally the Commission appears to take a censorious attitude to big pharma companies resorting to litigation to attempt to delay generic competition. The old French proverb comes to mind: 'Ce chien est très méchant. Quand on l'attaque, il se défend'. There is nothing new in any of this. It has been suggested that the Commission has discovered conduct which is 'shocking'. On the contrary, it has 'discovered' conduct which is normal and has been an inevitable feature of the industry for many, many years. All that is new are the numbers—none of which are particularly surprising.
7. One thing is clear—and again this is by no means confined to the pharma sector—the need for a strong and fast Central Patents Court for Europe sticks out a mile. And in this connection it should be noted that proposals for 'bifurcation'—for a court splitting the issue of validity and infringement in the current proposals—will not help that speed. Under the proposal if a patentee starts a case in a regional court and the defendant raises invalidity, the question of validity can be transferred to a central

[6] eg *Hoffman-La Roche v Secretary of State for Trade and Industry* [1975] AC 295—a failed attempt at attacking a price control order by an interim injunction to restrain its coming into force.

court. All that will take time. And the longer a patentee can keep uncertainty going even for a patent ultimately shown to be invalid, the worse.

8. Do competition authorities have a part to play where a patent is obviously invalid? Should a company be punished for applying for (or if not that at least attempting to enforce) such a patent? I do not know, and even if I did, as a judge I could not comment, but the question is worth asking. I can say this: it would be seriously dangerous to have a rule that applying for or seeking to enforce a patent of doubtful validity was a violation of competition law: most companies in the world would be guilty on that basis. Courts are the basic places for deciding on the validity of rights—to punish someone for going to court may involve conflict with Art 6 of the European Convention on Human Rights. And besides the true remedy for really bad patents is their swift demise in speedy revocation proceedings brought before the patent can do any damage.
9. So therefore I suggest that what is needed is (a) forgetting about all changes to the law of grant, (b) a serious look at current opposition procedures within the EPO and (c) above all the creation of a respected, fast, and reliable European Patent Court. That is as true in the pharma sector as in any other. It is particularly that last proposal which matters for European industry as a whole. Evergreening by bad patents can in the end only be dealt with by courts knocking them out swiftly. That has always been true.
10. Finally, although there have been bad patents in the pharma sector, it is important to keep things in perspective. As a whole patents for pharmaceuticals have greatly benefitted and continue to benefit mankind greatly. Changes to the system should be viewed with great care—on the whole it works very, very well. One should be very careful to avoid panic-driven or emotion-led changes which could damage an important and beneficial part of industry. The Commission repeatedly says that it does not want to damage the pharmaceutical industry and that it recognises how important patents are to it—it sounds to me a bit like Mark Anthony emphasising that Brutus was an honourable man. The big truth is that if you damage the income stream of research companies, you are going to imperil future research at the expense of European—indeed world—citizens. Yes, you will save money now, but at the cost of fewer future medicines.

POSTSCRIPT

I think the Commission invited me to speak because it thought I was some sort of anti-patent (especially pharma-patent) judge. I had recently delivered a judgment about a patent for a particular crystalline form of a known medicine in which I had said 'It is the sort of patent which can give the patent system a bad name' (Servier v Apotex)[7]. *The preliminary report was given in a huge hall in Brussels. All morning the Commission officials, very pleased with themselves, expounded what they had 'discovered' and that what pharma companies were doing was terribly evil. I had been emailed the draft report only the evening before and had to put this together very fast. I was first on in the afternoon. The mood was very tense—many were from pharma companies and were appalled at this attack on the industry. They were frightened too. The Commission had in my view abused its powers throughout the inquiry—dawn raids and repeated questioning of industry with peremptory demands for immediate answers. One story I was told later by a patent attorney typifies this probably lawless behaviour. He was away from his office on one raid. He returned to find his desk had been searched even to the point that they had unwrapped Christmas presents he was keeping there to bring home. I still chill at the thought this could happen as though it were 'normal', to use a Commission official's word. I am told that the video of my speech shows the Commission officials behind me reacting in horror. We have the podcast on the Institute of Brand and Innovation Law website but the Commission took it down early.*

[7] Servier v Apotex *[2008] EWCA Civ 445.*

21

FRAND: A Legal Analysis

1. The European Telecommunications Standards Institute (ETSI) FRAND declaration reads:

   > 6.1 When an ESSENTIAL IPR relating to a particular STANDARD OR TECHNICAL SPECIFICATION is brought to the attention of ETSI, the Director-General shall immediately request the owner to give within three months an irrevocable undertaking in writing that it is prepared to grant irrevocable licences on fair, reasonable and non-discriminatory ('FRAND') terms and conditions under such IPR to at least the following extent: [details omitted]

2. It is generally accepted that this commitment, although given to ETSI, is enforceable by third parties. It is governed by French law, which allows enforcement by a third party of a contract by which one of the parties agrees to confer a benefit on third parties. Actually most other laws do. And in practice no SEP holder would argue to the contrary.
3. The FRAND declaration is that the patentee will grant licences. As a practical matter that means to offer licences on FRAND terms—the patentee cannot compel anyone actually to take up the offer.
4. So the patentee has complied with its declaration to ETSI and contractual obligation to a third party if it makes a FRAND offer to that party.
5. What if the patentee sues on an SEP? As I see it, when the court comes to decide whether an injunction should be granted (and not before) the questions will be:
   a. Is the defendant relying on the declaration to enforce his third party rights conferred by that declaration? If he is not, that is his choice, but there will be no FRAND defence.

b. Assuming the realistic situation that the defendant does rely on the declaration, the next question is whether the patentee has made what it considers to be a FRAND offer and what that offer is. If the patentee has not made such an offer, or the offer which it has made is clearly not FRAND ($50 per phone for example) then there is a defence. The defence arises not as a matter of competition law, but as a result of contract law. The defendant is contractually entitled to receive a FRAND licence and the patentee cannot rely upon his breach of contract to say there is no licence.
c. In the real world the most likely—almost certain—scenario is that the patentee will say it has made a FRAND offer and the defendant will say it has not. There is a FRAND dispute. The court (or arbitrators) would be adjudicating as a matter of contract law—one side (the defendant) says the other (the patentee) is in breach of its contractual obligation to offer a FRAND licence. It is not a matter of competition law.
d. There are now two questions: how the dispute should be resolved and what, if anything, should be done in the meantime.
e. As to resolution of the dispute, if the parties cannot agree on arbitration, then the court will have to adjudicate. In practice sensible parties will agree on arbitration for a variety of reasons (skill of the tribunal, international acceptance of the award, possibility of choosing arbitrators of appropriate skills).
f. As to what is to be done in the meantime, the court (if the patentee asks) could order the defendant to pay money in escrow—to remove the incentive for 'reverse hold-up' while he stalls the resolution of the dispute. The court could even order the defendant to pay what he says is the appropriate amount direct to the patentee with the balance (or a proportion of it) going into escrow.

6. What if the defendant says the patents sued upon are invalid, or he is not using any of them? Firstly he is and must be at liberty so to contend—I side with competition law and public policy in saying that anyone must be at liberty to apply to revoke a patent. Resolving these questions will take time—the court may be asked to grant an interim injunction meantime. If it is so asked, then the sensible way forward is to put in place an interim regime as above with payments in escrow.

7. Very probably in this case the defendant will also say the offer is not FRAND. In which case the FRAND dispute and the patent dispute will have to run in parallel.
8. If the defendant wins the patent dispute that is the end of the case. But what if he loses? Can he just take the patentee's original offer or contend in the FRAND dispute that he should pay the same as if he had not challenged the patent? No—for two good reasons:
    a. Firstly, as a matter of business sense, a patent of established validity is worth more than one which has not been challenged. Any realistic notional negotiation for a licence will take into account the likelihood of the patent being held valid.
    b. Secondly there is the patentee's FRAND commitment itself to consider. In particular it will very probably have other licensees that have accepted its offers of a licence. They did not challenge validity. It would be wrong—discriminatory—to treat the party that unsuccessfully challenged just as if it had not. So the patentee is indeed obliged by its FRAND commitment to charge the unsuccessful challenger more.
9. This is a good thing. It encourages third parties to consider carefully before challenging validity and thus prevents spurious litigation and reverse hold-up.
10. Next there is the important question of whether a patentee can comply with its FRAND obligation by offering its entire portfolio of patents or just its entire portfolio of SEPs for licence as a package. I think the answer here is that it can do the latter (all SEPs) but not the former (all SEPs with all non-SEPs):
    a. Offering only a complete package of SEPs and non-SEPs is forcing the licensee to take more than the FRAND obligation (and duty) requires. Although this is a matter of French law, I doubt that any court would construe the duty as allowing an offer only with bundled non-SEPs.
    b. Moreover, there might be a competition law objection too. It has long been established, for instance, that a patentee may not use its monopoly to require a party to buy non-patented articles as a condition of sale of patented articles ('You can only have my patented boots if you buy socks from me too' is the sort of thing). I do not think it matters whether there is also a competition law objection—the ETSI commitment itself prevents bundling.

  c. But offering all a party's SEPs is a different thing. The ETSI obligation requires this—a patentee could not comply with it by offering licences only on some of its SEPs. Furthermore it is standard industry practice to offer all a patentees' SEPs and at the time the ETSI commitment was devised everyone would have known that.

11. Of course there is nothing to stop a patentee offering also its entire portfolio of patents (SEPs and non-SEPs). Many patentees do just that. But the licensee must have the option of SEPs only.
12. What is a court do to when the patentee says it has complied with the obligation by offering a package of all its SEPs? The answer is that it must go to a determination by arbitration or a court, as described above. What the court should not embark upon is an evaluation of the royalty merely of the patents sued upon:
  a. That is not how it works in negotiated licences and the court should follow the practice of commerce.
  b. Moreover it is in truth impractical. The American decisions where courts have tried to apply American principles of patent damages (*Georgia Pacific*) show this. In any event the American principles of patent damages cannot be what the parties to an ETSI commitment governed by French law had in mind.
13. How is FRAND to be determined? Essentially this is a valuation exercise. And a far from easy one. Valuation exercises have to be carried out by tribunals in all sorts of circumstances—including IP cases. For instance tribunals may have to settle royalties (compulsory licences under patents, or copyright tribunals setting rates and so on). All these exercises are difficult and in their nature rather imprecise.

    In the case of FRAND one would start by looking for comparables. If the patentee had a number of other licensees who had willingly paid what he is seeking from this defendant that would be a good measure. In reality that may well not be so—for in the real world the patentees' other licensees may be cross-licensors and the licences may well be for non-SEPs too.

    The tribunal would want evidence from licensing experts and particularly from people with experience of FRAND licensing. In the end it will have to decide whether the patentee's offer was or was not FRAND based on the evidence before it. That was what was happening in Australia before *Apple v Samsung* settled. It is happening in at least one ongoing arbitration.

14. Three final points:
    a. It does not matter whether the defendant is a 'willing licensee'. That is an amorphous concept. It does not matter if he says he is 'willing to negotiate'. For all that matters is whether or not the patentee has made a FRAND offer.
    b. All of this works as a matter of law without any need for competition law to intervene.
    c. And it remains the case that attempts by competition law authorities to penalise a patentee for even suing upon an SEP are wrong and probably unlawful for the reasons I set out in my 'Grasshoppers and Ants' article (Chapter 19). See also the view of Tim Eicke QC at www.verfassungsblog.de/eu-commissions-contempt-national-courts/#.VDVcLb4kO9s. October 2014

POSTSCRIPT

A Commission official told me that he agreed with this analysis. And, if courts could be relied upon to apply it, there would indeed be no need for competition law. He expressed concern that they would not. There is something in what he says about courts not applying it—certainly I have heard that a lower-level German court took the view that the FRAND commitment was, as far as German patents are concerned, governed by German law. This is commercial madness—the commitment must be the same for all countries. If that is the concern, the Commission should intervene in such proceedings rather than fine people for going to court.

22

*Patent Trolls in Europe—Does Patent Law Require New Barriers?**

DEFINITION AND LANGUAGE. WHAT IS A 'PATENT TROLL'?

THE PHRASE 'PATENT troll' is quite new. It is not quite clear who first used it. According to that fount of all knowledge, Wikipedia, it was popularised in about 2000 by an American called Peter Detkin, assistant general counsel of the chip-maker Intel. According to Wikipedia there are earlier uses, the earliest being in 1993.

There is some dispute as to what the phrase means. Here is what Wikipedia says:

> 'Patent troll' is a controversial neologism susceptible to multiple definitions. Among them is a party that:
>
> — 'Purchases a patent, often from a bankrupt firm, and then sues another company by claiming that one of its products infringes on the purchased patent;
> — Enforces patents against purported infringers without itself intending to manufacture the patented product or supply the patented service;
> — Enforces patents but has no manufacturing or research base; or
> — Focuses its efforts solely on enforcing patent rights.'

If you go to an English dictionary there are a whole variety of meanings, most of which I had never heard of. But two of the best known are these. First from Scandinavian mythology: 'one of a race of supernatural beings formerly conceived as giants and, now, in Denmark and Sweden, as dwarfs or imps, supposed to inhabit caves or subterranean dwellings'. Many will know the nursery story from Norway

* For the May 2008 GRUR Meeting, Stuttgart.

about the three Billy-Goats Gruff and the troll under the bridge who threatens to eat them up. He is finally kicked into the river and away by the third and largest Billy Goat Gruff. The other well-known meaning is for a method of fishing in which a hooked line is dragged from behind a boat.

Word-Spy says this: 'So a "patent troll" is, officially, someone who fishes around for unused patents, but is also, unofficially, a low, inhuman creature that only uses those patents for litigious purposes'. All this is emotive stuff. It suggests the troll—a non-self-exploiting patentee—is a bad thing and should be treated as the third Billy Goat Gruff treated the troll under the bridge.

You can see how emotive it all is by asking whether a university which has patents it seeks to exploit by licensing is a troll. Or a lone inventor who tries to make money by licensing his invention. The perspective changes depending on the commercial nature of the patentee.

WHY HAS DISCUSSION ABOUT TROLLS BECOME SO TOPICAL?

The reason is clear. It comes from the US. And is a direct result of a combination of factors:[1]

(a) The pro-patentee attitude of US juries.[2]
(b) The preposterous awards of damages which are often made, quite apart from triple damages for wilful infringement.[3]
(c) The possibility of lawyer-driven litigation by virtue of the contingency fee system of the US—lawyers can take up to 50 per cent of the damages for taking a case as a speculation. It is an

[1] *There are two I missed. Firstly, wholly disproportionate discovery (both documentary and oral—many US lawyers make very good livings out of depositions). Secondly the fact that the US practice, unlike anywhere else in the world, is to try damages with infringement and validity. Bringing in damages with liability means practically doubling the costs of a trial, involving, as it does, different issues, different discovery and different factual and expert witnesses.*

[2] Currently about one-fifth of US patent infringement suits are started in the small town of Marshall, Texas, where the perception, at least, is that the jury will find for the plaintiff. *Marshall is still a much favoured venue by patentees, though the Court of Appeals for the Federal Circuit (CAFC) has managed to allow venue challenge in cases which have nothing to do with Texas.*

[3] *Although damages under US law are meant to be compensatory, they are generally much more than that. One of the troubles is that the jury will assume the lawyers are getting a cut and up the award (very human). Another is the fact that losses caused to a practising entity by competition from an infringement are not reasoned well. There is too much reliance on so-called expert evidence. Actually in my experience, save where the expert can provide factual evidence of comparables (generally difficult) they largely indulge in advocacy rather than in providing genuine expertise.*

advantage to lawyers on contingency fees to have a system where even if the action fails, the defendants' legal costs will not normally be paid.[4] Quite apart from its inherent injustices, that fact is, at the very least, a weapon in negotiation: 'It will cost you $5m and a lot of grief and trouble to win, I will settle for $3m.'

(d) The widening scope of patentability—particularly patents for software and business methods.[5] These are often of uncertain scope—and it has been possible to get bad patents which are nonetheless powerful weapons because of the risk factor.

Trolls have been less prominent in Europe[6]—because it does not have these factors at all or, to the extent it does, nowhere to the same degree.

WHAT, IF ANYTHING, SHOULD THE LAW DO ABOUT TROLLS?

First is not to get too excited about them. For legal purposes any patent holder who himself does not manufacture or use the patented invention should be treated the same. There is nothing new about such patentees—the problem of the non-exploiting patentee has always been with us.

Second is to be firm that the basic issues of infringement and validity have nothing to do with whether the patentee is a troll or not.

Third is to appreciate that a non-exploiting patentee is inherently much less likely to be awarded any provisional measure, especially

[4] *The House of Representatives voted in favour of a Bill in 2013 that would encourage judges hearing a patent case to award fees to the winner of an infringement lawsuit. This legislation was backed by technology companies (such as Google, Apple and Cisco) but it was not possible to achieve any progress in the Senate amid opposition both from pharma companies and the Senate Majority Leader. In the last midterms (November 2014), the Republicans took over the Senate so there is renewed hope for legislative progress.*

[5] *The patentability of these has recently been cut back by the Supreme Court in* Alice v CLS Bank, *which held that patents for finance trading systems were invalid for lack of patent eligibility. I applaud the result because I think inventions of ways of doing business do not need a patent incentive. Suppose the Lombard traders had patented the system of double-entry bookkeeping. If they could they could have controlled all kinds of business. As regards patents for computer programs, again I am very doubtful that they incentivise the creation of new programs. Certainly the early years of computer programs saw rapid innovation without the patent system. Copyright protection was enough.*

[6] *They are not wholly absent. Of the many battles between Nokia and IPComm in Europe, I think I am right in saying they cost of the order of £70m and Nokia prevailed in all save one—and even in that case the EPO revoked the patent.*

one by way of an injunction. Why? Because such a party only holds the patent so as to extract money from others—money is his only desired remedy. He has no business to be protected by his patent. So he can wait for his money until his rights have been finally determined. In an appropriate case[7] the court may say, by way of an interim order, that an alleged infringer must make safeguarded 'royalty' payments (eg into a joint bank account) pending the ultimate decision as to whether the patent is valid and infringed,[8] but it would require very unusual circumstances for a court to grant a troll a full interim injunction restraining infringement.

Fourth is to appreciate that although the 'troll problem'—to the extent there is one—may be exacerbated by the inability of patent offices to turn down many bad patents, the problem is fundamentally not about bad patents. A troll may hold a patent which is both valid and infringed. 'Raising the bar' of the standard of patentability by patent offices will stop both trolls and 'ordinary' patentees from waving bad patents at others. That will be a good thing (if it can be done, as to which I am not sure)[9] but cannot provide an answer to the fundamental 'troll problem'.

I now come to that—the hard bit—the case where a patent has been held valid and infringed and there is no escape via a finding of non-infringement or invalidity. I start with a story about George Bernard Shaw, the Irish playwright. He sat next to a lady at dinner. He asked if she would sleep with him for a hundred thousand pounds. She said yes. He then asked if she would for a shilling. She said, 'Of course not, what do you take me for!' Said GBS, 'We've already established that. Now we're just haggling over the price.'

What has that got to do with trolls you ask? Well it comes out of a little discussion I had with a prominent German lawyer. He said to me, 'For us, there is no problem.' 'Why?' I asked. 'Because if a valid patent is infringed, there will be an injunction.' 'Suppose,' I asked, 'the patent was for a life-saving drug and the patentee had not enough product to supply the market. Would a German court really stop the supply of an infringer's product?' 'Well,' he said, conceding

[7] eg where the alleged infringer may not be good for a later financial award.

[8] Such as was done in *Brupat v Sandford* [1983] RPC 61.

[9] *See my essay about this (Chapter 27). People continue to talk about this: they seem unable to grasp the real world of patent examination. Possibly doubling the costs of examination would help (in this life you get what you pay for) but though that is rational it is politically impossible.*

the point, 'maybe not. But it would have to be a very extreme case.' The same with George Bernard Shaw's lady.

Take another example. As many of you will know there is litigation about the anti-photocopy security system built into the Euro banknotes. An American non-manufacturing company is claiming, in about nine different European countries, that the Euro notes infringe its patent for such a system. Thus far, in France and the UK, the patent has been held invalid. In Germany and Holland there are first instance findings of validity which are under appeal. Infringement is in any event contested. But, suppose, in the end, that in one country the patent is held valid and infringed. Can the patentee not only demand but insist in that country upon an injunction to restrain infringement. Must the court of that country grant an injunction, despite the enormous consequences? Will the citizens of that country have to deliver up the contents of their wallets?[10]

Now some have the view that 'Property is property is property'. I call them absolutists. My German friend was an absolutist until challenged with the extreme consequences. But there are absolutists who say a patent right is much like that of the owner of a ransom strip of land. Such an owner simply says: 'Buy me off or you can't build.' Absolutists say that to withhold the injunction and award only a financial remedy amounts to compulsory purchase or licence.

And so it does. But saying so, or abstract appeals to the word 'property', do not provide an answer based on rationalism. To decide what to do about the non-exploiting patentee you really need to know the unknowable—what *economic* difference does it make to grant, or withhold, an injunction in such cases? Does it encourage or discourage innovation? Is the damage to competition worth it? What is the effect on the public interest?

Now we have not really had to face up to the problem in Europe yet. The Americans have. At one point the absolutist view had a real prospect of prevailing. In *NTP v RIM* in 2005 following a decision by the CAFC upholding a jury finding of infringement, the US government itself was asking that the possible injunction against Research in Motion, which would have stopped Blackberrys working all over the US, should have an exception in favour of Government Blackberrys. *NTP* was a non-working patentee—a troll. In the end the case settled for a vast payment by RIM, US$612 million. RIM could not afford the risk, even though by then the USPTO [United States

[10] *In the end the patents were held invalid everywhere, so the point never arose.*

Patent and Trademark Office] had made a first instance ruling in re-examination that all three of the patents sued upon were invalid.

Shortly thereafter, in *eBay v MercExchange*,[11] the Supreme Court rejected the absolutist approach. But it did not provide much by way of a clear rule as to when an injunction will be granted and when refused. It said:

> A plaintiff must demonstrate: (1) that it has suffered an irreparable injury; (2) that remedies available at law, such as monetary damages, are inadequate to compensate for that injury; (3) that, considering the balance of hardships between the plaintiff and defendant, a remedy in equity is warranted; and (4) that the public interest would not be disserved by a permanent injunction.

This is a pretty vague test. Maybe a clearer one cannot be devised. The Supreme Court remitted consideration of what to do to the District Court. That court refused a permanent injunction. The case then settled.

Of course saying 'award damages instead of an injunction' itself may provide problems. How much would be a major question. And how should they be paid? After all a defendant who is allowed to infringe for a number of years may have no idea of the scale of his future activity—or may not have the money for an up-front payment. So the court may find itself drawn into some quasi-compulsory licence proceedings. It could say, for instance, that an injunction will be granted unless the defendant abides by certain terms, eg accounting, up-front payments and so on. Much remains to be worked out here, and may have to be if parties do not settle.

I turn to what Europe should do. Well, at present it will be down to various national courts to decide whether an injunction can be refused and if so on what terms. Obviously the sooner we have a common approach through a common court the better. What should such an approach be?

A good starting position is the Enforcement Directive.[12] Article 3 says that enforcement measures shall be 'effective, proportionate and dissuasive and shall be applied in such a manner as to avoid the creation of barriers to legitimate trade and to provide for safeguards against their abuse'. That is not an absolutist approach to remedies—far from it. A court is not compelled to grant an injunction, however

[11] *eBay v MercExchange*, US No 05–131 (2006).
[12] 2004/48/EC.

disproportionate a measure it may be or how abusively the patent owner has behaved.

So I think the answer is reasonably clear. We must leave it to the judges. Any attempt to lay down detailed rules would be a mistake. Why? Because you cannot cater in advance for all types of case. A non-exploiting patentee may have a good reason for not exploiting—eg he has another patented product which does the job. Or he may have a perfectly fair licensing programme in operation. Or the defendant may have deliberately flouted the patent without any reasonable excuse.

The common law countries would have no real difficulty with the remedy being left to the judges. For due to our legal history, we have traditionally held the remedy of an injunction to be what we call 'discretionary'. We have never been absolutists about injunctions.[13] Of course where there is a threatened infringement of a right an injunction will be granted. But the court has always had the right to say no—damages will be an adequate remedy. In the field of intellectual property we have applied that in the case of a breach of confidence—where an inventor wanted to sell his idea for money, money is what he got.[14] Similarly in 1995 I refused an injunction and awarded damages in a case where a record had been on the market for 11 years before the writer of the lyrics complained of copyright infringement. The writer wanted money—that is what he got.[15]

Now I know that the notion of 'judicial discretion' is anathema to some continental jurists. But unless you take the absolutist position—which I believe I have shown is absurd—there is no alternative. The experience of the common law countries shows that a judicial discretion is workable. It will have to be adopted. It may mean in some cases the court having to decide what a reasonable royalty is, and what the terms of a licence are, but that would not be the end of the world.

Before concluding I should mention one other possible answer to the 'troll problem'. It could be argued that a troll which asks 'too much' as the price of buying off an injunction is abusing its monopoly contrary to Art 82 of the EU Treaty. So instead of using a judicial discretion to withhold an injunction on terms, one asks whether there

[13] Save, perhaps, in the case of an injunction to restrain a defendant from doing that which by contract he has agreed not to do.

[14] *Seager v Copydex* [1967] 1 WLR 923.

[15] *Banks v EMI Songs* [1996] EMLR 452.

is an abuse of monopoly instead, and only if there is does one refuse an injunction. I think this would be a bad solution to the problem. It is likely to be complicated, roundabout and involve the impossible question of whether the patentee is asking 'too much'. Competition law is not the answer or at least not the only answer.

So in the end my answers to the question posed by the title of this talk are (1) no patentee has an absolute right to an injunction; (2) normally he will get one; (3) the court should always have a reserve power to refuse an injunction and to fashion a financial and/or other remedy appropriate to the circumstances of the case and the public interest; and (4) the matter should be left to the courts—attempts to legislate for the problem are almost certain to lead to trouble.[16]

[16] *It seems that this solution will be adopted for the forthcoming Unitary Patent Court within the EU. Argument has raged about whether rules for this court should contain more explicit rules about withholding injunctions—see eg the open letter from 17 major companies (including Apple, Samsung, Microsoft and Cisco) to the Preparatory Committee, the EU Commission and others. The reasons why detailed rules are not wise are that you cannot foresee all situations which might arise and such rules may be inflexible. Personally I favour a general approach that an injunction will be granted unless that remedy is substantially disproportionate in all the circumstances. I do wish that the Rules referred to the public interest as a potential ground for withholding both for interim and final injunctions. Common lawyers would not need it, but some continental lawyers with their black-letter-law disposition may need it.*

23

*Patent Thickets: A Paper for the European Patent Office Economic and Scientific Advisory Board (ESAB) Meeting at the University of Leuven (26 September 2012)**

THE PURPOSE OF this paper is to outline the factual basis upon which any rational discussion of 'patent thickets' can take place. Although I will use this term, it should be recognised that it is emotive, suggesting that there is something wrong with the present position. Another emotive expression is 'barriers to entry', which carries the unspoken implication that the barriers are somehow unjustified. A less emotive expression would be 'the problems of patent compliance'. A rational approach to the study should not proceed on any emotional basis. The focus of the discussion should be on whether there is anything wrong with the present system and, if so, how far it can be fixed.

Patents come in many sorts. Some have wide claims, some narrow and some in between. Some are valid, others not. Some cover matter which would be essential for any new entrant to an industry to use, others not. Some cover valuable commercial products or processes, many do not. Patent Offices do their best to examine patent applications and to grant only those which are valid and with claims which do not have undue width. But it is inherent in the system (and always has been) that there will be a lot of invalid granted patents, the proportion varying from industry to industry.

* *This piece was published subsequently in (2013) 8(3)* Journal of Intellectual Property Law & Practice 203–06.

Further, quite apart from granted patents there are large (and growing) numbers of as-yet unexamined patent applications. These are published quickly (18 months from application) and it is possible for them to turn into multiple applications by the divisional procedure. So the discussion must include not only 'patent thickets' but also 'patent application thickets'.

There is also the so-called problem of 'royalty stacking'. In some industries, even when the patents relevant to a proposed activity have been identified, so many are in the hands of a number of proprietors who all want royalties, with the consequence that the total amount of royalties demanded makes the proposed activity unprofitable

I turn to consider each of these matters in more detail.

WIDTH OF CLAIM

A few inventions are so important that they lead to entire new industries. An old example would be the pneumatic tyre. The transistor would be another. These are wholly exceptional. They certainly provide a barrier to entry into that industry. That is what the patent system is for. They do not form any part of a 'thicket' problem.

But there are lesser patents too, patents which can monopolise important areas of commercial interest within an industry. They too are barriers to entry. Again, they do not form part of a 'thicket' problem, though they may in some cases raise problems as to whether their use is essential for anyone trading in a particular market.

The reason why both these types of patent are irrelevant to the present discussion is that they do not involve multiplicity of patents. They are essentially lone, important, patents. Most typically they are to be found in the pharma and biotech fields. Industry- and industry-sector-dominating valid patents of wide and commercially dominating scope are less common in other industries.

There is also a problem of how patent law itself copes with claims of undue width. We can all agree that no one should be able to claim more than he or she has invented. There is no explicit ground of invalidity in the European Patent Convention (EPC) to address this,[1] but necessity has harnessed two other objections, obviousness and

[1] Unfortunately the creators of the EPC ignored the British suggestion that there should be such a ground of objection to validity.

sufficiency, to cover it. The reasoning is rather convoluted, but does the job. For present purposes it is not necessary to go into the detail, it being sufficient to note that a number of patents have claims of undue width which produce a compliance problem.

PATENT VALIDITY AND QUALITY

The assessment of validity of a granted patent, and the potential validity (and probable ultimate scope of a valid claim of an application) are often troublesome, expensive and time-consuming to determine. A would-be new entrant to a commercial activity therefore, in theory, if he wants to be sure of being safe, has to consider not only the claims of all the patents and patent applications which he might infringe but also their validity. Obviously the higher the standard of examination by the Patent Office, the less attention to validity need be paid by the would-be new entrant. However, the reality is that it is impossible for standards to be raised very substantially: Patent Offices cannot be perfect, prior art may be missed or not fully appreciated. And, in any event, the standards of Patent Offices are simply irrelevant to as-yet unexamined patent applications.

ESSENTIALITY

Some patents cover matter which must be used by any entrant: essential patents. There are, in general, two sorts of essential patent: those essential by reason of the natural world and those essential to comply with man-made standards. Examples of the former are gene patents; examples of the latter are patents the use of which is necessary to comply with some man-defined standard, eg 3G. In either case it is simply not possible to design around.

Essentiality is not in itself part of the so-called thicket problem, but can be a contributory factor in those industries where an entrant is faced with a large number of essential patents. That is particularly the case with industries concerned with man-made essentiality, because very large numbers of patents may be essential. The thicket problem there is generally ameliorated by industry-wide agreements to pool patents, making licences available on fair, reasonable and non-discriminatory (FRAND) terms. But such a solution has its own problems (eg what rate of royalty is FRAND?) and can lead to royalty stacking problems for a new entrant. Often in this sort of industry the proportion of invalid patents is very high.[2]

PATENT APPLICATIONS AND DIVISIONALS

It must be understood that any well-drafted patent application will have claims wider than those which will eventually be granted. No competent patent attorney would claim narrowly in the first instance. He goes wide to see what prior art is found and shapes his eventual widest claim around that. It would be negligent for him not to do so. There is no sanction for applying for claims which would be unduly wide and are unlikely to be granted.

Sometimes a basic application will be broken up into a number of applications for different patents, each having the same priority date and date of application. Division can take place either as a result of the Office requiring it or voluntarily on the part of the applicant. The Office will require it where the patentee has included in his initial application so much matter that the Office says the application should be divided up into several patents. The original application is said by the Office to be for more than one invention. Such forms of divisional patents are comparatively rare, compared with divisionals resulting from the voluntary action of the patentee. Patentees frequently divide their original applications into one or more divisional patents. They may do this for perfectly rational reasons. For instance there may be parts of the application which the Office finds acceptable and other parts which it does not. The patentee can divide out the uncontroversial part and get early protection for that, while leaving the controversial part for argument, evidence and possible appeal. There are other reasons for voluntary division, for instance attempts to draft claims which read on to competing products which have already come onto the market. The game is to create a patent with narrow claims (hence easier to defend) covering the product—but which does not offend the 'no added matter' rule.

Any would-be entrant must therefore consider not only all pending applications but also divisional application, as well as potential

[2] See the widely circulated paper by Richard Vary of Nokia, *Bifurcation: Bad for Business*. It is not formally published anywhere as of the time of writing. It was made available on IPKat on 20 April 2012 (where it can be found) and may be formally published elsewhere by the time of publication of this article.

divisionals from these. What valid claims *could* be obtained on the basis of the application is seldom an easy question to answer.

SUMMARY

It follows from the above, from the way the system works, that anyone wanting to start a new commercial activity of the sort which can or might be patented has a patent compliance problem. That is so whether he wishes to make something of (or import) a design which is less than 20 years old or whether it is of a new design which is itself the subject of a patent or patent application. The compliance problem applies to all innovators. A mere intermediary such as a dealer may be able by contract to shift the consequences of non-compliance, of being the subject of a patent action, particularly a successful one, onto his supplier but even then he has to be sure he has an effective remedy. Is the supplier likely to be solvent? And can an effective remedy be obtained against him (especially if the supplier is outside the territory of the EU or the Lugano agreement)? These are often important commercial questions.

Patent compliance is expensive. In theory all patents and patent applications which are potentially relevant to the proposed activity have to be identified and their scope compared with the product or process concerned. Once those which cover that product or process or arguably do so have been identified, an inquiry as to their validity will (or may, some companies may stop before then) be conducted. This entire process requires skilled patent attorneys or lawyers, who themselves are expensive.

Big companies spend a lot on patent compliance. Some years back, the chief patent attorney of BP estimated that about half his department was involved with issues of compliance rather than in patenting new BP inventions. Other companies may spend less, or even choose not to bother, wait until a problem emerges and expect to solve it then. Smaller companies often cannot afford to do a compliance exercise thoroughly. And, as I have explained, even big companies in some industrial sectors (eg mobile phones) simply pool their patents, agreeing to cross-license each other, the amounts payable themselves often being roughly calculated by numbers (rather than validity) of so-called 'essential' patents (though there can be dispute about what is really essential).

It is particularly the position of small companies which excites some commentators. The suggestion is that there are so many patents 'out there' that they are deterred from entry into the market. The sharpest criticism is directed in favour of the small innovative company. The critics say that the problem of patent compliance is so great that innovation itself is deterred.

Over the course of my professional life as a lawyer I have never come across that. I have never heard of anyone actually being deterred to innovate by the formidable-sounding difficulties of compliance I have outlined above. People seem simply to get on with inventing, inventing around, and worrying about the difficulties later. Perhaps worthy of research is to find out how much the so-called thicket problem deters innovation, particularly by small companies. The UK's Intellectual Property Office made a stab at this and found no real deterrence, as I understand it.

Nonetheless patent compliance is expensive and ways should be considered of reducing the costs. Basically there are two possibilities, both aimed at reducing the numbers of patents that fall within the scope of any compliance exercise. The first is to increase the official fees for examination and grant and the second is to increase the fees for renewal. The fewer the trees, the thinner is the thicket. Other possible measures might include (a) making sure that there are really speedy and efficient ways of attacking patents—the current EPO opposition procedure is far too slow to clear a thicket commercially and amounts almost to chopping trees with a penknife; (b) introducing some sort of penalty or sanction for holding a patent which is invalid; (c) setting up a licensing body to deal with problems of royalty stacking.

One possible conclusion may be no more than that the thicket problem is simply a natural consequence and cost of the patent system as a whole, that nothing can really be done about it. There is nothing new about the problem. Mr Blanco White put it this way in his book in 1947:[3]

> There is … a way in which a monopoly in an important invention may be kept alive after the patent has come to an end, and that is by patenting large numbers of minor improvements to the original invention … Provided the patented improvements represent genuine development over the period during which the original patent is in force, and provided they are patented with determination and persistence, by the time the original

[3] TA Blanco White, *Patents and Registered Designs* (This is the Law Series, Stevens, 1947)

> patent expires a would-be imitator should be faced with this situation: that the article described in the original specification is too inferior to contemporary designs to be commercially saleable, while he cannot imitate the newer models without risking an action for infringement of so many of the improvement patents, that he would almost certainly lose in respect of some patent or other. Even if he were to win the action on enough of the patents to let him go on manufacturing without any fundamental change in his design, the cost of fighting and losing the action as a whole would still take much of the profit out of his venture. For this reason the existence of a mass of improvement patents is often a sufficient deterrent to would-be imitators. The original manufacturer's position need not deteriorate with further lapse of time: he should always be some years ahead in design so far as patentable improvements are concerned, while the longer he keeps the field to himself the greater the advantage he has in manufacturing experience. His monopoly will last until some competitor comes along with the skill needed to 'design round' the more dangerous patents and the courage to fight a patent action if necessary; how long this will be will depend as usual on the importance of the market covered by the monopoly, as well as on the rate at which he continues to devise new patentable improvements. In the past, such monopolies have sometimes lasted a long time.

I used the quotation in my speech at the Commission when it introduced its preliminary findings in the Pharma Inquiry.[4] The Commission thought it had found something new and reprehensible—what it called 'patent clusters'. But that was in relation to the pharma industry, which has relatively few patents compared with other (eg electronics) industries.

Actually I suspect the 'problem' goes back to the very beginning of significant use of the patent system. Boulton and Watt used walls of patents to keep others out. A really good study would be of Edison's patents. I have long suspected that most of these were for minor improvements rather than major inventions and some of doubtful validity: he would have understood the patent system well enough to protect his businesses as far as possible by a thicket. A good area of research would be, for instance, to study all Edison's patents to see the extent to which he was creating thickets.

More generally I do not think it is helpful or useful to get excited about any specific 'thicket' problem. Such problems as there are part

[4] See Chapter 20, *Patents and Pharmaceuticals*, a paper given in November 2008 at the Presentation of the Directorate-General of Competition's Preliminary Report of the Pharm-sector inquiry, CIPA, December 2008 p 711.

of the very patent system itself. All attention should be focussed on improving all aspects of that.

POSTSCRIPT

EPO's Economic and Scientific Advisory Board (ESAB) produced a report on the Thicket Workshop.[5] *It is quite a good discussion of the alleged problem. What did emerge is that there is no consensus that 'thickets' are really a problem at all and that they are 'closely related to the management of innovation and its complexity'. To me at least that means that thickets are a sign of innovation, not an impediment.*

There are allegations that thickets cause 'hold-up'. This economists' buzzword is actually used in two senses. The first is that thickets actually impede innovation—preventing possible new entrants from themselves innovating. The second is a market sense—impeding new entrants or causing 'royalty stacking' to a point where the would-be new entrant has to pay so much in royalties to the various owners of the patents forming the 'thicket' that it is not worthwhile entering. I don't believe either theory is true—see the next chapter.

[5] *On the EPO website.*

24

Don't Attack Patent Law but Improve it[*]

THERE IS A school of thought among some economists and legal academics who espouse the hypothesis that patent rights, although intended to stimulate innovation, actually threaten it. The hypothesis goes something like this. First, that patents expire 20 years from the date of application. From the time of grant, the patentee has an exclusive right over the subject-matter of the patent. Second, that an exclusive right means what it says, the right to exclude. The patentee can exclude others from any commercial activity over that subject-matter. This exclusive right does not, though, stop others from merely doing research about the invention that is the subject of the main patent. Later inventors can patent any improvements provided they are new and inventive. But because the main patent excludes any commercialisation of the improvement, the reality is that people will not try to make improvements whilst the main patent remains in force.

Until it expires, the main patent is therefore seen as a disincentive to any innovation that comes within its scope. People will be less willing to try to make improvements, particularly if the scope of the main patent is wide, in other words, a big invention. And a further problem arises if there are lots of overlapping patents for minor inventions in the same field, known as 'patent thickets'. In a report to the UK government, Professor Ian Hargreaves asserted that patent thickets 'obstruct entry to some markets and so impede innovation'.

This hypothesis may sound plausible enough, but is it true? Let's consider it as a natural scientist would when developing a theory from a hypothesis. Only when a hypothesis is found to accord with

[*] *First published by* Europe's World *in June 2014.*

observation and experiment can it be treated as valid—as a theory. Economists' hypotheses can sometimes be tested by observation, but seldom by experiment. So the test for converting an economist's hypothesis to theory ought to be largely observation.

Does the hold-up hypothesis I have described stand up to observation? Nearly 200 years have passed since the beginning of the industrial age, so there should be some solid supporting evidence by now if it is correct. As there is none, the answer must be a clear 'no'; there is no credible observation, or evidence that patents threaten innovation or have ever done so.

First, observation of the real commercial world shows that patents provide a major incentive to innovate. Why spend billions on research and development, much of which will be fruitless, if the results of success can be copied by someone without sharing those costs? Ask innovative companies how they fund their research, and the answer is always the same—with the profits from other successful research efforts. The telecom innovator Qualcomm, for instance, invests 20 per cent of its profits in further research. Consider what happened where there was no patent system: neither the Soviet Union nor Communist China produced a single new class of pharmaceutical compound. Yet since introducing market reforms, China has now built a patent system with amazing success in such a short time.

Second, consider the history of patent abolitionism. Arguments for abolishing patents were loud in the mid-nineteenth century. The Netherlands, then a backward non-innovative economy, even abolished patents for 35 years. That enabled a Mr Philips to set up a copycat electric lamp company free from the Edison and Swan patents—but Philips, once it became an innovator in the twentieth century, then emerged as one of the great innovation and patenting companies. Switzerland also had weak patent laws, while the German patent laws of that time did not protect products manufactured abroad, but when they strengthened those laws, the great and ever-innovative Swiss patent-based pharmaceutical industry came into being. As such, I believe that just as those old abolitionists lost, the new abolitionists that exist and the quasi-abolitionists—those trying to water down the patent system, such as competition authorities—should now lose.

Does the evidence of history bear out the hypothesis? I cannot think of a single example to support it. There are several supposed examples, some of almost mythical status. *The* first is the proposal that the Boulton and Watt patent (for condensing the steam of a steam engine in a separate condenser) held up the development of 'strong steam'—using much higher pressure cylinders and not bothering to condense steam at all. Detailed research has shown the story isn't true. Studies of the sewing machine wars of the mid-1900s likewise show anything but hold-up as rival inventors fought in the courts and in the market: sewing machine technology burst on consumers much as mobile phone technology has done today. Other examples recent scholarship has shown of supposed patent hold-up that have no basis in reality are the supposed hold-up of electric light technology by Edison's patents, the supposed hold-up of Ford after he lost a patent action in the 1900s and the supposed hold-up of aeroplane development by the Wright brothers' patents in the First World War. Examination of the facts, including descending into the technology and examining the scope of the patents concerned and finding out what really was happening, has exploded all these myths.[1]

What then of the thicket part of the hypothesis? Again, the evidence doesn't support it. The best supposed modern example of this is that of mobile phone technology, where in reality innovation is extremely rapid: new models with new features appear so fast that one can hardly keep up. And prices are falling—especially considering the increasing number of features with every new model from competing companies. If you look without any preconception at actual technology, you will find that 'thickets' are a sign of fast-moving innovation, quite the reverse of what the hypothesis predicts.[2]

As well as this, the hypothesis ignores the reality of evidence from companies whose business depends on innovation. These companies know that their patents are time limited, so unless they can innovate

[1] *Some sensible researchers decided to investigate these properly. That involved considering things like the actual protection conferred by patents and what really happened. See R Katznelson and J Howells, 'Inventing- around Edison's Incandescent Lamp Patent: Evidence of Patents' Role in Stimulating Downstream Development'; R Katznelson and J Howells, 'The Myth of the Early Aviation Patent Hold-Up—How a US Government Monopsony Commandeered Pioneer Airplane Patents'* (2015) 24(1) Industrial and Corporate Change *1–64, doi: 10.1093/icc/dtu003; G Selgin and J Turner,*

'Strong Steam, Weak Patents, or, the Myth of Watt's Innovation-Blocking Monopoly, Exploded' 2011 54(4) Journal of Law and Economics *841; J Howells and R Katznelson, 'The Coordination of Independently-Owned Vacuum Tube Patents in the Early Radio Alleged Patent "Thicket"'*, http://j.mp/Radio-Thicket. *I commend those who are inclined to believe in hold-up or that the patent system impedes innovation to read these with care. It does mean you have to understand the technology.*

[2] *Recently and very notably, the CAFC affirmed at trial Judge's decision to reject arguments based on alleged royalty stacking and hold-up*, D-Link v Ericsson, *4 December 2014: ' The district court need not instruct the jury on hold-up or stacking unless the accused infringer presents actual evidence of hold-up or stacking'. Certainly something more than a general argument that these phenomena are possibilities is necessary.*

their businesses will fail. There is competition in innovation itself—a competition which depends on the patent system to make it possible. You need only ask pharmaceutical companies or telecom companies such as Qualcomm how much their business models and their investment in R&D depend on the patent system to explode the hypothesis.

A final reality check is the fact that patent law provides limited protection for patents developing new uses of old and known medicines. It is inherently unlikely that the first use of a new medicine developed at a huge cost of time and money is the only, or even the best, use of that medicine. Yet because of a lack of patent incentive, there isn't nearly enough research into new uses of old medicines. Again, this can be examined by asking pharmaceutical companies what they are doing—and in the case of new uses for old medicines, there is a huge reluctance to invest in research. A striking and seriously alarming example is that of the bisphosphonates. Developed for treating loss of bone density, there are good indications that they may have valuable uses in rheumatoid arthritis, certain cancers and heart disease. But no one is following up because they cannot get a useful patent if they do the research.

This is not to say the patent system is perfect; far from it. There are real problems with the proportion of invalid patents granted, with expensive litigation systems (especially that of the US with its jury trial, preposterously over-elaborate discovery system and over-compensatory awards of damages partly fuelled by lawyers on contingency fees taking large proportions of any damages). But only a man blinded to the evidence by his own hypothesis would say that patents threaten innovation. All attention should move away from attacks on the principle behind patent law, and concentrate on improving its machinery.

25

The Perfect Patent Court[*]

WHEN I WAS asked to write for this Festschrift I accepted at once. Who could fail to respond for such men as Dieter and Gert? They belong to the generation of pioneers: those who took the EPO from infancy to the mighty enterprise it is today. I count both of them as friends—and it is difficult to imagine the EPO without them.

The success of enterprise EPO is all the more striking when compared with the failure of Europe to produce a European patent court—either as an EU court or any other kind of supra-national court. For enforcement[1] one still has to go to national jurisdictions with all their varied and quite different approaches.[2] Why is this? The answer is complex. At its heart lies the fact that legal *procedure* is a much harder subject than the uninitiated (which I am afraid includes

[*] An essay in '… *und sie bewegt sich doch!' Patent Law on the Move, a Festschrift for Gert Kolle and Dieter Stauder* (Carl Heymanns Verlag, 2005).

[1] Subject perhaps to pan-European enforcement by a national court. We await the decision of the ECJ in *GAT v Luk*, but pan-European jurisdiction for national courts if available would almost certainly lead to forum shopping of the worst kind—particularly attempts to be first to start in what is perceived to be a pro-patentee jurisdiction. *In GAT Case C-539/03 the ECJ ruled against pan-European enforcement by national courts at least where validity is in issue. Some (particularly the Dutch) say this does not apply to (a) preliminary relief or (b) where the court can conclude that there is no serious attack on validity. In Case C-616-10* Solvay v Honeywell *the ECJ gave one of its 'ça depend' answers—the national court must embark on the task of deciding whether there is a risk of irreconcilable decisions. That means trying to predict the result of parallel cases in other jurisdictions, case which will be tried by different procedures and very likely on different evidence. In reality pan-European enforcement of patents no longer has the enthusiasm it had in the heyday of Dutch Rambo lawyers (a phrase I think invented by Jan Brinkhof) going round the world saying 'we can get you a Europe-wide injunction—come to us'. All this will fade away with the forthcoming UPC.*

[2] To draw a distinction between 'common law' and 'civil law' approaches is crude: in reality the differences between systems in different countries is enormous—particularly between the so-called civil law countries. For instance German litigation is procedurally wildly different from that in France, which itself differs markedly from that in Italy or Sweden. In truth each country is very different from all the others.

politicians and civil servants who draft laws and rules) would begin to suppose. All too often legal procedure is treated as a 'Cinderella' subject—a minor detail to be added on at the end. Some would say (and that includes me) that the opposition and appeal procedure of the EPO is an example of just that. It has become so slow and cumbersome that it seems certain that, sooner rather than later, it will be subject to successful attack for breach of Art 6 of the European Convention on Human Rights. I think it is high time that the whole procedure was reviewed from top to bottom.[3]

The problems of creating a European patent court and of the EPO procedures led me to my chosen title. Suppose one was given a free hand to create the perfect patent court. Where would one start? I started by setting out a list of requirements.

The court should be:

1. capable of providing a speedy resolution;
2. cheap;
3. capable of dealing with highly complex technical issues;
4. accessible to SMEs,[4] both plaintiffs' and defendants';
5. capable of dealing with many different languages;
6. predictable;
7. equipped with a respected judiciary;
8. fair in its procedures;
9. readily accessible—hence a local presence;
10. able to deal with questions of interim relief very quickly;
11. able to enforce its orders readily.

I thought of adding that it would nice if there were also World Peace, Freedom from Poverty and Disease, and Goodwill to all Men. I will, however, confine myself to considering the points in my list. But before I do so, I have a number of general remarks.

First, many of the requirements apply equally to other courts which deal with the resolution and enforcement of civil disputes. But the requirements for a patent court are more stringent than those for the general run of courts. Thus the very nature of the dispute is such that a court staffed by a lawyer judge (or judges) will very likely be unable to resolve a dispute on its own. Substantive patent law itself brings in the notional 'person skilled in the art' at a variety of key points: as

[3] By a group with much experience of real, hostile, litigation. It is no good the job being done by amateurs—that was the trouble in the first place.

[4] Small and medium-sized enterprises.

the person to whom the claims are directed, the person to whom the invention must be non-obvious and the person who must be capable of performing the invention. A mere lawyer simply does not have the background to be able to make judgments on these matters—indeed in many cases the very words used in the claims are not part of his vocabulary at all. So a lawyer-judge needs teaching in a way that is far from usual in other civil disputes.

Second, patent law itself draws some none-too-precise lines—for instance as to what is obvious.[5]

Third, the problem of language arises at least to some degree in nearly all cases. This is because even if the language of both parties and the court is the same, there is very likely to be prior art in some other language. Currently the three official languages of the EPO mean that the patent must be translated into other languages if it is to take effect outside English-, German- or French-speaking countries. The proposals for translating only the claims will save some money but in reality if litigation or its prospect comes into play, the whole patent will have to be translated.[6]

Fourth, it is obvious that the various requirements are, very often, in conflict with each other. You can achieve a speedy resolution and very cheaply by a toss of a coin but you will be very short on the other requirements (save, perhaps, language!). The more deeply you go into the case, the more expensive and slower it is likely to be.

REQUIREMENT 1—SPEED

This is very important. Commercially a position of uncertainty nearly always favours a patentee. In some cases the mere fact of pending litigation operates as a de facto injunction.[7] It is inevitably the case that a significant proportion of patents which are granted are nonetheless invalid. Grant is obtained at the behest of the inventor

[5] That is why in the UK the House of Lords has said that the trial judge's views on this should not be overruled unless he has made a clear error, *Biogen v Medeva* [1997] RPC 1. You have to give the decision to someone—and although it is possible that another may take a different view, it is not sensible to have appeals purely on that basis—the first instance judge has a 'margin of appreciation' to use a phrase from the field of human rights law.

[6] Not least because the claims alone are at best only a guide—they have to be construed in context as Art 69 of the EPC makes clear.

[7] Would you buy a machine if you knew it might be held to infringe so that your supplier would cease to maintain it?

without intervention by third parties—a busy patent examiner is simply bound to miss points which a hostile third party would make or press hard. Besides, patent searches can miss material within the scope of the search and are bound to miss other things such as prior uses or commercial brochures.

It is the opinion of many that the standard of the EPO is too low.[8] There are many patent agents who feel a quiet sense of triumph when they have got what they think is a dodgy case past the Office. It is no good wishing all this were not so[9]—it is an inevitable and, so far as I can see, unavoidable consequence of the system.[10] Given that is so, it is all the more important the courts, the ultimate arbiters of both scope and validity, reach their answer quickly.

How is that to be achieved? Well, in my experience by setting a fair but tight timetable. This cannot be done by the application of more or less rigid rules but by an early case management conference. And it requires that there be a court to hear the case when it is ready. This involves resources but those who provide courts—states or groups of states—should understand that money is not saved by letting a court's case-load build up. On the contrary the longer a case takes the more resources all (parties and court) have to put into it.[11] In my opinion courts should run hard timetables—even putting themselves at risk of having to work hard! Cases should be double-booked in the diary or nearly so to allow for those that settle. If they do not and one has to be adjourned, the parties should be compensated and a new date fixed quickly.

REQUIREMENT 2—CHEAPNESS

Costs are made up of two elements, court fees and those of the lawyers, patent agents and experts (whether party or court experts).

[8] And I have heard it said that the British Office is even lower—not my experience. *Can Patent Offices do better? Not unless they are paid more and even then there can be no guarantee—see 'Raising the Bar' Chapter 27. A realist would ignore the pompous, own-trumpet-blowing, self-congratulatory stuff which appears from time to time on the EPO President's blog.*

[9] As, for instance, the recently formed British 'Patent Reform Group' say. *This group has turned out to be only a small lobby group, in my opinion at least rather naïve about how the system really works.*

[10] It has the unfortunate consequence that, in some inexperienced jurisdictions, courts are apt to take the line 'if it is good enough for the EPO, it is good enough for me', in effect failing to address validity properly.

[11] This is not least because whenever anything happens it is necessary to get up to speed on the case. If the file has been closed for six month then it has to be re-read—a real waste of time.

The biggest element in most systems is the latter, the people the parties have to hire. The more they do the more they cost. So to keep costs down the system must aim to cut out unnecessary work. Take the English system and obviousness. We allow discovery of the inventors' work and of what work (if any) was being done on the problem by he who is attacking the patent.[12] The theory justifying this is that it is important when considering obviousness to consider how real people were working at the time. But there is scarcely any logic in this—one is concerned with the notional skilled man who was necessarily not the patentee. And why discovery just from the parties when the logical (but impossible) thing would be to get the documents of all those anywhere in the world who were working on the problem? I think that, save in exceptional cases,[13] discovery on obviousness is a waste of time and expense in nearly all cases. I do not say 'all' for I can think of one or two cases over my entire career where discovery really did make a difference on obviousness.[14] I do not think that giving up discovery on obviousness save in rare cases would be too high a price for the savings to be made in most cases. So in my perfect court, at the price of justice in isolated cases, we do not have it, unless there is a very special reason.

Next consider experiments done for the purpose of the case. The English courts take this much more seriously than do most others. We have detailed rules about the admission of evidence. If a litigation experiment is to be admitted it must be shown to the other side. We find that far too often the wrong experiment is done[15] wasting

[12] Subject to a 'window' of two years around the priority date—see CPR Part 63 Practice Direction 5.1.

[13] eg where the patentee starts giving evidence of how he made the invention. *I dissented in the Court of Appeal about discovery on obviousness in* Nichia v Argos *[2007] EWCA 741. I reviewed the value of such discovery in some detail and thought it not worth it in a case which I thought could be seen to be as not worth much. The other members of the court thought there should have been some evidence about the value. I like to think my approach was right—discovery would be disproportionate. All that was needed was a short bit of evidence showing that, but unfortunately the patentees did not provide it. People know better now.*

[14] One celebrated case (which I was not in) formed part of the *Du Pont/Akzo* litigation. A Du Pont copy of Akzo's patent revealing their invention had written on it by a Du Pont scientist 'Hot Rats'—so struck was he by the idea said later to be obvious. Another was *Molynke v P&G* [1992] FSR 487 where the defendant's own discovery showed their concern and difficulty over the problem solved by the patent—see p 588 for a quotation from a key discovery document.

[15] For a recent pair of examples see *SKB v Apotex*, 29 November 2004 and *SmithKline Beecham's patent (No 2)* [2003] RPC 607, 624–25 (reversed on appeal, but not on this point—a further appeal to the House of Lords is pending). *The HL reversed the CA on the point of law involved.*

very much money. In my perfect patent court this sort of thing will not happen. Nor, on the other hand, will unobserved experiments be allowed—I have seen too many cases (in parallel litigation to that going on in England) where casual evidence of an experiment is admitted—almost without any details of what was supposed to have been done. Experiments done for litigation are quite unlike normal science—they are done to prove something, not to find something out. Bias by way of 'tweaking' is all too common. In my perfect court, experiments will largely be done by the court's own expert[16]—and only if strictly necessary.

More generally in relation to party costs my court would be very careful when I came to awarding full costs to the winning party.[17] You cannot stop a party hiring lots of very expensive lawyers, patent attorneys and experts—but if they do the other side should not be penalised. And my court would constantly remind everyone that the best teams are small.[18]

What about court costs? How much should this perfect court charge the parties? Well in an ideal world courts, like policemen, should come free to the individual users—part of the very fabric of a civilised society. But I have never heard of a fee-less court. So how should court fees be charged? The German (or Swiss) model of charging by the notional worth of the case has something to be said for it in principle. The court fee is kept somewhat in proportion to what is at stake. But of course in reality it is often well-nigh impossible to put a rational value on a case. Take the small-scale alleged infringer of a pharmaceutical patent who counterclaims for invalidity. Although his sales are small, if he breaks the patent the cost to the patentee is vast. What is the 'value' of the case? Despite this, I think my court would have some attempt to base its own fees on 'value'—rather than for instance either near nominal fees (the current British system) or fees which depend in part on court time (as is proposed for England and Wales).[19]

[16] About how he or she is found, see below.

[17] I have no doubt that this is what a court should do—the American method of no attorney costs save in exceptional cases leads to the well-known injustice that it is often cheaper to pay the plaintiff off than win the case.

[18] When I was a barrister I used to rejoice if the other side had an army. Even better was a case with two defendants who insisted on each having their own lawyers—they always got at cross-purposes and marred their case.

[19] *The UPC is to have a fee system based on the value of the case. I still do not understand how this works because it is in reality impossible to value an injunction or the future market for a patented product. However, as in Germany now (where the busy* Länder *courts make a*

Can the costs of the perfect court be brought down to a level which all can afford? Obviously not—unless the state pays for everyone. There will always be some who are too poor to litigate. Nor do I think it necessarily a good idea that costs are too low. Patent litigation is not in itself a Good Thing. Far from it. It is a Necessary Evil. Even if there were no fees at all the parties would have to put time and effort into their cases—all of which are part of the costs of industry. So I think a reasonable cost is actually important to the system. You need an entry fee so that people only litigate when a matter is sufficiently important. On the other hand you must not have an entry fee which is so high that only the very wealthy can afford it.

I would make one other observation: it is important, whatever the level of costs, that there are good mechanisms for encouraging settlement of cases. The recent growth of alternative dispute resolution (ADR) in the common law countries has yet to be followed by a similar pattern on the Continent (save where ADR is used to settle worldwide litigation). My perfect court will have associated with it an ADR scheme. It would not be compulsory[20] as in some US States, but it would be encouraged.

REQUIREMENT 3—CAPACITY TO DEAL WITH HIGHLY COMPLEX ISSUES

This is a major problem. One can put aside obviously silly ideas—such as a jury of housewives, vacuum-cleaner salesmen etc.[21] Seriously,

lot of money out of fees) I suppose some sort of measure will emerge—rather like tables of values for injuries in personal injury cases. There is a legal 'value' for a lost eye, even though in reality there is none.

[20] Most studies show that compulsory ADR does not work—and in any event there are some sorts of case (eg those of counterfeit goods) which are really about invoking the coercive power of a court order rather than resolving a dispute. It is truly said that you can take a horse to water but you can't make him drink.

[21] The rest of the world is astonished by the US system. Because (for historical and constitutional reasons) they have jury trial is no reason for anyone else to do so. It is disappointing to learn that the Japanese are considering it. *Fortunately that idea seems to have been dropped.* And, in the US, systems have had to be devised to deal with the problems of irrational jury verdicts—the 'judgment notwithstanding verdict' and the CAFC itself are essential safeguards. *Others are the Markman hearing (claim construction a matter of law and so for the judge), the many applications for summary judgment (again for the judge), the new inter partes review system which can annul or restrict a patent without a jury and perhaps other devices).* One is reminded of the White Knight in *Alice*—'But I was thinking of a plan to dye one's whiskers green, and always use so large a fan that they could not be seen'. The jury system is the green whiskers and the judgment, notwithstanding verdict and the CAFC *plus the other devices*, are the fan.

how is the court to understand the case? Broadly there are two approaches on offer: party experts or court-appointed experts. It is no good, as the European Commission appeared to think, expecting the court to be able to provide its own expertise.[22] Party experts have two problems: potential bias and cost. My friend Dieter Braendle[23] cynically says of party experts 'They always lie'. On the other hand, court-appointed experts are all too apt to answer questions of their own choosing, fail to report in time, or otherwise go wrong. And in reality the court-appointed expert will often become, in reality,[24] the judge, with no opportunity for either side even to address him.

Dieter is both right and wrong about bias. If the expert thinks he can 'get away with it' I agree that there is a real risk of bias. But if he is told that his answers will be fiercely tested by hostile questioning from the other side he is likely to be careful before giving a biased opinion. One of the great advantages of cross-examination of an expert witness is that the charlatan will be exposed. The price is cost—particularly if the court does not exert tight control over time.

So what does my ideal court do? Well I think it has to go for a mixture. If what is at stake is a lot, then I would allow party experts. If not then I would often go for a court expert.[25] But I would make them meet to agree what they can and what they cannot. And I would make them focus on why they disagree.[26] They must give their reasons. As I often said, what matters is not so much the opinion, but the reasons on which it is based. My ideal court will have rules telling experts how to construct their reports. And it will make sure they answer the question(s) that matter. It will also have rules requiring the parties to set out what they say the common general knowledge of the skilled man is.

[22] The suggestion of different panels, one for engineering, one for electronics, one for chemistry etc is a nonsense. Technology is much too specialist for this sort of approach. All you can expect in a judge is some broad technical knowledge, coming perhaps from an original science degree coupled with experience in patent law for some time. *The UPC will have technical judges, but it is not envisaged that they will provide the specialised knowledge of the particular subject-matter of the patent. They will largely be patent attorneys and will be able to understand the evidence more readily and help the legal judges understand the technical aspects of the case. I am optimistic that this will work well.*

[23] Of the Zurich Commercial court. *Now Chief Judge of the Swiss Federal Patent Court.*

[24] For what else can the court do but follow him?

[25] To be appointed, where possible, by agreement of the parties. What is no good is expecting the court to find an expert—for many fields a judge would not have the first idea as to where to go.

[26] We have started doing this in England—not so much in patent as in other cases. It often works and the whole case settles. There is room for more use of this in patent cases.

REQUIREMENT 4—ACCESSIBILITY TO SMEs

This is all bound up with cost. So there is little to add. But one thing I would say is the court ought not to cheapen its procedures so much that the justice becomes rough and ready. If you do, then you will sacrifice predictability. And a court where anything can happen is a recipe for encouraging litigation of weak cases.[27] Making the court so simple and cheap and 'friendly' to SMEs carries with it the danger of making their life a misery. Remember they are often defendants.

REQUIREMENT 5—LANGUAGE

This one is near intractable. What is obviously silly is to have rigid rules about this. The Commission's (or politicians') idea that the defendant should be sued in his own language was clearly a non-starter. It merely showed lack of contact with the real world. I think the only sensible thing is for this court to have its own control over the language(s) to be used.[28] Some cases could be worked entirely in English. Others entirely in German or French. Sometimes a mixture of language would be necessary. What is essential is that the trial is fair to all sides—and language(s) should be chosen on that basis by the court itself.[29] In that way preconceived governmental prejudices can be put on one side.

One other word: much of patent law actually depends on precision of language. Translation always carries with it the danger of blurring meaning—especially when the result of routine work. I think it would be important that there is only one official document to work from—the language of the patent itself.[30]

[27] Any practising lawyer knows the rule: if you have a good case try to find a solid, sound, predictable court; if your case is weak, try to find a judge who won't see through it. *I suspect the unpredictability of juries is one of the reasons (there are others) why 'troll' litigation is so much more common in the US than anywhere else in the world.*

[28] *The politicians stupidly tried to legislate for this, putting rules about language in the difficult-to-change UPC Agreement itself (Art 49) It looks like you have to start the proceedings in the language of a local division (it might be possible for parties to agree a language in advance, but not all parties co-operate—not surprising since they are having a legal war. It is possible by consent to change to the language of the patent. There is provision for an application by one side for the case to be heard in the language of the patent, but the procedure is daft. You don't go to the court deciding the case but to the President of the Court of First Instance. The language provisions may prove a significant factor in increasing legal costs and delay.*

[29] When the parties cannot agree—though I suspect they often would.

[30] *That will not always be the case. One hopes that if and when the court gets going in practice most if not all cases will be in the international language called English.*

REQUIREMENTS 6 AND 7—PREDICTABILITY AND EXPERIENCED JUDGES

I have already touched on this. Better than litigation is none. It is better that people know where they stand without having to go to court. It is for that reason (though I stray slightly outside my subject) that I welcome Art 69 of the EPC and its Protocol as interpreted by the House of Lords in *Kirin-Amgen*.[31] The plain fact is that a doctrine of equivalents is bound to be uncertain—it involves the court finding infringement even though the defendant is outside the claim as properly read in context—a sort of sympathy vote.

How then is predictability to be achieved? Well it involves the use of experienced judges—and judges who meet frequently enough to discuss the law and form a common approach.[32] So requirement 6 runs hand-in-hand with the next. Clearly there will have to be a number of judges—it would be a mistake to let them sit in the same panels. They would have to mix and change panels as much as is practicable—otherwise there would be a real risk of different approaches developing.[33]

Who should be eligible to be a judge? Well in an ideal world I think the judges should be chosen from the best of the practising lawyers. This is because it is practice which brings you close to clients—both plaintiffs and defendants. This gives you an understanding of the needs of industry—of the dangers of courts which are 'pro-patentee' as well as those which are 'anti-patentee'. I do not rule out judges from a career judiciary[34] but it is my experience talking to both lawyers and judges from France and Germany that both would welcome the possibility of experienced lawyers going on the Bench.[35]

What about appeal judges? Does this court need a separate group? I think not. In Australia the Federal Court operates perfectly satisfactorily using the same judges for first instance and appeal—one sits at first instance and three others on appeal. I think that is what is needed for my perfect patent court.[36]

[31] *Kirin-Amgen Inc & Ors v Hoechst Marion Roussel Ltd & Ors* [2004] UKHL 46.

[32] The EPO biennual conference has done much for this—but a real court would need much more. The German Richterakademie is the sort of thing needed—perhaps for Europe the patent judges of the perfect court would have a school in Venice or Prague.

[33] Again the politicians overlook this sort of thing—proposals for different panels in different places will not do.

[34] Far from it—there are some first-class judges in France and Germany, for instance.

[35] I can name a number of lawyers in France and Germany who should be judges!

[36] *I never could persuade anyone about this one. No one would even look at it—but then there was a general failure to look around the world at other federal systems.*

Who should appoint the judges? Well there is a real danger if it is left to politicians—the court could be a parking place for failed politicians or people to whom a favour was owed. We do not want any of that. So I think it will have to be an independent appointments board. On that should sit representatives of industry as well as of governments—people with real reputations and stature are needed for this perfect court.[37]

REQUIREMENT 8—FAIR PROCEDURES

This is perhaps self-evident. But it is not self-evident what the procedures should be. I have already commented on speed. I do not think cross-examination should be as of right, though the threat of it should always be there as an inducement to truth.

Discovery should be possible but only for cases that really need it. As much should be done on paper as possible—but there remains a real need for a hearing of the main case which is more than derisory.[38] The rules of the court should not be too prescriptive—and the judges should be in command of the procedure for the case, always driving it forward.[39]

REQUIREMENT 9—ACCESSIBILITY

It is self-evident that the perfect court should be readily accessible. It follows as night follows day that where possible it should be close to the parties. Of course there will be cases where this is not possible (eg a South African party suing a Finn). Flexibility is what is needed.

[37] *We haven't got that—but at least we haven't got appointment by politicians (unlike the CJEU, which has a ludicrous system of appointment—at least four of the judges are ex-politicians and only a minor proportion have had real experience either as judges or lawyers. The actual system is yet to be settled in detail. The politicians have done their best to mess things up providing for an unwieldy appointing body with a member from every state even though there is no requirement for every Member State to have a judge. I hope sense will see the appointing body acting on a recommendation of a small sub-committee. What matters is the quality of the court for that is what matters to European industry, not petty national interests.*

[38] A lot can be done in a defined short time as anyone who has appeared before the ECJ will know. I used to appear for the UK government in quite a few cases some time ago (25 years, actually!). We said a lot in the time allowed for a government (20 minutes). More would be needed for a patent case, but ideally hearings of a day or so would be about rights unless the technology is very high or there was some other complication. *That is the aim of the UPC Rules.*

[39] A notion completely absent, for instance, in the EPO.

A single seat will not do—though as a practical matter there will have to be a main HQ. This should be in somewhere accessible. The current European model is, not to put too fine a point on it, daft.[40] If this perfect court is European its seat will be in one of the great European capitals[41] but it will be able to take hearings anywhere. And it will make enormous use of modern technology—electronic filing and video hearings (particularly for short matters) should be the norm.

REQUIREMENT 10—SPEEDY INTERIM RELIEF

There are some cases which need this. How much this is needed actually depends on other things too—particularly how quickly a full trial on the merits could be heard. If the latter can be achieved in a year or less (as I think should be the norm) then the need for speedy interim relief is less than if it takes years to get to trial. Some say this does not matter because cases very often settle if an interim injunction is granted. That is true—but not necessarily for good reasons: an injuncted defendant may not find it worthwhile to go to a full trial, even if he has good prospects of success.

Speedy relief should, however, be possible in days, or even, in a particularly urgent case, hours.[42] A particular problem in patent cases is that it is often not possible to form a reasonable estimate of who is likely to win the main trial. This may be because the technology is high and the court simply cannot get to grips with it in a short time, or because it is difficult to evaluate particular issues. So my perfect court is careful about granting interim relief save in cases where there will be real damage before trial.[43]

[40] Luxembourg is very difficult to get to from most Member States. So also Alicante. These sites show what happens when politicians have too much say. *They've done it again! Luxembourg is the site of the Court of Appeal of the forthcoming UPC—and agreed without even a counter-proposal. I cannot think that anyone in industry or any user is happy with this. It poses a further real difficulty. Many (not merely English) experienced patent judges may not apply for the Court of Appeal if, as it probably does, it involves uprooting the family and living there.*

[41] Personally, I prefer Paris. *At least the seat of the Central Division will be there—forming a balance between Germany and the UK which will be good for Europe. But I loathe the politicians' decision that the first President must be French, not because of anything against the French but because this is a European court which should be free from petty nationality rules. The judges should have had the complete choice of first President.*

[42] Necessarily for only a holding period, eg where an infringing machine is about to leave the jurisdiction.

[43] eg the collapse of the market price for a pharmaceutical.

REQUIREMENT 11—READY ENFORCEMENT OF ORDERS

This is also self-evident. But courts alone cannot, in the ultimate analysis, actually single-handedly enforce their orders. For that, policemen or access to bank accounts and so on is necessary—in short, other arms of the 'state' are likely to be involved. This perfect court must mesh seamlessly with those—and if it is court for several states, the machinery must be there. It is all too easy to see how paperwork could get in the way.

CONCLUSION

Well, this rough canter over the requirements for the perfect court shows how hard the problem is. All we can really do is to reach a compromise—emphasising some requirements at the expense of others. Most important of all in reaching any such compromise is to remember that the court is for industry—not for the judges or lawyers or patent agents or experts. Just as plumbers and drains engineers are important for our daily living environment, so this court and all who operate in it would be important for industry and innovation. It and those who work in it should be the servants, not the masters.

POSTSCRIPT

This was in 2005, shortly before the European Commission became engaged again in the project. It had done so in 1975 and 1989, formulating the Community Patent Convention and its revision—so badly received by users that neither came into force. It is worth recounting a little history from my perspective.

In 1998, at the Madrid European Patent Judges' Symposium, the judges discussed the idea of a common court for litigating parallel European patents. The then President of the Bundespatentgericht, the visionary Antje Sedemund-Treiber, proposed that we form what she called 'The Madrid Group' to advance the idea of a European patent court. In the event we were able to do little collective work (I have put those documents I have about it in the IP Library at the Institute of Advanced Legal Studies) but it was not easy—not least because not all judges had email then! Besides, the next year the EPO became involved and European patent litigators joined in. I went, with a Lord Chancellor's Department official, to an early discussion about the proposal in Berne (note the Swiss were involved—the young Swiss Stefan Luginbühl, now at the EPO, was an enthusiastic supporter and has written an excellent book on the story). The proposal became called the 'European Patent Litigation Agreement' (EPLA). Work was supported by the EPO and draft rules and a draft Protocol were in being by the early 2000s. The idea was simple: a coalition of the willing. The willing countries (whether of the EU or not) would in effect pool their patent courts so that all the parallel patents could be litigated in one go. There was no proposal to create a Unitary patent. The solution proposed was to the actual real problem—unnecessary and possibly conflicting national decisions.

The EPLA proposal was frustrated. This is not the place to set out the detail. Professor Arnull and I set out some of it in a paper called 'European patent litigation: out of the impasse' [2007] European Intellectual Property Review 1*. Here it suffices to say that the European Parliament's legal service gave an opinion on 1 February 2007 to the effect Member States were not entitled to enter into the EPLA. It went too far in saying it could not be done at all (after all the ECJ approved the principle in the first Spanish challenge)—though in retrospect I can see that because EU law had started intruding on patent law (eg the Enforcement Directive), albeit at the edges, you could not have a court with non-EU judges. I still think the EPLA proposal was viable for EU-only states. I regret that its basic structure was not simply carried into an only-EU-Member-State EPLA. The EPLA was a great deal more practical, cheaper and less prone to forum shopping than the future UPC we will now have.*

After the demise of the EPLA the Commission became involved. Margot Frölinger, one of the best civil servants I have met, was given the job. But with ridiculously meagre resources. Here was a project of creating the first Federal Court of Europe—a mighty enterprise. Courts need a structure, a system of judge appointment, pay and conditions, rules of procedure, a bureaucracy, an IT system and so on. Margot was given two assistants from within the Commission and someone from the EPO and hardly any money. No lawyer was involved apart from herself. I contrast that now with the huge amount of money that must be being spent on the Commission's review of the Biotech Directive. I am one of a large expert panel of about 30 advising the Commission. We are about to have our ninth meeting in less than two years with more to come. They must have spent at least three times more on this minor (compared with the whole) aspect of the patent system. Towards the end of the Commission consultation on the patent court we had got to the point when the Commission would not even pay for meals.

At the very outset of the Commission involvement, Margot visited me in the Royal Courts of Justice in June 2007. Before she came I set out in an email my 'red lines'. This is the text:

1. *There must be at least one experienced judge on the panel at first instance.*
2. *The Court must have power to revoke a patent—we can never get back to the days when you can rely upon patent office examination reliably to reject unworthy applications.*
3. *The language regime should be tailored for the case. If Nokia sue Erikson they do it in English; if two small Italians sue, then things will have to be in Italian. Such a system will keep costs down and be more acceptable to users.*
4. *There should be no permanent panels. So local presence (which is important) does not mean a fixed panel—otherwise there will be forum shopping.*
5. *The Court should run with an electronic dossier and video linking wherever possible.*
6. *The procedure should be à la Venice 2—with the judges having as much control over the rules as possible. We cannot have an EPO-type system with cases taking up to 15 years.*
7. *Judges must be borrowed from the national courts to start with.*
8. *The ECJ must not be allowed to rule even on questions of patent law. If it does (a) delays will be introduced but (b) more significantly, uncertainty will follow. The ECJ is not really designed for commercial disputes. Interestingly that was the first thing Antje Sedemund-Treiber said to me at the conference. A wise woman.*
9. *Scientific advice/input. This is a real problem. For many important patents are in fields of technology where the number of real experts are few. (I had one recently about computer modelling the design of rock drill bits—we sat with a scientific advisor—the British Patent Office said it had no one who really understood the stuff). I favour scientific advisors who do not have a vote picked on a more or less ad hoc basis—simple cases will need none, the parties can generally be made to agree an advisor.*
10. *Appeal court—based not in Luxembourg—I have always favoured Paris.*

We sort of have (1) but the politicians' notion that you can be 'experienced' by a week or so training in Budapest is fiction and a danger to the system. The real problem is that the legal judge of the court will be on his or her own. It is not like the German system where the young ones learn from their seniors. We have to hope that the technical judges—who will largely be patent attorneys—will in fact know enough patent law. We have (2) but not really (3) though in the real world it may turn out to be so—see above. We do not have (4), which I regret hugely—the whole structure of divisions is bound to promote forum shopping, different practices and so on. It was unnecessary and yet may dominate the litigation system. We are not yet sure about (5) but it looks possible. The UK government, which has been given the job of sorting this, did not do the obviously sensible thing, namely to go round the world looking at other systems already in use (USA, including different States, Canada and Australia were particular places to look at because they are for big places and for essentially federal systems). We do have (6)—and this may be the saving grace—mainly thanks to Kevin Mooney and his Committee who are the only people to have put sustained, consistent and hard work into the project. We have (7)—really important. As to (8) it is not entirely clear. Already the EU has stepped in with its own rules about patentability of biotech inventions, which has led to the stupid, anti-human rights decision of the CJEU in Brüstle*—the Court seems incapable of grasping the elementary concept of what a patent claim is for and how it is to be interpreted, see also its Supplementary Protection Certificate (SPC) decision in* HGS v Lilly, *Case C-493/12. There remains a danger that the Court will use TRIPS to assert a power to rule on substantive patent law, bypassing the EPC—see* Daichi Sankyo v DEMO, *Case C-414/1. (9) I think the solution of technical judges with a legal judge may work—provided the Court really pays attention to party experts too. The danger is that the technical judges may think they know more than they really do—being an experienced patent attorney or patent lawyer does not make you a true expert, all it does is to equip the court to understand true experts. Finally as to (10) I foresaw the danger of Luxembourg back then in 2007 but no amount of practical common sense could stop it.*

Margot asked me to suggest names for a committee of judges and industry experts to help on the project. I provided some, many of whom ended up on her committee. We met from time to time in the Cassis de Dijon *room in the Commission building on the rue de Spa in Brussels. All went well but rather slowly for some time—with such scant resources what would you expect? Presidencies came and went. By July 2009 a proposal for the main agreement—an international patent court outside the EU structure—was thought sufficient for the Council and Commission to send to the Court of Justice for an opinion as to its lawfulness. Personally I thought it was probably premature—not enough detail existed—but in the event the Court thought otherwise by an opinion of March 2011 (Opinion 1/09). On the main point the ECJ said that the proposal was not compatible with the EU Treaties—because the Court would include non-EU states. Quite obvious in retrospect.*

Thereafter the proposal was amended. Spain and Italy said they would not join. The proposed scheme then became one of enhanced co-operation. That had a very damaging effect for two reasons: first it meant that it was no longer an EU scheme and did not qualify for EU funding. The result is that the Court is very likely to be strapped for cash. In its early years it will have to be funded by participating national governments but there are signs that some are not paying up or are doing so slowly. Secondly, it meant there could no longer be formal Commission involvement in preparations for the Court. In the end it is being put together by a large amount of goodwill and free input (particularly by Kevin's team).

For reasons that completely defy common sense the politicians then became very excited by the project even though it was obviously not ready. Like a bus with no brakes and wonky steering it rushed along wildly. Consultation with users and judges was lost or ignored. We (judges and lawyers) had to fight to keep the definition of infringement (Arts 6–8) out of the Unitary Patent proposal and confine it to the international agreement (otherwise the industry-opposed CJEU involvement in patents would come about). At one point an MEP called Berhard Rapkay, Chairman of the Legal Affairs Committee of the European Parliament, said, 'You know I am something of a legal layman—I am happy to listen to legal experts, but the point is that there are all sorts of differing legal viewpoints but at the end of the day our job is to take a political decision.' What, one asks, is a non-lawyer doing chairing the Legal Affairs Committee? And what kind of 'political decision' was sensible when the opinions of users, judges and practitioners were virtually unanimously against it? And why was it necessary to make any decision at all when so much was not ready? In the event it took the final Ministers' meeting to keep Arts 6–8 out of the Regulation. But the final structure is far from ideal.

Will it work people ask? That is the wrong question. Of course it will work—all legal systems work one way or another—you have little choice. The real questions are will it work well? Will it be better than the system we now have? As to that the position is, I am afraid, doubtful. There are good bits and bad bits.

Main Bad Bits

1. *The split structure of local divisions and a central division was never asked for by anybody. It was devised by the Polish Presidency (it is ironic that Poland will not be participating in the enhanced co-operation). It poses real threats by way of forum shopping and delays. The Rules Committee has done its best to deal with the worst bits. For instance patentees cannot ask for bifurcation until the pleadings are in, by which time it is unlikely that a local division will send off half the case to central on the basis that it itself is not up to the job. Moreover even if bifurcated there is a rule that the two courts should try to reach a result at the same time.*
2. *The split structure with divisions will not help the judges to form a cohesive and predictable whole. One of the great advantages of the English and Welsh Court of Appeal system is that we do not sit in permanent panels but rotate. The continental practice of permanent panels* (cf *the General Court, the Alicante Boards and, largely, the EPO Boards of Appeal) surely leads to divisions. To rotate you need a system for changing. The court should have one.*
3. *The costs are unknown but likely to be high—much to the disadvantage of SMEs.*
4. *The language rules are unnecessarily complex leading to increased costs and delay.*
5. *Luxembourg!*

Main Good Bits

1. *Rules of Procedure. A small group of judges and practitioners (from France, Switzerland, Germany, Italy, Holland, Sweden. Austria and Portugal) gathered together for three days before the*

second San Servolo[44] meeting of November 2006. Our purpose was to formulate principles of procedure for a future patent court. The Venice II principles were accepted by all at the full meeting. They have formed the basis of the new rules and have almost wholly been untouched by politicians. They could well work better than anywhere else in the world. It is vital the judges keep proper control—and that big cases really are treated differently from small ones. Big cases more English style, little ones more German style.

2. *The judges: As Chairman of the Advisory Committee on selection and training of judges I am happy to say that we are spoilt for choice and have the best patent judges of Europe applying. If anyone can make this disjointed system work it is going to be the judges. Keep your fingers crossed!*

What patenting strategy should people follow? There is no short answer. It is obvious to all but the Rapkays of this world that things are much more complex than they were before. Complexity's joined-at-the-body companion, much greater time and cost, is with us in force. It will be necessary to increase the patenting budget for the best patenting strategy. European patent attorneys and lawyers have a rosy future.

The formal options are:

1. *Purely national applications. These result in national patents with only national protection and to be litigated in national courts.*
2. *'Classical' European applications, which will result in a bundle of parallel national patents but which are to be litigated together in the new UPC with the possibility of (a) central revocation (which some see as a disadvantage, (b) near-EU-wide injunctions and (c) good prospect of forum shopping. You can also hedge your bets by 'opting out' for the present, but it may come at a fee.*
3. *Unitary Patent—for nearly the whole of the EU. This will cost—we do not know how much but the betting is about the cost of five parallel classical patents.*

[44] *The rather spartan island in the middle of the Venice lagoon where the Venice meetings take place. Lennie Hoffmann called it 'Alcatraz'. Once it was a lunatic asylum—some say appropriate for patent lawyers and judges but I could not possibly comment.*

These are not all incompatible with each other—particularly at the application stage, which can (and often does) take a long time in the EPO. You can begin by mixing and matching! If you have an invention which you expect will both be big and early to market with the prospect of early infringers, then it will probably make sense to go for both for national patents and in the EPO.[45] *Although there is a rule that you cannot simultaneously have a European patent (or Unitary Patent) for the same invention, it does not come into play until the second of the two is granted. That will inevitably be by the ponderous EPO. Also you can play around with the 'same invention' rule, breaking up your invention into lots of sub-inventions thereby probably getting protection by national patents, classical patents and even Unitary Patents all at the same time. And because national Patent Offices (particularly the UK) will be much faster, if you include the national patent option you will be able to go after the infringer early on.*

As you can see, patenting in Europe is up there with three- (or perhaps n-) dimensional chess. No doubt when it becomes apparent that the system is more expensive and complex than before, the politicians will try to blame the lawyers—but it is the lawyers' job to serve his client and if it serves the client's purpose the tools by the politicians must be used.

[45] *The UK Intellectual Property Office is particularly fast—my last case at the Bar involved this tactic. The case was over in the Court of Appeal before the EPO had finished the grant process.*

26

*To Bifurcate or Not to Bifurcate: That is the Question**

I STARTED WRITING this flying from Irkutsk to Moscow on my way back from an IP conference of the Supreme Court of Russia. President Lutz went too. Such a thing could not have happened in the world where I started the practice of IP law in 1967. IP as we know it hardly existed in Russia. And in the West each country did its own IP thing, near oblivious of what was going on anywhere else. How things have changed. No country is an IP island any more.[1] For Europe that has been and will increasingly be, wholly beneficial.[2] For IP law can no longer be a purely national matter—the demands of a common market require that there be common IP laws across the market. And those laws and the procedures enabling their enforcement must be fashioned so as to serve the needs of commerce and industry—not the private interests of lawyers or the ingrained ways of judges. Lawyers and judges are, and should be regarded as, the servants not the masters.

It is with that in mind that I approach my subject: one that has been rather divisive on the long, road towards a European Patent Court. Europe[3] is split between those countries which treat the issues of patent infringement and patent validity in quite distinct and separate

* *First published for the 50th Birthday of the Bundespatentgericht (Hermans, 2011) and subsequently by CIPA (June 2012) p 328.*

[1] The expression is taken from the opening words of the poem by John Donne (1572–1621). He particularly had Europe in mind: the opening words are: 'No man is an island entire of itself; every man is a piece of the continent, a part of the main; if a clod be washed away by the sea, Europe is the less'.

[2] Provided the law is not made too uncertain by poor legislation or indeed poor judicial decisions.

[3] Whether one takes the 27 countries of the European Union or the 38 of the European Patent Union.

courts and those which do not. The former I shall call the 'bifurcators'. The majority of European countries are non-bifurcators, but there is a significant and important minority, led by Germany, which is not. My purpose here is to discuss the divergence and what to do about it for a future European Patent Court.

I make my position plain at the outset. I am an anti-bifurcator, albeit tempered with pragmatism. Starting from scratch and with no baggage of history, constitutional law, ingrained ways or vested interests, one would naturally say that a patent dispute should be decided by a single court. Other civil disputes are tried in a single court. No one would say, for instance, that you should have one court for deciding that a contract was validly made and another for deciding whether the contract had been broken.[4] Whilst, because of scientific technicalities, a patent court has to be rather specially constructed, that is no reason for compulsory bifurcation into two separate court systems.

Let us begin at the beginning. Why then is there bifurcation in Germany? Was it because at some point the legislators decided that bifurcation was the best way to deal with patent disputes? I believe the answer is a firm no. It happened, and is so, for quite different reasons. I am no expert on the German Constitution. My limited understanding goes back to what I can remember from a brilliant lecture given on 12 June 1974 by the then President of the Bundespatentgericht, Dr Ernst Pakuscher. It was given to a meeting of the Chartered Institute of Patent Agents. My head of chambers, Thomas Blanco White QC, said I should go along because it would do me good. He was right. In the space of an hour Dr Pakuscher not only described the history and structure of his court and of the court system generally but also many other aspects of the German system—including the then competing theories for determining the scope of patent protection.[5] I have located a shortened copy of the lecture.[6] It does not contain what I recall was the explanation for bifurcation, a purely jurisdictional matter arising from Germany's federal nature. What I recall was simply this: that the grant of a patent was a matter for the nation, a federal matter, whereas infringement of patent was a

[4] *Still less deciding whether a contract was broken before deciding whether there was one.*

[5] Dreiteilungslehre and Zweiteilungslehre. With Art 69 and its Protocol these have long gone—though some might say there are vestiges of one or the other in the still extant, but in practice very limited in scope, notion that despite the fact that Art 69 says the scope of protection is determined by the claims as interpreted by the description and drawings, that scope can extend beyond the meaning of the claim by virtue of a 'doctrine of equivalents'.

[6] CIPA, November 1974, p, 35.

civil wrong and civil wrongs were tried in the courts of the individual *Länder*. I hope I have got that basically right. Certainly none of my many German friends have ever told me that bifurcation was *devised* as the best way to litigate patent disputes.

It does not follow that because bifurcation was not devised as the best way to litigate patent disputes it is not in fact the best. And it is certainly perceived by many in Germany as being very satisfactory. But there are German dissentients, whereas I have never heard of any judge or lawyer from a non-bifurcating country speak in favour of bifurcation. The German dissentients I have in mind in particular are Professor Josef Straus who has told me directly that he is not a bifurcator,[7] and President Pakuscher. Here is what he said in that 1974 lecture:

> [T]he extension of the jurisdiction of the FPC ['Federal Patent Court'] to a comprehensive court for patent litigation seems desirable. As first step, therefore, it might suffice to extend the jurisdiction of the FPC by giving it power to decide upon appeals in infringement cases. At the same time the procedural split of competence between nullity and infringement should be abolished by admitting the counterclaim of nullity of the patent in an infringement suit.

These days, however, the majority German opinion is clearly in favour of bifurcation. President Lutz, in what I believe to be only the second lecture ever given in the UK[8] since the foundation of the Court whose 50th birthday we now celebrate, gave three reasons in its favour:

> **First argument:**
>
> — The questions of infringement are freed from the burden of the frequently very difficult technical questions related to the examination of the validity of the patent, especially the questions of novelty and inventive step.
> — These questions can only be answered with the aid of technical expert opinion in most cases.
> — The consultation of a technical expert opinion in civil proceedings however makes the civil proceedings much longer and much more expensive.
> — We can avoid this in Germany in most cases because of our bifurcation system.

[7] I asked whether he had written on the subject. Sadly the answer is no. A pity because his wisdom is needed on this subject.

[8] The Sir Hugh Laddie lecture given on 15 June 2010 at University College London.

Second argument:

— The question of the validity of the patent is ruled on centrally for all of Germany by one court, namely the Federal Patent Court.
— The judges at the Federal Patent Court are specialised in ruling on questions of the patentability of an invention.
— And the technical expertise is also available among the judges.
— The Federal Patent Court rules on nullity suits in a configuration of five judges, three of whom are so-called technical judges.
— The technical judges have special expertise in the technical field to which the patent relates.
— For this reason, it is possible in most cases to rule on the nullity suit very quickly without consulting an external expert opinion.
— Roughly 60 technical judges work at the Federal Patent Court who are experts in the fields of mechanical engineering, electrical engineering or chemistry.
— The technical judges are assigned to the nullity proceedings in whose technical sphere they have particular expertise.
— The consultation of an external expert is hence only rarely required.
— This makes the proceedings shorter and cheaper.

Third argument:

— Roughly 1,000 patent infringement suits are filed in Germany per year.
— Having said that, only roughly 250 nullity suits are lodged. This means that 75% of infringement suits do not question the validity of the patent, at least not by lodging a nullity suit.
— I dare to presume that the question of the legal validity of the patent would be questioned in nearly all 1,000 cases if we had an integrated system in Germany in which patent infringement proceedings also permitted the question of the validity of the patent to be asserted by an objection or counter-suit to the Regional Court.
— The consequence of this would be that an external expert witness would have to be consulted on the infringement process in almost all 1,000 sets of infringement proceedings.
— This would massively extend the length of the proceedings and vastly increase the costs.
— If however the defendant has to lodge a separate nullity suit, they will think twice as to whether they have adequate arguments for the nullity of the patent in order to file such a suit.
— Experience shows that the infringer only questions the validity of the patent by means of a suit in one set of proceedings out of four.
— I consider this to be a massive reduction in the burden of the infringement proceedings and of the courts overall.

I do not agree with any of these reasons!

Start with the first. It is based on a false premise: that issues of infringement are essentially not technical and do not need considerable expertise whereas issues of validity are. That is not right. The real distinction is between high- and low-technology cases. Thus the subject matter of some patents is technically easy (the Epilady patent is a paradigm example) and that of others technically very difficult, for instance many genetic engineering patents, most cellular phone patents and so on.[9] Where the subject matter is technically easy, the issues of infringement and validity can be resolved by no or very little technical input. Where the subject matter is technically difficult a mere lawyer judge will need technical assistance, whether the issue is infringement or validity or both.

I pause here to say a defendant may essentially take one of three positions—that what he does is outside the scope of protection, that what he does falls within the scope of protection but the patent is invalid, or a mixture of the two, namely that if the scope of protection is wide enough to cover what he does, then the patent is invalid. Experience (or at least my experience) shows that all three types of defence are common.

I would add a word about patent validity. I note that President Lutz's justifications for bifurcation did not include reliance upon an assertion that granted patents were probably valid. He was right. There was a time when the German office had a very high reputation as an examining office. You only got good inventions past it. That is still by and large true but it would be a mistake these days to have a strong presumption of validity given the enormous pressures on offices. Anecdotally it is said that it is easier to get a patent past the EPO than the German office. In reality a significant proportion of granted patents are invalid. That will continue to be so for the foreseeable future, however much talk or effort goes into 'raising the bar'. Any litigation system must recognise that.

Turning back to the first reason, therefore, since validity is really an issue in most proceedings you do not really cheapen things and avoid the need for expert assistance by bifurcation. What you may do, if you decide infringement first and grant an injunction is to put a defendant at a real commercial disadvantage. Does he carry on with litigation taking the fight to the Bundespatentgericht or does he give

[9] Even the very words used in the claims of such patents require technical education.

up the commercial activity held to infringe? Many a businessman would choose the latter, just as most defendants subject to an interim junction give up and do something else rather than go to a full trial. Moreover, in practice he simply may not be able to sell pending determination of the nullity suit: customers for some kinds of goods will simply stay away when they hear that the infringement court says the patent is infringed.

President Lutz's second reason is really about the virtues of a patent court having technical judges, not a reason for bifurcation. Technical judges would be as competent to handle infringement issues as those of validity, as indeed President Pakuscher recognised all those years ago. Whether having 'technical judges' is always enough is itself open to debate.[10]

The third reason was put more pithily to me and Robert van Peursem[11] (another convinced anti-bifurcator) by our mutual and greatly respected friend Klaus Grabinski.[12] He said, 'It works.' President Lutz puts figures on it. He says in only 25 per cent of the 1,000 cases of alleged patent infringement do defendants bring nullity suits in the Bundespatentgericht. I am not surprised and do not regard this as evidence favouring bifurcation. Firstly one must discount those cases where the defendant wins in the infringement court: few such defendants are concerned about validity after winning. So the proportion where the defendant goes on to challenge validity is greater than one in four. Secondly the figures do not show the reasons why defendants do not pursue a nullity claim. As I have said, there are good commercial reasons why the figures are likely to be as they are.

The question is not so much does it work—of course it does. The real question is whether it works as well as a non-bifurcated system. In that regard it is worth emphasising that even the German courts do not apply 'pure' bifurcation. The infringement court does not simply say to a defendant who says 'but the patent is invalid' 'Go away; it is none of our business.' On the contrary it makes a 'cursory

[10] A science or engineering degree or even a doctorate obtained some time ago hardly makes anyone a real expert in the small corners of real expertise where so many patents lie. I suppose some might regard me, having a degree in science from many, years ago and many years of work in patents with a great range of different fields of technology as qualified to be a 'technical judge'. I do not. I have enough technology to be scientifically numerate—to understand what the real experts are saying—but no more. There is a major difference between a real expert in a subject and an outsider who can, with instruction, get to understand the technology sufficiently for the limited purpose of a patent case.

[11] An eminent patent judge of the District Court of the Hague.

[12] Recently rightly elevated to the Bundesgerichtshof.

examination'[13] of validity and if it thinks there is a good prospect of nullification by the BPG [Bundespatentgericht] it will stay proceedings rather than grant an injunction. This, to my mind, is close to what the courts of most non-bifurcating countries do when asked to grant an interim injunction. They ask who is most likely to win the case at full trial.[14] So the German system implicitly accepts that 'pure' bifurcation is unsatisfactory.

Before I come to any future European system, I should say something about how British courts handle what might be seen as bifurcation issues. For I think it could provide useful guidance for the future. Pragmatism rules. Generally at first instance the judge will decide all the issues before him both of infringement and the various attacks on validity which have been advanced. In that way everything is decided. Of course if the defendant advances too many attacks, he will be put under pressure to say which he thinks are his best.[15] But even at first instance it sometimes makes sense to 'bifurcate'—not in the sense of sending the issue of validity to another court but instead leaving it to be decided by the same court at a later time, if necessary.

A good recent example was Nicholas Pumfrey's last case. Interdigital claimed that 29 of its patents were essential to comply with the 3G standard. Nokia said none of them were. My court decided that this was a real commercial issue fit for the declaratory powers of the court.[16] So Nokia asked Pumfrey J for a declaration that none of the Interdigital patents were essential. That was an issue about the scope of the patents, not their validity. Pumfrey J embarked on the potentially daunting task of comparing the technical 3G standard with each of the main claims of each of the 29 patents.[17] As often happens things narrowed down. Fairly early on Interdigital dropped 21 of the patents. By the time of trial it had dropped another three, leaving Pumfrey J with just four. Two of these were virtually the same,[18] so he had three to deal with. He held, in a judgment given just three

[13] President Lutz's phrase.

[14] My own country has a lesser test imposed by *American Cyanamid v Ethicon* [1975] AC 396. I do not agree with it save where the complexity of the case means you cannot really form a provisional view as to the ultimate winner.

[15] Good advocates appreciate that taking too many points makes their case weaker—the judge is apt to think that the case is being run on the hope that something might work rather than on the basis that the advocate has a killer punch. In addition we have costs sanctions which can be used against parties who take too many points.

[16] *Nokia v Interdigital* [2006] EWCA Civ 1618.

[17] Incidentally itself a task involving considerable technical input—as scope of claim is apt to be with high-tech patents.

[18] A parent and a divisional.

days before he died, only one of these was essential, that is to say you had to fall within its claims to comply with the 3G standard.[19] Whether or not the patent was valid was never in issue and was never decided. Pragmatic bifurcation worked.

On appeal we sometimes 'bifurcate' too. Actually what we do is to prioritise. We had two good examples this year, both about heart valves. In the earlier case[20] the first instance judge had found the patent invalid although it would have been infringed if valid. We decided to consider validity first, for if we upheld the judge the issue about the scope of the patent fell away. And that is what happened. In the later case[21] the position was the other way round. The first instance judge held the patent not infringed but valid. We decided to hear the infringement issue first because the defendant was not concerned to attack validity if he did not infringe. We decided the patent was clearly not infringed and so did not go on to hear the validity appeal.

It is important to realise that what we have been doing is essentially case management and no more. It is trying to find the fastest and most economical way of deciding the whole dispute between the parties. Sometimes that leads us to other short cuts—for instance one can 'bifurcate' validity attacks too. Suppose, for instance, there are conventional obviousness attacks but also an alleged prior public use. It may make sense to try the latter as a preliminary point. I say 'may' because there is always a danger with going for any possible short cut—what we call a 'preliminary point'. It will be decisive of the case if it goes one way. But if it goes the other then time and cost is apt to be lost.

The lesson I suggest for the proposed future European Patent Court is be pragmatic. Under the current proposals[22] a regional court or local division can either decide the whole case for itself or 'bifurcate', sending the validity issue off to the central division. The thinking still seems to be 'infringement easy, validity hard'. A better solution would have been to say 'hard cases for central, easier ones local'.[23] However

[19] *Nokia v Interdigital* [2007] EWHC 3077 (Pat).

[20] *Cook Biotech v Edwards Life Sciences* [2010] EWCA Civ 718.

[21] *Medtronic Core Valve v Edwards Life Sciences* [2010] EWCA Civ 704.

[22] Art 15a(7) of the Draft Agreement on the EU Patent Judiciary 9124/08 allows a regional division to decide the whole case, infringement and validity. Or it can send a counterclaim for infringement to the central division, or, if the parties agree, the whole case to the central division.

[23] Actually I was never in favour of local or regional divisions as such at all. All cases should start centrally (though there could be regional filing offices. Once a claim is filed and a defence entered, then the place of hearing can be decided, taking into account where the parties are and the necessary language requirements. All judges of the Court should be able to sit anywhere.

given the proposal much will turn on how the judges work it out. If one regional or local court 'bifurcates' and others do not, then there could be forum shopping of the worst kind: Europe-wide injunctions might be regularly granted solely on the basis of the infringement issue. If so unjustified patents will prove to be commercially worthwhile to their holders and a detriment to European industry. If, however, the judges decide in the end only to bifurcate where that makes case management sense, then all could be well. In the end I suspect the judges, given the power, will get it right. I certainly hope so. And my belief is that German judges, given the power to decide the whole case, will do just that as often as they can—thereby fulfilling President Pakuscher's ideas many, many years later.

I end by this: concerns about the future should not let us, on this happy occasion, fail to realise just how much the Bundespatentgericht has achieved in its first 50 years. Congratulations and Happy Birthday!

POSTSCRIPT

1. *Whether the new Unified Patent Court should bifurcate or at least have the possibility of bifurcation formed a significant matter of debate during the period of discussions. I believe the German insistence on bifurcation did damage: it was, I think, a major reason for the creation of the flawed basic structure—a central division and regional divisions with the possibility of the latter bifurcating by sending validity to the central division. A pity. And all the more so because most people now think that the German divisions will either not bifurcate or will hardly do so. There are several reasons. First, unlike the mandated position in the German courts, there is no in-built compulsory bifurcation. Secondly, the first point at which bifurcation can be considered is rather a long way down in the procedure—full pleadings on infringement and validity will already be in. Thirdly, it seems rather unlikely that a German division will say, 'Oh validity is a very difficult matter—so much beyond our own skills that we will send it to the specialists in the Central Division.' Fourthly, it will be up to the parties to apply for bifurcation. Any sensible court will realise that a patentee who so asks is really saying, 'I think the defendant is within my claim, but I am worried about validity.' The real worry is that perhaps less skilled divisions may*

bifurcate and grant a pan-European injunction before validity is tested. I hope the judges of the new court will simply regard the possibility of bifurcation as a historical artefact of no practical value, rather like junk DNA.

2. *Bifurcation can and does lead to real injustice—an injunction on an invalid patent. As practised by the German courts an injunction is only withheld if there is a high chance of the patent being held invalid—almost a knock-out. That does not reflect the reality that a very substantial proportion of patents are invalid and inevitably so—see Chapter 27, 'Raising the Bar'. A very important paper, 'Invalid but Infringed',[24] was published recently. So far as I know this is the first time anyone has done a detailed analysis of cases where the German infringement court has granted an injunction on a patent which subsequently is found invalid. The headline is in the abstract: 'Our conservative estimates indicate that 12% of infringement cases in which the patent's validity is challenged produce such 'invalid but infringed' decisions'. The 12 per cent are only the ones you can measure—anyone who has any experience of litigation knows that where a temporary injunction is granted, defendants often do not fight on, not because they have a weak case but because commercially it is not worthwhile.*

   Anecdotally I add this. At the European Patent Office Economic and Scientific Advisory Board meeting on the Unitary Patent and Unitary Patent Court in December 2013 I sat next to Heiner Flocke, President of an association of German SMEs. His association is against bifurcation and he told me that an injunction on a patent later held invalid had cost his company €1 million.

[24] *K Cremers, F Gaessler, D Hahoff and C Helmers, 'Invalid but Infringed', Max Planck Institute for Innovation & Competition Research Paper No 14-14, 13 September 2014.*

27

Raising the Bar: A Mistaken Chimera?[*]

'RAISING THE BAR' has become a fashionable expression. It is in vogue. It conveys the perception that Patent Offices, and most particularly the European Patent Office (EPO), are letting through to grant too many bad patents. And that something ought to be done about it. The analogy is with the high jump. One raises the bar so that fewer competitors can get over. The European Commission is disturbed by the perception of too many defective patents. The pharma inquiry was permeated by it.[1] The Commission's Directorate-General for Internal Market and Services is even inviting tenders for a study to 'propose effective policy solutions for the effective functioning of the future patent system in Europe'. The implication is that there is something seriously wrong at present.

I suggest that the whole notion of 'raising the bar' and trying to do something about it is mistaken. It does not understand or take into account realities. And there is a better and more practical way to deal with the problem of bad patents. And of making the European patent system more effective. No study is needed and I fear it will be not only a waste of resources, but a distraction.

Make no mistake. I accept that a substantial proportion of granted patents are invalid or are at the least too wide in scope. I have no

[*] *First published as a chapter in Marie-Anne Frison-Roche (ed),* Concurrence santé publique, innovation et médicament *(LGDJ, 2010).*

[1] For instance, note the interest in the degree of success in oppositions by generic companies—an interest which shows a depressing failure to understand what success actually means. The inquiry counted as a success any limitation of the patent under opposition. But anyone with only a bit of experience of patents should know that the important question is not whether a patent has been limited, but whether its scope has been limited to exclude that which matters commercially. That question the pharma inquiry never tried to answer. So all its numbers about success in opposition are a waste of time and space.

idea what the proportion is.[2] And I do not see any practical way of finding out to any degree of useful precision. For example, it would be pointless to look at the proportion of patents invalidated or curtailed by court-based revocation proceedings. In my country nearly half the patents litigated have, over recent years, been found invalid. But the reason is not that the court is anti-patent. It is that the court system is quick and reliable. That makes it a forum of choice for a party wishing to attack a patent. An early victory in England is a very useful negotiating weapon—and the evidence used can be of great value if there is a parallel EPO opposition going on and/or litigation elsewhere in the world. So we have quite a lot of pure revocation actions—even more since it was decided that a generic drug company wishing to come on the market with a product falling within a patent which it contended was invalid would most likely have an interim injunction granted against it. After all the generic company could have 'cleared the way' by applying earlier for revocation. Now that is what the do.

Nor is there any value in looking at the results of EPO oppositions. This is so for several reasons. You need to know why people oppose a particular patent; how hard they oppose will be important here. Some, perhaps most, oppositions are probably entered into as a precaution, not necessarily because the opponent has concrete plans which might be affected by the patent.[3] In other cases oppositions are used as bargaining tools. Simply going by the number of oppositions or whole or partial success in them is likely to be misleading.[4]

Having said that I have the subjective impression that a substantial proportion of granted patents are invalid or at least faulty. I would add that I think the proportion has probably stabilised.[5] But at a

[2] My own private guess is that at least 15% of patents are wholly invalid and another 30% have claims which are too wide. I could not substantiate these numbers—they come from a lifetime of experience and nothing else.

[3] That is one of the unintended consequences of the 9-month period from grant within which an opposition must be started. In my country when a similar limitation period was abolished in 1977, the rate of oppositions in the Patent Office almost completely collapsed—precisely the opposite of what the Patent Office expected!

[4] Another thing the Pharma inquiry missed was the commercial nature of oppositions: big pharma v big pharma for patents for new kinds of drug which have not yet reached the market; generic v big pharma for variants of products already on the market. Generic companies in their nature need an established market to enter—a market at the high price previously commanded by a patent. Only then is it in their interest to enter the market, preferably at a price a little short of the previously patent-protected price.

[5] In the first 20 or so years of the EPO it was a common perception that it would accept almost anything. More recently the perception is that it has tightened up somewhat.

higher proportion, and again this is a matter of impression, compared with the old national systems, particularly those of Germany and Holland.[6]

To a naïve outside observer[7] this sounds shocking. So many bad patents? But in reality it is inevitable. Moreover it has long been so. This is what Mr Blanco White (later QC) wrote as long ago as 1947: 'The great majority of patents go through their lives in peace, with nobody really convinced they are valid but nobody prepared to take the risk of infringing them'.[8] Importantly there is a way for dealing with a particular problem caused by a particularly bad or too wide patent. It is upon this that Europe (and indeed other countries—for the 'problem' of invalid or too wide patents is worldwide) needs to concentrate. General solutions, such as 'raising the bar' for all patent applications, are simply impractical and not worth it.

I begin by explaining why a substantial proportion of granted patents will be invalid or at least faulty and why little can be done about it. It comes from the very nature of the patenting process. The applicant drafts and files his specification describing and claiming what he says is his invention. The Office searches, examines and reports to the applicant who then responds. In the nature of things, however good the examiner is—and by and large the EPO searchers and examiners are very good—things may go wrong for a number of reasons:

(1) Searching is never perfect: either something may be missed or relevant prior art simply may not be in any of the databases searched. After all, the prior art consists of anything made available to the public. That includes prior public uses and oral disclosures and a wealth of literature (eg textbooks) not normally searched. Moreover the searched material may be in any language—prior art in Japanese or Chinese (the latter is becoming very important). An EPO searcher processing this application just in the same way as she does others cannot possibly hope to achieve a perfect result every time. The wonder of it is that the searchers do so well—especially since they have limited time for each application.

[6] When I was a young lawyer (in the late '60s and '70s) it was the common view that the German office was tough but that the Dutch office was toughest of all. The trouble was that both offices suffered from large delays—most particularly the Dutch office which often took more than 10 years to reach a decision about grant or not.

[7] Which sadly seems to include some parts of the Commission.

[8] TA Blanco White, *Patents and Registered Designs* (Stevens, 1947).

(2) Next, there are things which a search, however perfect, could not reveal. A recent instance is that of the invalid Servier patent.[9] It claimed what it said was a new crystalline form of a drug, giving a recipe for making it and a means of identifying it. In reality the published prior art method of making the drug would produce this very crystalline form unless you took the special precaution of fast freezing the solution containing the drug. No examiner could have known that. Examiners cannot do experiments to find out the crystalline form of the prior art.

(3) Another thing an examiner cannot deal with readily is insufficiency—the need to disclose the invention clearly enough and completely enough for it to be performed by the person skilled in the art. The specification may set out a recipe for making the product. Just reading the recipe cannot tell you whether it really works. An examiner perforce must take it on trust that it does.

(4) Then there comes the examiner's report. She will in all probability point out defects and aspects of why the original claim is too broad. The patentee will respond and a correspondence ensues. Consider the resources on either side. Although the examiner will be reasonably familiar with the art, she is unlikely to be as skilled in it as the patentee. After all the latter is working directly in the particular field of technology. Moreover the patentee will generally be armed with skilled advisors, who, subject to money, can spend a great deal of effort on getting the patent. The examiner on the other hand has but limited resources and time—and the pressure on examiners continues to grow as the stream of patent applications turns into a torrent.

(5) Nor is it simply a question of relative resources. In the nature of things the examiner is at a disadvantage in another important way. Unless the position is clear, questions of technical fact which are in dispute will have to go unresolved—the applicant gets the benefit of the doubt.

The consequence of all this is simply that a Patent Office can only ever be a coarse filter—all it can do is to perform the very useful task of eliminating clearly bad applications and refusing obviously over-wide claims. Talk of 'raising the bar' can be seen to be impractical if by that is meant asking the Patent Office to do more to reject bad applications.

[9] *Servier v Apotex* [2008] EWCA Civ 445.

How is it to do it? Search harder? Who is to pay? Spend longer on each patent? Who is to pay? And what about the delays and uncertainties which protracted examination will cause? Bear in mind how many patents are processed every year. What exactly is the Office supposed to do that it is not doing now? I actually think the criticism the EPO gets is quite unfair. It can only come from those with no or little understanding of the patent system. By and large it is working well—its problems are those of success and of increasing numbers of applications. Any solution which involves spending more time on each application is bound to be a disaster. There will be more appeals against rejection leading to more delay and more uncertainty. Leave well alone.

What about a different sort of 'raising the bar', namely changing the legal standards of patentability, and particularly that of obviousness? Some may think (the preliminary report of the Pharma inquiry is an example) that patents should only be granted for 'big' inventions. But that is not the system we have in Europe or internationally. And, if we made new, non-obvious but only incremental improvements unpatentable, I think we would do very great damage to the incentives for research.

Does it matter that the Office is a coarse filter? Not really. It has always been so as the quote from Mr Blanco White shows. What can and does matter in some cases, but not others, is the quality of a particular patent. In some industries for instance—those of electronics and mobile telephony—individual patents are seldom of great importance in themselves. So their individual quality seldom matters. Companies file for, own and cross-license patents in bulk. This is not new either—patent pool licensing has gone on probably since the 1930s and was certainly endemic by the 1950s.[10] No one actually goes through all the claims of the masses of patents involved, still less considers the validity of each of them.

In other industries patents are more specific: a product is covered by only one or, at the most, a few patents: pharma is a paradigm instance. Then an individual patent can, and probably will, make all the difference. And when that is so, why then the parties involved can concentrate on that patent. And that is what they do and have always done.

[10] My late brother, an electronics engineer, described to me patent pooling agreements made in the late '50s by his employers, the English General Electric Company, with others. People would turn up to a meeting with piles of patents—you measured the height of the pile to assess a company's strength. The same sort of thing goes on today. *It applies both to pools and standard essential patents.*

So what is to be done about bad patents? The answer is not to worry about most of them. Most patents do not matter commercially so 'raising the bar' for all patents, besides being impossible, would be a largely wasted exercise if it could be done.

Nor would it be right, legal or practical to pick a particular type of patent—pharma patents are currently being suggested—for some sort of special 'raising the bar' treatment. Indeed there is no evidence that there are more bad patents in the field of pharma than in other fields. Nor is there any reason why there should be.

The system should concentrate on the relatively few patents which do matter. Which these are is for the market to decide. What is needed is a better system to enable a party potentially affected by a particular bad patent to get rid of it. An individual party can devote firepower on that patent in a way that the Patent Office could not hope to do. A better and more widespread search can be done. Real experts can be consulted. Experiments can be done. In short a tailored and serious attack can be prepared and launched.

The trouble with the present set-up is where? The courts of all the 27 Member States of the EU or the 34 Member States of the European Patent Convention are not a suitable set of places. Some are fast, some slow. Some are experienced in patents, others not. And it is all ridiculously expensive, quite apart from the inevitable translation costs and delays.

What is needed is the creation of a European patent court staffed by judges who understand the system and particularly who recognise that a patent granted by the Office is no more than a patent which has passed the coarse filter of the Patent Office. There should be no strong presumption of validity.[11] The court must be able to work fast, and particularly to respond with speed to applications for revocation when that matters commercially A patentee whose patent is found invalid after a fight ought to pay all the legal and technical costs of the other side—that will serve as a part deterrent to obtaining or defending bogus monopolies.[12]

[11] The American 'clear and convincing proof' test for invalidation is too pro-patentee given the reality of patent examination. By all accounts, the standard is worse than in Europe, and perhaps understandably so given that many US patent office examiners do not stay in the job very long.

[12] Whether there should be more to pay where the patentee knew or ought to have known that his patent is invalid is a question worthy of debate.

If Europe devotes proper resources to creating and maintaining such a court, there will be little value at best to obtaining, and more especially maintaining, a bogus patent which has a scope of commercial importance. Bogus patents of apparent commercial importance will simply be ignored. And the 'raising the bar' idea will fade away into history as having been an irrelevant distraction. There is no need for the Commission's 'effective policy study'. The answer is staring us all in the face—the court. All resources should be aimed at implementing it.

POSTSCRIPT

The 'effective policy study', which must have cost a lot (why, oh why is how much not publicly available?), duly emerged in March 2011: 'Study on the quality of the patent system in Europe' Tender MARKT/2009/11/D. There was no attempt to test the quality of searching or examination as such. Instead there was an opinion poll which produced little of value. Much of the long report is in newspeak and, just as I predicted, nothing or nothing much has come of it.

The real question now is what will happen when the Unitary Patent Court starts with its revocation jurisdiction available at any time to anyone and a loser-pays rule. Will patentees bother to defend very bad patents? Certainly this Court has a better prospect of dealing with real problems than mere resort to a slogan, 'raising the bar'.

28

Law and the Human Genome Project[*]

MARK TWAIN'S CONNECTICUT Yank went to Warwick Castle, England. There he was magically transported back to the time of King Arthur. He did well. He was made First Minister. He was called Sir Boss. What was the first thing he did in power?

> The very first official thing I did, in my administration—and it was on the very first day of it, too—was to start a patent office; for I knew that a country without a patent office and good patent laws was just a crab, and couldn't travel anyway but sideways or backwards.[1]

Was Sir Boss right? Or, more specifically, was he right for modern-day conditions, for all technologies and for all countries?

I do not propose to answer that question in detail. It is a very big one. All that I can say is that it does seem inherently unlikely that 'One size fits all' is a correct analysis of the benefits of patents (or other IP rights, for that matter) for all peoples everywhere. Certainly that was not the view of many now-advanced industrial countries at earlier stages of their development. Let me give just two examples:

(a) In my country, one of the first to have a patent system, you could get a patent for stealing ideas from foreigners and bringing them into the Realm for the first time. The first recorded British patent

* *Delivered at Washington University, Missouri, Colloquium April 2002 and published as a chapter in F Scott Kieff (ed),* Perspectives on Properties of The Human Genome Project *(Elsevier, 2003) 449–58.*

[1] I have always wanted to use this quote in a lecture. How fortunate to be able to do so on the banks of the Mississippi—it was from the call of the men who measured the depth of the river for the pilots that Mr Clemens took his nom-de-plume. 'Mark Twain' meant that the depth was 2 fathoms—dangerously close to the bottom.

for an invention was indeed for that—it was granted in 1449 to John of Uthnam, a Dutchman who had special techniques for making stained glass windows. He was given a monopoly, plus tax breaks, in return for which he had to do the stained glass windows for Eton College and a Cambridge College. He also had to train apprentices in the new techniques:

> and because the said art has never been used in England and John intends to instruct divers lieges of the king in many other arts never used in the realm beside the said art of making glass, the king retains him therefor for life at his wages and fees and grants that no liege of the King learned in such arts shall use them for a term of twenty years against the will and assent of John, under a penalty of £200, whereof two parts shall be rendered to the king and one part to John, any liege who cannot levy that sum to suffer imprisonment without delivery save by the king's special command.

(b) In your country you refused to accord copyright to foreign authors unless their works were first published in the US. In practice for the whole of the nineteenth century and much of the twentieth, your country was a world centre of piracy. An English judge put it this way in 1880:

> Persons in the position of the defendants, that is of agents for an American publisher, must be taken to know that Americans are in the habit of printing and exporting piratical works and they must therefore know that they import books from America at the risk of their containing what is piratical and are thus committing an unlawful act and of being liable to be sued without notice.[2]

In those early days national interests—and particularly the interest in encouraging national industry—prevailed over international equality. The growth of an international system, commencing with the great Treaty of Paris in 1883, began to change things. But it did so slowly. National interests still prevailed. For instance in many countries failure to exploit a patented invention by local manufacture was a ground for an exclusive licence. TRIPS has largely changed that. But no one should underestimate the resentment it causes in under-developed and developing countries. I have had the benefit of attending two WIPO [World Intellectual Property Organization] seminars, one in Egypt for Arab nations in 1996 and, most recently, this year, in India

[2] *Per* Sir George Jessel MR (1880) 15 Ch D 501.

for judges from Asia. The common complaints were two-fold: that TRIPS would destroy local pharmaceutical industries and would keep the price of medicines beyond the reach of the people. Make no mistake, these are complaints which not only have force, but also are deep seated. They cannot be ignored. They cannot be answered by words like 'property'. Nor can they be answered by vague promises of economic benefit. If you ask how Westerners would react if the boot were on the other foot, you may understand better. Look how fast people in the US reacted when the anthrax scare was on—Cipro was patented by a foreign company and there was instantly much talk of compulsory licensing. That was just a scare—think how people in poor countries weigh respect for patents against a shortage of, or impossibly high prices for, drugs for large-scale actual diseases.

And in no field is the complaint more acute than in patents on, or related to, human genes. It becomes coupled not only with a pressing need for cheap medicines but with emotional appeals to 'natural law'—how can anyone 'own' genes? The complaint has added force from the hard fact that no one can design around gene patents. One of the driving forces—the incentive to design around—relied upon to justify the patent system is gone. Another man's gene patent is an absolute bar in relation to whatever that gene does. This is a very important fact about such patents—a fact which has important effects and creates important conceptions in the first world.

Moreover gene patents are apt to have a very long reach. Take the breast cancer gene patents on BRCA1 and BRCA2. These appear to reach through to touch all those researching those diseases—again with much resentment, this time in the world of research scientists and doctors. Can it really be right that only one commercial concern should have control over any use of these genes—whether by way of testing for breast cancer, treatment or even, suppose it to be the case, other cancers affected by those genes? Can the patent system justify a monopoly over all testing for these cancers? I am told that Myriad, who own the patents, are trying to insist not merely on a monopoly on testing kits, but on conducting the tests—to the exclusion of hospitals and doctors. To outsiders that sort of reach may well bring the patent system as it stands into question.[3]

[3] *I felt in my bones even then that the Myriad patents would cause trouble. The US Supreme Court ultimately held that isolated genes could not be patentable:* Association for Molecular Pathology v Myriad Genetics *569 U.S.—(2013). It was probably really troubled by the width of the claim. I am sure the answer lies not in adjusting substantive patent law but in creating some sort of abuse of monopoly rule.*

This brings me to the first subject I wish to discuss, the partly allied topics of compulsory licences and parallel imports. First compulsory licences. I believe that most considerations of these have been and are superficial and ill-informed. I propose to generalise from my own experience of these.

In my experience as a practising lawyer there were two periods when they were available in the UK. When I came into practice in the late 1960s, importers of generic drugs from non-patent countries (mainly Italy at the time) were beginning to make use of a provision of our patent law which had been introduced as a result of experience during the First World War. The pre-War success of the great German dye and chemical industry was seen to have been partly based on a successful use of patents to confine industrial know-how to Germany, to the disadvantage of home manufacture. The 'solution' was to provide that anyone could, on application to the Patent Office, have a licence 'on such terms as seems fit'.

In the early 1960s would-be importers sought to use this provision[4] to obtain compulsory licences for already-successful drugs. The earliest targets were the early psychotropic drugs,[5] shortly followed by the benzodiazapines.[6] The battles about these largely raged over the royalty rate—should it be enough to recompense the companies for ongoing research and promotion costs as well as profit? Should it be fixed or should it fall with prices? Not only did patentees look to fair royalties (which I do not think they got), but they also used the procedural system for delay. Under the law as it stood the licensee had no licence until all the terms were settled—so the more you could find to argue about the greater the delay. Looking back I think it fair to conclude that the whole business was essentially a failure from society's point of view. Some middlemen made money. The State (which in the UK pays for most pharmaceuticals, at least patented ones) saved a little but not much, I think. Research and risk money were adversely affected.

In 1977 this type of licence was abolished. But another emerged later as a result of the extension of term of a patent from 16 to 20 years and the removal of any possibility of extension of patent term.[7]

[4] Which by this time had been re-enacted as s 41 of the Patents Act 1949.

[5] eg Smith Kline and French's Stelazine (trifluoperazine).

[6] First Hoffmann-La Roche's Librium (chlordiazepoxide) and Valium (diazepam) and then a number of follow-ups.

[7] Until 1977 a patentee who could show that he had had 'inadequate remuneration' could obtain an extension of his patent for up to 10 years. Drug companies could often do this—demonstrating many 'lost years' and only late recompense for early, mainly abortive, research.

By way of transition, 'new existing patents' (those which had more than 11 years to run) got an automatic extension of term to 20 years but were subject to 'licences of right' for the last four of these. Again the middlemen emerged. Again the battles were about rates of royalty. This time the drug companies did rather better legally,[8] though in practice I think the middlemen made a lot more money because their sales were so much more than under the prior regime.

What is to be concluded about compulsory licences? First and foremost, unless they are well thought out, they are not likely to be effective in the way intended. In particular they are a very poor way of dealing with drug prices—and especially so if they are available to middlemen rather than being confined to promoting local manufacture. Middlemen are not interested in low prices—what they want is a high price so they can sell at that price minus a little bit. Compulsory licences are, on the other hand, a very good way for lawyers and accountants to make money. No doubt better systems can be devised than we had in the UK. But I very much doubt that rewarding unproductive middlemen is the best way to get cheaper drugs—even for markets which, by any practical or moral standard, should have them.

Compulsory licences for local manufacture, on the other hand, may have a proper purpose. Whether such licences should be available is a real and important question—one allied to the subject of parallel imports as I shall show later.

What about compulsory licences for research tools? I here speak not of patents on scanners, stethoscopes and such like—artefacts in themselves. It is patents on probes—tools employing a genetic code—that may cause problems. On the one hand some legal systems provide an exception to the scope of protection for research. This may be wide or narrow, but it is an all-or-nothing solution. Surely better is an approach which recognises the patentee should have some reward but which also controls the size of that reward—a compulsory licence. There are many that say that a complete monopoly over a gene, just because you were first to isolate it, or even if you are first to isolate it and know what it is for, goes too far. It may well be that well-designed compulsory licence provisions would be helpful in this

[8] SmithKline got 46% of their pre-licence price for Tagamet (cimetidine). Contrast that with 26%, which was about the highest achieved under the s 41 regime. Even at 46%, the generic companies, within a few months, took the entire 'generic' market (ie that met by doctors prescribing generically rather than by the trade mark).

area. It is not as though compulsory licence provisions cannot be made to work—they in fact work very well, for instance in relation to musical copyrights.[9] There is, I think, too great a danger in calling patents 'property' and arguing on from that they must be inviolate. A lot depends on the nature of the invention—one that is not only high risk but involves billions in research, and ages in time to bring to market, stands in a different economic case from an isolated gene—especially one isolated by more or less standard techniques.

I turn to parallel imports. The old English rule was that the patentee was taken to have consented to his product being on the market anywhere in the world if he sold it without any fetter. Only if he labelled the product in such a way as to bring home to those who dealt in it (including subsequent purchasers) that the product was licensed for sale in limited territories could he use his patents outside those territories to prevent parallel imports. Other countries have different rules. And there may be different rules about other IP rights: the European Union, for instance, has settled on a rule for trade marks—that unless there is express consent or conduct unequivocally indicating such consent, no trade-marked goods can be imported into the EU without the trade mark owner's consent.[10] So, Kodak film made in Rochester NY by Kodak and sold in the US will, if imported into the EU, infringe Kodak's EU trade marks.

What I have to suggest is that rational world—or at least regional—rules for parallel imports are seriously needed. This is particularly so in the case of pharmaceuticals. Drug companies cannot expect to make serious money by sales in poor countries. No one in such places can afford Western prices. So either the companies sell at a much lower price, or not at all. But they cannot afford to sell at lower prices if the drugs immediately leave the poor country and reappear as parallel imports in high-price developed countries—which is exactly what middlemen will do if they can. Strong barriers to parallel imports are needed in the name of humanity in this kind of case. If they are not available then either the drugs will not be sold at all in the poor

[9] Cases about these before the Copyright Tribunal in the UK show that they are, or can be, just as complex as compulsory licences for patents. It would not be right to dismiss the compulsory licences in copyright as an inappropriate analogy because they are just a question of a 'penny a play'.

[10] A purist would say this is bizarre because it is contrary to a central function of a trade mark—to denote trade origin. If a mark does that it fulfils its task and in a global market it is irrelevant where the goods are actually made or sold.

countries or will only be sold at a high price. Either situation is a strong incentive for local manufacture via compulsory licensing. Putting it bluntly if the drugs are not made available cheaply the case for compulsory licensing becomes unanswerable. And they can only be sold cheaply if they are confined to the markets where they are sold.

That makes it important to put in place two systems to ensure such confinement: first one can reasonably ask that some sort of system in the country or region of import to prevent export be put in place. No one can expect that to work on its own—that would be to expect too much of local court and administrative systems. So the first-world countries need to amend their own laws to ensure that patent enforcement against 'grey' drugs from third-world countries works well. The old British rule for patents is not likely to be enough. Something like the EU's rule for trade marks is what is wanted—proof positive that consent was given for resale in the first world when drugs were sold in the third world. Otherwise there is infringement.

I turn to my next main topic, again alluded to by Sir Boss. He wanted 'good patent laws'. If one stands back and takes a world view, the differences in substantive patent law are, in principle, not that great. This is because the main objections to validity are lack of novelty and obviousness. Things like first to invent/first to file or grace periods and restrictions on the sort of thing that can be patented (computer programs, methods of medical treatment), important though they are, are second order compared with that great duo, novelty and obviousness.

I said 'in principle' because what matters in practice is how the rules are worked. Mary Mack, in her biography of Jeremy Bentham, said two things of penetrating wisdom: 'Substantive laws are not self-enforcing. They pre-suppose an efficient adjectival law' and 'The law is everything and in it procedure and evidence come first'. I venture to suggest that the various systems devised for judging whether patents are valid or infringed are, frankly, not very good. No one outside your country, for instance, regards the use of jury trial as remotely sensible. William Penn and his collaborator, Mead, were put on trial in London for sedition. Having heard the case the jury retired to consider their verdict. They were for an acquittal. The judge refused to accept the verdict and directed them to convict. They refused. The judge had them locked up without food or water. They held out. Eventually the impasse was overcome by an application to the Court of King's Bench, which overruled the judge, thus establishing the right of a jury to come to its own verdict—if it chooses—in the face of the evidence. That lesson was brought to your country.[11] It remains an important bastion of freedom. But you have taken it to its illogical conclusion—the right of man to have his case tried by a body of people who cannot possibly understand.[12]

Of course you have created the Federal Court of Appeal, which can, within limits, put things right. But only after a wrong verdict and all the damage it can do. And even that Court is likely to be severely tested in high-technology cases. After all, its judges (and law clerks) are themselves not experts. Some things which seem to outsiders as clever and thus inventive are actually pretty mundane to those who really understand the art. Some might say, for instance, that it is wrong to hold that it is 'inventive' to ascertain a gene sequence by standard techniques so as to confer patentability on what is really no more than the predictable result of routine research.

We in England use specialist patent judges. They have to give reasons. They can be assisted to understand the case by a scientific advisor—not a member of the court. In high-technology cases I think we are at the limit of what is doable. It is not easy even for an experienced patent lawyer-judge unaided to understand new and very complex technologies loaded with jargon.

On both sides of the Atlantic in the common law courts we use party-appointed experts, the expensive process of discovery and extended (and thus expensive) cross-examination. The costs of this are not merely financial. Large cases take scientists off their proper job. I had one case, for instance, where the clients reckoned that fighting it cost them three months' research time.

There is also the problem of party experts—some scientists will say anything for money. We in England are trying to keep them under control—by saying their first duty is to the court and a number of other things I do not have time to go into here. You, in the US, are often looking for performance rather than solidity of expert view—as

[11] *My friend Martin Adelman says there was a much baser reason for the 7th Amendment, which provides: 'In Suits at common law, where the value in controversy shall exceed twenty dollars, the right of trial by jury shall be preserved, and no fact tried by a jury, shall be otherwise re-examined in any Court of the United States, than according to the rules of the common law'. It was that quite a lot of Americans had taken over British-owned land and feared claims by the original owners. The thought was that a US jury would reject those claims. However, I still intuit that part of the reason, at least, for the amendment was the spirit of liberty.*

[12] I am aware that many US trial lawyers express some confidence in trial by jury even for patent cases. I have to say that that confidence is not shared by any foreign lawyer I have ever met, whether from the common law or inquisitorial systems, whether in Europe or Asia or Australasia. Nor have I met a scientist who is happy to have high-technology questions judged by laymen.

I would do if I were aiming for jury trial or even a trial before a non-specialist judge.

But even if you do have experts who are trying to be fair and non-partisan there is a basic problem in the adversarial system. It is an old problem. The young Learned Hand said, in 1901: 'The trouble with all this is that it is setting the jury to decide where doctors disagree'.[13] And it is not much better if it is 'setting' a judge alone to decide really complex matters.

That great jurist James Fitzjames Stephens articulated the problem in a different way even earlier:

> Few spectacles, it might be said, can be more absurd and incongruous that that of a jury composed of twelve persons who, without any previous scientific knowledge or training, are suddenly called upon to adjudicate in controversies in which the most eminent scientific men flatly contradict each other's assertions.[14]

Further there is the problem of expert selection—a problem which is very old and again gives one an uneasy feeling that we are not getting it right. An English judge put the point fair and square as long ago as 1873:[15]

> Now, in the present instance, I have the evidence of experts on the one side, and on the other, and, as usual, the experts do not agree in their opinion. There is no reason why they should. As I have often explained, since I have the honour of a seat on this bench, the opinion of an expert may be honestly obtained, and it may be quite different from the opinion of another expert, also honestly obtained. But the mode in which evidence is obtained is such as not to give the fair result of scientific opinion to the court. A man may go, and does, sometimes, to half a dozen experts. He takes their honest opinion: he finds three in his favour and three against him; he says to the three in his favour: 'Will you be kind enough to give evidence?' He pays the ones against him their fees and leaves them alone; the other side does the same. It may not be three out of six, it may be three out of fifty ... I am sorry to say the result is that the court does not get the assistance from the experts, which, if they were unbiased and fairly chosen, it would have a right to expect.

On the continent of Europe the tendency is to use a comparatively inexpert tribunal, which itself consults an 'expert'. Whether that individual is really an expert is often questionable. And he may often

[13] [1901] *Harvard Law Review*.
[14] Address to the Juridical Society, 1859.
[15] Sir George Jessel MR in *Thorne v Worthington Skating Rink Co.*, LR 6 Ch D n at p 415.

answer the 'wrong' question or take ages to come up with any answer at all. He is effectively the judge, which has lots of attendant dangers, especially where there is no opportunity of testing his views.

It is further unsatisfactory to have different tribunals judging what is in substance the same case in different countries. You can get a world patchwork of decisions at great expense and delay. There are two sorts of problem—different national jurisdictions and getting an adequate tribunal. I think the problems can be linked—and ultimately should be linked for high-technology cases such as gene patents.

What then is the answer? So far as the different jurisdiction problem goes there are three in principle. We carry on as we are, or we let the courts of one country decide for other countries, or an international tribunal. I put aside 'carry on as we are' for the moment to look at the other two solutions. The second solution confers extra-territorial jurisdiction on national courts. The recent drafts for a new Hague treaty go down that line. I think it is wrong and dangerous. You cannot have German or English or Estonian or Greek courts deciding that an American patent is being infringed in the US and ordering an American defendant to stop manufacture in America. And vice versa. Especially unacceptable would be enforcement abroad of US jury verdicts.

What then about the third solution? This would involve a treaty—and it would crucially require that a proper tribunal be set up. That is why there is link between the two problems of a modern judicial system for patents and the cross-border difficulties. Is it possible to do better than any of the existing models? I think so. I think a court with experienced patent lawyer judges, assisted (as members of the court or possibly as a specialist jury) by scientists can be made to work. I do not think, however, that scientists should be permanent members of the court. In a field such as genetics you really need people who are, or who have recently been, active. Otherwise they are not really experts themselves and could be dangerous—witness the sort of problem to be had in the European Patent Office where the Office relies too much on its own expertise and not enough on properly prepared, impartial, party-provided expert evidence.

Is such a solution likely? I think in the very long run yes. We in Europe are gingerly going down that line—possibly in the next few years. If not this time, then next time round, say 10 years—language is an enormous complication. Gradually English as the language of business and technology will be sufficiently widespread to make this possible. But the European solution is likely to be modelled on the sort of court I have mentioned—it is a hybrid of the common law and continental approaches.

Looking at the problem more widely, the needs of international trade are more and more requiring regulation at a supranational level. The WTO [World Trade Organization] tribunals deal with international trade—disputes between states. I suspect there will one day be international patent courts—that the WTO tribunals are just precursors of things to come. The days of the nation state for big patent disputes are numbered. The number of days is big but finite.

Postscript (*to the original article when published*): The above is substantially as I gave the talk in St Louis in April 2002. Not much has changed since, but readers might like to note that some of the problems I discuss are addressed in a discussion paper published by the Nuffield Council on Bioethics (www.nufffieldbioethics.org) and the Report of the Commission on Intellectual Property Rights (www.iprcommission.org). Both these documents (and the resulting discussions) are well worth reading. There has been some progress along the lines I predicted as regards international patent litigation in that the EU is aiming to bring in a fully fledged EU patents court by the year 2010.

POSTSCRIPT

So much for 2010! More like 2017. And a truly international patent court still remains a dream.

29

*In Honour of Rüdiger Rogge**

RÜDIGER ROGGE AND I we were in the bar (is anyone surprised!) of the hotel where the European patent judges were staying. He told me the following story. When a law student he went to stay with a family in Scotland. It was all a little formal and his English was not that good. Early on he was asked what he intended to do. He said, 'I am going to be a judge'. There was a complete and utter silence. The family was horrified. Rüdiger could not understand what he had said wrong—maybe it was his imperfect English and he had said something rude. Of course there was a complete misunderstanding. To be a judge in Scotland (as in England) you had to have had a successful career as a lawyer first. So what he was understood as saying is 'I will be a very good and successful lawyer, so successful that in due course I will be one of the few who is asked to become a judge'. Monstrous arrogance. In reality of course, Rüdiger knew that he would leave university soon and, after training, start his career as a judge. It was not the language which divided him and his hosts but the unimaginably different legal systems—one with career judges and one with judges chosen from established practising lawyers.

We now know, of course, that the Scottish family was partly right after all—Rüdiger did become a great lawyer though only as judge. He is far too modest to have imagined that at the time but we now have his judgments to prove it. The loss to the German legal profession was the gain of the German judiciary. In the future things may be different. I have asked many successful German lawyers this question: 'Would you like to be a judge?' Nearly always the answer, after a startled pause, has been 'yes'. The reason for the pause is that

* *First published by GRUR 2001, vol 10–11, pp 937–39.*

to become a judge is not open to them in Germany. So it is just not a thing they have ever thought about. Of course becoming a judge means less money, at least that is so in every country which can make lawyers judges. But lawyers (particularly successful ones) are willing to sacrifice that for a job well worth doing.

Certainly I would hope that membership of any future European patent court could include some of the best European patent lawyers. Whether it will remains to be seen. Speaking of that future court, my crystal ball has vouchsafed me part of the Reporting Judge's Report for a hearing in that court. It is dated 1 April 2015 and reads as follows:

'My Lords. This case raises for the first time what the European rule regarding equivalents is to be. To assist you in this regard I propose to review various solutions reached in the past.

I begin with the United Kingdom. It has had a patent law going back to the seventeenth century. Originally there were no claims at all—it was left to a jury to decide whether the defendant had taken the invention. By the nineteenth century such a vague rule had gone and the modern system of claims began. And they became more important as claims became more and more precise. Before the 1960s the courts had basically taken the view that a patent claim was the definition of the monopoly claimed. The meaning of a patent claim was to be decided by the words used *when read in the context of the specification and drawings*.[1] In two important decisions in the 1960s the House of Lords almost settled the matter once and for all—there was no doctrine of equivalents: if you were outside the meaning of the claims (properly construed in context) you did not infringe. However, there were still those who asserted that a defendant also infringed if, although just outside the claim, he had taken the 'pith and marrow of the invention'. And the House of Lords had not quite closed off that argument.

Argument raged as to whether the 'doctrine of pith and marrow' was dead. In 1980 came the infamous *Catnic* case. Lord Diplock, like Stalin, rewrote history. He asserted that it was all just a question of construction—there was no separate doctrine of equivalents or pith

[1] Incidentally those who drafted the Protocol to Art 69 of the EPC seem, wrongly, to have thought English law was more restrictive; that English law required the claims to be read in the abstract, almost as though there were no specification or drawings. So, although the Protocol says the extreme of literal, out-of-context interpretation is to be avoided, it helps no one because no one ever wished to go that far.

and marrow. He created his famous 'Catnic' test which the British then treated as *via media* of the Protocol for some 25 years. The English Court of Appeal even called the 'Catnic' questions the 'Protocol' questions, even though no other European country used the Catnic test. In the year 2004 the House of Lords consigned *Catnic* to the dustbin of history. It proposed a new test which was ...'

[Here the crystal ball has clouded.]

'I turn to another common law country, the US. Of course that country has a right to jury trial, though in the late twentieth century that right was curtailed by the courts as far as possible consistently with the Constitution. That procedural absurdity did not affect substantive law. The US has always had an explicit doctrine of equivalents. But the scope of the doctrine has varied greatly. At one point it was very generous to the patentee, but as time passed the courts rendered the doctrine narrower and narrower. The 'notice function' of a claim (ie telling third parties what they could not do) received more emphasis. In particular, by the beginning of this century, the courts held that the doctrine only applied where an equivalent of a claimed element was used (thus excluding any more general equivalence from infringement). And then they went further and excluded equivalents which could clearly have been claimed at the time. Only equivalents unforeseeable to the skilled man at the time of filing were held to infringe. Thus if the patentee claimed 'element A *nailed* to element B' screwing, gluing or riveting A to B would not infringe but a wholly novel method of fixation would.

On top of that the Americans have a doctrine of 'file-wrapper estoppel'. The basic idea behind this is that where a man, in making his patent application, represents that his claim has a limited scope (normally of course to avoid prior art), he may not assert a greater width thereafter. It is a fine idea in principle but experience shows it is not particularly helpful: seldom does one get a clear representation as to scope of claim with the result that horrendous arguments rage over the whole of the patent application file. In the early part of this century the Americans went so far as to assume, unless the contrary could be proved, that any amendment by way of claim limitation was intended to meet prior art. The consequence was that the doctrine of equivalents could not apply to any amended element of a claim unless the patentee could show he had amended for some reason unconnected with an objection to patentability.

No one suggests we in Europe should have a file-wrapper doctrine: it would mean that no lawyer could safely advise on infringement without reading the whole EPO file—at vast increase in cost and for very little benefit. On the other hand the American experience of a very limited doctrine of equivalents may be instructive. It tells us ...'

[Here again the crystal ball went dark.]

'What then of the Germans? Before the EPC, claims did not have the same significance as in the UK—attention focussed on the inventive concept to which the claims were a guide. When Art 69 of the EPC became part of German law it is not surprising that the Germans retained a fairly liberal doctrine of equivalents. But, under the guidance of that great judge Rogge, the doctrine narrowed: general equivalence was not enough—you had to have equivalence of an element of the claim. Moreover the equivalent had to be one which the skilled man could discover from the claims. So in the above example, riveting, welding or gluing would infringe.

As to other countries ...'

[Again the ball went dark.]

'Next I should mention the amendment to the Protocol which took place in 2003. It says that 'due account' should be taken of equivalents. That is a politician's document. It could mean anything: you could take 'due account' of an obvious equivalent by saying the patentee must have meant to exclude it. Or you could take 'due account' by saying that any equivalent will infringe—or that any non-obvious equivalent will infringe. The fact is that the amendment left it to the courts, ultimately to this court, to decide what to do.

Which, if any, of the above solutions should Europe adopt? Before I suggest an answer I think it is worth summarising some important factors:

(1) Patent claims are monopolies defined by the patentee—it is sensible to construe the monopoly in the context of the specification.
(2) Industry spends a great deal of time and money studying patent claims—most patent departments spend at least as much on patent avoidance as on patent prosecution, if not more. Whatever doctrine of equivalents you adopt, it must be as certain as possible. Otherwise the costs to European industry and research will be horrendous. The notice function of a patent claim is indeed very important.

(3) A critical decision is whether the German solution is to be adopted. Should a patent claim be extended by the doctrine of equivalents to cover solutions which the patentee could have foreseen but did not (perhaps deliberately) choose to claim?
(4) If the doctrine of equivalents is wide, one is likely to find more patents invalid—for one must, for the purpose of validity, consider both the meaning of the claim and any extension produced by the doctrine. Patent offices are not apt to do that—they operate on the claim as such.
(5) Any adoption of issue estoppel would have the consequences I mention above.

So, the choices to be made by this court are essentially one of the following:

(a) No infringement by equivalents of what is claimed. All the court must do is to ascertain the meaning of the claim in the context of the drawings and text.
(b) A doctrine of equivalents, which is:
    (i) infringement by any equivalent of an element of the claim; or
    (ii) infringement by an equivalent of an element of the claim only if that equivalent would have been obvious at the date of application (?publication); or
    (iii) infringement by an equivalent of an element of the claim only if that equivalent would not have been obvious at the date of application (?publication); or
    (iv) some other, wider doctrine.'

POSTSCRIPT

1. *I never did like (or really understand) the Catnic questions, either in their original form or as re-formulated by Hoffmann J in* Improver v Remington.[2] *In this piece I forecast that the 'Protocol Questions' would be superseded (a polite way of*

[2] [1990] FSR 181

saying 'dumped'). I prophesied 2004. And so it came to pass. In Kirin-Amgen,[3] *Lord Hoffmann described the 'Protocol' questions as 'only guidelines, more useful in some cases than others'. I had made an attempt in the Court of Appeal to put them on one side in Rockwater*[4] *but that Court could not formally do so. Since* Kirin-Amgen *the Protocol questions have faded almost into complete obscurity. A good thing too.*

2. *My forecast date for a European patent court was 2015. My bet now is that it will start on 1 January 2017—so the first case reaching the Court of Appeal will be about 2019. I hope the question of equivalents comes later rather than sooner so that the court will have bedded in before it commits itself on such a big question.*
3. *I was wrong about file-wrapper estoppel in Europe. The Germans still stoutly resist it on the rational ground that the scope of protection is, by Art 69 of the EPC (current version), 'determined by the claims'. Nothing in Art 69 or its Protocol mentions the file, so the file is not relevant. (You can pull their legs about why the same logic does not apply to a doctrine of equivalents. Sometimes they answer that the amended Protocol says you must take due account of equivalents. But that overlooks the fact that the Protocol is not a protocol on claim construction but a protocol on the construction of Art 69 itself.)*

   The Dutch espouse reference to the file. It is not clear whether that is only for restricting the patentee from espousing a wider interpretation than one he relied upon to get his patent or more generally so that it could be used to support a wide construction. Logic says if you use the file as a kind of travaux préparatoires *then it could go either way, but that offends common sense.*

   The British have been trying to keep the file out, but some recent decisions are becoming ambiguous on the point.

[3] [2004] UKHL 46.

[4] *Rockwater v Technip France* [2004] EWCA (Civ) 381.

Personally I think it better to keep it out—patents are complicated enough without having to read the whole file—and generally if you do, you either get nothing or something only arguably in your favour, which leads to a satellite argument not about the meaning of the claims but about the meaning of the patent office correspondence.

4. *As regards equivalents, the Germans have been continuing to narrow their doctrine—see* Occlutech.[5] *And no one has yet been able to tell me what the French, Italian etc, etc versions of the doctrine are. I really hope that the new UPC will simply do away with it altogether and use purposive construction. Above all a clear rule is needed.*

[5] *DE-AGA Medical Corp v Occlutech, Case X ZR 16/09, 10 May 2011.*

30

Abolish Patents?

CATRIONA HAMMER[1] *ASKED me to write a short piece following the publication of anti-patent material by Boldrin and Levine. I came up with this, which I still think is really all that needs to be said! I can't see any answer.*

> 'I knew that a country without a patent office and good patent laws was just a crab, and couldn't travel anyway but sideways or backwards. (Mark Twain's Connecticut Yankee at the Court of King Arthur)
>
> So long as men are governed by unexamined prejudices and led away by sounds, it is natural for them to regard Patents as unfavourable to the encrease of wealth. So soon as they obtain clear ideas to annex to these sounds, it is impossible for them to do otherwise than recognize them to be favourable to that encrease: and that in so essential a degree, that the security given to property can not be said to be compleat without it. (Jeremy Bentham in the late eighteenth century)
>
> Floods of patents are issued … the validity of which is uncertain. At the meeting of the British Association, held in 1931, we hear patents described as 'lottery tickets.' Manufacturers can never tell whether they are infringing on some patent and becoming liable to heavy damages. 'A bad patents system,' writes Nature in connection with this point, is 'a fetter on the hands of industry and an instrument of blackmail.' (Michael Polanyi, scientist, in 1944 (I am grateful to Rosemarie Ziedonis for this quote))
>
> The best solution is to abolish patents entirely through strong constitutional measures and find other legislative instruments, less open to lobbying and rent-seeking, to foster innovation whenever there is clear evidence that laissez-faire under-supplies it. (Boldrin and Levine, *The Case against Patents*, September 2012)

[1] *Of GE Healthcare and now also President of the Chartered Institute of Patent Attorneys.*

Who is right, Twain and Bentham or Polyani and Boldrin/Levine? One side or the other must be wrong. I think the answer is easy. Twain and Bentham. And not just because they write better. I think you can prove it by asking yourself a few simple questions:

1. How many major new medicines did the command economy of the Soviet Empire produce? (Answer: None).
2. Imagine you thought you had a new good idea and wanted to develop it for the market. But, as is usually the case, quite a bit of work, time and expense would be needed to do that, you had not got a lot of money and you could not be sure the product would sell though it has prospects. So you go to a potential investor or bank for some money. They ask. 'Well suppose it works, what's to stop others copying?' You answer: 'Nothing, people will easily be able to undercut because they do no research.' Question: 'Will you get the money?'
3. Does the development of mobile phone and computer technology seem very fast to you? Does it look like patents have impeded that development?[2]
4. Why do big pharma and high-tech companies often spend as much as 17 per cent of their *turnover* in patented medicines on research? Has it anything to do with the fact that the patents on their existing products are going to expire?
5. Why have the Chinese, a communist country, invested so much in creating a patent system since 1994? Are they stupid or something?
6. Are you likely to change your mind because some economists have produced some equations based on simplistic assumptions with no way of knowing reliably or at all what numbers to put into them?

Finally there is a different question. Could the patent system be improved, for instance in the US, by abolishing jury trial, keeping damages rational and introducing the English rule as to legal expenses—'loser pays'?[3]

[2] *See also Chapter 23, 'Patent Thickets'.*
[3] *See also Chapter 25, 'The Perfect Patent Court'.*

31

Patent Litigation: Why Everyone Gets it Wrong and What Should We do?[*]

IF A MAN from Mars came down and looked at how we resolve patent disputes, he would be amazed. Almost for sure he would go home and say, we have nothing to learn from these Earthlings, except how not to do it. The Martian patent system could only look at Earth's various mistakes to see what could be done better.

The Martian will start with what the Earthlings are trying to achieve with a patent system. It is for encouraging people to have and to find out good ideas. And to encourage them to invest in their development. Both having the idea and the development are important. He would learn that Earthlings do not allow patents for ideas that are old or obvious. Our Martian might think that is very odd—why, he might ask, is there no protection for an old, neglected idea, which will need millions on development just to find out if it is really good? A prior published drug compound which needs $500m risk money to bring it to market is a good example. No one will do it without protection. But let that pass (for another Fordham conference) for there is more to amaze our Martian.

He will, I suggest, think that naturally there are mechanisms for obtaining protection. But why so many in different places? After all the objective is supposed to be same all over Earth (though he might question whether that is rational—less-developed areas do not self-evidently need the same rules as highly developed areas). But is it really useful for *Homo sapiens* to have different mechanisms in the

[*] *Paper given at the Fordham IP Conference, Easter 2005.*

shape of parallel examining patent offices? Well, says our Martian. I suppose this shows how primitive Earthlings are. But surely once the patent is granted the rules about how you decide what is protected by the patent will be more or less the same—Earthlings could not be so silly as to have different basic rules in different places? Wrong. We do—the debate about claim interpretation and equivalents is about as old as the patent system and shows no sign of going away. Some favour a reasonably certain system—going by the meaning of the words in context (the British rule), others favour reading a whole prosecution file (the Americans), others favour adding to the meaning of the words in context a little, indefinable, fuzzy extra, which may go by the name of the 'doctrine of equivalents' or the more colourful old English expression 'doctrine of pith and marrow'. The Martian will note that, for those that have it, no one seems to know or agree how to define the limits of this fuzzy edge. So it has inherently the seeds of much dispute—as indeed it has proved. He might ask whether it is worth having it—does it encourage litigation rather than innovation?

Well then, says the Martian, coming to expect the answer, I expect the Earthlings have a whole bunch of ways of dealing with patent disputes, even though Earth has increasingly a global economy with corresponding global patent problems and disputes. But even he would be astonished at what he found. I suppose he would first identify what it is that is needed in a sensible patent dispute resolution system. A list something like this would occur to him:

1. capable of providing a speedy resolution;
2. cheap;
3. capable of dealing with highly complex technical issues;
4. accessible to SMEs[1] both as plaintiffs and defendants;
5. capable of dealing with many different languages;
6. predictable;
7. equipped with a respected judiciary;
8. fair in its procedures;
9. readily accessible—hence a local presence;
10. able to deal with questions of interim relief very quickly;
11. able to enforce its orders readily.

[1] Small and medium-sized enterprises.

He would then go on to see how the various nations match up to these requirements. I fear he would not be surprised to learn that the answer is: not very well.

Let us examine some of the requirements. Our Martian would, I suggest, be likely to expect that the body which takes the decision would at least have some reasonable technical background. This is needed at the most basic level because pure laymen or lawyers will, at the very best, have to struggle and learn, just to understand what the dispute is about, still less decide it. So our Martian would be amazed to discover that in the most powerful nation on earth, the primary tribunal need not have any technical qualification at all—however complex the technology. I think he would be even more amazed to learn that questions of fact, which apparently also include questions about the fuzzy boundary called equivalents, are left to a bunch of ordinary people, called a jury. Can it really be that a case about, for instance, digital image compression is heard before a group which might consist of a typist, a greengrocer, a policeman, a fisherman, a cowboy and so on? It is for them to decide whether an idea in that field is 'obvious'? Why, he would say to himself, to that lot nothing about digital image compression is obvious.

Then he might look at Germany. Ah, he says, they do have technically qualified people in their Federal Patent Court. That makes sense. But then he finds out that infringement is not dealt with in that court—even though infringement is frequently technical too. He could not understand a system where the whole case was not done in one court.

If he moved on to France, he would find no jury but again no technical expertise. And so for most countries in the world.

He would, I think, not be surprised to find that in many countries without necessary technical expertise in its courts, various devices were introduced to try to ameliorate matters—in the US, for instance, the rule that the meaning of the claim is a question of law gets at least that question away from the jury, as does the device of judgment notwithstanding verdict. And the creation of some expertise by experience rather than technical training is apparent in the use of particular courts (eg the Federal Court of Appeals or the use of experienced judges (eg Delaware) in the US, Düsseldorf and Mannheim in Germany, specially designated judges in France and so on. In some places he would note the use of specialist patent courts staffed by judges with a basic technical training and years of experience in patent law. He might note that in such places you can get a result very fast. But even these places do not have detailed relevant experience on the bench—the judge is asked to decide what would have been obvious to the skilled man when he is not one himself.

So I think the Martian would ask himself why no court in the world consists of a panel consisting of a lawyer with two real experts in the particular field concerned—one selected by each side. Surely that would be better and faster and cheaper?

Next he would look at speed of decision. He would understand that this is vital for a fair patent system. If a patentee could spin things out for years, the defendant, even if he is right, will suffer greatly as a commercial matter. So our Martian would look at the current state of affairs in the European Patent Office in utter amazement—it takes five years minimum to resolve things and often much longer. I observed recently that waiting for the EPO is like waiting for Godot. Our Martian might learn about Art 6 of the European Convention on Human Rights—the right to a fair trial—and conclude that no one in the EPO had heard of it. Nor would he be impressed with most countries. He would, I think, expect a case to be over within two Earth years and in urgent cases faster. A rational litigation system needs maximum time limits.

What then of predictability? This I have dealt with in relation to scope of the monopoly and in relation to the tribunal itself. Other subjects, particularly obviousness, he would recognise as inherently woolly but he would wonder why one did not aim to narrow this by the use of skilled tribunals. Our Martian would surely say to himself—better than litigation of great cost, time and trouble is knowing where everyone stands from the outset.

Next costs. Let us start with court fees. The Martian might expect courts to come for free—civil justice systems are as much a part of a civilised democratic system as policemen or city lights. But our Martian would find that governments charge fees all over the world. What would surprise him are the big differences in different places. Court fees in the US are not far from nominal—and are independent of the value of the case. In Germany and Switzerland court fees depend on the value of the case. Our Martian would not understand how you can realistically value a patent case where the primary remedy is an injunction. But he would understand that the *Länder* in Germany at least regard patent actions as serious revenue raisers. He would look at England and Wales and say the Treasury-inspired proposals to increase court fees are mad.

But of course the really big costs are not court fees: they are the lawyers. Next to them, at least in some cases, the experts. Our Martian would be really puzzled by this—what is it that they all do? He might particularly ask what discovery is for—particularly for some topics. Take the English system and obviousness. We allow discovery of the inventors' work and of what work (if any) was being done on the problem by he who is attacking the patent.[2] The theory justifying this is that it is important when considering obviousness to consider how real people were working at the time. But there is scarcely any logic in this—one is concerned with the notional skilled man who was necessarily not the patentee. And why discovery just from the parties when the logical (but impossible) thing would be to get the documents of all those anywhere in the world who were working on the problem? I think that, save in exceptional cases,[3] discovery on obviousness is a waste of time and expense in nearly all cases.[4] I do not say 'all' for I can think of one or two cases over my entire career where discovery really did make a difference on obviousness.[5] I am pretty sure the Martian would think that no discovery on obviousness would be sensible. And the same would go for insufficiency. Indeed our Martian might well think that the only subject needing discovery was infringement (if what the defendant was doing was in doubt) and prior use. Be sure, our Martian would wonder why we have not all simplified things a lot more.

Next, experiments done for the purpose of the case. Anyone who has ever done much experimental work knows that they often go wrong. And it is equally easy to overlook something which may bias

[2] Subject to a 'window' of two years around the priority date—see CPR Part 63 Practice Direction 5.1.

[3] eg where the patentee starts giving evidence of how he made the invention.

[4] *Two years later I had to consider this further in* Nichia v Argos *[2007] EWCA Civ 741. I am still a bit cross that the other two did not agree—there was no evidence that the costs of discovery would be disproportionate but, as I believe I showed in the judgment, it was obviously so even though the others could not see it. Moral: if you can, prove it. Do not rely on the court to have common sense! I am glad that discovery will be very much restricted in the future UPC.*

[5] One celebrated case (which I was not in) formed part of the *Du Pont/Akzo* litigation. A Du Pont copy of Akzo's patent revealing their invention had, written on it by a Du Pont scientist, 'Hot Rats'—so struck was he by the idea said later to be obvious. Another was *Molynke v P&G* [1992] FSR 487 where the defendant's own discovery showed their concern and difficulty over the problem solved by the patent—see p 588 for a quotation from a key discovery document.

the result. That is so even when you want to be truly scientific and objective. Learning to be a good experimental scientist takes a lot, including especially the development of the faculty of discerning flaws. So it is odd that experiments to prove something for the purposes of a case—litigation experiments—are generally treated with much less care than 'proper' scientific experiments. Very few legal systems handle experiments well—with that same rigour that scientists use. Our Martian would recognise as only fair that an experiment should, if possible, be reproducible. He would see the English system of not allowing a party to give evidence of experiments without first having given notice to the other side of the experiment, what it is supposed to prove and an opportunity of seeing it performed as fair. It costs (especially if it is unnecessarily overloaded with lots of lawyers) but is necessary in many cases.

Languages. Our Martian would note that Earth has many languages—but only a limited number for science and engineering. He would wonder why courts do not just use those—adapting in a pragmatic way for cases where parties speak different languages. He could hardly believe that there was a massive translation industry producing unwanted translations.

Looking at the world as a whole, our Martian might well conclude that there is not much he can learn, except what not to do.

Suppose now he was asked by Earth to make recommendations—what would they be?

1. Be as precise as possible—forget 'equivalents' and 'fairness'. Patents are an economic instrument where certainty matters.
2. Abolish national courts—set up transnational courts. In these use experienced patent judges assisted by true experts as a sort of jury.
3. Keep costs down—but have the rule that loser pays a reasonable amount.
4. Do not have unnecessary discovery.
5. Be pragmatic about language—use what language(s) are necessary for the case.
6. Make sure experiments are done fairly.
7. Impose strict time limits so that people get a result in a year to first instance and two to appeal maximum.
8. Allow but limited cross-examination—essentially on fact and limited in time.

POSTSCRIPT

1. *Quite a lot of this (but not (1) or (5)) are features of the UPC. Whether (1) will be a feature will have to be resolved by the Court itself.*
2. *The absence of most of these features from the US system is why it does not work well. I keep a list of solutions to all this in my Dropbox account. Here it is:*
   - *(a) Introduce a basic procedural rule that the loser pays the other side's legal costs (attorneys and expert fees). The Court can be given a discretion, eg where the party is a relatively small entity and had reasonable cause for suing or defending.*
   - *(b) Allow anyone to attack the validity of a patent at any time. Abolish the requirement for standing to attack. The new post-grant inter partes review procedure does not have a standing requirement. A very good thing and enables a party to remove or cut down the scope of a patent before actually doing anything commercially.*
   - *(c) Develop more precise rules for withholding a final injunction.* eBay[6] *is hopelessly vague, and rather muddles interim injunction considerations (are damages an adequate remedy?) with final injunction considerations. The best test is probably 'would a final injunction be a wholly disproportionate remedy?'. I rather expect the new UPC to come up with this or something very close to it.*
   - *(d) Damages:*
     - *(i) Get rid of the wilful infringement rule—it leads to more legal costs and is unnecessary. No one else has it.*
     - *(ii) Make them properly compensatory and no more. In the case of non-practising entities (NPEs) reasonable royalty only. I still think we basically get this right in the UK—I tried to set it out in one of my early judgments,* Gerber v Lectra.[7]
   - *(e) Get rid of discovery save for key issues of fact eg prior use.*

[6] eBay v MercExchange *547 US 388.*
[7] Gerber v Lectra *[1995] RPC 383.*

- (f) *(In your dreams) abolish jury trial. One can go a long way to understanding the US system if one appreciates that it has a range of devices to get round constitutionally mandated jury trial. Markman hearings, frequent summary judgment motions, applications for judgment notwithstanding verdict, arguments about deference to jury verdicts and even the new post-grant inter parties review are all really ways of avoiding a jury.*
- (g) *Try compensation only after and if patent is found valid and infringed. This is important. Given juries and discovery, having a trial about damages with the trial about validity and infringement greatly increases legal costs. Do the Americans not notice that no one else in the world tries the amount of compensation at the same time as liability, at least not unless there is a very special reason?*

These defects combine to produce the toxic mix which has led to the current criticism of the patent system itself. For example, the fact that a patentee can sue with no risk of paying the other side's costs, added to contingency fees, creates lawyer-driven litigation. Discovery (vast written) and prolix oral drives up costs and so on.

These procedural *defects of the US litigation system are in my opinion a major reason why the patent system itself is being queried so much more now than in the past. And for reasons I explain elsewhere in this volume, attacks on the system as such may put innovation itself at risk. I really wish the Americans would pull their socks up—if they don't they may find within the foreseeable future that China has overtaken them as an innovating country. For the Chinese, with astonishing speed, have created a patent system and have already started turning their hand to creating specialist patent courts.*

32

The Community Patent or a European Patent Court? Is it Time to Choose?[*]

WHEN I WAS first asked to come to this Fordham conference I wondered what, in the field of European patent court procedure and structure, I could talk about. Things appeared to be stuck in the mud or, worse, moving deeper into it, as a man struggling in quicksand. My last talk on this subject at Fordham, three years ago, ended with the following gloomy conclusion:

> Whether we continue with the existing convention or a new convention, it does look like we have entered a new era: one in which people litigate mainly about where they are to litigate rather than just getting on with their cases.

But at last it may be that things are changing: that the awful mess we are in now will not persist.

I begin with a brief review of where we are. European patent law is largely harmonised so far as substantive law is concerned (though there is clearly some unfinished business as regards definition of scope of monopoly). The harmonisation was as a result of the EPC. But this Treaty was essentially directed at the Member States. They were to bring their national patent laws into line one with another. The EPC did not seek to, and did not, set up a supranational law. In truth there is no European patent law, just a set of national but identical patent laws. The nearest the EPC came to supranational provision was to set up the European Patent Office as a supranational body and require Member States to recognise the patents it granted and the results

[*] *A paper for the 2000 Fordham University Law School Conference.*

of its 'opposition' procedure. At the last conference I criticised that procedure—a criticism which remains substantially as valid today as it was then.[1] All I would say is that since then I have reflected more on the problem. I think it would be a thoroughly good thing if the opposition were:

(a) characterised as a judicial process rather than as a continuation of an 'administrative process' (only a Sophist would say otherwise);[2]
(b) given clear judicial rules, which included treating the members of the division as first instance patent judges—ideally they would not sit in Munich but away from the Office; and the same goes for the Boards of Appeal;
(c) given time limits for the end of the process.

These are matters which deserve more debate, and I believe one day will get it.[3] However there are other, more pressing problems, to which I now turn.

As you will know from the time of the EPC in 1973, people have been trying to do something about parallel national litigation. There was a draft Convention to create a patent for the entire Community—the CPC. Juridically, such a patent is quite different from a series of national patents. It would be an essentially EU legal creature, taking effect as a matter of European law. The proposal foundered in 1975—essentially for two reasons: language and a court system. Revived in the late1980s it foundered again—for the same two reasons.

Following that or about the same time, the Dutch read the Brussels Convention on Enforcement and Recognition of Judgments. It is startling that no one realised its potential impact on intellectual property

[1] *It remains valid: (a) It is far too slow. It is true that the Boards of Appeal will upon request by a national judge speed up appeals somewhat (though real speed, such forcing the parties to hearing within a month or so, is well beyond achievable). But that does not speed up oppositions. In truth there is no perception within the EPO of the need for real expedition in those relatively few cases where commercial considerations require a quick, final answer.*

[2] Boards of Appeal still largely consider that they are courts of first instance—hence the willingness to admit evidence which could perfectly well have been admitted below. Of course if they are really a first instance judicial body, then there is no right of appeal, which puts the whole system (and hence all members of the European Patent Union in breach of TRIPS. Art 41(4) of this provides 'Parties to a proceeding shall have an opportunity for review by a judicial authority of ... at least the legal aspects of initial *judicial* [my emphasis] decisions on the merits of the case'.

[3] *Not yet, however! I am afraid the Boards and their procedure remain largely the same, and the delays are now just as bad as they were in 2000. A thorough overhaul is necessary. I have a number of ideas but this is not the place for them.*

rights enforcement before—after all it was in force amongst the original members from 1968. The UK, Denmark and Ireland joined in 1982. Its rules, so far as they apply to intellectual property, are, frankly, dreadful. In broad terms it is an allocation Treaty. It set its face against the notion of *forum conveniens*—you do not decide on the most sensible forum for a dispute, you apply the rules woodenly. Moreover no one realised that in the case of parallel rights in different countries, the basic rules of the Treaty (sue the defendant in his home country) could be turned on their head in IP cases by suing his customer in the country of his choice and joining in the 'true' defendant in those proceedings. To some extent the recent Dutch notion of the 'spider in the web' ameliorates the position. It has some intellectual justification from the *Shevill* case though the intellectual foundations of that case are themselves not easy to follow. What has really been happening is that the courts have been trying to find a way of reintroducing *forum conveniens*.

I do not want to say more about Brussels now. Much of what I would have said is likely to have been said in the session on multinational IP litigation. The fact is that Brussels is no good for patents and every user says so.

What then are the alternatives? Well, clearly the CPC model, having failed twice, is no good. The heart of its scheme was what was called COPAC—the 'Community Patent Court of Appeal'. The idea was that one would use national courts as Community courts of first instance with an appeal to a common court of appeal. There was an add-on idea: the latter could be linked to the European Court of Justice with a further appeal to that. Patent holders disliked the idea. The fact is that not all European countries have civil legal systems which work well. Some countries take years to get a result (people speak of Belgian or Italian torpedoes under the Brussels system). Moreover, and this is even more significant, not all countries have specialist patent judges or have civil procedures well designed for patent cases. Take the often key question of whether an invention was obvious. Some countries leave that to a court expert who will virtually decide the case himself—often without argument and irrespective of how skilled in the art he really is.

The plain fact is that you could not create a workable system along the COPAC model. Nor, I think, can you make it workable by tinkering with it. Until recently that seemed to be the thinking within the EU. The idea was that Member States should create specialist patent courts from which appeal would lie to the Court of First Instance of the European Court of Justice. This seemed to me like the man struggling in mud or quicksand—it would make things worse. I put aside the problems that many countries might have constitutional problems (what do you do, for instance, in a federal country where the courts are essentially state rather than federal?). The real problem is that you would be back to forum shopping, torpedoes and the real problems of inexperienced judges. Some countries have no patent actions. Making a specialist court for that country would be pointless.

Thus it is that one is driven inexorably towards the notion of a supranational court both of first instance and appeal. It is either that or continue with the current situation. Two models have recently begun to emerge: one is the EPC Protocol model and the other is the EU model.

The EPC Protocol idea is that there should be an add-on Treaty to the EPC. (For some unknown reason add-on Treaties are called 'Protocols'.) This Protocol would create a court for litigating patents granted by the EPO for all the members of the EPC who joined the scheme. There would be a court of first instance and appeal. Brussels would be excluded. The judges would be chosen from available specialist judges from national courts along with expertise from the EPO Boards of Appeal. An advantage of this scheme is that it would readily incorporate non-EU EPC countries, particularly Switzerland, which has rather a good stock of specialist patent judges. A disadvantage, at least in theory, is that it would notionally divide the EU between those countries litigating under the Protocol system and those outside it who would still be under the Brussels model.[4]

Until recently the Protocol idea was the only realistic idea in town. As I have said, the EU was fiddling with the COPAC model—as the follow-up to the Green Paper showed. But I can tell you that the Commission has now come to realise that that way will not work. It has accepted the logic of the necessity of a full court, first instance and appeal, both on pragmatic grounds and, I understand, on constitutional grounds (the idea of an appeal to a Community court from a national court may be unconstitutional, though I am not sure why). The pragmatism accepts the problem of appeals from wildly different national systems and the problem of overloading the CFI [Court

[4] *I missed the problem that some comparatively minor bits of patent law and procedure are or could be EU law. That surely meant that you could not have non-EU participation in a court—see Chapter 25, 'The Perfect Patent Court'.*

of First Instance]. The Commission recently took up an offer from interested judges to discuss the question in principle. They are now actively looking at what needs to be in legislation by way of fundamental rules of the proposed court. Indeed this very day my brother judge, Sir Nicholas Pumfrey, along with others, is assisting the Commission in this endeavour.

I have to say I welcome the Commission's new and realistic position and the vigour which they are putting into it. A paper outlining the proposals is likely this summer. European industry will applaud—it is what they have been asking for for years.

Quite what the impact of the Commission's new position will be on the Protocol idea is hard to say. One view is that it will supersede it. If a working EU litigation system is put in place there would hardly be an incentive for any EU Member State to join the Protocol. But the very existence of the proposal is a spur to the EU to get on with it. The idea of the Protocol would hardly have emerged if the EU had not seemed so stuck in the mud. And the Protocol may yet have its uses—what about the non-EU countries? So although I pose the question is it time to choose?, I think the answer is not yet, if at all. Let us keep them in competition for a while longer. And in the end, there may be ways for both schemes to work. For instance, it may be that non-EU members of the EPC would agree to use the EU court for litigation (that is likely to be the practical result). The only thing I fear from that is that excellent non-EU judges might be excluded from the court. But it may be possible to allow for this in implementing legislation. In my own country, for instance, it is not a rule of law that you have to be a UK citizen to be a judge. We have several senior ones who are South Africans.

Of course once one has decided to create a supranational court under either model formidable problems remain to be solved. Let me list some of them here:

(a) The 'clash' between the common law system and the Civil law system. Some gloomy types suggest this is too difficult to overcome but I do not think so. Indeed a meld is what is actually being carried out in the War Crimes Tribunal at the Hague.
(b) Discovery of documents or a saisie?
(c) Expert evidence—how much court based how much external experts—single experts or each side having their own?
(d) How much oral procedure should there be? Should there be cross-examination common law style? Should there be limited cross-examination or none?

(e) How will the court's orders be enforced? It would seem ultimately by making them take effect as orders of a national court for each Member State.
(f) What matters should be reserved for the jurisdiction of the court? Infringement and validity obviously but what about amendment of the patent, damages, consequences of breach of an order etc, etc?
(g) Who should sit on the court? National judges of experience, but who else? Technical judges of the kind found in the Federal Patent Court of Germany?
(h) What about the Court of Appeal? Should or could one use the same pool of judges as those who sit at first instance as is done in Australia and was done for a while in England in the last century? I think that would work at least for a transitional period.
(i) Where should the court sit? Can it have a local presence? I think it should have an HQ and be prepared to move. The analogy with the old English Assize system is good. To create a uniform legal code across the country Henry II sent his judges out to try big cases. That was 700 years ago when crossing England was much harder than travelling across Europe is now.
(j) What about small companies? Will they have to travel? Not necessarily if the court can move.
(k) Who can appear before the court? Lawyers yes, but what about patent attorneys?
(l) What are the court fees to be? And what controls should the court have over lawyers' fees? What orders for costs can be made?
(m) Should the court grant provisional measures for the whole EU?
(n) Can national courts play a part, for instance granting provisional measures effective until the court can hear the matter?
(o) Should there be a period of limitation, if so what?
(p) What about language? This was one of the great stumbling blocks of the CPC and this proposal does not address it. In the real world people would probably be happy to work just in English (quite a few non-English favour this on cost grounds) but can you really say to a Spaniard, say, that whether or not he can make and sell something in the EU is to be decided in English? I think there may be a pragmatic way out here—and as English is becoming more and more the lingua franca of Europeans the problem may dissolve.
(q) How many of the procedural rules can be worked out by the court and what must be done by implementing rules?

Who could be the losers under either system? Well, an often suggested candidate is the SME. If a man only has a local business in one Member State why should he become involved in this 'federal' court? As plaintiff he would not have to, for no one is suggesting he cannot have a purely national patent. But if he elects for a full European monopoly then I see no reason why he should not have to face a fully European court if his monopoly is challenged. As a defendant the problem is perhaps greater, though once he wants to challenge validity he is putting the whole European market into play.

Who else could be losers? I will be blunt—it could be, and is intended to be, lawyers. We are genuinely trying to get rid of multiplicity of litigation. That means using fewer lawyers, at least per case. And if language is restricted, those who make a living by translation may find less to do. In the real world I doubt if anyone will lose significant work. There is so much IP that really there are not enough lawyers to do it. But in the end the lawyers do not matter. Legal systems and machinery are not there for the benefit of lawyers.

You can see that there is much to be done. The challenge for Europe is to produce a really good litigation system for patents. I believe it can be done. We Europeans can produce a model for the world. And if we fall short of that ideal, I console myself with the proposition that things could be much worse than they are now. And at least we are not proposing to send patent disputes to juries!

POSTSCRIPT

This was 14 years ago. Much has happened. So this talk is really of value only historically—I hope interesting for all that. See Chapter 25, 'The Perfect Patent Court', for more.

33

*The Harmonisation of Patent Litigation**

MY ALTERNATIVE TITLE is 'unfinished business'. And I begin with a story told to me by my father. When he was in the War Office a fellow officer had on his desk not two, but three trays. There were the usual two, labelled 'in' and 'out'. The third was labelled 'too difficult'.

The founders of the modern European law of patents, in creating the EPC of 1973, strictly observed this principle. They concentrated on substantive law. They left the vital questions of procedure largely for another time. And, as will be seen, so far as they had to and so did deal with procedure, what they have left us is unsatisfactory.

What they left us, in short, is not only unfinished business, but by much the hardest part of that business. As Mary Mack said in her Biography of Jeremy Bentham: 'The law is everything, and in it procedure and evidence come first'. I make no complaint about what the founders did. They had no choice. It was too early even to try to tackle procedure. But the time has now come for this generation of Europeans to try and finish the unfinished business. The task is formidable. It involves lawyers from each country concerned really trying to understand what is done in other countries. It is no good saying 'we do it this way. So, if they do it different in some other country, they must be wrong.' What we need to do is find the good bits of procedure from all around Europe, and create a coherent, economical, fast and fair system.

* *Based on a lecture given to the Dutch AIPPI Group in Zeist, Holland (1997) and first published in [1997]* Intellectual Property Quarterly *142–50.*

I do not expect us to succeed in finding a perfect system of justice. I do not believe it can exist on this earth. But we need to strive towards that summit of perfection, even though we can never reach it. At present we are hardly even in the foothills of the mountain labelled 'perfect procedure'. And for many years no one seemed to be interested in going anywhere nearer the mountain. It is entirely understandable that it was you, in Holland, who, after so many years, tried to take some independent steps towards the foothills. I refer to your courts' assertion of a power to assert cross-border rights. After all you have always been great internationalists—it is not a coincidence that Grotius was Dutch.

Let me therefore outline some of the present problems and what I see as possible solutions and future problems.

THE EUROPEAN PATENT OFFICE

As Things Stand

I start here. I am going to say some critical things. I want no one to think that I thereby am hostile to the EPO or to those in it. On the contrary, I have many friends there and I believe it can and ultimately must play an even more significant role in European patent matters. It is either that or chaos.

Running through what I say will be two themes: speed and fairness. Let me begin with speed.

The processing of applications takes two stages—pre-grant and opposition—between the Office and the applicant. Why do some cases take so long at this stage—when matters are solely between the applicant and the Office?

Look at what applicants want first. A naïve view might be that they want their patent as quickly as possible. But that is true only for a small proportion of cases—cases where the invention is commercialised quickly and copyists are likely. But generally no one knows for a long time how important an invention is. It is the rare case where there is a commercial hurry for the grant of the patent. In most cases a patentee wants to wait for a host of reasons. First he can wait to see whether his idea is any good at all. The longer his patent takes to process, the better. He can avoid expensive translations and designation fees for as long as possible. Next he can keep his competitors guessing. Until grant they do not know what the maximum scope of protection may be. That may be enough to deter the competition.

Finally it is the case that there is no real pressure on the Office. It gets the renewal fees while the patent is pending so it might be said that it even has an interest in delay.

So in many cases there is a built-in bias towards inertia. I believe that the Office needs to tackle this. Both pre- and post-grant it must set real deadlines—dates by which the applicant or opponent must reply. And those dates should not be extended without good reason. It might be said that there is a lot of work for the examiners to do. This is true—but delay always increases the work involved.

Next consider oppositions. I have to say that the Office's idea of a fast track—both in the Opposition Division and in the Boards of Appeal—is not good enough. Let me give you a recent example. Last September or thereabouts I fixed a case for trial next December. I was told that the patent is also in litigation in Italy, Germany and, I think, France. I was told that the matter was before a Board of Appeal already. I asked the EPO whether it could get on with the case. I was told there would not be a result before the end of 1997. I will be blunt. I do not think that will do. I can think of no good reason why the case could not be done within six months from my request. It would mean putting the parties under strict time limits but where is the difficulty in that? They had already been through opposition and were preparing for battle in four countries. Why should we all have to wait to know whether there will be a patent and what its claims might be?

What are my solutions? I have already talked of fixed times without extensions. I also think fixed hearing dates are important. It was Dr Samuel Johnson who said that 'there is nothing like a hanging for concentrating a man's mind wonderfully'. That is true. A fixed hearing date has just that effect. I think the Office should aim to fix a hearing date soon after battle is joined in an opposition. Experience in our courts and US courts suggests that what is wanted is a Listing Official—someone within the Office whose job it is to drive both the examiners and Boards of Appeal and the parties. Moreover, the Office should do away with the practice of doing nothing if an opposition is entered early in the nine-month period. The current practice is to wait until the end of the period in case anyone else joins in. I do not see why late joiners should not be made to speed up. Suppose the nine-month period were abolished? What would the Office do then? Wait until the patent expired?

I also think the Office should consider a system for expedited applications and oppositions—which can be initiated by any party, a third party who gives reasons, or a national court. I hope my friends in the Office will listen: for the ancient maxim of Magna Carta is as true in patent matters as in any other: 'justice delayed is justice denied'. I can say that in our courts we are too often hearing cases about patents which are still somewhere in the opposition process of the EPO. What we will not do is to wait and see what happens unless both sides want that. Incidentally, you may be interested to know that our Court of Appeal has just, in *Beloit v Valmet*, held that our courts have jurisdiction to hear a case whilst an opposition or appeal is pending in the EPO. In fact I heard the case, and our Court of Appeal heard the appeal a year or so later. The matter is still pending in the EPO. If we had not got on with the case the defendants, who wanted to build a $350 million paper-making plant in Kent, would not have got the legal certainty which mattered.

Next fairness. I think the time has come for a review of some of the procedures. The manner in which matters are proved in the EPO is, in some areas, inadequate. Take prior use. I think the Office ought to require sworn statements coupled with documentary or other significant corroboration before accepting a prior use. It does not always do so. And in all cases the substance of evidence should be supplied to the other side well before the hearing. Likewise last-minute auxiliary requests changing the claims significantly should be ruled out. The patentee has had plenty of time to formulate his claims—by subsidiary claims when he files and early on in the court of any opposition procedure. Times for filing evidence and such requests should be set at an early stage. No one should be taken by surprise, either by an opponent or indeed the Office.

Consider another matter: transcripts and open access to hearings. It is, I suggest, quite wrong that there is no public access to hearings. Of course in most cases no one but the parties is interested. But should the press really be excluded from hearings about the oncomouse and like cases? Moreover not even the alternative is available—recordings. Why are there are no recordings of hearings before the Opposition Division and still more so the Boards of Appeal? I recently held, in *Lenzing's Application*, that national courts could not review decisions of the Boards of Appeal. Moreover, I held that the Boards did provide a means of judicial review within the meaning of Art 21 of TRIPS. I described the members of the Boards as 'judges in all but name'. Well, it is a feature of the proper administration of justice that courts operate openly and transparently. Justice must not only be done but be seen to be done. The scrutiny of the public is indispensable to the proper administration of justice. It is publicity which enables us all to judge the judges. I cannot do better than quote Jeremy Bentham: 'Publicity is the very soul of justice. It is the keenest spur to exertion and the surest of all guards against improbity. It keeps the judge himself while trying under trial'.[1]

I do not know why recordings are not made or even permitted to be made, as I understand is the position. What is there to fear? Even if actual access of the public to hearings is impractical I do think everyone present should know that what they say is taken down and can be looked at later. As a national judge, I would like to know if a fact, technical or otherwise, has been misrepresented to the Office. The mere fact of the existence of a recording can have a great deterrent on such misrepresentation.

Another thing is the strange practice of giving results within an hour or so of the hearing and the reasons later—in extreme cases, nearly a year later. Why? It gives the impression that the hearing is only a formality: hanging first, trial later. It serves no useful purpose. It may mean that when the decision is written the real reasons have been forgotten or only half remembered. Judges do not have this practice. They do not do it because in writing, or giving the decision orally, they reason to the result. So should the EPO.

Thus far I have spoken about ordinary oppositions and appeals and matters which need no more than administrative action. Now I turn to a more radical proposal.

The Enlarged Board and National Judges: A Proposal

The EPO organises a biennual conference of European patent judges. I believe all those who attend find these of enormous benefit. Not only do we learn how others do things, but we learn to think together more. And, frankly, we make friends and learn to respect one another.

The time has now come to move further. I have put forward a proposal that the Enlarged Board should contain a significant number of national judges. It is making and shaping the European law

[1] Quoted by Lord Shaw in *Scott v Scott* [1913] AC 417, 477. This case is the leading English authority on the need for the administration of justice to be open.

of patents. It is vital that the national judges who enforce and consider the validity of patents should take a significant hand in this exercise. By so doing a convergence of approach will be aided. My proposal is no secret. It is necessarily in general terms and there are obvious problems such as how you choose which judges to sit. But I am glad to say that all but one of the European judges to whom I wrote support the idea. I look forward to the day when judges from around Europe, judges with practical experience of patent enforcement, form, in effect, the final court of appeal of the EPO.

Amendment of the EPC

In the end the proposal may involve an amendment of the EPC. I do not shrink from that. It has worked well for 20 years but the time is coming to see what can be done to improve procedures. I think we need a full court of appeal for the EPO staffed at least in the majority by actual national judges or persons qualified to be national judges in their own countries. I do not say such a court should take all appeals. But it should take all questions of law or procedure of importance. Moreover, I think, as Judge Sylvie Mandel of the Court of Appeal of France suggests, that such a court could take references from national courts. Even if that were not its initial function that could come. The ECJ is not a suitable forum for two reasons: first, it would be impossible given that the EPC covers non-EU states and second, its judges, with all due respect, might find the technicalities of some patents unattractive to deal with. Let us see how they get on with trade marks first.

Incidentally, if there were an amendment of the EPC one of the things that must be addressed is amendment of patent—limitation of claims particularly. Currently, once a patent enters the national phase national procedures for amendment of the patent apply. Some countries do not allow amendment. Others do, but by different procedures and criteria. It is entirely possible for different amendments to be allowed in different countries. I understand that you in Holland have no amendment procedure as such—instead you have the concept of partial validity of a claim, allowing the valid bit to be enforced. None of these differences makes sense. The whole point is to have a patent of the same scope throughout the countries of designation. If it is amended it should be amended everywhere and the grounds for allowing or refusing an amendment should be the same everywhere.

Currently, for example, we in the UK are more careful about allowing an amendment than they are in the EPO. We retain a rule that if the patentee was late in applying for an amendment when he knows or ought to have known his claims as they stood were bad, then he will not be allowed to amend and will lose his patent. We think it is a good rule—stopping people holding onto monopolies they know to be bad. Should that be the general rule? In a sense the difference is understandable. In theory the EPO is dealing with a patent at an early stage in its life. But even so if it emerged that a patentee had deliberately tried to get a patent when he knew it was bad (eg deliberately suppressed his own prior use saying 'no one will catch me') surely he should not be allowed to amend to get out of what he had done?

PATENT LITIGATION

I avoid talking about the CPC. Experience rather suggests that at present this is in the 'too hard' tray. It has been there for 20 years and looks as though it is staying there, though the Commission says in its First Action Plan for Innovation in Europe[2] that it is planning a Green Paper for 1997. I do think, however, that the Commission would do well to consult national patent judges about any proposal. We cannot advise on the politics of the matter but we can advise on practicalities. I wish the Commission well with the plan. But at present it is likely to require translation into all the Community languages. My clear impression is that in reality industry—the customers—will not want it on that basis. I advise the Commission to consider this problem at the beginning. It is no good setting up a system which costs too much. Moreover, I think the direct approach of a Community Court of Patent Appeal—COPAC—logical though it might be, has real problems. Who would sit on it? Who would want to sit on it? How much work would it have—a deluge or a trickle, and so on? I think there are other ways to be considered. One I propose above—more involvement of national judges in the EPO.

Another is the most important development by way of the direct involvement of national judges in Europe-wide disputes. You in Holland have pioneered the cross-border injunction. I rather think Jan Brinkhof, in asking me, was hoping that I would make a forecast

[2] 20.11.1996 Com(96) 589 final.

of what the English courts will do, or at least give my views on what you have done. I do not intend to do that for two reasons. First I think it difficult for a judge to indicate his views on a matter which may well come before him. But second I can give you some news.

Last week Lloyd J held that, by virtue of Art 2 of the Brussels Convention, the English court has jurisdiction to hear a question of infringement of a Dutch copyright. The plaintiff was an architect called Pearce. When he was a student he did a project by way of a design for a town hall in Docklands London. Of course the design would have not only a UK copyright, but copyright in the all the Berne countries, including Holland. He claimed that two Dutch architecture firms had access to his work and had copied it in Holland to design the Kunsthal in Rotterdam. Other defendants were also joined, namely the engineers Ove Arup, and the owners of the building, the City of Rotterdam. Only infringement of Dutch copyright was asserted.

Ove Arup were domiciled in England. The judge held that by virtue of Art 2 they could be sued in England for breach of the Dutch copyright. All other English rules of law and procedure preventing this were overcome by Art 2. Moreover he held that there was no discretion. The English courts were obliged to accept jurisdiction, even though the key events all happened in Holland. The other defendants were then brought in under Art 6(1).

The judge went on to hold, however, that the plaintiff's case was so weak that it should be struck out. This is unfortunate, for only a court of appeal can refer a question under the Brussels Convention and this case may never get there. I dare say another will before too long. If the Convention really requires national courts to hear cases of infringement of foreign intellectual property rights, provided a defendant can be found within the territorial jurisdiction of the national court, then I believe we will be in for a period of forum shopping on a large scale. Let me mention some of the considerations, starting from the plaintiff's point of view. He will ask questions in the following order:

(1) Where am I most likely to win? Make no mistake, this is much the most important question.
(2) His next question will be where is quickest?
(3) And where is cheapest?

Many other considerations may arise. For instance, which country's courts give the most damages? Can I get damages for what the

Americans call 'conveyed goods', for instance lost sales of spares for the patented article? Can I get punitive damages? Can I get legal aid? I suspect that was a big motive in *Pearce v Ove Arup*—especially since we have the strange and unjust rule that a successful defendant cannot get his legal costs from the Legal Aid Fund. Other considerations may be: can I get (or avoid) discovery? Will there be cross-examination? Can I call my own expert? 'Is my case weak, but commercially worthwhile, so I should try to find an inexperienced judge and hope that he/she will not find out?

Nor will it only be plaintiffs who forum shop. Many potential defendants may try pre-emptive strikes, particularly for declaratory or similar relief. It has already been tried in Belgium (see the decision of 6 February 1997 in *Smithkline Beecham Pharma v Chiron*). The court held that it had jurisdiction to grant cross-border relief but declined, in summary proceedings, to grant an order suspending the effects of the defendant's patents until the basic action could be tried. A less ambitious attempt failed in England (see *Organon Technica v F Hoffmann-La Roche*),[3] but only on a technicality which could no longer apply because of a change in the rules. Others may try so to organise their affairs so as to avoid countries which are seen as too pro-plaintiff. For instance, a few years ago when your *kort geding* procedure was seen as a near certain passport to a Europe-wide injunction, I heard the chief patent agent of Akzo say at a conference that he advised his own company not to start new activities in Holland. Other companies will certainly react the same way about any country whose judges are, or are thought to be, pro-plaintiff.

How should the judges react to all this? I believe that we should be careful. We should be astute as to what is really going on, we should keep in touch with one another and we should remember that the interests of you intellectual property lawyers come second: what matters is European industry. That will not be served by chaos. It will be served by orderly, just resolution of disputes. And that must be achieved quickly: industry cannot afford uncertainty.

The beauty of a point based on copyright, from a scholar's point of view, is that it is not complicated by the exclusive jurisdiction provision of Art 16. Patents are. Before I go on to consider them, you may be interested to know that on the same day as *Pearce v Ove Arup* was decided, last Friday, I refused to stay an English passing-off action where there was a dispute about the same trade mark in Germany.

[3] *Organon Technica v F Hoffmann-La Roche* [1996] FSR 383.

I do not have time to go into that here, though you may find the case, called *Mecklermedia v DC*, interesting. I must return to patents.

The next bit of news is that my brother judge, Laddie J, was hearing a question of cross-border jurisdiction in patent matters yesterday. He was being asked to enjoin, on a provisional basis, a Dutch company from infringing a British, Spanish and German patent and a German company from infringing a German patent. It was being contended, by virtue of Art 21, that he had to deal with the claim against the Dutch defendant because it is admittedly properly before the court along with a British defendant. Obviously I cannot predict what he will do.

But I can say this: patents have the real complication of Art 16. The truth is that you cannot infringe an invalid patent. The UK Act, by s 74(1)(a), specifically provides that a defendant can put validity in issue by way of defence. But that only makes explicit that which is self-evident as a matter of logic. Now Art 16 confers exclusive jurisdiction in proceedings concerned with the validity of patents. Some countries hear infringement and validity in different courts. I cannot believe that it would be right to treat infringement in those countries simply as subject to Art 2. In other words it would be wrong to say that infringement proceedings are not concerned with validity because validity is dealt with in a different court. Does all this mean that so far as final relief is concerned, only national courts have jurisdiction if validity is in issue? I do not know, but the Court of Justice is certainly going to have to decide that one.

I turn to provisional relief—'protective measures'—under Art 24. You have decided that such measures may be given Europe wide. I do not know what the UK position is. But I do want to put forward some important considerations.

(1) What if the claim is bad, eg the patent is invalid? Justice requires that the defendant who was stopped be fully compensated. How is that to be secured? A bond in some cases may be necessary. In cases where the plaintiff is obviously solvent—a BP or Akzo—it may be sufficient to have a legally binding obligation to compensate.

(2) What about the case where it is simply too difficult to form a provisional view on the merits? The fact is that the subject-matter of many patents is too complex for the court to understand enough to form any reasonable assessment of the ultimate merits. Then there are real problems.

(3) How long before a full trial can be had? If it is fast enough then you need not go into the merits. In the UK we have by and large been finding it possible to push cases to trial quickly. Generally it takes a year, but both Laddie J and I have found it possible to order shorter times than that. Often of course the parties settle—there is the Dr Johnson hanging effect at work for you.
(4) What is to be the position in other countries pending trial? Suppose the validity of the patent is attacked in those countries? Should the provisional measure continue? Should the parties (or at least the plaintiff if the defendant so demands) be required to start infringement proceedings in other countries if validity is attacked? What if the patent is found valid in some countries and not in others?
(5) How should the court regard the fact that the patent has been examined, and possibly opposed unsuccessfully? Does that strengthen the case? I have my doubts. You in Holland have been used to a strong patent office. When I was young it was said to be the toughest office in the world. It would be a mistake to assume that other offices, including the EPO, are that strict. The fact is that although there must be something of a presumption that a patent has been examined well, I would not, myself, regard that as too strong. An office is seldom as effective at devising an attack as a hostile opponent or defendant. Moreover, it is likely to accept assertions of technical fact by a patentee—there is no one to challenge them So I think it is more important to form one's own view on the strength of the attack In this connection I give a word to lawyers. Only put your best case. If a judge sees a patent attacked on the basis of 15 bits of prior art he instinctively asks, 'Why so many, have they not got a good one?'
(6) What about the defendants' ability to pay damages for infringement? And will those damages include conveyed goods (eg damages for lost sales of spares) and so on?

For myself I think the above considerations lead to the conclusion that it is only in cases which are reasonably clear on both infringement and validity that a court should take the step of granting a Europe-wide injunction. A lesser standard may well put European industry under too monopolistic a grip.

Finally I turn to another subject. What should courts do about prior findings of fact by other courts? Suppose you in Holland decide that a prior use happened—for instance, that a device was shown to a member of the public and that what was seen was enabling. Should, or must, another court accept that finding? We in England have a doctrine called *res judicata by issue estoppel* which may lead to that result. It is a very international doctrine. Provided one is sure that the point was fairly before, and tried on the merits, by the foreign tribunal with any appeal decided or foreclosed, we accept that finding. I do not know whether any other European countries have such a rule. Even if not, I rather suspect that as we converge we are likely to pay more and more respect to each other's findings. So here is another area where the interplay between courts is likely to be of significance. Thus far *issue estoppel* has not had much significance in UK patent litigation. It was rejected as between our courts and the US courts in one case, *Kirin-Amgen v Boehringer Mannheim*,[4] but the relevant facts were not critical to the US decision.

All these complexities show just how much unfinished business there is. It is our generation's job to help finish it—to produce a rational, just, fair and effective system of patent dispute resolution in Europe. All of us, judges, legislators and lawyers, must work together to that end.

[4] *Kirin-Amgen v Boehringer Mannheim* 31.7.1996, CA.

34

Paper for the Ninth (Madrid) Symposium of the European Patent Judges 1998

SINCE OUR LAST meeting, and inspired by it, many of you will know that some of us have actively tried to find a way forward for a more integrated patent litigation system for Europe. I, and others, have lectured and written about the subject. I have been fortunate enough to attend meetings in a variety of places, for instance I have been the guest of the President of the Federal Patent Court of Germany and of the Richterakadamie. I gave a lecture in Holland[1] and a short presentation to the Richterakadamie in April this year. Copies of these are made available (along with two other lectures). In these papers I sought to outline the problems of patent litigation in Europe and how the cross-border injunction is not a solution. Many of you will also know that in response to the Green Paper some of us sent a letter to the Commission offering the assistance of the judges. A copy of that letter is also annexed. I am surprised we have not heard anything from the Commission as a result.[2]

I do not wish to go back to what I said in those papers. It is sufficient for me to say today that the future lies not in cross-border injunctions granted by national courts, but in a European Patent Court. The major difficulties in the way of such a court are partly political (language and other reasons) and partly simply because the

[1] Bijblad Industriële Eigendom No 5 1997, [1997] IPQ. It is Chapter 33.

[2] *That was putting it mildly—it was a disgrace. The civil servants were not only rude but obviously of a similar mind to an architect who thinks he can design a mighty building without consulting a structural engineer. In the end it was the judges and practitioners who built the best bits of the Unified Patent Court (the Rules of Procedure). The parts built with no or little consultation are those which imperil the scheme—see Chapter 25, 'The Perfect Patent Court'.*

task of making such a court is so hard. Judges cannot do anything about the political problems, but they can at least assist in making the task easier. They can do that in two ways: first by providing practical advice on setting up a judicial system which will be both workable and reliable. The politicians and civil servants cannot do that on their own. With all due respect, for instance, the judicial arrangements of the EPO, set up by the Munich Diplomatic Conference, are not satisfactory in principle and have become cumbersome and in practice less and less respected by industry. Secondly I believe there are practical steps which can and should be taken now to help produce a rational and cohesive patent system for Europe.

A WORKABLE SYSTEM

Here I repeat part of my paper to the Richterakadamie.

> If I am right that no solution under the existing provisions is acceptable and that the current position is unstable, then an alternative solution must be found. Many agree with this, but what is the solution and how do we get there?
>
> As you will know there has been a Commission Green Paper and subsequent consultation. The way forward is clearly some sort of European solution. Some points seem to be largely agreed:
>
> First it is agreed that infringement and validity should be tried together. This is not the German national way, but I confess I have met few German lawyers prepared to defend split trial. It is the result of history and politics. Next it is agreed that the EPO cannot be made the final arbiter of validity. There are many reasons for this—its current inadequate dispute resolution procedures and the fact that it is essentially a Patent Office are but two.
>
> Next it is agreed that there should be a European Patent Court of Appeal. Whether it is a free-standing court set up by Treaty or introduced by the Community as part of the Court of First Instance is not clear. It may not matter, but certainly it would be good to have the Swiss in the system—they have reliable and experienced patent judges. There are not that many of them around Europe.
>
> But after that the glass goes dark. Should there be Community courts which are really national courts with Community hats on—as has been set up for European Trade Marks. Or should there be a court of first instance which is set up de novo? I favour the latter.

> And in any event what is the procedure of the court of first instance to be? Different countries have different notions of what is meant by an 'appeal'. In common law countries the court of first instance is the place where essentially *all* the evidence is gathered. Appeals are heard on the materials before the court of first instance and only in exceptional cases is fresh evidence admitted. I think we will have to have such a rule within Europe. The system will be no good unless it can work quickly. Any period of more than 2 years to trial will be very bad for industry (currently we have 1 year in England). Appeals should be heard and determined within a year thereafter as a maximum. If the Court of Appeal can admit fresh material that sort of objective could not be met. For once fresh material can be admitted, the other party must be able to deal with it and so you get into fresh rounds of evidence and submissions. Moreover the work of the court will get bogged down.
>
> Now if the Court of Appeal is to work on the material from the court of first instance, then there must be a proper way of getting that material recorded and set. I favour uniform rules of procedure. The creation of a working set of these is an enormous challenge. The biggest difference between Roman and common law countries is not substantive law, it lies in procedure and legal institutions. Yet I think the job can be done. Some aspects of English procedure are good, and others are bad. For instance in some areas of law (particularly those concerned with fact, such as prior use) our procedures are good. Discovery of documents and cross-examination by a lawyer from the other side is a good way of getting at the truth. But in other areas (especially that major area, obviousness) I think it is not a particularly good way—and it is certainly expensive.

Now I have said the task is immense. In the UK the Commission's Green Paper caused a Committee of the Upper Chamber of our Parliament to set up a Committee to look into the question. It took evidence from right across British industry, the professions, the judges and indeed invited Judge Brinkhof to give evidence. I think its conclusion[3] is accurate. It reads as follows:

> The Committee believes the Community patent, a single patent which is valid throughout the Community, would have advantages over the present system of European and national patents. The success of the system depends firstly … on keeping the costs down. A practical solution has to be found to the question of the number and extent of translations. There must also be judicial arrangements which will command the confidence of industry. The Community patent has to be sufficiently attrac-

[3] The full report is worth reading. It is called 'The Community Patent and the Patent System in Europe' 26th Report of Session 1997–98 HL Paper 15.

tive to industry and able to compete alongside national patents and the European patent. If not, it will remain a white elephant which no-one will want. It is clear to the Committee that there is substantial interest and support for a Community Patent within industry at the present time. A major political push and preparedness to compromise on the language question are needed if the idea is to become a reality.

Now I believe that the judges have done all they can at this stage to assist in the idea. The question is how hard industry will push—and how much the politicians can respond. We can do no more than stand ready to assist.

PRACTICAL STEPS

Having so concluded, however, I do not think we should be doing nothing until the politicians call upon us. On the contrary there are a number of small, but I think nonetheless practical steps we can be taking now. I outline some of them:

1. First, we should write our judgments with a view to them being intelligible to courts across Europe. We are increasingly being invited to read judgments of other national courts (and of course of the EPO). Translation is often necessary, but even in translation it is not always easy to understand what other judges say. There are two reasons for this:
   (a) There are often many procedural unspoken assumptions, assumptions which a judge would expect anyone acquainted with his or her national system to know. We must all remember that others do not have this basic knowledge. So it is better to make those matters explicit—for instance by recording how the court came by the information which forms the basis of its judgment.
   (b) In our judgments we should endeavour to use the Articles of the EPC directly. The Parliaments of many countries chose to implement the provisions of the EPC either by rewriting it or by renumbering it or both. In the UK our Parliament did both. If in our judgments we refer to our national sections or articles and not those of the EPC we immediately make our judgments much more difficult to understand for outsiders. We are all supposed to be implementing the law of the EPC, let us use its actual language and its actual

provisions. Just as Art 85 conveys instant meaning to all competition lawyers throughout Europe, so should Art 54 EPC. For myself I have just decided so to do and have said so in a judgment.[4]

(c) I also think we should try and use convenient case names. The time has long past when one can pretend that the law is not in part judge-made. It is made, albeit 'interstitially' (the great US Justice Holmes' word) in decided cases. Reference to cases should therefore be 'user-friendly'. This involves abandoning in part some existing traditions. For instance the EPO Boards of Appeal still refer to the case we all call '*Mobil*/Friction reducing additive' simply by the unmemorable name Case G02/88. The European Court of Justice took this step a long time ago. Everyone responds to *Cassis de Dijon*[5] but no one knows what the official case number is.

2. We should see that important judgments of patent courts of each of our countries are disseminated. Following discussions at the last Symposium, Hugh Laddie and I have persuaded some publishers to commence a series of law reports of European Patent cases. The publishers (Sweet & Maxwell) will need to be supplied with the cases and for that purpose it would be invaluable to have judges in each country who send cases in for possible reporting. Initially at least the reports will only be in English—they will be modelled on the European Trade Mark Reports, which started a couple of years ago. I do not think we should underestimate the significance of a set of European patent reports. The natural tendency of judges is to keep the law cohesive and this will be an invaluable tool for that purpose. I unashamedly intend to act as a recruiting agent for the editorial board of this journal at this Symposium. The publishers want to start at the end of this year, so this is no mere visionary dream of the future.[6]

[4] *Bristol-Myers v Baker Norton* [1998] EWHC Patents 300. 20 August 1998.

[5] Case 120/78, *Rewe-Zentral v Bundesmonoopolverwaltung für Branntwein.*

[6] *It ran for a few years but was overtaken by the Internet.*

3. We should increasingly be willing to consult each other. The Internet is a powerful tool for this purpose. I would like to see a European Patent Judges' forum set up. Maybe the EPO could help in this regard.

4. We should all do our best to find out how colleagues in other countries actually go about their jobs. In the real world procedural law is not just some sort of handmaiden to substantive law: it determines most of what happens. So we must all try to learn what we each do—and indeed what part lawyers, experts and others play in the differing judicial procedures across Europe. Only by a better understanding of the strengths and weaknesses of our various national procedures will we be able to help produce, when the time comes, a really good European procedural code. There are all sorts of ways of learning—I mention just one: I extend a welcome to any and all of you to come and see the Patents Court in London if ever you are there. I know my brother judges, Hugh Laddie and Nicholas Pumfrey extend the same warm welcome.

POSTSCRIPT

1. *The first part of this shows early thinking about the project. It was at this symposium that the 'Madrid Group' was formed—see Chapter 25*
2. *The second part, about what could be done now, largely happened. However, there was a moment of drama after I gave the paper. During discussion time one of the French judges, Sylvie Mandel, said it was not possible in France to refer to foreign decisions. She said that French judges could not refer to previous cases even French cases. All the other judges were surprised and shocked for they agreed with me.*

Apparently the theory is that 'La Loi' must be only the law as made by the people—statute. There is in French legal theory no such thing as judge-made law. Part of the reason comes from the Revolution—under the Ancien Régime *the judges were appointed by the King and so 'law' made by them was something like a sovereign command and contrary to the spirit of the Revolution. Very Enlightenment. Jeremy Bentham thought the same thing.*

Of course in the real world judge-made law is inevitable. The French get round their rule by simply copying without acknowledgment passages from earlier judgments. That is also the explanation for the fact that ECJ judgments, until the UK and others arrived, never referred to its own earlier judgments. I do not know whether the French rule is actually a rule of law or is a rule of practice. I think I have more recently seen a few French judgments which do refer to other judgments (of the ECJ). But I still wish they would pay more attention to what other European courts decide.

35

*Objectionable Narrowness of Claim, a 'Side Bar'**

I WISH TO throw open a problem that has long niggled me. Can a claim be too narrow and if not, does it matter? If it matters what is the legal objection to the claim?

The paradigm and most general form of the claim I have in mind is: 'the World[1] when supporting my invention?' A more concrete example runs as follows: claim 1 is to an improved steam whistle. It is a perfectly ordinary sort of claim, specifying by integers (or 'features' in the new European terminology) the new whistle. But claim 2 is to a battleship fitted with the new steam whistle. Claim 3 is to a navy which includes one or more such battleships. Claim 4 is to a navy which includes any ship fitted with such a whistle. And so on.

It is not all that easy to find a good objection to such a claim. Assume that the whistle is new and non-obvious. Further there are perfectly good instructions on how to construct the whistle. The skilled man already knows how to construct battleships and navies. The claim is not ambiguous. The ordinary everyday grounds of attack are irrelevant. Nor can you say that claims are too wide. On the contrary claims 2 and 3 are *narrower* than claim 1, which is itself unobjectionable. In England we used to have an objection that the claim was 'not fairly based' on the matter disclosed in the specification. It was intended to be a codification of the common law. But it seldom worked—and when it did it was in circumstances where

* *First published in D Chisum et al (eds),* Principles of Patent Law *(Foundation Press, 1999). I invited comments, wrongly in the event, expecting none. When I got some from Richard Stern, a Washington lawyer, the piece along with our email correspondence was published in [1999] EIPR 40. These were very early days of the Internet.*

1 I suppose 'the universe containing …' is even more general and even narrower.

the claim was too wide. In the case of the battleships and so on you could easily disclose the idea of fitting the whistle to a battleship. There is no recorded instance under the old law of a claim having been defeated for being too narrow. There is nothing in the European Patent Convention which seems directly in point and I know of no European case which deals with the point. I am not a US lawyer, but I would be surprised if you have anything either.[2] The problem needs thinking out from first principles.

Should there be an objection that a claim is too narrow? Test this pragmatically. How could it matter? Does a man who has claim 1 get any advantage from claims 2 or 3? He gets nothing by way of strengthened validity: if claim 1 fell, claims 2–4 would go with it.

However, remedies may possibly be affected by this kind of claim. I do not suppose that the level of damages would be affected by infringement of claim 3 rather than claim 1 in the rather absurd steam whistle case. But a steam kettle might be different. You can have a claim to an improved kettle (an obvious example is the invention of the gadget which turned it off when it boiled). Can you have a claim to tea when made from water boiled in the improved kettle? If so, then the patentee would want to claim damages on (or perhaps profits from) the tea as well as the kettle. Could he sell his kettle with a limited licence requiring royalties on tea?

This last example is not so unreal. Some years ago the patentee of the device for electrostatic spraying was clever enough to include claims for the use of his device also. He made money not only from selling the device but from licensing its use—he charged by amount of paint consumed. That is close to charging for articles painted with his process.

I have an uneasy feeling that somehow the patentee ought not to be better off by this sort of claim but that he could be. It may be that he could not get any more damages directly out of a court (he'd have trouble with me, for instance). But there would be other advantages: it would probably be easier to assert claims against people down the line (café proprietors for instance). And the patentee might be in a better position vis-à-vis anti-trust law. For example he would say that, in charging royalties on tea (or painted articles), he was doing no more than claiming them on what he had actually patented. Thus he would avoid any charge of 'bundling' unpatented articles with

[2] If you do, let me know: rjacob@lix.compulink.co.uk. *This is the first kind of judicial email address, now long defunct.*

patented ones. Moreover it might be easier to justify what are in reality unreasonable royalty rates.

So I think there should be an objection. What is wanted is one directed at including within a claim that which has no or no sufficient nexus to what the patentee has really invented. Whether such an objection can be constructed out of existing laws is, I think, something of a challenge. I leave it to the reader to consider the problem further.

'Date: Tue, 11 Aug 1998 16:39:23 -0400

From: Richard Stern

'... I would be surprised if you have anything else either. If you do, let me know ...' Side Bar for Princ. of Pat. Law.

There is a substantial body of US law on this. See, for example, the US Supreme Court opinion in *Lincoln Engineering v. Stewart-Warner*, 303 U.S. 545 (1938). The CCPA, predecessor to the Fed. Cir., considered this body of law no longer authoritative after the 1952 Patent Act.

A pertinent portion of the *Lincoln Engineering* opinion is shown below [303 U.S. at 549]:

> The petitioner's principal contention is that our decision in the Rogers Case is controlling. We so hold. As has been said, the combination of elements disclosed is old in the art. As the Circuit Court of Appeals held, a headed nipple or fitting connected with the bearing, and to be coupled to the conduit from the grease gun, is old and unpatentable. A compressor or pump for propelling lubricant is old and unpatentable as such. The invention, if any, which Butler made was an improvement in what he styles in his specifications the 'chuck' and in his claim a 'coupling member.' It is not denied that multi-jawed chucks had been used in industry and as couplers in lubricating apparatus. Butler may have devised a patentable improvement in such a chuck in the respect that the multiple jaws in his device are closed over the nipple by the pressure of the grease, but we think he did no more than this. As we said of Gullborg in the Rogers Case, having hit upon this improvement he did not patent it as such but attempted to claim it in combination with other old elements which performed no new function in his claimed combination. The patent is therefore void as claiming more than the applicant invented. The mere aggregation of a number of old parts or elements which, in the aggregation, perform or produce no new or different function or operation than that theretofore performed or produced by them, is not patentable

> invention. And the improvement of one part of an old combination gives no right to claim that improvement in combination with other old parts which perform no new function in the combination. The same argument was unavailing in the Rogers case. It was there contended that the pin fitting of the Gullborg patent performed a new function in causing the beneficial operation of the coupler at the moment of disengagement. We commented upon the matter thus: 'The design of the bayonet slots is such that, in uncoupling, the coupling member of the gun will at first be moved slightly forward on the pin fitting thus backing up the perforated washer in the bore of the coupler.' But there, as in the present case, it was the peculiar and improved mechanism of the coupler which brought about the result and not the form of the fitting. We suppose that a headed nipple has always been so headed in order that the jaws of the chuck may slip over the head in the coupling and uncoupling operation. The weakness of the respondent's position is well illustrated by what developed at argument. When interrogated as to how in the claimed combination the function of the nipple could be thought novel in any different sense than the function of the pump, counsel replied that the pump performed a novel function because the pressure it generated forced forward the piston in the coupler and caused the movable jaws to engage the fitting. If this argument is sound, the respondent may convict every one who sells a grease pump of contributory infringement. The answer is the same as in the case of the headed nipple. The function of a pump has always been to force a fluid or a grease through a conduit. The fact that this function of the pump is utilized in Butler's improved form of coupler not only to convey the lubricant to the bearing but to operate the jaws of the chuck does not alter the function of the pump. The invention, if any, lies in the improvement in the coupling device alone.

Narrow claiming in this manner is common in the US for a number of practical reasons. One reason is as you suggest, to inflate the royalty base. Another reason is to overcome the contention that the claimed subject matter is 'non-statutory'—an abstract idea or business scheme or mathematical computation. The skilled claims draftsman embeds the non-statutory subject matter in apparatus elements that cannot be avoided when using the idea or scheme. For a discussion of this, see my article *Tales From The Algorithm War*, 18 AIPLA Q.J. 371, 382–83 (1991).

Another reason is to circumvent the exhaustion doctrine. (Or non-derogation from grants, per decision of the House of Lords in *British Leyland v. Armstrong*.)

Litigation is now pending in the US (one of several such cases is *Minebea v. Papst*, USDC for the District of Columbia) on one such group of patents. The inventor Papst invented new motors. He claimed them as motors and separately as disc drives containing the new motors but otherwise acting in a conventional manner. Papst licensed the motor patents to motor manufacturers. Then he demanded further royalties from disc drive manufacturers. (The motors have no use except in disc drives.) Litigation ensued. The adversaries of Papst assert the exhaustion doctrine and equitable estoppel (estoppel in pais).

Best wishes,

Richard H. Stern

Date: Thu, 13 Aug 98

Well—I never really expected an answer. Thank you very much.

Of course estoppel (or as we Europeans say exhaustion) or antitrust arguments are very much secondary remedies. Your old Supreme Court case (saying you have claimed more than you have invented) is sort of satisfactory. But think of the full implications—nearly every patent has subsidiary claims with trivial integers which the patentee has not really invented. We usually regard these as valid if the main claim is valid, do we not?

Thanks again

Robin Jacob

Date: Thu, 13 Aug 1998

The current thinking in the CAFC is definitely Yes, especially per Judge Rich.

You might be interested in writing a short comment on this for the European Intellectual Property Review.

Best wishes,

Richard H. Stern

Date: Sat, 15 Aug 98 08:32 BST-1

I thought of asking whether the editors of the book minded if I sent the same article to EIPR. I could now add to our little discussion. I will try and get round to it after holidays. France is where God takes his and so do I.

Could you give a me a quote from Judge Rich? Then I will just send my piece and some of our correspondence to EIPR.

Robin Jacob

Date: Mon, 17 Aug 1998 11:38:31 -0400

Yes. It will take me a little time to look up something suitable for the purpose.

Date: Mon, 17 Aug 1998 20:12:15 -0400

From: 'Richard Stern' RSTERN@Ablondifoster.com

Perhaps this will do? (Taken from Chisum on Patents, sec. 5.04[5] at 5-425)

In re Bernhart (CCPA 1969), 417 F2d 1395, 1402:

> Many cases have said that the combination claim reciting only one new element with no new result is overclaiming or claiming more than the applicant invented. Such statements are indeed puzzling in view of the fact that the addition of elements to a claim narrows its scope and thereby creates a lesser monopoly. Others have said the combination is not new, or is obvious, if no new co-action or result is obtained. This too is unsound, since it is not the result which is to be patented but the recited machine, composition, etc. If the prior art does not show or suggest the improved element itself, it defies logical reasoning to say that the same prior art suggests the use of that improved element in a combination

This seems to miss the point of the Supreme Court's opinion in *Hotchkiss v Greenwood* in 1850, which is that if making wood doorknobs in a particular shape is old, then once porcelain is discovered it is obvious to use it to make the same kind of doorknobs. Query: Should it make a difference if you are the inventor of porcelain?

The CCPA then goes on to hold that the 1952 patent act put an end to the foregoing form of analysis about 'old or exhausted combinations' and instead requires examination of the claimed combination as a gestalt. The court also complained about 'Jepson' (German) claiming as making claims less intelligible rather than more intelligible, so that patentees were really doing everybody a favor by claiming new carburetors as entire automobiles with new carburetors in them (my gloss!), rather than 'in a car having such and such elements, the improvement comprising using such and such a new carburetor in the engine.'

The only CAFC decision I found that seemed in point was *Radio Steel & Mfg. Co v MTD Products*, 731 F2d 840 (CAFC 1984), which approves and follows *Bernhart.* Id at 845. There is also a CA2 decision to the same effect, like the other decisions, refusing to follow Lincoln Engineering. The CA2 decision is *Jamesburg Corp v Litton Industrial Products,* 586 F2d 917, 924 (2d Cir 1978).

Best wishes,

Richard H. Stern

The problems caused by too-narrow claims continue. For instance, I suppose the true explanation of the Supreme Court decision in Schütz v Werit *[2013] UKSC 16 is that the Court instinctively felt the claim (to bottle plus cage when the clever bit was just the cage) was too narrow. Certainly that was Floyd J's view. Since a 'too-narrow' claim cannot be invalidated on that ground, courts have to find work-arounds when problems of the sort here are discussed. But my guess is that such claims will still have value—for instance, drafting claims to cover more than has been invented may be a way of increasing revenue attributable to a patent for the purpose of the 'patent box' tax exemption—taxmen will never understand this sort of thing!*

Part V

Trade Marks

36

*Trade Marks: Reality or Illusion?**

IN MY OPINION no one can truly answer the question 'what is a trade mark?'. Nor do I think the answer to that question, if there were one, would tell us what legal rights should be conferred on a trade mark. That is why there are so many questions courts send to the CJEU and why its answers are so often opaque and not infrequently inconsistent with one another. Indeed, although patent law has its complexities, deep down I think trade mark law is more difficult and inherently full of self-inconsistencies.

The main purpose of this talk is to ask what values trade mark law does or should protect. Is trade mark law promoting a better society or is it supporting less attractive aspects of human nature? Does it or should it support investment into conspicuous consumerism? Does it divert investment away from matters of true value to humanity? Does it or should it encourage investment in the ephemeral, the meretricious? I like this latter word, derived from the Latin *meretrix* meaning prostitute. 'Meretricious' is defined in the *Oxford English Dictionary* as 'apparently attractive but having no real value'.[1] The dictionary goes on to provide a host of synonyms, some of which are 'flashy, pretentious, garish, chintzy, tinselly' and one the English language stole from German, 'kitschy'. Does or should trade mark law protect illusion, false or overvalued image?

I begin by adapting quite a lot from a talk I gave at the Fordham University IP conference in 1997.

> There are basically two sides, whom I will personify as two characters called 'Free Trader' and 'Protectionist'. Free Trader calls intellectual property

* *A paper for the Bundespatentgericht Conference, April 2014.*

[1] *I learnt the word from Anthony Walton who said, when I was at the Bar, 'If you see a case about something meretricious, you'll find Robin Jacob there.' I did have quite a few cases about things like Toilet Ducks.*

rights 'monopolies'. Protectionist, as his name indicates, regards such rights as 'protective'.

He also likes the name 'intellectual property' he seeks to derive justification for his views from the use of the word 'property'. And 'intellectual' adds a real notion of class—of rights worthy of protection.

Free Trader's basic stance is against any rights which prevent or restrict competition unless a case can be made for their existence. He is happy to accept that a legal right to prevent traders from deceiving the public should exist. Such a right is embodied, for instance, in the English law of passing off. It is included within other laws of unfair competition. Few would doubt that it is unfair to sell goods by telling lies. Free Trader is unwilling for the law of trade marks (registered or unregistered) to go further than preventing deception. He agrees that a system of properly controlled trade mark registration can serve a useful purpose. He accepts that such a system serves the same end of stopping dishonest trading. Second Free Trader recognises that it is legitimate for a party to get his mark registered—get his protection—a little way in advance of actually commencing use. That has an administrative and commercial convenience. Thirdly he accepts that the registered mark system is a convenient way of his finding out what marks are claimed by others.

But Free Trader does not go further than this. He objects to marks being registered on the off chance of later use or, still worse, with a view to compelling others to take a licence or for some other reason pay him money—he dislikes those aspects of the European system of trade marks which encourage trade mark trolls. He objects to registration of descriptive marks. He objects to specifications of goods or services which are too wide and give us a cluttered register. He wants unused marks to be readily removable, much more so than now.[2] He would like an affidavit verifying substantial commercial use before a registration can be renewed.

Free Trader objects to registrations of marks which are not, in his view, trade marks at all, for instance the names of performers. Thus, for example, he thoroughly supports the decision[3] of Laddie J that 'Elvis Presley' is not a trade mark. He, like Laddie J, thinks that it is the name of a dead rock and roll star and that is that. Anyone can make memorabilia referring to Elvis. He sees no reason why anyone should get a monopoly on such items. Nor does he sympathise with live people, e.g. sportsmen, registering their names as trade marks for goods or services with which they have no real connection. If the law is to give protection to a name and likeness (which Free Trader doubts) then at least that should be a separate right: it is a nonsense to try and bring it under the rubric 'trade mark'.

[2] Under the old British system it could be done in a couple of months.
[3] 18 March 1997.

Free Trader also objects to attempts to dress up as a trade mark or trade dress any aspect of the appearance of an article which is functional or simply decorative. He applauds my decision in *Hodgkinson & Corby v Wards Mobility*.[4] There the defendants were selling a copy of an article of highly distinctive appearance (an anti bed-sore cushion for the immobile) but I refused to find passing off in the absence of any evidence of deception. Free Trader reacts with horror when he is told that in some jurisdictions the sale of copies which are unnecessarily close to an original is regarded as 'unfair competition'. 'Why is it unfair if there is no deception, no patent, no registered design and no copyright?' he asks. He loves what I said in *Hodgkinson*:

> There is no tort of copying. There is no tort of taking a man's market or customers. Neither the market nor the customers are the plaintiff's to own. There is no tort of making use of another's goodwill as such. There is no tort of competition.

Free Trader likewise objects to trade mark rights going further than he thinks they need to. Free Trader objected, for instance, to the old British Trade Marks Act provision, s.4 of the 1938 Act. This got into the Act via pressure from the drug companies. There was a case[5] in the 1930s which gave rise to the pressure. A wily merchant decided to trade on the back of a well-known health pill. The pill was called 'Yeast-Vite'. He said his yeast pills were 'a substitute for Yeast-Vite'. He was sued both for passing off and infringement of the registered mark Yeast Vite. He won.[6]

Free Trader says comparative advertising, unless it is dishonest, is all right. He is happy with 'My washing powder produces results as good as Persil but half the price' or with 'my perfumes smell like *Trésor* or *Miracle* or some other well-known brand—provided always the statements are true.

I turn to Protectionist. He starts from a wholly different vision: that a trade mark is a creation of the owner. It is created by being devised, and it is brought up and maintained by promotion. It is the result of investment—often considerable investment. It is an icon, to be valued in itself. If you walk along Maximilianstrasse with Protectionist by your side his eyes will light up at the great international brands glitzily on display. Thus, he says, a trade mark should be regarded as property and the law should treat it is such. Protectionist endorses an analogy given by Prof. Hugh Hansen: 'You can't use a man's car without his permission because it belongs to him. So also with his trade mark.' Protectionist invokes other ideas: he claims a moral high ground. He says: 'It is wrong for a trader to use the

[4] *Hodgkinson & Corby v Wards Mobility* [1995] FSR 169.

[5] *Irvings Yeast-Vite v Horsenail* (1934) 51 RPC 110.

[6] On registered trade mark. However, there was evidence that he had sold his pills as Yeast Vite and at first instance a passing-off injunction was granted.

trade mark of his rival howsoever. Doing so is to give the trader a "free ride"'. He even claims authority from the Bible, referring to a passage in the Gospel according to St. John: 'I sent you to reap that whereon ye bestowed no labour: other men laboured, and ye are entered into their labours'.[7] Protectionist often appeals to the adage 'Anything worth copying is worth protecting'.

Protectionist is particularly concerned for famous marks. He thinks they are especially worthy of protection—after all they are the result of vast investment. He would not, for instance, go along with the English case of *Stringfellows*,[8] where the owner of a famous nightclub of that name was held unable to stop the sale of oven-ready chips of especial thinness. This was so even though there was some confusion. The court said it did not matter: there was no damage. Not so says Protectionist. All confusion is damaging: it dilutes the mark he asserts.

The extreme Protectionist view goes even further. He says that even a non-confusing association will damage the mark and ought to be stopped. He applauds the *Claeryn/Klarein* case.[9] The plaintiff used Claeryn for gin; the defendant Klarein for washing up liquid. The defendant lost. The idea is that those who drink the gin do not want an association with the washing up liquid.

Protectionist has no sympathy for the views of the Free Trader. He says to him, 'You are just bleating about competition. I am just as much in favour of proper competition as you. All I say is that one trader should steer well clear of the mark of another. He does not have to try and come close. Let him invent his own mark and build it up himself. He is certainly free to do that, and if he does so he is not reaping where others have sown, he is reaping his own crops.'

My fictional characters Free Trader and Protectionist have their real counterparts. They represent views passionately held. My first question is, why so passionate? The protagonists for each side are strident.[10] I have begun to think that it is because, to many, it has become not so much a matter of rational argument: it has become a matter of belief, almost a religious question. Moreover the Protectionist side has been getting a louder and louder voice. Why? I am bound to say that I think it is because they have

[7] John 4:38.

[8] *Stringfellow v McCain Foods (GB) Ltd* [1984] RPC 501.

[9] *Colgate-Palmolive v Royal Distillers Erven Lucas Bols* (1976) IIC 420.

[10] See, for instance, the fierce (and highly readable) debate between Kamperman Sanders and Peter Prescott QC on the *Wagamama* case. The articles are 'Back to the Dark Ages' [1996] 1 EIPR 3; 'Think Before You Waga Finger' [1996] 1 EIPR 317; 'The Return to Wagamama' [1996] 1 EIPR 521; and 'Has the Benelux Trade Mark Law been Written into the Directive?' [1997] EIPR 99.

the richest and most organised lobby. The public have no real voice in any of the debates.

I concluded my 1997 lecture in this way:

> I suspect the debate will continue for ever: there is never going to be reconciliation between Protectionist and Free Trader. They talk different languages. The courts will sit at the interface, inclining one way and then the other depending, I suspect, on innate views as to how competitive the commercial world should be.

My talk was rather prophetic. I even used the word 'free ride' for the Protectionist point of view. In Europe (but not elsewhere—most notably in the USA) Protectionist has largely won, for the time being at least. The high point is the ECJ decision of 2009 *L'Oréal v Bellure*.[11] The defendant was honestly telling the truth: I found[12] the facts to be:

> [55] (i) It is lawful to make and sell a smell-alike product.
> (ii) The best and only practical way to describe its smell is to inform people that it smells like X.
> (iii) That is done by the use of the comparison lists.
> (iv) The Defendants get a major promotional advantage from using such lists.
> (v) Neither customers nor ultimate consumers are deceived as a result of the use of the lists.
> (vi) Neither the image nor the distinctiveness of the trade mark for the comparable fine fragrance is impaired by the use of the lists—there is no tarnishment or blurring.
> (vii) Sales of the corresponding fine fragrance are not affected by the use of the lists.

And:

> [63] I would add that a touch of reality is called for here. Consumers are not stupid. They will not see the cheap copy as being the same in quality as the original. They will see it for what it is and no more.

The Court in its reply said the following:

> [58] These functions [i.e. of a trade mark] include not only the essential function of the trade mark, which is to guarantee to consumers the origin of the goods or services, but also its other functions, in particular that of guaranteeing the quality of the goods or services in question and those of communication, investment or advertising.

[11] Case C-487/07 *L'Oréal v Bellure*.
[12] *L'Oréal v Bellure (No 1)* [2007] EWCA Civ 968.

It said the comparative use was not 'purely descriptive' because it was used for advertising. I don't understand that. The defendant in *Hölterhoff v Freiesleben*[13] was using the plaintiff's registered mark not only to describe what he could supply but to get a sale—he was advertising just as much as a market trader would be advertising when he told a customer that a particular member of the Stitch range of perfumes smelt like *Miracle*.

As regards Art 5(2) infringement the court was particularly sanctimonious. It said:

> [41] As regards the concept of 'taking unfair advantage of the distinctive character or the repute of the trade mark', also referred to as 'parasitism' or 'free-riding', that concept relates not to the detriment caused to the mark but to the advantage taken by the third party as a result of the use of the identical or similar sign. *It covers, in particular, cases where, by reason of a transfer of the image of the mark or of the characteristics which it projects to the goods identified by the identical or similar sign, there is clear exploitation on the coat-tails of the mark with a reputation.*
>
> [49] ... where a third party attempts, *through the use of a sign similar to a mark with a reputation, to ride on the coat-tails of that mark in order to benefit from its power of attraction*, its reputation and its prestige, and to exploit, without paying any financial compensation and without being required to make efforts of his own in that regard, the marketing effort expended by the proprietor of that mark in order to create and maintain the image of that mark, the advantage resulting from such use must be considered to be an advantage that has been unfairly taken of the distinctive character or the repute of that mark.

In my judgment applying the Court's decision[14] I said:

> [49] So far as I can see this is saying if there is 'clear exploitation on the coat-tails' that is ipso facto not only an advantage but an unfair one at that. In short, the provision should be read as though the word 'unfair' was simply not there. No line between 'permissible free riding' and 'impermissible free riding' is to be drawn. All free-riding is 'unfair.' It is a conclusion high in moral content (the thought is clearly that copyists, even of lawful products should be condemned) rather than on economic content.

So we see the Court saying the 'image' of a trade mark is to be protected. It is that I call into question.

[13] Case C-2/00 *Hölterhoff v Freiesleben* [2002] ECR I-4187.
[14] *L'Oréal v Bellure (No 2)* [2010] EWCA Civ 535.

In my first judgment in a paragraph which has had no or little comment I said:

> [21] Moreover there is no harm to the trade mark owner—other than possibly a 'harm' which, to be fair, L'Oréal has never asserted. That 'harm' would be letting the truth out—that it is possible to produce cheap perfumes which smell somewhat like a famous original. I can understand that a purveyor of a product sold at a very high price as an exclusive luxury item would not like the public to know that it can be imitated, albeit not to the same quality, cheaply—there is a bit of a message that the price of the real thing may be excessive and that the 'luxury image' may be a bit of a delusion. But an uncomfortable (from the point of view of the trade mark owner) truth is still the truth: it surely needs a strong reason to suppress it.

This paragraph is about image versus reality. I once edited the leading textbook on UK trade marks. I noticed something significant: that if you took out all the cases dealing with cigarettes and other smoking things and those concerned with drinks, especially alcoholic drinks, the book would be about half the size! Actually the rival products were much the same: it was advertising which sought to promote a difference—an image—when in reality there was little to choose between them. One brand of cigarette was much the same as another. What made Marlborough famous and successful was the image of the healthy young cowboy—miles from the reality of what smoking does.[15]

So I question the Court's protection for these 'functions'. It seems to me that it is encouraging investment—advertising investment—in things which do not really matter to mankind. True it is that some people like to wear Gucci or Rolex watches or carry Mulberry handbags, but their motive is image. 'Look at me, ' they say, 'I am one of the exclusive wealthy, I am like a celebrity.' It is part of human nature, but it is not its best side and I think trade mark law should simply keep away. So called 'luxury goods' industries often pay as much as 30 to 40 per cent of revenue on advertising and promotion, but in the great scheme of things luxury goods are essentially meretricious.

[15] *That reminds me of some advice I gave in the 1970s to a company which sold a brand of anti-smoking chewing gum. Marlboro used to put huge advertisements of their cowboy along the Cromwell Road. My client asked whether it was safe to put up an equally huge advert showing a healthy-looking cowboy in the foreground, but in the background an obviously sick and coughing cowboy with the strapline 'I crossed the border into Tabmint Country'. I advise that the client would be safe, but almost surely would be sued and if it was that would provide lots of free publicity. The client did not have the guts to press ahead. Wimpishly, it asked Marlboro whether it would object and when told it would, backed down.*

Trade mark law should protect them from deception or confusion, not go further. To do so is to pander to illusion, image and human vanity. The extent of protection should be limited to reality.

I should say I am grateful to Professor Barton Beebe of New York University who has written a major article on this subject.[16] His main thesis is that humankind has always valued scarcity—Roman emperors and senators wore purple togas because purple was such an expensive dye. Trade mark law is being used to create artificial scarcity and thus to pander to this meretricious side of human nature.

European trade mark law should be amended in two ways:

(1) it should be lawful to tell the truth in commerce;
(2) the only function of a trade mark which should be protected is the origin function.[17]

[16] 'Intellectual Property and the Sumptuary Code' (2010) 123 *Harvard Law Review* 809.

[17] *There are current Commission proposals for amendment of the law. The proposals suggest that the same mark/same goods rule should be so limited, but that makes little sense unless it applies to all forms of infringement. The court is quite capable of saying that its elusive other 'function' notions continue to apply and that the proposed amendment (assuming it is adopted) makes no difference. The proposals are not imbued with the spirit of competition that IP rights need to be justifiable.*

37

*Trade Marks and the Olympic Games Throughout the Years**

BLUE, YELLOW, BLACK, green and red. Few can recite the colours of the Olympic Symbol, in their correct order, starting from the flagpole outwards. And I suppose even fewer know what the colours stand for—the five continents (blue—Europe, yellow—Asia, black—Africa, green—Australasia, and red—the Americas). Or that the borderless plain white background itself has symbolism. It stands for peace during the Games. Yet the Olympic Symbol is universally recognised—perhaps, outside of those of the great religions (and maybe not even that), the most universally recognised of all symbols. What can we learn from it? When I was given the topic of Trade Marks and the Games, I wondered what I could say. As I thought more I realised that the Symbol, the flame and the inspiration behind the Games can provide insights into almost every fundamental problem or question of trade mark law—one might say the eternal questions of trade mark law.

I begin with that which I have touched upon already—recognition and imperfect recollection. It is a remarkable thing that so much of the detail of such a well-known symbol is not itself memorable. That is not normally a characteristic of well-known trade marks. Most of these are so well known that small deviations are enough for the public to notice the difference. There is a world of difference between water associated with Chanel and water associated with a canal. Or between 'Harrods' and 'Horrids'. Why is the Symbol different? I think it is probably because it is purely visual—a mark consisting of graphics alone. Other visual marks may be similar in that respect, though there are limits here—for instance most people can tell the

* *Delivered at the Marques Annual Conference (Athens, August 2000).*

difference between three stripes (Adidas) and two stripes (imitators). Word marks in the real world are generally more precise of definition and of recognition. They are generally more important than purely visual marks.

You will know that, without distinguishing between word and graphic marks, the European Court of Justice has said 'the more distinctive the earlier mark, the greater the risk of confusion'.[1] It added that 'marks with a highly distinctive character, either per se or because of the reputation they possess in the market, enjoy broader protection than marks with a less distinctive character'.

So far as variants of a distinctive mark are concerned, that statement, I say, (a) is plain wrong and (b) is not and cannot be a statement of law. Whether one mark is confusingly similar with another is not a question of law. I can understand the factual proposition that the more distinctive a mark is, the more its use on different sorts of goods may confuse—Kodak[2] for socks or almost anything else probably does. But try making a small difference to the word—substituting a 'j' for the 'd' for instance. You get Kojak. I doubt whether anyone made the slightest association between a bald-headed lollipop-sucking American policeman, or the actor Telly Savalas, and Kodak, still less whether anyone was deceived or confused. One letter can make a big difference—and the more so the more famous the mark because there is less, not more, room for imperfect recollection. Thus the Olympic Symbol provokes an interesting discussion about distinctive marks and what degrees of similarity are permissible and what not. It points up a significant factual matter—that variations to graphical marks are less acceptable than variations to word marks. That is a fact about human perception, not a rule of law.

Turning back to the Olympic Symbol itself, what deviation is enough before there is no deception or confusion? And how much further a deviation is needed before there is no 'association' in the widest sense of the term? Few would doubt that a monochrome version of the Symbol does not go far enough to avoid deception. How about five interlinked rings in a straight line? Or only four? The latter of course is actually a trade mark of another: it is the Audi badge. Many would say it is reminiscent of the Olympic Symbol. And so it

[1] *SABEL v Puma* [1997] ECR I-6191, para 22; *Canon v MGM* [1999] ETMR 1 para 17.

[2] *Kodak, even at the time of this talk, was a mighty brand. And it was the perfect utterly distinctive trade mark to be used in examples. How the mighty have fallen.*

is. But few would say the law should stop it. We come to the next 'trade mark' problem whose discussion is provoked by the Symbol. For it was precisely this sort of non-commercial 'association' which briefly drifted across the face of European trade mark law. It was the so-called Benelux view of infringement. The idea was that trade marks are such delicate things that they would crumble if anyone so much as touched them. The Dutch decision of *Klarein* was based on the notion that anyone drinking the gin would not want any association with a lavatory cleaner of a similar name. This was so much nonsense. You can perfectly well have similar names for different products which cause neither damage nor damaging association. In my country we have Kit-Kat for a very successful chocolate product and Kitekat for cat food. We have Jif for lemon juice and Jif for bathroom cleaner. Not to say Jiffy for padded envelopes and, independently, for condoms. Particularly appropriate for this conference is another pair of marks: Total for Greek yoghurt and for petroleum products. I have to say I think the ECJ's decision in *Puma* and subsequent cases, that trade mark confusion is about confusion as to commercial origin, is a good thing. I do not think trade mark owners need more protection than that. I suspect many here will disagree. Let us have a lively debate on the topic.[3]

That debate can include a focus on a real case: *New Zealand and Commonwealth Games Assn v Telecom New Zealand and Saatchi & Saatchi*.[4] New Zealand does not, or did not at the relevant time (1996), seem to have any special law for protecting the Olympic Symbol. New Zealand Telecom put out an advertisement on television. A visual play was made of the Olympic Symbol. Instead of circles, the word 'ring' was used—five times in the positions where the circles would be and in the same colours and order as the Symbol. The voiceover said 'with Telecom Mobile you can take your own phone to the Olympics'. A claim for an interim injunction failed. The judge thought the public would be 'mildly amused' by the pun but was not impressed by the idea that the public would assume a business association between the plaintiff and NZ Telecom. One can go further. Suppose the public did so think. The most the association could be

[3] *That is all just history. After Puma the ECJ went overboard in favour of protection using Art 5(2). As if Europe can only survive in a competitive world by clinging on to brands which promote image rather than reality—see Chapter 36, 'Trade Marks: Reality or Illusion?'.*

[4] *New Zealand and Commonwealth Games Assn v Telecom New Zealand and Saatchi & Saatchi*, unreported, 2 May 1996.

is that Telecom had paid some money to the Association. Would that be enough to amount to passing off? I do not stay for an answer now, though I have some ideas.

Next the Olympic Symbol can make us think about that most elusive question of all, what actually is a trade mark? Most people think they know but it gets pretty tricky at times. If you see the Olympic Symbol used on a variety of goods what does it denote? You can buy, for example, or at least you could for the Games, an Olympic windsock. You can buy official clothing, posters and mugs. Almost anything can carry the Olympic flag. Sadly, and to its shame, the International Olympic Committee [IOC] in 1936 permitted the use of the symbol on Nazi hunter-killer submarines. Is the symbol a trade mark or is it something else—just a mark which you need permission to use? Real trade marks denote a commercial association between the goods or services bearing the mark and the owner. The only association between the Olympic Symbol and any goods or services bearing the mark is that permission has been given by the IOC.

It is, I suggest, precisely because the Symbol is not a trade mark that it was considered necessary to give the IOC a very special right, separately recognised in many countries pursuant to a special Treaty—the Nairobi Treaty of 1981. In my own country that protection is via the 'Olympic Symbol etc. (Protection) Act 1995. This is a whole Act of Parliament just for the Symbol. It is 19 sections long. It protects the Symbol and indeed the Olympic motto and even the words 'Olympic' and 'Olympics' (amongst others). Infringement consists of use of the Symbol or protected motto or words 'in the course of trade'. Unlike a trade mark, it does not matter what the trade may be. It can be in any goods or any services.

The width of protection is also wider than that for a trade mark. It extends to a 'representation of something so similar to the Symbol or motto as to create in the public mind an association with it'. That is remarkable—maybe Benelux-type association is enough. Having created the right, there have to be all sorts of exceptions—including protection for what people were already doing. Some of us flew here via Olympic Airways. Its right to use the name 'Olympic' now depends on an exception. Suppose the exception did not exist and so it was necessary for the airline to get permission from the IOC. And suppose the permission had been given. Would the use be a trade mark use? Many say that for trade mark use the proprietor should have some responsibility for the quality of the goods or services under the mark. I doubt anyone would fly Olympic Airways if they thought it was the IOC, which was responsible for the quality of the airline. Certainly I would prefer to go by an airline run by people who knew how to fly planes than by the IOC. The trade-mark idea that the owner of the mark should have control over the quality of the goods or services of the mark is inapposite to the use of the Symbol or the name. It is striking that its permission to use the name Olympic is by virtue of an exception to the general rule. Possibly Audi's four rings are only saved by the exception.

The width of the protection given can be seen also in the context of a real case. A company called Olympic Oils Ltd tried in the UK to register OLYMPIC and the word in combination with a flaming torch for cooking oils. The Registry rejected the application out of hand, as it had to do. The 1995 Act had amended the Trade Marks Act so as to make registration of any controlled word for any goods or services objectionable.[5]

So the Symbol has wider protection than any ordinary trade mark. It is a merchandising right, pure and simple. When you see the mark used it denotes 'a chink in the distant cash register of the IOC and no more'. Putting it another way, you know by the use of the Symbol that the IOC is getting a cut from this product. The IOC is not responsible for the quality of the goods. No one buys an Olympic tee shirt because they think the IOC knows anything about tee shirts, let alone is responsible for its quality or design. Of course it might refuse permission for some disreputable trade, but one would only think less of it for granting such permission because it has the power to withhold it.

Now, how does the protection given to the IOC compare with that given by actual registrations of trade marks for the purpose of merchandising? Are these registrations good and can you use the trade mark system for the same sort of operation as that carried out by the IOC? Take some actual examples. First UK trade mark No 2050596. It consists of three close-up photographs of Jacques Villeneuve. They are registered as a series for a wide range of goods in each of seven different classes. Some of the goods are bizarre: for instance 'satellite apparatus' in class 9, paper knives in class 16. What Jacques Villeneuve wants from the registration, of course, is to license it.

[5] TM Appn No 2165204.

He wants, in short, a merchandising right. And he may have got it. Or take another example, Arsenal[6] or Real Madrid or their respective crests, registered for a wide range of goods in many classes. I suppose vast sums are received for the licensing of marks such as these. Are these truly trade marks? One view is that they are not, they are really something different—badges to be merchandised.

What may be needed for those who want such rights is a separate merchandising right such as that of the IOC. Whether such rights should exist is a matter for debate. What one finds now is some intellectually dishonest stretching of the concept of a trade mark. It occurred, for instance, in relation to the 'Duff Beer' case in Australia.[7] Students of *The Simpsons* will know that Homer drinks a brand called 'Duff Beer'. The defendants made a real beer of that name. They were enjoined, on the theory that the public would think that the makers of *The Simpsons* had licensed the beer. Contrast that with the *Wombles* case in England in 1975, where the makers of *The Wombles* TV series failed to stop a skip hire business calling itself Wombles Skips.[8] Of course it is fair to remember that Australia has the short but immensely fertile s 52 of the Trade Practices Act 1974, which makes actionable 'misleading or deceptive conduct in trade', irrespective of goodwill or any damage.

The Symbol of course is used to make a great deal of money: merchandising rights do. Its internationally agreed protection guarantees that. One may wonder what the founder of the modern Olympic Games, Baron Pierre de Coubertin, would have thought. He devised the Games for their first modern incarnation in 1896. They ran every four years without a symbol until he devised the flag. It was first made for him in a Parisian shop in 1913. The flag, two metres high and

[6] *When I wrote that in the summer of 2000 I had no idea that a real Arsenal case was on foot, decided the first time around by Hugh Laddie who rejected the passing off claim and indeed doubted whether the crest was a trade mark, and sent the case off to Luxembourg. What happened thereafter is so well known that there is no point in adding anything—save for a comic story. Because the status of rights in the crest was uncertain, Arsenal decided to create a new one, which of course would have copyright rights even if not as a trade mark. At a party I met an Arsenal director. He asked, 'Do you like the new crest?' I said, 'No, it's horrible.' He said, 'I designed it.' Well, he had asked. It was the end of the conversation though. There is one other question: why did Arsenal bother to sue in passing off? They could have gone for summary judgment saying 'same mark, same goods, Art 5(1) ergo judgment for us'. All the evidence about the public seeing the badge only as a badge of allegiance would never have come in.*

[7] *Twentieth Century Fox v S. Australian Brewing Co.*, 17th May 1996, Federal Court of Australia.

[8] *Wombles Ltd v Womble Skips Ltd* [1997] RPC 9.

three metres long, continued to fly from the first Games thereafter, 1920 Antwerp. It was replaced by a Korean silk version for the Seoul Olympics of 1988.

At the time of their creation Baron Coubertin said this:

> These five rings represent the five parts of the world now won over to the Olympism and ready to accept its fertile rivalries. Also the six colours thus combined represent those of all nations, with no exceptions. This is a real international emblem.

There was no doubt that he had the vision and intention to create a truly international symbol. I very much doubt whether, if he had been asked, he would have agreed with the proposition that he was creating a truly international trade mark or even a device from which money was to be made. His 'Olympism' ideal was far removed from commerce. In 1908 the Baron heard the sermon of the Bishop of Pennsylvania in a service marking the Games. From that sermon he took the message which is displayed on the scoreboard at every Games since: 'The most important thing in the Olympic Games is not to win but to take part. Just as the most important thing in life is not the triumph but the struggle'.

The athletes were not competing for money then. Ostensibly they do not do so now. The Olympic Oath is far from commerce or money. This is what is proclaimed by a chosen athlete from the host nation:

> In the name of all competitors, I promise that we will take part in these Olympic Games, respecting and abiding by all the results which govern them in the true spirit of sportsmanship, for the glory of sport and the honour of our teams.

No one adds: 'And for all the cash we can make!' Would the Baron have approved of what the modern IOC say about the Symbol?: 'The Olympic symbol, the Olympic flag and the Olympic motto are the exclusive intellectual property of the IOC and may not be used without its prior written authorisation'.

No one can answer. It may be the Baron would have said that making money was a necessary evil if the Games are to be run as they are now, with vast investment and vast management structures. Or he may have deplored the modern commercialism of the Games.

Let me turn to another symbol of the Olympic Games—the Olympic torch. A torch was first used for the 1928 Amsterdam Games. The idea of a relay was first used for the notorious 1936 Games. For each Games it is lit by the light of the sun at Olympia. Then it is carried by relay to the host city to light the Olympic torch, which burns throughout the Games and is extinguished as part of the closing ceremony. What rights exist in this potent ritual? It would seem none—though I would not be surprised to see the modern IOC trying to find a way of exploiting it—but how do you sell or license a flame?

What can the Olympic motto teach us about trade marks? The motto is 'Citius, Altius, Fortius'—Faster, Higher, Stronger. It seems entirely apt to describe the growth in intellectual property rights over the last 30 years or so. But it was not devised for that purpose. Father Henri Didon, a friend of Baron de Courbetin, devised it. It was first used along with the Symbol of the 1920 Antwerp Games. As far as I know no one complained that it was in Latin rather than Greek. There was no comparable row to that about the Coliseum being on the medals for the Sydney Games. I do not know whether the absence of such a fuss then and the fuss now tells us anything instructive about changes in the world generally. I do not think it tells us anything constructive about trade marks.

Of course it does not matter what language the motto is in—the Act provides that the motto and any protected word are included when translated into any language. Think of that. Faster, Higher, Stronger is protected for any trade use. So is something likely in the public mind to create an association with it. Compare the position with trade marks. Registries and courts have been very wary of protecting slogans—'Still Going Strong' 'the Real Thing' 'Have a Break' 'Is Good For You' all have doubtful or no protection. Should that be or should the owner of a well-known slogan get protection? Let that be another matter for debate at this conference.

I believe I have proved that those who chose the title for this talk chose wisely. The juxtaposition of the Games and trade marks shows that in protection the Games are ahead of the game. Whether that will always be so remains to be seen. I add only one word of warning. It is said that the ancient Games fell into disrepute and ultimately ceased because they became too commercial. Let us hope that the diversion of Baron de Courbetin's ideal to more commercialism does not have the same effect.

38

Product Shape and Trade Dress: A Critical Analysis[*]

THE BEAUTY AND purpose of conferences like this is that one debates principles. The fine detail of the legislation or case law of any particular country, whilst it of course matters in the country concerned, often obscures the wood from the trees. Here we debate the wood, using trees only to illustrate the debate.

In 1997 my paper to this Conference[1] was entitled 'When is a trade mark not a trade mark?' I gave it the alternative title 'trade mark wars'. I described the two sides of what I saw as a debate between two characters I called 'Protectionist' and 'Free Trader'. I concluded that the debate would go on for ever. On the one hand are ranged those who think trade-mark and like rights should protect traders from any form of imitation—the 'anything worth copying is worth protecting' school. On the other are the minimalists—those who believe that one starts from the proposition that 'all is fair in love, war and market competition'. They say that every exception to that rule in the form of intellectual property rights must be justified—the justification coming from economic considerations (encouragement of research and investment) or the need for honest trading. The minimalist accepts trade mark rights essentially because he believes in an honest market.

Nearly all debates about trade mark and unfair competition law are versions of that fundamental debate. This year's topic is no exception. What I propose to do is to examine a few cases, some old and some new, and then try to draw some broad conclusions.

[*] *A paper for the 2000 Fordham University Law School Conference.*

[1] Largely set out in Chapter 36.

I start with a case exactly 100 years old, *Payton v Snelling, Lampard*.[2] It illustrates the 'no deception, no injunction' school of thought perfectly. The plaintiff sold coffee under the mark 'Royal'. The defendant used the mark 'Flag'. But otherwise the defendant copied the plaintiff's coffee tins for each of three sizes. Each were round and coloured red, blue and green to denote particular qualities of coffee. It was obvious that the defendant's tins were based on those of the plaintiff. But the claim in passing off failed. It failed because the words 'Royal' and 'Flag' did the job of distinguishing. Lord MacNaghten put it this way:

> We know what would happen if a man came into a shop and asked for Royal Coffee and the tradesman had no Royal Coffee upon his shelf ... He would say:- 'I have not got Royal Coffee, but I have some coffee quite as good; will you take Flag Coffee at just the same price, or a very little dearer? It is quite as good or perhaps a little better.' In 99 cases out of 100 the customer would take it. There is no deception there.

Another old case shows an attempt as early as 1877 by a trader to get a monopoly in shape by way of trade mark registration. The case was *James' TM*.[3] I do not think it has satisfactory reasoning but it shows that questions or problems of registration of trade dress are far from new. The plaintiffs made 'black lead'—a substance used for blacking fire grates. They sold it in the form of a cylinder with a dome and originally it was the subject of registered design protection but that had expired. It was in 1877 that they registered as a trade mark a picture of the black dome. The Court of Appeal said the registration was good. They found on the evidence that the shape was distinctive of the trade mark owner and that that justified the registration. They appeared to think, however, that the registration could not stop a defendant selling black lead in the shape of dome-topped cylinders—all it could stop was a defendant who used the picture—the 2D representation. I think that is ridiculous: it meant a defendant could make his lead in that shape but could not put a picture of what he sold on the wrapping. The case would have been much more interesting if the court had proceeded on the basis that the registration would stop another man making lead in that shape. In principle I do not see why it should not—the dome shape was purely adventitious and had nothing to do with the material as such. I think Free Trader

[2] *Payton v Snelling, Lampard* (1900) 17 RPC 628.
[3] *James' TM* (1886) 3 RPC 340.

would agree. The registration would not interfere with any trade in black lead. In more recent times the courts have readily treated registration of a picture as a registration of the shape of thing pictured. I did so myself, in *Philips v Remington*:[4] 'It would be quite artificial to regard a straight picture of a thing, and the thing itself, as significantly different under a law of trade marks which permits shapes to be registered'.

I come to more modern times, pausing to mention only briefly that in 1911 the House of Lords had protected, by a passing-off action, the physical shape of the thing sold on the market—a 'dolly blue' then used in washing clothes. It consisted of a bag containing the chemical on a stick: *Edge v Niccolls*.[5] The House accepted the evidence (poor by modern standards) that 'washerwomen, cottagers, and other persons in a humble station of life' would be deceived. What is interesting is that the House accepted that to differentiate (by using a fancier stick, for example) might cost more but that did not matter.

It was in the 1970s that the pharmaceutical companies realised that the appearance of their tablets or pills mattered. It mattered because any patient on a repeat prescription would be bound to notice a difference in his pills. This is vividly illustrated by a case that never came to court: Parke Davis were in the habit of putting a band round the middle of their capsules. One capsule was white with a white band. The imitator felt it necessary to copy this. A case that did come to court was concerned with black and green capsules, *Hoffman-la-Roche v DDSA*.[6] Roche put out a tranquilliser in these distinctive colours. It was very successful:

> It would seem that the average citizen of the welfare state is never, or rarely, in a condition of what the late President Harding used to call 'normalcy': either he needs stimulation, in the form of what is called a 'pep' pill, or he needs sedation, and for that he has to have a tranquilliser. So up and down he goes but never remains stable. At least that is the natural inference from the fact that of this particular tranquilliser no less than three and quarter hundred millions were prescribed and sold in 1968 alone.

Although the tranquilliser concerned was still under patent, the defendants had obtained a compulsory licence. They threatened to

[4] *Philips v Remington* [1998] RPC, 290.
[5] *Edge v Niccolls* [1911] AC 693.
[6] *Hoffman-la-Roche v DDSA* [1972] RPC 1.

sell using the same coloured capsule and were restrained. Harman LJ said this:

> Now I myself never received from the defendants a satisfactory answer to the plain question why do they wish to market their goods in green and black? I can only answer that they wish so to do in order to attract to themselves some part of the plaintiffs' goodwill and trade on their reputation and in fact to represent to the public that their goods are the goods of the plaintiffs.

There is trouble with that question—even though it is one that is nearly always asked in a passing-off case. Before identifying that trouble I should mention that the coloration of capsules became registrable as a trade mark, *SK&F's Appn.*[7] SK&F sold a range of capsules which had one end coloured and one transparent. Through the transparent end you could see individual pellets, some of which were white and the others coloured. There was a different combination for each particular medicine. For reasons which baffled me the opponents argued their case principally on the meaning of the word 'mark' (under the legislation you could only register a mark, though that was not fully defined). They said that there had to be a difference between the mark and the thing marked and so, since you could not have the 'mark' absent the capsule, there was no mark. This was a metaphysical and abstract kind of argument. It did not appeal to the House of Lords who accepted SK&F's argument most pithily put by my leading counsel, Mr TA Blanco White QC: 'A thing marked all over is nonetheless marked'. They were right to do so. In trade dress cases (whether trade mark registration or passing off or unfair competition) what matters is the effect on the market. Metaphysics has no place here.

But were the House of Lords in *SK&F* and the Court of Appeal in *Hoffmann-La Roche* right? Was the coloration of the capsules truly 'distinctive' of the plaintiffs? Take the green and black capsules. It was of course true that the defendant wanted to use those colours because otherwise the patients would query their pills. But is it not equally plausible that the patient would take the colours as denoting the *kind and dosage* of medicine?—after all the defendant's pill did have the right dose of the right medicine and the patient was getting exactly what had been prescribed. The position might be the

[7] *SK&F's Appn* [1976] 511.

same for SK&F's fancy-coloured pills. In neither case was there any investigation of what the patients actually understood from the colours. And after all they were simply getting what the doctors had prescribed. The courts have realised there was something fishy going on—for when it came to a single colour they went the other way *Roche Products v Berk*[8] (yellow and white tablets), *Boots v APS*[9] (a pink pill); *John Wyeth v M&A*[10] (a blue lozenge). The alleged distinction between the cases is the highly distinctive black and green compared with the commonplace pills. But in both kinds of case the defendant was seeking to get exactly the same advantage—avoidance of patient queries. Harman LJ's question—why are they doing it?—is as good for one kind of case as the other. There is a moral, however. It is this: the fancier a trade dress the more readily will courts protect it, never mind the logic!

Before turning to functional articles I wish to mention one other case which may surprise non-UK members of the audience. It is the plastic lemon case, *Reckitt & Colman v Borden*.[11] By means of a passing-off case the plaintiffs succeeded in preventing the defendants from selling lemon juice in a lemon-shaped plastic bottle—moreover a bottle that was not particularly like that used by the plaintiffs. The fact was that the plaintiffs were able to prove that the defendants' product, if put out on supermarket shelves, would deceive a substantial proportion of the public. They proved that the shape of the bottle had become distinctive not only in the sense that it was widely recognised, but also that the customers *cared* about the maker of the lemon juice. The fact that defendants' shape was somewhat different and that they used a red and yellow label and a red top as opposed to a green and yellow label and a green top as used by the plaintiffs was not enough to prevent deception. In practice in supermarkets the customer relied on the shape to buy the lemon juice of the manufacturer they wanted—the one they knew and loved. Let me show you an interesting exhibit. It was a poster of some packaging designers unconnected with either side who were advertising their services.

This vividly shows how much trade dress—what we in England call 'get up'—matters in the commercial world. I do not think Free Trader would have any problem with a monopoly in any of them—

[8] *Roche Products v Berk* [1973] RPC 461.
[9] *Boots v APS* [1988] RPC 45.
[10] *John Wyeth v M&A* [1988] FSR 26.
[11] *Reckitt & Colman v Borden* [1990] RPC 341.

even the lemon is all right by him given the finding of deceptiveness (which would, I admit, surprise him).[12]

You will notice that I talked about 'what the customer will go by'. I think this is a very important question in trade dress or get up cases. It was touched upon as long ago as 1917 by the new young judge, Judge Learned Hand, in *Crescent Tool v Kilborn & Bishop*.[13] The plaintiffs made a spanner of an unusual shape. The defendants copied but clearly used their own name. The plaintiffs lost, Judge Hand asking 'what moves the public to buy?'

Let us race forward to the new world of the European Directive and Regulation. You already know my views in *Philips*. I think there is a real danger in perpetual monopolies of what are, in substance, articles. That danger can manifest itself in many ways. Take the esoteric and over-debated subject of smell marks. I disregard the technical problems of 'capable of graphical representation'. That is a side issue like the question of 'mark' in the case of SK&F's coloured capsules. No one would have a problem of allowing a perpetual monopoly in the smell of roses for automobile tyres (I gather a real case, though I doubt whether any customer would rely upon the smell to get the make he wants). With the 'smell of fresh cut grass' for tennis balls I do have a problem. The debate was all about whether that is 'capable of being represented graphically' (Art 2 of the Directive). But that is not the point. Suppose it is, is this the sort of thing for which an applicant should have a trade mark monopoly? It may be a clever idea, but that does not make it a trade mark. If people buy the balls, do they do so because the smell tells them who made the balls or just because of the novelty—because they *like* the balls to smell that way? If it is the latter (as I suspect it is) then no trade mark monopoly should be given. Only if over time the owner can show that it is the smell which moves people to buy because they rely upon the smell to get the make they want should it be registered. Otherwise what you have done is confer a perpetual monopoly in a desirable commercial product.[14]

[12] *It did me—I never thought we could prove substantial deception, especially by the second version with a red top and red and yellow (as opposed to green and yellow) tag label. But we did, and I have always taken the view since that it is a mistake for a lawyer to advise definitively on whether or not two things are confusingly similar. That is a question of fact, not law.*

[13] *Crescent Tool v Kilborn & Bishop* (1917) 147 F 299.

[14] *In the end it was refused, I believe. One exotic point: suppose it had been registered, would any tennis ball used on a grass court infringe after the first service?*

Take some other cases. People are applying to the Office for registration of unusually shaped containers. I do not think they should be allowed just because the shape is unusual. Why do I say this? It is because an unusual shape is not necessarily a sign of commercial origin. It may well be an attractive shape which people will buy for the shape. In some cases the applicants are bottle makers, not makers of the liquids to be sold under the mark. That shows what's afoot—bottle makers seeking a perpetual monopoly in a bottle shape. Again take a perfume. I expect many a man has chosen a perfume on the basis that the smell seems all right and the bottle looks nice. The bottle is in substance part of the product sold, not its trade mark. Of course over time a bottle may come to be distinctive (*in the trade mark sense*) of its contents—so that you can rely on it. Coca-Cola of course comes to mind, but even lesser-known bottles can be protected. There is a brand of whisky, for instance, sold in a distinctive and well-recognised shaped bottle—the dimple bottle. It was protected in a passing-off action a long time ago, *Haig v Forth Blending*.[15] But, note this well, the plaintiff proved that people asked for their whisky as 'dimple' whisky.

Let me now turn to a paradigm problem, that of Lego. I must make an admission and confess an interest. I was counsel for Tyco in its long-running copyright battle with Lego, both in Hong Kong and Australia. In the end the spirit of competition prevailed and Tyco were entitled to sell exact copies of Lego bricks in those countries and the UK. Corresponding US proceedings (based on unfair competition and passing off) also failed. But Lego prevailed (not against Tyco but another copyist) under the unfair competition law of Germany in *Klemmbausten*.[16] That was a long time ago and I wonder whether the same would be true if the case came up in Germany today. They also prevailed in Denmark in *Lego v Byggi*.[17] Lego have also recently won on unfair competition grounds before the Supreme Court in Italy (*Lego v Tyco*), though it is worth noting that Tyco has gone out of the brick business[18] and did not defend the appeal. It was the

15 *Haig v Forth Blending* (1952) 70 RPC 259.

16 *Klemmbausten* [1964] GRUR 621.

17 *Lego v Byggi* [1995] EIPR D65.

18 *I was told that Tyco was bought by Hasbro who did a commercial deal with Lego—one that included Lego buying the moulds used by Tyco and in fact then later used by Lego for making Lego bricks. I have no first-hand knowledge of this but it is possible—I do know that Tyco's copies of Lego were the best ever copies—better than Lego's own copying of Kiddicraft bricks in the early days!*

case that in none of the common law countries could Lego show any form of passing off or deception. Tyco's products were clearly packaged as such—indeed they made a virtue of the fact that they were compatible with Lego but were not Lego. I assume the same is true for Germany and Italy. Why then did those tribunals find the competition unfair? Frankly I cannot understand why. Why should someone who makes a modular product be entitled to protection against someone who makes things to fit his modules? I do think this is a deep and important question. It shows a different philosophy operating as between the common law and the continental legal worlds. I would like this problem to be one of the subjects of the ensuing debate. Before parting from Lego, however, I should mention that the OHIM have accepted a Lego brick as a trade mark. It is under opposition but I have to say that I think the fact of acceptance is astonishing from the competition point of view.[19]

OHIM are generally proving quite careful about monopolies—particularly word marks. I am not sure they have quite the same care about get-up cases. For instance, recently the First Board of Appeal accepted an application for a snack product shaped like a flower with six non-uniform petals.[20] They thought the shape was sufficiently arbitrary that it had the minimum degree of distinctiveness required by Art 7(1(e) of the Regulation. But were they not applying an insufficient test? 'Distinctive' in trade mark law does not mean just 'unusual'—it means indicating trade origin. If people want to buy the biscuits because of their fancy shape, that is not a trade mark reason for purchase. It was not even shown that anyone thought the shape of a snack denoted trade origin. It is not for the Office to assume that it does or will do so; it is for the applicant to prove it.

Perhaps I can sum up in this way. Trade dress or get-up cases are no different in principle from other sorts of case. However, courts called upon to protect them, and trade mark registries called upon to grant monopolies in them should be particularly careful in not

[19] *In the end a perpetual monopoly by way of trade mark registration in a functional brick-shape was refused by a grand chamber of the ECJ, Case C-48/09* Lego v OHIM and Megabrands *(2010). The reasoning (functional features are just that, even if the function could be achieved in a different way) and result are to be applauded. The only things to add are (a) it is astonishing that such a common-sense result had to go all the way to the ECJ and (b) that but for the resistance of a commercial party, Megabrands, Lego might have achieved a permanent monopoly—the Office should have refused from the outset. It is the function of an examining Office to refuse this sort of thing, to protect the public from unjustified monopolies. Commercial opponents may not have the resources to fight this sort of claim.*

[20] Case R467/1999-1 15 December 1999.

enforcing or creating monopolies in articles or things as such. If you require all the proof that winning the *Jif* lemon case required, namely proof that the get-up is widely recognised by the public as indicating trade source and relied upon for that purpose, then no harm will be done. But, if you accept a lesser standard (eg merely recognition of a three-headed razor), then competition will be harmed and the public, in the end, will be the loser. If in doubt, protection should be refused.

POSTSCRIPT

There is a difference between 'distinctive' meaning simply unusual or striking to the eye and 'distinctive' for the purposes of trade mark law, ie a sign which the public relies upon *as indicative of trade source. If the difference is allowed to blur you turn the Trade Mark Registry into a design registry. That has two consequences, a perpetual and a wider monopoly—better than design registration! It is perpetual because, subject to use, it can be perpetually renewed. It is wider because the test for infringement of a registered design (scope includes 'any design which does not produce on the informed user a different overall impression) is narrower than for a registered trade mark (the average consumer) test. The informed user can compare side by side whereas the average consumer can be confused by imperfect recollection.*

There have been other attempts to get a perpetual monopoly for what is really a design. I am glad to say they have largely failed, eg Bang & Olufsen's attempt to register a new striking design of speaker as a trade mark.[21] *Note that the court's reason here, ie that the shape gave substantial value to the goods, would apply even if the design had become famous by use. Another failed attempt was chocolate bunnies,* Lindt[22]*—devoid of distinctive character. The long-term observer will see much the same sort of thing being played out now as was played out in the old cases under the old law which I discuss in the article. Big companies never change their spots when it comes to seeking design protection under trade mark law!*

I had early involvement with this sort of problem in European trade mark law. In Philips (the three-headed electric razor) I held the registration (of a picture of the razor) invalid for a variety of reasons.[23]

[21] Bang & Olufsen, *Case 7-508/8 (2011)*.
[22] *Case* C-98/11 Lindt *(2012)*.
[23] Phillips Electronics NV v Remington Consumer Products Ltd *[1998] RPC 283*.

It went to the Court of Appeal who referred questions to the ECJ, though not very good ones.[24] *The ECJ took four years to answer—on the very narrow (but quite right) point that the features were all engineering features and so barred by Article 3e(ii) of the Directive ('necessary to obtain a technical result', it making no difference that the same result could be achieved by other shapes).*[25] *Then in 2002 I referred to the ECJ questions about whether Walls could register the appearance of its well-known Viennetta ice cream. I expressed the view it could not but the case sadly settled. If it had not, many of the points raised in later cases would have been raised earlier—who knows whether or not with the same result? Finally, in the Court of Appeal I wrote the judgment upholding Pumfrey J's refusal to register as a trade mark a fancy shape for a cheese.* Bongrain.[26]

24 *[1999] RPC 809.*
25 *[2003] RPC 2 and [2003] Ch 159.*
26 Bongrain *[2005] RPC 14.*

Part VI

Copyright

39

Parody and IP Claims: A Defence?—A Right to Parody?[*]

Figure 1: Laugh-it-Off T-shirt

Does the law have a sense of humour? This question is raised whenever the irresistible force of free expression, in the form of parody, meets the immovable object of property rights in the form of trademark protection.

[*] This was first published as a chapter in 'Intellectual Property at the Edge: The Contested Contours of IP' (Cambridge University Press) (June 2014), Dreyfuss and Ginsburg. Prior to that it was sent to the last of the many consultation of the UK IPO on copyright—see below.

SO BEGINS JUSTICE Albie Sachs' glorious assenting judgment in the Constitutional Court of South Africa.[1] The Court reversed the Supreme Court's finding that the slogans on this T-shirt (see Figure 1) infringed Carling's famous registered trade mark for its Black Label beer. He asked his question in the context of trade marks[2] but the same question arises, more frequently, with copyright. Indeed I suppose the Carling registered mark must also be the subject of copyright[3] and the complaint could have included a copyright claim.

What Laugh-it-Off did was offensive. It changed 'Black Label' to 'Black Labour', 'Carling Beer' to 'White Guilt', 'America's Lusty, Lively Beer' to 'Africa's lusty lively exploitation since 1652' and 'enjoyed by men all around the world' to 'No regard given worldwide'. Laugh-it-Off contended that the T-shirt 'either criticises the way SAB markets its beer by targeting black workers, or generally criticises the exploitation of blacks by whites'.[4] Crude, not particularly funny, slightly unclear in what was being parodied, but a parody nonetheless.[5]

Laugh-it-Off was a small business and the sales of this T-shirt were very small. But instead of just ignoring it, Carling sued and created a cause célèbre. A wiser course would almost certainly have been to have done nothing.[6] Not only can we be grateful to the obdurate and rigid line taken by Carling which gave us the splendid judgments of the Constitutional Court, but there is a lesson from that too. It is not merely that people do not like being parodied (which is hardly

[1] Case CCT 42-04, 27 May 2005. This is a must-read for anyone interested in parody and IP.

[2] Very oddly no one in the case seems to have considered whether there was a straightforward defence: that although the attacked use resembled the Carling mark it was not confusingly similar to it. It could have been argued that 'similar' within the meaning of s 34(1)(c) of the South African Trade Marks Act means 'confusingly similar'. The whole point of the parody would have been missed if Laugh-it-off's 'mark' was confusingly similar. South Africa does not need to go down the overprotective European approach to trade marks, which treats them as precious icons to be cosseted, venerated and treated like sacred cows.

[3] Unless it was too old. The company is indeed old, but the device marks on which it sued, judging by their date of registration in the early 1990s, were probably well in copyright. Device trade marks are regularly updated with a consequent new copyright.

[4] Media Summary, *Laugh it Off Promotions v South African Breweries* CCT 42/04.

[5] I remember a much wittier T-shirt. It had 'Horrids' written in the characteristic script and green colour of the Harrods department store. It was duly injuncted on the basis of copyright in the absence of a parody exception (not reported but I was in court at the time, around the mid-1970s).

[6] In the early days of the Internet I asked Coca-Cola's chief trade mark counsel what they were going to do about 'Coke sucks' sites. He said, with refreshing realism: 'Nothing—if we sued we'd give publicity and make things worse'.

surprising) but that some are so touchy they will sue for the slightest 'insult'. There are a significant number of powerful IP owners who definitely do not have a sense of humour.[7]

Another example of a humourless, but this time successful, plaintiff comes from the time when I was doing my Bar Finals. In 1963 Twentieth Century Fox launched the epic film *Cleopatra*, starring Elizabeth Taylor, Richard Burton and Rex Harrison. A famous poster for the movie is shown in Figure 2.

Figure 2: Poster for the film *Cleopatra*

[7] Sometimes it may be the legal department. I am reminded of part of the correspondence between Warner Bros' legal department and Groucho Marx when the former (whose film *Casablanca* had recently been a success) threatened legal action against *A Night in Casablanca*: Groucho wrote: 'I have a hunch that this attempt to prevent us from using the title is the brainchild of some ferret-faced shyster, serving a brief apprenticeship in your legal department. I know the type well—hot out of law school, hungry for success, and too ambitious to follow the natural laws of promotion. This bar sinister probably needled your attorneys, most of whom are fine fellows with curly black hair, double-breasted suits, etc., into attempting to enjoin us. Well, he won't get away with it! We'll fight him to the highest court! No pasty-faced legal adventurer is going to cause bad blood between the Warners and the Marxes. We are all brothers under the skin, and we'll remain friends till the last reel of 'A Night in Casablanca' goes tumbling over the spool'. Available at http://archive.org/details/Groucho_Marx_Letter_to_Warner_Brothers .

In early 1964 the 'Carry on Team' came out with *Carry On Cleo*, starring Amanda Barrie, Sidney James and Kenneth Williams. To put it into context for Americans and others who do not understand the British psyche,[8] the *Carry On* films were a series of smutty, humorous films with absurd plots and characters. The lines were replete with double entendres and dreadful puns.[9] The poster which Twentieth Century got injuncted for copyright infringement is shown in Figure 3.[10]

Figure 3: Poster for the film *Carry On Cleo*

[8] Understanding a *Carry On* is a bit like trying to understand not only how cricket is played but why.

[9] eg when Caesar is attacked, he cries out, 'Infamy! Infamy! They've all got it in for me!'

[10] *Twentieth Century Fox v Anglo-Amalgamated Film Distributors* (1965) 109 SJ 107. A short report of the judgment granting an interlocutory injunction. The judge, amazingly enough, thought that the poster was damaging.

I thought then and think now that was ridiculous.[11] There is a good case for saying this was not an infringement at all.[12] But assuming it prima facie was, it seems obvious that there should have been a defence of parody. Few really dispute that, and that the defence should apply both to copyright and trade mark infringement.[13] Putting it another way, the right of 'property'—a word which carries with it the automatic implication of the right to exclude—should be circumscribed to allow for some sorts of parody. And I think it should not matter what kind of intellectual property[14] is in play.

Unlike in the United States,[15] parody is not currently an exception to copyright in the UK. The Hargreaves Report on Intellectual Property, however, included in its recommendations that such an exemption be created. The problem is what sorts of parody should be allowed? In the EU, which increasingly has legislative power over IP,[16] the position is that each Member State can do its own thing about this as far as copyright is concerned. Article 5(3) of the Information Society Directive (ISD)[17] says 'Member States may provide for exceptions or limitations to the rights provided for in Articles 2 and 3 [ie the reproduction and communication rights] in the following cases: (k) use for the purpose of caricature, parody or pastiche'.

The permissibility of parody is clearly an issue which has plagued the courts for some time. By their very nature, parody exceptions contest the scope of protection of intellectual property. They are at the edge of what is permissible and even now many courts have trouble deciding what is permissible and what steps over that precarious edge into infringement.

The French have legislated.[18] Article L122-5 of the French IP code says: 'Once a work has been disclosed, the author may not prohibit ...

[11] Mr Bumble comes to mind.

[12] The judge applied the 'so near as to suggest the original' test which is not the same as the statutory test of 'reproduce a substantial part'.

[13] Particularly, as the European cases and *Carling* show, that these days the prima facie scope of trade mark rights extends so far.

[14] Copyrights, trade marks, design rights or moral rights can all potentially get in the way of parody.

[15] Where 'fair use' generally allows parody—see Rebecca Tushnet's chapter in *Intellectual Property at the Edge: The Contested Contours of IP* (Cambridge University Press, 2014), Dreyfuss and Ginsburg.

[16] Art 118 of the Lisbon Treaty on the functioning of the EU says so, but what is now called the EU has been making IP laws at least since the Trade Marks Directive 93/89.

[17] The Information Society Directive 2001/29.EC.

[18] So have a number of others. The current Consultation (see below) wants 'evidence' and does not seem to have had the wit to try to find out how the parody exceptions are actually working in other countries.

(4) parody, pastiche and caricature, observing the rules of the genre'. I doubt whether the last bit of this is helpful. For when it comes to parody 'the genre' has no rules, making application of this legislation problematical. Parody ranges from the downright brutally offensive to the respectful *homage*. I cannot imagine any way of determining the 'rules of genre'. It would be left to the court to make them up—in effect to read these words as if they meant 'fair'.[19]

As far as trade marks are concerned, there is no provision for parody in the current EU legislation.[20] But the recent Max Planck study[21] has recommended[22] that:

> It should also be specified that parodies, as particular form of criticism or comment, also fall into the ambit of the provision [ie of a 'referential use' defence]. The use would be allowed to the extent that it does not contravene principles of honest practices in industrial and commercial matters.

Any implementing legislation, if comes to pass, and it probably will, will be EU wide, unlike copyright where currently Member States may do their own thing. Of course 'honest practices etc'. also probably amounts to a rather fuzzy 'what the court thinks fair'. And of course everyone knows the US has 'fair use', leaving it all to the courts. I do not suppose anyone thinks that thereby a clear bright line has been achieved.

Can one do better? Or must one simply leave an appeal to fairness to define a parody exception to IP rights? Well the British government thinks one can do better. I suspect it is wrong. Let us examine what it is up to more closely. The December 2006 Gowers Review of Intellectual Property[23] recommended[24] after consultation that there should be created an 'exception to copyright for the purpose of caricature, parody or pastiche by 2008'. The government, instead of then

[19] Professor Ginsburg tells me that French case law has indeed done just that. The courts have articulated some rules. These include that the parody not be confusing; that the parody not intend personally to harm the author; and—somewhat uncertainly—that the parody is intended to be funny.

[20] Hardly surprising. I do not suppose that at the time of the original Trade Marks Directive (1989) anyone ever thought that trade mark right could extend to parody in the first place. And so it shouldn't.

[21] Study on the Overall Functioning of the European Trade Mark System for the EU Commission, 5.2.2011.

[22] ibid, para 5.262.

[23] Andrew Gowers, an ex-editor of the *Financial Times*, was asked to produce a review of the whole of IP law within 6 months—an obviously impossible task, not least for someone with no IP background.

[24] Recommendation 12, see paras 4.89–4.90.

just getting on with it, put it out to consultation again, as if Gowers had not already done so. This was by a 'newspeakly' named document called 'Taking Forward the Gowers Review, Proposed Changes to the Copyright Exceptions' published in December 2007 (so much for 'by 2008'). I do not know what happened to that consultation, for the next event, under the new Coalition Government, was another review of IP law by another distinguished journalist, Professor Ian Hargreaves. Like Gowers he was given just six months to cover the whole of IP. As far as parody and copyright were concerned he said: 'Government should deliver [more newspeak!] copyright exceptions at national level to realise all the opportunities within the EU framework, including format shifting, parody, non-commercial research, and library archiving'.[25] He noted that 'After two consultations the only concrete action has been the abandonment of efforts to bring in … an exception to cover parody'.[26]

The government published a response to Hargreaves in August 2011. It said it would 'bring forward proposals in autumn 2011 for a substantial opening up of the UKJ's copyright exceptions regime'.[27] 'This will include proposals … to introduce an exception for parody'. The next step was, the reader will now not be surprised to learn, was a document called 'Consultation on proposals to change the UK copyright system'.[28]

To that I now turn. Hargreaves said decisions on IP policy should be 'evidence based'. I do not know what he had in mind as to what constitutes 'evidence'. I do not suppose the government knows either but it says it agrees. I rather think 'evidence' is, and can only be, either material put forward by various lobbying groups, or so-called 'economic' evidence based on tenuous or speculative data. As far as parody is concerned, it is impossible to see how there can be any real concrete 'evidence'. The Consultation has four-and-a-half pages[29] on the subject. It consists mainly of statements of the blindingly obvious or questions which cannot possibly be answered either at all or quantitatively.

[25] *Digita; Opportunity: A Review of Intellectual Property and Growth, May 2011*, para 5.40.

[26] ibid, para 10.5.

[27] *The Government Response to the Hargreaves Review of Intellectual Property and Growth*, p7. It was published on 3 August 2011. It contains lovely pictures of the Ministers but is so sloppy that does not actually bear a date!

[28] Ref 2011-004.

[29] 'Consultation on proposals to change the UK copyright system', pp 83–88, paras 7. 100–7.122.

Here is an example of the blindly obvious: under the heading 'Impact on creators of original works'. It says:[30]

> Four potential effects of a parody exception on the sales of original works have been identified: 1) lost sales due to confusion between a parody and an original work; 2) increased sales due to greater publicity and awareness for the original; 3) lost sales due to negative reputational effects on the original; 4) increased sales due to positive reputational effects on the original.

But even this is inadequate. Thus it ignores what can be one of the key reasons why some people sue for copyright infringement—damage to *amour propre*, a real matter of concern to touchy—too touchy—copyright owners as I have observed above. And it devotes quite a bit of space (not only here, but elsewhere) to 'lost sales due to confusion'. That is rather ridiculous for two reasons. A parody which is liable to be taken for the original is an unsuccessful parody: because the whole point of parody is that the audience recognises it for what it is. Secondly, if a work is deceptive, the law has an independent remedy—passing off. For instance in *Clark v Associated Newspapers*[31] a well-known colourful politician successfully sued the *London Evening Standard* which published a spoof 'Alan Clark Diary'. He proved[32] that a substantial number of people thought the diary was actually his, that they were confused or deceived. No one suggests that a parody which deceives should be allowed. You do not have to consult about such a self-evident matter. So also for parody which is defamatory: defamation has its own causes of action, most relevantly for libel.

Incidentally it is interesting to observe that the parody in the *Clark* case, a literary parody, did not involve any question of copyright infringement. It is an odd fact that it is much more possible to parody a literary work, or an author's literary style, without substantially reproducing a copyright work, than it is to parody a visual or musical work. The *Oxford Book of Parodies*[33] is full of parodies down the ages which could never have amounted to prima facie copyright infringement which needed a defence. That fact ought to inform the government. If literary authors have to put up with parody, why not authors of other types of work?

[30] Para 7.111.
[31] *Clark v Associated Newspapers* [1998] 1 WLR 1558, [1998] RPC 261.
[32] Or at least the judge held he proved—many of us doubt he was right on the facts.
[33] Gross, J (ed), *The Oxford Book of Parodies* (Oxford University Press, 2012).

I turn to exemplify some obviously unanswerable questions (or at least not usefully answerable questions) posed by the Consultation:

78. Do you agree that a parody exception could create new opportunities for economic growth?
79. What is the value of the market for parody works in the UK and globally?
80. How might a parody exception impact on creators of original works and creators of parodies? What would be the costs and benefits of such an exception?

And:

82. How should an exception for parody, caricature and pastiche be framed in order to mitigate some of the potential costs described above?
83. Would making this a 'fair dealing' exception sufficiently minimise negative impacts to copyright owners, or would more specific measures need to be taken?
84. Are you able to provide evidence of the costs and benefits of such an exception?

Did those who wrote this, in their desire for 'evidence', seriously expect that anyone could give concrete reliable answers to these questions?[34]

I have another concern about this Consultation. Nowhere does it mention free speech—yet parody often involves just this. The notion that one is concerned solely with market economics mistakenly confines the debate. Article 10(1) of the European Convention on Human Rights says: 'Everyone has the right to freedom of expression'. It is qualified by Art 10(2), which includes 'the protection of the reputation or the rights of others'. But the qualification is not so extensive as to prevent reasonable criticism—which is just what a parody may be. Free speech really matters: it should in some cases trump IP rights, as it did in the *Carling* case.

Further, the Consultation explicitly refused to address another way in which parody may be restricted by IP rights—no qualification of the so-called 'moral right' is proposed. The Consultation says:

> As well as economic rights, the Copyright Act provides certain moral rights to creators, which derive from international law, including the

[34] Professor Barton Beebe suggests the questions themselves are parodies. Actually there is a small exercise by Erickson, Kretschmer and Mendis which examines parodies of pop songs on YouTube (*Copyright and the Economic Effects of Parody: An empirical study of music videos on the YouTube platform, and an assessment of regulatory options*). It was published on 19 May 2013. It concludes they are harmless and even could help promote the original. Such parodies of course only form a small part of the universe of parodies—and are all essentially non-commercial. The self-evident reality is that the IPO's questions are unanswerable—and in any event parody is self-evidently more about free speech than economics or markets.

> right to be identified as the author of a work and the right to object to derogatory treatment of a work. These rights, deriving from international law, include the right to object to derogatory treatment applies to any use of a work that amounts to distortion or mutilation of the work, or is otherwise prejudicial to the honour or reputation of its creator. Moral rights therefore clearly place limits on the extent of any parody exception. However, many parodies will not constitute derogatory treatment of a work and moral rights and parody exceptions coexist in many other European countries, including those that provide much stronger moral rights than in the UK.[35]

It is not much use providing a defence of parody to copyright infringement if the author has another weapon. The Consultation blithely asserts that 'many parodies will not constitute derogatory treatment of a work'. I doubt that. In particular the so-called 'integrity right' could well get in the way. The Copyright, Designs and Patents Act 1988 gives an author a right 'not to have his work subjected to derogatory treatment'.[36] That is defined as follows:

> (2) For the purposes of this section—
>
> (a) 'treatment' of a work means any addition to, deletion from or alteration to or adaptation of the work, other than ... [minor exception];
>
> (b) the treatment of a work is derogatory if it amounts to distortion or mutilation of the work or is otherwise prejudicial to the honour or reputation of the author or director...

Consider a parody of an artistic work, say a photograph or a poster. Almost certainly that will involve something by way of *addition to, deletion from or alteration to or adaption of it.* I cannot conceive of a parody which would not amount to at least one of these things. Some courts may consider that enough. A better reading is that there is an overall requirement too: whether the parody *is otherwise prejudicial to the honour or reputation of the author.* Note that the basic test is *prejudicial to the honour or reputation of the author.* Is not all adverse criticism prejudicial to the person criticised? Adverse criticism may be entirely justified but harmful to the author's reputation—indeed a justified criticism may be more harmful than one which has no justification.

35 Para 7-105.
36 Section 8(1).

Remember as I have said twice before, authors can be ever so touchy. Perhaps the most famous daft example of this in the context of the integrity right comes from Canada. In *Snow v The Eaton Centre*[37] a sculptor had made some models of Canada Geese to hang in the atrium of the Eaton Centre shopping mall like a flight of geese. To jolly up the mall for Christmas, its owners put red ribbons round the necks of the geese. The sculptor took umbrage, sued and won. He persuaded the court that the sculpture's integrity was 'distorted, mutilated or otherwise modified' and that was 'to the prejudice of the honour or reputation of the author' contrary to s 28.2 of the Canadian Copyright Act. Most people think the decision silly on its facts, but for present purposes it illustrates how powerful the 'moral right' can be.

So I think the Consultation underestimates the potential of moral rights to allow for parody where the author is the subject of it. The real reason why some parodies may escape the integrity right is different: that the parody does not attack the reputation of the author but someone else. Thus Laugh-it-Off would escape being caught by this provision. It was prejudicial to Carling's reputation, not that of the unknown author of the trade mark itself.

The Consultation says nothing can be done about providing a parody exception to moral rights because there is an international obligation to provide for the moral right which does not have any express such exception.[38] Technically this so: the UK Act was copied from Art 6*bis* of the Berne Convention.[39] But it would surely be worth exploring how far the obligation has been 'written down' in the jurisprudence of other countries.

Moreover Art 10 of the European Convention on Human Rights may itself provide a right of parody where free speech is involved. It did so, for instance, when Louis Vuitton sued the artist Nadia Plesner for depicting a poor African child carrying a Chihuahua dog and its 'Audra' handbag. She had used it originally on a T-shirt and agreed

[37] *Snow v The Eaton Centre* (1982) 70 CPR (2d) 105.

[38] S Ricketson and J Ginsburg argue that parodies do not harm honour or reputation within the meaning of Art 6*bis*, *International Copyright and Neighbouring Rights: The Berne Convention and Beyond* (Oxford University Press, 2006) para 10.29. But one can easily foresee that a powerful offended parody victim might want to argue otherwise. And that depending on how offensive the parody was, a court might rule otherwise.

[39] Introduced by the Rome Act of 1928.

to give up after threats by Vuitton. Then she used the same figure again in a picture she called *Darfurnica*, a protest about genocide in Darfur (see Figure 4).

Figure 4: *Darfurnica* by Nadia Plesner

Vuitton got an ex parte injunction from the Dutch Court to restrain its depiction anywhere in the EU. Plesner retaliated by seeking, in effect, a declaration that Art 10 trumped Vuitton's right (actually it was a registered design right, but the type of right should make no difference). Vuitton was equivocal about whether it actually wanted to suppress the whole picture and in the end said it did not—even though it was the picture that provoked the claim. Judge Edgar Brinkman ruled[40] in Plesner's favour, irrespective of whether the figure was in the whole picture or not. He held that Art 10 did prevail over Vuitton's 'property'[41] right. Judge Brinkman records that there was a parallel ex parte injunction in France. Researches do not show that anything happened after that, so presumably the little boy remains injuncted in France.

A similar use of Art 10 was made by the German Federal Court in a silly trade mark infringement case about a postcard. The card ridiculed Milka chocolate's idyllic advertising theme using cows and mountains using a purple background corresponding to Milka's colour mark registered for, inter alia, chocolate. The Court held it

[40] 4 May 2011.
[41] Note again the invocation of 'property' as a justification for an oppressive injunction.

was prima facie an infringement[42] but that free speech and Art 10 rights meant that the use was with 'due cause'.[43] What a convoluted way of reaching the only sensible result!

I do not think anyone could complain if the moral rights legislation were made expressly subject to the provisions of the ECHR, which indeed is probably the legal position under the Human Rights Act 1998.[44] Indeed I would go further and make all IP rights expressly subject to the Convention.

I turn to what I think the government should do in relation to copyright. I have little to say, for it is not complicated. It should put forward legislation for an additional exception to copyright infringement (of all types of work). This could simply provide:

(1) It is not an infringement of the copyright in any type of work to make a fair parody, caricature or pastiche[45] of it.

I am not sure that any more is worth adding to try to define 'fair'. But if it is, it should be woolly. Something like:

(2) In considering what is 'fair' the court shall take into account all relevant circumstances, including the extent, if at all, to which the work complained of is competitive with that work, the degree, if any, of the offensiveness of the parody, or the degree to which the parody may constitute fair comment on the work, its author or any matter of public interest.

And I would add an express provision:

(3) All rights provided for in this Act and any other intellectual property right are subject to the provisions of the European Convention on Human Rights and in particular any fair parody caricature or pastiche shall be permitted if it is an exercise of the right of freedom of expression provided for by Art 10(1) of that Convention.

Finally the government should get on with it. No more consulting or wishing for an impossible 'evidence' base.

[42] Another example of how protective European trade mark law has become, cf. the point I made about the Black labour case.

[43] Case I ZR 159/02, 3 February 2005. Under Art 9(1)(c) of the Community Trade mark Regulation as amended (EC 207/2009) and national law implementing Art 5(2) of the Trade Marks Directive as amended, (08/95/EC) in the case of dissimilar goods the proprietor must show that the use of the defendant's sign is 'without due cause'.

[44] Section 3(1) provides: 'So far as it is possible to do so, primary legislation and subordinate legislation must be read and given effect in a way which is compatible with the Convention rights'.

[45] I use the phrase in the Information Society Directive 2001/29/EC. There can be absolutely no point in trying to define these more. The Consultation asks whether there should be a further definition. That is obviously a pointless question.

Postscript [to original chapter]. After this chapter was sent in draft to the last of the UK IPO's 'calls for evidence' the UK IPO announced that a 'fair dealing' for parody would be provided.[46] It said:

> The Government will legislate to allow limited copying on a fair dealing basis for parody, caricature and pastiche, while leaving the existing moral rights regime unchanged. It considers that this permitted act will provide economic and cultural benefits by removing unnecessary restrictions on the activity of some creators, reducing administrative costs, and encouraging creators, without causing any significant economic harm to holders of rights in the parodied content. The requirement that any parody use of a work be 'fair dealing' is an additional restriction which ensures that the exception is not misused, and will preclude the copying of entire works where such taking would not be considered fair (for example if such works are already licensable for a fee). The existing moral rights regime will be maintained unchanged, so that creators will be protected from damage to their reputation or image through the use of works for parody.
>
> In addition to the benefits to parodists outlined above, of allowing easier production of parody works, there are compelling social and cultural benefits such as the development of free speech and the fostering of creative talent. The wider public would also benefit from increased legal clarity and opportunities for freedom of expression when creating parody for non-commercial reasons. The Government agrees with the Business, Innovation and Skills Select Committee that genuine political and satirical comment should be protected.

So something should happen. I would be pleased to see them adopt all my proposals included in (3) above, but I doubt they will do anything so sensible.

POSTSCRIPT

1. *The UK IPO finally got the legislation done in October 2014—nearly the eighth anniversary of the recommendation of Gowers.*[47] *This is what was provided:*

   (1) *Fair dealing with a work for the purposes of caricature, parody or pastiche does not infringe copyright in the work.*[48]

[46] Under the Orwellian title 'Modernising Copyright. A Modern Robust and Flexible Framework', 17 December 2012.

[47] *The Gowers Review of Intellectual Property (December 2006).*

[48] *Reg 5(1) of the Copyright and Rights in Performances (Quotation and Parody) Regulations 2014 No 2356. There is no rational reason for the delay. It could be and was all done by a Statutory Instrument made pursuant to the European Communities Act 1972. No Act of Parliament was needed.*

This is probably the same as my proposal—there is no real difference between 'fair dealing with a work' and 'to make a fair parody'. I am glad they did not try to spell out what 'fair' meant. Judges will have to work it out on a case-by-case basis—though I anticipate that most parodies will be adjudged 'fair dealing'.

But sadly they did not do anything about moral rights, which may undercut the freedom provided by this defence as explained above.

The UK IPO has a pamphlet called 'Exception to copyright: Guidance for creators and copyright lawyers',[49] *which has a bit about the parody exception. It is probably all right as far as it goes.*[50] *At the very back it contains a health warning: 'This guidance sets out the general principles of the changes to copyright law, it is not legal advice. It is recommended that you obtain legal advice in circumstances where you have specific questions relating to the law'. But I think it would be much better and more certain if the warning was (a) much more upfront and (b) made it clear that this is only the Office view of the law and that the actual law is set out in the Act as amended. The danger of this sort of pamphlet from government is that it is taken as the law. Other departments are much worse at this sort of thing—pamphlets about tax, planning, and the Home Office guidance on immigration law for example. When I was Nigel Bridge's pupil in 1966–67 he regularly was asked to advise on the legal meaning of Customs pamphlets and always answered to the effect that there was no point, the law is set out in the statute not the pamphlet. (Nigel was the 'Treasury Devil' ie the junior barrister appointed to handle most government legal questions—it could largely be done by one man in those days.) On the whole I favour government departments refraining from writing commentaries on the law.*

2. *The CJEU has had its Delphic say on the subject in* Deckmyn v Banderstreen.[51] *Totally predictably the Court said parody was an autonomous EU law concept. But then (predictably again) it proceeded to muddled reasoning. The parody/pastiche in question was a well-known cartoon character called Lambic who*

[49] www.gov.uk/government/uploads/system/uploads/attachment_data/file/375953/Guidance_for_creators_and_copyright_owners.pdf.

[50] *Though I doubt that the unambiguous assertion: 'it would not be considered "fair" to use an entire musical track on a spoof video' is necessarily right in all circumstances.*

[51] *Case C-201/13* Deckmyn v Banderstreen, *3 September 2014.*

distributed money by throwing coins to the populace. A Flemish political party took the image, substituted the face of Lambic with that of the mayor of Ghent and changed the populace so as to have dark-coloured skin and women with headscarves. The political point being made was that taxpayers' money was going to immigrants. Instead of saying, as it should have done, that this was indeed a parody or pastiche, albeit offensive, the Court went on to add that in the application of the parody exception there must be a fair balance between the right of the copyright owner not to be discriminated against and the freedom of expression of the user. I just do not understand that—however offensive a parody may be, it remains a parody. You need another mechanism to take it out of the exception. UK law has it in the qualification 'fair dealing'. If Belgian law does not, the solution lies in changing Belgian law, not distorting what is meant by parody.

40

The Globalisation of Copyright[*]

AS I SAT down to write this talk I said to myself—don't mention the cricket, directly or indirectly—especially don't mention the Ashes.[1] So, if I am not to talk about these unmentionable subjects what should I talk about?

John MacPhail told me I had a free hand—a kind of no ball. I could try to hit anywhere. But I have spent all my life working to a brief. Argue for this, or for that at the bar, decide the answer to this or that case as a judge. Now I was being asked to brief myself. To invent a case to advance and then to advance it. At first I was stumped. Oops. I knew my audience would be one of the most sophisticated in the world. I was going to say that anyone who can understand the laws of cricket is by definition sophisticated. But I won't.

What was clear is that I could not talk about the Australian law of copyright, for increasingly Australian law has differed from that of other countries—not just because your law has changed, though it has, but because we have all changed. There have been quite a lot of nation states doing their own thing in copyright.

It was that thought which inspired my topic—is that the way things will be for the future—or does the future hold the opposite—a convergence of copyright laws across the world? Does it do any good for a country to do its own thing?

The first part of my talk will be about this. The second will be about mechanisms for enforcement—what does globalisation mean for these?

[*] A Paper for the Conference of the Australian Copyright Society, November 2005.

[1] England had just won the dramatic series 2.1, returning the Ashes to England after 8 years. The remainder of this paragraph, indeed whole talk, has more cricket references. They will be incomprehensible to Americans, continental Europeans, Chinese and many others.

SUBSTANTIVE LAW

To make predictions about the future it is generally valuable first to look back to see what forces and mechanisms got us to where we are. So it is worth making explicit some of the driving forces for copyright.

Firstly it is trite that a major driving force for the creation and extension of copyright laws has been a need to respond to technology. You do not really need a law of copyright unless there are cheap and available means for copying or exploiting things and a corresponding large-scale demand from consumers. So the Statute of Anne was a response to the demand for engravings. The various eighteenth- and nineteenth-century extensions of copyright in both fields of application and term were a response to the lowering of the cost of reproduction coupled with the rise in size and affluence of the middle classes. We are mostly aware of the Commonwealth developments, but there were corresponding developments on the continent of Europe. The battles over copyright creation and extensions were tough. Perhaps the most famous opponent was Lord Macaulay. Here is what he said in 1841, opposing an extension of term from 28 years from publication to 60 years from the death of the author: 'It is good that authors should be remunerated, and the least exceptionable way of remunerating them is by a monopoly. Yet monopoly is an evil. For the sake of the good we must submit to the evil: but the evil ought not to last a day longer than is necessary for the purpose of securing the good'.

Macaulay's famous phrase is that copyright is a 'tax on knowledge'. This view of copyright is that of an economic free trader. IP rights should only be given when they are necessary. By and large that is the prevailing philosophy of the common law, though no one can doubt that sometimes judges want to stop people just because they have copied.

That is the notion behind another driver for copyright: that creative work *ought* to belong to the author. The notion came out of or at least was greatly reinforced by the Age of Enlightenment. The quotation from Lawrence Sterne in Chapter 1 of Laddie et al[2] summarises the view: 'The sweat of a man's brows, and the exudations of a man's brains are much a man's own property as the breeches

[2] *Laddie, Prescott and Vitoria*, The Modern Law of Copyright and Designs (*LexisNexis 4th Edn 2011, 1st edn 1995*).

on his backside'. Make no mistake—this has deep emotional appeal. Copyright is seen not merely as an economic tool, a property right, but as something like an extension of the personality of the author—something for his benefit and that of his heirs.

The recent European creation of a *droit de suite* ('re-sale right') for all of Europe shows this notion is alive and well. The idea is that the creator of an artistic work should have a share in all subsequent sales of his work. The emotional appeal is driven by the picture of the young artist in a garret selling his work for a pittance and later seeing it fetching zillions at Sotheby's. The EU Directive[3] pursuant to which we in Europe must have this law starts:

> Whereas in the field of copyright, the resale right is an unassignable and inalienable right, enjoyed by the author of an original work of graphic or plastic art, to an economic interest in successive sales of the work concerned.

This is set forth as an article of faith, not one of reason—as a result of a natural law. Personally I think no good will come of it. Some rich artists will get more, poor artists will get nothing and the bureaucrats who administer it will make a comfortable living for doing a boring job.

Will Australia have a *droit de suite* one day?[4] Well that will in part depend on a third driver which has emerged and will I think be increasingly important—harmonisation of IP in the global world.

We have already had one major example of this—the extension of the term of copyright to 70 years from the year of death of the author. For reasons which are not clear, the Austrians and Germans, but no one else in Europe or elsewhere, had settled on a term of copyright which was 70 years from the year of death of the author. The rest of the world had, for most of the last century, had life plus 50 years. I have never found the justification for that period, still less the German one. The latter is supposed to have something to do with giving a reward not just to the author, but to his children and grandchildren on the grounds that his children somehow lost out due to the Great War. Whatever the reason, the disparity in term was seen as distorting the Common Market, as it did. The solution was to ratchet up all copyrights to life plus 70 years. It was done with hardly any debate at the time. No doubt so far as the UK was concerned it was worthwhile—British copyrights, what with British

[3] 2001/84/EC.

[4] It does! See the Postscript to this chapter.

pop music and the predominance of English as an author's language, are worth proportionately more than continental copyrights. No one cared about Joe Public.

No one has justified, or could, justify this on the grounds of encouragement of authors. It is a pity that Lord Macaulay was not around to oppose any of this. Actually, so far as I can see, no one was—not even to oppose the fact that the extension was retrospective with only a limited exception for those who had started exploiting a work whilst it was out of copyright. Thus, for instance, James Joyce came back into copyright—enabling the Joyce estate to suppress copies and preserve what it thinks (others do not) the purity of his work. One day people will be able to do with it as they want, but they can't now.

The US followed this ratcheting-up by the EU. It too extended copyright term to 70 years. Promotion of this was largely by the vested interests of Hollywood and the record industry—the inheritors of the mantles of Lord Macaulay's booksellers. The thought of Mickey Mouse running out—oops—of copyright, was too much. And the Supreme Court duly endorsed the extension, notwithstanding the powerful Macaulay-type argument to the contrary.[5]

Will there be a further ratcheting-up of copyright term? Possibly—what happens when Mickey Mouse finds himself with only a few overs to go? He will want a timeless test.[6] And he will want never to be given out.[7] There will be pressures for this. Whether the US Supreme Court could reconcile that with Section 8.8 of the Constitution ('for a Limited Time') is an interesting question.[8]

Globalisation of substantive law was given a great boost by TRIPS in 1994. For the first time states who signed (and in practice they had to or find themselves with what would in effect be trade sanctions applied to them) were obliged to have IP laws and of a prescribed basic content. How different from how things were once. Here is Sir George Jessel in 1880:

> Persons in the position of the defendants, that is of agents for an American publisher, must be taken to know that Americans are in the habit of printing and exporting piratical works and they must therefore know that they

[5] *Eldred v Ashcroft* 537 US 186 (2003) 1.

[6] Another cricket reference.

[7] And another.

[8] This confers powers on Congress 'to promote the Progress of Science and the Useful Arts by securing for Limited Times to Authors and Inventors the exclusive Right to their respective Writings and Discoveries'.

> import books from America at the risk of their containing what is piratical and are thus committing an unlawful act and of being liable to be sued without notice.[9]

That old US law—of not according copyright to foreigners and later only to do so if there was first or simultaneous publication in the US—was made for US economic interests. Even by the 1950s it was unsustainable because of the increasing worldwide nature of the publishing business.[10]

Increasingly it is going to be difficult for countries to make IP laws which just suit them. Increasingly there will be pressure—rational in part—for laws to be uniform. We are seeing that in a big way in Europe—patent law and trade mark law has been harmonised, design law largely so, and copyright in part. More will come. I think the same sort of thing will happen on a growing scale on a world basis. Notice, for instance, that even the US is trying to change its patent laws so as to be more in harmony with the rest of the world—there is a Bill before Congress aiming to introduced first to file, early publication and elimination of the best-mode requirement, all changes which would bring the US more in line with other countries.

Whether harmonisation is a good thing must depend partly on how well it is done. But whether it is done well or not, what is clear is that nation states will have less and less real individual choice as to what they put in their copyright laws. In reality what will matter are international norms. There will be less and less point in having special national laws of copyright in a world market. I question, for instance rules like s 7 of your Patent Act. The rest of the world has a rule that a prior published document, no matter how obscure, must be considered for the purposes of invalidating a patent for obviousness. It may not be sensible—a document in Sanskrit in the children's section of Alice Springs public library in reality will not come to the attention of a notional skilled man.[11] Your rule is that such a document will not count unless it is shown that the skilled man would have 'ascertained, understood and regarded as relevant' the document concerned. A rational rule. But it means that in some cases an Australian patent

[9] Per Sir George Jessel MR (1880) 15 Ch D 501.

[10] The US joined the Berne Convention in 1957.

[11] I had just invented this example in Unilin v Berry [2007] EWCA Civ 2007 and was so proud of it that I repeated it in Green Lane Products v PMS International [2008] EWCA Civ 358. CIPA, the Chartered Patent Attorneys' journal, later contained a lovely follow-up—a purported letter from the librarian of Alice Springs public library saying that no book had ever been wrongly shelved and strongly objecting to the suggestion that this was even possible.

would survive an obviousness attack which would succeed in the rest of the world. Is that sensible from the point of view of Australia's economy? Or is it just better to line up with the rest of the world—even if the law is cruder and a little less 'fair'?

So I foresee increasing moves for harmonisation. With it, as we have found in Europe, there is likely to be increasing opacity in the legislation. European trade mark law is a good example of the danger—we have masses of litigation going to the European Court of Justice on what a trade mark is or is for—70 cases in 10 years—and there seems no respite. Curiously, in some ways harmonisation will be a move back to the past for the Commonwealth. After all the first real international copyright Act was the Imperial Copyright Act of 1911—which served the whole Commonwealth well for a long time.

Let me turn back to another driver—technology, particularly the Internet. Works protected by copyright are, by and large, deliverable digitally (not paintings or sculptures—yet—though who knows what will be possible by way of digital holograms in the future).[12] How will courts and legislatures respond?

So far as courts are concerned, we can again find a lesson in history. Before the 1911 Act there was no copyright in a sound recording. Only copyright in musical works—the law lagged behind the technology. To produce a gramophone record of a now long forgotten song called *Where my caravan has rested*, the Columbia Graphophone (what was a 'graphophone'?) Company bought one copy of the sheet music for the song with piano accompaniment. In infringement of copyright, orchestral arrangements were made. The English Court of Appeal granted a remedy which went well beyond delivery up of the infringing copies—the defendants were injuncted from selling the records and made to deliver up the matrix used for making them. We would now call this a 'reach through' remedy. The court did not consider quantum of damage—but I suppose applying modern principles, damages would cover sales of the records too—as flowing foreseeably from the infringement. The case was *Chappel v Columbia Graphophone Co.*[13]

I am surprised that the implications of *Chappel* have not been more widely exploited. There have been patent cases where a small-scale infringement was used so as to produce a product which could be shown to be equivalent to the patentees' product for marketing

[12] I missed digital printing which has made this problem come alive now.
[13] Chappel v Columbia Graphophone Co [1914] 2 Ch 745.

authorisation purposes. The court 'reached through' to require the defendant to have his authorisation cancelled. I once had a case against Hugh Laddie where Sega, a computer game console manufacturer, had a little program which normally had to be run before you could access a game. So by virtue of this it had control over all games which could run on the console. The defendant, in infringement of copyright, decompiled this little program. Using the information thereby obtained, he created a way of playing games on the console *without further use of the program*. And wrote his own games for Sega consoles. I argued that this was a *Chappel* case. Hugh struggled before Aldous J. Before he decided it we settled—principally because there was a new EU Directive allowing decompiling in this sort of case.

Willie Aldous later told us that he thought I was right. But I am not so sure. What was sought to be protected commercially was the right of access to Sega consoles, not the little access program itself. Bill Gummow was kind enough to send me a copy of the recent High Court decision in *Stevens v Sony*.[14] Although the facts and law were different (no one-time-only copyright infringement of a distinct program), the same worries were at work.

However I think *Chappel*-type reach-through relief may have a significant part to play in the future of IP. What its limits are remains to be explored. How far, for instance, can a reach-through claim for damages go?[15] In the case of copyright, suppose a man sends, by email or post, one pirate copy of work out of the jurisdiction in the knowledge that it will be copied and disseminated by the recipient. Is that damage which can be recovered for the single infringement? And can an injunction be granted restraining further dissemination? Such an injunction would not depend on the law of copyright abroad. It would not involve extra-territorial enforcement of copyright, which I will come to later. The *Chappell* game is one which we may find played out across the world.[16]

The courts have also become involved in another field, where also there has been and I expect will be more, legislative activity. Broadly I would call it the field of 'shoot the messenger'. The general idea is

[14] *Stevens v Sony* [205] HCA 58.

[15] A question raised more often in patents, see eg *Gerber v Lectra* [1997] RPC 433 (damages for patent infringement to include foreseeable consequential loss, including for sales of spares, post-expiry sales which would not have been made if the defendant had not established an infringing business when the patent was in force).

[16] It hasn't happened yet, which still surprises me.

that those who provide facilities to enable others to infringe should be liable for those infringements. Copyprotect legislation is an example of this. But of even more significance will be legislation and judicial decisions aimed at making Internet providers and deliverers liable.

It seems hard to have to make the postman liable for what he delivers, but I can see no other realistic way of preserving copyright in music, computer programs and other kinds of digitally deliverable works. Pictures and words will come next—already Google wants to put all books on the Web. Recent litigation shows the future trend. I refer of course to *Grokster* in the US Supreme Court[17] and the *KaZaa* decisions in Holland and here.[18] Earlier cases, eg *Sony v Universal City*[19] and *Amstrad v BPI*[20] went the other way, but I suspect that necessity will drive legislation and the courts. I suspect also that the postman's defence—how can I know what is in the letters—may technically be invalid. Copyright law may drive the technology to find ways to prevent infringement.[21]

ENFORCEMENT

Of course making the postman, or indeed the sender himself, liable is not an end of the matter. Actually it is only the beginning. How and where are rights to be enforced? This is my second major topic. Since IP rights are territorial in nature there are just three basic models for adjudication of disputes or the invocation of a restraining court order:

1. Enforcement country by country. This is the classical model upon which I grew up. It meant and means that the same essential dispute can be run in parallel or re-run country by country.

[17] *MGM v Grokster* US 125 SCt 2764 (2005).

[18] Holland [2004] ECDR 16; 2003 WL 23508845 (HR(NL)). Note that this case failed essentially for procedural and evidential reasons.

[19] *Sony v Universal City* 464 US 417, 104 S Ct 774 (maker of video recording machines not liable for infringements made by consumers); Australia, *Universal Music v Sharman*, 5 September 2005.

[20] *Amstrad v BPI* [1986] FSR 159 (sale of double-headed tape recorders lawful even though some consumers would use the machines for infringement).

[21] Things have moved on a little. You can get injunctions against ISPs requiring them to block pirate sites of which they have notice, Twentieth Century Fox v BT (No 2) [2011] EWHC 2714 (Ch). But the full story (involving potential liability) of both sites that facilitate downloading (or streaming) of infringing material and sites that facilitate the sale of counterfeit goods has some way to go.

My admission to the Bar of NSW was part of the classical model. Lego had sued Tyco in Hong Kong. After a fully fought Titanic battle (two rounds of interlocutory injunction, three rounds to the Privy Council) Tyco won. Lego turned to sue Tyco's Australian customers here[22] (They did not, though they could have, played the further game of joining in Tyco. That game is to find a defendant within the jurisdiction, sue him and bring in other parties, especially the foreign supplier.) Tyco got me to come here, since I knew all the evidence by heart. The law was a bit different but the evidence was much the same.[23] As was the result.[24]

2. Enforcement by the courts of one country enforcing the laws of other countries. This is what the Europeans call 'cross-border jurisdiction'.
3. Enforcement by some sort of international tribunal—a supranational tribunal.

I think these are the only possibilities. But there is an important variant of the first: where some aspect of a first litigation in country A is carried over to subsequent parallel litigation in country B. I have in mind the doctrine of estoppel, issue estoppel or some variant of it. By and large courts have been resistant to this, and litigators have, perhaps surprisingly, not pressed it.[25] A recent attempt in the US to have a judgment of mine as to the obviousness of a patent applied as an estoppel failed.[26] The reasoning was that such a question is one of mixed fact and law. And so it was, sort of. A more specific factual finding—eg as to a prior use—would, it seems, have attracted the doctrine.

Expect more of this in the future—it is difficult to suppose, for instance, that a factual finding of copying by a court of country A could not be the subject of an issue estoppel in country B, under

[22] *Interlego v Croner* (1991) 102 ALR 379, (1992) 111 ALR 597—the clients, rightly, thought that in view of their representation by David Catterns, QC, there was no point in paying more vast sums for me on the appeal!

[23] Actually I was surprised by how difficult it was simply to put the transcripts before the Court. Key witnesses (eg the Lego draftsman) were called all over again—to no useful effect. At that point Australian procedural rules seemed unduly technical compared with what I was used to. I gather they have changed since.

[24] I loved it—and realised all the more that it doesn't make much difference where a barrister appears.

[25] It was not tried in *Interlego v Croner.*

[26] *Merck v Teva.* Patent held invalid by me [2003] FSR 29, upheld [2004] FSR 16. US Court decisions 288 F Supp 2d 601. Actually the trial court (with a jury) held the patent valid in the end but the CAFC reversed that. So the parallel litigation ended with the same result—a result also reached in Holland.

our common law notions of this doctrine.[27] But this would be a bit odd. Some countries (eg most European continental countries) do not have any, or any developed, notion of issue estoppel. Should common law countries apply issue estoppel in respect of issues decided by the courts of a country which knows no such doctrine? I ask, but do not answer the question. There is a comity/reciprocity problem to be resolved here.[28]

And even if there is no issue estoppel, the classical model is bound to involve and does involve complicated procedural manoeuvres whereby one side wants to get material (evidence, discovery documents) obtained in one jurisdiction into litigation in another. This forms a whole sub-industry—French lawyers, for example, offer their *saisie contrafaçon*—a kind of Anton Piller without the need to show a dishonest defendant and with few procedural safeguards—as a means of obtaining evidence for foreign proceedings. Likewise we are all familiar, particularly in patent cases, with tedious battles over disclosure of documents obtained in one jurisdiction for use in a corresponding or related battle elsewhere.

I return to the second of the basic modes—the assertion of cross-border jurisdiction by the courts of one country over IP rights in another. I begin with rights, such as copyright, which do not require registration. The common law has actually asserted this for some time in trade marks—without, I think, realising the full implications of what it has been up to.

The basic rule of private international law so far as the common law was concerned is that in *Chaplin v Boys*[29]—the so-called double actionability rule.[30] Given that the court has jurisdiction over a defendant, eg because he is within the jurisdiction, he can be sued for a tort he has committed abroad provided it is also actionable within the jurisdiction if done there (I skip detailed trimmings as discussed in *Boys*). Now that rule has in fact been applied in passing-off cases. An old one is the *Two Elephants* case, *Orr-Ewing v Johnston*[31] where a defendant was restrained from exporting to India yarn under a trade mark deceptive in India.[32] Clearer is *John Walker v*

[27] See Carl Zeiss v Raynor and Keeler [1967] 1 AC 853.
[28] Still not resolved.
[29] *Chaplin v Boys* [1971] AC 356.
[30] Abolished in the UK by the Private International Law (Miscellaneous Provisions) Act 1995, s 10.
[31] *Orr-Ewing v Johnston* (1880) 7 App Cas 219.
[32] Now it is the Indians who export yarn!

Ost[33] where the distinction between an action based on an English tort (of sending instruments of deception abroad) and that based on the foreign tort is made clear. Other trade mark cases followed, for instance *Dunhill v Sunoptic*[34] where the Court of Appeal injuncted the defendants from passing off in Switzerland (where the law was proved) but would not accept the suggestion that all parties to the Paris Convention had laws to prevent passing off, and thus refused a near worldwide injunction.

Now all this seemed to apply to copyright as much as to passing off. But a first try to make it work was too ambitious. In *Tynan Productions v Conan Doyle*[35] a bold attempt to get the English court to say that no rights in the US would be infringed by a Sherlock Holmes film failed. A variety of reasons was given. Some would probably apply today (eg that the exercise was pointless because the US courts would not abide by the decision). But a main plank—the so-called *Moçambique* rule[36]—has been swept away in England by the Court of Appeal decision in *Pearce v Ove Arup*.[37]

It is worth discussing the implications of this in more detail. Pearce claimed that a world-famous architect, Rem Koolhaus, had infringed his Dutch copyright in designing the Kunsthal (Art Gallery) in Rotterdam. He had trouble in suing in Holland, but managed to get the opinion of English counsel that there was an infringement of the Dutch copyright. He sued the English consulting engineers, Ove Arup. He then joined in Koolhaus—and, for no apparent reason—the Rotterdam Town Council. The first instance judge held he had jurisdiction by reason of the Brussels Convention (as to which, more anon), but struck the action out as hopeless on the facts. The Court of Appeal held that there was jurisdiction on a much wider basis. So far as I can understand it (and I am afraid it is not a model of clarity) it has held that the *Moçambique* reason for not entertaining foreign IP cases is no longer valid. That rule was that English courts should not exercise jurisdiction over matters (such as land law) which are the particular province and competence of a foreign country. That left, in the *Pearce* case, only the double actionability rule to be satisfied, which it was.[38]

[33] *John Walker v Ost* [1970] RPC 489.
[34] *Dunhill v Sunoptic* [1979] FSR 337.
[35] Tynan Productions v Conan Doyle [1990] RPC 185.
[36] British South Africa Co v Companhia de Moçambique [1893] AC 602.
[37] *Pearce v Ove Arup* [1999] FSR 525.
[38] As I have said the rule was abolished in 1995, but it had to be satisfied in the *Pearce* case because the Kunsthal was built before then.

What the case does not consider is what it was really about—forum shopping. The real reason for suing in England was that under the English system of legal aid, once you got a positive counsel's opinion, it was not only granted, but, if the legally aided plaintiff won, the defendant did not normally get his costs—even from the legal aid fund.[39]

Now the reason forum shopping was not considered was because it is an irrelevant concept under the peculiar European rules contained in the Brussels Convention. This has been replaced by the 'Brussels Regulation'[40]—which in practice means the same thing though they have renumbered the provisions as all legislators do just to annoy users and put up costs.

Continental jurisdictions do not like the notion of judicial discretion—which lies at the heart of the doctrine of *forum non conveniens*. So by Brussels a strict system of forum allocation was set up. I will describe it briefly. The basic rule is that a defendant is to be sued in the courts of his domicile.[41] But in the case of 'tort delict or quasi-delict' the courts for the place where the harmful event occurred or may occuralso have jurisdiction.[42] Moreover, once there is jurisdiction over one defendant, it is possible to join in others 'provided the claims are so closely connected that it expedient to hear and determine them together to avoid the risk of irreconcilable judgments resulting from separate proceedings'. Add to this the *lis pendens* rule: that 'where proceedings involving the same cause of action and between the same parties are brought in the courts of different Member States, any court other than the court first seised, shall of its own motion stay proceedings until such time as the jurisdiction of the first court seised is established.[43]

Now those academics who drafted this stuff had very little idea about, and no feel for, intellectual property. They were basically thinking about where a particular dispute should go—not realising that IP disputes not only can run across borders but that if they do there are *parallel* claims in each country where there is alleged

[39] Actually in the end Koolhaus won hands down and was later able to satisfy the special rule for getting his costs from the legal aid fund—that he had suffered 'undue financial hardship'.

[40] EC 44/2004.

[41] Art 2.

[42] Art 5.3.

[43] Art 27(1).

infringement or threatened infringement. And they most crucially overlooked that an IP right holder can sue not only the originator of the alleged infringement—the manufacturer for instance—but also his customers. So, far from providing a clear allocation system, what was in fact set up for IP was a forum shopper's delight.

In its most extreme form it goes like this: choose your favoured jurisdiction, find a defendant there, eg a vendor of the alleged infringing goods, sue him and then use the joining-in rule to bring in other defendants, including the principal defendant such as the manufacturer or main importer into Europe. *Pearce* was an example of this. Note particularly that there is no element of discretion here—no notion of *forum non conveniens.*

It was the Dutch who first realised the potential for all this—a breed of what one Dutch judge called 'Rambo Lawyers' went round the world saying: 'sue in Holland, we have a quick procedure (called a *kort geding*—a bit like a super summary judgment) and can get plaintiffs judgment readily'. At first it worked very well—though some plaintiffs realised that if they enforced the judgment (you need to do that in Holland—a court order does not take automatic effect) they would have to put up a bond and were unwilling to do so. In patents at least, the same Dutch judge, Jan Brinkhof, came to realise that this jurisdiction was exorbitant and tried to rein it in. He invented a doctrine of 'the spider in the web' whereby you only sue for pan-European injunctions if the real defendant was in Holland.[44] That has been swept away by the Dutch Supreme Court.[45]

So the position really seems to be, for IP rights that need no registration, as decided by the Dutch and by the English Court of Appeal in *Pearce*, forum shopping rules. French and German courts have been granting cross-border injunctions for some time without any real deep consideration of the implications.[46]

Naturally potential defendants started to find ways round. The principal way round in Europe is the 'Italian torpedo'. The potential defendant sues for a declaration of non-infringement in a country whose courts are very slow. He says the *lis pendens* rule applies. So no other court can touch the dispute. Some say that it does not

[44] *Expandable Grafts v Boston Scientific*, Court of Appeal of the Hague, 23 April 1998.

[45] *Primus v Roche*, 19 December 2004.

[46] See P Véron, in Journal du Droit International 128 (2001) 805, English translation (2002) 84 Journal of the Patent and Trademark Office Society 421.

work—that non-infringement is not the same *lis* as infringement, but that seems very artificial. It is another point for the ECJ.

Another unsolved problem relates to rights which have to be registered, such as patents, registered trade marks and designs. For there is exclusive jurisdiction to the courts of a country 'in proceedings concerned with the registration or validity of' such rights.[47] What if the defendant in a patent action says the patent is invalid—does that exclude cross-border jurisdiction? The English say it does. So does the Commission—probably for the devious reason that it wants a Community Patent and Patent Court. The Dutch, French and German say invalidity is irrelevant to the question of infringement. We do not know and await the answer of the ECJ in a pair of cases.[48]

Thus far I have described the parochial European position. But make no mistake cross-border jurisdiction is a subject which is going worldwide—or may do so. I elaborate. First, some countries just assert a worldwide jurisdiction over a defendant properly before the court (and perhaps others brought in because one is properly before the court). The Dutch, again, seem to think nothing of this in principle. But there has yet to be a Dutch case where a US corporation with a Dutch subsidiary has been ordered not to do things in the US by infringing the US patent. Any attempt to do so might be met by an anti-suit injunction in the US—not least because, for reasons no one else in the world can understand, there is a constitutional right to trial by jury for any case which would have been heard by a jury in England in 1792.[49]

So at least one smallish country asserts the right to enforce foreign IP rights. It was only a matter of time before this happened the other way round—in the US. Judge Tim Leonard of the US District Court in Oklahoma, not a name heretofore known in the world of intellectual property, has caused a stir. A Dr Voda was suing a company called Cordis for infringement of a US patent. Discovery revealed that Cordis had moved its manufacture out of the jurisdiction of the

[47] Art 22.4.

[48] C-539/03 Roche v Primus and Case C-4/03 Gat v Luk. The ECJ said no, at least for cases where validity was properly in issue. It is not settled what the position is where it is not, or where there is an application for a pan-European interim injunction. The Dutch say the ruling does not apply for interim injunctions or where there is no reasonable challenge to validity.

[49] Seventh Amendment. The right to jury trial is one of the burdens the US patent system has to endure!

US courts—to Europe and Canada. So Dr Cordis applied to amend to sue for infringement of five foreign patents claiming this fell within the 'supplemental jurisdiction' of the US courts. Judge Tim Leonard allowed the amendment. The decision is one-and-a-half pages long. The first page is mainly the title and the long list of counsel and the even longer names of their firms. The reasoning is rather short 'the court finds that it would have supplemental jurisdiction of the foreign patents claim'.

Well it is on its way to appeal. Lots of amicus briefs have been submitted. I will list them: the Federal Circuit Bar Association (against international jurisdiction), the Intellectual Property Owners Association (against), the American Intellectual Property Law Association (against), the US government (against), US law professors (for). So only the academics are for. And of course it is they who, perhaps, are less able to sense the international consequences of a 'for' decision. Notably, but such is the way of the world, no foreign government has intervened.

It is worth considering the possible consequences. Obviously if the US courts start on this line,[50] the courts of other countries will respond. There will be a war of competing jurisdictions. Anti-suit injunctions and applications for stays *lis alibi pendens* will proliferate. Being a good lawyer will involve being a good forum shopper. And if this is the position for patents, why should it not also be so for copyright?

Some might say that even if you get a decision of a foreign court it will not be recognised or enforceable outside the country asserting long-arm jurisdiction. And that may be so—few would want to enforce a US jury damages award for instance. But in reality that will not matter—for there could be enforcement against the defendant's assets in the country concerned—in the real global world of commerce people have to do business everywhere and have assets of some sort everywhere. So enforcement problems are unlikely to be a major obstacle to long-arm enforcement.

Well I do not know which way things will go—unseemly and unproductive international scrambles for jurisdiction—or a continuation of

[50] The CAFC held there was no jurisdiction 2007-1297, -1343. It gave cogent reasons why—reasons which in my opinion the UK Supreme Court at the very least ought to have considered in Lucasfilm, below.

the classical model.[51] What I think will increasingly occur is pressure for some sort of multi-national court. We, in Europe, are exploring the idea for patents now. The need for this is more pressing than for copyright.[52] But in the long term I can see that happening, particularly as between countries whose laws have harmonised. And particularly also for international and web-based businesses such as Kazaa.

Well I have not presented a particularly ordered talk; it is messy and full of disparate bits—I make no apology—for that is what the globalisation of copyright is like: messy and full of disparate bits. We are all standing on a sticky wicket.[53] And it is now time to draw stumps.[54]

POSTSCRIPT

This as it was given in 2005. A lot has happened since. I have a few comments on some things. I have put these into footnotes. But what I said about Artist's Resale Right (droit de suite*) needs a larger comment.*

The international pressure for this right made Australia give in by the Resale Royalty Right for Visual Artists Act 2009. It costs rather a lot to administer (10 per cent) at present, with the Australian

[51] In the UK our Supreme Court came up with the to my mind oppressive and ridiculous decision that the English court, where it has personal jurisdiction (because the defendant is in England) has subject-matter jurisdiction over copyright and other unregistered IP right infringements carried out by the defendant abroad, Lucasfilm v Ainsworth [2011] UKSC 29. The defendant in Twickenham lawfully made Star Wars stormtrooper helmets—their copyright protection in the UK had expired. He sold about £10,000 worth to a few American customers—just exporting from here without doing any act in the US. By long-arm US law that was an infringement of American copyright. The SC held he could be sued here for that. Astonishingly, to my mind the SC (Lords Walker and Collins) said 'There are no issues of policy which militate against the enforcement of foreign copyright'. *Did they not realise the self-evident burden imposed on a British manufacturer who might want to sell goods abroad? Is he supposed to check the copyright laws of each and every country to which he might send his goods? Did it make no difference that the rule was not even based on reciprocity—you can't sue someone in America for infringing a non-American copyright. And it is perfectly silly (as the SC did) to distinguish between registered and unregistered rights. In some cases, indeed, registered and unregistered rights go hand in hand—for instance registered design right and unregistered design right or registered trade mark and passing off (unfair competition in some countries). To have different jurisdictional rules for registered and unregistered rights makes no business sense.*

[52] Europe is moving ahead with this. But as usual in IP the politicians have blundered around. They have created an elaborate system with local, regional and central divisions, with over-elaborate language provisions and so on—see Chapter 25 If they had left it to Europe's patent judges and litigators a much better system would have emerged.

[53] More cricket.

[54] And more.

government itself putting up money for some of the administration. Whether it is a worthwhile scheme remains moot and there is currently a review of the scheme taking place.

As far as Europe is concerned it has come into force—though, in the UK, only for works of dead artists since the beginning of 2013. The European Commission reported on the scheme in December 2011.[55] *The conclusions reflect anxiety about the costs of administration (is anyone surprised?*[56] *There is some evidence that artists like it (after all who doesn't like a cheque from time to time?). But I think they are naïve: overall living artists lose out. Re-sale right is not a good thing for art—particularly for young artists. I can't refrain from saying why:*

(1) The world art market at any one point of time is the total sum people are paying for artworks at that time. No one will pay more to cover the costs of administration of the resale right system. So that total sum, although it will vary from moment to moment, is invariant as regards the presence or absence of a resale right. Absent the system, the money goes to sellers (by artists and subsequent owners, or agents (galleries) and auctioneers). With the system some of the total sum also has to go on its administration. The system is in effect a tax with a rather expensive administration added.

(2) The system only benefits artists who have achieved some success in their lifetime or thereafter. There is a lower cap—in the UK works have to fetch at least £1,000 to qualify. In the nature of things it will be largely those artists who have become famous, and perhaps even more so their heirs, who get significant returns. In France, for example, as much as 70 per cent of all resale payments go to the heirs of the nation's most famous artists—eg Matisse (d. 1954, in copyright until 2025) or Braque (d. 1963, in copyright until 2034).

(3) There is something of a deterrent to buying works from young artists whose prices will normally be low. Many buyers may have in the back of their minds the hope that the artist may

[55] Report from the Commission to the European Parliament, the Council and the European Economic and Social Committee COM (2011) 878.

[56] The Commission report suggests €50 per transaction. My own guess is that is an underestimate: think of what is involved—the costs of finding an artist or still worse his/her heirs could be huge. The same problem as with orphan works.

become famous one day—there is a bit of a gamble. If there is to be tax levied on the work if ever it is sold, the incentive to buy is somewhat reduced.

(4) *The right bears particularly hard on small galleries as all the evidence submitted to the European Commission and the Australian review shows. Yet it is through smaller galleries that most artists start. They will incur their own administration fees quite apart from the costs of the collecting societies (currently in the UK these keep 15 per cent of the royalty). If you impose administrative costs on, and a tax on the artworks sold by, galleries, you will surely reduce their number—and thus the part of the art market most important to young artists. The UK Intellectual Property Office makes this point in its response to the Commission's consultation on implementation of the Directive, saying: 'Many smaller galleries claim that the introduction of ARR has adversely affected their business and they cannot afford the associated costs'.*[57]

(5) *Because the right is only conferred on a reciprocal basis (eg US artists currently do not get royalties on their works sold in Europe) there is a pressure for the right to spread.*[58] *That will mean increasing complexity for administration with greater costs.*

(6) *This is another example of the spread of bad ideas in copyright eg basic term extended from 50 to 70 years from year of death of author, increase of copyright in sound recordings from 50 to 90 years from publication—as if Cliff Richard and the Beatles hadn't got enough already.*

[57] Intellectual Property Office (IPO) response to consultation in preparation of a Commission report on the implementation and effect of the Resale Right Directive (2001/84/EC) 3.

[58] There was a Bill before Congress for an 'American Royalties Too Act 2014'! It failed but I would be surprised if it did not try to return.

Part VII

Forewords and Prefaces

41

Foreword to the CIPA Guide to the Patents Act*

WHEN STEPHEN JONES asked me to write a foreword for this edition, I thought 'Blimey, haven't I just done it?'. Well it was not so long ago—the last edition was 2009. In the Foreword to that I wrote in praise of the emergence of the patent agent/scholar. I withdraw none of that. The Black Book is the work of scholars—not scholars of an abstract, too-theoretical-to-be-useful bent, but learned writers who seek to set out the law as it really is so that the reader knows where he or she stands. Some like Stephen have dual qualification as both patent agents and solicitors, but the bulk of the writing has been by 'pure' patent agents.

None of that has changed so there is no point in repeating what I said then on that topic. This time I want to add something else—what about the patent agent/cunning schemer? I illustrate what I mean by what happened about this very Foreword. Stephen asked me to do it some time ago and I forgot and might not have got round to doing it. But then he told me that Paul Cole had asked Chief Judge Randall Rader of the Court of Appeal for the Federal Circuit to write an introduction from a US standpoint. Paul told Randy that I was writing the Foreword to induce him to write. Randy said he would be happy to be associated with anything in which I was involved and agreed. And because Randy had agreed, I got on with my bit. The cunning patent agent/scholars played one of us off against the other. Well done! And, more seriously, I hope and expect that Randy will commend the work to US readers. I do, as well as to anyone else

* *Paul Cole and Stephen Jones (eds),* CIPA Guide to the Patents Act, *7th edn (Sweet & Maxwell, 2011).*

concerned with European patents. Note that I say 'European Patents' rather than British Patents—for in essence, despite its title, that is what this book is about.

I have used the expression 'patent agent/scholars' although I know that patent agents are now called 'attorneys'. I carry on saying patent agent. I know it sounds a bit old fashioned, but I have a good reason to wonder whether the change to 'attorney' was an altogether good idea. For 'attorney' not only means something like legal agent, but it once, at least, had overtones. As, for instance, when Dr Johnson said that 'he did not seek to speak ill of any man behind his back, but he believed the gentleman was an attorney'. And when Thomas Carlyle said 'attorney cunning is a kind of thing that fancies itself to be talent'.

Enough of that. Where are we now? Well the first thing to observe is how fast the new edition has come round. It will appear in 2011, just three years after the previous edition. That is a reflection of how much is happening in the world of patents. The Enlarged Board continues to produce decisions of more or less opacity and the Black Book covers all this well.

More alarmingly, indeed most alarmingly, the Court of Justice of the European Union is beginning to assume patent jurisdiction. We now have two decisions based on the Biotech Directive. Looking back, I am far from convinced that any Directives touching patentability were within the EU's competence. Patents are governed by the EPC, a non-EU Treaty. What business is it of the EU by a Directive to attempt to override this Treaty? And both decisions are unsatisfactory. *Monsanto* (Case C-428/08) has the Court telling us that soya meal which contains bits of broken up genes which could no longer work are not protected. I do not quarrel with that as an ultimate conclusion, but it was not arrived at, as it could have been, by claim construction (which is how Pumfrey J did it in the corresponding English case). That would have been consistent with Art 69 of the EPC. Instead we find the Court adding EU law to patent law—a dangerous precedent for the future because it is entirely foreseeable that there will be conflict between the EPC and EU law leading to fuzzy edges and uncertainty. Even more serious is *Brüstle v Greenpeace* (C-3410) where the Court set back European stem-cell research. It should have read the Directive down to its irreducible minimum. The result is not to stop the research, which is perfectly lawful, but to remove the patent incentive for it. Humanity is the loser. It is all tied up with 'ethical', perhaps religious, considerations—as if an acorn were a tree.

It is decisions like these (and the chaotic tsunami of ECJ and CJEU trade mark cases) which have made it clear to all industry that the CJEU should not have competence in patents. The proposed Unitary Patent and European Patent Court—perhaps now rushing to a premature realisation—stand in danger of this threat as I write. I am alarmed more generally about the current proposals: they do not stand the acid test—are they better than what Europe has now? Forum shopping will remain high on the agenda of patentees. In particular the possibility of bifurcation with entrenched local divisions which may favour patentees of doubtful patents would tip the balance in favour of enforcing arguably invalid patents at least provisionally.

Another, much to be welcomed, development, is the changes to the Patents County Court. When Judge Fysh took it over it was more or less moribund. He breathed life into but before long found himself shackled by Lord Woolf's one-size-fits-all idea for civil procedure—that the rules should be the same everywhere. That made no sense for a court which was for small patent cases and which needed special rules to ensure swift and cheap resolution. Well that shackle has now gone—and the court has fit-for-purpose rules. It has also been fortunate that Colin Birss QC was willing to take on the job. I commend the court to patent agents—and I repeat the message I gave last time: one of the best ways to run a small patent case is by a patent agent working with a junior barrister.

Where will we be by the time of the next edition? I do not know. It is possible there will be a patent court for all of the EU or all of the EU except Spain and Italy. And there may be a 'unitary patent'. On the other hand, it may be that the current proposals will fail—if they proceed as they stand at present, I frankly hope that they do. But if some key changes are made then it should all come to pass. If they do not, then next time it will happen. Whatever happens this time, the Black Book will set it all out clearly—or, given the problems of obscurity which increasingly affect all IP law, as clearly as possible.

I shall continue to keep the book within easy reach. So should anyone else concerned with European or British patents.

26 October 2011

42

Foreword to Bullen & Leake & Jacob's Precedents of Pleadings Hong Kong*

I AM HUGELY pleased and gratified to be asked to write this Foreword. For the name Bullen and Leake and Jacob means a lot not only to the common law, but also to me personally. I turn to explain each of these.

First the place of pleadings in the common law. A, perhaps *the*, defining feature of the common law is its manner of conducting a civil action. A bedrock component of that is the system of 'pleadings'. This has a technical meaning in the common law—it does not mean a general mix of evidence and argument as most civilian lawyers take it to mean—or even the oral argument. The common law is more precise. A 'pleading' is a document setting out what facts the party intends to prove at a later stage—the stage we call the trial when the parties join battle in open court. A pleading is not proof in itself (In England and Wales the pointless Woolfian addition of a 'statement of truth' has modified that somewhat—but not so as to make any significant difference.) The responsive pleading sets out what facts the party admits, those he denies (or challenges the other party to prove) and those he intends to prove for himself. The pleadings do not say how any of the facts are to be proved. The pleadings set the battle lines—they are not the battle itself.

Drawing a pleading is an art. The pleader must think clearly. He or she has to know the substantive law which applies to the case and to work out each fact that must be proved to win. Then those facts

* *K Bokhary (ed),* Bullen & Leake & Jacob's Precedents of Pleadings Hong Kong *(Sweet & Maxwell, 2013).*

must be set out in a logical and clear order. A long rambling legal and factual argument/evidence document is not the way of a common law pleading. That is not to say a pleading cannot also be a piece of advocacy. My late father used to say that a Statement of Claim should in effect say 'The defendant is a s..t'. And a favourite story of the late Sir James Comyn was of a Statement of Claim which began 'Prior to the matters complained of herein there stood, in its own grounds laid out by Capability Brown, a beautiful Georgian Manor'. The defendant is condemned before one even knows who he is or what it is alleged he did.

Bullen and Leake on Pleadings (as it was until my father's name was added) is one of the oldest trade marks in the common law. The first edition was in 1860. My father had a copy of the third edition of 1868. I have it now. It once belonged to Scrutton LJ and has the bookplate 'Mr Justice Scrutton and a stamp 'Lord Justice Scrutton'. It was the last edition by Bullen & Leake themselves and was the last edition before the Judicature Acts. Its full title was *Precedents of Pleadings in Personal Actions in the Superior Courts of Common Law*.

B&L was and is a vital tool in any litigator's armoury. It shows you by example just how to do it. For each subject there is first a section on the law—a summary rather than a detailed exposition. The summary is just what is needed. Then you get the detailed precedents. From these you can work out how to plead the case you yourself have. The teaching value is immense—familiarity with other legal systems which do not have books of precedents at all, still less one as good as this, shows a much less organised approach.

Now to more personal matters. My father's connection with Bullen and Leake was immense. Editing it is an immense task. He joined the team for the 11th (1959) edition but I guess could not have done much for that. Sweet and Maxwell asked him to take on the next edition in about 1960. He was 15 years late in delivering it! There was a good reason: over the years the book had become encrusted with additions and amendments. It was a muddle and it was time for an almost total re-write. That my father achieved. By way of tribute Sweet and Maxwell offered to add his name to that of the original authors. Not even Alfred T Denning, lead author of the 1935 ninth edition achieved that! Almost the last thing my father saw before he died was the 14th edition. I was able to show it to him in his nursing home.

The fact there is to be a specific Hong Kong edition of B&L&J is exciting and important. It shows the common law is alive and well in Hong Kong. I have been allowed to see a few chapters—they are well-tailored for Hong Kong. Every litigator should have a copy to hand. The result will surely be a better litigation process in Hong Kong—both for cases that come to trial and for the many more which settle on the way once the parties can see how the pleadings have defined the lines of the proposed battle. Hong Kong's prosperity in part depends on the working of its legal system. A better litigation process contributes to prosperity and this book will in its own way help.

My father would have been really pleased too. For he was born in Shanghai, first saw a common law court in the British Consulate there, saw Hong Kong in the 1920s and always had a huge respect for China and the Chinese people. I wish this book well. May there be many subsequent editions.

43

Foreword to Software Patents Worldwide*

'IT IS IMPORTANT to doubt and doubt is not a fearful thing, but a thing of very great value'. So wrote the late, great, Richard Feynman.[1] He was speaking of everything, not, of course, specifically of the value of the patent system, still less of any of the exceptions to it. Yet his lesson is a valuable reminder that nothing should be taken for granted; that we should approach things with a rational and questioning mind. That applies as much to the subject matter of this valuable and interesting collection of essays as to anything else.

Historically, with the growth of free enterprise, the notion of private monopolies came into question. Before that, Kings could sell what they wanted. In my own country, when the King started selling monopolies in anything, the judges said the law would not allow it. That was the great *Case of Monopolies* in 1602[2] (the monopoly which was held invalid was in the sale of playing cards). But the judges would allow, and the Statute of Monopolies in 1624 confirmed, that some private monopolies should be allowed. The Statute expressed those as being in 'any manner of new manufacture'. There was the requirement of novelty (which in due course was held to embrace obviousness too). And a requirement that the monopoly should be for a 'manner of manufacture'. So a divide was set up between the sort of thing which could be patented (ie a 'manner of manufacture') and the sort of thing that could not. What constituted a 'manner of manufacture' was a woolly, a fuzzy question. The borderline between

* *Gregory A Stobbs (ed),* Software Patents Worldwide (*Wolters Kluwer, 2007).*

1 Richard Feynman, *The Meaning of It All* (Addison-Weslty, 1998) 28.

2 *Darcy v Allen* 1 WPC 1; Noy 173, Moore KB 11 Co Rep 84b.

that which was patentable and that not was left to 'interpretation' by the judges.

Of course in reality it was a policy question: what sort of thing would it be good for the economy if it were patentable? This was decided by what was in reality no more than a 'gut' feeling. Over the years the judges expanded the notion of 'manner of new manufacture'. At one point (in the 1950s) they fastened on the idea of a 'vendible product' or a process for making such a product. At times Parliament interfered (particularly from 1919 to 1932 only processes for making pharmaceuticals were patentable). In the 1960s the notion of 'manner of manufacture' expanded to include agricultural and related ideas including microbiological entities. But it never went as far as methods of medical treatment (which I think personally should be patentable—of course no judge would actually injunct a doctor from treating a patient, but it would never come to that).

In Australia they have carried on with this judge-made drawing of the line based on the words of that old 1623 statute. But the UK did not. Other European countries had their own lines drawn about patentability. I know little about those lines, though enough to know that often the touchstone was 'is there something technical about the invention?' In 1972 Europe tried to standardise things via the European Patent Convention. Possibly deliberately there is no definition of 'invention'. But there are exclusions. An examination of the *travaux préparatoires* shows a complete absence of any clear thinking about these. It was going to be left to the judges (including the EPO in this context) to decide what the limits were. Have they done a good job? It is not for me, a judge, to opine definitively. The EPO thinks it is doing a good job. I, like Professor Feynmann, have doubts—not only as to whether the EPO is getting it right, but as to whether anyone is. I think the line is fuzzy: what is 'technical' (a test often asked) is an easy question to ask but not to answer. Nor is there any clear policy thinking by the judges who have to draw the lines. Or much in the way of evidence to assist them in their policy decisions. Are patents for business methods or computer programs a good way of encouraging progress or do they stand in the way of it? I do not actually know and I do not think anyone else does either. All too often you hear the assertions of those who do not doubt—believers that patents for such things are, or are not, good.

Meanwhile in the USA things ran amok. From at least the Second World War to the early 1980s patents were not considered important. By and large, if a patentee sued, he lost. Thing changed mightily with the creation of the Court of Appeals for the Federal Circuit in 1982. And more so as jury trial in patent actions and oversized damage awards became the order of the day. Until recently the pendulum has swung mightily in favour of patentability. The US, like many a convert to a new religion, once it became in favour of patentability, adopted it with a zealous fervour. 'Anything under the sun made by man' seemed almost the test: business methods and computer programs fell into place in the 1990s. And the US brought pressure on others to follow its lead.

Now, I detect a period of caution arriving. People are beginning to doubt. Even in the US.[3] We have so-called 'green' and 'open source' movements (often those who support non-patentability do so with as much religious zeal as those who support the opposite). But even putting these aside, questions about the patent system and its value are increasingly being asked.

For myself I prefer evidence-based rational debate. I think that debate starts by placing the onus on those who favour patentability. For the patent system is a cost to industry: only if that cost can be justified is the system justifiable. More specifically it is that test which I think should be the real, underlying approach to the interpretation of exclusions to patentability.

It is in that context that this collection of essays is likely to be useful. In most countries there is some sort of exclusion for software as patentable subject-matter. This lies in part, perhaps, in the notion that somehow computer programs are not 'technical' and that patent law should be confined to that which is. And there are other considerations too: the fact that there is likely to be considerable alternative protection via the law of copyright, the inherent problems in defining a software invention, the problems in searching for prior art and so on.

Whatever the reason, the position arrived at (insofar as any clear position has been reached) in important patent jurisdictions is a topic worthy of study. That is what this book seeks to investigate and describe. It covers China, the EPO, France, Japan, the UK and the US. I do not propose to comment on individual pieces—a Foreword is not a book review. What I can say is that they form a helpful contribution to policy makers around the world. If only they would read works like this before making laws rather than after.

[3] *More than doubt now, see eg* Alice Corporation Pty Ltd v CLS Bank International, et al *573 US __ (2014).*

44

Preface to Intellectual Property Rights and the EC Competition Rules*

WHEN VAL KORAH wrote to ask whether I would write a Preface for this book, I straightaway e-mailed a 'yes'. I had not, of course, even seen so much as a draft paragraph, let alone a chapter. Was I taking a risk? Was there a chance I might be writing a preface to a dull but worthy book, or even worse, a bad one? No, not a bit. For I knew both how clearly Val thinks and how clearly she writes. And of course her store of knowledge of competition law must be unequalled. Following my acceptance she e-mailed me the book in draft. I thought I would dip into it and that would be enough for a Preface. Wrong. It is really a bit of a page-turner.

The conflict between intellectual property (laws for stopping people doing things) and competition laws (laws for allowing people to do things) is obvious—the monopolists v the anti-monopolists. Moreover, by its very nature the key areas of competition law are apt to be fuzzy both in law and on the facts. How do you decide whether someone has a dominant position, and what amounts to abuse of such a position when the law has given you a monopoly anyway? These and similar questions are perennial. And it is all too easy to say it is one big muddle with no clear rules.

Well, there is something in that, but it is not true to say that no guidance can be given. This book proves it. Val Korah not only tells you what has been going on, what can be predicted and what not, but also she identifies the key economic and other thinking (in some

* *Valentine Korah*, Intellectual Property Rights and the EC Competition Rules *(Hart Publishing, 2006).*

cases 'thinking' is too kind a word) which lies behind some of what has gone on. And she is not slow in directing astute criticism.

Let me give some examples. Look at her criticism of what happened in *Merck v Stephar*—where the Court said exhaustion of patent rights applied even in a country where there was no patent to exhaust (see Chapter 2). 'That is not a reason, but a conclusion' is about as pithy a way of condemning judicial reasoning as you can get. Or take her discussion of the Commission's attitude to IPR licensing in the '70s and early '80s to be found in Chapter 4. She points out about as clearly as anyone could that the Commission and Court have not really understood the problems from a practical, commercial point of view. It would be, and would have been, so much better, if the approach is that in a licence the parties are basically free to decide what they like—and that competition law should only interfere where one is sure that it is necessary to do so. The onus should lie on he who seeks to upset a commercial agreement. If that had always been the approach, I rather think that EU companies would have found life much easier; and EU economies would have been more competitive rather than less, for overregulation by a wooden, rule-of-thumb approach to competition law impedes industry and commerce, rather than stimulating competition.

I could go on, but this a Preface, not a review. What shines out at every point is an intelligent discussion of the issues. If I were teaching competition law, this book would be mandatory. And I think the student/teacher discussions it would provoke would be intelligent and lively. As it is, I do not teach competition law. But as soon as a competition case reaches a court in which I sit, I shall reach for this book. It will surely give the key thinking about the area of law in which the problem has arisen. Often it will provide enough for the answer.

POSTSCRIPT

The book is five years old but I recommend it still to anyone who wants to understand competition law and have the good and bad, the rational and the irrational, parts explained. Val says a new edition is on its way. I hope it will be just as short for there are plenty of long books about the subject, books which provide less insight.

45

Foreword to Decisions of the UK Performing Rights Tribunal and Copyright Tribunal 1957–1996*

WHEN I STARTED at the Bar I had never heard of the Performing Rights Tribunal (PRT). As time went on I learned, through gossip, that there was this thing. Distinguished members of the Bar appeared before it in cases which went on for ages. It was presided over by even more distinguished members of the Bar. I had no idea what went on or what the cases were about or even who they were between. It was a subject shrouded in deep and dark mystery.

My state of ignorance continued for many years. In 1989 I knew that the 1988 Act had renamed it the Copyright Tribunal. I still had not much idea what went on. I was asked to be a Deputy Chairman. I accepted with some worries—what if I got myself into some mammoth dispute? How would I know what it was about? And what procedures were there? I asked around and discovered that Anthony Walton QC had copies of all or nearly all previous decisions of the PRT. I had a kit of these made. Also, the then Chairman, Michael Bowers, had the brilliant idea of a one-day meeting for all the members of the Tribunal. He got a former distinguished member of the Bar who had experience of the Tribunal (then a Law Commissioner and now a High Court judge)[1] to come and tell us what went on. After that (apart from some trivial interlocutory hearings, nearly all of which settled) I found myself chairing a full Tribunal dispute. I was fortunate to have experienced members with me. And I was fortunate to discover that William Aldous QC had invented a practice

* *M Freegard and J Black,* Decisions of the UK Performing Rights Tribunal and Copyright Tribunal 1957–1996 *(LexisNexis and Tottel Publishing, 1997).*

[1] *It was Richard Buxton.*

direction (of course printed here as amended) which made it unnecessary for every tiny point made by one side to be put to the other. We got through the case. But I wished I had understood the Tribunal and its procedures better before getting into that position.

None of that can happen again. Michael Freegard and Jack Black have decided to reveal all. The mystery has gone. Anyone who wants to know what the Tribunal does, how it does it and what it might do in the future has only to turn to this ground-breaking book. It will be invaluable. No one concerned with the Tribunal will be able to do without it. One gets much more than the detailed summaries of past cases contained in Chapter 2. The discussion in the later chapters puts the Tribunal's work and functions into a wider context. That context is not only national and the authors have provided a really useful summary of the position in other countries. Plainly in the future there will be more international matters to be considered—one day there may even be a European Union Copyright Tribunal.[2]

Another way in which the book will be valuable is in its compilation of all relevant procedural materials. To have the relevant bits of the Act and Rules, the practice directions and so on all in one place will be very handy. I used to have a home-made file of this stuff. People will not need such a thing in the future, save for any amendments. I believe that there will be amendments—amendments to ensure tighter control over the proceedings by way of limiting the time for cross-examination and other methods of stopping cases getting bogged down in detail. I do not suppose, however, there will be an amendment by which it is deemed that each side has called an economist and the two economists have cancelled each other out. We will have to see. The next edition of this book (which will surely become a standard) will contain it if it happens.

POSTSCRIPT

There never was another edition—probably because work in the Copyright Tribunal almost died away. That is not necessarily a bad thing. One cannot tell whether matters are simply being resolved without recourse to the Tribunal. Perhaps they are, for the second-hand price of this book is around £80, which suggests people still need it. They would only do that if the subject-matter were still live.

[2] *Still only in the mid-distance.*

46

Foreword to Trade Mark Law: A Practical Anatomy*

I AM HONOURED TO be asked to write this Foreword. And it is a great pleasure. I will tell you why. Many years ago a Chancery judge (Eve, Clauson, Romer?) heard a wholly unmemorable appeal about the registrability of a mark—was it the sort of thing that was too descriptive was the kind of question before him. He began with words to the effect that he had to decide a matter 'in this not very interesting branch of the law'. I can't actually re-find the case—an interesting task for a diligent pupil or trainee. Whoever the judge was, he was completely wrong. For trade mark law is astonishingly deceptive. Curiously, the less you know about it the more you think it must be simple—we all know what a trade mark is, obviously you cannot register descriptive words and people mustn't use someone else's mark or something confusingly similar. That's about all there is to it, isn't it? Well that view could hardly be more wrong. Anyone who has had to delve into the subject discovers, astonishingly, that it is fraught with genuine intellectual difficulties. That was true under the old law, as my late pupil master, Anthony Walton QC, so comically indicated in his address of welcome to me when I was appointed.[1] One of the points he described as Gödel Undecidable points is 'what is a trade mark actually for?'. And there were several other such trade mark points, all of which have resurfaced under the new law. He begged me not to decide such points because they gave much work to lawyers.

Anthony would have been glad to know that none of these points, in their new form, have been decided. On the contrary, I think it is

* *Jeremy Phillips*, Trade Mark Law: A Practical Anatomy *(Oxford University Press, 2003).*
[1] Chapter 1 of this volume.

fair to say that notwithstanding a mass of decisions from the ECJ since the Directive came into effect (was it really only nine years ago?) trade mark law is more confusing, more uncertain, than it has been for years—indeed more so than when there were not so many 'helpful' interpretations from the Court. New concepts or at least forms of words have appeared—'global appreciation', 'lexical invention', 'guarantee of origin' and so on, but we are no closer to having clearly defined rules of law.

What has Jeremy Philips done about this? Has he provided clear answers to the problems of trade mark law? By reading this book can we know what a trade mark is or is not for? Most decidedly not. What we can and do get is something much more exciting. We get deep insight into the intellectual problems involved. This book makes you think. And it makes you understand at a profound level why some basic questions of trade mark law remain uncertain and probably always will be. He makes you understand that trade mark law has a lot in common with quantum mechanics. Each have at their heart an uncertainty principle.

Not only has Jeremy done this, but he has done it with a deceptively light touch. Unlike most law books, if you open this book at almost any page you are likely positively to enjoy what you read and often you will have a silent chuckle. And because Jeremy is essentially dealing with principles, this book should be of interest to trade mark lawyers everywhere—it does not matter what the details of your legal system are, the underlying intellectual problems find their way to the surface. I do not say the reader will necessary agree with what he says. They may well not—but they will be provoked to think and to work out their own answers. This is not the sort of law book which sends you to sleep. Read it and enjoy.

Royal Courts of Justice,
October 2003

Part VIII

Personal

47

To Dieter Stauder

For his Festschrift*

I WAS ONCE A young barrister in practice in the chambers of that great intellectual property lawyer, Thomas Blanco White QC. I had been a pupil there (of another great lawyer, Anthony Walton) in 1967–78. The year before that, Bill Cornish, my first law teacher at LSE had been Blanco's pupil. Bill went back to academia, starting at LSE the first teaching of IP in any British university. Before long he formed an association with the Max Planck Institute in Munich and spent some time there.

What, you ask, has this got to do with Dieter Stauder? Well, early in the seventies I got a call from Bill. Would I see this young lawyer from Max Planck who was in England and interested in comparative patent law and particularly procedure. I of course said yes (you do if Bill asks). So this young man with wild woolly hair, enormous enthusiasm and a strikingly animated manner came to tea.[1] He wanted to try to understand how we did patent actions in England. Could I help him to see the court files for some patent cases? Dieter expected that such a thing as the court file for the case—what the French call a *dossier*—would surely exist. But I had no idea. I did not know (and rather doubted) whether such a thing existed at all. Investigations were made and it turned out that only a very rudimentary file existed. What you would get would be merely a copy of the starting document (the Writ as it was called in those days), a few official

* *Horst-Peter Götting and Claudia Schlüter (eds),* Nourriture de l'esprit: Festschrift für Dieter Stauder zum 70. Geburtstag *(Nomos Verlagsges.Mbh + Co, 2011).*

[1] Only the colour of the hair has changed. True he is older—but his extraordinary enthusiasm remains completely unabated.

procedural forms, and any sworn statements (affidavits) which happened to come into existence during the procedure to trial. The real documents, namely the pleadings[2] and the evidence, were not there. The latter is hardly surprising: in those days nearly all evidence at a full trial on the merits was given orally, both factual and expert.

Nowadays a young Dieter would find rather more—English procedure now provides for written evidence (both factual and expert) to be exchanged prior to the trial. We also have written arguments (what the Americans call briefs and we call 'skeleton arguments' both prior to trial and after the evidence is closed). Some of this material (but I doubt all, especially the skeleton arguments) finds its way into a court file.[3] But even now the key material will not be there. The documents disclosed by each side pursuant to discovery (what we now call disclosure) will not be there.[4] For under the English way of doing things what really matters is the live factual and expert evidence given at trial and tested by cross-examination.[5] Expensive it is, but it remains the best humans can devise for ascertaining the truth and testing of opinions. Big, but not small or even medium, patent cases justify the procedure.[6] So the vital evidence is in no court file.

What Dieter could not find from files back in the seventies, and the young Dieter could not find now, is how the system really works. We were all a bit innocent then. We had the idea that if you could speak another's language it would be but a small step to understand their legal system. Not so. You can read about the procedural rules of the courts of another country, but you will have no or little idea of how it all really works. I like to draw the analogy with chess: knowing the rules and how the pieces move would tell you nothing of chess. So also with legal procedure.

Dieter, of course, was undeterred by the absence of any court files. He set about understanding English procedure in other ways—and got a good grasp from lawyers of how it really worked. He put all this to good use—the European Patent Office from its early days has

[2] A technical English term for documents setting out what the party intends to prove by evidence, if not admitted, at the trial. 'Pleadings' is often used by continental lawyers in a different sense—the lawyers' arguments.

[3] One day, maybe, there will be a full electronic file. I rather guess it is about 10 years away. Government IT is ponderous and very expensive!

[4] I would like to see a lot less of these—discovery should be ordered only on narrowly defined issues, if ordered at all.

[5] Asking of questions by the lawyer for the other side.

[6] We are just about to try a much abbreviated procedure for small cases in the Patents County Court.

had the benefit of advice from Dieter. Actually it would have been much better if they had simply asked him to draft their entire 'court' structure[7] and rules of procedure.

Well now I gather Dieter is to be 70 though he shows no sign of growing up. He remains as challenging and controversial as ever. Earlier this year, at a Symposium in Utrecht in honour of Jan Brinkhof who was retiring as a professor there, Dieter gave a most startling speech. His theme was simple: that continental judges, and most especially German judges, ought to write their judgments more in the way English judges do! I have since wondered about that. German judgments are often written essentially only for the parties—there is an assumption of knowledge about the background to the case. Also, sometimes, the reasoning, in translation at least, can appear to be a little opaque. English judges are generally more explicit. And they do try, perhaps harder than German judges who assume an informed audience, to set out clearly the legal principles being applied. So there is something in what Dieter said. But I think it only applies to cases of importance. The judgments in these will be widely read. Every European judge should try to write important judgments so that they can be understood by judges and lawyers of other European countries. That is what Dieter was saying. What else could you expect from a great European?

Happy birthday Dieter,

Really sorry not to have time to write more,

From your friend, Robin.

[7] The current notion that an 'opposition' is some kind of administrative procedure and that it is all right to have the examiner who granted the patent on the Board is manifestly daft, for 'oppositions' are hostile litigation and are inherently judicial in nature.

48

Speech at the CIPA President's Dinner on HMS Belfast, *3 June 2009*

Mr President,[1] ladies and gentlemen,

Hello Sailors.

Joseph Henry,[2] one of the foremost American scientists of the nineteenth century, in his old age, said: 'If I could live my life all over again ... I might have taken out more patents'. When young, he held the view that patents were the sort of thing that held Europe back. Also when young, he invented the telegraph and realised that different arrangements of clicks could be used to represent different letters. He patented none of it.

He willingly explained all this to the young Samuel Morse, a failed artist and religious zealot who believed that America was the subject of secret plots by Negroes, Jews and above all Catholics. The Jesuits, he thought, were fanning out across America storing guns in nunneries—all was ultimately controlled by the Emperor of Austria. Morse thought that the telegraph would be a way for the forces of good to combat this—and incidentally that he could make a lot of money. Working largely with stolen ideas, he patented much, made a lot and spent many years in excruciating litigation defending his stolen ideas—even having to explain how it was that some crucial documents had mysteriously burnt just before they were due to be produced on discovery.

Henry had the happier life, loved and respected everywhere.

What Mr President, are the lessons of all this? It is simple. Henry should have had a good patent agent.

[1] *The President of CIPA (Chartered Institute of Patent Attorneys) was John Brown.*
[2] *The unit of capacitance is named after him.*

And that not a lot changes deep down. The laws of human nature apply just as much to IP as anything else. There are good guys and bad guys, clever and stupid ones, male and female.

I said not a lot changes, but attempted change is on the way. This year has seen some.

First is the extraordinary attack on the patent system from the Competition Directorate of the European Commission.

[Omitted from here—see Chapter 20 on the Pharma-sector Inquiry.]

Next, and in marked contrast to DG Competition, has been the work of Margot Fröhlinger and her small team in moving forward the European Patent Court project. Before long the ECJ will be asked to pronounce on the legality of a separate court set up by separate treaty. Since they know what a mess they have made of trade marks and most definitely do not want patents, it is a fair bet that the Court will rule that it is okay. That will itself undermine the objecting nations, particularly Spain and that bit of France consisting of its Justice Ministry. The project will move on—perhaps in the end operating for only some Member States by way of enhanced co-operation.

As you know I have been a supporter of this project and am one of the judicial consultees—I am off to Brussels again for a Friday session on the first draft of the proposed Rules. We do not have lunch all day.

On the home front, change is also in the air. Notwithstanding its cost, patent litigation here is at the highest level I have ever seen. And IP (mainly patent) appeals are increasing—I have about 16 to be heard in the next nine months.

Of potential great importance is Jackson LJ's review about legal costs. I have long taken the view that a lot of time is wasted in patent actions on things like discovery.

Jackson LJ has produced his interim report. Kitchin and Arnold JJ have had a constructive meeting and ideas such as cost-capping are coming to the fore.[3]

I have also long taken the view that your profession could play a great part in reducing costs—smaller cases can and should be run by a patent agent and junior barrister. Indeed I go further: you have achieved the right to instruct barristers direct, and rights of advocacy. You seldom use them. Sooner rather than later, if you do not use your

[3] *As they did for the County Court, newspeakly renamed Intellectual Property Enterprise Court.*

rights, you may lose them. Already some non-patent people in the judiciary and the MoJ [Ministry of Justice] are asking 'What is the Patents County Court for?'

And things are changing on the education front. The days when once you passed your exams you went into practice and education ceased are gone. Now we all teach each other. Your profession has become active in this. The CIPA journal of today is a much more formidable thing than the little publications of yesteryear. The Black Book is at everyone's side.

The last thing I wish to mention, Mr President, is a matter of great sadness. We have lost two great patent lawyers too young, first Nicholas Pumfrey and then Hugh Laddie, within a single year. It is Hugh I particularly want to mention. At UCL, in the short period he had, he set about creating the most exciting centre for IP law and practice—IBIL [Institute of Brand and Innovation Law]. His idea was special: bring in key players from around the world, bring in top practitioners (judges, barristers, solicitors and patent agents) and make a melange—a European centre of enormous power and influence. It has worked thus far: the evening seminars have been sold out even though they use a lecture theatre for 400 people.[4]

Mr President we, that is all the professions, need to carry on that work. You have kindly joined the Board. One of your jobs this year will be to twist the arm of this great profession to make IBIL the success this country needs.

Well, Mr President, I have wondered why you chose the *Belfast*, for your profession is not one that can be said to be all at sea.

I could offer you a toast with a nautical flavour: 'to CIPA and all who sail in her'.

[4] *When I wrote this I had not the slightest idea (consciously at least) that I would go to IBIL!*

49

Mr Justice Jacob Interview for Managing Intellectual Property*

What have been the big changes in the past 20 years?

In 1990, in the Patents Court we had just passed the era of Mr Justice Whitford and Mr Justice Falconer—they both served in the War and belonged to a time past. The Court of Appeal had not had any experienced patent judges. Mr Justice Aldous (as he was) had proved to be a good first-instance judge and had moved things on.

Since then, things have moved on a lot more. The length of trials has gone down by about two-thirds since the 1970s and by possibly a third since Aldous's time. The length depends partly on the judge. The other complication is the technology. You hesitate to think how long some of today's high-tech cases would have taken in the 1970s.

Why is that?

Partly witness statements, partly a change in the culture of judging and of the Bar. There's still room for improvement there. There's a time coming when we'll say: a trial will take so many hours or days and that's that. The new proposed County Court[1] procedures may lead the way to that. They're not far from the procedures agreed by a group of judges in Venice a couple of years ago for a proposed European Patent Court.

* May 2003.
[1] *Renamed the Intellectual Property Enterprise Court.*

And costs?

Costs have gone up. To some extent that's a feature of the trial time going down. Witness statements and so on cut out actual hearing days but take time to prepare. The other change is skeleton arguments didn't really exist in 1990 and nor did post-trial submissions.

Other changes?

The other change was the Court of Appeal acquiring a specialist patent judge. It should now have had two and would have done but for the loss of Pumfrey LJ. Patent work has never been busier in our courts.

What do you put that down to?

I don't know entirely. To some extent it's a reflection of the worldwide increase in IP litigation. It also a reflection on the influence of the English Court. Someone in industry said to me, 'We do our small cases in Germany and our big cases in the UK.' There are now more big cases.

At one point it used to be said the High Court was anti-patentee because it was knocking out a lot of patents. That was unfair and irrational. There were quite a lot of patents knocked out but why were the cases brought here? The answer was these were weak patents granted by the EPO, you could get a fast trial here, and go directly for revocation. People were doing just that. It was a strong tactic, could lead to settlement worldwide and could possibly be of some significance in the EPO proceedings themselves.

Fast courts attract work and that is another reason, for our courts are fast. That can be slightly self-defeating: if too many cases come there will be delays. So far we have kept up, however.

At the same time you had pan-European injunctions in the Netherlands.

Some of that may have been connected. At one point the Dutch judges seemed more ready to find the patent valid at the preliminary injunction stage so people started revocation actions here to forestall Dutch action. Actually now it's difficult to put a cigarette paper between their judges and ours. We get different results sometimes but that's different.

Another significant development is there was virtually no contact with other judges in Europe. Now there's lots. It's mainly between the Netherlands, Germany and the UK. Beyond that there's a language barrier but we do our best. I pay attention to judgments in France for example. In general the European judges have got closer. That is a reflection of the times too.

How does it manifest itself?

Formally we meet in the European Patent Judges Symposium organised by the EPO every two years. Every off year is the Venice symposium, which is more confined to the big patent countries than the European Patent Symposium. On top of that we have informal contacts in various ways. For instance, at the beginning of this year there was a goodbye to Jan Brinkhof as a Professor in Utrecht. I, Lennie Hoffmann and Simon Thorley were some of the people who spoke at that.

Email's made a difference too. If you get a case, you can send an email to a Dutch or German judge saying: have you got this one? Sometimes we agree and sometimes we don't agree; it's much closer than it was. They're the main patent countries and when you're talking about a European system, unless the Commission or a big coalition of willing countries come up with something better, we'll stick with what we've got. It's got better on its own anyway.

People have noted in your judgments that you take account of decisions in Europe.

Yes, the contact we have has produced a more cohesive system for Europe. In trade marks nearly everything has changed. In the UK we had a very stable system, very few cases going to the House of Lords or even Court of Appeal. Now it's impossible to keep up with the references to the ECJ. European trade mark law is very, very confused. The legislation is not good—there was little consultation about it. The contrast with the European patent is significant. The substantive provisions of the EPC were produced by a brilliant group of experts with no time constraints in the Strasbourg Convention. The trade mark system is peculiar. I once wrote that it had ignored a hundred years of experience of trade mark law in different Member States, experience which had identified some of the basic problems of trade mark law such as does it have to be trade mark use to infringe? Or how do you deal with comparative advertising? These sorts of straightforward questions were not addressed as they should have been. Everything went into the melting pot. Industry has had to pay and continues to pay for it and the courts cost governments too.

Do you think the issues are being clarified?

No, it's getting worse. I don't think the ECJ is a good commercial court. Its work on other subjects, such as VAT, is much better and its constitutional or quasi-constitutional decisions are vital for the very being of the EU. But most members of the ECJ have not been commercial lawyers and I think it shows.

What would be the solution?

It's very difficult. You've got to start from here, with all the cases we have already decided. So even if you now made a specialist panel—which has its difficulties in itself—it would be difficult to get back to a rational picture.

The problem with trade marks is one of the reasons why we don't want the same system for patents If one had the ECJ pronouncing on claims of obviousness, claim construction and similar questions and judgments taking two or three years, anything could happen but slowly. That would be very bad for European industry. It's a bit concerning. Industry is dead against it.

There is the Biotech Directive saying what is patentable and not patentable. There's a bit of encroachment into patent law by the ECJ that I think is uncomfortable and could lead to trouble. The Enforcement Directive could also affect the enforcement of patents, though not substantive patent law. There is an argument that IP is becoming part of the *acquis communitaire*, which could become a constitutional problem. If the EU signs the EPC then it becomes part of European law and the ECJ could make rulings. How would that affect non-EU countries who are members of the EPC?

That's all still to be resolved?

That's all developments for the future. This current shove may or may not work. Some countries are not keen, such as the Spanish. In France it depends on the department.

If it fails, I think this time it is unlikely that there would be Community opposition to the original EPLA project of a coalition of the willing. You'd have to have a critical mass—the Germans, the Dutch, UK and the Scandinavian countries could have a crack at creating a court for all their cases and hopefully France would join too. You'd treat it as the national court and litigate all the corresponding national patents in that. I've never seen a constitutional objection to that. In the real world, if you decided a patent dispute for those countries you've covered most of the EU. I think it would be cheaper and more efficient.

I'm worried about the current compromises though—the Germans have gone back on bifurcation. They're worried about losing what they see as the good aspects of their system. I think flexible bifurcation makes sense. The default position should be you don't do it, but there are cases where you should.

Do all these developments make cases more complicated?

We're beginning to get scientific advisers more. It was a power created by the 1949 Act but it wasn't used for many years. The original idea was to get the world's greatest experts. The tendency now is not to go for the Nobel prize winner, and I think that's better. Get a good academic—I've just been sitting with one, I had a good experience with another and it's been excellent.

I think it could become commonplace in higher-tech cases, though the cost is a problem. In some cases it's been mooted to use a patent office examiner. I think that could work in appropriate cases. As long as the parties don't make a fuss the scientific advisor is all right.

Parties are worried that they could influence the judge but none of the scientific advisers have tried to do that. They can explain things: in some cases without help, you can't even figure out what the dispute's about never mind who are the good and bad guys. The parties have found it quite good. I hope it doesn't get interfered with. You get to the point quicker and better and have more confidence that you're at the point.

The distressing tendency of judges, and I include myself, is the length of judgments. We're all writing too much. Some of it is just putting in unnecessary detail. It is hard to leave out detail. I don't put in dates that don't matter, addresses, full names, full case names that don't matter. Do you always need to know that the company's a limited company? The White Book could lose 50 pages by dropping 'limited' or its equivalent.

Do you look back at old judgments?

Yes. Sometimes you think: that sounded pretty good—did I write that? But other times you think: I wish I hadn't said that. Sometimes you have to say: I got it wrong. When you get reversed, there's always two reactions. One is: I got it wrong and I can now see why. Another is: Lord forgive them for they know not what they do. When you've made a mistake, you have to admit it's silly, though sometimes it's down to the way it's argued. A case on appeal often looks very difficult to the case below.

Has the standard of advocacy risen?

Yes I think it has. The patent Bar is excellent, world-beating. They're precise, they know their tribunals well. Undoubtedly some of the solicitors seem to do an awful lot of unnecessary work, which is another big difference that has come in over the years. Barristers' fees used to be half of the case and now they're more like 10 per cent. That's where the costs have gone up. Some of it is complexity, some of it is too many people on the team. Once, on a one one-day application I decided, the solicitors used 15 people—a rugby team! Clients are getting a Rolls-Royce job. The problem is there are rather a lot of people who can't afford Rolls-Royces.

We'll see how the Patents County Court develops under the new rules and the new judge who succeeds His Honour Judge Fysh. The Court has been under an enormous handicap. The Woolf reforms said everyone will have the same rules, so there ceased to be any difference at the County Court. I've never agreed with the Woolf same one-size-fits-all approach: horses-for-courses is a better way.

The streamlined procedure was introduced, but by consent only—the side that wanted it would very likely be the winner. It's not been used too much for that reason.

It's going to be a hard task for the judge and he/she will have to be tough on the litigants. You have to say: focus on your best point or points. That's what's wrong with the EPO procedure—they need some judicial training: how to handle cases that are full-blooded commercial fights. The EPO or someone should produce courses and a handbook on how to litigate before the EPO. I know some advocates would favour that.

The standard of advocacy at the EPO is said to be awful. Far too many points are taken, far too many pieces of prior art cited. English lawyers are trained in court by doing trials before becoming judges: our experience brings to bear in different ways. There are some very good people at the EPO—you'll see in my recent judgments they have done very well on keeping things stable, even if everything's not perfect. If they hadn't done what they've done, European patent law would be in a right mess. They've done a much better job for patents than the ECJ has for trade marks.

What skills does a good advocate have?

There's a basic requirement to speak, to deliver. Then there is the ability to focus on one or only a very few points. Of course there's the old-fashioned skill of telling them what you're going to tell, tell it, then tell them what you've told them. And an ability to debate with the court: to be prepared for difficult questions. A big difference since 1990 is skeleton arguments. We don't now come into court with blank minds—we have initial views but they are just that. I frequently change my mind in the course of a case: oral arguments really matter, particularly when they're clashed against each other and you have to choose between them. The strength of the litigator has some influence but cases are basically decided in our system on the evidence. The most important function of all is to get the right evidence in front of the court.

Do you also follow cases in other jurisdictions beyond Europe?

Yes. I think the next generations will have much more to do with what the Chinese courts decide. They have put enormous investment into the IP system.

In the US their system is distorted by the jury trial and the things they do to try and get round it. The whole approach to the law is different. I've never met anyone outside the US who thinks it's rational to try a patent case 'to' (as the Americans say) a jury . Trade mark cases I can see: juries are consumers, they might be better than judges.

In 2030, where will we be?

I think we'll have a European patent court by then. One reason is people will be more willing to recognise English as the working language of Europe. What keeps India together with 200 languages? The common language of English. The language of patents is not the language of Goethe and Shakespeare. It's hardly a language at all. All the scientists are using English.

Machine translations too will be much better. How good they'll be it's not for me to say. You can get a general idea but getting the nuance—which is what matters in a patent claim—is hard.

Courtrooms will be more electronic. We've had one or two part-electronic trials already. Judges' IT systems are very slow. We're pretty backward here. We still have members of the Court of Appeal who don't use email, which is a pain. Emails allow you to circulate judgments straightaway.

That'll be another feature of the European patent court—more video screenings and links. We did it the other day—counsel was stuck in South Africa by volcanic ash and appeared in an all-day case by video link. It worked and was very effective. He won. I think documents will be more electronic too, I have wondered about that. Judges and litigators will adapt—it will be a gradual development—just as everyone types now, which they didn't used to.

Will there still be wigs and gowns?

I expect so.

50

Interrogatories Answered by the Treasurer[*]

1. **Which judge(s) or member(s) of the Bar (excluding Sir Jack Jacob) had the greatest influence on you and why?**

   Anthony Walton QC, my second pupil master. Besides being a true comic (unbelievably funny yet deeply pessimistic), he saw further and deeper in intellectual property than any other person I have known. Much of his thinking appears in my work even today. Anyone who would like a flavour of this great man should read his speech of welcome to me when I became a judge.[1]

2. **Is there another career you would have enjoyed and why?**

   Well, I wanted to be a physicist but wasn't clever enough. And, when a boy, a photographer (I built my own enlarger and dark-room). I still think scientists are in general cleverer than lawyers.

3. **What one piece of advice would you give to someone appearing in the Court of Appeal (Civil Division) for the first time?**

   Keep it simple—treat us as a high-class jury.[2]

[*] *First published in* Graya News *(the magazine for and about Gray's Inn and its members), Summer 2007, pp 5–6.*

[1] *Chapter 1.*

[2] *When I took silk in 1981 Desmond Ackner, then in the Court of Appeal, advised me to do that to the Court of Appeal. Once, when I was before Fred Lawton (Lawton LJ) I told him that. His reply was 'And how do you treat the House of Lords? As an ordinary Jury?'*

4. **What changes in the law and the legal profession during your career do you most welcome and which do you most deplore?**

   The greater diversity of the Bar is a joy to see. The only thing that really matters is how good you are. I deplore the introduction of hourly billing. It is supposed to control costs but I think it has precisely the opposite effect. Would anyone employ a builder on the basis that he decides all the detail of what work is done, how many do it and how long they each spend on the job? I sometimes see bills for summary assessment of costs where solicitors have put a whole rugby team on the case. Noticeably, since I left the Bar, the proportion of costs which are counsel's fees has fallen (sometimes to below 10 per cent). This is not because counsel do less (often it is the barrister who has done the only real work) but because of the hours claimed by the solicitors' team. Generally, I wonder what they were all doing.

5. **What is your idea of the perfect weekend?**

   First, that is at least three days long. (Someone once said: 'The trouble with working on Wednesdays is that it interferes with both weekends.') Second, that the next working day will not be hard. Ideally the Saturday would have an early kick-off with Arsenal beating MU by three goals. Then to a show with friends and a really good dinner. Next two days to the country with lots of biking and walking and family and good food and wine. Some might think it is a bit boring but as you get older you like that sort of thing more.

6. **What is your favourite city in the world?**

   Apart from London (now the world's first city and a place you can never get bored in), Sydney. Why? Because it is very handsome, full of life and culture, and full of mates (I am still a member of chambers there, in name at least).

7. **Which book have you most enjoyed reading during the last year?**

   The Third Policeman by Flann O'Brien. This has that rare quality (shared by only a few, PG Wodehouse, Jerome K Jerome) of having passages which send you into uncontrollable fits of laughter—you can't read on until you recover.

8. **What is the most memorable sporting event you have witnessed?**

   By radio, Arsenal beating Spurs 1-0 in 1971; on television, Arsenal beating Liverpool 2-1 in 1989; actually being there, England v Australia Lords Test 1956.

9. **What would you like to do when you stop being a Lord Justice?**

   This is difficult to imagine. More bike riding in France. Earn a few bob as an arbitrator, teach and write about law—I expect to do all until I am incapable.

10. **What would be one thing our readers would be surprised to learn about you?**

    My wife says there is nothing. So I will tell a story instead. I went to visit a friend in hospital. He was in a ward with several others and conversation got a bit general (about things like football). When I had gone, my friend said to the chap next to him (a window cleaner who had fallen and hurt himself) 'that was a High Court Judge'. The reply was: 'Go on? They make all sorts of riff-raff judges these days.' In a way I see that as a compliment.

51

*Three Little Ships (Treasurers' Trip to New World, Jamestown)**

I WAS TREASURER of Grays Inn in 2007. One of my jobs was to go with the Treasurers of the other three Inns to the celebrations of the first British settlement in the New World, Jamestown (named after the King), in what became Virginia. This is the piece I wrote about it.

On 26 April 1607 three little ships, the *Susan Constant*, the *Godspeed* and the *Discovery*, made landfall in America. On 14 May the crew went ashore at the site of Jamestown in what was to become the State of Virginia. Jamestown was the first English-speaking colony in America. The venture was essentially commercial. It had none of the religious fervour accompanying the *Mayflower*, which sailed some 13 years later.

The new little colony went through much misery and disease, but eventually survived. The settlers brought with them the common law and with it the notion of the rule of law, rather than the rule of Kings.

Some 400 years later the four Inns of Court were invited to celebrate this first settlement by coming to a conference on the rule of law run jointly by Richmond University and COMBAR [Commercial Bar Association]. This we did with enormous pleasure.

We found ourselves staying in a bizarre, gigantic hotel in Richmond called the Jefferson. Built with tobacco money in the 1890s, the interior looked like a mixture of the Reform Club and the Titanic. On Saturday 14 April we all piled into three buses. Preceding the buses were several limousines containing our Lord Chief Justice, Lord

* Graya News, *Summer 2007 issue.*

Phillips, Chief Justice Roberts of the United States and the Governor of Virginia. Blue lights flashed from a host of police cars and motor cycle outriders as we proceeded in a stately way to the site of the old colony. There we found some brilliant archaeological work being done. Those early colonists, notwithstanding the malaria and all their other tribulations, were men (and the first were all men—women only came out later) of great ingenuity.

The two Chief Justices and our Honorary Bencher, Sandra Day-O'Connor, made delightful speeches and then went on to unveil a plaque provided as a gift by the four Inns. Thereafter we visited the really clever and very interesting museum which was full of tales of those early days and of artefacts found by the archaeologists.

The trip ended with some terrific nibbles, accompanied by a drink known as a 'Godspeed'—a mixture of rum, grenadine and pink grapefruit juice—all poured into a glass of crushed ice. It grows on you.

52

*On Going to the Bar**

IN APRIL YOUR dynamic President[1] organised a reception for ITMA [Institute of Trade Mark Attorneys] members, the Bar and judges. It was in an early kind of trade marks registry—the College of Arms. It was a jolly event for all. Your President collared me and somehow lured me into writing this.

Actually it wasn't very difficult for I am very glad to do it. I have long regretted that relations between the Bar and trade mark attorneys (and patent attorneys) are not as close as they were when I started in IP all those years ago (1967 would you believe?!). Things were very different. Not merely was the law all domestic but the way people went about was different too. The Bar was smaller than it is now and had a reputation for being a very boring place to be. I was told not to go to the Patent Bar (no use of 'IP' then) for that very reason—indeed the only reason I went to the Patent Bar was because it seemed no one else wanted me.

Anyway what I found was a profession which was largely engaged in what might be called shadow-boxing. Most patent work was by way of oppositions or belated oppositions in the Patent Office; most trade mark work was by way of oppositions in the Trade Marks Registry. Design and copyright work hardly existed at all. Actual claims in the courts for injunctions, damages and so on were rare—look at the thickness of [1967] RPC [*Reports of Patent, Design and Trade Mark Cases*] and you are looking at all the cases for the year that had even slight significance (the FSR [Fleet Street Reports] had just started but was essentially no more than an early print of what was to come later in the RPC).

* *This was first published in* ITMA Review *(July/August 2013).*

1 *Catherine Wolfe of Boult Wade Tennant.*

This world, odd though it was by today's in-your-face standards, was a good school. And one of the reasons for that was the close relationships the Bar had with trade mark and patent agents (as they were then called). The general pattern of 'litigation' as I found it was something like this: the proceedings were started by the agent who drafted the pleadings and evidence. A few months before the hearing counsel was instructed directly—when all the evidence was in. You had a con[2] the week before and then argued it before a hearing officer. There were appeals to the Patents Appeal Tribunal (the only patent judge, Lloyd-Jacob J) in the case of patents. There were hardly any trade mark appeals. Occasionally there was a bit of passing off in the courts, but not a lot—we are speaking of pre-piracy days.

It was because the Bar was instructed direct that barristers came to know trade mark and patent agents. We worked together—and there is nothing like working against a common enemy (the other side) to make good friendships. Astonishingly, agents were willing to instruct even a very junior barrister—I started getting my own work I suppose in 1968–69. Before that as a 'devil' I sat in on my Master's conferences—and there met young agents learning their trade from their seniors in much the same way as I was (though they were paid, but not a lot).

The result of all this was good for both sides. As I learned more and grew in confidence I began to understand significant differences between the approach of a barrister and that of an agent—particularly of those agents who did opposition work rather rarely. There were two differences: first the barrister would concentrate on finding the strongest points of attack (or defence). And second the barrister had a much more acute sense of the significance of evidence. The difference could be exemplified thus, for instance, in a case where evidence that a mark had become distinctive was required. The agent would ask the client for figures of sales under the mark and largely be content with that. The barrister would want more—proof that the sales had actually been under the mark, invoices, evidence of customer recognition. The idea was to bury the point beyond argument. I suspect the same sometimes still happens—trade mark registries (home and OHIM) are apt not to be too critical and you can often get away with less than overwhelming evidence. But one should never count on it.

[2] Barristers' term for a conference.

Thus I began to be less satisfied with the 'advocacy only' role. I needed to be in at the beginning—and was able to get my agents increasingly to understand that. It meant focussing early on the winning (or at least best) points and having the courage to drop arguable, but lesser, ones. It meant working on the evidence to overwhelm the other side if it could be done. It also meant that it was possible to head off, before it happened, the running of two inconsistent points (eg in patents, the largely incompatible cases of obviousness and insufficiency). The forming—one might even say crafting—of a case at an early stage working with an agent was hugely enjoyable and I believe resulted in more wins (or good settlements—which count as wins) than would have happened with the late instruction model.

One other thing I did learn is that trade mark agents in those days were not good if a case was, or was likely to be, a serious fight. Far too many never really understood what is almost a law of nature: that trade mark cases get worse with delay. The agents' usual mode of working in oppositions was rather relaxed—the Office allowed it and there was no real hurry. That is likely to be fine for the general run of case. However there are others where, from the outset, there is potentially a big fight. As soon as that appears to be the case, a good trade mark attorney will go to the Bar. Even a few days' delay may matter. A change of gear is vital. And all the points I made about evidence become even more important.

I hope that has changed—though I can think of at least one case we heard in the Court of Appeal recently where the attorney who started a fight in the registry obviously did not go to counsel and put some rather weedy evidence in on a point he or she had obviously not thought through. Remember it is no good trying to get your case right on appeal—under the UK system if you need evidence the time to put it in is first time round and that is the time to try to make it overwhelming.

What then of present-day relations between the Bar and attorneys? Well contact by working on cases together has become rarer and consequently relations are apt to be more distant and less satisfactory than when I started. I think attorneys should change that and they can easily do so. Going to the Bar is not difficult. It is dead easy. And need not be expensive (though some of the 'top' barristers naturally command high fees). Even if you do not have a particular barrister in mind, all you have to do is to ring up the clerk to one of the well-known sets and say you want to instruct a barrister. There is no need to go to a senior one—there are a host of very good young juniors.

You need not go only by the clerk's recommendation—you can see what cases the prospect has been in, you can ask your friends about whom they have found is good. It is all very simple—the Bar is no longer stand-offish—indeed if you were to find a stuck-up barrister I suggest you drop him or her. Don't be afraid to negotiate fees—the clerk's first ask is unlikely to be his last! Get your conference early. In that conference work out who is going to do what and when by.

One other thing. Going to Bar means you can widen your experience beyond that of your firm—get ideas from a variety of minds. An old solicitor I knew used to say that going to different members of the Bar was rather like a bee going from flower to flower—there was fertilisation of ideas. And indeed within a firm there is a danger of a monoculture of ideas.

So, thanks to your President for asking me to write this. And go to the Bar not just on Friday nights.

53

Thomas Blanco White QC 1915–2006

A Personal Reminiscence by Robin Jacob*

YOUR EDITOR ASKED me to write an obituary. But one appeared in *The Times* of 11 February. I thought I would write something different—just tell stories about 'Blanco' as he was known to the entire IP world. Doing something different is very appropriate—he was always his own man. So a different 'obituary' fits him well. Here it is, from one who will be forever grateful to this delightful, eccentric man.

Blanco was a giant. From the late '40s to the '80s—about 40 years in all—he was *the* authority on IP. Not just in the UK, but all over the Commonwealth. Even today, in places where the law is based on the old British law, his writings are one of the first things lawyers go to. The last (green) full edition of his book *Patents for Inventions and the Protection of Industrial Designs* (for which he always used the acronym PIRD), the 4th edition, is still a must for the shelf of any serious Australian patent lawyer. And whenever one comes across a bit of our current Act which has come down from the ages, go to see what Blanco had to say about it. That is what I do. So also for trade marks. He was the chief editor of *Kerly*[1] from the 8th to 12th editions. He wrote *Halsbury* on patents. He invented and wrote most of what became the *Guidebook to Intellectual Property*. He was the editor of the RPC for ages—most of the headnotes of the 1950s and early '60s are his.

* CIPA Journal, *March 2006*.

[1] Kerly's Law of Trade Marks and Trade Names.

I joined Blanco's set as a pupil in September 1967. It was on its uppers. The head of chambers, a top junior and the senior clerk had retired. Another member had dropped dead outside the Rotunda in the Patent Office just two years earlier. Yet another had left permanently sick. There were just four left—no silks. Blanco was the new head of chambers, the job having fallen to him the previous Easter. Despite his writings he had just been refused silk and was to be refused twice more before he finally got it. The whole place needed painting and was covered in dust. Old papers lay everywhere. They said the chambers would fold. It was Blanco, along with Anthony Walton (my pupil master), Kynric Lewis and Julian Jeffs that I joined. It was the best thing that happened in my professional life.

The first thing that Blanco did as head of chambers was to institute the chambers tea party. Before then, in the way of the Bar at the time, clerks took tea to individual members of chambers in their rooms. Blanco said that in times past that happened even if the barrister was in conference—the clients were not offered any. Blanco's tea party was, I truly believe, one of the foremost IP centres in the world—certainly the common law world. Blanco's pupil, Bill Cornish, went to it when it was started during the year before I joined. Of course it included the usual gossip. And it was a true democracy—the means of governance of chambers. It continued to be so until he retired (against our wishes) in about 1989. But above all it was a place of debate. You could take any problem there. Blanco would start a discussion of any point arising in one of his cases by saying 'Do any of you act for some crooks called X'?[2] The debates were often fierce—Anthony Walton and Blanco, the two most senior, were ferocious intellects. And they often did not agree. We learned. More than that we were entitled and encouraged to join in. There was nothing of the arrogance of experience about Blanco—however junior you were, you could pipe up and he listened to the point on its merits.

Sometimes Blanco would talk about what to us was a long distant past. He was brought up amongst Fabians. His mother was a formidable early feminist and intellectual. He had, just by the door on the way in to his room in chambers, a framed letter dated 1915. It was from the President of the Board of Trade. It said: 'The following *gentlemen* [my emphasis] have been appointed to inquire into the recent rise in prices'. There followed a list of the names of about 10 people. One of them was 'Mrs Amber Blanco White'. He was proud

[2] To avoid any conflict of interest.

of his mother—she lived to a great age and he used to visit her on the way home almost every day until she died—he never said so himself but the clerks told us.

Another story about his youth. He remembered Beatrice Webb feeding (he illustrated with an outstretched hand) a biscuit to a dog: 'Now eat it up ... slowly, and enjoy it.' In the 1930s Blanco was one of those Hampstead left-wing intellectuals who, along with others of a quite different political view, particularly Churchill, could see what dark clouds were rising in Germany. But he went further—he actually went to observe a Nuremberg rally and could speak with authority about what he saw—and heard—for, of course, he could speak German (along with Russian and a few other languages—I remember him saying his Serbo-Croat was not that good).

Blanco, to those who did not know him well, seemed distant. He was shy, awkward. He was not one to say things twice—nor to make much of an allowance for the intellectually challenged. He did not shake hands with clients—and sometimes sat in silence in conference fiddling with some red tape or paper clips. So it was one of my functions as his junior in consultation[3] to say, 'Say it again Blanco, I haven't understood.' Even if I had, I was pretty sure the client and his solicitor or patent agent hadn't. So another go would help.

He spoke a perfect English—transcripts of his argument, whether in the Office or the courts never needed correction. And he wrote perfect English with precision. Again you have to go to his books to see. Here is an example of his written advocacy. In 1975 we were appearing for SK&F in the groundbreaking registration of the colours of medicinal capsules as trade marks. The other side's main point (we never thought it their best) was that what we were trying to do was to register the overall appearance of the article and this could not be a 'mark' within the 1938 Act. In the 'Blue Book'—as the printed case to the House of Lords was called—Blanco destroyed the point thus: 'a thing marked all over is marked nonetheless'.

On one thing he was wrong: he said in about 1980 'This racket will see me out and it will probably see you out, but it can't last longer than that'. Well the worldwide swing for IP was not foreseeable then. He was rather amused by it—though he was not in favour of more and more IP as became the trend in the '80s and '90s. After the swing towards plaintiffs in the UK started in earnest in the 1970s he

[3] The word used for a meeting with leading counsel—a QC. A junior barrister only had a conference ('con').

once said: 'Well I had got used to the idea that there is an irrebuttable presumption that all patents were valid: what I had not expected is that there was also an irrebuttable presumption they were infringed'.

Part of that swing was the realisation that copyright in engineering drawings could probably prevent most copying. Shortly after the Design Copyright Act 1968 was passed, the Chartered Institute did something of a kind I have never heard of it doing before or since. It asked Blanco to write an opinion for it to circulate to all members about the significance of the Act. In just a few pages he set out with astonishing clarity not only what was to become the new basic rule, but also its ramifications. Instead of 'you can copy anything unless it is patented or registered as a design' the rule was to be 'you can't copy anything because it is likely to have been made from drawings'. He foresaw the significance as regards spare parts. It was all there. He even said 'a lot of minor patenting will probably be unnecessary'. I am not sure the profession really understood or believed his opinion at the time—certainly it took a few years for cases to come to court and even longer for patent agents to take a serious interest in copyright.

Blanco liked being a little cryptic. He once said that you should always have a few footnotes which hint, darkly, that you know more than you have had space to say here. Anthony Walton made up this story, of Blanco saying 'Ah, we know the result in the House of Lords, but the question is: who really won?' Blanco himself often told another apocryphal story: of the man who, having just lost in the House of Lords, said 'that will teach them'. He could aggravate clients greatly: he liked to tell them, particularly Americans, that the prospects of success were '50/50 with a margin of error of 100%'. Another saying of his was 'once an impossible case gets on its feet, there is no stopping it'. And this: 'cases that are wrongly decided should always be reported'. More seriously he used to say 'one of our main functions is to keep the clients out of court'. I rather think that too many lawyers have lost that ethos—though the best still have it.

His working methods were remarkable. He so arranged things that he hardly ever came in on Mondays, for Mondays were his writing days. Later he took Fridays too. Yet he always had an impeccable typed note. It consisted essentially of single words or phrases and page references. That was all he needed. One of the fields in which he excelled—indeed was head and shoulders above all others—was patent term extension, for war loss and particularly for inadequate remuneration. He really understood accounts and could understand accountants. Many an apparent profit turned into a vast loss under the skilled yet fair hands of Blanco and the accountants. His advocacy here was formidable if you understood the case.

To the uninitiated it seemed distant, abstract and less than compelling. One client (I think ICI) thought he had done a terrible job when they were granted an extension of 10 years (the maximum possible). And that was often so—he was far from a 'jury' advocate, seeking to win by logic, not performance. Yet there were times when he was compelling—I remember well how he had the House of Lords eating out of his hand in the *SK&F* trade mark case for example.

Blanco was a great friend of the profession of patent agent. He invented the first course for actually teaching patent law in the 1950s. It was not aimed at any particular exam, but some of the brightest students of the day would go. The course was taken over by successive members of chambers—indeed I did it for a few years. Blanco attracted some of the cleverest patent agents of his time to instruct him. Sitting in consultation as a junior listening to him debate some difficulty with one of these giants was again a learning curve. His son, Henry, became a patent agent with his encouragement. So there is still a Blanco White doing patent law, though Henry now does this in Philadelphia.

We have all lost a great man.

54

Hugh Laddie Memorial[*]

WE ARE HERE to celebrate Hugh Laddie. We are not here to mourn—though mourn we all do. We are not here to mourn because Hugh would have been against it. He passionately—everything he did was with passion—looked forward, not backward. Even in our last conversations—when the doctors had said nothing could be done, he was quite unsorry for himself. Yes he was sorry for others—for his beloved family, for his friends and for not being able to carry on all the things he so much wanted to do. He could have given up well before then—but far from it. He was telling me all the things he wanted UCL and his creation at UCL, IBIL, to do. He knew he would not be there to see it happen—his exact words were 'I'm not going to live to be a 100' but it made no difference to his vision or excitement.

I first met Hugh nearly 40 years ago. He came into the chambers tea party as a new pupil in 1969, the year he was called to the Bar. There were then just six members of chambers. The daily tea party was not only a ritual and a centre of gossip, but also the management committee and above all for Hugh and me, and for those who came later, a law school. From the moment he arrived, Hugh joined in. Shy and retiring he was not ...

Hugh and I soon became friends—and also the rivals we were to be thereafter. We were much closer in age than the others, which brought us together. We developed a rapport—almost like twins. The Chancery judges sometimes could not tell the difference between us. On motion day quite often one of them would say 'Yes Mr Laddie' to me and 'Yes Mr Jacob' to him. And to the end, when I rang him

[*] *A Thanksgiving to celebrate the life and work of Professor Sir Hugh Laddie (Middle Temple Hall, 4 March 2009).*

at home, if Stecia answered she would call him saying, 'It's your twin on the line.' We could read each other's minds—sentences seldom needed completing. And rivals though we were, when we found ourselves on opposite sides, as we often did, we settled nearly everything. Only twice, from 1969 to 1993, the years in chambers together, did we actually appear against each other—on each occasion we were given no choice and on each the result we both expected came about.

It seems implausible now, but Hugh did not get going quickly. He did not have his own room for some time—he was placed in what was called 'the pupil's room'. It was, to put it kindly, dilapidated. It had three carpets, one on top of the other, each with a large hole in the same place as the other holes—so the wood floor showed through. On a hot day in the summer vacation of 1971 I remember him sitting, head down, despondent and unshaven, at an old desk in that dilapidated room. He said he was never going to make it, that he would join his uncle's scrap metal business. I told him not to give up. He didn't, but it was a close-run thing. The scrap metal business was the loser,

The case that really changed him happened shortly thereafter. The Church of Scientology brought an action against a very small publisher. The Church was trying to use copyright to suppress criticism. Hugh got the job for a pittance. His sense of justice took fire. Suddenly he was fighting. The Scientologists had a silk—Jeremiah Harman—who was not unknown for heavy-handed tactics. Hugh knew it was all down to him—he fought hard and precisely and delivered a knock-out blow. That was his real beginning—the moment when he realised he really could do it. He was on his way. Record pirates and *Anton Piller* were not far behind. The rest is well known.

He was given his own proper room, my former very small room, shortly thereafter. I had built the bookshelves there and since he was inheriting these he repaid by helping me build the bookshelves in the larger room that I was going to, that very same former 'pupils' room'. We worked by gaslight in the non-working days of the three-day week—we calculated no one would know if we used electric drills.

Hugh loved good people—of all races and beliefs. He had close friends around the world. His reason told him there was no chosen people and he refused to believe in a God. Stecia told me that just two days before he died, a rabbi came to see him. As soon as the rabbi entered the room, Hugh said 'You know I don't believe a word of it'.

But what he did believe in was people and justice and, when he was a fighting barrister, in fighting for his client. The money and his own position or health did not come into it. Here is an example never publicly told before. When he was offered a job on the Bench it was known that the rules about judicial pensions and time of service were about to be changed. And for the worse. Hugh could have beaten the change but at the time he was defending a particular client who, although of no particular personal merit, was one he thought needed defending. He postponed his appointment until the case was over even though it meant he came under the new rules.

And of course he was funny. A source of jokes of all kinds, even about himself. He loved engineering and making things and I suppose that is partly why, when he eventually could afford it, he bought that Meccano-like thing, a Morgan sports car One morning he bounced into chambers with this story. His Morgan was parked outside some shops whilst he was on the other side of the road. From there he saw a couple of girls admiring it before walking on. He got into the car a little later and drove off. He stopped at some red lights. The same girls came by on the pavement. He heard one say to the other, 'What a shame, it's an old geyser.'

We all miss the old geyser very much.

55

Sir Hugh Laddie Obituary[*]

FEW LAWYERS CAN claim to have contributed significantly to a piece of development in the practice of the law. Hugh Laddie, who has died of cancer aged 62, was certainly one of that exclusive breed of barristers who relish the opportunity for creativity in their legal practice. In the early 1970s, as a member of the Patent Bar in the burgeoning era of intellectual property, he invented means of helping recording companies and artistic performers protect their rights. Record pirates had begun to be a significant problem. They made, or imported, pirate copies, so they thought out of sight and reach of rights owners. Whenever infringement of intellectual property rights was detected, it had been insufficient just to sue them: before the court could make any order, the pirates simply, surreptitiously and speedily disposed of infringing material and all documents which would show what they had really been up to. What was needed was a procedure whereby the right holder could gain access to the pirate's premises before he could destroy or make away with documents and pirate copies. The order which was needed had to be made ex parte—made without prior notice to the defendant. Hugh Laddie, having first made a vast search of nineteenth-century cases, boldly tried out the pre-emptive strike, asking judges to make ex parte orders requiring the pirates to give immediate access to their premises and to allow an instant search for documents and infringing copies. After a number of successful such orders at first instance, the Chancery judges wondered whether this deceptively enchanting advocate had beguiled them. So an order was refused and Laddie had to take the point on appeal. It succeeded. The case is known

[*] *First published in* The Guardian *and co-written with Sir Louis Blom-Cooper (2 December 2008).*

around the world as *Anton Piller*, even to this day. Laddie's inventiveness also aided performers, who had no explicit property right in their performances, to gain protection for their work in an equally ground-breaking case called *Island Records*. It is worth recording that he did all this as still quite a junior member of the Bar.

Hugh Laddie was educated at Aldenham School and St Catherine's College, Cambridge, where he read medicine before turning to the law, called to the Bar by Middle Temple in 1969 (bencher 1993), taking silk in 1986. He was made a High Court judge in 1995 as one of the then two patent judges in the Chancery Division. His 10 years as a judge of first instance were never tranquil, although the early years continued his creativity. Possessed of a profound sense of justice he found the procedural rules inhibiting. Increasingly he railed against the handicap of a trial judge to do justice given the restraints of elaborate rules of court. He found the Woolf reforms of 1998 as 'not very impressive'. He thought the reforms merely gave new names to old procedures: 'my view is you don't turn a dog into a cat by calling it "Kitty".' He found access to justice for the citizen insufficient. He boldly tried to enhance the cost-effective resolution of disputes. The restraints of judgeship became more and more irksome. This led him to resign from the Bench in 2005. No one since Sir Henry Fisher, in 1970, had done such a thing. He declared publicly that he had become bored. Boredom, in a judge, he explained, was the best reason for standing down, if only because the public could not be assured that justice in his court could be seen to be done. He made his departure as public as possible, which perhaps deserved some adverse comment. That may explain why the legal establishment received the manner of his departure coolly. But many in the legal profession quietly applauded the honesty and integrity of Mr Justice Laddie.

Hugh's devotion to the promotion, and proper control, of intellectual property law was kept very much alive with his dual position as a consultant to a firm of solicitors (itself considered by many to be inappropriate for an ex-High Court judge) and Professor of Intellectual Property Law at University College (an appointment which was an inspirational idea coming from Lord Woolf). At UCL Hugh set about creating a department unlike anything that had been seen before so far as UK academia is concerned. He shamelessly canvassed and received considerable sums of money from the legal profession. He exploited his friendships in this country and around the world to make the new 'Institute of Brand and Innovation Law' not only a reality, but also the leading academic centre for the subject in this country. No one he roped in resisted. His genial and warm friendship was irresistible. These characteristics were the more noticeable once the aura of the judicial robes had faded.

Outside the law Hugh Laddie had a remarkable appetite for knowledge. His father-in-law once observed that he had never met anyone who could pick up a book and learn its content and meaning so powerfully.

A tragically early death has deprived the intellectual property world of an outstanding thinker and reformer. But his contribution to the law will always be remembered by his link to *Anton Piller* and similar innovations.

Notwithstanding all his public achievements, Hugh Laddie's family was the core of his life. He leaves a widow, Stecia, two sons and a daughter. His mother has survived him.

Hugh Ian Lang Laddie, born 15 April 1946, died 28 November 2008.

56

*In Memoriam: Nicholas Pumfrey**

22 May 1951–24 December 2007

'THE HONEY JUDGE' is what Mary Fysh[1] called Nicholas. That was not merely because he kept bees at his beloved house, surrounded by lavender fields, in the Haut Provence. Indeed he did keep bees and at some point usually just before Christmas he was apt to appear in your room grinning and bearing a giant pot of honey in a plastic bag. But the name 'honey judge' was more appropriate than just because of that—it correctly summarised what he was—a really, really sweet man.

It is an inevitable feature of life that people die. But it is ever so hard when it happens to one so young, so full of life, so life-enhancing. Even though it is now nearly a year since he died, people keep saying to me they feel the same way as I do about his death—that they go on missing him very badly. I still cannot bear to take the name 'Pumfrey' off one of the quick-dial buttons on my phone. I still miss those phone calls at about 9.30: 'Good morning. Here is your wake-up call' was how he often started these. The conversation was 95 per cent gossip and 5 per cent law.

But that 5 per cent was serious—though never solemn. If we disagreed about a point, Nicholas would say: 'Now look here' and proceed to expose any weakness I had. Of course after I had gone to the Court of Appeal we could not talk about any pending appeal—though I would get told why I was wrong in those rare cases (I can only think of one) where I was party to reversing him. Nor could we talk about cases pending before him in case they came my way later. But that left plenty to discuss—whatever the problem which he or I had had.

* *For the Fordham 2008 Conference.*

[1] Michael Fysh QC, SC's wife.

Nicholas's funeral service took place in the ancient Temple Church. The place was crowded out—how many is anyone's guess but it can't have been much less than 1,000. He himself had no religion—many of our jokes were about it.

Nicholas had just come to the Court of Appeal before he died. His breathtaking knowledge of so many areas of the law beyond intellectual property itself was about to be deployed in judgments which would have been wise, readable and humane. Many are losers by his death—his friends, his colleagues, both intellectual property law and the law in general, and not just in my country but well beyond. The Fordham conference itself will be the poorer—many at it will miss that great shock of white hair, the incisive comments and that enormous grin.

57

Sir Nicholas Pumfrey[*]

SIR NICHOLAS PUMFREY (Lord Justice Pumfrey) died of a massive stroke on Christmas Eve. He was only 56. He had just been appointed to the Court of Appeal, having served as a Chancery judge for a little over 10 years. He died before the honour of membership of the Privy Council (which goes with membership of the Court of Appeal) could be conferred upon him.

The bare facts of his career seem unremarkable. The son of a solicitor he went to St Edmund's School, Oxford and on to St Edmund Hall. He read physics, followed by a one-year degree in law (the BCL). Then on to the Bar, being called by Middle Temple in 1975. There followed a search for pupillage at the Patent Bar. One prominent set of chambers (or at least a particular member of that set—things like chambers pupillage committees did not exist then) rejected him, to its permanent sorrow and chagrin. Wiser counsel prevailed in the chambers of Stephen Gratwick QC, the then doyen of the Patent Bar. He was taken on as pupil. His master was not particularly busy or successful so Nicholas largely had to teach himself. But that is just what he was really good at. It was not long before Stephen Gratwick said to the senior clerk, 'There is your next silk.' That proved to be so. Nicholas took silk in 1990 and was appointed a High Court judge in 1997 at the early age of 46. He was a nominated judge of the Patents Court from then until his appointment to the Court of Appeal last November.

Those are the bare facts. But they do not reveal anything about this extraordinary man. He was an extraordinarily private sort of person—he had many friends within the law and outside and much

[*] *First published in* The Guardian *(5 January 2008) and jointly written with Sir Louis Blom-Cooper.*

affection for his family (his mother and sister). But he kept his relationships in distinct compartments. There were his old non-lawyer friends from university, his lawyer friends, his French friends in his beloved village in France high in the Haut-Provence, his family and perhaps other compartments too. Somehow he kept them all distinct from the others, yet without in any way being secretive or furtive. He never married nor formed any sort of close relationship with anyone. The consensus was that despite his enormous warmth, humour and generosity he was afflicted by a deep-rooted, and wholly unjustified, lack of self-confidence—he was too shy to come or allow anyone to come too close. Whatever the reason, one could fairly call Nicholas an old-fashioned bachelor. Like some Victorian uncle he had a number of godchildren (though unlike such an uncle he was himself an atheist), nephews and nieces, and quasi-nephews and nieces, who adored him. You only had to see the children of summer visitors in France following him around with excitement and joy to realise that they could see through his shyness—to the man of fun and interest.

It goes without saying that Nicholas was a superb intellectual property (patents, trade marks, designs, copyright and such like) lawyer. But he was much more of an all-rounder than that. There was hardly an area of law where he did not have an insight and wisdom. For instance when he had only been a judge for a short while he found himself having to decide whether the mighty firm of accountants KPMG should be restrained from acting for the Brunei Investment Authority on the grounds that it also acted for Prince Jefri. The Prince's contention, that there was a risk of a conflict of interest, was upheld by Pumfrey J. The Court of Appeal (presided over by Lord Woolf) reversed him but was in turn reversed by the House of Lords. It was a resounding vindication of Nicholas's inbuilt sense of what is fair. I rang him up when the report of the House of Lords decision appeared, saying 'I bet you are grinning from ear to ear.' 'Well yes I am, actually,' was the answer.

His command of technology was extraordinary. He could do his own plumbing, fix his motorbike, make honey (he kept bees) and find truffles unaided by dog or pig. He was a first class cook—it was well worth being his guest. In one complex computer program case, one of the experts asked 'does he program in C or C+?' When younger he crossed France several times by bike—it would have been better for his health if had continued to ride rather than always use his powerful BMW bike, and what he called his 'bread delivery van' in France. He was proud to have cycled up Mont Ventoux both from the North and South.

Nicholas was known throughout the world by the intellectual property community. He was a regular speaker at the largest IP conference, that held annually at Fordham University, New York and for the last few years taught patent law for a week at the prestigious Max Plank Institute in Munich. He was the first British judge to be made a member of the Enlarged Board of Appeal (the top tribunal) of the European Patent Office in Munich. He will be much missed around the world, not only here.

He was also a prominent and active member of his beloved Inn, Middle Temple, chairing in succession the Catering and Finance Committees. Although he said he did not want the job, it seems unlikely that his fellow Benchers would have allowed him to refuse to become Treasurer in due course.

Publicly his loss will matter a lot. The Court of Appeal needed another IP judge, especially for the heavy, highly complex technical patent cases which have recently become more common—to the existing regular diet of pharmaceuticals has been added much litigation about electronics, particularly telephone and communication systems (his last judgment at first instance, handed down on 20 December, was about patents said to be essential for 3G mobile telephones). And Europe will miss his wisdom too. The European Commission is currently engaged in a project to create a European Patent Court and possibly a true EU-wide patent. The project has failed several times before, generally for lack of consultation. This time it is consulting both industry and judges and the court may really come to pass. Nicholas was taking an active part in the discussions (he was, for instance, a participant and speaker at the meeting held in October 2006 by the French Conseil d'Etat on the subject) and with his wisdom, experience and near fluent French, was much wanted. He would have been freer to take part in this work in the Court of Appeal than in the Chancery Division.

Privately those in each of his compartments will miss him greatly—and the Court of Appeal has lost what surely would have been an outstanding member on a personal basis as well as a legally.

Nicholas Richard Pumfrey,

Barrister and Judge.

Born 22 May 1951; died 24 December 2007.

58

My Friend Cyril[*]

MY ACTUAL FIRST memory of Cyril is of a moment in the LSE refectory (then on the third floor of the main building, serving food which, fortunately, was of a quality hard to find these days). It was Yom Kippur. Cyril joined a group of us with his tray and sat down. 'What's that you're eating?' asked someone. 'Pork sausages,' said Cyril. 'Given him his foreskin back,' cried one bright spark. It still makes me laugh, as do so many other memories of Cyril.

Although a year younger than me, Cyril was older in the law, having been in the year above me at LSE. (I was actually an evening student.) Quite how we met and became friends I do not know. I think he had actually left LSE before I got to know him: he kept coming back when he was in articles (to Bernard Sheridan). I know he was a student of my father, who had invented an LLM course at UCL in civil procedure. (Many years later Cyril was to give the course himself.) I can almost remember the moment when he became interested in civil procedure. One evening, again in the refectory, Cyril came in from the office and said: 'You know what I've discovered? You can murder the other side if you know your White Book.'

Cyril and I became close friends. I imagine I was one of few invited to his parents' flat in the East End. It was in Jamaica Street and I think I can still remember the number, 141, later to be renumbered 341 (Cyril was annoyed about the renumbering). He was proud and intensely fond of his parents. When his father (an East End tailor)

[*] *A speech given on 29 June 2011 at the LSE Law Faculty party to celebrate Cyril's donation of his legal biography library. Cyril Glasser was an East End working class Jewish boy ('Everyone in my school went into the law: as a policeman, solicitor or criminal)'. He was known to and loved by so many, including the Lard Chancellor's Private Secretary (Sir Tom Legge) and Nelson Mandela (Cyril said Mr Mandela told him about a Presidential visit to a court: 'the last time I was here I thought I might be hanged').*

was getting very old and his eyesight was failing, Cyril told me how his Dad had, the night before, beaten him at dominos—he described, with pride and joy, the old man's look of cunning glee as he put down his last piece.

Later our legal paths took different directions, Cyril with his amazing career at Sheridans and me with my more ordered path at the patent Bar. Others will have more to say about what Cyril did professionally. What remained with him at all times until he died was a fierce sense of justice—indeed it is a pity he did not live to see the Strasbourg court, in the Naomi Campbell case, condemn contingency fee uplifts being visited upon the losing party. Cyril had maintained from the outset that this was a form of confiscation of property: the loser was paying *more* than the winner had spent on costs. Of course this was but one aspect of the dismantling of legal aid—a matter which troubled Cyril hugely in those later years when Parkinson's was upon him. Every month or so I used to bike over to his house in Kentish Town and he would hold forth—with increasing physical difficulty—about this.

He held forth about other things too—his Jewish roots and Jewish judges became more important to him—though he never showed any sign of becoming religious. And he was particularly interested in all legal biography—for it was always through people that he saw the law. LSE is lucky to have the considerable collection he built up over the years.

Part IX

Conclusion

VALEDICTORY REMARKS ON THE RETIREMENT OF THE RT HON LORD JUSTICE JACOB

IN THE COURT OF APPEAL

Royal Courts of Justice
Strand, London, WC2A 2LL

Date: 22nd March 2011

Before:

THE LORD CHIEF JUSTICE OF ENGLAND AND WALES
THE MASTER OF THE ROLLS
THE CHANCELLOR OF THE HIGH COURT
THE VICE PRESIDENT OF THE QUEEN'S BENCH DIVISION
LORD JUSTICE JACOB

- -

Present in the (packed) Court of the Lord Chief Justice of England and Wales:
Judges of the Court of Appeal and the High Court of Justice
Judges' Clerks
Staff of the Royal Courts of Justice
Members of the Bar
Solicitors
Patent Agents
Trade Mark Agents
and
Members of the Public

Transcript of the Shorthand Notes of Marten Walsh Cherer Ltd
1st Floor, Quality House, 6-9 Quality Court, Chancery Lane,
London WC2A 1HP. Telephone No: 020 7067 2900.
Fax No: 020 7831 6864
DX 410 LDE info@martenwalshcherer.com

THE LORD CHIEF JUSTICE: What a happy occasion! It is an amazing turn-out. How nice to see you all. I was going to do some character assassination on Lord Justice Jacob, but I have been told to hold my peace and say nothing and invite the Master of the Rolls to go first. So I shall. *(Laughter)*

THE MASTER OF THE ROLLS: This is an application by Lord Justice Jacob for permission to retire. *(Laughter)* If there was any ground for dismissing the application, I would unhesitatingly do so. I know that all his and my colleagues in the Court of Appeal wholeheartedly agree. Accordingly, this is the judgment of the court.

I turn to consider the arguments which can be advanced to support the contention that the Lord Justice's application should be dismissed.

First, although one can well understand the applicant's wish to spend more time with his splendid wife and family, the notion of 'retiring' and 'Jacob' are not exactly natural bedfellows. There is no more energetic or committed judge, whether in or out of court, than Lord Justice Jacob.

However, unfortunately, this point is met by the applicant's intention to lecture, write, bicycle, arbitrate, mediate, travel, teach, sit occasionally and watch Arsenal Football Club. So he will be as busy as ever.

Secondly, it is clear from the appearance of the applicant that he is far too young to retire. However, I have been referred to the case of *Who v Who*, which establishes that, despite his appearance, he is 70 years old, or virtually 70. So that point falls away.

Thirdly, the Lord Justice's written judgments are far too stylish and clear to permit him to step down. Consider the first two sentences of his judgment in *Ferguson v British Gas*, where he said this:

> It is one of the glories of this country that every now and then one of its citizens is prepared to take a stand against the big battalions of government or industry. Such a person is Lisa Ferguson, the claimant in this case.

I wonder who won! *(Laughter)* It is pure Denning in style.

But this point falls away because the Lord Justice will continue to write, sit and teach, and so his outstanding style will continue to be available despite his retirement.

The next ground that is raised is that the court cannot possibly lose his administrative abilities. He ran the Patents Court at first instance extremely well. He was an excellent Chancery supervisory judge on the Western, Midland and Welsh Circuits. As his successor, I can tell you that he was a very hard act to follow. In the Court of Appeal, he runs the IP appeals list brilliantly. He even lets me sit on the occasional appeal. I was a bit mystified why I was sitting on an appeal a few weeks ago which involved machinery that makes lavatory rolls and kitchen towel rolls. I only realised during the course of the first morning that, of course, he decided I should hear it because of my job as Master of the Rolls. *(Laughter)*

Unfortunately, this fourth ground falls away because, thanks to his guidance and leadership, the excellent team in the Court of Appeal consisting of Kim, Rob, Sally and Anne Marie has now learned how to manage appeals in IP cases.

Fifthly, it is said that his wonderful sense of humour and his engaging and idiosyncratic character cannot be lost to the Court of Appeal. Consider his judgment in *Rockwater v Technip* where he described that figure, familiar to patent practitioners, a man skilled in the art. 'It is settled,' said Lord Justice Jacob, 'that this man, if real, would be very boring—a nerd.' Later, he said: 'The man can, in appropriate cases, be a team—an assembly of nerds. But,' he continued, 'the skilled man is not a complete android.' The other members of the Court of Appeal agreed.[1]

But this fifth ground cannot be sustained because his humour will be deployed for the benefit of his students and his audiences.

Sixthly, it is said that the Lord Justice is probably the most popular member of the Court of Appeal, with his sense of humour, quizzical stare, expressive eyebrows, and his lack of pomposity and side. He currently presides over what he calls 'the bad boys' corridor'. I shall spare the blushes of Lord Justice Hooper and Lord Justice Moses by not identifying the other members of that corridor. *(Laughter)* However, that point is unfortunately met by the fact that he has promised to come and see us very often.

Seventhly, there is the fact that he is the UK intellectual property supremo and we, therefore, cannot afford to lose him. He has tirelessly worked on difficult and technical judgments, and travelled to conferences throughout the world in support of IP, and, in particular, support of IP in the UK.

[1] *Not quite right. Pill LJ agreed with everything except the nerd/android bit, saying ' Jacob LJ will think me less than supportive of the development of the language of the law but I do respectfully prefer, for its clarity, Lord Reid's terminology cited at paragraph 7 of the judgment'. He apparently had to look up 'nerd' and 'android' in a dictionary. John Mummery, delightfully and diplomatically, said he agreed with both judgments!*

As a new boy in the area, I benefited enormously from Robin's education and advice on my first few IP judgments. I should like to take the opportunity of thanking him for all his help on my early IP judgments, but I should make it clear that any errors in those judgments are entirely his. *(Laughter)* As to this ground, the truth is that his contribution to IP will continue as Professor at UCL and as a legal adviser and arbitrator.

The final ground that is put forward is the fact that we may lose his wonderful clerk Lorraine. However, this provides no basis for dismissing the application, as she will, I am happy to say, carry on working as a clerk in the Royal Courts.

In these circumstances, I have regretfully concluded that none of these arguments can be sustained and that Lord Justice Jacob should be entitled to retire. But he can only do so on his firm undertaking that he will have a long and happy retirement and that he will come and visit us frequently.

His application is therefore allowed but he will have to pay the costs on an indemnity basis. *(Laughter)*

THE LORD CHIEF JUSTICE: Mr Thorley, do you want to make any submissions about the order that has just been made in relation to costs? Normally we like to hear the argument before we give the judgment. *(Laughter)*

MR SIMON THORLEY QC (3 New Square): My Lords, Alice in Wonderland has always had a place in this court! *(Laughter)*

My Lords, the Master of the Rolls has given me eight minutes on which to eulogise on the subject of Lord Justice Jacob, who has just looked at his watch. My Lords, I think I could do it in eight words: Lord Justice Jacob is a thoroughly good bloke.

May I just amplify on that a little. The world of intellectual property owes him a very great debt for channelling his undoubted talents into this field, both as a practitioner and as a judge. The contribution that he has made over the last 45 years is immense.

I have had the privilege of observing the major part of this. I sat down on Sunday to write these notes and sent an e-mail to the Master of the Rolls to assure him that I was going to stay within the eight minutes because, having written it, I felt constrained to cross out the anecdotes and there was very little left. *(Laughter)*

My Lords, the first seriously contested application I had in these courts was before Mr Justice Walton in the prefabricated courts which used to be in the courtyard behind. There was no question of the air-conditioning failing because there was none. It was against Mr Robin Jacob. The case was called *Wombles Skips v Wombles Ltd*, a passing off case, and he won. He has never let me forget it. *(Laughter)*

Robin Jacob the barrister possessed many of the recognised virtues of our profession. He was quick to assimilate facts and to understand complex technology. He was decisive in forming an opinion, clear in his advice, with a ready ability to sort out the good arguments from the bad, and to pursue the good with succinct vigour. He had an infinite capacity for hard work and, above all, good health.

THE LORD CHIEF JUSTICE: I am sorry to interrupt, Mr Thorley. It sounds as though grandson Max is being removed from the court! *(Laughter)* He obviously takes after his grandfather, insisting on being heard. I am sorry to interrupt you.

MR SIMON THORLEY QC: Insisting on being heard by interrupting, not an unknown family characteristic! *(Laughter)*

My Lords, you may have noted that I said he possessed many of the required virtues of being a barrister—but not all. I understand there were occasions when his instructing solicitors, whilst duly grateful for his clear advice, were a little surprised that it had been given without unduly disturbing the pristine condition of the papers that had been sent to him.

Above all, Robin Jacob the barrister was held in the highest esteem by his colleagues, particularly by his juniors which I was once—only once—and his opponents alike for the straightforward and good-natured way in which he conducted litigation. There was none of the wholly unnecessary carping, waspish, point-scoring advocacy which can render litigation tedious, unpleasant and, above all, expensive.

He would tease his opponents—usually me—usually unmercifully, but always with the great good humour that is an integral part of his make-up.

Time moved on and the Bar was deprived of the vibrancy of Robin Jacob QC. Would Mr Justice Jacob lose the ebullience and good humour of our erstwhile colleague? Would he suffer from that dread disease of judgitis? Would he heck? The late Charles Sparrow once observed that he was unable to understand why his Lordship was only comfortable when conducting his court in the atmosphere of the music hall. A little exaggerated perhaps, but, provided you were well prepared, focused and short-winded (woe betide you if you were not), the addition of a little humour was welcome.

My Lords, as you all know, one of the greatest qualities of a judge is to conduct litigation in a way that leaves the losing party happy—in the sense that he has had a fair trial.

I was once instructed indirectly by a US lawyer from the deep South, whose drawl I can't possibly imitate. When we left court, he said, 'That judge has comprehended the technology. He has listened to both sides of the argument. He appears to have understood them. Win or lose, I could not ask for anything more.' My Lords, that is a tribute, I think, to a judge.

Mr Justice Jacob as a trial judge was a great reformer, well in advance of the Woolf reforms. Timetables were streamlined, discovery was minimised and issues were crystallised. Patent trials in the 1970s and 1980s, and indeed early in the 1990s, regularly lasted for six weeks or more. My first big trial as a Silk against Robin Jacob QC was in front of a youthful Mr Justice Morritt, which took just over five weeks to argue a fairly simple patent about, quite appropriately, babies' nappies. By the time Mr Justice Jacob had left, trials were taking five to six days, and, what is more, he gave every impression on occasions of having read the papers in advance.

We then lost Mr Justice Jacob to the Court of Appeal. Would his spontaneity be lost in the cerebral world of this court? Those responsible for listing know, however, how to bring the best out of their judges, and the newly elevated Lord Justice Jacob was assigned to a court presided over by Lord Justice Ward. The rest is history. *(Laughter)*

My Lord, may I take this opportunity to pay tribute to my Lord's clerk Lorraine Bennett, to whom first and foremost many happy returns, who has been more than equal to the daunting task of keeping you on the straight and narrow. Her methods were many and varied, including ringing me up one morning to ask if I would take you out to lunch because you were being a nuisance. *(Laughter)*

Now, my Lord, the time has come for you to ride off, no doubt on a rickety bicycle, into the colourful retirement sunset of academia. I know that when Treasurer of Gray's Inn you greatly enjoyed the company of the students. All I can say is that the students at UCL will be both fortunate and privileged when their paths cross with yours. Whether their vision of the Rt Hon Professor Sir Robin Jacob will entirely accord with reality is another matter.

My Lord, my time is up. I have spoken for eight minutes without interruption by you—a record. May I, on behalf of the Bar, wish your Lordship the most happy, fulfilled and lengthy retirement from the Bench.

THE LORD CHIEF JUSTICE: Thank you, Mr Thorley. Miss May?

MISS CHARLOTTE MAY (8 New Square): My Lords.

It is an honour and a privilege to say a few words to my Lord, Lord Justice Jacob, on behalf of the Junior Bar.

Unlike Mr Thorley, I am only allowed four minutes. But, just like Mr Thorley, I rejoice in the fact that it will probably be the longest period a member of the Junior Bar will ever get to address my Lord without interruption, so I intend to make the most of it. Of course, whether or not your Lordship can resist temptation this time remains to be seen.

I have summarised my speech into three short points. And before you ask, my Lord, yes—they are my best points! *(Laughter)*

First, I must thank my Lord on behalf of the Junior Bar for the benefit of 18 years of my Lord's judging. Right from the very beginning, my Lord, you firmly stamped your personality on proceedings in your court. As a result, they were fast, efficient and full of good humour. Always commercially minded, your Lordship actively managed your cases to keep costs down—even before the days of CPR[2] and openly encouraged parties to settle if there was an obvious way out.

Mr Thorley has already referred to your Lordship's legendary knack, when in practice, to pick out the crucial document in the instructions without reading them. Your Lordship's ability to get right to the heart of the issue never diminished as a judge. Within virtually the first five minutes of any hearing before my Lord, you would always ask the killer question. As an advocate, one merely hoped that it was to be fired at the opposition!

Thanks to my Lord's style and influence we now have a litigation system that is significantly more streamlined and efficient, and IP courts that are respected across Europe and internationally.

My second point is to thank my Lord on behalf of the Junior Bar for the benefit of 18 years of your Lordship's judgments. As a body of

[2] Civil Procedure Rules.

works, they comprise a masterpiece of learning in IP. No matter how complex, your Lordship has always had the ability to express the issue succinctly and to reason upon it in clear and straightforward language. Your Lordship manages to say what everyone else is thinking. Only recently your Lordship honestly described the excluded matter provisions in the EPC as something which does your head in! *(Laughter)*

But it is not only IP cases where your Lordship has left your mark. Over the years my Lord has given judgments on issues ranging from family law to planning to pensions to immigration, always with the same clarity and Denning-esque approach to justice. Like Lord Neuberger, I consider one of the more memorable decisions was the case of *Ferguson v British Gas* in which my Lord praised the courage of Ms Ferguson to take a stand against one of the big battalions of industry in what can only be described as a cracking read!

Now, they say that behind every successful man is a successful woman, and my Lord is no exception. I refer of course, to my Lord's wonderful wife Wendy, who has contributed to my Lord's success by providing constant support and encouragement whilst running the family home and pursuing her own talent as an artist. We are very grateful to her too.

My third and last point is to wish my Lord well for the future. The Junior Bar is delighted that my Lord has been appointed as the first Sir Hugh Laddie Chair in IP at UCL, not least so that we can continue to benefit from my Lord's deep knowledge and understanding of the subject. According to the UCL website, it is my Lord's intention to make UCL one of the key world centres for *practical* IP law, research and teaching. There is no one better placed than my Lord to achieve this endeavour, and we wish you the very best.

THE LORD CHIEF JUSTICE: Thank you very much. Mr Westmacott?

MR PHILIP WESTMACOTT (Intellectual Property Lawyers' Association): My Lords.

I have instructions to speak without hesitation, deviation or repetition for no more than two minutes, but, unlike the radio panel game, the topic, Lord Justice Jacob, does not change from round to round. *(Laughter)*

So I asked my fellow solicitors—what should I say? There was no shortage of material, but, even applying a coarse filter, of the type to be found in Patent Offices around the world, I discovered that rather more than 12/14ths of the material they so kindly supplied had to be discarded as highly entertaining but entirely unsuitable for repetition in open court—rather like the infamous bundle 50 in the HCV litigation.[3]

I hope I may be permitted to address my remarks primarily to Lord Justice Jacob. We are here to thank you, my Lord. First, for your undeniable energy and enthusiasm—as an effective junior barrister you earned the sobriquet 'Bobbin' Robin'. *(Laughter)*

Secondly, for your undoubted determination that 'the mode of conducting the law in a patent case' was capable of remedy. Your method was to focus on essentials. This included reducing the number of documents. After all, as counsel, you personally had no wish to plough through volumes of documents. Why should the court? So, when in the HCV case the defendant noticed frequent references to a gentleman by the name of Rodney in the claimant's discovery, they demanded immediate disclosure of all Rodney's invention notebooks. You were delighted at your solicitors' reply: 'Dear Sirs, Rodney is a chimpanzee'.[4] *(Laughter)*

In mid-December 2008 a patent infringement case was started. The defendants decided to rely on just their best bit of prior art. Mr Justice Lewison gave directions: the High Court tried the case before Easter 2009. You gave directions: the Court of Appeal decided the case by the end of July. A full decision of an appellate court on a patent in some seven months—I believe that is a world record. Maybe the proper recipients of the Lawyer Award for that case should have been you and Mr Justice Lewison.

You have consistently been clear, maybe almost impatient, that IP cases should be conducted quickly, efficiently and at the minimum cost consistent with a fair outcome. Our clients are grateful for that.

[3] *This needs explanation. It was my last case. My juniors were David Kitchin and Richard Meade. On one of the many days of preparation, Richard came in with a thin paperback called* The World's Filthiest Jokes. *He said we should have a reading of one every hour and so we did. After that he punched holes in the book, took a spare file, labelled it Vol. 50 and took it up to the clerks' room asking them to include this in the next set of* Chiron *papers coming in for Peter Prescott QC, the leader for one of our two defendants. In the course of the trial, Simon Thorley QC for the other sought to put a new bundle of scientific papers to one of our experts. He said, 'My Lord, may we call this Volume 50?' Neither the judge nor our opponents could understand why we thought that so funny.*

[4] *I told the solicitors they should have got a plain exercise book, scrawled the pages with coloured crayons and sent that as Rodney's notebook.*

One of the qualities we all seek in a judge is predictability. You have been known to describe certain pharmaceutical patents as ones which give the patent system a bad name and for which the only solution is a rapid and efficient method for obtaining revocation.

When the European Commission invited you to give an address when they presented preliminary views during the pharmaceutical sector inquiry, they may not have expected that you would start your speech with a quotation from the Pied Piper of Hamelin, or the almost equally famous writings of Mr Thomas Blanco White. It turned out you had no problem with pharmaceutical patents as such—only with bad ones. An outcome is predictable only when all the evidence is considered. It appeared that the European Commission official who sat behind you, and whose face told a thousand words, had just discovered this—to his cost.

On the subject of eloquence, we are grateful for the amusing turns of phrase found in your many judgments. It is no coincidence that in no less than five of the last ten years, one of your remarks has been selected as the quotation of the year in the Annual Patent Review.

I cannot let this morning pass without remarking on your considerable loyalty: to your fellow judges, both in this country and abroad; to fellow members of the Bar and, in particular, junior members starting out on their careers. Indeed I can even, on occasion, recall your saying something really quite complimentary about select members of my own branch of the profession! *(Laughter)*

So (and, to misquote your judgment in *Gerber*, I hope that it will not be thought that I have built towers of appreciation on sands of unreliable evidence) you have shown yourself thus far—and, as has been said, your career is far from complete—as intelligent, enthusiastic, focused, a moderniser, knowledgeable, committed, witty and loyal. But there is one last virtue I should mention—humility.

In *Gerber*, you said: 'Quantification of damage in a case such as the present is a much harder, less certain, task than I had hitherto thought. Although I have had to reach an answer I do not pretend it is an accurate measure of the damage ... It is just the best assessment I can make.'

My Lord we know that you have consistently done your best for your clients when you appeared as counsel, for litigants when a judge and for all those who use the courts in which you have sat.

For all of this, we, the IP solicitors, thank you.

THE LORD CHIEF JUSTICE: Thank you. Mr Poore?

MR ALASDAIR POORE (Chartered Institute of Patent Attorneys): My Lords, I am speaking on behalf of the Chartered Institute of Patent Attorneys, and I am pleased to say that this is not a geometric progression because in one minute I would find it hard to do justice to your Lordship's extreme service to the intellectual property community.

Your Lordship was appointed to the Bench at a time when reform was in the air. I remember a fresh wind blowing through the Patents Court Users' Committee, as it was then called, before reform got its name changed, with a genuine desire to see change. I thought that the fresh wind would blow itself out on the rocks of the Lord Chancellor's Department. Maybe it was the effect of competition from the Patents County Court, but, more likely, it was your real interest in change.

We are now seeing the real benefit of that change, both in the Patents Court, and more widely, and even perhaps in the European Patents Court in due course, and, indeed, also your support (and challenges) to patent attorneys playing roles in those courts.

At the Bar, as you have heard, I guess, there were rumours—and I stress rumours—that, if you wanted Mr Jacob QC to read the papers, there would of course be an extra charge. *(Laughter)*

Likewise, on the Bench, it would have been a mistake always to allow facts to detract from a good judgment. For example, what about *Aerotel*? The facts (as they later turned out) showed that the patent was bad for excluded subject matter. If the facts had taken their toll initially, we might have missed your incisive analysis of the patentability of computer-implemented inventions.

Aerotel was followed in *Symbian*—a patent attorney litigator case, reported in CIPA in the following terms: 'The clear and authoritative guidance from the Court of Appeal will end a difficult period of uncertainty and confusion for UK inventors', which just goes to shows that one should not let facts get in the way of a good press release. *(Laughter)*

These cases illustrate your often outspoken desire to ensure that intellectual property law is always subject to rigorous challenges, whether patents, trade marks or in other matters, and, incidentally, creates all the more work for patent attorneys.

Good things have to come to an end. But this one, we hope, will not. The intellectual zeal with which you have challenged a European view, especially the European Court of Justice (or CJEU, as we are now required to call it), can now be applied with all the more vigour in an academic environment, an environment untrammelled by any facts—or by the constraints of the law. Your challenging ideas and intellectual stimulus are something our members will relish, as will your students.

All our members will sincerely appreciate your service and regret your departure but look forward to a very stimulating future.

THE LORD CHIEF JUSTICE: Thank you very much. Mrs Ramage?

MRS MAGGIE RAMAGE (The Institute of Trade Mark Attorneys): My Lords, Lord Justice Jacob.

I have the pleasure to appear before you today on behalf of The Institute of Trade Mark Attorneys, as its President.

Lord Justice Jacob is known to us all as having strong views, and handing down strongly worded judgments, for example, as recently seen in the Decision of *L'Oréal v Bellure*.

In the early 1990s, I instructed Lord Justice Jacob, when he was in Chambers. At the time I was acting for Yellow Pages, as part of British Telecom, against Thomson Directories. Indeed, I remember visiting Lord Justice Jacob, or Robin Jacob, as he then was, on two separate occasions. On the first occasion, we had a lengthy conference in Chambers about strategy on the case at issue. Some months later, at the second conference, Lord Justice Jacob kicked off the discussion with the criticism, 'You do not appear to have done anything I advised you to previously.' *(Laughter)* This rather put us in our place, but it is a piece of advice I have always remembered. Listen to advice and act upon it.

Over the years, Lord Justice Jacob has been particularly supportive of our Institute and has been very keen to speak to our members at evening seminars and to attend various social events we have run. Indeed, when I became President of the Institute last spring, the Institute had an evening reception, to mark the occasion. This was the first time I had spoken on behalf of my Institute to the various distinguished guests, and one overriding memory I do have is of addressing all the guests, but being aware of one person in particular standing centre right, directly in my field of vision, grinning his head off, and generally willing me on. I certainly felt, on that occasion, that I had Lord Justice Jacob behind me.

My Institute has always had an excellent relationship with you, and I think it is fair to say that our members are grateful for the encouragement you have shown, particularly with what is now very much a growing group of trade mark litigators.

We in the Institute are indebted to you for your help over the years, and appreciate the encouragement you have given, both to our members generally, but also to me personally. We join together to wish you all the best in your new position as the first Sir Hugh Laddie Chair in Intellectual Property Law at UCL, as Director of the Institute of Brand and Innovation Law. Indeed, I am sure that my members would join me in saying that we could not think of anybody better equipped to take on this role. We wish you all the very best for the future.

THE LORD CHIEF JUSTICE: Thank you very much. Lord Justice Jacob?

LORD JUSTICE JACOB: Lord Chief, Master of the Rolls, other members of the court, Mr Thorley, Miss May, Mr Westmacott, Mr Poore, Mrs Ramage.

Seventeen-and-a-half years ago, in thanking everyone for their speeches of welcome to me as a new judge, I ended by promising to do my best.

Well, I tried. *(Laughter)*

But sometimes higher courts—*(Laughter)*—and the European Courts of Justice said that my best wasn't good enough.

Lord Chief, for the purposes of today at least, I forgive them. *(Laughter)* They knew not what they were doing. *(Laughter)*

What I did not know 17½ years ago was how much I was going to enjoy the job. That enjoyment came, above all, from the people behind the scenes.

Of course I expected to meet other judges. What I did not expect was to find as much warmth and friendship as I did. I came out of the rather closed world of IP into the wider world—especially when I went on circuit.

That was all rather unexpected.

But what was totally unexpected was the staff here and on Circuit. What marvellous people! It is they who keep the great ship of the law on the road, if you see what I mean. *(Laughter)* They did it and do it unstintingly and with devotion. Thank you all, those who are present and those who are not.

May I mention a few.

Just before I started, I met Doug Noon, the greatest Superintendent ever of this mighty building. He gave me my first, very crummy room. It was small, filthy and cut off from all the other Chancery judges. He said he would sort it in due course—and he did, in spades. Others of his team are here—Dave Reynolds and Margaret Barrett in particular. This building has been so lucky to have them.

On my first morning in came Doug Bell with his then boss. Doug is one of the two greatest listing officers ever. The other is, of course, Anne Marie Munn.

Roger Little took me to a vast, dark cavern below—I still wonder whether it is there. It was full of furniture covered in dust and very dark. He said, 'Have a chair.' *(Laughter)* Steve Burrows made sure that we were all safe and still does.

Then there have been the ushers, who keep every court running like clockwork. I thank you all. I can't name them all, but I give special thanks to Penny McNulty, who looked after me for so many years in Chancery.

And then there have been the judges' clerks. They are an absolutely amazing body of people, both here and on circuit. If anything is even slightly going wrong, it is sorted. Thank you all so much.

Thus I come to Lorraine, the power. Don, I hope you don't mind if I tell the absolute truth. Lorraine is the best clerk of them all. *(Laughter)* She has been with me for over 13 of my 17½ years as judge. Through all that time she has been my guardian angel—always thinking ahead of me, always alert, always seeing trouble well before it even begins to surface. She is very cross with me for leaving and it is one of the things I regret most.

She will in due course be going to a new judge. He or she is probably here. I say to you now: if you get her, you have drawn first prize. Look after her well. She will repay in spades. If you don't, I know where you live! *(Laughter)* Today is her birthday. Happy birthday, Lorraine, and thank you, thank you, thank you.

I am leaving this job with a very heavy heart, with huge misgivings, and wondering whether I have done the right thing. I am going to miss you all so so much. However, the new job does fill me with excitement and it is an opportunity not to be missed.

I hope to see you all at UCL early and often.

I hope I am going to have more time at home. Wendy is very worried about that. *(Laughter)* Either I am, in which case maybe she'll wish I wasn't, or, if I don't, she'll get cross. She has made so much possible.

I was warned by a fellow judge not to blub and I have just about done it.

Thank you all.

THE LORD CHIEF JUSTICE: Thank you. Thank you all very much for coming. It is an occasion which will be warm in Robin's mind.

Index

www.ingramcontent.com/pod-product-compliance
Ingram Content Group UK Ltd.
Pitfield, Milton Keynes, MK11 3LW, UK
UKHW020130290926
15471UKWH00003B/386

9 781509 918386